Business Law

Henry R. Cheeseman

Custom Edition for the City University of New York, Borough of Manhattan Community College

Percy L. Lambert J.D.
Stephen Larrington J.D.
Senior Editors

Editors–Law Faculty
Borough of Manhattan Community (

Honorable Pam Jackman-Brown
Judge, New York State Supreme Court

Ann Marie Basic, J.D.
Joel Evans J.D.
John Johnson J.D.
Juan Lopez J.D.
Bridgett McMillian J.D.
Gary Smoke J.D.

Moyee Huei-Lambert, M.L.S.
Senior Researcher

Taken from:

Business Law: Legal Environment, Online Commerce, Business Ethics, and International Issues, Seventh Edition, by Henry R. Cheeseman

Learning Solutions

New York Boston San Francisco
London Toronto Sydney Tokyo Singapore Madrid
Mexico City Munich Paris Cape Town Hong Kong Montreal

Taken from:

Business Law: Legal Environment, Online Commerce, Business Ethics, and International Issues, Seventh Edition
by Henry R. Cheeseman
Copyright © 2010, 2007, 2004, 2001, 1998, 1995 by Pearson Education, Inc.
Published by Prentice Hall
Upper Saddle River, New Jersey 07458

Copyright © 2010, 2009, 2007, 2006, 2005, 2004 by Pearson Learning Solutions
All rights reserved.

Pearson Learning Solutions, 501 Boylston Street, Suite 900, Boston, MA 02116
A Pearson Education Company
www.pearsoned.com

Printed in the United States of America

1 2 3 4 5 6 7 8 9 10 V036 15 14 13 12 11 10

000200010270575702

NM/CA

ISBN 10: 0-558-83521-X
ISBN 13: 978-0-558-83521-7

Copyright Acknowledgments

Contents in Brief

Contents

Borough of Manhattan Community College

City University of New York

Business Management Department

Business Law
BUS 110
3 Credits

3 hours

Course Description

This course surveys briefly the American legal system and the basic law of contracts. Reference is made to typical business transactions and, by a study of pertinent cases, how the various principles of contract law apply to them.

Purpose of Course

The primary purpose of a course in Business Law is to develop an understanding of the legal framework of business. In our society, political, social and economic forces continually interact. To avoid confusion and chaos, we have developed a legal system. The laws derived from this system apply both to individuals and business. Knowledge of the legal system and how it operates is essential to any successful business endeavor. Students will engage in problem solving exercises as well.

Prerequisites/Co-requisites

Students must have passed ENG 088, ESL 094, RDG 062, and MAT 010/011.

Student Learning Outcomes

1. To give students an understanding of the general principles of law, and how it affects conduct in society.
2. To develop an overall understanding of the federal and state court systems, and the jurisdictional authority of the courts in society.
3. To learn the principles involved with the law of contracts.
4. To learn specific laws relating to business in the area of tort, agency, property and bankruptcy.

Upon completion of this course, students should be able to demonstrate and perform the following:

1. Understand the legal framework of business and the principles of the law that apply to business transactions.
2. Understand the logic and purpose of law.
3. Understand the legal decision making process as it relates to specific business transactions.
4. Develop a vocabulary that will be helpful in the legal problem solving process.

Required Text & Readings

Cheeseman, Lambert, *Business Law City University of New York-Borough of Manhattan Community College*, Pearson Custom Publishing (Prentice Hall) Copyright 2007

Recommended: *The Blessings of Liberty: A Concise History of the Constitution of the United States*, Michael Les Benedict, D.C. Heath & Company, Copyright 2006

Outline of Topics

Topical Outline

PLEASE NOTE: The appendix includes Spanish equivalents for important legal terms in English. The instructor may assign additional reading materials.

College Attendance Policy

At BMCC, the maximum number of absences is limited to one more hour than the number of hours a class meets in one week. For example, you may be enrolled in a three-hour class. In that class, you would be allowed 4 <u>hours</u> of absence (not 4 days). In the case of excessive absences, the instructor has the option to lower the grade or assign an F or WU grade.

Academic Adjustments for Students with Disabilities

Students with disabilities who require reasonable accommodations or academic adjustments for this course must contact the Office of Services for Students with Disabilities (Room N320; Telephone # 212-220-8180). BMCC is committed to providing equal access to all programs and curricula to all students.

BMCC Policy on Plagiarism and Academic Integrity Statement

Plagiarism is the presentation of someone else's ideas, words or artistic, scientific, or technical work as one's own creation. Using the idea or work of another is permissible only when the original author is identified. Paraphrasing and summarizing, as well as direct quotations, require citations to the original source. Plagiarism may be intentional or unintentional. Lack of dishonest intent does not necessarily absolve a student of responsibility for plagiarism.

Students who are unsure how and when to provide documentation are advised to consult with their instructors. The library has guides designed to help students to appropriately identify a cited work. The full policy can be found on BMCC's web site, www.bmcc.cuny.edu. For further information on integrity and behavior, please consult the college bulletin (also available online).

I have read the above and understand its terms completely and accept same.

Name: _____

Student ID: _____

Section: _____

Signature: _____

CHAPTER 1

"Where there is no law, there is no freedom."

—John Locke
Second Treatise of Government, Sec. 57

Legal Heritage and the Information Age

Chapter Objectives

After studying this chapter, you should be able to:

1. Define *law*.
2. Describe the functions of law.
3. List and describe the sources of law in the United States.
4. Explain the development of the U.S. legal system.

Chapter Contents

- **Introduction to Legal Heritage and the Information Age**

- **What Is Law?**
  Landmark U.S. Supreme Court Case · *Brown v. Board of Education*

- **Schools of Jurisprudential Thought**
  International Law · *Immigration to the United States of America*

- **History of American Law**
  International Law · *Adoption of English Common Law in America*
  International Law · *The Civil Law System*

- **Sources of Law in the United States**

Introduction to Legal Heritage and the Information Age

Every society makes and enforces laws that govern the conduct of the individuals, businesses, and other organizations that function within it. In the words of Judge Learned Hand, "Without law we cannot live; only with it can we insure the future which by right is ours. The best of men's hopes are enmeshed in its success."[1]

Although the law of the United States is primarily based on English common law, other legal systems, such as Spanish and French civil law, also influenced it. The sources of law in this country are the U.S. Constitution, state constitutions, federal and state statutes, ordinances, administrative agency rules and regulations, executive orders, and judicial decisions by federal and state courts.

Businesses that are organized in the United States are subject to its laws. They are also subject to the laws of other countries in which they operate. Businesses organized in other countries must obey the laws of the United States when doing business here. In addition, businesspeople owe a duty to act ethically in the conduct of their affairs, and businesses owe a responsibility not to harm society.

This chapter discusses the nature and definition of law, theories about the development of law, the history and sources of law in the United States.

What Is Law?

A lawyer without history or literature is a mechanic, a mere working mason: if he possesses some knowledge of these, he may venture to call himself an architect.

Sir Walter Scott
Guy Mannering, Ch. 37 (1815)

The law consists of rules that regulate the conduct of individuals, businesses, and other organizations within society. It is intended to protect persons and their property against unwanted interference from others. In other words, the law forbids persons from engaging in certain undesirable activities. Consider the following passage:

> Hardly anyone living in a civilized society has not at some time been told to do something or to refrain from doing something, because there is a law requiring it, or because it is against the law. What do we mean when we say such things? Most generally, how are we to understand statements of the form "x is law"? This is an ancient question. In his Memorabilia (I, ii), Xenophon reports a statement of the young Alcibiades, companion of Socrates, who in conversation with the great Pericles remarked that "no one can really deserve praise unless he knows what a law is."
>
> At the end of the 18th century, Immanuel Kant wrote of the question "What is law?" that it "may be said to be about as embarrassing to the jurist as the well-known question 'What is truth?' is to the logician."[2]

Definition of *Law*

law
That which must be obeyed and followed by citizens, subject to sanctions or legal consequences; a body of rules of action or conduct prescribed by controlling authority and having binding legal force.

The concept of **law** is broad. Although it is difficult to state a precise definition, *Black's Law Dictionary* gives one that is sufficient for this text:

> Law, in its generic sense, is a body of rules of action or conduct prescribed by controlling authority, and having binding legal force. That which must be obeyed and followed by citizens subject to sanctions or legal consequences is a law.[3]

Functions of the Law

The law is often described by the function it serves within a society. The primary *functions* served by the law in this country are:

1. Keeping the peace

   Example Laws that make certain activities crimes.

2. Shaping moral standards

   Example Laws that discourage drug and alcohol abuse.

3. Promoting social justice

   Example Laws that prohibit discrimination in employment.

4. Maintaining the status quo

   Example Laws that prevent the forceful overthrow of the government.

5. Facilitating orderly change

   Example Laws enacted only after considerable study, debate, and public input.

6. Facilitating planning

   Example Well-designed commercial laws that allow businesses to plan their activities, allocate their productive resources, and assess the risks they take.

7. Providing a basis for compromise

   Example Allowing for the settlement of cases prior to trial. Approximately 90 percent of all lawsuits are settled in this manner.

8. Maximizing individual freedom

   Example The rights of freedom of speech, religion, and association granted by the First Amendment to the U.S. Constitution.

Commercial law lies within a narrow compass, and is far purer and freer from defects than any other part of the system.

Henry Peter Brougham
House of Commons,
February 7, 1828

Concept Summary
Functions of the Law

1. Keep the peace	5. Facilitate orderly change
2. Shape moral standards	6. Facilitate planning
3. Promote social justice	7. Provide a basis for compromise
4. Maintain the status quo	8. Maximize individual freedom

Fairness of the Law

On the whole, the U.S. legal system is one of the most comprehensive, fair, and democratic systems of law ever developed and enforced. Nevertheless, some misuses and oversights of our legal system—including abuses of discretion and mistakes by judges and juries, unequal applications of the law, and procedural mishaps—allow some guilty parties to go unpunished.

The law, in its majestic equality, forbids the rich as well as the poor to sleep under bridges.

Anatole France

Example

In *Standefer v. United States*[4] the Supreme Court of the United States *affirmed* (let stand) the criminal conviction of a Gulf Oil Corporation executive for aiding and abetting the bribery of an Internal Revenue Service agent. The agent had been acquitted in a separate trial. In writing the opinion of the Court, Chief Justice Warren Burger stated, "This case does no more than manifest the simple, if discomforting, reality that different juries may reach different results under any criminal statute. That is one of the consequences we accept under our jury system."

Flexibility of the Law

U.S. law evolves and changes along with the norms of society, technology, and the growth and expansion of commerce in the United States and the world. The following quote by Judge Jerome Frank discusses the value of the adaptability of law:

Law must be stable and yet it cannot stand still.

Roscoe Pound
Interpretations of
Legal History (1923)

> The law always has been, is now, and will ever continue to be, largely vague and variable. And how could this be otherwise? The law deals with human relations in their most complicated aspects. The whole confused, shifting helter-skelter of life parades before it—more confused than ever, in our kaleidoscopic age.

"We conclude that in the field of public education the doctrine of 'separate but equal' has no place."

—Justice Warren

When the original 13 states ratified the Constitution of the United States of America in 1788, it created a democratic form of government and granted certain rights to its people. But all persons were not treated equally, as many people, including drafters of the Constitution such as Thomas Jefferson, owned African American slaves. It was more than 75 years before the Civil War was fought between the northern states and the southern Confederate states over the preservation of the Union and slavery. Slavery was abolished by the Thirteenth Amendment to the Constitution in 1865. The Fourteenth Amendment, added to the Constitution in 1868, contains the Equal Protection Clause, which provides that no state shall "deny to any person within its jurisdiction the equal protection of the laws." The original intent of this amendment was to guarantee equality to freed African Americans.

But equality was denied to African Americans for years to come. This included discrimination in housing, transportation, education, jobs, service at restaurants, and other activities. In 1896, the U.S. Supreme Court decided the case *Plessy v. Ferguson.*[6] In that case, the state of Louisiana had a law that provided for separate but equal accommodations for African American and white railway passengers. An African American passenger challenged the state law. The Supreme Court held that the "separate but equal" state law did not violate the Equal Protection Clause of the Fourteenth Amendment. The "separate but equal" doctrine was then applied to all areas of life, including public education. Thus, African American and white children attended separate schools, often with unequal facilities.

It was not until 1954 that the U.S. Supreme Court decided a case that challenged the separate but equal doctrine as it applied to public elementary and high schools. In *Brown v. Board of Education,*[7] a consolidated case that challenged the separate school systems of four states—Kansas, South Carolina, Virginia, and Delaware—the Supreme Court decided to revisit the separate but equal doctrine announced by its forbearers in another century. This time, a unanimous Supreme Court, in an opinion written by Chief Justice Earl Warren, reversed prior precedent and held that the separate but equal doctrine violated the Equal Protection Clause of the Fourteenth Amendment to the Constitution. In its opinion, the Court stated:

> We cannot turn the clock back to 1868 when the Amendment was adopted, or even to 1896 when Plessy v. Ferguson *was written. Today, education is perhaps the most important function of state and local governments.*
>
> *We conclude that in the field of public education the doctrine of "separate but equal" has no place. Separate edu-*

cational facilities are inherently unequal. Therefore, we hold that the plaintiffs and others similarly situated for whom actions have been brought are, by reason of the segregation complained of, deprived of the equal protection of the laws guaranteed by the Fourteenth Amendment.

After *Brown v. Board of Education* was decided, it took court orders as well as U.S. Army enforcement to integrate many of the public schools in this country. The *Brown v. Board of Education* case demonstrates that one Supreme Court case can overrule prior Supreme Court cases to promote justice. The U.S. Supreme Court's *Brown v. Board of Education* opinion is set forth in Exhibit 1.1. *Brown v. Board of Education*, 347 U.S. 483, 74 S.Ct. 686, 98 L.Ed. 873, **Web** 1954 U.S. Lexis 2094 (Supreme Court of the United States, 1954)

Case Questions

Critical Legal Thinking What does the Equal Protection Clause of the Fourteenth Amendment to the U.S. Constitution provide?

Business Ethics Was the Equal Protection Clause properly applied in the early U.S. Supreme Court decision *Plessy v. Ferguson*? Explain.

Contemporary Business It has been said that the U.S. Constitution is a "living document"—that is, one that can adapt to changing times. Do you think this is a good policy? Or should the U.S. Constitution be interpreted narrowly and literally, as originally written?

■ **EXHIBIT 1.1** Opinion of the U.S. Supreme Court: *Brown v. Board of Education*

Supreme Court of the United States

No. 1 ——— , *October Term, 19* 54

Oliver Brown, Mrs. Richard Lawton, Mrs. Sadie Emmanuel et al.,

Appellants,

vs.

Board of Education of Topeka, Shawnee County, Kansas, et al.

Appeal from *the United States District Court for the* ——————————— *District of Kansas.*

This cause *came on to be heard on the transcript of the record from the United States District Court for the* ——————— *District of* Kansas, ——————— *and was argued by counsel.*

On consideration whereof, *It is ordered and adjudged by this Court that the judgment of the said* District ——————— *Court in this cause be, and the same is hereby,* reversed with costs; and that this cause be, and the same is hereby, remanded to the said District Court to take such proceedings and enter such orders and decrees consistent with the opinions of this Court as are necessary and proper to admit to public schools on a racially nondiscriminatory basis with all deliberate speed the parties to this case.

Per Mr. Chief Justice Warren,

May 31, 1955.

Men have never been able to construct a comprehensive, eternalized set of rules anticipating all possible legal disputes and formulating in advance the rules which would apply to them. Situations are bound to occur which were never contemplated when the original rules were made. How much less is such a frozen legal system possible in modern times?

The constant development of unprecedented problems requires a legal system capable of fluidity and pliancy. Our society would be straightjacketed were not the courts, with the able assistance of the lawyers, constantly overhauling the law and adapting it to the realities of ever-changing social, industrial, and political conditions; although changes cannot be made lightly, yet rules of law must be more or less impermanent, experimental and therefore not nicely calculable.

Much of the uncertainty of law is not an unfortunate accident; it is of immense social value.[5]

Schools of Jurisprudential Thought

jurisprudence
The philosophy or science of law.

The philosophy or science of the law is referred to as **jurisprudence**. There are several different philosophies about how the law developed, ranging from the classical natural theory to modern theories of law and economics and critical legal studies. Classical legal philosophies are discussed in the following paragraphs.

Natural Law School

The **Natural Law School** of jurisprudence postulates that the law is based on what is "correct." Natural law philosophers emphasize a **moral theory of law**—that is, law should be based on morality and ethics. Natural law is "discovered" by humans through the use of reason and choosing between good and evil.

Examples
Documents such as the U.S. Constitution, the Magna Carta, and the United Nations Charter reflect this theory.

Historical School

The law is not a series of calculating machines where definitions and answers come tumbling out when the right levers are pushed.

William O. Douglas
The Dissent, A Safeguard of Democracy (1948)

The **Historical School** of jurisprudence believes that the law is an aggregate of social traditions and customs that have developed over the centuries. It believes that changes in the norms of society will gradually be reflected in the law. To these legal philosophers, the law is an evolutionary process.

Example
Historical legal scholars look to past legal decisions (precedent) to solve contemporary problems.

Analytical School

The **Analytical School** of jurisprudence maintains that the law is shaped by logic. Analytical philosophers believe that results are reached by applying principles of logic to the specific facts of the case. The emphasis is on the logic of the result rather than on how the result is reached.

Sociological School

The **Sociological School** of jurisprudence asserts that the law is a means of achieving and advancing certain sociological goals. The followers of this philosophy, known as *realists*, believe that the purpose of law is to shape social behavior. Sociological philosophers are unlikely to adhere to past law as precedent.

Command School

The philosophers of the **Command School** of jurisprudence believe that the law is a set of rules developed, communicated, and enforced by the ruling party rather than a reflection of

Pyongyang, North Korea.
This is the Kim Il Sung statue and Mount Paekto–Mansudae Grand Monument in Pyongyang, North Korea. North Korea—the Democratic People's Republic of Korea (or DPRK)—is a communist dictatorship, first commanded by the late Kim Il Sung. North Koreans pay homage to the Dear Leader's statue in Pyongyang, the capital of North Korea.

the society's morality, history, logic, or sociology. This school maintains that the law changes when the ruling class changes.

Critical Legal Studies School

The **Critical Legal Studies School** proposes that legal rules are unnecessary and are used as an obstacle by the powerful to maintain the status quo. Critical legal theorists (the *Crits*) argue that legal disputes should be solved by applying arbitrary rules that are based on broad notions of what is "fair" in each circumstance. Under this theory, subjective decision making by judges would be permitted.

Law and Economics School

The **Law and Economics School** (or the **"Chicago School,"** named after the University of Chicago, where it was first developed) believes that promoting market efficiency should be the central goal of legal decision making.

Example

Proponents of law and economics theory suggest that the practice of appointing counsel, free of charge, to prisoners who bring civil rights cases should be abolished. They believe that if a prisoner cannot find a lawyer who will take the case on a contingency-fee basis or *pro bono* (free of charge), the case is probably not worth bringing.

Concept Summary
Schools of Jurisprudential Thought

School	Philosophy
Natural Law	Postulates that law is based on what is "correct." It emphasizes a moral theory of law—that is, law should be based on morality and ethics.
Historical	Believes that law is an aggregate of social traditions and customs.
Analytical	Maintains that law is shaped by logic.
Sociological	Asserts that the law is a means of achieving and advancing certain sociological goals.
Command	Believes that the law is a set of rules developed, communicated, and enforced by the ruling party.
Critical Legal Studies	Maintains that legal rules are unnecessary and that legal disputes should be solved by applying arbitrary rules based on fairness.
Law and Economics	Believes that promoting market efficiency should be the central concern of legal decision making.

International Law

Immigration to the United States of America

"That I will support and defend the Constitution and laws of the United States of America against all enemies, . . ."

—Oath of Citizenship
United States of America

The United States of America was originally founded by immigrants, primarily those from western Europe. Many sought wealth and prosperity; some sought religious freedom, and others were running from their debts. But no matter the reason, during the sixteenth, seventeenth, and eighteenth centuries, the immigrants kept coming, and they moved increasingly further inland from the Atlantic Ocean. Many immigrants also came from the continent of Africa, most forcibly to become slaves.

After winning a bloody revolution and gaining freedom from Great Britain, immigrants continued to pour into the country during the nineteenth and twentieth centuries, and they continue to do so in the twenty-first century. Immigrants to the United States come from all over the world.

In 1921, the United States enacted its first immigration quota law, setting a limit on the number of immigrants that could be admitted to the United States from each foreign country each year. During different times, the quotas for each foreign country have been raised or lowered, depending on the world situation. For example, after World War II, the United States increased the quotas dramatically to accept many persons who had been displaced by the war. This quota system is still in effect today.

Currently, the immigration laws of this country are administered by the **United States Citizenship and Immigration Services (USCIS)**, which is part of the U.S. Department of Homeland Security.

Foreign nationals who qualify, and have met the requirements to do so, may become citizens of the United States. During their swearing-in ceremony, they must swear the following Oath of Citizenship:

The Oath of Citizenship

I hereby declare, on oath, that I absolutely and entirely renounce and adjure all allegiance and fidelity to any foreign prince, potentate, state, or sovereignty of whom or which I have heretofore been a subject or citizen; that I will support and defend the Constitution and laws of the United States of America against all enemies, foreign and domestic; that I will bear true faith and allegiance to the same; that I will bear arms on behalf of the United States when required by law; that I will perform noncombatant service in the Armed Forces of the United States when required by the law; that I will perform work of national importance under civilian direction when required by the law; and that I take this obligation freely without any mental reservation or purpose of evasion; so help me God. In acknowledgement whereof I have hereunto affixed my signature.

History of American Law

When the American colonies were first settled, the English system of law was generally adopted as the system of jurisprudence. This was the foundation from which American judges developed a common law in America.

English Common Law

common law
Law developed by judges who issued their opinions when deciding a case. The principles announced in these cases became precedent for later judges deciding similar cases.

English common law was law developed by judges who issued their opinions when deciding cases. The principles announced in these cases became *precedent* for later judges deciding similar cases. The English common law can be divided into cases decided by the *law courts*, *equity courts*, and *merchant courts*.

Law Courts   Prior to the Norman Conquest of England in 1066, each locality in England was subject to local laws, as established by the lord or chieftain in control of the

Ellis Island, New York.
Ellis Island, New York, was the primary entry point for immigrants entering the United States from the late 1800s until 1954.

International Law

Adoption of English Common Law in America

All the states of the United States of America (except Louisiana) base their legal systems primarily on the English common law. In the United States, the law, equity, and merchant courts have been merged. Thus, most U.S. courts permit the aggrieved party to seek both law and equitable orders and remedies.

The importance of common law to the American legal system is described in the following excerpt from

Justice Douglas's opinion in the 1841 case *Penny v. Little*:

The common law is a beautiful system, containing the wisdom and experiences of ages. Like the people it ruled and protected, it was simple and crude in its infancy and became enlarged, improved, and polished as the nation advanced in civilization, virtue, and intelligence. Adapting itself to the conditions and circumstances of the people and relying upon them for its administration, it necessarily improved as the condition of the people was elevated. The inhabitants of this country always claimed the common law as their birthright, and at an early period established it as the basis of their jurisprudence.[8]

local area. There was no countrywide system of law. After 1066, William the Conqueror and his successors to the throne of England began to replace the various local laws with one uniform system of law. To accomplish this, the king or queen appointed loyal followers as judges in all local areas. These judges were charged with administering the law in a uniform manner, in courts that were called **law courts**. Law at that time tended to emphasize the form (legal procedure) over the substance (merit) of a case. The only relief available at law courts was a monetary award for damages.

Chancery (Equity) Courts Because of the unfair results and the limited remedy available in the law courts, a second set of courts—the **Court of Chancery** (or **equity court**)—was established. These courts were under the authority of the lord chancellor. Persons who

Two things most people should never see made: sausages and laws.

An old saying

International Law

The Civil Law System

One of the major legal systems that has developed in the world in addition to the Anglo-American common law system is the **Romano-Germanic civil law system**. This legal system, which is commonly called the **civil law**, dates to 450 B.C., when Rome adopted the Twelve Tables, a code of laws applicable to the Romans. A compilation of Roman law, called the *Corpus Juris Civilis* ("Body of Civil Law"),

was completed in A.D. 534. Later, two national codes—the French Civil Code of 1804 (the Napoleonic Code) and the German Civil Code of 1896—became models for countries that adopted civil codes.

In contrast to the Anglo-American common law, in which laws are created by the judicial system as well as by congressional legislation, the Civil Code and parliamentary statutes that expand and interpret it are the sole sources of the law in most civil law countries. Thus, the adjudication of a case is simply the application of the code or the statutes to a particular set of facts. In some civil law countries, court decisions do not have the force of law.

Many countries in Europe still follow the civil law system.

believed that the decision of the law court was unfair or believed that the law court could not grant an appropriate remedy could seek relief in the Court of Chancery. Rather than emphasize legal procedure, the chancery court inquired into the merits of the case. The chancellor's remedies were called *equitable remedies* because they were shaped to fit each situation. Equitable orders and remedies of the Court of Chancery took precedence over the legal decisions and remedies of the law courts.

Merchant Courts   As trade developed in the Middle Ages, the merchants who traveled about England and Europe developed certain rules to solve their commercial disputes. These rules, known as the "law of merchants," or the **Law Merchant**, were based on common trade practices and usage. Eventually, a separate set of courts was established to administer these rules. This court was called the **Merchant Court**. In the early 1900s, the Merchant Court was absorbed into the regular law court system of England.

Sources of Law in the United States

In the more than 200 years since the founding of the United States and adoption of the English common law, the lawmakers of this country have developed a substantial body of law. The *sources of modern law* in the United States are discussed in the paragraphs that follow.

Constitutions

Constitution of the United States of America
The supreme law of the United States.

The Constitution of the United States is not a mere lawyers' document: it is a vehicle of life, and its spirit is always the spirit of age.

Woodrow Wilson
Constitutional Government in the United States (1927)

The **Constitution of the United States of America** is the *supreme law of the land*. This means that any law—whether federal, state, or local—that conflicts with the U.S. Constitution is unconstitutional and, therefore, unenforceable.

The principles enumerated in the Constitution are extremely broad because the founding fathers intended them to be applied to evolving social, technological, and economic conditions. The U.S. Constitution is often referred to as a "living document" because it is so adaptable.

The U.S. Constitution established the structure of the federal government. It created the following three branches of government and gave them the following powers:

- The **legislative branch (Congress)** has the power to make (enact) the law.
- The **executive branch (president)** has the power to enforce the law.
- The **judicial branch (courts)** has the power to interpret and determine the validity of the law.

Powers not given to the federal government by the Constitution are reserved for the states. States also have their own **constitutions**. These are often patterned after the U.S. Constitution, although many are more detailed. State constitutions establish the legislative, executive, and judicial branches of state government and establish the powers of each branch. Provisions of state constitutions are valid unless they conflict with the U.S. Constitution or any valid federal law.

Treaties

The U.S. Constitution provides that the president, with the advice and consent of two-thirds of the Senate, may enter into **treaties** with foreign governments. Treaties become part of the supreme law of the land. With increasing international economic relations among nations, treaties will become an even more important source of law that will affect business in the future.

treaty
A compact made between two or more nations.

Codified Law

Statutes are written laws that establish certain courses of conduct that must be adhered to by covered parties. The U.S. Congress is empowered by the Commerce Clause and other provisions of the U.S. Constitution to enact **federal statutes** to regulate foreign and interstate commerce. State legislatures enact **state statutes**. The statutes enacted by the legislative branches of the federal and state governments are organized by topic into code books. This is often called **codified law**.

State legislatures often delegate lawmaking authority to local government bodies, including cities and municipalities, counties, school districts, water districts, and such. These governmental units are empowered to adopt **ordinances**. Ordinances are also codified.

statute
Written law enacted by the legislative branch of the federal and state governments that establishes certain courses of conduct that must be adhered to by covered parties.

ordinance
Law enacted by local government bodies, such as cities and municipalities, counties, school districts, and water districts.

U.S. Congress, Washington, DC. *The U.S. Congress, which is a bicameral system made up of the U.S. Senate and the U.S. House of Representatives, creates federal law by enacting statutes. Each state has two senators and is allocated a certain number of representatives, based on population.*

Executive Orders

The executive branch of government, which includes the president of the United States and state governors, is empowered to issue **executive orders**. This power is derived from express delegation from the legislative branch and is implied from the U.S. Constitution and state constitutions.

Example

When the United States is at war with another country, the president of the United States usually issues executive orders prohibiting U.S. companies from selling goods or services to that country.

Regulations and Orders of Administrative Agencies

The legislative and executive branches of federal and state governments are empowered to establish **administrative agencies** to enforce and interpret statutes enacted by Congress and state legislatures. Many of these agencies regulate business.

Examples

Congress has created the Securities and Exchange Commission (SEC) to enforce federal securities laws and the Federal Trade Commission (FTC) to enforce consumer protection statutes.

Congress or the state legislatures usually empower these agencies to adopt **administrative rules and regulations** to interpret the statutes that the agency is authorized to enforce. These rules and regulations have the force of law. Administrative agencies usually have the power to hear and decide disputes. Their decisions are called **orders**. Because of their power, administrative agencies are often informally referred to as the "fourth branch of government."

Judicial Decisions

When deciding individual lawsuits, federal and state courts issue **judicial decisions**. In these written opinions, a judge or justice usually explains the legal reasoning used to decide the case. These opinions often include interpretations of statutes, ordinances, and administrative regulations and the announcement of legal principles used to decide the case. Many court decisions are printed (reported) in books that are available in law libraries.

***Doctrine of* Stare Decisis**   Based on the common law tradition, past court decisions become **precedent** for deciding future cases. Lower courts must follow the precedent established by higher courts. That is why all federal and state courts in the United States must follow the precedents established by U.S. Supreme Court decisions.

The courts of one jurisdiction are not bound by the precedent established by the courts of another jurisdiction, although they may look to each other for guidance.

Example

State courts of one state are not required to follow the legal precedent established by the courts of another state.

Adherence to precedent is called the **doctrine of *stare decisis*** ("to stand by the decision"). The doctrine of *stare decisis* promotes uniformity of law within a jurisdiction, makes the court system more efficient, and makes the law more predictable for individuals and businesses. A court may later change or reverse its legal reasoning if a new case is presented to it and change is warranted. The doctrine of *stare decisis* is discussed in the following excerpt from Justice Musmanno's decision in *Flagiello v. Pennsylvania*:

> Without *stare decisis*, there would be no stability in our system of jurisprudence. Stare decisis channels the law. It erects lighthouses and flies the signal of safety. The ships of jurisprudence must follow that well-defined channel which, over the years, has been proved to be secure and worthy.[9]

Concept Summary

Sources of Law in the United States

Source of Law	Description
Constitutions	The U.S. Constitution establishes the federal government and enumerates its powers. Powers not given to the federal government are reserved to the states. State constitutions establish state governments and enumerate their powers.
Treaties	The president, with the advice and consent of two-thirds of the Senate, may enter into treaties with foreign countries.
Codified law: statutes and ordinances	Statutes are enacted by Congress and state legislatures. Ordinances are enacted by municipalities and local government bodies. They establish courses of conduct that covered parties must follow.
Executive orders	Issued by the president and governors of states. Executive orders regulate the conduct of covered parties.
Regulations and orders of administrative agencies	Administrative agencies are created by the legislative and executive branches of government. They may adopt rules and regulations that regulate the conduct of covered parties as well as issue orders.
Judicial decisions	Courts decide controversies. In doing so, a court issues an opinion that states the decision of the court and the rationale used in reaching that decision.

Priority of Law in the United States

As mentioned previously, the U.S. Constitution and treaties take precedence over all other laws in the United States. Federal statutes take precedence over federal regulations. Valid federal law takes precedence over any conflicting state or local law. State constitutions rank as the highest state law. State statutes take precedence over state regulations. Valid state law takes precedence over local laws.

Where law ends, there tyranny begins.

William Pitt,
First Earl of Chatham

Test Review Terms and Concepts

Administrative agency
Administrative rules and regulations
Analytical School
Civil law
Codified law
Command School
Constitution
Constitution of the United States of America
Court of Chancery (equity courts)
Critical Legal Studies School
Doctrine of *stare decisis*
English common law

Executive branch (president)
Executive order
Federal statutes
Historical School
Judicial branch (courts)
Judicial decision
Jurisprudence
Law
Law courts
Law and Economics School ("Chicago School")
Law Merchant
Legislative branch (Congress)

Merchant Court
Moral theory of law
Natural Law School
Order
Ordinance
Precedent
Romano-Germanic civil law system
Sociological School
State statute
Statute
Treaty
United States Citizenship and Immigration Services (USCIS)

Case Problem

1.1 Fairness of the Law: In 1909, the state legislature of Illinois enacted a statute called the "Woman's 10-Hour Law." The law prohibited women who were employed in factories and other manufacturing facilities from working more than 10 hours per day. The law did not apply to men. W. C. Ritchie & Co., an employer, brought a lawsuit that challenged the statute as being unconstitutional, in violation of the Equal Protection Clause of the Illinois constitution. In upholding the statute, the Illinois supreme court stated:

It is known to all men (and what we know as men we cannot profess to be ignorant of as judges) that woman's physical structure and the performance of maternal functions place her at a great disadvantage in the battle of life; that while a man can work for more than 10 hours a day without injury to himself, a woman, especially when the burdens of motherhood are upon her, cannot; that while a man can work standing upon his feet for more than 10 hours a day, day after day, without injury to himself, a woman cannot; and that to require a woman to stand upon her feet for more than 10 hours in any one day and perform severe manual labor while thus standing, day after day, has the effect to impair her health, and that as weakly and sickly women cannot be mothers of vigorous children.

We think the general consensus of opinion, not only in this country but in the civilized countries of Europe, is, that a working day of not more than 10 hours for women is justified for the following reasons: (1) the physical organization of women, (2) her maternal function, (3) the rearing and education of children, (4) the maintenance of the home; and these conditions are, so far, matters of general knowledge that the courts will take judicial cognizance of their existence.

Surrounded as women are by changing conditions of society, and the evolution of employment which environs them, we agree fully with what is said by the Supreme Court of Washington in the Buchanan case; "law is, or ought to be, a progressive science."

Is the statute fair? Would the statute be lawful today? Should the law be a "progressive science"? *W. C. Ritchie & Co. v. Wayman, Attorney for Cook County, Illinois*, 244 Ill. 509, 91 N.E. 695, **Web** 1910 Ill. Lexis 1958 (Supreme Court of Illinois)

Business Ethics Case

1.2 Business Ethics: In 1975, after the war in Vietnam, the U.S. Government discontinued draft registration for men in this country. In 1980, after the Soviet Union invaded Afghanistan, President Jimmy Carter asked Congress for funds to reactivate draft registration. President Carter suggested that both males and females be required to register. Congress allocated funds only for the registration of males. Several men who were subject to draft registration brought a lawsuit that challenged the law as being unconstitutional, in violation of the Equal Protection Clause of the U.S. Constitution. The U.S. Supreme Court upheld the constitutionality of the draft registration law, reasoning as follows:

The question of registering women for the draft not only received considerable national attention and was the subject of wide-ranging public debate, but also was extensively considered by Congress in hearings, floor debate, and in committee. The foregoing clearly establishes that the decision to exempt women from registration was not the "accidental by-product of a traditional way of thinking about women."

This is not a case of Congress arbitrarily choosing to burden one of two similarly situated groups, such as would be the case with an all-black or all-white, or an all-Catholic or all-Lutheran, or an all-Republican or all-Democratic registration. Men and women are simply not similarly situated for purposes of a draft or registration for a draft.

Justice Marshall dissented, stating:

The Court today places its imprimatur on one of the most potent remaining public expressions of "ancient canards about the proper role of women." It upholds a statute that requires males but not females to register for the draft, and which thereby categorically excludes women from a fundamental civil obligation. I dissent.

Is the decision fair? Is the law a "progressive science" in this case? Is it ethical for males but not females to have to register for the draft? *Rostker, Director of Selective Service v. Goldberg*, 453 U.S. 57, 101 S.Ct. 2646, 69 L.Ed. 2d 478, **Web** 1981 U.S. Lexis 126 (Supreme Court of the United States)

Endnotes

1. *The Spirit of Liberty*, 3rd ed. (New York: Alfred A. Knopf, 1960).
2. "Introduction," *The Nature of Law: Readings in Legal Philosophy*, ed. M. P. Golding (New York: Random House, 1966).
3. *Black's Law Dictionary*, 5th ed. (St. Paul, MN: West).
4. 447 U.S. 10, 100 S.Ct. 1999, 64 L.Ed.2d 689, **Web** 1980 U.S. Lexis 127 (Supreme Court of the United States).
5. *Law and the Modern Mind* (New York: Brentano's, 1930).
6. 163 U.S. 537, 16 S.C. 1138, 141 L.Ed 256, **Web** 1896 U.S. Lexis 3390 (Supreme Court of the United States, 1896).
7. 347 U.S. 483, 74 S.Ct. 686, 98 L.Ed. 873, **Web** 1954 U.S. Lexis 2094 (Supreme Court of the United States, 1954).
8. 4 Ill. 301, 1841 Ill. Lexis 98 (Ill.).
9. 417 Pa. 486, 208 A.2d 193, **Web** 1965 Pa. Lexis 442 (Supreme Court of Pennsylvania).

CHAPTER 2

"I was never ruined but twice; once when I lost a lawsuit, and once when I won one."

—Voltaire

Court Systems and Jurisdiction

Chapter Objectives

After studying this chapter, you should be able to:

1. Describe state court systems.
2. Describe the federal court system.
3. List and describe the types of decisions that are issued by the U.S. Supreme Court.
4. Compare the jurisdiction of state courts with that of federal courts.
5. Define *standing to sue* and *venue*.

Chapter Contents

Introduction to Court Systems and Jurisdiction

There are two major court systems in the United States: (1) the federal court system and (2) the court systems of the 50 states, the District of Columbia, and territories of the United States. Each of these systems has jurisdiction to hear different types of lawsuits. This chapter discusses the various court systems and the jurisdiction of different courts to hear and decide cases.

State, District of Columbia, and Territory Court Systems

Each state, the District of Columbia, and each territory of the United States has its own separate court system (hereafter collectively referred to as "**state courts**"). Most state court systems include the following: *limited-jurisdiction trial courts, general-jurisdiction trial courts, intermediate appellate courts,* and a *supreme court.*

Limited-Jurisdiction Trial Courts

limited-jurisdiction trial court
A court that hears matters of a specialized or limited nature.

State **limited-jurisdiction trial courts**, which are sometimes referred to as **inferior trial courts**, hear matters of a specialized or limited nature.

Examples
Traffic courts, juvenile courts, justice-of-the-peace courts, probate courts, family law courts, courts that hear misdemeanor criminal law cases, and courts that hear misdemeanor criminal law cases are limited-jurisdiction courts in many states.

Because limited-jurisdiction courts are trial courts, evidence can be introduced and testimony can be given. Most limited-jurisdiction courts keep records of their proceedings. Their decisions can usually be appealed to a general-jurisdiction court or an appellate court.

small claims court
A court that hears civil cases involving small dollar amounts.

Many states have also created **small claims courts** to hear civil cases involving small dollar amounts (e.g., $5,000 or less). Generally, the parties must appear individually and cannot have lawyers represent them. The decisions of small claims courts are often appealable to general-jurisdiction trial courts or appellate courts.

General-Jurisdiction Trial Courts

general-jurisdiction trial court
A court that hears cases of a general nature that are not within the jurisdiction of limited-jurisdiction trial courts. Testimony and evidence at trial are recorded and stored for future reference.

Every state has a **general-jurisdiction trial court**. These courts are often referred to as **courts of record** because the testimony and evidence at trial are recorded and stored for future reference. These courts hear cases that are not within the jurisdiction of limited-jurisdiction trial courts, such as felonies, civil cases over a certain dollar amount, and so on.

Some states divide their general-jurisdiction courts into two divisions, one for criminal cases and another for civil cases. Evidence and testimony are given at general-jurisdiction trial courts. The decisions handed down by these courts are appealable to an intermediate appellate court or the state supreme court, depending on the circumstances.

Intermediate Appellate Courts

intermediate appellate court
An intermediate court that hears appeals from trial courts.

In many states, **intermediate appellate courts** (also called **appellate courts** or **courts of appeals**) hear appeals from trial courts. They review the trial court record to determine whether there have been any errors at trial that would require reversal or modification of the trial court's decision. Thus, an appellate court reviews either pertinent parts or the whole trial court record from the lower court. No new evidence or testimony is permitted.

The parties usually file legal *briefs* with the appellate court, stating the law and facts that support their positions. Appellate courts usually grant a brief oral hearing to the parties.

Appellate court decisions are appealable to the state's highest court. In sparsely populated states that do not have an intermediate appellate court, trial court decisions can be appealed directly to the state's highest court.

Highest State Court

Each state has a highest court in its court system. Most states call this highest court the **state supreme court**. Some states use other names for their highest courts. The function of a state's highest court is to hear appeals from intermediate appellate state courts and certain trial courts. No new evidence or testimony is heard. The parties usually submit pertinent parts of or the entire lower court record for review. The parties also submit legal briefs to the court and are usually granted a brief oral hearing. Decisions of highest state courts are final unless a question of law is involved that is appealable to the U.S. Supreme Court.

Exhibit 2.1 portrays a typical state court system. Exhibit 2.2 lists the websites for the court systems of 50 states and 4 jurisdictions associated with the United States.

state supreme court
The highest court in a state court system; it hears appeals from intermediate appellate state courts and certain trial courts.

■ EXHIBIT 2.1 Typical State Court System

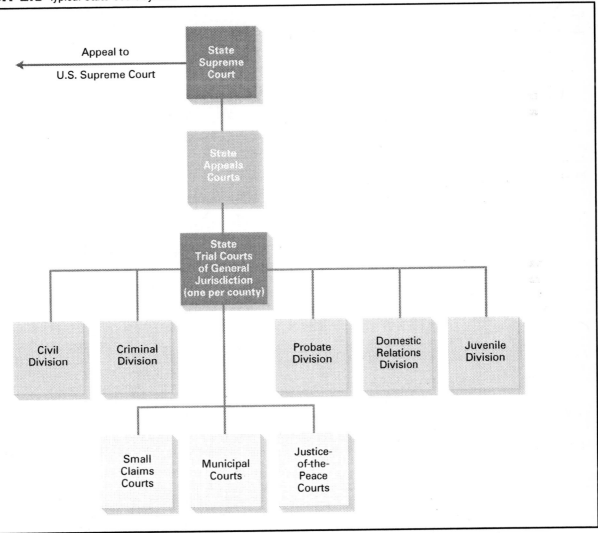

■ EXHIBIT 2.2 State Court Systems

State	Website	State	Website
Alabama	www.judicial.state.al.us	Montana	www.montanacourts.org
Alaska	www.state.ak.us/courts	Nebraska	court.nol.org
Arizona	www.supreme.state.az.us	Nevada	www.nvsupremecourt.us
Arkansas	www.courts.state.ar.us	New Hampshire	www.courts.state.nh.us
California	www.courtinfo.ca.gov/courts	New Jersey	www.judiciary.state.nj.us
Colorado	www.courts.state.co.us	New Mexico	www.nmcourts.com
Connecticut	www.jud.state.ct.us	New York	www.courts.state.ny.us
Delaware	www.courts.state.de.us	North Carolina	www.nccourts.org
District of Columbia	www.dccourts.gov	North Dakota	www.ndcourts.com
Florida	www.flcourts.org	Ohio	www.sconet.state.oh.us
Georgia	georgiacourts.org	Oklahoma	www.oscn.net/oscn/schome
Guam	www.guamsupremecourt.com	Oregon	www.ojd.state.or.us
Hawaii	www.courts.state.hi.us	Pennsylvania	www.courts.state.pa.us
Idaho	www.isc.idaho.gov	Puerto Rico	www.tribunalpr.org
Illinois	www.state.il.us/court	Rhode Island	www.courts.state.ri.us
Indiana	www.in.gov/judiciary	South Carolina	www.judicial.state.sc.us
Iowa	www.judicial.state.ia.us	South Dakota	www.sdjudicial.com
Kansas	www.kscourts.org	Tennessee	www.tsc.state.tn.us
Kentucky	www.courts.ky.gov	Texas	www.courts.state.tx.us
Louisiana	www.lasc.org	Utah	www.utcourts.gov
Maine	www.courts.state.me.us	Vermont	www.vermontjudiciary.org
Maryland	www.courts.state.md.us	Virginia	www.courts.state.va.us
Massachusetts	www.mass.gov/courts	Virgin Islands	www.visuperiorcourt.org
Michigan	www.courts.michigan.gov	Washington	www.courts.wa.gov
Minnesota	www.courts.state.mn.us	West Virginia	www.wv.gov
Mississippi	www.mssc.state.ms.us	Wisconsin	www.wicourts.gov
Missouri	www.courts.mo.gov	Wyoming	www.courts.state.wy.us

Contemporary Environment

Specialized Courts Hear Commercial Disputes

In most states, business and commercial disputes are heard by the same courts that hear and decide criminal, landlord–tenant, matrimonial, medical malpractice, and other non-business-related cases. The one major exception to this standard has been the state of Delaware, where a special chancery court hears and decides business litigation. The chancery court, which deals mainly with cases involving corporate government disputes, has earned a reputation for its expertise in handling and deciding corporate matters. Perhaps the existence of this special court and a corporation code that tends to favor corporate management are the primary reasons that more than 60 percent of the corporations listed on the New York Stock Exchange are incorporated in Delaware.

Businesses tend to favor special commercial courts because the judges presiding over them are expected to have the expertise to handle complex commercial lawsuits. The courts are also expected to be more efficient in deciding business-related cases, thus saving time and money for the parties. Other states are also establishing courts that specialize in commercial matters.

Federal Court System

Article III of the U.S. Constitution provides that the federal government's judicial power is vested in one "Supreme Court." This court is the U.S. Supreme Court. The Constitution also authorizes Congress to establish "inferior" federal courts. Pursuant to this power, Congress has established special federal courts, the U.S. district courts, and the U.S. courts of appeals. Federal judges are appointed for life by the president, with the advice and consent of the Senate (except bankruptcy court judges, who are appointed for 14-year terms).

Special Federal Courts

The **special federal courts** established by Congress have limited jurisdiction. They include the following:

special federal courts
Federal courts that hear matters of specialized or limited jurisdiction.

- **U.S. Tax Court.** The **U.S. Tax Court** hears cases that involve federal tax laws.
- **U.S. Court of Federal Claims.** The **U.S. Court of Federal Claims** hears cases brought against the United States.
- **U.S. Court of International Trade.** The **U.S. Court of International Trade** hears appeals of rulings of the U.S. Customs offices that involve tariffs and international commercial disputes.
- **U.S. Bankruptcy Court.** The **U.S. Bankruptcy Court** hears cases that involve federal bankruptcy laws.
- **U.S. Court of Appeals for the Armed Services.** The **U.S. Court of Appeals for the Armed Services** exercises appellate jurisdiction over members of the armed services.
- **U.S. Court of Appeals for Veterans Claims.** The **U.S. Court of Appeals for Veterans Claims** exercises jurisdiction over decisions of the Department of Veterans Affairs.

U.S. District Courts

The **U.S. district courts** are the federal court system's trial courts of general jurisdiction. There are 94 U.S. district courts. There is at least one federal district court in each state and the District of Columbia, and heavily populated states have more than one district court. The geographical area served by each court is referred to as a **district**. The federal district courts are empowered to impanel juries, receive evidence, hear testimony, and decide cases. Most federal cases originate in federal district courts.

U.S. district courts
The federal court system's trial courts of general jurisdiction.

U.S. Courts of Appeals

The **U.S. courts of appeals** are the federal court system's intermediate appellate courts. There are 13 circuits in the federal court system. The first 12 are geographical. Eleven are designated by numbers, such as the "First Circuit," "Second Circuit," and so on. The geographical area served by each court is referred to as a **circuit**. The 12th circuit court, located in Washington, DC, is called the **District of Columbia Circuit**.

Congress created the 13th court of appeals in 1982. It is called the **Court of Appeals for the Federal Circuit** and is located in Washington, DC.[1] This court has

U.S. courts of appeals
The federal court system's intermediate appellate courts.

Court of Appeals for the Federal Circuit
A U.S. Court of Appeals in Washington, DC, that has special appellate jurisdiction to review the decisions of the Court of Federal Claims, the Patent and Trademark Office, and the Court of International Trade.

■ **EXHIBIT 2.3**   Map of the Federal Circuit Courts

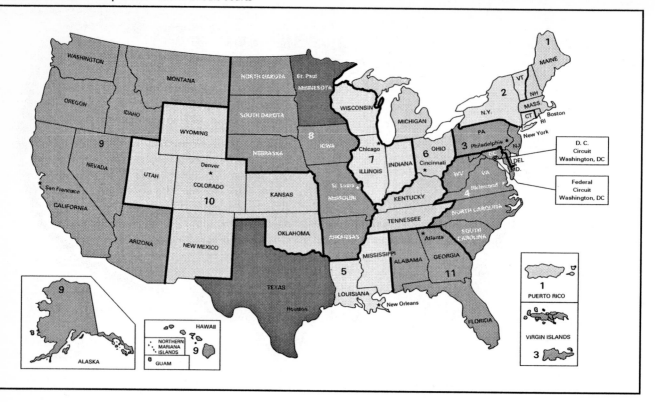

special appellate jurisdiction to review the decisions of the Court of Federal Claims, the Patent and Trademark Office, and the Court of International Trade. This court was created to provide uniformity in the application of federal law in certain areas, particularly patent law.

As an appellate court, each of these courts hears appeals from the district courts located in its circuit as well as from certain special courts and federal administrative agencies. An appellate court reviews the record of the lower court or administrative agency proceedings to determine whether there has been any error that would warrant reversal or modification of the lower court decision. No new evidence or testimony is heard. The parties file legal briefs with the court and are given a short oral hearing. Appeals are usually heard by a three-judge panel. After a decision is rendered by the three-judge panel, a petitioner can request a review *en banc* by the full court.

Exhibit 2.3 shows a map of the 13 federal circuit courts of appeals. Exhibit 2.4 lists the websites of the 13 U.S. courts of appeals.

■ **EXHIBIT 2.4** Federal Court of Appeals

United States Court of Appeals	Main Office	Website
First Circuit	Boston, Massachusetts	www.ca1.uscourts.gov
Second Circuit	New York, New York	www.ca2.uscourts.gov
Third Circuit	Philadelphia, Pennsylvania	www.ca3.uscourts.gov
Fourth Circuit	Richmond, Virginia	www.ca4.uscourts.gov
Fifth Circuit	Houston, Texas	www.ca5.uscourts.gov
Sixth Circuit	Cincinnati, Ohio	www.ca6.uscourts.gov
Seventh Circuit	Chicago, Illinois	www.ca7.uscourts.gov
Eighth Circuit	St. Paul, Minnesota	www.ca8.uscourts.gov
Ninth Circuit	San Francisco, California	www.ca9.uscourts.gov
Tenth Circuit	Denver, Colorado	www.ca10.uscourts.gov
Eleventh Circuit	Atlanta, Georgia	www.ca11.uscourts.gov
District of Columbia	Washington, DC	www.dcd.uscourts.gov
Court of Appeals for the Federal Circuit	Washington, DC	www.cafc.uscourts.gov

United States Supreme Court

The highest court in the land is the **U.S. Supreme Court**, located in Washington, DC. The Court is composed of nine justices who are nominated by the president and confirmed by the Senate. The president appoints one justice as **chief justice**, who is responsible for the administration of the Supreme Court. The other eight justices are **associate justices**.

Following is Alexis de Tocqueville's description of the Supreme Court's role in U.S. society:

> The peace, the prosperity, and the very existence of the Union are vested in the hands of the justices of the Supreme Court. Without them, the Constitution would be a dead letter: the executive appeals to them for assistance against the encroachments of the legislative power; the legislature demands their protection against the assaults of the executive; they defend the Union from the disobedience of the states, the states from the exaggerated claims of the Union; the public interest against private interests, and the conservative spirit of stability against the fickleness of the democracy.

Jurisdiction of the U.S. Supreme Court

The Supreme Court, which is an appellate court, hears appeals from federal circuit courts of appeals and, under certain circumstances, from federal district courts, special federal courts, and the highest state courts. No new evidence or testimony is heard. As with other

U.S. Supreme Court
The highest court in the United States, located in Washington, DC. The Supreme Court was created by Article III of the U.S. Constitution.

Supreme Court of the United States, Washington, DC. *The highest court in the land is the Supreme Court of the United States, located in Washington, DC. The U.S. Supreme Court decides the most important constitutional law cases and other important issues it deems ripe for review and decision. The Supreme Court's unanimous and majority decisions are precedent for all the other courts in the country.*

Contemporary Environment

The Process of Choosing Supreme Court Justices

In an effort to strike a balance of power between the executive and legislative branches of government, Article II, Section 2, of the U.S. Constitution gives the president the power to appoint Supreme Court justices "with the advice and consent of the Senate." This means that the majority of the 50 senators must approve the president's nominee in order for that nominee to become a justice of the U.S. Supreme Court.

President George W. Bush, a Republican, was given the chance to cast a conservative shadow over the Court's decisions when Justice Thurgood Marshall retired in 1991. Marshall, who served 24 years, was one of the most liberal members of the Court. President Bush nominated Clarence Thomas, an African American conservative, who was confirmed by the U.S. Senate with a 52–48 vote.

The election of Bill Clinton as president swung the pendulum back to the Democrats. President Clinton, with the consent of the Senate, replaced Justice Byron White, a Democrat-appointed liberal, with Ruth Bader Ginsburg, a moderate liberal.

President George W. Bush, a Republican, became president of the United States in January 2001 and served two terms. In 2005, then presiding Chief Justice Rehnquist died. President Bush nominated John G. Roberts, Jr., to be the next chief justice of the Supreme Court. Justice Roberts, a conservative, was easily confirmed by the Senate. In the same year, Justice Sandra Day O'Connor, the centrist vote on the Court, resigned from the Supreme Court. President Bush nominated Samuel A. Alito, Jr., a conservative, to fill the vacancy. Justice Alito was confirmed by a 58–42 vote of the Senate.

President Barack Obama, who was inaugurated in 2009, nominated two persons to the Court in 2010, Sonia Sotomayor (who was confirmed) and Elena Kagan.

■ EXHIBIT 2.5 Federal Court System

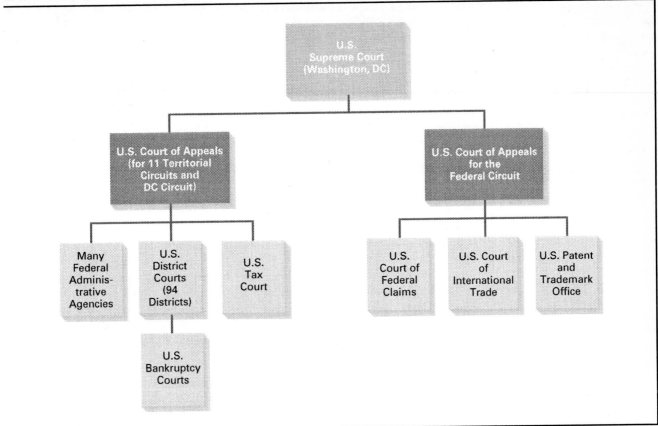

appellate courts, the lower court record is reviewed to determine whether there has been an error that warrants a reversal or modification of the decision. Legal briefs are filed, and the parties are granted a brief oral hearing. The Supreme Court's decision is final.

The federal court system is illustrated in Exhibit 2.5.

Decisions of the U.S. Supreme Court

The U.S. Constitution gives Congress the authority to establish rules for the appellate review of cases by the Supreme Court, except in the rare case in which mandatory review is required. Congress has given the Supreme Court discretion to decide what cases it will hear.[2]

A petitioner must file a **petition for certiorari**, asking the Supreme Court to hear the case. If the Court decides to review a case, it issues a **writ of certiorari**. Because the Court issues only about 100 opinions each year, writs are granted only in cases involving constitutional and other important issues.

Each justice of the Supreme Court, including the chief justice, has an equal vote. The Supreme Court can issue several types of decisions, as described in the following paragraphs.

Unanimous Decision   If all the justices voting agree as to the outcome and reasoning used to decide a case, it is a **unanimous decision**. Unanimous decisions are precedent for later cases.

Example
Suppose all nine justices hear a case, and all nine agree to the outcome (e.g., the petitioner wins) and the reason why (e.g., the Equal Protection Clause of the U.S. Constitution had been violated); this is a unanimous decision. This unanimous decision becomes precedent for later cases.

petition for certiorari
A petition asking the Supreme Court to hear a case.
writ of certiorari
An official notice that the Supreme Court will review a case.

Majority Decision   If a majority of the justices agree as to the outcome and reasoning used to decide a case, it is a **majority decision**. Majority decisions are precedent for later cases. A majority decision occurs if five, six, seven, or eight justices vote for the same outcome for the same reason.

Example

If all nine justices hear a case, and five of them agree as to the outcome (e.g., the petitioner wins) and all of these five justices agree to the same reason why (e.g., the Equal Protection Clause of the U.S. Constitution has been violated), it is a majority opinion. The majority opinion becomes precedent for later cases and has the same force of law as a unanimous decision. The remaining four justices' vote for the respondent has no legal effect whatsoever.

Plurality Decision   If a majority of the justices agree as to the outcome of a case but not as to the reasoning for reaching the outcome, it is a **plurality decision**. A plurality decision settles the case but is not precedent for later cases.

Example

If all nine justices hear a case, and five of them agree as to the outcome (e.g., the petitioner wins), but not all of these five agree to the reason why (e.g., three base their vote on a violation of the Equal Protection Clause and two base their vote on a violation of the Freedom of Speech Clause of the U.S. Constitution), it is a plurality decision. Five justices have agreed to the same outcome, but those five have not agreed for the same reason. The petitioner wins his or her case, but the decision is not precedent for later cases. The remaining four justices' votes for the respondent have no legal effect whatsoever.

Tie Decision   Sometimes the Supreme Court sits without all nine justices being present. This could happen because of illness, conflict of interest, or a justice not having been confirmed to fill a vacant seat on the Court. If there is a **tie decision**, the lower court decision is affirmed. Such votes are not precedent for later cases.

Example

A petitioner wins her case at the U.S. Court of Appeals. At the U.S. Supreme Court, only eight justices hear the case. Four justices vote for the petitioner, and four justices vote for the respondent. This is a tie vote. The petitioner remains the winner because she won at the Court of Appeals. This decision of the Supreme Court sets no precedent for later cases.

Contemporary Environment

"I'll Take You to the U.S. Supreme Court!"

In reality, the chance of ever having your case heard by the highest court is slim to none. Each year, more than 7,000 petitioners ask the Supreme Court to hear their cases. These petitioners usually pay big law firms from $30,000 to $200,000 or more to write the appeal petition. In recent years, the Supreme Court has accepted only fewer than 100 of these cases for full review each term.

Each of the nine Supreme Court justices has three law clerks—recent law school graduates usually chosen from elite law schools across the country—who assist them. The justices rarely read the appellate petitions but instead delegate this task to their law clerks. A clerk writes a short memorandum, discussing the key issues raised by the appeal, and recommends to the justices whether they should grant or deny a review. The justices meet once a week to discuss what cases merit review. The votes of four justices are necessary to grant an appeal and schedule an oral argument before the Court ("**rule of four**"). Written opinions by the justices are usually issued many months later.

So what does it take to win a review by the Supreme Court? The U.S. Supreme Court usually decides to hear cases involving major constitutional questions, such as freedom of speech, freedom of religion, equal protection, and due process. The Supreme Court also hears many cases involving the interpretation of statutes enacted by Congress. The Court rarely decides day-to-day legal issues such as breach of contract, tort liability, or corporations law unless they involve more important constitutional or federal law questions.

So the next time you hear someone say, "I'll take you to the U.S. Supreme Court!" just say, "Probably not!"

Concurring Opinion   A justice who agrees with the outcome of a case but not the reason proffered by other justices can issue a **concurring opinion** that sets forth his or her reasons for deciding the case.

Dissenting Opinion   A justice who does not agree with a decision can file a **dissenting opinion** that sets forth the reasons for his or her dissent.

Jurisdiction of Federal and State Courts

Federal courts and state courts each have jurisdiction to hear and decide certain types of cases.

Jurisdiction of Federal Courts

Article III, Section 2, of the U.S. Constitution sets forth the jurisdiction of federal courts. Federal courts have *limited jurisdiction* to hear cases involving a federal question or based on diversity of citizenship.

Federal Question   The federal courts have jurisdiction to hear cases involving "federal questions." **Federal question cases** are cases arising under the U.S. Constitution, treaties, and federal statutes and regulations. There is no dollar-amount limit on federal question cases that can be brought in federal court.[3]

Diversity of Citizenship   A case may be brought in federal court if there is diversity of citizenship. **Diversity of citizenship** occurs if a lawsuit involves (1) citizens of different states or (2) a citizen of a state and a citizen or subject of a foreign country. Diversity of citizenship is used to bring or maintain a lawsuit in federal court when the subject matter of the lawsuit involves a nonfederal question. A corporation is considered to be a citizen of the state in which it is incorporated and in which it has its principal place of business.

The reason for providing diversity of citizenship jurisdiction to federal courts was to prevent state court bias against nonresidents. The federal court must apply the appropriate state's law in deciding the case. The dollar amount of the controversy must exceed $75,000.[4] If this requirement is not met, action must be brought in the appropriate state court.

Exclusive Jurisdiction   Federal courts have **exclusive jurisdiction** to hear cases involving federal crimes, antitrust, bankruptcy, patent and copyright cases, suits against the United States, and most admiralty cases. State courts cannot hear these cases.

federal question case
A case arising under the U.S. Constitution, treaties, or federal statutes and regulations.

diversity of citizenship
A means for bringing a lawsuit in federal court that involves a nonfederal question if the parties are (1) citizens of different states or (2) a citizen of a state and a citizen or subject of a foreign country.

exclusive jurisdiction
Jurisdiction held by only one court.

Concept Summary
Jurisdiction of Federal Courts

Type of Jurisdiction	Description
Federal question	Cases arising under the U.S. Constitution, treaties, and federal statutes and regulations. There is no dollar-amount limit in federal question cases.
Diversity of citizenship	Cases between citizens of different states or between a citizen of a state and a citizen or subject of a foreign country. Federal courts must apply the appropriate state law in such cases. The controversy must exceed $75,000 for the federal court to hear the case.

Jurisdiction of State Courts

State courts have jurisdiction to hear cases that federal courts do not have jurisdiction to hear. These usually involve state laws.

Examples
Real estate, corporations, partnerships, limited liability companies, contracts, sales and lease contracts, and negotiable instruments are state law subject matters. (Remember that state law cases that involve diversity of citizenship can be heard by federal courts.)

■ EXHIBIT 2.6 Jurisdiction of Federal and State Courts

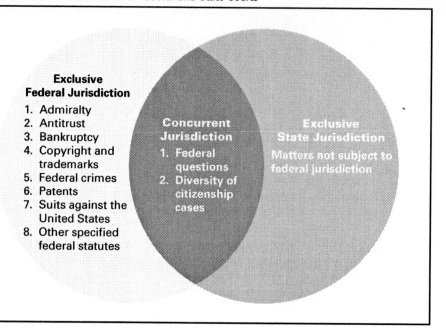

Exclusive Federal Jurisdiction
1. Admiralty
2. Antitrust
3. Bankruptcy
4. Copyright and trademarks
5. Federal crimes
6. Patents
7. Suits against the United States
8. Other specified federal statutes

Concurrent Jurisdiction
1. Federal questions
2. Diversity of citizenship cases

Exclusive State Jurisdiction
Matters not subject to federal jurisdiction

concurrent jurisdiction
Jurisdiction shared by two or more courts.

State courts have **concurrent jurisdiction** with federal courts to hear cases involving diversity of citizenship and federal questions over which federal courts do not have exclusive jurisdiction.

If a case involving concurrent jurisdiction is brought by a plaintiff in federal court, the case remains in federal court. If the plaintiff brings a case involving concurrent jurisdiction in state court, the defendant can either let the case be decided by the state court or remove the case to federal court.

If a case does not qualify to be brought in federal court, it must be brought in the appropriate state court.

Exhibit 2.6 illustrates the jurisdiction of federal and state courts.

In the following case, the court had to decide which state's law applied to a case.

Personal Jurisdiction of Courts

Not every court has the authority to hear all types of cases. First, to bring a lawsuit in a court, the plaintiff must have *standing to sue*. In addition, the court must have *personal jurisdiction* to hear the case, and the case must be brought in the proper *venue*. These topics are discussed in the following paragraphs.

Standing to Sue

standing to sue
Some stake in the outcome of a lawsuit.

To bring a lawsuit, a plaintiff must have **standing to sue**. This means the plaintiff must have some stake in the outcome of the lawsuit.

Example

Linda's friend Jon is injured in an accident caused by Emily. Jon refuses to sue. Linda cannot sue Emily on Jon's behalf because she does not have an interest in the result of the case.

A few states now permit investors to invest money in a lawsuit for a percentage return of any award of judgment. Courts hear and decide actual disputes involving specific controversies. Hypothetical questions will not be heard, and trivial lawsuits will be dismissed.

In the following case, the court had to decide which state's law applied to a case.

CASE 2.1
Jurisdiction of Courts

Bertram v. Norden, et al.

159 Ohio App.3d 171, 823 N.E.2d 478,
Web 2004 Ohio App. Lexis 5500 (2004)
Court of Appeals of Ohio

"We note that Michigan is a known snowmobiling destination, and, as such, Michigan lawmakers have taken steps to deal with the liability issues that go along with the dangers of snowmobiling."

—Judge Rogers

Facts

Four friends, John Bertram, Matt Norden, Scott Olson, and Tony Harvey, all residents of Ohio, traveled to the Upper Peninsula of Michigan to go snowmobiling. On their first day of snowmobiling, after going about 135 miles, the lead snowmobiler, Olson, came to a stop sign on the snowmobile trail, where it intersected a private driveway. As Olson approached the sign, he gave the customary hand signal and stopped his snowmobile. Harvey, second in line, was going too fast to stop, so Olson pulled his snowmobile to the right side of the private driveway. Harvey, to avoid hitting Olson, pulled his snowmobile to the left and went over a five- or six-foot snow embankment. Bertram, third in line, going about 30 miles per hour, slammed on his break, turned 45 degrees, and slammed into Olson's snowmobile. Bertram was thrown from his snowmobile. Norden, fourth in line, could not stop, and his snowmobile hit Bertram's leg. Bertram's tibia and fibula were both fractured and protruded through his skin. Bertram underwent surgery to repair the broken bones.

Bertram filed a lawsuit against Olson, Harvey, and Norden in a trial court in Ohio, claiming that each of his friends was liable to him for their negligent snowmobile operation. The Ohio court held that Michigan law applied and that a Michigan statute specifically stated that snowmobilers assumed the risks associated with snowmobiling. The court therefore held that the three friends were not liable to Bertram and granted their motions for summary judgment. Ohio law did not contain an assumption of the risk rule regarding snowmobiling. Bertram appealed, alleging that Ohio law applied to the case because all of the parties were from Ohio.

Issue

Does Michigan or Ohio law apply to this case?

Language of the Court

Because the accident took place in Michigan, we must presume that Michigan law applies absent any other jurisdiction having more substantial contacts. Bertram, however, contends that Ohio law should apply, because all of the parties were residents of Ohio at the time of the accident and all consequences flowing from his injury occurred in Ohio. We disagree.

Because the snowmobiling accident took place in Michigan, the place where the conduct causing Bertram's injury occurred in Michigan and Michigan has enacted specific legislation involving the risks of snowmobiling, we find that Michigan law clearly controls in this case. While all parties are residents of and have their relationships in the State of Ohio, we are not persuaded by Bertram's argument that this issue should control.

Decision

The Court of Appeals of Ohio held that the law of the state of Michigan, where the accident occurred, and not the law of the state of Ohio, the state of the residence of the parties, should apply. The court upheld the trial court's application of Michigan assumption of the risk statute to this case and affirmed the trial court's grant of summary judgment to the three defendant friends of plaintiff Bertram.

Case Questions

Critical Legal Thinking What does the doctrine of assumption of the risk provide? Explain.

Business Ethics Was it ethical for Bertram to sue his three friends for negligence? Why or why not?

Contemporary Business Why did Bertram want Ohio law, and not Michigan law, to apply to the case?

In Personam Jurisdiction

in personam jurisdiction
Jurisdiction over the parties to a lawsuit.

service of process
A summons being served on the defendant to obtain personal jurisdiction over him or her.

Jurisdiction over a person is called ***in personam* jurisdiction**, or **personal jurisdiction**. A *plaintiff*, by filing a lawsuit with a court, gives the court *in personam* jurisdiction over himself or herself. The court must also have *in personam* jurisdiction over the *defendant*, which is usually obtained by having a summons served to that person within the territorial boundaries of the state (i.e., **service of process**). Service of process is usually accomplished by personal service of the summons and complaint on the defendant.

If personal service is not possible, alternative forms of notice, such as mailing of the summons or publication of a notice in a newspaper, may be permitted. A corporation is subject to personal jurisdiction in the state in which it is incorporated, has its principal office, and is doing business.

A party who disputes the jurisdiction of a court can make a *special appearance* in that court to argue against imposition of jurisdiction. Service of process is not permitted during such an appearance.

Landmark U.S. Supreme Court Case

International Shoe Company v. State of Washington

How far can a state go to require a person or business to defend himself or itself in a court of law in that state? That question was present to the Supreme Court of the United States in the landmark case **International Shoe Company v. State of Washington**.[5]

The International Shoe Company was a Delaware corporation that had its principal place of business in St. Louis, Missouri. The company manufactured and distributed shoes throughout the United States. The company maintained a sales force throughout the United States. In the state of Washington, its sales representative did not have a specific office but sold shoes door-to-door and sometimes at temporary locations. The sales representatives were paid commissions based on the number of shoes they sold.

The state of Washington assessed an unemployment tax on International Shoe for the sales representative it had in the state. When International Shoe failed to pay, Washington served personal service on a sales representative of the company in Washington and mailed the service of process to the company's headquarters in St. Louis. International Shoe appeared specially to argue that it did not do sufficient business in Washington to warrant having to pay unemployment taxes in that state. The office of unemployment ruled against International Shoe, and the appeals tribunal, the superior court, and supreme court of Washington agreed. International Shoe appealed to the U.S. Supreme Court.

In its decision, the U.S. Supreme Court noted, "due process requires only that in order to subject a defendant to

a judgment in personam, if he be not present within the territory of the forum, he have certain minimum contacts with it such that the maintenance of that suit does not offend 'traditional notions of fair play and substantial justice.'"

The Supreme Court stated:

Applying these standards, the activities carried on in behalf of International Shoe in the state of Washington were neither irregular nor causal. They were systematic and continuous throughout the years in question. They resulted in a large volume of interstate business, in the course of which International Shoe received the benefits and protection of the laws of the state, including the right to resort to the courts for the enforcement of its rights. The obligation which is here sued upon arose out of those very activities. It is evident that these operations establish sufficient contacts or ties with the state of the forum to make it reasonable and just, according to our traditional conception of fair play and substantial justice, to permit the state to enforce the obligations which International Shoe has incurred there. Hence, we cannot say that the maintenance of the present suit in the state of Washington involves an unreasonable or undue procedure.

Thus, the famous "minimum contacts" test and "traditional notions of fair play and substantial justice" establish when a state may subject a person or business to the walls of its courtrooms. Obviously, this is not a bright-line test, so battles of in personam jurisdiction abound to this day.

In Rem Jurisdiction

A court may have jurisdiction to hear and decide a case because it has jurisdiction over the property of the lawsuit. This is called *in rem* **jurisdiction** ("jurisdiction over the thing"). For example, a state court would have jurisdiction to hear a dispute over the ownership of a piece of real estate located within the state. This is so even if one or more of the disputing parties live in another state or states.

in rem **jurisdiction**
Jurisdiction to hear a case because of jurisdiction over the property of the lawsuit.

Quasi In Rem Jurisdiction

Sometimes a plaintiff who obtains a judgment against a defendant in one state will try to collect the judgment by attaching property of the defendant that is located in another state. This is permitted under *quasi in rem* **jurisdiction**, or **attachment jurisdiction**. Under the **Full Faith and Credit Clause** of the U.S. Constitution (Article IV, Section 1), a judgment of a court of one state must be given "full faith and credit" by the courts of another state.

quasi in rem **jurisdiction**
Jurisdiction that allows a plaintiff who obtains a judgment in one state to try to collect the judgment by attaching property of the defendant located in another state.

Concept Summary
In personam, In Rem, and *Quasi In Rem* Jurisdiction

Type of Jurisdiction	Description
In personam jurisdiction	With *in personam* jurisdiction, a court has jurisdiction over the parties to the lawsuit. The plaintiff submits to the jurisdiction of the court by filing the lawsuit there. Personal jurisdiction is obtained over the defendant through *service of process* to that person.
In rem jurisdiction	With *in rem* jurisdiction, a court has jurisdiction to hear and decide a case because it has jurisdiction over the property at issue in the lawsuit (e.g., real property located in the state).
Quasi in rem jurisdiction	A plaintiff who obtains a judgment against a defendant in one state may utilize the court system of another state to attach property of the defendant that is located in the second state.

Long-Arm Statute

In most states, a state court can obtain jurisdiction over persons and businesses located in another state or country through the state's **long-arm statute**. These statutes extend a state's jurisdiction to nonresidents who were not served a summons within the state. The nonresident must have had some **minimum contact** with the state.[6] In addition, the maintenance of the suit must uphold the traditional notions of fair play and substantial justice.

The exercise of long-arm jurisdiction is generally permitted over nonresidents who have (1) committed torts within the state (e.g., caused an automobile accident in the state), (2) entered into a contract either in the state or that affects the state (and allegedly breached the contract), or (3) transacted other business in the state that allegedly caused injury to another person.

long-arm statute
A statue that extends a stat's jurisdiction to nonresidents who were not served as summons within the state.

Venue

Venue requires lawsuits to be heard by the court with jurisdiction nearest the location in which the incident occurred or where the parties reside.

venue
A concept that requires lawsuits to be heard by the court with jurisdiction that is nearest the location in which the incident occurred or where the parties reside.

Example

Harry, a resident of the state of Georgia, commits a felony crime in Los Angeles County, California. The California state Superior Court located in Los Angeles is the proper venue because the crime was committed there, the witnesses are probably from the area, and so on. Although Harry lives in Georgia, the state of Georgia is not the proper venue for this case.

Occasionally, pretrial publicity may prejudice jurors located in the proper venue. In such cases, a **change of venue** may be requested so that a more impartial jury can be found. The courts generally frown upon **forum shopping** (i.e., looking for a favorable court without a valid reason).

Forum-Selection and Choice-of-Law Clauses

forum-selection clause

A contract provision that designates a certain court to hear any dispute concerning nonperformance of the contract.

choice-of-law clause

A contract provision that designates a certain state's law or country's law that will be applied in any dispute concerning nonperformance of the contract.

One issue that often comes up when parties from different states have a legal dispute is which state's court will be used, or which federal courts in either of the states will hear the case. When the parties have not agreed in advance, courts must make the decision about which court has jurisdiction. Also, sometimes there is a dispute as to which state's laws apply to a case. If there is a dispute regarding the correct court to hear the case, or what law applies to the case, a court will make that decision. This will cost time and money.

Therefore, parties sometimes agree in their contract as to what state's courts, what federal courts, or what country's court will have jurisdiction to hear a legal dispute should one arise. Such clauses in contracts are called **forum-selection clauses**.

In addition to agreeing to a forum, the parties also often agree in contracts as to what state's law or country's law will apply in resolving a dispute. These clauses are called **choice-of-law clauses**.

Test Review Terms and Concepts

Associate justice
Change of venue
Chief justice
Choice-of-law clause
Circuit
Concurrent jurisdiction
Concurring opinion
Court of Appeals for the Federal Circuit
Dissenting opinion
District
District of Columbia circuit
Diversity of citizenship
Exclusive jurisdiction
Federal question case
Forum shopping
Forum-selection clause
Full Faith and Credit Clause
General-jurisdiction trial court (court of record)

In personam jurisdiction (personal jurisdiction)
In rem jurisdiction
Intermediate appellate court (appellate court or court of appeals)
International Shoe Company v. State of Washington
Limited-jurisdiction trial court (inferior trial court)
Long-arm statute
Majority decision
Minimum contact
Petition for certiorari
Plurality decision
Quasi in rem jurisdiction (attachment jurisdiction)
"Rule of four"
Service of process
Small claims court

Special federal court
Standing to sue
State courts
State supreme court
Tie decision
Unanimous decision
U.S. Bankruptcy Court
U.S. Court of Appeals
U.S. Court of Appeals for the Armed Services
U.S. Court of Appeals for Veterans Claims
U.S. Court of Federal Claims
U.S. Court of International Trade
U.S. District Court
U.S. Supreme Court
U.S. Tax Court
Venue
Writ of certiorari

Case Problems

2.1 Federal Question: Nutrilab, Inc., manufactures and markets a product known as "Starch Blockers." The purpose of the product is to block the human body's digestion of starch as an aid in controlling weight. The U.S. FDA classified Starch Blockers as a drug and requested that it be removed from the market until the FDA approved its use. The FDA claimed that it had the right to classify new products as drugs and prevent their distribution until their safety is determined. Nutrilab disputed the FDA's decision and wanted to bring suit to halt the FDA's actions. Do the federal courts have jurisdiction to hear this case? *Nutrilab, Inc. v. Schweiker*, 713 F.2d 335, **Web** 1983 U.S. App. Lexis 25121 (United States Court of Appeals for the Seventh Circuit)

2.2 Jurisdiction: James Clayton Allison, a resident of the state of Mississippi, was employed by the Tru-Amp Corporation as a circuit breaker tester. As part of his employment, Allison was sent to inspect, clean, and test a switch gear located at the South Central Bell Telephone Facility in Brentwood, Tennessee. One day, when he attempted to remove a circuit breaker manufactured by ITE Corporation (ITE) from a bank of breakers, a portion of the breaker fell off. The broken piece fell behind a switching bank and, according to Allison, caused an electrical fire and explosion. Allison was severely burned in the accident. Allison brought suit against ITE in a Mississippi state court, claiming more than $50,000 in damages. Can this suit be removed to federal court? *Allison v. ITE Imperial Corp.*, 729 F.Supp. 45, **Web** 1990 U.S. Dist. Lexis 607 (United States District Court for the Southern District of Mississippi)

2.3 Long-Arm Statute: Sean O'Grady, a professional boxer, was managed by his father, Pat. Sean was a contender for the world featherweight title. Pat entered into a contract with Magna Verde Corporation, a Los Angeles–based business, to co-promote a fight between Sean and the then-current featherweight champion. The fight was scheduled to take place in Oklahoma City, Oklahoma. To promote the fight, Pat O'Grady scheduled a press conference. At the conference, Pat was involved in a confrontation with a sportswriter named Brooks. He allegedly struck Brooks in the face. Brooks brought suit against Pat O'Grady and Magna Verde Corporation in an Oklahoma state court. Court records showed that the only contact Magna Verde had with Oklahoma was that a few of its employees had taken several trips to Oklahoma to plan the title fight. The fight was never held. Oklahoma has a long-arm statute. Magna Verde was served by mail and made a special appearance in Oklahoma state court to argue that Oklahoma does not have personal jurisdiction over it. Does Oklahoma have jurisdiction over Magna Verde Corporation? *Brooks v. Magna Verde Corp.*, 1980 Ok. Civ. App. 40, 619 P.2d 1271, **Web** 1980 Okla. Civ. App. Lexis 118 (Court of Appeals of Oklahoma)

2.4 Minimum Contacts: The National Enquirer, Inc., is a Florida corporation with its principal place of business in Florida. It publishes the *National Enquirer*, a national weekly newspaper with a total circulation of more than 5 million copies. About 600,000 copies, almost twice the level in the next highest state, are sold in California. The *Enquirer* published an article about Shirley Jones, an entertainer. Jones, a California resident, filed a lawsuit in California state court against the *Enquirer* and its president, who was a resident of Florida. The suit sought damages for alleged defamation, invasion of privacy, and intentional infliction of emotional distress. Are the defendants subject to suit in California? *Calder v. Jones*, 465 U.S. 783, 104 S.Ct. 1482, 79 L.Ed.2d 804, **Web** 1984 U.S. Lexis 4 (Supreme Court of the United States)

Business Ethics Case

2.5 Business Ethics: One day, Joshua Gnaizda, a three-year-old, received what he (or his mother) thought was a tantalizing offer in the mail from Time, Inc. The front of the envelope contained a see-through window that revealed the following statement: "Joshua Gnaizda, I'll give you this versatile new calculator watch free just for opening this envelope." Beneath the offer was a picture of the calculator watch itself. When Joshua's mother opened the envelope, she realized that the see-through window had not revealed the full text of Time's offer. Not viewable through the see-through window were the following words: "And mailing this Certificate today." The certificate required Joshua to purchase a subscription to *Fortune* magazine in order to receive the free calculator watch. Joshua (through his father, a lawyer) sued Time in a class action, seeking compensatory damages in an amount equal to the value of the calculator watch and $15 million in punitive damages. The trial court dismissed the lawsuit as being too trivial for the court to hear. Joshua appealed. Should Joshua be permitted to maintain his lawsuit against Time, Inc.? Did Time act ethically? Should Joshua's father have sued for $15 million? *Harris v. Time, Inc.*, 191 Cal.App.3d 449, 237 Cal.Rptr. 584, **Web** 1987 Cal.App. Lexis 1619 (Court of Appeals of California)

Endnotes

1. Federal Courts Improvement Act of 1982. Public Law 97–164, 96 Stat. 25, 28 U.S.C. Section 1292 and Section 1295.
2. Effective September 25, 1988, mandatory appeals were all but eliminated, except for reapportionment cases and cases brought under the Civil Rights Act and Voting Rights Act, antitrust laws, and the Presidential Election Campaign Fund Act.
3. Prior to 1980, there was a minimum dollar amount controversy requirement of $10,000 to bring a federal question action in federal court. This minimum amount was eliminated by the Federal Question Jurisdictional Amendment Act of 1980, Public Law 96–486.
4. The amount was raised to $75,000 by the 1996 Federal Courts Improvement Act. Title 28 U.S.C. Section 1332(a).
5. 326 U.S. 310, 66 S.Ct. 154, 90 L.Ed 95, **Web** 1945 U.S. Lexis 1447 (Supreme Court of the United States).
6. *International Shoe Co. v. Washington*, 326 U.S. 310, 66 S.Ct. 154, 90 L.Ed. 95, **Web** 1945 U.S. Lexis 1447 (Supreme Court of the United States).

The Courts of New York

By Percy L. Lambert J.D.

The present New York court system has its genesis in the New York constitution of 1895. Article VI of the constitution describes and explains the role and power of the judiciary and the extent of each court's jurisdiction. The courts operated under the 1895 constitution for sixty-five years with minor changes coming in 1925 and major changes occurring in 1961 and 1977 by amendments to the constitution. The amendments of 1961 provided for a unified court system and those enacted in 1977 provided for a streamlined administrative structure, the appointment of the state's highest judges and the creation of a commission to oversee and regulate judicial conduct.

All New York courts are constitutionally established. They are courts of limited jurisdiction, with the competence of particular courts specified in the provisions of the state constitution and various legislative statutes. The courts are limited by precluding them from granting certain types of relief to litigants, from entertaining certain kinds of actions, geographically, monetarily, and, as the text explains, its jurisdiction is equally limited by the paramount authority of the federal courts to exercise exclusive jurisdiction over certain matters. Where federal law preempts state court action, no state court can exercise jurisdiction whether the parties consent or desire it.

In New York the court of last resort is the Court of Appeals. The intermediate appellate courts are the Appellate Divisions of the Supreme Court. Also, where established, the Appellate Terms of the Supreme Court has jurisdiction over appeals from District, City, Town and Village Courts.

The state court of general jurisdiction is the New York Supreme Court, which is state-wide. The New York County Court has general criminal jurisdiction but otherwise limited jurisdiction. Those other courts in New York possessed of limited jurisdictions are: Family Courts, Court of Claims, Surrogate Courts, Civil Court of New York City, Criminal Courts of New York City, District Courts, City Courts, Town Courts and Village Courts.

Under the unified court system, standards and policy of state-wide application are promulgated and supervised by the Chief Administrator on behalf of the Court of Appeals. These standards are promulgated by the Chief Judge *after* consultation with the Administrative Board of the Judicial Conference and approve of the Court of Appeals. With the exception of town and village justices, all judges or justices of the state must be admitted to the Bar of New York. They must have been members of the Bar for at least five years, excluding those serving on the Appellate Courts, the Supreme Court and the Court of Claims, who must have been members for at least ten years. Non-lawyers may serve as town and village justices.

New York courts in civil matters are governed by the Civil Practice Law and Rules; in criminal matters it is governed by the Criminal Procedure Act.

New York courts, with the exception of justice courts, are financed by the state and are administered by the Office of Court Administration under the authority of the Chief Judge of the State of New York. Each of these courts is discussed more fully below.

An understanding of the court structure of New York begins with the court of last resort:

Court of Appeals

The Court of Appeals is the highest court in the state and the court of last resort for most cases. It is generally the ultimate authority on questions of law in New York State. Although a few cases, involving questions of federal law or the United States Constitution, eventually may be taken to the United States Supreme Court, these are rare. The Court of Appeals hears both criminal and civil appeals. (The distinctions between criminal and civil cases are discussed in later sections.)

This court, which convenes in Albany, consists of six associate judges and one Chief Judge, who also serves as Chief Judge of the State and chief judicial officer of the unified court system. All judges of this court are appointed by the Governor, with the advice and consent of the senate, from a list prepared by a nonpartisan nominating commission.

Appeals in civil cases must first be heard in one of the appellate divisions of the state's Supreme Court before being taken to the Court of Appeals. However, cases involving only questions of statute's constitutionality may go directly to the Court of Appeals from the trial court. In cases that come through the Appellate Division, the appellant generally must obtain permission to appeal to the Court of Appeals. The only instances in which a case will automatically be sent to the Court of Appeals are when two justices of the Appellate Division dissent or a state or federal constitutional question is presented.

Criminal cases must be appealed to the Appellate Division or the Appellate Term first, and special permission must be obtained before the case may be taken to the Court of Appeals. The death penalty was declared unconstitutional as written in People v. Stephen Yaboll.

In addition to hearing appeals, the Court of Appeals is responsible for determining policy for the administration of the state's court system and for adopting rules governing the admission of attorneys to the bar.

Appellate Division of Supreme Court

The Appellate Division of the Supreme Court is the intermediate appellate court of the state. It hears civil and criminal appeals, reviewing the record established at trial in lower Courts. The Appellate Division is divided geographically into four departments throughout the state; each department is responsible for hearing most appeals from the courts within its geographical area.

Justices of the Appellate Division are appointed by the Governor from among Supreme Court justices. The number of justices in each department will vary between four and five, depending on the caseload. Each department of the Appellate Division is responsible for admitting to practice and disciplining attorneys within its respective geographical region.

Appellate Term of Supreme Court

The four departments of the Appellate Division are divided further into 12 judicial districts (see chart). The Appellate Term of the Supreme Court is unique to the First and Second Judicial Departments (New York City; Nassau, Suffolk, Rockland, Westchester, Putnam, Dutchess and Orange Counties). The Appellate Term, which is composed of justices of the Supreme Court chosen by the Chief Administrator of the Courts with approval of the presiding of the Appellate Division, hears appeals from local and county courts. At least two and no more than three justices will preside in any case.

Supreme Court

The Supreme Court is the statewide trial court with the broadest jurisdiction, both criminal and civil. It can hear virtually any type of case brought before it, with the exception of claims against the state, which must be brought in the Court of Claims.

The Supreme Court's practically unlimited jurisdiction makes its caseload correspondingly heavier than that of other courts. Consequently, attempts are generally made throughout the state to divide the workload among the Supreme Court and the lower courts of limited jurisdiction.

One area in which the Supreme Court must be involved, however, is in proceedings to end a marriage since it is the only court that can grant a divorce, annulment or separation.

As noted above, the Supreme Court is divided into 12 judicial districts statewide, and justices are elected in each district for terms of 14 years.

Judges of the Court of Claims have the sole responsibility for hearing claims brought against the state of New York or certain state agencies.

Judges of the Court of Claims are appointed by the Governor, with the advice and consent of the state senate, for terms of nine years.

Family Court

The Family Court was established in 1962 to replace the Children's Court and New York City's Domestic Relations Court. The Family Court handles most cases involving youths between the ages of 8 and 16 who are charged with offenses that would be crimes if committed by adults.

It also hears cases involving family disputes and child custody, determines support payments for families, handles adoptions, and may even determine the parentage of a child through paternity proceedings.

Family Court deals with all types of family problems except termination of a marriage, which the Supreme Court handles (see above). Family Court judges serve for ten-year terms. Outside New York City, they are elected; within the city of New York, such judges are appointed by the Mayor.

Civil Court of the City of New York

The Civil Court hears civil cases in the City of New York involving amounts up to $25,000 exclusive of interest and costs. It includes a small claims part for the informal disposition of minor matters, and a landlord tenant part. The New York City Civil Court does not have general jurisdiction in equitable matters, but has unlimited jurisdiction over proceedings to recover real property located in New York City and landlord-tenant matters regardless of amount. There is no monetary limitation on counterclaims in this court. Appeals from the NYC Civil Court are heard in the Appellate Terms of the Supreme Court.

Surrogate's Court

The Surrogate's Court is responsible for all matters relating to the property of deceased persons and to guardianships. Whether or not a person leaves a valid will all claims on the estate brought by heirs, legatees or creditors are handled by the Surrogate's Court.

Judges of this court are elected in each county for terms of 10 years (14 years in New York City). Matters commonly dealt with in the Surrogate's Court include the probate of wills; the appointment and control of executors, administrator and trustees; adoptions; and the final settlement of estates.

County Court

A County Court exists in each county of the state outside New York City (see "LOCAL COURTS" below for equivalent in New York City). Judges are elected for ten-year terms, with the number of judges varying according to population. County Court judges preside over both criminal and civil cases.

Although the County court's jurisdiction over criminal matters is almost unlimited (as is the Supreme Court's), its jurisdiction in civil cases is more restricted. Money claims in cases to be tried in this court may not exceed $25,000.

In sparsely populated counties, a single judge may be responsible for the Family Court. They need not be lawyers, although they must meet special training requirements. They are elected to four-year terms by the locality they serve.

Justice Court   Justice courts can hear both criminal and civil cases, but their jurisdiction in both instances is severely limited. In criminal matters, justice courts can try misdemeanors, traffic cases and minor violations and conduct preliminary proceedings in felony cases.

In civil matters, justice courts may hear where no more than $3,000 worth of property or money is in dispute. Also, landlord-tenant cases may be heard there, regardless of the amount of rent involved. A justice court may not decide a case involving title to real property.

New York City Criminal Court   This court's jurisdiction is limited to all misdemeanors and lesser offenses occurring in New York City. It also handles felony arraignments and preliminary hearings.

Judicial Conduct Commission

The state constitution provides for a Commission on Judicial Conduct, which has the authority to impose sanctions, from admonition to removal, on judges and justices of state and local courts and to retire them for disability, subject to review by the Court of Appeals.

Alternative Methods of Dispute Resolution   *Alternative dispute resolution ("ADR")* is an umbrella term used to describe a variety of processes and techniques to resolve disputes. The unified Court system has developed a number of pilot ADR programs for different types of cases throughout the state. Experimentation has been encouraged in the courts at every level using mediation, arbitration, neutral evaluation and summary jury trials. Furthermore, given New York's extraordinary size and diverse regions, each of these initiatives is tailored to the particular community and court environment in which it operates.

The Community Dispute Resolution Centers program, administered by the Office of Court Administration, and available in all 62 counties of the state, provides financial support to nonprofit organizations that offer dispute resolution centers offer mediation and some arbitration services as an alternative to criminal, civil and family court litigation. In addition to providing dispute resolution services, many of the centers offer a variety of educational, facilitative and preventive services in their communities that help people to manage and resolve conflicts before they reach the court system.

Outline of New York State Court System

Highest Court—Court of Appeals

Appellate Division—One in each department *(4)*

Appellate Term—1st and 2nd Dept. Only Supreme Court—Statewide

Court of Claims—Statewide Family Court—1 each county except one for NYC (5 counties in NYC)

Surrogate Court—1 in each county (62)

County Court—1 in each county outside NYC (57)

Lower Courts

New York City Civil Court

New York City Criminal Court

District Court—Nassau and Suffolk County

City Court—Outside New York City

Town Court

Village Court

Case Problems

Question I

Robert Jackson (Robert), a citizen of New Jersey, enrolled as a student at the Borough of Manhattan Community College in New York City. To finance his education, Robert performed a wild animal act with a trained bear. The bear was known to be pesky and had to be under constant watch and control while performing a charity benefit at Omega Psi Phi Fraternity House for drinks and the attention of a beautiful young lady named Jasmin from Atlanta, Georgia. The fraternity house had no liquor or cabaret license. Next to Jasmin was Paul Brock, a student from Philadelphia, Pennsylvania, who was invited to the charity event. When Robert momentarily diverted his attention from the bear to wink at Jasmin, the neglected bear attacked Paul. Angry at the attack by the bear, Paul hit the bear and attacked Robert and Jasmin. The bear, angry with all three, attacked in return. Robert, Jasmin, and Paul received severe injuries and required serious hospitalization. During Robert's stay and as a result of hospital negligence he developed an infection, which required a longer hospital stay than the others. He was forced to drop out of school and was unable to work. Both Paul and Jasmin were forced to stay three months in New York for treatment.

Discuss what claim if any the parties have and against whom. Describe which New York court would have jurisdiction to hear such claims and why.

Question II

Mary Elizabeth and Jherusha Asbury were injured when the car in which they were riding was stuck by a car driven by Grace, a minor, whose father Kyle was teaching her to drive. The accident took place on the New York-Vermont border.

Following the accident Mary Elizabeth and Kyle got into an argument during which they exchanged physical blows. If Mary Elizabeth and Jherusha sue for negligence, may Mary Elizabeth, also in the same action, sue for assault and battery? Which court is the most likely forum to hear this case and why?

Question III

Paul Roberts, a 12th grade student, entered a department store one afternoon to return a shirt he had purchased. The shirt did not fit him, and he wanted to replace it with one that did. He told the salesperson in the shirt department that he wanted to exchange the shirt. The salesperson, who was busy waiting on another customer, told Paul to leave the shirt, go to the shirt counter two aisles away, and take one that was the proper size. Paul found the proper-sized shirt and left the store with it. Outside the store, Paul was approached by the store detective who told Paul that he was suspected of theft and must come to the manager's office with him.

When they got to the manager's office, the detective locked Paul in a room while he went to investigate the alleged theft. Two hours later, the detective returned. He said that he had learned Paul had in fact exchanged the shirt for one of the proper size and had not stolen it. He apologized to Paul and told him he was free to leave the store.

Paul brought an action against the department store for false imprisonment.

The Trial

During the trial, the storeowner testified that shoplifting at the store had become a major problem, increasing 100 percent in the past year. The detective testified that he saw Paul pick a shirt up from the counter and walk out of the store with it without paying for it. He said that Paul didn't have a bag for the shirt and couldn't produce a receipt. He further testified that he kept Paul locked up for two hours because the sales-clerk Paul had talked to had gone to lunch. It took that long to check with the salesperson about what had happened, to check the store records, and to check with the police to see if Paul had a criminal record.

During the trial, the attorney for the store argued that detaining a person suspected of theft was necessary to determine whether a theft had actually taken place and that stores cannot stay in business if they cannot prevent shoplifting. The store's attorney further argued that Paul's activities indicated that he had committed a theft and that two hours was not an unreasonable period of time to detain someone under those circumstances.

Paul's attorney argued that the detective should have had positive proof that Paul had committed the crime before detaining him, that two hours was an unreasonable time to detain anyone even if suspected of having committed a crime, and that there are other ways to prevent shoplifting without resorting to detention.

Questions to Discuss

1. Who has the stronger argument, the store or Paul? Why?
2. Do you need any additional information to determine the facts?
3. If you were the judge or jury hearing this case, for whom would you decide and why?
4. What steps do you think the store detective could have taken to prevent the lawsuit for false imprisonment?
5. Which New York court would have jurisdiction over this matter and why?

Borough of Manhattan Community College
Business Management Department

OUTLINE OF NEW YORK STATE COURT SYSTEM

Court of Appeals

Appellate Divisions—
one in each department
(4)

Appellate Term
1st and 2nd Depts. only

Supreme Court—Statewide

Court of Claims
Statewide

Family Court
1 in each county except
one for New York City
(5 counties in N.Y.C.)

Surrogate's Court
1 in each county
(62)

County Court
1 in each county outside
of N.Y.C.
(57)

New York City
Civil Court

New York City
Criminal Court

District Court
Nassau and
Suffolk

City Courts
outside
New York City

Town Court

Village Court

CHAPTER 3

"We're the jury, dread our fury!"

—William S. Gilbert
Trial by Jury

Judicial, Alternative, and Online Dispute Resolution

Chapter Objectives

After studying this chapter, you should be able to:

1. Describe the pretrial litigation process.
2. Describe how a case proceeds through trial.
3. Describe how a trial court decision is appealed.
4. Explain the use of arbitration and other nonjudicial methods of alternative dispute resolution.
5. Describe *online dispute resolution*.

Chapter Contents

Introduction to Judicial, Alternative, and Online Dispute Resolution

The process of bringing, maintaining, and defending a lawsuit is called *litigation*. This is also called *judicial dispute resolution* because courts are used to decide the case. Litigation is a difficult, time-consuming, and costly process that must comply with complex procedural rules. Although it is not required, most parties employ a lawyer to represent them when they are involved in a lawsuit.

Several forms of **nonjudicial dispute resolution** have developed in response to the expense and difficulty of bringing a lawsuit. These methods, collectively called *alternative dispute resolution*, are being used more and more often to resolve contract and commercial disputes. In addition, arbitration is often used to solve Internet and e-commerce disputes. This is called **online dispute resolution**.

This chapter discusses the judicial litigation process, alternative dispute resolution, and online dispute resolution.

Pretrial Litigation Process

The bringing, maintaining, and defense of a lawsuit are generally referred to as the *litigation process*, or **litigation**. The pretrial litigation process can be divided into the following major phases: *pleadings, discovery, dismissals and pretrial judgments*, and *settlement conference*. Each of these phases is discussed in the paragraphs that follow.

Pleadings

The paperwork that is filed with the court to initiate and respond to a lawsuit is referred to as the **pleadings**. The major pleadings are the *complaint*, the *answer*, the *cross-complaint*, and the *reply*.

Complaint and Summons

To initiate a lawsuit, the party who is suing (the **plaintiff**) must file a **complaint** in the proper court. The complaint must name the parties to the lawsuit, alleges the ultimate facts and law violated, and contains a "prayer for relief" for a remedy to be awarded by the court. The complaint can be as long as necessary, depending on the case's complexity. A sample complaint appears in Exhibit 3.1.

Once a complaint has been filed with the court, the court will issue a summons. A **summons** is a court order directing the defendant to appear in court and answer the complaint. The complaint and summons are served on the defendant by a sheriff, another government official, or a private process server.

Answer

The defendant must file an **answer** to the plaintiff's complaint. The defendant's answer is filed with the court and served on the plaintiff. In the answer, the defendant admits or denies the allegations contained in the plaintiff's complaint. A judgment is entered against a defendant who admits all of the allegations in the complaint. The case proceeds if the defendant denies all or some of the allegations.

If the defendant does not answer the complaint, a **default judgment** is entered against him or her. A default judgment establishes the defendant's liability. The plaintiff then has only to prove damages.

In addition to answering the complaint, a defendant's answer can assert **affirmative defenses**.

Examples

If a complaint alleges that the plaintiff was personally injured by the defendant, the defendant's answer could state that he or she acted in self-defense. Another affirmative defense

---

litigation
The process of bringing, maintaining, and defending a lawsuit.

pleadings
The paperwork that is filed with the court to initiate and respond to a lawsuit.

plaintiff
The party who files a complaint.

complaint
The document a plaintiff files with the court and serves on the defendant to initiate a lawsuit.

summons
A court order directing the defendant to appear in court and answer the complaint.

answer
The defendant's written response to a plaintiff's complaint that is filed with the court and served on the plaintiff.

Pieces of evidence, each by itself insufficient, may together constitute a significant whole and justify by their combined effect a conclusion.

Lord Wright
Grant v. Australian Knitting Mills, Ltd. (1936)

■ EXHIBIT 3.1 Sample Complaint

In the United States District Court for the District of Idaho

John Doe   Civil No. 2-1001
          Plaintiff

          v.   COMPLAINT

Jane Roe

          Defendant

The plaintiff, by and through his attorney, alleges:

1. The plaintiff is a resident of the State of Idaho, the defendant is a resident of the State of Washington, and there is diversity of citizenship between the parties.
2. The amount in controversy exceeds the sum of $75,000, exclusive of interest and costs.
3. On January 10, 2008, plaintiff was exercising reasonable care while walking across the intersection of Sun Valley Road and Main Street, Ketchum, Idaho when defendant negligently drove her car through a red light at the intersection and struck plaintiff.
4. As a result of the defendant's negligence, plaintiff has incurred medical expenses of $104,000 and suffered severe physical injury and mental distress.

WHEREFORE, plaintiff claims judgment in the amount of $1,000,000 interest at the maximum legal rate, and costs of this action.

By _____
          Edward Lawson
          Attorney for Plaintiff
          100 Main Street
          Ketchum, Idaho

---

would be an assertion that the plaintiff's lawsuit is barred because the *statute of limitations* (time within which to bring the lawsuit) has expired.

Cross-Complaint and Reply

A defendant who believes that he or she has been injured by the plaintiff can file a **cross-complaint** against the plaintiff in addition to an answer. In the cross-complaint, the defendant (now the **cross-complainant**) sues the plaintiff (now the **cross-defendant**) for damages or some other remedy. The original plaintiff must file a **reply** (answer) to the cross-complaint. The reply, which can include affirmative defenses, must be filed with the court and served on the original defendant.

Intervention and Consolidation

If other persons have an interest in a lawsuit, they may **intervene** and become parties to the lawsuit.

Example

A bank that has made a secured loan on a piece of real estate can intervene in a lawsuit between parties who are litigating ownership of the property.

cross-complaint
A document filed by the defendant against the plaintiff to seek damages or some other remedy.

reply
A document filed by the original plaintiff to answer the defendant's cross-complaint.

intervention
The act of others to join as parties to an existing lawsuit.

Cyber Law

Internet Law and Online Commerce

E-Filings

When litigation takes place, the clients, lawyers, and judges involved in the case are usually buried in papers. These papers include pleadings, interrogatories, documents, motions to the court, briefs, and memorandums; the list goes on and on. By the time a case is over, reams of paper are stored in dozens, if not hundreds, of boxes. In addition, court appearances, for no matter how small the matter, must be made in person.

Example

Lawyers often wait hours for a 10-minute scheduling conference or other conference with a judge. The time it takes to drive to and from court also has to be taken into account, which in some areas may amount to hours.

Today, because of the Internet and other technologies, a **virtual courthouse** is being developed. Technology allows for the electronic filing—**e-filing**—of pleadings, briefs, and other documents related to a lawsuit. E-filing includes using CD-ROMs for briefs, scanning evidence and documents into a computer for storage and retrieval, and e-mailing correspondence and documents to the court and the opposing counsel. Scheduling and other conferences with the judge or opposing counsel are held via telephone conferences and e-mail.

Many courts have instituted e-filing and electronic document filing and tracking. In some courts, e-filing is now mandatory. Companies such as Microsoft and LexisNexis have developed systems to manage e-filings of court documents.

Concept Summary
Pleadings

Type of Pleading	Description
Complaint	A document filed by a plaintiff with a court and served with a *summons* on the defendant. It sets forth the basis of the lawsuit.
Answer	A document filed by a defendant with a court and served on the plaintiff. It usually denies most allegations of the complaint.
Cross-complaint and reply	A document filed and served by a defendant if he or she countersues the plaintiff. The defendant is the *cross-complainant*, and the plaintiff is the *cross-defendant*. The cross-defendant must file and serve a *reply* (answer).

consolidation

The act of a court to combine two or more separate lawsuits into one lawsuit.

If several plaintiffs have filed separate lawsuits stemming from the same fact situation against the same defendant, the court can **consolidate** the cases into one case if doing so would not cause undue prejudice to the parties.

Example

If a commercial airplane crashes, killing and injuring many people, the court could consolidate all the lawsuits against the defendant airplane company. This is because the deaths and injuries all relate to the same fact situation.

Statute of Limitations

statute of limitations

A statute that establishes the period during which a plaintiff must bring a lawsuit against a defendant.

A **statute of limitations** establishes the period during which a plaintiff must bring a lawsuit against a defendant. If a lawsuit is not filed within this time period, the plaintiff loses his or her right to sue. A statute of limitations begins to "run" at the time the plaintiff first has the right to sue the defendant (e.g., when the accident happens or when the breach of contract occurs).

Federal and state governments have established statutes of limitations for each type of lawsuit. Most are from one to four years, depending on the type of lawsuit.

Example

The state of Idaho has a two-year statute of limitations for negligence actions. On July 1, 2009, Otis negligently causes an automobile accident in Sun Valley, Idaho, in which Cha-Yen is injured. Cha-Yen has until July 1, 2011, to bring a negligence lawsuit against Otis. If she waits longer than that, she loses her right to sue him.

Discovery

The legal process provides for a detailed pretrial procedure called **discovery**. During discovery, each party engages in various activities to discover facts of the case from the other party and witnesses prior to trial. Discovery serves several functions, including preventing surprises, allowing parties to thoroughly prepare for trial, preserving evidence, saving court time, and promoting the settlement of cases. The major forms of discovery are discussed in the following paragraphs.

discovery
A legal process during which each party engages in various activities to discover facts of the case from the other party and witnesses prior to trial.

Deposition

A **deposition** is the oral testimony given by a party or witness prior to trial. The person giving a deposition is called the **deponent**. A *party* to the lawsuit must give a deposition, if called upon by the other party to do so. The deposition of a *witness* can be given voluntarily or pursuant to a subpoena (court order). The deponent can be required to bring documents to the deposition. Most depositions are taken at the office of one of the attorneys. The deponent is placed under oath and then asked oral questions by one or both of the attorneys. The questions and answers are recorded in written form by a court reporter. Depositions can also be videotaped. The deponent is given an opportunity to correct his or her answers prior to signing the deposition. Depositions are used to preserve evidence (e.g., if the deponent is deceased, ill, or not otherwise available at trial) and impeach testimony given by witnesses at trial.

deposition
Oral testimony given by a party or witness prior to trial. The testimony is given under oath and is transcribed.

deponent
A party who gives his or her deposition.

Interrogatories

Interrogatories are written questions submitted by one party to a lawsuit to another party. The questions can be very detailed. In addition, certain documents might be attached to the answers. A party is required to answer the interrogatories in writing within a specified time period (e.g., 60 to 90 days). An attorney usually helps with the preparation of the answers. The answers are signed under oath.

interrogatories
Written questions submitted by one party to another party. The questions must be answered in writing within a stipulated time.

Production of Documents

Often, particularly in complex business cases, a substantial portion of a lawsuit may be based on information contained in documents (e.g., memorandums, correspondence, and company records). One party to a lawsuit may request that the other party produce all documents that are relevant to the case prior to trial. This is called **production of documents**. If the documents sought are too voluminous to be moved or are in permanent storage, or if their movement would disrupt the ongoing business of the party who is to produce them, the requesting party may be required to examine the documents at the other party's premises.

production of documents
A request by one party to another party to produce all documents relevant to the case prior to the trial.

Physical or Mental Examination

In cases that concern the physical or mental condition of a party, a court can order the party to submit to certain **physical or mental examinations** to determine the extent of the alleged injuries. This would occur, for example, where the plaintiff has been injured in an accident and is seeking damages for physical injury and mental distress.

physical or mental examination
A court-ordered examination of a party to a lawsuit before trial to determine the extent of the alleged injuries.

Concept Summary
Discovery

Type	Description
Deposition	Oral testimony given by a *deponent*, either a party or witness. Depositions are transcribed.
Interrogatories	Written questions submitted by one party to the other party of a lawsuit. They must be answered within a specified period of time.
Production of documents	Copies of all relevant documents obtained by a party to a lawsuit from another party upon order of the court.
Physical or mental examination	Court-ordered examination of a party where injuries are alleged that could be verified or disputed by such examination.

Dismissals and Pretrial Judgments

pretrial motion
A motion a party can make to try to dispose of all or part of a lawsuit prior to trial.

There are several **pretrial motions** that parties to a lawsuit can make to try to dispose of all or part of a lawsuit prior to trial. The two major pretrial motions are *motion for judgment on the pleadings* and *motion for summary judgment*.

Motion for Judgment on the Pleadings

motion for judgment on the pleadings
A motion which alleges that if all the facts presented in the pleadings are taken as true, the party making the motion would win the lawsuit when the proper law is applied to these asserted facts.

A **motion for judgment on the pleadings** can be made by either party once the pleadings are complete. This motion alleges that if all the facts presented in the pleadings are true, the party making the motion would win the lawsuit when the proper law is applied to these facts. In deciding this motion, the judge cannot consider any facts outside the pleadings.

Motion for Summary Judgment

motion for summary judgment
A motion which asserts that there are no factual disputes to be decided by the jury and that the judge can apply the proper law to the undisputed facts and decide the case without a jury. These motions are supported by affidavits, documents, and deposition testimony.

The trier of fact (i.e., the jury or, if there is no jury, the judge) determines factual issues. A **motion for summary judgment** asserts that there are no factual disputes to be decided by the jury and that the judge should apply the relevant law to the undisputed facts and decide the case. Thus, the case can be decided before trial by a judge who comes to a conclusion and issues a summary judgment in the moving party's favor. Motions for summary judgment, which can be made by either party, are supported by evidence outside the pleadings. Affidavits from the parties and witnesses, documents (e.g., a written contract between the parties), depositions, and such are common forms of evidence.

If, after examining the evidence, the court finds no factual dispute, it can decide the issue or issues raised in the summary judgment motion. This may dispense with the entire case or with part of the case. If the judge finds that a factual dispute exists, the motion will be denied, and the case will go to trial.

In the following case, the court did not grant a motion for summary judgment because it found that there were factual disputes for the jury to decide.

Settlement Conference

settlement conference
A hearing before a trial in order to facilitate the settlement of a case. Also called a *pretrial hearing*.

Federal court rules and most state court rules permit the court to direct the attorneys or parties to appear before the court for a **settlement conference**, or **pretrial hearing**. One of the major purposes of such hearings is to facilitate the settlement of a case. Pretrial conferences are often held informally in the judge's chambers. If no settlement is reached, the pretrial hearing is used to identify the major trial issues and other relevant factors. More than 95 percent of all cases are settled before they go to trial.

CASE 3.1
Summary Judgment

Toote v. Canada Dry Bottling Company of New York, Inc. and Pathmark Stores, Inc.

7 A.D.3d 251, 776 N.Y.S.2d 42, Web 2004
N.Y. App. Div. Lexis 6470 (2004)
Supreme Court of New York, Appellate Division

"Plaintiff alleges that she tripped over cases of soda that were stacked on the floor of defendant's supermarket."

—Judge Lerner

Facts

Plaintiff Phyllis Toote filed a lawsuit against Pathmark Stores, Inc., a grocery store, and Canada Dry Bottling Company of New York, a bottler and distributor of soda. In her complaint, plaintiff alleged that the defendants were liable for negligence for injuries she suffered when she fell over cases of soda that were stacked on the floor of the supermarket when she was shopping at the supermarket.

Defendant Pathmark took plaintiff Toote's deposition, in which she stated that she had entered the supermarket, and upon entering the store, she immediately walked to the soda aisle. Toote stated that she did not see the soda stacked on the floor before she fell over the soda. In the deposition, Toote stated that she did not know how long the soda had been on the floor before she tripped and fell. Pathmark made a motion for summary judgment, alleging that plaintiff Toote could not establish how long the soda had been on the floor before she fell. The motion court denied Pathmark's motion for summary judgment, finding that there were questions of fact to be decided by the jury. Pathmark appealed.

Issue

Should the motion court have granted Pathmark's motion for summary judgment?

Language of the Court

Plaintiff alleges that she tripped over cases of soda that were stacked on the floor of defendant's supermarket. It appears that at the time of the accident, the supermarket's shelves, in accordance with usual practice, were being "packed out" with soda by an employee of either defen- *dant bottling company or defendant soda distributor. The supermarket moved for summary judgment, contending that it did not create the alleged dangerous condition and that plaintiff's deposition testimony, to the effect that she walked to the soda aisle immediately after entering the store and did not see any soda on the floor before falling, shows that she cannot establish how long the soda had been on the floor before she fell. The motion court correctly held that such testimony does not establish, prima facie, the supermarket's lack of prior actual or constructive notice of the soda on the floor, or that it may not be held liable for an independent contractor's negligence on the basis of the supermarket's non-delegable duty to keep the public areas of its premises reasonably safe.*

Decision

The appellate court decided that there were issues of fact to be decided by a jury and affirmed the motion court's denial of Pathmark's motion for summary judgment.

Case Questions

Critical Legal Thinking What is a motion for summary judgment? When is a motion for summary judgment granted?

Business Ethics Was it ethical for Pathmark, the supermarket, to make a motion for summary judgment based on the facts of this case? Explain.

Contemporary Business Do you think supermarkets have to face a significant number of "faked" slip-and-fall cases?

Contemporary Environment

Cost–Benefit Analysis of a Lawsuit

The choice of whether to bring or defend a lawsuit should be analyzed like any other business decision. This includes performing a **cost–benefit analysis** of the lawsuit. For the plaintiff, it may be wise not to sue. For the defendant, it may be wise to settle. The following factors should be considered in deciding whether to bring or settle a lawsuit:

- The probability of winning or losing
- The amount of money to be won or lost

- Lawyers' fees and other costs of litigation
- Loss of time by managers and other personnel
- The long-term effects on the relationship and reputation of the parties
- The amount of prejudgment interest provided by law
- The aggravation and psychological costs associated with a lawsuit
- The unpredictability of the legal system and the possibility of error
- Other factors peculiar to the parties and lawsuit

Trial

Pursuant to the Seventh Amendment to the U.S. Constitution, a party to an action at law is guaranteed the right to a **jury trial** in a case in federal court.[1] Most state constitutions contain a similar guarantee for state court actions. If either party requests a jury, the trial will be by jury. If both parties waive their right to a jury, the trial will occur without a jury. The judge sits as the **trier of fact** in nonjury trials. At the time of trial, each party usually submits to the judge a **trial brief** that contains legal support for its side of the case.

A trial can last less than one day to many months, depending on the type and complexity of the case. A typical trial is divided into stages. The stages of a trial are discussed in the following paragraphs.

Jury Selection

The pool of potential jurors is usually selected from voter or automobile registration lists. Individuals are selected to hear specific cases through a process called **voir dire** ("to speak the truth"). Lawyers for each party and the judge can ask prospective jurors questions to determine whether they would be biased in their decisions. Biased jurors can be prevented from sitting on a particular case. Once the appropriate number of jurors is selected (usually 6 to 12 jurors), they are **impaneled** to hear the case and are sworn in. The trial is ready to begin. A jury can be **sequestered** (i.e., separated from family, etc.) in important cases. Jurors are paid fees for their service.

Opening Statements

Each party's attorney is allowed to make an **opening statement** to the jury. In opening statements, an attorney usually summarizes the main factual and legal issues of the case and describes why he or she believes the client's position is valid. The information given in this statement is not considered as evidence.

The Plaintiff's Case

A plaintiff bears the **burden of proof** to persuade the trier of fact of the merits of his or her case. This is called the **plaintiff's case**. The plaintiff's attorney calls witnesses to give testimony. After a witness has been sworn in, the plaintiff's attorney examines (i.e., questions) the witness. This is called **direct examination**. Documents and other evidence can be introduced through each witness. After the plaintiff's attorney has completed his or her questions, the defendant's attorney can question the witness. This is called **cross-examination**. The defendant's attorney can ask questions only about the subjects that were brought up during the

---

trier of fact

The jury in a jury trial; the judge where there is not a jury trial.

voir dire

The process whereby prospective jurors are asked questions by the judge and attorneys to determine whether they would be biased in their decisions.

Courts of appeals should be constantly alert to the trial judge's firsthand knowledge of witnesses, testimony, and issues; in other words, appellate courts should give due consideration to the first-instance decision maker's "feel" for the overall case.

Justice Ginsburg
Weisgram v. Marley Company 528 U.S. 440, 120 S.Ct. (2000)

direct examination. After the defendant's attorney completes his or her questions, the plaintiff's attorney can ask questions of the witness. This is called **re-direct examination**.

The Defendant's Case

The **defendant's case** proceeds after the plaintiff has concluded his or her case. The defendant's case must (1) rebut the plaintiff's evidence, (2) prove any affirmative defenses asserted by the defendant, and (3) prove any allegations contained in the defendant's cross-complaint. The defendant's witnesses are examined by the defendant's attorney. The plaintiff's attorney can cross-examine each witness. This is followed by re-direct by the defendant and re-cross-examination by the plaintiff.

Rebuttal and Rejoinder

After the defendant's attorney has finished calling witnesses, the plaintiff's attorney can call witnesses and put forth evidence to rebut the defendant's case. This is called a **rebuttal**. The defendant's attorney can call additional witnesses and introduce other evidence to counter the rebuttal. This is called the **rejoinder**.

Closing Arguments

At the conclusion of the presentation of the evidence, each party's attorney is allowed to make a **closing argument** to the jury. Both attorneys try to convince the jury to render a verdict for their clients by pointing out the strengths in the client's case and the weaknesses in the other side's case. Information given by the attorneys in their closing statements is not evidence.

Jury Instructions

Once the closing arguments are completed, the judge reads **jury instructions** (or **charges**) to the jury. These instructions inform the jury about what law to apply when they decide the case. For example, in a criminal trial, the judge reads the jury the statutory definition of the crime charged. In an accident case, the judge reads the jury the legal definition of *negligence*.

jury instructions
Instructions given by the judge to the jury that inform them of the law to be applied in the case.

Jury Deliberation and Verdict

After the judge reads the jury instructions, the jury retires to the jury room to **deliberate** its findings. This can take from a few minutes to many weeks. After deliberation, the jury reaches a **verdict**. In civil cases, the jury will assess damages against the defendant if they have held in favor of the plaintiff. The jury often assesses penalties in criminal cases.

Entry of Judgment

After the jury has returned its verdict, in most cases the judge will enter a **judgment** to the successful party, based on the verdict. This is the official decision of the court.

The court may, however, overturn the verdict if it finds bias or jury misconduct. This is called a **judgment notwithstanding the verdict** or **judgment n.o.v.** or **j.n.o.v.**

In a civil case, the judge may reduce the amount of monetary damages awarded by the jury if he or she finds the jury to have been biased, emotional, or inflamed. This is called **remittitur**.

The trial court usually issues a **written memorandum** that sets forth the reasons for the judgment. This memorandum, together with the trial transcript and evidence introduced at trial, constitutes the permanent **record** of the trial court proceeding.

Appeal

In a civil case, either party can **appeal** the trial court's decision once a **final judgment** is entered. Only the defendant can appeal in a criminal case. The appeal is made to the

appeal
The act of asking an appellate court to overturn a decision after the trial court's final judgment has been entered.

Ethics Spotlight

Frivolous Lawsuit

Although most lawsuits that are filed have some merit, some lawsuits do not. These are called frivolous lawsuits. Consider the following case. The Chungs are Korean residents who came to the United States in 1992. The Chungs opened a dry-cleaning store and eventually owned three dry-cleaning stores in the Washington, DC (DC) area. Roy L. Pearson was a DC administrative judge who was a customer at one of the Chungs' dry-cleaning stores. Pearson walked to the Chungs' store because he did not have a car.

The Chungs had signs in the window of their store that stated "Satisfaction Guaranteed" and "Same Day Service." Pearson claimed that the Chungs lost a pair of his pants. He sued the Chungs for $67 million in damages, alleging that they violated the DC Consumer Protection Act. Pearson later reduced his demand to $54 million. Pearson demanded $3 million for violation of the "Satisfaction Guaranteed" sign, $2 million for mental suffering and inconvenience, $500,000 in legal fees for representing himself, $6 million for 10 years of rental car fees to drive to another dry-cleaning shop, and $51 million to help similarly dissatisfied DC customers. Pearson stated that he had no choice but to take on "the awesome

responsibility" for suing the Chungs on behalf of every DC resident.

The court, in denying class action status, stated "The court has significant concerns that the plaintiff is acting in bad faith." After hearing testimony of witnesses, the trial court judge ruled in favor of the Chungs. Pearson made a motion to reconsider to the trial court, which was denied. A website was set up to accept donations for the Chungs' legal fees of $83,000, which were eventually paid by donations.

A DC commission voted against reappointing Pearson for a 10-year term as an administrative law judge in part because his lawsuit against the Chungs demonstrated a lack of "judicial temperament." Pearson lost a $100,000-per-year salary. The Chungs sold the dry-cleaning store involved in the dispute. Pearson filed a notice of appeal.

Business Ethics

What is a frivolous lawsuit? Explain. Do you think Pearson's lawsuit had any merit? Do you think Pearson acted in "bad faith" in this case? How much emotional distress do you think the Chungs suffered because of this lawsuit?

---

appellant

The appealing party in an appeal. Also known as the *petitioner*.

appellee

The responding party in an appeal. Also known as the *respondent*.

appropriate appellate court. A **notice of appeal** must be filed within a prescribed time after judgment is entered (usually within 60 or 90 days).

The appealing party is called the **appellant**, or **petitioner**. The responding party is called the **appellee**, or **respondent**. The appellant is often required to post a bond (e.g., one-and-one-half times the judgment) on appeal.

The parties may designate all or relevant portions of the trial record to be submitted to the appellate court for review. The appellant's attorney may file an **opening brief** with the court that sets forth legal research and other information to support his or her contentions on appeal. The appellee can file a **responding brief**, answering the appellant's contentions. Appellate courts usually permit a brief oral argument at which each party's attorney is heard.

An appellate court will reverse a lower court decision if it finds an **error of law** in the record.

An appellate court will not reverse a **finding of fact** unless such finding is unsupported by the evidence or is contradicted by the evidence. Very few trial court decisions are reversed because most findings of fact are supported by the evidence. In rare occasions, an appellate court will overturn a jury verdict if the appellate court cannot, from the record of the trial court, find sufficient evidence to support the trier of fact's findings.

Alternative Dispute Resolution

The use of the court system to resolve business and other disputes can take years and cost thousands, or even millions, of dollars in legal fees and expenses. In commercial litigation, the normal business operations of the parties are often disrupted. To avoid or reduce these problems, businesses are increasingly turning to methods of **alternative dispute resolution (ADR)** and other aids to resolving disputes. The most common form of ADR is *arbitration*. Other forms of ADR are *negotiation, mediation, conciliation, mini-trial, fact-finding,* and using a *judicial referee*.

alternative dispute resolution (ADR)
Methods of resolving disputes other than litigation.

Negotiation

The simplest form of alternative dispute resolution is engaging in negotiations between the parties to try to settle a dispute. **Negotiation** is a procedure whereby the parties to a dispute engage in negotiations to try to reach a voluntary settlement of their dispute. Negotiation may take place either before a lawsuit is filed, after a lawsuit is filed, or before other forms of alternative dispute resolution are engaged in.

In a negotiation, the parties, who are often represented by attorneys, negotiate with each other to try to reach an agreeable solution to their dispute. During negotiation proceedings, the parties usually make offers and counteroffers to one another. The parties or their attorneys also may provide information to the other side that would assist the other side in reaching an amicable settlement.

Many courts require that the parties to a lawsuit engage in settlement discussions prior to trial to try to negotiate a settlement of the case. In such a case, the judge must be assured that a settlement of the case is not possible before he or she permits the case to go to trial. A judge may convince the parties to engage in further negotiations if he or she determines that the parties are not too far apart in the negotiations of a settlement.

If a settlement of the dispute is reached through negotiation, a settlement agreement is drafted that contains the terms of the agreement. A **settlement agreement** is an agreement that is voluntarily entered into by the parties to a dispute that settles the dispute. Each side must sign the settlement agreement for it to be effective. The settlement agreement is usually submitted to the court, and the case will be dismissed based on the execution of the settlement agreement.

Arbitration

In **arbitration**, the parties choose an impartial third party to hear and decide the dispute. This neutral party is called the **arbitrator**. Arbitrators are usually members of the American Arbitration Association (AAA) or another arbitration association. Labor union

arbitration
A form of ADR in which the parties choose an impartial third party to hear and decide the dispute.

Landmark Law

Federal Arbitration Act

"By agreeing to arbitrate a statutory claim, a party does not forgo the substantive rights afforded by the statute, it only submits to their resolution in an arbitral, rather than a judicial, forum."

—Justice White

The **Federal Arbitration Act (FAA)** was originally enacted in 1925 to reverse the long-standing judicial hostility to arbitration agreements that had existed at English common law and had been adopted by U.S. courts. The FAA provides that arbitration agreements involving commerce are valid, irrevocable, and enforceable contracts, unless some grounds exist at law or equity (e.g., fraud, duress) to revoke them. The FAA permits one party to obtain a court order to compel arbitration if the other party has failed, neglected, or refused to comply with an arbitration agreement.

Since the FAA's enactment, the courts have wrestled with the problem of which types of disputes should be arbitrated. Breach of contract cases, tort claims, and such are clearly candidates for arbitration if there is a valid arbitration agreement. In addition, the U.S. Supreme Court has enforced arbitration agreements that call for the resolution of disputes arising under federal statutes. The Supreme Court has stated, "By agreeing to arbitrate a statutory claim, a party does not forgo the substantive rights afforded by the statute, it only submits to their resolution in an arbitral, rather than a judicial, forum."[3]

arbitration clause

A clause in a contract that requires disputes arising out of the contract to be submitted to arbitration.

Federal Arbitration Act (FAA)

A federal statute that provides for the enforcement of most arbitration agreements.

agreements, franchise agreements, leases, and other commercial contracts often contain **arbitration clauses** that require disputes arising out of the contract to be submitted to arbitration. If there is no arbitration clause, the parties can enter into a **submission agreement** whereby they agree to submit a dispute to arbitration after the dispute arises.

Congress enacted the *Federal Arbitration Act* to promote the arbitration of disputes.[2] About half of the states have adopted the **Uniform Arbitration Act**, which promotes the arbitration of disputes at the state level. Many federal and state courts have instituted programs to refer legal disputes to arbitration or another form of ADR.

Arbitration Providers   ADR services are usually provided by private organizations or individuals who qualify to hear and decide certain disputes.

Arbitration Procedure   An arbitration agreement often describes the specific procedures that must be followed for a case to proceed to and through arbitration. If one party seeks to enforce an arbitration clause, that party must give notice to the other party. The parties then select an arbitration association or arbitrator, as provided in the agreement. The parties usually agree on the date, time, and place of the arbitration (e.g., at the arbitrator's office, at a law office, or at any other agreed-upon location).

At the arbitration, the parties can call witnesses to give testimony and introduce evidence to support their case and refute the other side's case. Rules similar to those followed by federal courts are usually followed at an arbitration. Often, each party pays a filing fee and other fees for the arbitration. Sometimes the agreement provides that one party will pay all the costs of the arbitration. Arbitrators are paid by the hour, day, or other agreed-upon method of compensation.

Decision and Award   After an arbitration hearing is complete, the arbitrator reaches a decision and issues an award. The parties often agree in advance to be bound by the arbitrator's decision and remedy. This is called **binding arbitration**. In this situation, the decision and award of the arbitrator cannot be appealed to the courts. If the arbitration is not binding, the decision and award of the arbitrator can be appealed to the courts. This is called *non-binding arbitration*. Courts usually give great deference to an arbitrator's decision and award.

If an arbitrator has rendered a decision and an award, but a party refuses to abide by the arbitrator's decision, the other party may file an action in court to have the arbitrator's decision enforced.

Mediation

mediation

A form of ADR in which the parties use a mediator to propose a settlement of their dispute.

Mediation is a form of negotiation in which a neutral third party assists the disputing parties in reaching a settlement of their dispute. The neutral third party is called a **mediator**. The mediator is usually a person who is an expert in the area of the dispute, or a lawyer or retired judge. The mediator is selected by the parties as provided in their agreement, or as otherwise selected by the parties. Unlike an arbitrator, however, a mediator does not make a decision or an award.

A mediator's role is to assist the parties in reaching a settlement. The mediator usually acts as an intermediary between the parties. In many cases, the mediator will meet with the two parties at an agreed-upon location, often the mediator's office or one of the offices of the parties. The mediator will then meet with both parties, usually separately, to discuss each side of the case.

After discussing the facts of the case with both sides, the mediator will encourage settlement of the dispute and will transmit settlement offers from one side to the other. In doing so, the mediator points out the strengths and weaknesses of each party's case and gives his or her opinion to each side about why they should decrease or increase their settlement offers. The mediator's job is to facilitate settlement of the case.

If the parties agree to a settlement, a settlement agreement is drafted that expresses their agreement. Execution of the settlement agreement ends the dispute. The parties, of course, must perform their duties under the settlement agreement. If an agreement is not reached, the parties may proceed to a judicial resolution of their case.

Conciliation

Conciliation is a form of alternative dispute resolution in which an interested party, a **conciliator**, helps the parties try to reach a resolution of their dispute. Conciliation is often used when the parties do not want to face each other in an adversarial setting. The conciliator schedules meetings and appointments during which information can be transferred to the parties. A conciliator usually carries offers and counteroffers for a settlement back and forth between the disputing parties. A conciliator cannot make a decision or an award.

Although the role of a conciliator is not to propose a settlement of the case, many often do. In many cases, conciliators are neutral third parties, although in some circumstances, the parties may select an interested third party to act as the conciliator. If the parties reach a settlement of their dispute through the use of conciliation, a settlement agreement is drafted and executed by the parties.

conciliation
A form of ADR in which the parties use a third party to help them resolve their dispute.

Mini-trial

A **mini-trial** is a voluntary private proceeding in which lawyers for each side present a shortened version of their case to the representatives of both sides. The representatives of each side who attend the mini-trial have the authority to settle the dispute. In many cases, the parties also hire a neutral third party—often someone who is an expert in the field concerning the disputed matter or a legal expert—who presides over the mini-trial. After hearing the case, the neutral third party often is called upon to render an opinion as to how the court would most likely decide the case.

During a mini-trial, the parties get to see the strengths and weaknesses of their own position and that of the opposing side. Once the strengths and weaknesses of both sides are exposed, the parties to a mini-trial often settle the case. The parties also often settle a mini-trial based on the opinion rendered by the neutral third party. If the parties settle their dispute after a mini-trial, they enter into a settlement agreement that sets forth their agreement.

Mini-trials serve a useful purpose in that they act as a substitute for a real trial, but they are much briefer and not as complex and expensive to prepare for. Because the strengths and weaknesses of both sides' cases are exposed, the parties are usually more realistic regarding their own positions and the merits of settling the case prior to an expensive, and often risky, trial.

Fact-Finding

In some situations, called **fact-finding**, the parties to a dispute employ a neutral third party to act as a fact-finder to investigate the dispute. The fact-finder is authorized to investigate the dispute, gather evidence, prepare demonstrative evidence, and prepare reports of his or her findings.

A fact-finder is not authorized to make a decision or an award. In some cases, a fact-finder will recommend settlement of the case. The fact-finder presents the evidence and findings to the parties, who may then use the information in negotiating a settlement if they wish.

Judicial Referee

If the parties agree, the court may appoint a **judicial referee** to conduct a private trial and render a judgment. Referees, who are often retired judges, have most of the same powers as trial judges, and their decisions stand as judgments of the court. The parties usually reserve their right to appeal.

In the following case, the U.S. Supreme Court addressed the issue of alternative dispute resolution.

U.S. Supreme Court
Circuit City Stores, Inc. v. Adams

532 U.S. 105, 121 S.Ct. 1302, 149 L.Ed.2d 234,
Web 2001 U.S. Lexis 2459 (2001)
Supreme Court of the United States

"Congress enacted the Federal Arbitration Act (FAA) in 1925. The FAA was a response to hostility of American courts to the enforcement of arbitration agreements."

—Justice Kennedy

Facts

Saint Clair Adams was hired as a sales counselor by Circuit City Stores, Inc., a national retailer of consumer electronics. Adams signed an employment contract that included the following arbitration clause:

I agree that I will settle any and all previously unasserted claims, disputes or controversies arising out of or relating to my application or candidacy for employment, employment and/or cessation of employment with Circuit City, exclusively by final and binding arbitration before a neutral Arbitrator. By way of example only, such claims include claims under federal, state, and local statutory or common law, such as the Age Discrimination in Employment Act, Title VII of the Civil Rights Act of 1964, the Americans with Disabilities Act, the law of contract and the law of tort.

Two years later, Adams filed an employment discrimination lawsuit against Circuit City in court. Circuit City sought to enjoin the court proceeding and to compel arbitration, pursuant to the FAA. The U.S. District Court granted Circuit City's request. The U.S. Court of Appeals reversed, holding that employment contracts are not subject to arbitration. Adams appealed to the U.S. Supreme Court.

Issue

Are employment contracts subject to arbitration if a valid arbitration agreement has been entered into between the parties?

Language of the U.S. Supreme Court

Congress enacted the Federal Arbitration Act (FAA) in 1925. The FAA was a response to hostility of American courts to the enforcement of arbitration agreements. To give effect to this purpose, the FAA compels judicial enforcement of a wide range of written arbitration agreements. The FAA's coverage provision, Section 2, provides that "a written provision in any contract evidencing a transaction involving commerce to settle by arbitration a controversy thereafter arising out of such contract or transaction, or the refusal to perform the whole or any part thereof, shall be valid, irrevocable, and enforceable, save upon such grounds as exist at law or in equity for the revocation of any contract."

Decision

The U.S. Supreme Court held that employment contracts, including the one in this case between Circuit City and Adams, are subject to arbitration if a valid arbitration agreement has been executed. The Supreme Court reversed the decision of the Court of Appeals and remanded the case for further proceedings.

Case Questions

Critical Legal Thinking   What is arbitration? What does the Federal Arbitration Act provide?

Business Ethics   Is it ethical for employers to include arbitration clauses in employment contracts? Or should employers face judicial litigation? Explain.

Contemporary Business   Who do you think benefits most from arbitration clauses in employment contracts: employers or employees? Why?

Internet Law and Online Commerce

Cyber Law

Online Dispute Resolution

Many ADR service providers now offer **online arbitration.** Most of these services allow a party to a dispute to register the dispute with the service and then notify the other party by e-mail of the registration of the dispute. Most online arbitration requires the registering party to submit an amount that the party is willing to accept or pay to the other party in the online arbitration. The other party is afforded the opportunity to accept the offer. If that party accepts the offer, a settlement has been reached. The other party, however, may return a counteroffer. The process continues until a settlement is reached or one or both of the parties remove themselves from the online ADR process.

Also, several websites offer **online mediation** services. In an online mediation, the parties sit before their computers and sign onto the website. Two chat rooms are assigned to each party. One chat room is used for private conversations with the online mediator, and the other chat room is for conversations between both parties and the mediator.

Online arbitration and online mediation services charge fees, but the fees are reasonable. In an online arbitration or online mediation, a settlement can be reached rather quickly, without paying lawyers' fees and court costs. The parties also act through a more objective online process rather than meet face-to-face or negotiate over the telephone, either of which could involve verbal arguments.

Federal Courthouse, Orange County, California. *This is the U.S. District Court for the Central District of California, Southern Division, located in Santa Ana, California.*

Test Review Terms and Concepts

Affirmative defense
Alternative dispute resolution (ADR)
Answer
Appeal
Appellant (petitioner)
Appellee (respondent)
Arbitration
Arbitration clause
Arbitrator
Binding arbitration
Burden of proof
Closing argument
Complaint
Conciliation
Conciliator
Consolidation
Cost–benefit analysis
Cross-complainant
Cross-complaint
Cross-defendant
Cross-examination
Default judgment
Defendant's case
Deponent
Deposition
Direct examination
Discovery
E-filing

Error of law
Fact-finding
Federal Arbitration Act (FAA)
Final judgment
Finding of fact
Impaneled
Interrogatories
Intervention
Judgment
Judgment notwithstanding the verdict
     (judgment n.o.v. or j.n.o.v.)
Judicial referee
Jury deliberation
Jury instructions (charges)
Jury trial
Litigation
Mediation
Mediator
Mini-trial
Motion for judgment on the pleadings
Motion for summary judgment
Negotiation
Nonjudicial dispute resolution
Notice of appeal
Online arbitration
Online dispute resolution
Online mediation
Opening brief

Opening statement
Physical or mental examination
Plaintiff
Plaintiff's case
Pleadings
Pretrial motion
Production of documents
Rebuttal
Record
Re-direct examination
Rejoinder
Remittitur
Reply
Responding brief
Sequester
Settlement agreement
Settlement conference (pretrial
     hearing)
Statute of limitations
Submission agreement
Summons
Trial brief
Trier of fact
Uniform Arbitration Act
Verdict
Virtual courthouse
Voir dire
Written memorandum

Case Problems

3.1 Physical Examination: Robert Schlagenhauf worked as a bus driver for the Greyhound Corporation. One night the bus he was driving rear-ended a tractor-trailer. Seven passengers on the bus who were injured sued Schlagenhauf and Greyhound for damages. The complaint alleged that Greyhound was negligent for allowing Schlagenhauf to drive a bus when it knew that his eyes and vision "were impaired and deficient." The plaintiffs petitioned the court to order Schlagenhauf to be medically examined concerning these allegations. Schlagenhauf objected to the examination. Who wins? *Schlagenhauf v. Holder*, 379 U.S. 104, 85 S.Ct. 234, 13 L.Ed.2d 152, **Web** 1964 U.S. Lexis 152 (Supreme Court of the United States)

3.2 Interrogatories: Cine Forty-Second Street Theatre Corporation operates a movie theater in New York City's Times Square area. Cine filed a lawsuit against Allied Artists Pictures Corporation, alleging that Allied Artists and local theater owners illegally attempted to prevent Cine from opening its theater, in violation of federal antitrust law. The suit also alleged that once Cine opened the theater, the defendants conspired with motion picture distributors to prevent Cine from exhibiting first-run, quality films. Attorneys for Allied Artists served a set of written questions concerning the lawsuit on Cine. Does Cine have to answer these questions? *Cine Forty-Second Street Theatre Corp. v. Allied Artists Pictures Corp.*, 602 F.2d 1062, **Web** 1979 U.S. App. Lexis 13586 (United States Court of Appeals for the Second Circuit)

3.3 Judgment n.o.v.: Mr. Simblest was driving a car that collided with a fire engine at an intersection in Burlington, Vermont. The accident occurred on a night on which a power blackout had left most of the state without lights. Mr. Simblest, who was injured in the accident, sued the driver of the fire truck for damages. During the trial, Simblest testified that when he entered the intersection, the traffic light was green in his favor. All the other witnesses testified that the traffic light had gone dark at least 10 minutes before the accident. Simblest testified that the accident was caused by the fire truck's failure to use any warning lights or sirens. Simblest's testimony was contradicted by four witnesses, who testified that the fire truck had used both its lights and sirens. The jury found that the driver of the fire truck had been negligent and rendered a verdict for Simblest. The defense made a motion for judgment n.o.v. Who wins? *Simblest v. Maynard*, 427 F.2d 1, **Web** 1970 U.S. App. Lexis 9265 (United States Court of Appeals for the Second Circuit)

3.4 Arbitration: AMF Incorporated and Brunswick Corporation both manufacture electric and automatic bowling center equipment. In 1983, the two companies became involved in a dispute over whether Brunswick had advertised certain automatic scoring devices in a false and deceptive manner. The two parties settled the dispute by signing an agreement that any future problems between them involving advertising claims would be submitted to the National Advertising Council for arbitration. Brunswick advertised a new product, Armor Plate 3000, a synthetic laminated material used to make bowling lanes. Armor Plate 3000 competed with wooden lanes produced by AMF. Brunswick's advertisements claimed that bowling centers could save up to $500 per lane per year in maintenance and repair costs if they switched to Armor Plate 3000 from wooden lanes. AMF disputed this claim and requested arbitration. Is the arbitration agreement enforceable? *AMF Incorporated v. Brunswick Corp.,* 621 F.Supp. 456, **Web** 1985 U.S. Dist. Lexis 14205 (United States District Court for the Eastern District of New York)

Business Ethics Case

3.1 Business Ethics: Dennis and Francis Burnham were married in West Virginia in 1976. In 1977, the couple moved to New Jersey, where their two children were born. In July 1987, the Burnhams decided to separate. Mrs. Burnham, who intended to move to California, was to have custody of the children. Mr. Burnham agreed to file for divorce on grounds of irreconcilable differences. Mr. Burnham threatened to file for divorce in New Jersey on grounds of desertion. After unsuccessfully demanding that Mr. Burnham adhere to the prior agreement, Mrs. Burnham brought suit for divorce in California state court in early January 1988. In late January, Mr. Burnham visited California on a business trip. He then visited his children in the San Francisco Bay area, where his wife resided. He took the older child to San Francisco for the weekend. Upon returning the child to Mrs. Burnham's home, he was served with a California court summons and a copy of Mrs. Burnham's divorce petition. He then returned to New Jersey. Mr. Burnham made a special appearance in the California court and moved to quash the service of process. Did Mr. Burnham act ethically in trying to quash the service of process? Did Mrs. Burnham act ethically in having Mr. Burnham served on his visit to California? Is the service of process good? *Burnham v. Superior Court of California,* 495 U.S. 604, 110 S.Ct. 2105, 109 L.Ed.2d 631, **Web** 1990 U.S. Lexis 2700 (Supreme Court of the United States)

Endnotes

1. There is no right to a jury trial for actions in equity (e.g., injunctions, specific performance).
2. 9 U.S.C. Section 1 et seq.
3. *Gilmer v. Interstate/Johnson Lane Corporation*, 500 U.S. 20, 111 S.Ct. 1647, 114 L.Ed.2d 26, **Web** 1991 U.S. Lexis 2529 (Supreme Court of the United States).

CHAPTER 4

"Ethical considerations can no more be excluded from the administration of justice, which is the end and purpose of all civil laws, than one can exclude the vital air from his room and live."

—John F. Dillon
Laws and Jurisprudence of England and America Lecture I (1894)

Ethics and Social Responsibility of Business

Chapter Objectives

After studying this chapter, you should be able to:

1. Describe how law and ethics intertwine.
2. Describe the moral theories of business ethics.
3. Describe the theories of the social responsibility of business.
4. Examine the provisions of the Sarbanes-Oxley Act.
5. Describe corporate social audits.

Chapter Contents

Introduction to Ethics and Social Responsibility of Business

Businesses organized in the United States are subject to its laws. They are also subject to the laws of other countries in which they operate. In addition, businesspersons owe a duty to act ethically in the conduct of their affairs, and businesses owe a social responsibility not to harm society.

Although much of the law is based on ethical standards, not all ethical standards have been enacted as law. The law establishes a minimum degree of conduct expected by persons and businesses in society. Ethics demands more. This chapter discusses business ethics and the social responsibility of business.

Ethics and the Law

ethics
A set of moral principles or values that governs the conduct of an individual or a group.

Ethics precede laws as man precedes society.

Jason Alexander
Philosophy for Investors (1979)

Sometimes the rule of law and the golden rule of **ethics** demand the same response by a person confronted with a problem. For example, federal and state laws make bribery unlawful. A person violates the law if he or she bribes a judge for a favorable decision in a case. Ethics would also prohibit this conduct. However, the law may permit something that would be ethically wrong.

Example
Occupational safety laws set standards for emissions of dust from toxic chemicals in the workplace. Suppose a company can reduce the emission below the legal standard by spending additional money. The only benefit from the expenditure would be better employee health. Ethics would require the extra expenditure; the law would not.

Another alternative occurs where the law demands certain conduct but a person's ethical standards are contrary.

Example
Federal law prohibits employers from hiring certain illegal alien workers. Suppose an employer advertises the availability of a job and receives no response except from a person who cannot prove he or she is a citizen of this country or does not possess a required visa. The worker and his or her family are destitute. Should the employer hire him or her? The law says no, but ethics says yes (see Exhibit 4.1).

Business Ethics

He who seeks equality must do equity.

Joseph Story
Equity Jurisprudence (1836)

How can ethics be measured? The answer is very personal: What is considered ethical by one person may be considered unethical by another. However, there do seem to be some universal rules about what conduct is ethical and what conduct is not. The following discussion highlights five major theories of ethics.

■ **EXHIBIT 4.1** Law and Ethics

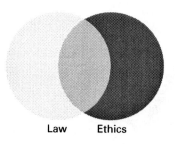

Law   Ethics

Ethics Spotlight

Wal-Mart Pays Big for Meal Break Violations

"At Wal-Mart, not only is there no such thing as a free lunch for employees but, in this sad case, there is no lunch at all."

—Wal-Mart Watch

In recent years, retail giant Wal-Mart has been the target of hundreds of lawsuits by employees in dozens of states, claiming the company violated wage-and-hour laws. In Colorado, Wal-Mart settled with a group of employees for $50 million because of denied meal break violations. In Oregon, workers were rewarded with nearly $2,000 each for similar violations.

A group of California Wal-Mart employees became the first in a series of class action lawsuits involving the denied meal breaks. In *Wal-Mart Stores v. S.C. (Savaglio)*, **Web** 2004 Cal. Lexis 3284 (Supreme Court of California, 2004), both current and former employees argued that Wal-Mart had violated California's meal period law. Wal-Mart fought back, saying that it didn't break any law.

The Oakland, California, jury watched four months of testimony and deliberated for three days before coming back with its verdict: 116,000 current and former Wal-

Mart employees were to receive $172 million in general and punitive damages. Wal-Mart employees and community activists felt vindicated and insisted that the company fix the broken system. Wal-Mart Watch, a union-backed group that keeps a very close eye on everything the company does, commented, "At Wal-Mart, not only is there no such thing as a free lunch for employees but, in this sad case, there is no lunch at all."

Less than a year after the meal break case, Wal-Mart was in court in Pennsylvania. This time, the jury hit the company with over $78 million in damages for forcing employees to work "off the clock" and during rest breaks.

Business Ethics

Did Wal-Mart act ethically in this case? Why do think Wal-Mart acted as it did in this case?

Ethical Fundamentalism

Under **ethical fundamentalism**, a person looks to an **outside source** for ethical rules or commands. This may be a book (e.g., the Bible, the Koran) or a person (e.g., Karl Marx). Critics argue that ethical fundamentalism does not permit people to determine right and wrong for themselves. Taken to an extreme, the result could be considered unethical under most other moral theories. For example, a literal interpretation of the maxim "an eye for an eye" would permit retaliation.

ethical fundamentalism
A theory of ethics that says a person looks to an outside source for ethical rules or commands.

Utilitarianism

Utilitarianism is a moral theory with origins in the works of Jeremy Bentham (1748–1832) and John Stuart Mill (1806–1873). This moral theory dictates that people must choose the actions or follow the rule that provides the **greatest good to society**. This does not mean the greatest good for the greatest number of people.

utilitarianism
A moral theory that dictates that people must choose the action or follow the rule that provides the greatest good to society.

Example
If an action would increase the good of 25 people by 1 unit each and an alternative action would increase the good of 1 person by 26 units, then the latter action should be taken.

Utilitarianism has been criticized because it is difficult to estimate the "good" that will result from different actions, it is hard to apply in an imperfect world, and it treats morality as if it were an impersonal mathematical calculation.

Example
A company is trying to determine whether it should close an unprofitable plant located in a small community. Utilitarianism would require that the benefits to shareholders from closing the plant be compared to the benefits to employees, their families, and others in the community in keeping it open.

Landmark Law

The Whistleblower Statute

The Bayer Corporation (Bayer) is a U.S. subsidiary corporation of the giant German-based Bayer A.G. Bayer is a large pharmaceutical company that produces prescription drugs, including its patented antibiotic Cipro. Bayer sold Cipro to private health providers and hospitals, including Kaiser Permanente Medical Care Program, the largest health maintenance organization in the United States. Bayer also sold Cipro to the federal government's Medicaid program, which provides medical insurance to the poor. Federal law contains a "best price" rule that prohibits a company that sells a drug to Medicaid from charging Medicaid a price higher than the lowest price for which it sells the drug to private purchasers.

Kaiser told Bayer that it would not purchase Cipro from Bayer—and would switch to a competitor's antibiotics—unless Bayer reduced the price of Cipro. Bayer's executives came up with a plan whereby Bayer would put a private label on its Cipro and not call it Cipro and sell the antibiotic to Kaiser at a 40 percent discount. Thus, Bayer continued to charge Medicaid the full price for Cipro while giving Kaiser a 40 percent discount through the private labeling program. One of Bayer's executives who negotiated this deal with Kaiser was corporate account manager George Couto.

Everything went well for Bayer until Couto attended a mandatory ethics training class at Bayer at which a video of Heige Wehmeier, then company chief executive, was shown. When the video stated that Bayer employees were to obey not only "the letter of the law but the spirit of the law as well," some of the Bayer executives laughed. Later that day, Couto attended a staff meeting at which it was disclosed that Bayer kept $97 million from Medicaid by using the discounted private labeling program for Kaiser and other health care companies. Two days later, Couto wrote a memorandum to his boss, questioning the legality of the private labeling program in light of Medicaid's "best price" law.

When he received no response to his memo, Couto contacted a lawyer. Couto filed a ***qui tam*** **lawsuit** under the federal **False Claims Act**—also known as the **Whistleblower Statute**—which permits private parties to sue companies for fraud on behalf of the government. The riches: The whistleblower can be awarded up to 25 percent of the amount recovered on behalf of the federal government, even if the informer has been a co-conspirator in perpetrating the fraud [31 U.S.C. Sections 3729-3733].

After the case was filed, the U.S. Department of Justice took over the case, as allowed by law, and filed criminal as well as civil charges against Bayer. After discovery was taken, Bayer pleaded guilty to one criminal felony and agreed to pay federal and state governments $257 million to settle the civil and criminal cases. Couto, age 39, died of pancreatic cancer three months prior to the settlement. Couto was awarded $34 million, which went to his three children. Did Bayer act ethically in this case? Did Couto act ethically in this case? *United States ex. rel. Estate of George Couto v. Bayer Corporation* (United States District Court for the District of Massachusetts, 2003).

Kantian Ethics

Kantian ethics

A moral theory which says that people owe moral duties that are based on universal rules, such as the categorical imperative "Do unto others as you would have them do unto you." Also known as *duty ethics*.

Immanuel Kant (1724–1804) is the best-known proponent of **duty ethics**, also called **Kantian ethics**. Kant believed that people owe moral duties that are based on **universal rules**. Kant's philosophy is based on the premise that people can use reasoning to reach ethical decisions. His ethical theory would have people behave according to the *categorical imperative* "Do unto others as you would have them do unto you."

Example

According to Kantian ethics, keeping a promise to abide by a contract is a moral duty even if that contract turns out to be detrimental to the obligated party.

The universal rules of Kantian ethics are based on two important principles: (1) consistency— that is, all cases are treated alike, with no exceptions—and (2) reversibility— that is, the actor must abide by the rule he or she uses to judge the morality of someone else's conduct. Thus, if you are going to make an exception for yourself, that exception becomes a universal rule that applies to all others. For example, if you rationalize that it is acceptable for you to engage in deceptive practices, it is acceptable for competitors to do so also. A criticism of Kantian ethics is that it is difficult to reach consensus as to what the universal rules should be.

In the following case, a company alleged that a competitor had engaged in false advertising.

CASE 4.1
Business Ethics

Pizza Hut, Inc. v. Papa John's International, Inc.

227 F.3d 489, Web 2000 U.S. App. Lexis 23444 (2000)
United States Court of Appeals for the Fifth Circuit

"This simple statement, 'Better Pizza.,' epitomizes the exaggerated advertising, blustering and boasting by a manufacturer upon which no consumer would reasonably rely."

—Judge Jolly

Facts

Papa John's International, Inc., is the third-largest pizza chain in the United States, with more than 2,050 locations. Papa John's adopted a new slogan—"Better Ingredients. Better Pizza."—and applied for and received a federal trademark for this slogan. Papa John's spent over $300 million building customer recognition and goodwill for this slogan. This slogan has appeared on millions of signs, shirts, menus, pizza boxes, napkins, and other items, and it has regularly appeared as the tag line at the end of Papa John's radio and television advertisements.

Pizza Hut, Inc., is the largest pizza chain in the United States, with more than 7,000 restaurants. Two years after the Papa John's advertisements began, Pizza Hut launched a new advertising campaign in which it declared "war" on poor-quality pizza. The advertisements touted the "better taste" of Pizza Hut's pizza and "dared" anyone to find a better pizza.

A few weeks later, Papa John's countered with a comparative advertising campaign that touted the superiority of Papa John's pizza over Pizza Hut's pizza. Papa John's claimed it had superior sauce and dough to Pizza Hut. Many of these advertisements were accompanied by the Papa John's slogan "Better Ingredients. Better Pizza."

Pizza Hut filed a civil action in U.S. District Court, charging Papa John's with false advertising in violation of Section 43(a) of the federal Lanham Act. The U.S. District Court found that the Papa John's slogan "Better Ingredients. Better Pizza." standing alone was mere puffery and did not constitute false advertising. The District Court found, however, that Papa John's claims of superior sauce and dough were misleading and that the Papa John's slogan "Better

Ingredients. Better Pizza." became tainted because it was associated with these misleading statements. The U.S. District Court enjoined Papa John's from using the slogan "Better Ingredients. Better Pizza." Papa John's appealed.

Issue

Is the Papa John's slogan "Better Ingredients. Better Pizza." false advertising?

Language of the Court

One form of non-actionable statements of general opinion under Section 43(a) of the Lanham Act has been referred to as "puffery." Prosser and Keeton on the Law of Torts (5th edition) define "puffing" as "a seller's privilege to lie his head off, so long as he says nothing specific, on the theory that no reasonable man would believe him, or that no reasonable man would be influenced by such talk."

We turn now to consider the case before us. Reduced to its essence, the question is whether the evidence established that Papa John's slogan "Better Ingredients. Better Pizza." is misleading and violative of Section 43(a) of the Lanham Act. Bisecting the slogan "Better Ingredients. Better Pizza.," it is clear that the assertion by Papa John's that it makes a "Better Pizza." is a general statement of opinion regarding the superiority of its product over all others. Consequently, it appears indisputable that Papa John's assertion "Better Pizza." is non-actionable puffery.

Moving next to consider the phrase "Better Ingredients," the same conclusion holds true. Like "Better Pizza." it is typical puffery. Thus, it is equally clear that Papa John's assertion that it uses "Better Ingredients." is one of opinion not

actionable under the Lanham Act. Consequently, the slogan as a whole is a statement of non-actionable opinion. Thus, there is no legally sufficient basis to support the jury's finding that the slogan is a "false or misleading" statement of fact.

Decision
The U.S. Court of Appeals held that the Papa John's trademarked slogan "Better Ingredients. Better Pizza." was mere puffery and a statement of opinion that was not false advertising and did not violate Section 43(a) of the Lanham Act. The U.S. Court of Appeals reversed the judgment of the U.S. District Court and remanded the case to the District Court for entry of judgment for Papa John's.

Case Questions

Critical Legal Thinking What is false advertising? What is puffery? How do they differ from one another?

Business Ethics Do businesses sometimes make exaggerated claims about their products? Are consumers smart enough to see through companies' puffery?

Contemporary Business If the Court of Appeals had found in favor of Pizza Hut, what would have been the effect on advertising in this country? Explain.

Rawls's Social Justice Theory

social contract
A moral theory that says each person is presumed to have entered into a social contract with all others in society to obey moral rules that are necessary for people to live in peace and harmony.

The notion that a business is clothed with a public interest and has been devoted to the public use is little more than a fiction intended to beautify what is disagreeable to the sufferers.

Justice Holmes
Tyson & Bro-United Theatre Ticket Officers v. Banton (1927)

John Locke (1632–1704) and Jean-Jacques Rousseau (1712–1778) proposed a **social contract** theory of morality. Under this theory, each person is presumed to have entered into a social contract with all others in society to obey moral rules that are necessary for people to live in peace and harmony. This implied contract states, "I will keep the rules if everyone else does." These moral rules are then used to solve conflicting interests in society.

The leading proponent of the modern justice theory was John Rawls (1921–2002), a philosopher at Harvard University. Under **Rawls's social justice theory**, fairness is considered the essence of justice. The principles of justice should be chosen by persons who do not yet know their station in society—thus, their "veil of ignorance" would permit the fairest possible principles to be selected.

Example
Under Rawls's social justice theory, the principle of equal opportunity in employment would be promulgated by people who would not yet know if they were in a favored class.

As a caveat, Rawls also proposed that the least advantaged in society must receive special assistance in order to realize their potential. Rawls's theory of social justice is criticized for two reasons. First, establishing the blind "original position" for choosing moral principles is impossible in the real world. Second, many persons in society would choose not to maximize the benefit to the least advantaged persons in society.

Ethical Relativism

ethical relativism
A moral theory which holds that individuals must decide what is ethical based on their own feelings about what is right and wrong.

Ethical relativism holds that individuals must decide what is ethical based on their own feelings about what is right and wrong. Under this moral theory, if a person meets his or her own moral standard in making a decision, no one can criticize him or her for it. Thus, there are no universal ethical rules to guide a person's conduct. This theory has been criticized because action that is usually thought to be unethical (e.g., committing fraud) would not be unethical if the perpetrator thought it was in fact ethical. Few philosophers advocate ethical relativism as an acceptable moral theory.

Concept Summary
Theories of Ethics

Theory	Description
Ethical fundamentalism	Persons look to an outside source (e.g., the Bible, the Koran) or a central figure for ethical guidelines.
Utilitarianism	Persons choose the alternative that would provide the greatest good to society.
Kantian ethics	A set of universal rules establishes ethical duties. The rules are based on reasoning and require (1) consistency in application and (2) reversibility.
Rawls's social justice theory	Moral duties are based on an implied social contract. Fairness is justice. The rules are established from an original position of a "veil of ignorance."
Ethical relativism	Individuals decide what is ethical based on their own feelings as to what is right or wrong.

Social Responsibility of Business

Businesses do not operate in a vacuum. Decisions made by businesses have far-reaching effects on society. In the past, many business decisions were based solely on a cost–benefit analysis and how they affected the "bottom line." Such decisions, however, may cause negative externalities for others. For example, the dumping of hazardous wastes from a manufacturing plant into a river affects the homeowners, farmers, and others who use the river's waters. Thus, corporations are considered to owe some degree of **social responsibility** for their actions. Four theories of the social responsibility of business are discussed in the following paragraphs.

The ultimate justification of the law is to be found, and can only be found, in moral considerations.

Lord MacMillan
Law and Other Things (1937)

Maximizing Profits

The traditional view of the social responsibility of business is that business should **maximize profits** for shareholders. This view, which dominated business and the law during the nineteenth century, holds that the interests of other constituencies (e.g., employees, suppliers, residents of the communities in which businesses are located) are not important in and of themselves.

maximizing profits
A theory of social responsibility that says a corporation owes a duty to take actions that maximize profits for shareholders.

Example

In the famous case *Dodge v. Ford Motor Company*,[1] a shareholder sued Ford Motor Company when its founder Henry Ford introduced a plan to reduce the prices of cars so that more people would be put to work and more people could own cars. The shareholders alleged that such a plan would not increase dividends. Mr. Ford testified, "My ambition is to employ still more men, to spread the benefits of this industrial system to the greatest number, to help them build up their lives and their homes." The court sided with the shareholders and stated that:

> [Mr. Ford's] testimony creates the impression that he thinks the Ford Motor company has made too much money, has had too large profits and that, although large profits might still be earned, a sharing of them with the public, by reducing the price of the output of the company, ought to be undertaken.
>
> There should be no confusion of the duties which Mr. Ford conceives that he and the stockholders owe to the general public and the duties which in law he and his codirectors owe to protesting, minority stockholders. A business corporation is organized and carried on primarily for the profit of the stockholders. The powers of the directors are to be employed for that end. The discretion of directors is to be exercised in the choice of means to attain that end and does not extend to a change in the end itself, to the reduction of profits, or to the nondistribution of profits among stockholders in order to devote them to other purposes.

Public policy: That principle of the law which holds that no subject can lawfully do that which has a tendency to be injurious to the public or against the public good.

Lord Truro
Egerton v. Brownlow (1853)

CASE 4.2
Business Ethics

U.S. Supreme Court
Wal-Mart Stores, Inc. v. Samara Brothers, Inc.

529 U.S. 205, 120 S.Ct. 1339, 146 L.Ed.2d 182, Web 2000 U.S. Lexis 2197 (2000)
Supreme Court of the United States

"Their suspicions aroused, however, Samara officials launched an investigation, which disclosed that Wal-Mart [was] selling the knockoffs of Samara's outfits."

—Justice Scalia

Facts

Samara Brothers, Inc. (Samara), is a designer and manufacturer of children's clothing. The core of Samara's business is its annual new line of spring and summer children's garments. Samara sold its clothing to retailers, who in turn sold the clothes to consumers. Wal-Mart Stores, Inc. (Wal-Mart), operates a large chain of budget warehouse stores that sell thousands of items at very low prices. Wal-Mart contacted one of its suppliers, Judy-Philippine, Inc. (JPI), about the possibility of making a line of children's clothes just like Samara's successful line. Wal-Mart sent photographs of Samara's children's clothes to JPI (the name "Samara" was readily discernible on the labels of the garments) and directed JPI to produce children's clothes exactly like those in the photographs. JPI produced a line of children's clothes for Wal-Mart that copied the designs, colors, and patterns of Samara's clothing. Wal-Mart then sold this line of children's clothing in its stores, making a gross profit of over $1.15 million on these clothes sales during the 1996 selling season.

Samara discovered that Wal-Mart was selling the knockoff clothes at a price that was lower than Samara's retailers were paying Samara for its clothes. After sending unsuccessful cease-and-desist letters to Wal-Mart, Samara sued Wal-Mart, alleging that Wal-Mart stole Samara's trade dress (i.e., look and feel) in violation of Section 43(a) of the Lanham Act. Although not finding that Samara's clothes had acquired a secondary meaning in the minds of the public, the U.S. District Court held in favor of Samara and awarded damages. The U.S. Court of Appeals affirmed the award to Samara. Wal-Mart appealed to the U.S. Supreme Court.

Issue

Must a product's design have acquired a secondary meaning before it is protected as trade dress?

Language of the U.S. Supreme Court

The Lanham Act, in Section 43(a), gives a producer a cause of action for the use by any person of "any word, term, name, symbol, or device, or any combination thereof which is likely to cause confusion as to the origin, sponsorship, or approval of his or her goods." The text of Section 43(a) provides little guidance as to the circumstances under which unregistered trade dress may be protected. It does require that a producer show that the allegedly infringing feature is likely to cause confusion with the product for which protection is sought. In an action for infringement of unregistered trade dress a product's design is protectable only upon a showing of secondary meaning.

Decision

The U.S. Supreme Court held that a product's design has to have acquired a secondary meaning in the public's eye before it is protected as trade dress under Section 43(a) of the Lanham Act. The Supreme Court reversed the decision of the U.S. Court of Appeals and remanded the case for further proceedings consistent with its opinion.

Case Questions

Critical Legal Thinking What is trade dress? Should it have been protected in this case?

Business Ethics Even if Wal-Mart's conduct was ruled legal, was it ethical?

Contemporary Business What can companies like Samara do to protect themselves from similar conduct by Wal-Mart or other larger companies? Explain.

Sarbanes-Oxley Act Prompts Public Companies to Adopt Codes of Ethics

In the late 1990s and early 2000s, many large corporations in the United States were found to have engaged in massive financial frauds. Many of these frauds were perpetrated by the chief executive officers and other senior officers of the companies. Financial officers, such as chief financial officers and controllers, were also found to have been instrumental in committing these frauds. In response, Congress enacted the **Sarbanes-Oxley Act** of 2002, which makes certain conduct illegal and establishes criminal penalties for violations. In addition, the Sarbanes-Oxley Act prompts companies to encourage senior officers of public companies to act ethi-cally in their dealings with shareholders, employees, and other constituents.

Section 406 of the Sarbanes-Oxley Act requires a public company to disclose whether it has adopted a **code of ethics** for senior financial officers, including its principal financial officer and principal accounting officer. In response, public companies have adopted codes of ethics for their senior financial officers. Many public companies have included all officers and employees in the coverage of their codes of ethics.

A typical code of ethics is illustrated in Exhibit 4.2.

Milton Friedman, who won the Nobel Prize in economics when he taught at the University of Chicago, advocated the theory of maximizing profits for shareholders. Friedman asserted that in a free society, "there is one and only one social responsibility of business—to use its resources and engage in activities designed to increase its profits as long as it stays within the rules of the game, which is to say, engages in open and free competition without deception and fraud."[2]

In the previous case, Wal-Mart was accused of unlawfully knocking off another company's product design.

Moral Minimum

Some proponents of corporate social responsibility argue that a corporation's duty is to **make a profit while avoiding causing harm to others**. This theory of social responsibility is called the **moral minimum**. Under this theory, as long as business avoids or corrects the social injury it causes, it has met its duty of social responsibility.

moral minimum
A theory of social responsibility that says a corporation's duty is to make a profit while avoiding causing harm to others.

Example
A corporation that pollutes the waters and then compensates those whom it injures has met its moral minimum duty of social responsibility.

The legislative and judicial branches of government have established laws that enforce the moral minimum of social responsibility on corporations.

Examples
Occupational safety laws establish minimum safety standards for protecting employees from injuries in the workplace. Consumer protection laws establish safety requirements for products and make manufacturers and sellers liable for injuries caused by defective products.

Stakeholder Interest

Businesses have relationships with all sorts of people besides their shareholders, including employees, suppliers, customers, creditors, and the local community. Under the **stakeholder interest** theory of social responsibility, a corporation must consider the effects its actions have on these *other stakeholders*. For example, a corporation would violate the stakeholder interest theory if it viewed employees solely as a means of maximizing shareholder wealth.

stakeholder interest
A theory of social responsibility that says a corporation must consider the effects its actions have on persons other than its shareholders.

The stakeholder interest theory is criticized because it is difficult to harmonize the conflicting interests of stakeholders.

■ EXHIBIT 4.2 Code of Ethics

**Big Cheese Corporation
Code of Ethics**

Big Cheese Corporation's mission includes the promotion of professional conduct in the practice of general management worldwide. Big Cheese's Chief Executive Officer (CEO), Chief Financial Officer (CFO), corporate Controller, and other employees of the finance organization and other employees of the corporation hold an important and elevated role in the corporate governance of the corporation. They are empowered and uniquely capable to ensure that all constituents' interests are appropriately balanced, protected, and preserved.

This Code of Ethics embodies principles to which we are expected to adhere and advocate. The CEO, CFO, finance organization employees, and other employees of the corporation are expected to abide by this Code of Ethics and all business conduct standards of the corporation relating to areas covered by this Code of Ethics. Any violation of the Code of Ethics may result in disciplinary action, up to and including termination of employment. All employees will:

- Act with honesty and integrity, avoiding actual or apparent conflicts of interest in their personal and professional relations.
- Provide stakeholders with information that is accurate, fair, complete, timely, objective, relevant, and understandable, including in our filings with and other submissions to the U.S. Securities and Exchange Commission.
- Comply with rules and regulations of federal, state, provincial, and local governments and other appropriate private and public regulatory agencies.
- Act in good faith, responsibly, with due care, competence, and diligence, without misrepresenting material facts or allowing one's independent judgment to be subordinated.
- Respect the confidentiality of information acquired in the course of one's work, except when authorized or otherwise legally obligated to disclose. Confidential information acquired in the course of one's work will not be used for personal advantage.
- Share knowledge and maintain professional skills important and relevant to stakeholders' needs.
- Proactively promote and be an example of ethical behavior as a responsible partner among peers, in the work environment and the community.
- Achieve responsible use, control, and stewardship over all Big Cheese's assets and resources that are employed or entrusted to us.
- Not unduly or fraudulently influence, coerce, manipulate, or mislead any authorized audit or interfere with any auditor engaged in the performance of an internal or independent audit of Big Cheese's financial statements or accounting books and records.

If you are aware of any suspected or known violations of this Code of Ethics or other Big Cheese policies or guidelines, you have a duty to promptly report such concerns either to your manager, another responsible member of management, a Human Resources representative, or the Director of Compliance or the 24-hour Business Conduct Line.

If you have a concern about a questionable accounting or auditing matter and wish to submit the concern confidentially or anonymously, you may do so by sending an e-mail to (bc.codeofethics@bigcheese.cc) or calling the Business Conduct Line 24-hour number at 1-888-666-BIGC (2442).

Big Cheese will handle all inquiries discreetly and make every effort to maintain, within the limits allowed by law, the confidentiality of anyone requesting guidance or reporting questionable behavior and/or a compliance concern.

It is Big Cheese's intention that this Code of Ethics to be its written code of ethics under Section 406 of the Sarbanes-Oxley Act of 2002 complying with the standards set forth in Securities and Exchange Commission Regulation S-K Item 406.

Example

In deciding to close an unprofitable manufacturing plant, certain stakeholders would benefit (e.g., shareholders and creditors), while other stakeholders would not (e.g., current employees and the local community).

Corporate Citizenship

corporate citizenship
A theory of responsibility that says a business has a responsibility to do good.

The **corporate citizenship** theory of social responsibility argues that business has a responsibility to do well. That is, business is responsible for helping to solve social problems that it did little, if anything, to cause.

Example

Under corporate citizenship theory of social responsibility, corporations owe a duty to subsidize schools and help educate children.

Contemporary Environment

The Corporate Social Audit

It has been suggested that corporate audits should be extended to include not only audits of the financial health of a corporation but also of its moral health. It is expected that corporations that conduct **corporate social audits** would be more apt to prevent unethical and illegal conduct by managers, employees, and agents. The audit would examine how well employees have adhered to the company's code of ethics and how well the corporation has met its duty of social responsibility.

Such audits would focus on the corporation's efforts to promote employment opportunities for members of protected classes, worker safety, environmental protection, consumer protection, and the like. Social audits are not easy. First, it may be difficult to conceptualize just what is being audited. Second, it may be difficult to measure results. Despite these factors, a growing number of companies are expected to undertake social audits.

Companies should institute the following procedures when conducting a social audit:

- An independent outside firm should be hired to conduct the audit. This ensures autonomy and objectivity in conducting the audit.
- The company's personnel should cooperate fully with the auditing firm while the audit is being conducted.
- The auditing firm should report its findings directly to the company's board of directors.
- The board of directors should review the results of the audit. The board of directors should determine how the company can better meet its duty of social responsibility and can use the audit to implement a program to correct any deficiencies it finds.

This theory contends that corporations owe a duty to promote the same social goals as individual members of society. Proponents of this "do good" theory argue that corporations owe a debt to society to make it a better place and that this duty arises because of the social power bestowed on them. That is, this social power is a gift from society and should be used to good ends.

A major criticism of this theory is that the duty of a corporation to do good cannot be expanded beyond certain limits. There is always some social problem that needs to be addressed, and corporate funds are limited. Further, if this theory were taken to its maximum limit, potential shareholders might be reluctant to invest in corporations.

In civilized life, law floats in a sea of ethics.

Earl Warren

Concept Summary
Theories of Social Responsibility

Theory	Social Responsibility
Maximizing profits	To maximize profits for stockholders.
Moral minimum	To avoid causing harm and to compensate for harm caused.
Stakeholder interest	To consider the interests of all stakeholders, including stockholders, employees, customers, suppliers, creditors, and the local community.
Corporate citizenship	To do well and solve social problems.

Test Review Terms and Concepts

Code of ethics
Corporate citizenship
Corporate social audit
Ethical fundamentalism
Ethical relativism
Ethics
False Claims Act (Whistleblower
    Statute)

Greatest good to society
Kantian ethics (duty ethics)
Maximizing profits
Moral minimum (make a profit while
    avoiding causing harm to others)
Outside source
Qui tam lawsuit
Rawls's social justice theory

Sarbanes-Oxley Act
Section 406
Social contract
Social responsibility of business
Stakeholder interest
Universal rules
Utilitarianism

Case Problems

4.1 Fraud: The Warner-Lambert Company has manufactured and distributed Listerine antiseptic mouthwash since 1879. Its formula has never changed. Ever since Listerine's introduction, the company has represented the product as being beneficial in preventing and curing colds and sore throats. Direct advertising of these claims to consumers began in 1921. Warner-Lambert spent millions of dollars annually advertising these claims in print media and in television commercials.

After 100 years of Warner-Lambert's making such claims, the Federal Trade Commission (FTC) filed a complaint against the company, alleging that it had engaged in false advertising in violation of federal law. Four months of hearings were held before an administrative law judge that produced an evidentiary record of more than 4,000 pages of documents from 46 witnesses. After examining the evidence, the FTC issued an opinion which held that the company's representations that Listerine prevented and cured colds and sore throats were false. The U.S. Court of Appeals affirmed. Is Warner-Lambert guilty of fraud? If so, what remedies should the court impose on the company? Did Warner-Lambert act ethically in making its claims for Listerine? *Warner-Lambert Company v. Federal Trade Commission*, 183 U.S. App. D.C. 230, 562 F.2d 749, **Web** 1977 U.S. App. Lexis 11599 (United States Court of Appeals for the District of Columbia Circuit)

4.2 Liability: The Johns-Manville Corporation was a profitable company that made a variety of building and other products. It was a major producer of asbestos, which was used for insulation in buildings and for a variety of other uses. It has been medically proven that excessive exposure to asbestos causes asbestosis, a fatal lung disease. Thousands of employees of the company and consumers who were exposed to asbestos and contracted this fatal disease sued the company for damages. Eventually, the lawsuits were being filed at a rate of more than 400 per week.

In response to the claims, Johns-Manville Corporation filed for reorganization bankruptcy. It argued that if it did not, an otherwise viable company that provided thousands of jobs and served a useful purpose in this country would be destroyed and that without the declaration of bankruptcy, a few of the plaintiffs who first filed their lawsuits would win awards of hundreds of millions of dollars, leaving nothing for the remainder of the plaintiffs. Under the bankruptcy court's protection, the company was restructured to survive. As part of the release from bankruptcy, the company contributed money to a fund to pay current and future claimants. The fund was not large enough to pay all injured persons the full amounts of their claims.

Is Johns-Manville liable for negligence? Was it ethical for Johns-Manville to declare bankruptcy? Did it meet its duty of social responsibility in this case? *In re Johns-Mansville Corporation*, 36 B.R. 727, **Web** 1984 Bankr. Lexis 6384 (United States Bankruptcy Court for the Southern District of New York)

Business Ethics Cases

4.3 Fraud: The Reverend Leon H. Sullivan, a Baptist minister from Philadelphia who was also a member of the board of directors of General Motors Corporation, proposed a set of rules to guide American-owned companies doing business in the Republic of South Africa. The *Sullivan Principles*, as they became known, call for the nonsegregation of races in South Africa. They call for employers to (a) provide equal and fair employment practices for all employees and (b) improve the quality of employees' lives outside the work environment in such areas as housing, education, transportation, recreation, and health facilities. The principles also require signatory companies to report regularly and to be graded on their conduct in South Africa.

Eventually, the Sullivan Principles were subscribed to by several hundred U.S. corporations with affiliates doing business in South Africa. Which of the following theories of social responsibility are the companies that subscribed to the Sullivan Principles following?

1. Maximizing profits
2. Moral minimum
3. Stakeholder interest
4. Corporate citizenship

To put additional pressure on the government of the Republic of South Africa to end apartheid, Reverend Sullivan called for the complete withdrawal of all U.S. companies from doing business in or with South Africa. Very few companies agreed to do so. Do companies owe a social duty to withdraw from South Africa? Should universities divest themselves of investments in companies that do not withdraw from South Africa?

4.4 Business Ethics: Kaiser Aluminum & Chemical Corporation entered into a collective bargaining agreement with the United Steelworkers of America, a union that represented employees at Kaiser's plants. The agreement contained an affirmative-action program to increase the representation of minorities in craft jobs. To enable plants to meet these goals, on-the-job training programs were established to teach unskilled production workers the skills necessary to become craft workers. Assignment to the training program was based on seniority, except that the plan reserved 50 percent of the openings for black employees.

Thirteen craft trainees were selected from Kaiser's Gramercy plant for the training program. Of these, 7 were black and 6 white. The most senior black trainee selected had less seniority than several white production workers who had applied for the positions but were rejected. Brian Weber, one of the white rejected employees, instituted a class action lawsuit, alleging that the affirmative action plan violated Title VII of the Civil Rights Act of 1964, which made it "unlawful to discriminate because of race" in hiring and selecting apprentices for training programs. The U.S. Supreme Court upheld the affirmative-action plan in this case. The decision stated:

We therefore hold that Title VII's prohibition against racial discrimination does not condemn all private,

voluntary, race-conscious affirmative action plans. At the same time, the plant does not unnecessarily trammel the interests of the white employees. Moreover, the plan is a temporary measure; it is not intended to maintain racial balance, but simply to eliminate a manifest racial imbalance.

Do companies owe a duty of social responsibility to provide affirmative-action programs? *United Steelworkers of America v. Weber*, 443 U.S. 193, 99 S.Ct. 2721, 61 L.Ed.2d 480, **Web** 1979 U.S. Lexis 40 (Supreme Court of the United States)

4.5 Business Ethics: Iroquois Brands, Ltd., a Delaware corporation, had $78 million in assets, $141 million in sales, and $6 million in profits. As part of its business, Iroquois imported pâté de foie gras (goose pâté) from France and sold it in the United States. Iroquois derived only $79,000 in revenues from sales of such pâté. The French force-fed the geese from which the pâté was made. Peter C. Lovenheim, who owned 200 shares of Iroquois common stock, proposed to include a shareholder proposal in Iroquois's annual proxy materials to be sent to shareholders. His proposal criticized the company because the force-feeding caused "undue stress, pain and suffering" to the geese and requested that shareholders vote to have Iroquois discontinue importing and selling pâté produced by this method.

Iroquois refused to allow the information to be included in its proxy materials. Iroquois asserted that its refusal was based on the fact that Lovenheim's proposal was "not economically significant" and had only "ethical and social" significance. The company reasoned that because a corporation is an economic entity, only an economic test applied to its activities, and Iroquois was therefore not subject to an ethical or a social responsibility test. Is Iroquois correct? That is, should only an economic test be applied in judging the activities of a corporation? Or should a corporation also be subject to an ethical or a social responsibility test? *Lovenheim v. Iroquois Brands, Ltd.*, 618 F.Supp. 554, **Web** 1985 U.S. Dist. Lexis 21259 (United States District Court for the District of Columbia)

Endnotes

1. 204 Mich. 459, 170 N.W. 668, Web 1919 Mich. Lexis 720 (Supreme Court of Michigan).

2. Milton Friedman, "The Social Responsibility of Business Is to Increase Its Profits," *New York Times Magazine*, September 13, 1970.

CHAPTER 5

"We the People of the United States, in Order to form a more perfect Union, establish Justice, insure domestic Tranquility, provide for the common defense, promote the general Welfare, and secure the Blessings of Liberty to ourselves and our Posterity, do ordain and establish this Constitution for the United States of America."

——Preamble to the Constitution of the United States of America

Constitutional Law for Business and E-Commerce

Chapter Objectives

After studying this chapter, you should be able to:

1. Describe the concept of federalism and the doctrine of separation of powers.
2. Define and apply the Supremacy Clause of the U.S. Constitution.
3. Explain the federal government's authority to regulate foreign commerce and interstate commerce.
4. Explain how speech is protected by the First Amendment.
5. Explain the doctrines of equal protection and due process.

Chapter Contents

Introduction to Constitutional Law for Business and E-Commerce

Prior to the American Revolution, each of the 13 original colonies operated as a separate sovereignty under the rule of England. In September 1774, representatives of the colonies met as a Continental Congress. In 1776, the colonies declared independence from England, and the American Revolution ensued. The **Declaration of Independence** was the document that declared independence from England.

This chapter examines the major provisions of the U.S. Constitution and the amendments that have been added to the Constitution. Of particular importance, this chapter discusses how these provisions affect the operations of business in this country. The Constitution, with amendments, is set forth as Appendix A to this book.

Constitution of the United States of America

In 1778, the Continental Congress formed a **federal government** and adopted the **Articles of Confederation**. The Articles of Confederation created a federal Congress composed of representatives of the 13 new states. The Articles of Confederation was a particularly weak document that gave limited power to the newly created federal government. It did not provide Congress with the power to levy and collect taxes, to regulate commerce with foreign countries, or to regulate interstate commerce.

The **Constitutional Convention** was convened in Philadelphia in May 1787. The primary purpose of the convention was to strengthen the federal government. After substantial debate, the delegates agreed to a new **U.S. Constitution**. The Constitution was reported to Congress in September 1787. State ratification of the Constitution was completed in 1788. Many amendments, including the Bill of Rights, have been added to the Constitution since that time.

> **U.S. Constitution**
> The fundamental law of the United States of America. It was ratified by the states in 1788.

The U.S. Constitution serves two major functions:

1. It creates the three branches of the federal government (i.e., the legislative, executive, and judicial branches) and allocates powers to these branches.
2. It protects individual rights by limiting the government's ability to restrict those rights.

The Constitution itself provides that it may be amended to address social and economic changes. Some important constitutional concepts are discussed in the following paragraphs. Exhibit 5.1 shows the U.S. Constitution.

> *The nation's armour of defence against the passions of men is the Constitution. Take that away, and the nation goes down into the field of its conflicts like a warrior without armour.*
>
> Henry Ward Beecher
> *Proverbs from Plymouth Pulpit, 1887*

Federalism and Delegated Powers

Our country's form of government is referred to as **federalism**. That means that the federal government and the 50 state governments share powers.

When the states ratified the Constitution, they **delegated** certain powers—called **enumerated powers**—to the federal government.

> **federalism**
> The U.S. form of government, in which the federal government and the 50 state governments share powers.
>
> **enumerated powers**
> Certain powers delegated to the federal government by the states.

Example
The federal government is authorized to deal with national and international affairs.

■ EXHIBIT 5.1 The Constitution of the United States of America

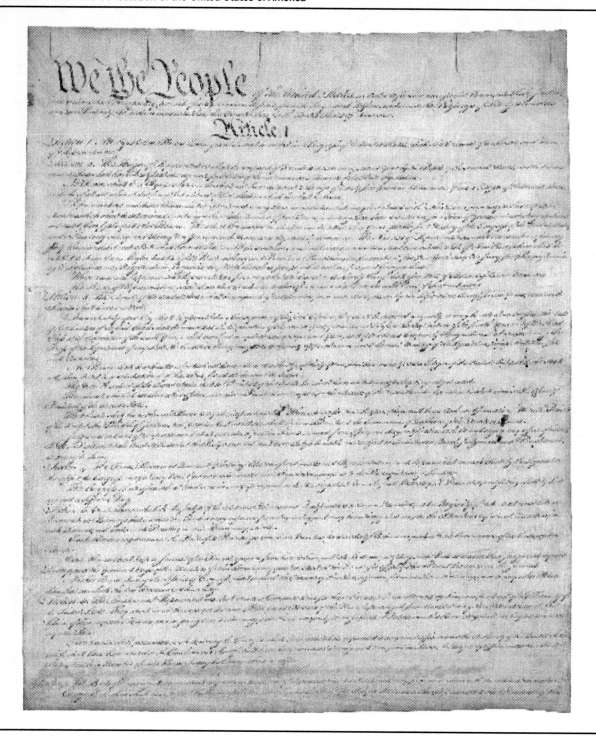

Any powers that are not specifically delegated to the federal government by the Constitution are **reserved** to the state governments. State governments are empowered to deal with local affairs.

Doctrine of Separation of Powers

As mentioned previously, the federal government is divided into three branches:

1. Article I of the Constitution establishes the **legislative branch** of government. The legislative branch is responsible for making federal law. This branch is **bicameral**; that is, it consists of the Senate and the House of Representatives. Collectively, they are referred to as **Congress**.[1] Each state has two senators. The number of representatives to the House of Representatives is determined according to the population of each state. The current number of representatives is determined by the most recent census.

2. Article II of the Constitution establishes the **executive branch** of government by providing for the election of the president and vice president. The president is not elected by popular vote but instead is selected by the **electoral college**, whose representatives are appointed by state delegations.[2] The executive branch of government is responsible for enforcing federal law.

3. Article III of the Constitution establishes the **judicial branch** of the government by establishing the U.S. Supreme Court and providing for the creation of other federal courts by Congress.[3] The judicial branch is responsible for interpreting the U.S Constitution and federal law.

legislative branch
The part of the U.S. government that makes federal laws. It is known as Congress (the Senate and the House of Representatives).

executive branch
The part of the U.S. government that enforces the federal law; it consists of the president and vice president.

judicial branch
The part of the U.S. government that interprets the law. It consists of the Supreme Court and other federal courts.

Checks and Balances

Certain **checks and balances** are built into the Constitution to ensure that no one branch of the federal government becomes too powerful.

checks and balances
A system built into the U.S. Constitution to prevent any one of the three branches of the government from becoming too powerful.

Example

The *judicial branch* has authority to examine the acts of the other two branches of government and determine whether those acts are constitutional.[4]

Example

The *executive branch* can enter into treaties with foreign governments only with the advice and consent of the Senate.

Example

The *legislative branch* is authorized to create federal courts and determine their jurisdiction and to enact statutes that change judicially made law.

Concept Summary
Basic Constitutional Concepts

Concept	Description
Federalism	The Constitution created the federal government. The federal government and the 50 state governments and Washington, DC, share powers in this country.
Delegated powers	When the states ratified the Constitution, they delegated certain powers to the federal government. These are called *enumerated powers*.
Reserved powers	Those powers not granted to the federal government by the Constitution are reserved to the state governments.
Separation of powers	Each branch of the federal government has separate powers. These powers are: a. Legislative branch—power to make the law. b. Executive branch—power to enforce the law. c. Judicial branch—power to interpret the law.
Checks and balances	Certain checks and balances are built into the Constitution to ensure that no one branch of the federal government becomes too powerful.

Supremacy Clause

The **Supremacy Clause** establishes that the U.S. Constitution and federal treaties, laws, and regulations are the supreme law of the land.[5] State and local laws that conflict with valid federal law are unconstitutional. The concept of federal law taking precedence over state or local law is commonly called the **preemption doctrine**.

Congress may expressly provide that a particular federal statute *exclusively* regulates a specific area or activity. No state or local law regulating the area or activity is valid if there is such a statute. More often, though, federal statutes do not expressly provide for exclusive jurisdiction. In these instances, state and local governments have *concurrent jurisdiction* to regulate the area or activity. However, any state or local law that "directly and substantially" conflicts with valid federal law is preempted under the Supremacy Clause.

In the following case, the U.S. Supreme Court applied the Supremacy Clause.

CASE 5.1
Supremacy Clause

U.S. Supreme Court

Rowe, Attorney General of Maine v. New Hampshire Motor Transport Association

128 S.Ct. 989, 169 L.Ed.2d 933, Web 2008 U.S. Lexis 2010 (2008)
Supreme Court of the United States

"And to allow Maine directly to regulate carrier services would permit other States to do the same. We find that federal law must preempt Maine's efforts directly to regulate carrier services."

—Justice Breyer

Facts

Prior to 1980, the trucking industry was subject to substantial federal government regulation that licensed routes, set pricing, and regulated other aspects of commercial trucking. The U.S. Congress enacted the federal Motor Carrier Act of 1980, which deregulated the trucking industry to make it competitively market oriented. In addition, Congress enacted two other federal statutes that preempted the regulation of trucking by the states.

Subsequently, the state of Maine adopted a state statute that regulated the trucking industry. One provision of the state statute forbids anyone other than a Maine-licensed tobacco retailer to accept an order for delivery of tobacco. Another provision forbids anyone knowingly to transport a tobacco product to a person in Maine unless either the sender or the receiver has a tobacco sales license issued by the state of Maine.

Several trucking associations brought a lawsuit in U.S. District Court, claiming that federal law preempted Maine's statute. The District Court held that federal law preempted the two provisions of the Maine statute. The U.S. Court of Appeals agreed. The state of Maine appealed to the U.S. Supreme Court.

Issue

Does federal law preempt the two provisions of the Maine state statute at issue in this case?

Language of the U.S. Supreme Court

The Court described Congress' overarching goal as helping assure transportation rates, routes, and services that reflect maximum reliance on competitive market forces, thereby stimulating efficiency, innovation, and low prices, as well as variety and quality. We find that federal law preempts the Maine laws at issue here. The Maine law thereby produces the very effect that the federal law sought to avoid, namely, a State's direct substitution of its own governmental commands for competitive market forces in determining the services that motor carriers will provide.

To allow Maine to insist that the carriers provide a special checking system would allow other States to do the same. And to interpret the federal law to permit these, and similar, state requirements could easily lead to a patchwork of state service-determining laws, rules, and regulations. That state regulatory patchwork is inconsistent with Congress' major legislative effort to leave such decisions, where federally unregulated, to the competitive marketplace. And to allow Maine directly to regulate carrier services would permit other States to do the same. We find that federal law must preempt Maine's efforts directly to regulate carrier services.

Decision

The U.S. Supreme Court affirmed the decisions of the U.S. District Court and the U.S. Court of Appeals, which held that federal law preempted the Maine statute that regulated the trucking industry.

Case Questions

Critical Legal Thinking What is the Supremacy Clause? Explain.

Business Ethics Why do you think the state of Maine passed these laws?

Contemporary Business What would be the consequences if there were no Supremacy Clause in the U.S. Constitution? Explain.

Commerce Clause

The **Commerce Clause** of the U.S. Constitution grants Congress the power "to regulate commerce with foreign nations, and among the several states, and with Indian tribes."[6] Because this clause authorizes the federal government to regulate commerce, it has a greater impact on business than any other provision in the Constitution. Among other things, this clause is intended to foster the development of a national market and free trade among the states.

The U.S. Constitution grants the federal government the power to regulate three types of commerce:

1. Commerce with Native American tribes
2. Foreign commerce
3. Interstate commerce

Each of these is discussed in the following paragraphs.

Commerce Clause
A clause of the U.S. Constitution that grants Congress the power "to regulate commerce with foreign nations, and among the several states, and with Indian tribes."

Commerce with Native Americans

Before Europeans arrived in the "New World," the land had been occupied for thousands of years by people we now refer to as Native Americans. There were many different Native American tribes, each having its own independent and self-governing system of laws.

When the United States was first founded over 200 years ago, it consisted of the original 13 colonies, all located in the east, primarily on the Atlantic Ocean. At that time, these colonies (states), in the U.S. Constitution, delegated to the federal government the authority to regulate commerce with the Native American tribes—in both the original 13 states and the territory that was to eventually become the United States of America.

Under its Commerce Clause powers, the federal government entered into treaties with many Native American nations. Most tribes, in the face of white settlers' encroachment on their land and federal government pressure, were forced to sell their lands to the federal government. The Native Americans received money and goods for land. The federal government obtained many treaties through unscrupulous means, cheating the Native Americans of their land. These tribes were then relocated to other, smaller, pieces of land called *reservations*, often outside their typical tribal lands. The federal government eventually broke many of the treaties.

Once Native Americans came under U.S. authority, they lost much of their political power. Most tribes were allowed to keep their own governments but were placed under the "protection" of the U.S. government. In general, the United States treats Native Americans as separate nations, similarly to the way it treats Spain or France; however, it still considers Native Americans "domestic dependent" nations with limited sovereignty.

Today, many Native Americans live on reservations set aside for various tribes. Others live and work outside reservations.

Indian Gaming Regulatory Act   In the late 1980s, the federal government authorized Native American tribes to operate gaming facilities. Congress passed the **Indian Gaming Regulatory Act,**[7] which sets the terms of casino gambling and other gaming activities on tribal land. This act allows Native Americans to negotiate with the states for gaming compacts and ensures that the states do so in good faith. If a state fails to do so, the tribe can bring suit in federal court, forcing the state to comply. Today, casinos operated by Native Americans can be found in many states. Profits from the casinos have become an important source of income for members of certain tribes.

Foreign Commerce

The Commerce Clause of the U.S. Constitution gives the federal government the *exclusive power* to regulate commerce with foreign nations.

Direct and indirect regulation of foreign commerce by state or local governments that unduly burdens foreign commerce violates the Commerce Clause and is therefore unconstitutional.

In the following case, the U.S. Supreme Court struck down a state law as violating the U.S. Constitution.

CASE 5.2
Foreign Commerce

U.S. Supreme Court

Crosby, Secretary of Administration and Finance of Massachusetts v. National Foreign Trade Council

530 U.S. 363, 120 S.Ct. 2288, 147 L.Ed.2d 352, Web 2000 U.S. Lexis 4153 (2000)
Supreme Court of the United States

"Within the sphere defined by Congress, then, the federal statute has placed the president in a position with as much discretion to exercise economic leverage against Burma, with an eye toward national security, as our law will admit."

—Justice Souter

Facts

The military regime of the country of Myanmar (called Burma prior to 1989) has been accused of major civil rights violations, including using forced and child labor, imprisoning and torturing political opponents, and harshly repressing ethnic minorities. These inhumane actions have been condemned by human rights organizations around the world. The state legislators of the state of Massachusetts were so appalled at these actions that in June 1996, they enacted a state statute banning the state government from purchasing goods and services from any company that did business with Myanmar.

In the meantime, the U.S. Congress enacted a federal statute that delegated power to the president of the United States to regulate U.S. dealings with Myanmar. The federal statute (1) banned all aid to the government of Myanmar except for humanitarian assistance, (2) authorized the president to impose economic sanctions against Myanmar, and (3) authorized the president to develop a comprehensive multilateral strategy to bring democracy to Myanmar.

The National Foreign Trade Council—a powerful Washington, DC–based trade association with more than 500 member companies—filed a lawsuit against Massachusetts to have the state law declared unconstitutional. The council argued that the Massachusetts "anti-Myanmar" statute conflicted with the federal statute and that under the Supremacy Clause that makes federal law the "supreme law of the land" the state statute was preempted by the federal statute. The U.S. District Court and U.S. Court of Appeals ruled in favor of the council. Massachusetts appealed to the U.S. Supreme Court.

Issue

Did the Massachusetts anti-Myanmar state statute violate the Supremacy Clause of the U.S. Constitution?

Language of the U.S. Supreme Court

Within the sphere defined by Congress, then, the federal statute has placed the president in a position with as much discretion to exercise economic leverage against Burma, with an eye toward national security, as our law will admit. And it is just this plenitude of executive authority that we think controls the issue of preemption here. The president has been given this authority not merely to make a political statement but to achieve a political result, and the fullness of his authority shows the importance in the congressional mind of reaching that result. It is simply implausible that Congress would have gone to such lengths to empower the president if it had been willing to compromise his effectiveness by deference to every provision of state statute or local ordinance that might, if enforced, blunt the consequences of discretionary presidential action.

We find it unlikely that Congress intended both to enable the president to protect national security by giving him the flexibility to suspend or terminate federal sanctions and simultaneously to allow Massachusetts to act at odds with the president's judgment of what national security requires. And that is just what the Massachusetts Burma law would do in imposing a different, state system of economic pressure against the Burmese political regime.

Decision

The U.S. Supreme Court held that the Massachusetts anti-Myanmar law conflicted with federal law and was therefore preempted by the Supremacy Clause of the Constitution. The Supreme Court affirmed the decisions of the U.S. District Court and U.S. Court of Appeals in favor of the National Foreign Trade Council.

Case Questions

Critical Legal Thinking What does the Supremacy Clause provide? Explain.

Business Ethics Do you think companies that have goods manufactured in Myanmar violate any ethical principles? Explain.

Contemporary Business Could the federal government enact an anti-Myanmar law such as the one Massachusetts enacted?

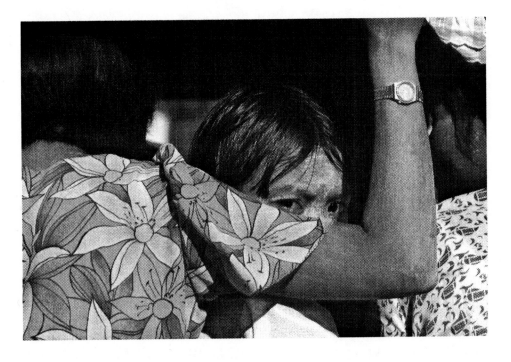

Myanmar. *The country of Myanmar (also called Burma) is ruled by a junta composed of its military generals. The country has been accused of human rights violations, including using child labor and forced labor, eliminating political dissidents, and strict censorship. The country, once a democracy, has been run by the military since 1962.*

Landmark U.S. Supreme Court Case
Heart of Atlanta Motel v. United States

"One need only examine the evidence which we have discussed ... to see that Congress may ... prohibit racial discrimination by motels serving travelers, however 'local' their operations may appear."

—Justice Clark

The Heart of Atlanta Motel, which was located in the state of Georgia, had 216 rooms available to guests. The motel was readily accessible to motorists using U.S. interstate highways 75 and 85 and Georgia state highways 23 and 41. The motel solicited patronage from outside the state of Georgia through various national advertising media, including magazines of national circulation. The motel maintained more than 50 billboards and highway signs within the state of Georgia. Approximately 75 percent of the motel's registered guests were from out of state. The Heart of Atlanta Motel refused to rent rooms to blacks.

Congress enacted the **Civil Rights Act of 1964**, which made it illegal for motels, hotels, and other public accommodations to discriminate against guests based on their race. After the act was passed, the Heart of Atlanta Motel continued to refuse to rent rooms to blacks. The owner-operator of the motel brought a declaratory relief action in U.S. District Court, **Heart of Atlanta Motel v. United States**, to have the Civil Rights Act of 1964 declared unconstitutional. The plaintiff argued that Congress, in passing the act, had exceeded its powers to regulate interstate commerce under the Commerce Clause of the U.S. Constitution. The U.S. District Court upheld the Civil Rights Act and enjoined the owner-operator of the Heart of Atlanta Motel from discriminating against blacks. The owner-operator of the motel appealed to the U.S. Supreme Court.

The U.S. Supreme Court held that the provisions of the Civil Rights Act of 1964 that prohibited discrimination in accommodations properly regulated interstate commerce. In reaching its decision, the U.S. Supreme Court stated:

The power of Congress over interstate commerce is not confined to the regulation of commerce among the states. It extends to those activities intrastate which so affect interstate commerce or the exercise of the power of Congress over it as to make regulation of them appropriate means to the attainment of a legitimate end, the exercise of the granted power of Congress to regulate interstate commerce.

Thus the power of Congress to promote interstate commerce also includes the power to regulate the local incidents thereof, including local activities in both the States of origin and destination, which might have a substantial and harmful effect upon that commerce. One need only examine the evidence which we have discussed above to see that Congress may—as it has—prohibit racial discrimination by motels serving travelers, however "local" their operations may appear.

The U.S. Supreme Court held that the challenged provisions of the Civil Rights Act of 1964 were constitutional as a proper exercise of the commerce power of the federal government. Heart of Atlanta Motel v. United States, 379 U.S. 241, 85 S.Ct. 348, 13 L.Ed.2d 258, Web 1964 U.S. Lexis 2187 (Supreme Court of the United States)

Interstate Commerce

interstate commerce
Commerce that moves between states or that affects commerce between states.

The American Constitution is, so far as I can see, the most wonderful work ever struck off at a given time by the brain and purpose of man.

W. E. Gladstone
Kin Beyond Sea (1878)

The Commerce Clause gives the federal government the authority to regulate **interstate commerce**. Originally, the courts interpreted this clause to mean that the federal government could only regulate commerce that moved *in* interstate commerce. The modern rule, however, allows the federal government to regulate activities that *affect* interstate commerce.

Under the **effects on interstate commerce test**, the regulated activity does not itself have to be in interstate commerce. Thus, any local (*intrastate*) activity that has an effect on interstate commerce is subject to federal regulation. Theoretically, this test subjects a substantial amount of business activity in the United States to federal regulation.

Example

In the famous case **Wickard, Secretary of Agriculture v. Filburn**,[8] a federal statute limited the amount of wheat that a farmer could plant and harvest for home consumption. Filburn, a farmer, violated the law. The U.S. Supreme Court upheld the federal statute on the grounds that it involved interstate commerce because the statute was designed to pre-

Internet Law and Online Commerce

E-Commerce and the Commerce Clause

Cyber Law

"State bans on interstate direct shipping represent the single largest regulatory barrier to expanded e-commerce in wine."

—Justice Kennedy

In this Information Age, federal and state governments have had to grapple with how to regulate the Internet and e-commerce. The federal government seems to be taking the upper hand in passing laws that regulate business conducted in cyberspace, thus creating laws that apply uniformly across the country. However, states have also enacted laws that regulate the Internet and e-commerce. State laws that unduly burden interstate e-commerce are unconstitutional, however. Consider the following case.

The state of Michigan regulates the sale of wine within its boundaries. Michigan law permits in-state wineries to sell wine directly to consumers, including by mail, Internet, and other means of sale. Michigan law prohibits out-of-state wineries from selling wine directly to Michigan consumers, including over the Internet. Michigan instead requires out-of-state wineries to sell their wine to Michigan wholesalers, who then sell the wine to Michigan retailers, who then sell the wine to Michigan consumers. Many small wineries across the country rely on the Internet to sell wine to residents in other states. Out-of-state wineries that are required by law to sell wine to Michigan wholesalers would incur a cost that in-state-wineries would not incur, thus making it more costly and often unprofitable for out-of-state wineries to sell to Michigan consumers.

Domaine Alfred, a small winery located in San Luis Obispo, California, and several other out-of-state wineries that were prohibited from selling wine directly to Michigan consumers, sued Michigan. The plaintiff wineries alleged that the Michigan law caused an undue burden on interstate e-commerce, in violation of the Commerce Clause of the U.S. Constitution. The U.S. District Court ruled in favor of Michigan. The U.S. Court of Appeals reversed and ruled in favor of the out-of-state wineries, finding that the Michigan law caused an undue burden on interstate e-commerce. The state of Michigan appealed to the U.S. Supreme Court.

The U.S. Supreme Court held that the Michigan state law that discriminated against out-of-state wineries in favor of in-state wineries caused an undue burden on interstate e-commerce, in violation of the Commerce Clause of the U.S. Constitution. The U.S. Supreme Court stated, "Technological improvements, in particular the ability of wineries to sell wine over the Internet, have helped make direct shipments an attractive sales channel. State bans on interstate direct shipping represent the single largest regulatory barrier to expanded e-commerce in wine." In this case, the U.S. Supreme Court saved e-commerce from a discriminatory state law. *Granholm, Governor of Michigan v. Heald,* 544 U.S. 460, 125 S.Ct. 1885, 161 L.Ed.2d 796, **Web** 2005 U.S. Lexis 4174 (Supreme Court of the United States, 2005)

vent nationwide surpluses and shortages of wheat during the Depression. The Court reasoned that wheat grown for home consumption would affect the supply of wheat available in interstate commerce.

State Police Power

The federal government does not retain sole power to regulate business. States retain the power to regulate *intrastate* business activity and much interstate business activity that occurs within their borders. This is commonly referred to as states' **police power.**

Police power permits states (and, by delegation, local governments) to enact laws to protect or promote the *public health, safety, morals, and general welfare.* This includes the authority to enact laws that regulate the conduct of business.

Examples
Zoning ordinances, state environmental laws, corporation and partnership laws, and property laws are enacted under state police power.

Dormant Commerce Clause

If the federal government has chosen not to regulate an area of interstate commerce that it has the power to regulate under its Commerce Clause powers, this area of commerce is subject to what is referred to as the **Dormant Commerce Clause**. A state, under its police

police power
Power that permits states and local governments to enact laws to protect or promote the public health, safety, morals, and general welfare.

unduly burden interstate commerce
A concept which says that states may enact laws that protect or promote the public health, safety, morals, and general welfare, as long as the laws do not unduly burden interstate commerce.

power, can enact laws to regulate that area of commerce. However, if a state enacts laws to regulate commerce that the federal government has the power to regulate but has chosen not to regulate, the Dormant Commerce Clause prohibits the state's regulation from unduly burdening interstate commerce.

Example

Assume that one state's corporations code permits only corporations from that state, but from no other state, to conduct business in that state. That state's law would unduly burden interstate commerce and would be unconstitutional.

Bill of Rights

Bill of Rights

The first 10 amendments to the Constitution, which were added to the U.S. Constitution in 1791.

The U.S. Constitution provides that it may be amended. In 1791, the 10 amendments that are commonly referred to as the **Bill of Rights** were approved by the states and became part of the U.S. Constitution. The Bill of Rights guarantees certain fundamental rights to natural persons and protects these rights from intrusive government action.

Examples

Fundamental rights guaranteed in the Bill of Rights include freedom of speech, freedom to assemble, freedom of the press, freedom of religion, and such. Most of these rights have also been found applicable to so-called artificial persons (i.e., corporations).

In addition to the Bill of Rights, 17 other **amendments** have been added to the Constitution. These amendments cover a variety of issues.

Examples

The additional 17 amendments to the Constitution have abolished slavery, prohibited discrimination, authorized the federal income tax, given women the right to vote, and specifically recognized that persons 18 years of age and older have the right to vote.

Originally, the Bill of Rights limited intrusive action by the *federal government* only. Intrusive actions by state and local governments were not limited until the *Due Process Clause of the Fourteenth Amendment* was added to the Constitution in 1868. The Supreme Court has applied the **incorporation doctrine** and held that most of the fundamental guarantees contained in the Bill of Rights are applicable to *state and local government* action. The amendments to the Constitution that are most applicable to business are discussed in the sections that follow.

Protest, Los Angeles, California. *The Freedom of Speech Clause of the First Amendment to the U.S. Constitution protects the right to engage in political speech. Freedom of speech is one of Americans' most highly prized rights.*

Freedom of Speech

One of the most honored freedoms guaranteed by the Bill of Rights is the **freedom of speech** of the First Amendment. Many other constitutional freedoms would be meaningless without it. The First Amendment's Freedom of Speech Clause protects speech only, not conduct. The First Amendment protects oral, written and symbolic speech.

The U.S. Supreme Court places speech into three categories: (1) *fully protected*, (2) *limited protected*, and (3) *unprotected speech*. These types of speech are discussed in the following paragraphs.

Fully Protected Speech

Fully protected speech is speech that the government cannot prohibit or regulate. The government cannot prohibit or regulate the content of fully protected speech.

Example

Political speech is an example of fully protected speech. Thus, the government could not enact a law that forbids citizens from criticizing the current president.

The First Amendment protects oral, written, and symbolic speech.

I disapprove of what you say, but I will defend to the death your right to say it.

Voltaire

Limited Protected Speech

The Supreme Court has held that certain types of speech have only **limited protection** under the First Amendment. The government cannot forbid this type of speech, but it can subject this speech to *time, place, and manner restrictions*. Two types of speech are accorded limited protection: *offensive speech* and *commercial speech*.

Offensive Speech   **Offensive speech** is speech that offends many members of society. (It is not the same as obscene speech, however.) The Supreme Court has held that the content of offensive speech may not be forbidden but that it may be restricted by the government under time, place, and manner restrictions.

Example

The Federal Communications Commission (FCC) is a federal administrative agency that regulates radio, television, and cable stations. Under its powers, the FCC has regulated the use of offensive language on television by limiting such language to time periods when children would be unlikely to be watching (e.g., late at night).

Commercial Speech   **Commercial speech**, such as advertising, was once considered unprotected by the First Amendment. However, today, because of U.S. Supreme Court decisions, the content of commercial speech is protected but is also subject to time, place, and manner restrictions.

Example

In *Virginia State Board of Pharmacy v. Virginia Citizens Consumer Council, Inc.*[9] the U.S. Supreme Court held that a state statute that prohibited a pharmacist from advertising the price of prescription drugs was unconstitutional because it violated the Freedom of Speech Clause. The U.S. Supreme Court held that this was commercial speech that was protected by the First Amendment.

Example

A city can prohibit billboards along its highways for safety and aesthetic reasons if other forms of advertising (e.g., print media) are available. This is a lawful place restriction.

In the following case, the court had to decide whether the government properly regulated commercial speech.

Mainstream Marketing Services, Inc. v. Federal Trade Commission and Federal Communications Commission

358 F.3d 1228, Web 2004 U.S. App. Lexis 2564 (2004)
United States Court of Appeals for the Tenth Circuit

"The national do-not-call registry offers consumers a tool with which they can protect their homes against intrusions that Congress has determined to be particularly invasive."

—Judge Ebel

Facts

Pursuant to enabling statutes, two federal administrative agencies—the Federal Trade Commission (FTC) and the Federal Communications Commission (FCC)—created the national do-not-call registry. The national do-not-call registry is a list that contains the personal telephone number of telephone users who have voluntarily placed themselves on this list, indicating that they do not want to receive unsolicited calls from commercial telemarketers. Commercial telemarketers are prohibited from calling phone numbers that have been placed on the do-not-call registry. Telemarketers must pay an annual fee to access the phone numbers on the registry so that they can delete those numbers from their solicitation lists. The national do-not-call registry restrictions apply only to telemarketers' calls made by or on behalf of sellers of goods or services. Charitable and fundraising calls are exempt from the do-not-call registry's restrictions. Persons who do not voluntarily place their phone numbers on the do-not-call registry may still receive unsolicited telemarketers' calls.

Mainstream Marketing Services, Inc., and other telemarketers sued the FTC and the FCC in several lawsuits, alleging that their free speech rights were violated and that the do-not-call registry was unconstitutional. The FTC and FCC defended, arguing that unsolicited telemarketing calls constituted commercial speech that could properly be regulated by the government's do-not-call registry's restrictions. The separate lawsuits were consolidated for appeal.

Issue

Are unsolicited telemarketing calls commercial speech that is constitutionally regulated by the do-not-call registry restrictions?

Language of the Court

Four key aspects of the do-not-call registry convince us that it is consistent with First Amendment requirements. First, the list restricts only core commercial speech—i.e., commercial sales calls. Second, the do-not-call registry targets speech that invades the privacy of the home, a personal sanctuary that enjoys a unique status in our constitutional jurisprudence. Third, the do-not-call registry is an opt-in program that puts the choice of whether or not to restrict commercial calls entirely in the hands of consumers. Fourth, the do-not-call registry materially furthers the government's interests in combating the danger of abusive telemarketing and preventing the invasion of consumer privacy, blocking a significant number of the calls that cause these problems.

A number of additional features of the national do-not-call registry, although not dispositive, further demonstrate that the list is consistent with the First Amendment rights of commercial speakers. The challenged regulations do not hinder any business' ability to contact consumers by other means, such as through direct mailings or other forms of advertising. Moreover, they give consumers a number of different options to avoid calls they do not want to receive. Namely, consumers who wish to restrict some but not all commercial sales calls can do so by using company-specific do-not-call lists or by granting some businesses express permission to call. In addition, the government chose to offer consumers broader options to restrict commercial sales calls than charitable and political calls after finding that commercial calls were more intrusive and posed a greater danger of consumer abuse.

The national do-not-call registry offers consumers a tool with which they can protect their homes against intrusions that Congress has determined to be particularly invasive. Just as a consumer can avoid door-to-door peddlers by placing a "No Solicitation" sign in his or her front yard, the do-not-call registry lets consumers avoid unwanted sales pitches that invade the home via telephone, if they choose to do so. We are convinced that the First Amendment does not prevent the government from giving consumers this option.

For the reasons discussed above, the government has asserted substantial interests to be served by the do-not-

call registry (privacy and consumer protection), the do-not-call registry will directly advance those interests by banning a substantial amount of unwanted telemarketing calls, and the regulation is narrowly tailored because its opt-in feature ensures that it does not restrict any speech directed at a willing listener. In other words, the do-not-call registry bears a reasonable fit with the purposes the government sought to advance. Therefore, it is consistent with the limits the First Amendment imposes on laws restricting commercial speech.

Decision

The U.S. Supreme Court held that unsolicited telemarketing calls constituted commercial speech that was subject to

government regulation and that the do-not-call registry restrictions did not violate the free speech rights of the plaintiff telemarketers.

Case Questions

Critical Legal Thinking   What is the do-not-call registry? How does it work?

Business Ethics   Is it ethical for telemarketers to make unsolicited phone calls to persons' houses? What time are some of these calls made? Is much fraud committed by telemarketers? Explain.

Contemporary Business   What is the economic effect on telemarketers of the do-not-call registry?

Cyber Law

Internet Law and Online Commerce

Broad Free Speech Rights Granted in Cyberspace

"As the most participatory form of mass speech yet developed, the Internet deserves the highest protection from government intrusion."

—Justice Stevens

Once or twice a century, a new medium comes along that presents new problems for applying freedom of speech rights. This time it is the Internet. In 1996 Congress enacted the **Computer Decency Act,** which made it a felony to knowingly make "indecent" or "patently offensive" materials available on computer systems, including the Internet, to persons under 18 years of age. Immediately, more than 50 cyberspace providers and users filed a lawsuit, challenging the act as a violation of their free speech rights granted under the First Amendment to the Constitution. The U.S. District Court agreed with the plaintiffs and declared the act an unconstitutional violation of the Freedom of Speech Clause.

On appeal, the U.S. Supreme Court agreed and held that the act was an unconstitutional violation of free speech rights. The Supreme Court concluded that the Internet allows an individual to reach an audience of millions at almost no cost, setting it apart from TV, radio, and print media, which are prohibitively expensive to use. The Court stated, "As the most participatory form of mass speech yet developed, the Internet deserves the highest protection

from government intrusion." The Court declared emphatically that the Internet must be given the highest possible level of First Amendment free speech protection.

Proponents of the Computer Decency Act argued that the act was necessary to protect children from indecent materials. The Supreme Court reasoned that limiting the content on the Internet to what is suitable for a child resulted in unconstitutionally limiting adult speech. The Court noted that children are far less likely to trip over indecent material on the Internet than on TV or radio because the information must be actively sought out on the Internet. The Court noted that less obtrusive means for protecting children are available, such as requiring parents to regulate their children's access to materials on the Internet and placing filtering and blocking software on computers to control what their children see on the Internet. It still remains a crime under existing laws to transmit *obscene* materials over the Internet. *Reno v. American Civil Liberties Union*, 521 U.S. 844, 117 S.Ct. 2329, 138 L.Ed.2d 874, **Web** 1997 U.S. Lexis 4037 (Supreme Court of the United States)

Unprotected Speech

unprotected speech
Speech that is not protected by the First Amendment and may be forbidden by the government.

The Supreme Court has held that the following types of speech are **unprotected speech** (i.e., they are not protected by the First Amendment and may be totally forbidden by the government):

1. **Dangerous speech.**

   Example Yelling "fire" in a crowded theater when there is no fire is not protected speech.

2. **Fighting words that are likely to provoke a hostile or violent response from an average person.**[10]

   Example Walking up to a person and intentionally calling that person names because of race or ethnicity would not be protected speech if it would likely cause the person being called the names to respond in a hostile manner.

3. **Speech that incites the violent or revolutionary overthrow of the government.** However, the mere abstract teaching of the morality and consequences of such action is protected.[11]

4. **Defamatory language.**[12]

   Examples Committing libel or slander by writing or telling untrue statements about another person or committing product disparagement or trade libel by writing or telling untrue statements about a company's products or services is not protected speech, and the injured party may bring a civil lawsuit to recover damages.

5. **Child pornography.**[13]

   Example Selling material depicting children engaged in sexual activity is unprotected speech.

6. **Obscene speech.**[14]   If speech is considered **obscene speech**, it has no protection under the Freedom of Speech Clause of the First Amendment and can be banned by the government.

   Examples Movies, videos, music, and other forms of speech that are obscene are unprotected speech.

obscene speech
Speech that (1) appeals to the prurient interest, (2) depicts sexual conduct in a patently offensive way, and (3) lacks serious literary, artistic, political, or scientific value.

The definition of *obscenity* has plagued the courts. The definition of *obscene speech* is quite subjective. One Supreme Court justice stated, "I know it when I see it."[15] In **Miller v. California**, the U.S. Supreme Court determined that speech is obscene when:

The Constitution of the United States is not a mere lawyers' document: It is a vehicle of life, and its spirit is always the spirit of the age.

Woodrow Wilson
Constitutional Government in the United States 69 (1927)

1. The average person, applying contemporary community standards, would find that the work, taken as a whole, appeals to the *prurient interest.*
2. The work depicts or describes, in a patently offensive way, sexual conduct specifically defined by the applicable state law.
3. The work, taken as a whole, lacks serious literary, artistic, political, or scientific value.[16]

States are free to define what constitutes obscene speech. Movie theaters, magazine publishers, and so on are often subject to challenges that the materials they display or sell are obscene and therefore not protected by the First Amendment. Over the years, the content of material that has been found to be obscene has shifted to a more liberal view as the general norms of society have become more liberal. Today, fewer obscenity cases are brought than have been in the past.

Freedom of Religion

Freedom of religion is a key concept addressed by the First Amendment. The First Amendment contains two separate religion clauses, the *Establishment Clause* and the *Free Exercise Clause.* These two clauses are discussed in the following paragraphs.

Establishment Clause

The U.S. Constitution requires federal, state, and local governments to be neutral toward religion. The **Establishment Clause** prohibits the government from either establishing a government-sponsored religion or promoting one religion over another. Thus, it guarantees that there will be no state-sponsored religion.

Establishment Clause
A clause to the First Amendment that prohibits the government from either establishing a state religion or promoting one religion over another.

Example
The U.S. Supreme Court ruled that an Alabama statute that authorized a one-minute period of silence in school for "meditation or voluntary prayer" was invalid.[17] The Court held that the statute endorsed religion.

Free Exercise Clause

The **Free Exercise Clause** prohibits the government from interfering with the free exercise of religion in the United States. Generally, this clause prevents the government from enacting laws that either prohibit or inhibit individuals from participating in or practicing their chosen religions.

Free Exercise Clause
A clause to the First Amendment that prohibits the government from interfering with the free exercise of religion in the United States.

Examples
Federal, state, or local governments could not enact a law that prohibits all religions. The government could not enact a law that prohibits churches, synagogues, mosques, or temples. The government could not prohibit religious practitioners from celebrating their major holidays and high holy days.

Example
In *Church of Lukumi Babalu Aye, Inc. v. City of Hialeah, Florida*,[18] the U.S. Supreme Court held that a city ordinance that prohibited ritual sacrifices of chickens during church services violated the Free Exercise Clause and that such sacrifices should be allowed.

Of course, the right to be free from government intervention in the practice of religion is not absolute.

Example
Human sacrifices are unlawful and are not protected by the First Amendment.

Concept Summary
Freedom of Religion

Clause	Description
Establishment Clause	Prohibits the government from establishing a government-sponsored religion and from promoting one religion over other religions.
Free Exercise Clause	Prohibits the government from enacting laws that either prohibit or inhibit individuals from participating in or practicing their chosen religions.

Equal Protection Clause

The **Fourteenth Amendment** was added to the U.S. Constitution in 1868. Its original purpose was to guarantee equal rights to all persons after the Civil War. The provisions of the Fourteenth Amendment prohibit discriminatory and unfair action by the government. Several of these provisions—namely, the *Equal Protection Clause*, the *Due Process Clause*, and the *Privileges and Immunities Clause*—have important implications for business. The Equal Protection Clause is discussed in this section. The Due Process Clause and the Privileges and Immunities Clause are discussed in following sections.

Fourteenth Amendment
An amendment added to the U.S. Constitution in 1868 that contains the Due Process, Equal Protection, and Privileges and Immunities clauses.

Federal, State, and Local Government Action

Equal Protection Clause
A clause which provides that a state cannot "deny to any person within its jurisdiction the equal protection of the laws."

The **Equal Protection Clause** provides that a state cannot "deny to any person within its jurisdiction the equal protection of the laws." Although this clause expressly applies to state and local government action, the Supreme Court has held that it also applies to federal government action.

This clause prohibits state, local, and federal governments from enacting laws that classify and treat "similarly situated" persons differently. Artificial persons, such as corporations, are also protected. Note that this clause is designed to prohibit invidious discrimination: It does not make the classification of individuals unlawful per se.

Standards of Review

The Supreme Court, over years of making decisions involving the Equal Protection Clause, has held that the government can treat people or businesses differently from one another if the government has sufficient justification for doing so. The Supreme Court has adopted three different standards of review for deciding whether the government's different treatment of people or businesses violates or does not violate the Equal Protection Clause:

1. **Strict scrutiny test.** Any government activity or regulation that classifies persons based on a *suspect class* (i.e., **race**) is reviewed for lawfulness using a **strict scrutiny test**. This means that the government must have an exceptionally important reason for treating persons differently because of their race in order for such unequal treatment to be lawful. Under this standard, many government classifications of persons based on race are found to be unconstitutional. Others are found lawful.

strict scrutiny test
A test that is applied to classifications based on race.

   Example A government rule that permits persons of one race but not of another race to receive government benefits such as Medicaid would violate this test.

   Example An affirmative action program that gives racial minorities a "plus factor" when considered for public university admission is lawful, as long as it does not constitute a quota system.[19]

2. **Intermediate scrutiny test.** The lawfulness of government classifications based on *protected classes* other than race (e.g., **sex**, **age**) is examined using an **intermediate scrutiny test**. This means that the government must have an important reason for treating persons differently because of their age or sex in order for such unequal treatment to be lawful. Under this standard, many government classifications of persons based on age or sex are found to be unconstitutional. Under this standard, the courts must determine whether the government classification is "reasonably related" to a legitimate government purpose.

intermediate scrutiny test
A test that is applied to classifications based on protected classes other than race (e.g., sex, age).

   Examples A rule prohibiting persons over a certain age from participating in military combat is lawful. The justification is that younger members of society are generally more physically fit for military service. However, a rule prohibiting persons over a certain age from being government engineers would not be lawful.

   Example The federal government's Social Security program, which pays benefits to older members of society but not to younger members of society, is lawful. The reason is that older members of society have earned this right during the course of their lifetimes.

   Example The federal government's requirement that males who reach the age of 18 must register for a military draft but that females do not have to register for the draft has been found constitutional by the U.S. Supreme Court.[20]

3. **Rational basis test.** The lawfulness of all government classifications that do not involve suspect or protected classes is examined using a **rational basis test**. Under this test, the courts will uphold government regulation as long as there is a justifiable reason for the law. This standard permits much of the government regulation of business.

rational basis test
A test that is applied to classifications not involving a suspect or protected class.

   Example Providing government subsidies to farmers but not to those in other occupations is permissible.

Due Process Clauses

The Fifth and Fourteenth Amendments to the U.S. Constitution both contain **Due Process Clauses**. These clauses provide that no person shall be deprived of "life, liberty, or property" without due process of the law. The Due Process Clause of the Fifth Amendment applies to federal government action; that of the Fourteenth Amendment applies to state and local government action. It is important to understand that the government is not prohibited from taking a person's life, liberty, or property. However, the government must follow due process to do so. There are two categories of due process: *substantive* and *procedural*.

Substantive Due Process

The **substantive due process** category of due process requires that government statutes, ordinances, regulations, and other laws be clear on their face and not overly broad in scope. The test of whether substantive due process is met is whether a "reasonable person" could understand the law to be able to comply with it. Laws that do not meet this test are declared *void for vagueness*.

Example
A city ordinance making it illegal for persons to wear "clothes of the opposite sex" would be held unconstitutional as void for vagueness because a reasonable person could not clearly determine whether his or her conduct violates the law.

Most government laws, although often written in "legalese," are considered not to violate substantive due process.

Procedural Due Process

The **procedural due process** form of due process requires that the government give a person proper *notice* and *hearing* of legal action before that person is deprived of his or her life, liberty, or property.

Example
If the federal government or a state government brings a criminal lawsuit against a defendant for the alleged commission of a crime, the government must notify the person of its intent (by charging the defendant with a crime) and provide the defendant with a proper hearing (a trial).

Privileges and Immunities Clause

The purpose of the U.S. Constitution is to promote nationalism. If the states were permitted to enact laws that favored their residents over out-of-state residents, the concept of nationalism would be defeated. Both Article IV of the Constitution and the Fourteenth Amendment contain **Privileges and Immunities Clauses** that prohibit states from enacting laws that unduly discriminate in favor of their residents. Note that the Privileges and Immunities Clause applies only to citizens; it does not protect corporations.

Example
A state cannot enact a law that prevents residents of other states from owning property or businesses in that state.

Courts have held that certain types of discrimination that favor state residents over nonresidents do not violate the Privileges and Immunities Clause.

Examples
State universities are permitted to charge out-of-state residents higher tuition than in-state residents. States are also permitted to charge higher fees to nonresidents for hunting and fishing licenses.

United States Post Office, Alhambra, California. *The United States has had many blemishes on its citizen's constitutional rights. For example, during World War II, Japanese Americans were involuntarily placed in camps. During the McCarthy hearings of the 1950s, citizens who were communists or associated with communists were "blackballed" from their occupations, most notably in the film industry. It was not until the mid-1960s that equal opportunity laws outlawed discrimination in the workplace based on race and sex.*

Test Review Terms and Concepts

Age
Amendments
Articles of Confederation
Bicameral
Bill of Rights
Checks and balances
Civil Rights Act of 1964
Commerce Clause
Commercial speech
Computer Decency Act
Congress
Constitutional Convention
Declaration of Independence
Delegated
Dormant Commerce Clause
Due Process Clause
Effects on interstate commerce test
Electoral college
Enumerated powers

Equal Protection Clause
Establishment Clause
Executive branch
Federal government
Federalism
Fourteenth Amendment
Free Exercise Clause
Freedom of religion
Freedom of speech
Fully protected speech
Heart of Atlanta Motel v. United States
Incorporation doctrine
Indian Gaming Regulatory Act
Intermediate scrutiny test
Interstate commerce
Judicial branch
Legislative branch
Limited protected speech

Miller v. California
Obscene speech
Offensive speech
Police power
Preemption doctrine
Privileges and Immunities Clause
Procedural due process
Race
Rational basis test
Sex
Strict scrutiny test
Substantive due process
Supremacy Clause
Unduly burden interstate commerce
Unprotected speech
Wickard, Secretary of Agriculture v. Filburn
U.S. Constitution

Case Problems

5.1 Separation of Powers: In 1951, a dispute arose between steel companies and their employees about the terms and conditions that should be included in a new labor contract. At the time, the United States was engaged in a military conflict in Korea that required substantial steel resources from which to make weapons and other military goods. On April 4, 1952, the steelworkers' union gave notice of a nationwide strike called to begin at 12:01 A.M. on April 9. The indispensability of steel as a component in weapons and other war materials led President Harry S. Truman to believe that the proposed strike would jeopardize the national defense and that governmental seizure of the steel mills was necessary in order to ensure the continued availability of steel. Therefore, a few hours before the strike was to begin, the president issued Executive Order 10340, which directed the secretary of commerce to take possession of most of the steel mills and keep them running. The steel companies obeyed the order under protest and brought proceedings against the president. Is this seizure of the steel mills constitutional? *Youngstown Co. v. Sawyer, Secretary of Commerce*, 343 U.S. 579, 72 S.Ct. 863, 96 L.Ed.2d 1153, **Web** 1952 U.S. Lexis 2625 (Supreme Court of the United States)

5.2 Commerce and Supremacy Clauses: Congress enacted a federal statute called the Ports and Waterways Safety Act that established uniform standards for the operation of boats on inland waterways in the United States. The act coordinated its provisions with those of foreign countries so that there was a uniform body of international rules that applied to vessels that traveled between countries. Pursuant to the act, a federal rule was adopted that regulated the design, length, and size of oil tankers, some of which traveled the waters of the Puget Sound area in the state of Washington. Oil tankers from various places entered Puget Sound to bring crude oil to refineries located in Washington. The state of Washington enacted a statute that established different designs, smaller lengths, and smaller sizes for oil tankers serving Puget Sound than allowed by the federal law. Oil tankers used by the Atlantic Richfield Company (ARCO) to bring oil into Puget Sound met the federal standards but not the state standards. ARCO sued to have the state statute declared unconstitutional. Who wins? *Ray, Governor of Washington v. Atlantic Richfield Co.*, 435 U.S. 151, 98 S.Ct. 988, 55 L.Ed.2d 179, **Web** 1978 U.S. Lexis 18 (Supreme Court of the United States)

5.3 Undue Burden on Interstate Commerce: Most trucking firms, including Consolidated Freightways Corporation, use 65-foot-long "double" trailer trucks to ship commodities on the highway system across the United States. Almost all states permit these vehicles on their highways. The federal government does not regulate the length of trucks that can use the nation's highways. The state of Iowa enacted a statute that restricted the length of trucks that could use highways in the state to 55 feet. This meant that if Consolidated wanted to move goods through Iowa, it needed to either use smaller trucks or detach the double trailers and shuttle them through the state separately. Its only other alternative was to divert its 65-foot doubles around Iowa. Consolidated filed suit against Iowa, alleging that the state statute was unconstitutional. Is it? *Kassel v. Consolidated Freightways Corporation*, 450 U.S. 662, 101 S.Ct. 1309, 67 L.Ed.2d 580, **Web** 1981 U.S. Lexis 17 (Supreme Court of the United States)

5.4 Privileges and Immunities Clause: During a period of a booming economy in Alaska, many residents of other states moved there in search of work. Construction work on the Trans-Alaska Pipeline was a major source of employment. The Alaska legislature enacted an act called the Local Hire Statute. This act required employers to hire Alaska residents in preference to nonresidents. Is this statute constitutional? *Hicklin v. Orbeck, Commissioner of the Department of Labor of Alaska*, 437 U.S. 518, 98 S.Ct. 2482, 57 L.Ed.2d 397, **Web** 1978 U.S. Lexis 36 (Supreme Court of the United States)

5.5 Commercial Speech: The city of San Diego, California, enacted a city zoning ordinance that prohibited outdoor advertising display signs—including billboards. On-site signs at a business location were exempted from this rule. The city based the restriction on traffic safety and aesthetics. Metromedia, Inc., a company in the business of leasing commercial billboards to advertisers, sued the city of San Diego, alleging that the zoning ordinance was unconstitutional. Is it? *Metromedia, Inc. v. City of San Diego*, 453 U.S. 490, 101 S.Ct. 2882, 69 L.Ed.2d 800, **Web** 1981 U.S. Lexis 50 (Supreme Court of the United States)

5.6 Substantive Due Process: The village of Hoffman Estates, Illinois, enacted an ordinance regulating drug paraphernalia. The ordinance made it unlawful for any person "to sell any items, effect, paraphernalia, accessory or thing which is designed or marketed for use with illegal cannabis or drugs as defined by Illinois Revised Statutes, without obtaining a license therefore." The license fee was $150. A violation was subject to a fine of not more than $500. The Flipside, a retail store located in the village, sold a variety of merchandise, including smoking accessories, clamps, roach clips, scales, water pipes, vials, cigarette rolling papers, and other items. Instead of applying for a license, Flipside filed a lawsuit against the village, alleging that the ordinance was unconstitutional, as a violation of substantive due process, because it was overly broad and vague. Who wins? *Village of Hoffman Estates v. Flipside, Hoffman Estates, Inc.*, 455 U.S. 489, 102 S.Ct. 1186, 71 L.Ed.2d 362, **Web** 1982 U.S. Lexis 78 (Supreme Court of the United States)

5.7 Equal Protection Clause: The state of Alabama enacted a statute that imposed a tax on premiums earned by insurance companies. The statute imposed a 1 percent tax on domestic insurance companies (i.e., insurance companies that were incorporated in Alabama and had their principal office in the state). The statute imposed a 4 percent tax on the premiums earned by out-of-state insurance companies that sold insurance in Alabama. Out-of-state insurance companies could reduce the premium tax by 1 percent by investing at least 10 percent of their assets in Alabama. Domestic insurance companies did not have to invest any of their assets in Alabama. Metropolitan Life Insurance Company, an out-of-state insurance company, sued the state of Alabama, alleging that the Alabama statute violated the Equal Protection Clause of the U.S. Constitution. Who wins? *Metropolitan Life Insurance Co. v. Ward, Commissioner of Insurance of Alabama*, 470 U.S. 869, 105 S.Ct. 1676, 84 L.Ed.2d 751, **Web** 1985 U.S. Lexis 80 (Supreme Court of the United States)

Business Ethics Cases

5.8 Business Ethics: The Raiders are a professional football team and a National Football League (NFL) franchise. Each NFL franchise is independently owned. Al Davis was an owner and the managing general partner of the Raiders. The NFL establishes schedules, negotiates television contracts, and otherwise promotes NFL football, including conducting the Super Bowl each year. The Raiders play home and away games against other NFL teams.

For years, the Raiders played their home games in Oakland, California. The owners of the Raiders decided to move the team from Oakland to Los Angeles, California, to take advantage of the greater seating capacity of the Los Angeles Coliseum, the larger television market of Los Angeles, and other economic factors. The renamed team was to be known as the Los Angeles Raiders. The city of Oakland brought an eminent domain proceeding in court to acquire the Raiders as a city-owned team. Can the city of Oakland acquire the Raiders through eminent domain? Is it socially responsible for a professional sports team to move to another location? *City of Oakland, California v. Oakland Raiders*, 174 Cal.App.3d 414, 220 Cal.Rptr. 153, **Web** 1985 Cal.App. Lexis 2751 (Court of Appeal of California)

5.9 Business Ethics: Congress enacted the Flag Protection Act, which made it a crime to knowingly mutilate, deface, physically defile, burn, or trample the U.S. flag. The law provided for fines and up to one year in prison upon conviction [18 U.S.C. Section 700]. Certain individuals set fire to several U.S. flags on the steps of the U.S. Capitol in Washington, DC, to protest various aspects of the federal government's foreign and domestic policy. In a separate incident, other individuals set fire to a U.S. flag to protest the act's passage. All these individuals were prosecuted for violating the act. The U.S. District Courts held the act unconstitutional, in violation of the defendants' First Amendment free speech rights, and dismissed the charges. The government appealed to the U.S. Supreme Court, which consolidated the two cases. Who wins? Does a flag burner exhibit moral behavior? *United States v. Eichman*, 496 U.S. 310, 110 S.Ct. 2404, 110 L.Ed.2d 287, **Web** 1990 U.S. Lexis 3087 (Supreme Court of the United States)

Endnotes

1. To be elected to Congress, an individual must be a U.S. citizen, either naturally born or granted citizenship. To serve in the Senate, a person must be 30 years of age or older. To serve in the House of Representatives, a person must be 25 years of age or older.

2. To be president, a person must be 35 years of age or older and a natural citizen of the United States. According to the Twenty-Second Amendment to the Constitution, a person can serve only two full terms as president.

3. Federal court judges and justices are appointed by the president, with the consent of the Senate.

4. The principle that the U.S. Supreme Court is the final arbiter of the U.S. Constitution evolved from *Marbury v. Madison*, 1 Cranch 137, 5 U.S. 137, 2 L.Ed. 60, **Web** 1803 U.S. Lexis 352 (Supreme Court of the United States, 1803). In that case, the Supreme Court held that a judiciary statute enacted by Congress was unconstitutional.

5. Article VI, Section 2.

6. Article I, Section 8, clause 3.

7. 25 U.S.C Sections 2701–2721.

8. 317 U.S. 111, 63 S.Ct. 82, 87 L.Ed.122, **Web** 1942 U.S. Lexis 1046 (Supreme Court of the United States).

9. 425 U.S. 748, 96 S.Ct. 1817, 48 L.Ed.2d 346, **Web** 1976 U.S. Lexis 55 (Supreme Court of the United States).

10. *Chaplinsky v. New Hampshire*, 315 U.S. 568, 62 S.Ct. 766, 86 L.Ed. 1031, **Web** 1942 U.S. Lexis 851 (Supreme Court of the United States).

11. *Brandenburg v. Ohio*, 395 U.S. 444, 89 S.Ct. 1827, 23 L.Ed.2d 430, **Web** 1969 U.S. Lexis 1367 (Supreme Court of the United States).

12. *Beauharnais v. Illinois*, 343 U.S. 250, 72 S.Ct. 725, 96 L.Ed. 919, **Web** 1952 U.S. Lexis 2799 (Supreme Court of the United States).

13. *New York v. Ferber*, 458 U.S. 747, 102 S.Ct. 334, 73 L.Ed.2d 1113, **Web** 1982 U.S. Lexis 12 (Supreme Court of the United States).

14. *Roth v. United States*, 354 U.S. 476, 77 S.Ct. 1304, 1 L.Ed.2d 1498, **Web** 1957 U.S. Lexis 587 (Supreme Court of the United States).

15. Justice Stewart in *Jacobellis v. Ohio*, 378 U.S. 184, 84 S.Ct. 1676, 12 L.Ed.2d 793, **Web** 1964 U.S. Lexis 822 (Supreme Court of the United States).

16. 413 U.S. 15, 93 S.Ct. 2607, 37 L.Ed.2d 419, **Web** 1973 U.S. Lexis 149 (Supreme Court of the United States).

17. *Wallace v. Jaffree*, 472 U.S. 38, 105 S.Ct. 2479, 86 L.Ed.2d 29, **Web** 1985 U.S. Lexis 91 (Supreme Court of the United States).

18. 508 U.S. 520, 113 S.Ct. 2217, 124 L.Ed.2d 472, **Web** 1993 U.S. Lexis 4022 (Supreme Court of the United States).

19. *Grutter v. Bollinger and the University of Michigan Law School*, 539 U.S. 306, 123 S.Ct. 2325, 156 L.Ed.2d 304, **Web** 2003 U.S. Lexis 4800 (Supreme Court of the United States, 2003).

20. *Rostker v. Goldberg*, 453 U.S. 57, 101 S.Ct. 2646, 69 L.Ed.2d 478, Web 1981 U.S. Lexis 126 (Supreme Court of the United States).

Key Excerpts from the Majority Opinion

Dred Scott v. Sandford (1857)

The decision was 7 to 2.

Chief Justice Roger B. Taney delivered the opinion of the Court.

. . . Can a negro, whose ancestors were imported into this country, and sold as slaves, become a member of the political community formed and brought into existence by the Constitution of the United States, and as such become entitled to all the rights, and privileges, and immunities, guarantied by that instrument to the citizen? One of which rights is the privilege of suing in a court of the United States in the cases specified in the Constitution.

We think they [people of African ancestry] are not [citizens], and that they are not included, and were not intended to be included, under the word "citizens" in the Constitution, and can therefore claim none of the rights and privileges which that instrument provides for and secures to citizens of the United States.

. . . [T]he legislation and histories of the times, and the language used in the Declaration of Independence, show, that neither the class of persons who had been imported as slaves, nor their descendants, whether they had become free or not, were then acknowledged as a part of the people, nor intended to be included in the general words used in that memorable instrument.

For if they were so received, and entitled to the privileges and immunities of citizens, it would exempt them from the operation of the special laws and from the police regulations which they considered to be necessary for their own safety. It would give to persons of the negro race, who were recognized as citizens in any one State of the Union, the right to enter every other State whenever they pleased . . . to go where they pleased at every hour of the day or night without molestation, unless they committed some violation of law for which a white man would be punished; and it would give them the full liberty of speech in public and in private upon all subjects upon which its own citizens might speak; to hold public meetings upon political affairs, and to keep and carry arms wherever they went. And all of this would be done in the face of the subject race of the same color, both free and slaves, and inevitably producing discontent and insubordination among them, and endangering the peace and safety of the State.

The act of Congress, upon which the plaintiff relies, declares that slavery and involuntary servitude, except as a punishment for crime, shall be forever prohibited in all that part of the territory ceded by France, under the name of Louisiana, which lies north of thirty-six degrees thirty minutes north latitude, and not included within the limits of Missouri. And the difficulty which meets us at the threshold of this part of the inquiry is, whether Congress was authorized to pass this law under any of the powers granted to it by the Constitution; for if the authority is not given by that instrument, it is the duty of this court to declare it void and inoperative, and incapable of conferring freedom upon any one who is held as a slave under the laws of any one of the States.

There is certainly no power given by the Constitution to the Federal Government to establish or maintain colonies bordering on the United States or at a distance, to be ruled and governed at its own pleasure; nor to enlarge its territorial limits in any way, except by the admission of new States. That power is plainly given; and if a new State is admitted, it needs no further legislation by Congress, because the Constitution itself defines the relative rights and powers, and duties of the State, and the citizens of the State, and the Federal Government. But no power is given to acquire a Territory to be held and governed permanently in that character.

. . . [I]t may be safely assumed that citizens of the United States who migrate to a Territory belonging to the people of the United States, cannot be ruled as mere colonists, dependent upon the will of the General Government, and to be governed by any laws it may think proper to impose. The principle upon which our Governments rests is the union of States, sovereign and independent within their own limits in . . . their internal and domestic concerns, and bound together as one people by a General Government, possessing certain enumerated and restricted powers, delegated to it by the people of the several States. . . .

But the power of Congress over the person or property of a citizen can never be a mere discretionary power under our Constitution and form of Government. The powers of the Government and the rights and privileges of the citizen are regulated and plainly defined by the Constitution itself. And when the Territory becomes a part of the United States, the Federal Government enters into possession in the character impressed upon it by those who created it. It enters upon it with its powers over the citizen strictly defined, and limited by the Constitution, from which it derives its own existence, and by virtue of which alone it continues to exist and act as a Government and sovereignty. It has no power of any kind beyond it; and it cannot, when it enters a Territory of the United States, put off its character, and assume discretionary or despotic powers which the Constitution has denied to it.

. . . [T]he rights of private property have been guarded with . . . care. Thus the rights of property are united with the rights of person, and placed on the same ground by the fifth amendment to the Constitution, which provides that no person shall be deprived of life, liberty, and property, without due process of law. And an act of Congress which deprives a citizen of the United States of his liberty or property, merely because he came himself or brought his property into a particular Territory of the United States, and who had committed no offence against the laws, could hardly be dignified with the name of due process of law.

Upon these considerations, it is the opinion of the court that the act of Congress which prohibited a citizen from holding and owning property of this kind in the territory of the United States north of the line therein mentioned, is not warranted by the Constitution, and is therefore void; and that neither Dred Scott himself, nor any of his family, were made free by being carried into this territory; even if they had been carried there by the owner, with the intention of becoming a permanent resident.

But there is another point in the case which depends on State power and State law. And it is contended, on the part of the plaintiff, that he is made free by being taken to Rock Island, in the State of Illinois, independently of his residence in the territory of the United States; and being so made free, he was not again reduced to a state of slavery by being brought back to Missouri.

. . . [I]n the case of *Strader et al. v. Graham* . . . the slaves had been taken from Kentucky to Ohio, with the consent of the owner, and afterwards brought back to Kentucky.

And this court held that their status or condition, as free or slave, depended upon the laws of Kentucky, when they were brought back into that State, and not of Ohio. . . .

So in this case. As Scott was a slave when taken into the State of Illinois by his owner, and was there held as such, and brought back in that character, his status, as free or slave, depended on the laws of Missouri, and not of Illinois.

Upon the whole, therefore, it is the judgment of this court, that it appears by the record before us that the plaintiff in error is not a citizen of Missouri, in the sense in which that word is used in the Constitution; and that the Circuit Court of the United States, for that reason, had no jurisdiction in the case, and could give no judgment in it. Its judgment for the defendant must, consequently, be reversed, and a mandate issued, directing the suit to be dismissed for want of jurisdiction.

Read the judgment in the Supreme Court case *Dred Scott v. John F. A. Sandford,* March 6, 1857 from the National Archives.

Key Excerpts from the Dissenting Opinion

Dred Scott v. Sandford (1857)

Justice McLean wrote the dissenting opinion.

. . . He [Scott] is averred to have had a negro ancestry, but this does not show that he is not a citizen of Missouri, within the meaning of the act of Congress authorizing him to sue in the Circuit Court. It has never been held necessary, to constitute a citizen within the act, that he should have the qualifications of an elector. Females and minors may sue in the Federal courts, and so may any individual who has a permanent domicile in the State under whose laws his rights are protected, and to which he owes allegiance.

Being born under our Constitution and laws, no naturalization is required, as one of foreign birth, to make him a citizen. The most general and appropriate definition of the term citizen is "a freeman." Being a freeman, and having his domicile in a State different from that of the defendant, he is a citizen within the act of Congress, and the courts of the Union are open to him.

In the discussion of the power of Congress to govern a Territory, in the case of the *Atlantic Insurance Company* v. *Canter,* (1Peters, 511; 7 Curtis, 685,) Chief Justice Marshall, speaking for the court, said, " . . . the power of governing a Territory belonging to the United States, which has not, by becoming a State, acquired the means of self-government, may result necessarily from the fact that it is not within the jurisdiction of any particular State, and is within the power and jurisdiction of the United States. The right to govern may be the inevitable consequence of the right to acquire territory; whichever may be the source whence the power is derived, the possession of it is unquestioned."

If Congress may establish a Territorial Government in the exercise of its discretion, it is a clear principle that a court cannot control that discretion. This being the case, I do not see on what ground the act [Missouri Compromise] is held [by the Supreme Court majority's opinion in the *Scott* case] to be void. It did not purport to forfeit property, or take it for public purposes. It only prohibited slavery; in doing which, it followed the ordinance of 1787.

Now, if a slave abscond, he may be reclaimed; but if he accompany his master into a State or Territory where slavery is prohibited, such slave cannot be said to have left the service of his master where his services were legalized. And if slavery be limited to the range of the territorial laws, how can the slave be coerced to serve in a State or Territory; not only without the authority of law, but against its express provisions? What gives the master the right to control the will of his slave? The local law, which exists in some form. But where there is no such law, can the master control the will of the slave by force? Where no slavery exists, the presumption, without regard to color, is in favor of freedom. Under such a jurisdiction, may the colored man be levied on as the property of his master by a creditor? On the decease of the master, does the slave descend to his heirs as property? Can the master sell him? Any one or all of these acts may be done to the slave, where he is legally held to service. But where the law does not confer this power, it cannot be exercised.

. . . Does the master carry with him the law of the State from which he removes into the Territory? and does that enable him to coerce his slave in the Territory? Let us test this theory. If this may be done by a master from one slave State, it may be done by a master from every other slave State. This right is supposed to be connected with the person of the master, by virtue of the local law. Is it transferable? May it be negotiated, as a promissory note or bill of exchange? If it be assigned to a man from a free State, may he coerce the slave by virtue of it? What shall this thing be denominated? Is it personal or real property?

Or is it an indefinable fragment of sovereignty, which every person carries with him from his late domicile? One thing is certain, that its origin has been very recent, and it is unknown to the laws of any civilized country. . . .

Key Excerpts from the Majority Opinion

Pleasant Grove City, Utah, et al. v. Summum

Certiorari to the United States Court of Appeals for the Tenth Circuit.

Argued November 12, 2008—Decided February 25,

No. 07-665. 2009

Pioneer Park (Park), a public park in petitioner Pleasant Grove City (City), has at least 11 permanent, privately donated displays, including a Ten Commandments monument. In rejecting the request of respondent Summum, a religious organization, to erect a monument containing the Seven Aphorisms of Summum, the City explained that it limited Park monuments to those either directly related to the City's history or donated by groups with longstanding community ties. After the City put that policy and other criteria into writing, respondent renewed its request, but did not describe the monument's historical significance or respondent's connection to the community. The City rejected the request, and respondent filed suit, claiming that the City and petitioner officials had violated the First Amendment's Free Speech Clause by accepting the Ten Commandments monument but rejecting respondent's proposed monument. The District Court denied respondent's preliminary injunction request, but the Tenth Circuit reversed. Noting that it had previously found the Ten Commandments monument to be private rather than government speech and that public parks have traditionally been regarded as public forums, the court held that, because the exclusion of the monument was unlikely to survive strict scrutiny, the City was required to erect it immediately.

Held: The placement of a permanent monument in a public park is a form of government speech and is therefore not subject to scrutiny under the Free Speech Clause. Pp. 4-18.

(a) Because that Clause restricts government regulation of private speech but not government speech, whether petitioners were engaging in their own expressive conduct or providing a forum for private speech determines which precedents govern here. Pp. 4-7.

(1) A government entity "is entitled to say what it wishes," *Rosenberger* v. *Rector and Visitors of Univ. of Va.*, 515 U.S. 819, 833, and to select the views that it wants to express, see, e.g., *Rust* v. *Sullivan*, 500 U.S. 173, 194. It may exercise this same freedom when it receives private assistance for the purpose of delivering a government-controlled message. See *Johanns* v. *Livestock Marketing Assn.*, 544 U.S. 550, 562. This does not mean that there are no restraints on government speech. For example, government speech must comport with the Establishment Clause. In addition, public officials' involvement in advocacy may be limited by law, regulation, or practice; and a government entity is ultimately "accountable to the electorate and the political process for its advocacy," *Board of Regents of Univ. of Wis. System* v. *Southworth*, 529 U.S. 217, 235. Pp. 4-6.

(2) In contrast, government entities are strictly limited in their ability to regulate private speech in "traditional public fora." *Cornelius* v. *NAACP Legal Defense & Ed. Fund, Inc.*, 473 U.S. 788, 800. Reasonable time, place, and manner restrictions are allowed, see *Perry Ed. Assn.* v. *Perry Local Educators' Assn.*, 460 U.S. 37, 45, but content-based restrictions must satisfy strict scrutiny, i.e., they must be narrowly tailored to serve a compelling government interest, see *Cornelius, supra,* at 800. Restrictions based on viewpoint are also prohibited. *Carey* v. *Brown*, 447 U.S. 455, 463. Government restrictions on speech in a "designated public forum" are subject to the same strict scrutiny as restrictions in a traditional public forum. *Cornelius, supra,* at 800. And where government creates a forum that is limited to use by certain groups or dedicated to the discussion of certain subjects, *Perry Ed. Assn., supra,* at 46, n. 7, it may impose reasonable and viewpoint-neutral restrictions, see *Good News Club* v. *Milford Central School*, 533 U.S. 98, 106-107. Pp. 6-7.

(b) Permanent monuments displayed on public property typically represent government speech. Governments have long used monuments to speak to the public. Thus, a government-commissioned and government-financed monument placed on public land constitutes government speech. So, too, are privately financed and donated monuments that the government accepts for public display on government land. While government entities regularly accept privately funded or donated monuments, their general practice has been one of selective receptivity. Because city parks play an important role in defining the identity that a city projects to its residents and the outside world, cities take care in accepting donated monuments, selecting those that portray what the government decisionmakers view as appropriate for the place in question, based on esthetics, history, and local culture. The accepted monuments are meant to convey and have the effect of conveying a government message and thus constitute government speech. Pp. 7-10.

(c) Here, the Park's monuments clearly represent government speech. Although many were donated in completed form by private entities, the City has "effectively controlled" their messages by exercising "final approval authority" over their selection. *Johanns, supra,* at 560-561. The City has selected monuments that present the image that the City wishes to project to Park visitors; it has taken ownership of most of the monuments in the Park, including the Ten Commandments monument; and it has now expressly set out selection criteria. P. 10.

(d) Respondent's legitimate concern that the government speech doctrine not be used as a subterfuge for favoring certain viewpoints does not mean that a government entity should be required to embrace publicly a privately donated monument's "message" in order to escape Free Speech Clause restrictions. A city engages in expressive conduct by accepting and displaying a privately donated monument, but it does not necessarily endorse the specific meaning that any particular donor sees in the monument. A government's message may be altered by the subsequent addition of other monuments in the same vicinity. It may also change over time. Pp. 10-15.

(e) "[P]ublic forum principles . . . are out of place in the context of this case." *United States* v. *American Library Assn., Inc.,* 539 U.S. 194, 205. The forum doctrine applies where a government property or program is capable of accommodating a large number of public speakers without defeating the essential function of the land or program, but public parks can accommodate only a limited number of permanent monuments. If governments must maintain viewpoint neutrality in selecting donated monuments, they must either prepare for cluttered parks or face pressure to remove longstanding and cherished monuments. Were public parks considered traditional public forums for the purpose of erecting privately donated monuments, most parks would have little choice but to refuse all such donations. And if forum analysis would lead almost inexorably to closing of the forum, forum analysis is out of place. *Capitol Square Review and Advisory Bd.* v. *Pinette,* 515 U.S. 753, distinguished. Pp. 15-18.

483 F. 3d 1044, reversed.

Alito, J., delivered the opinion of the Court, in which *Roberts, C. J.,* and *Stevens, Scalia, Kennedy, Thomas, Ginsburg,* and *Breyer, JJ.,* joined. *Stevens, J.,* filed a concurring opinion, in which *Ginsburg, J.,* joined. *Scalia, J.,* filed a concurring opinion, in which *Thomas, J.,* joined. *Breyer, J.,* filed a concurring opinion. *Souter, J.,* filed an opinion concurring in the judgment.

Key Excerpts from the Majority Opinion

Indiana v. Edwards

Certiorari to the Supreme Court of Indiana.
Argued March 26, 2008—Decided June 19, 2008

After Indiana charged respondent Edwards with attempted murder and other crimes for a shooting during his attempt to steal a pair of shoes, his mental condition became the subject of three competency proceedings and two self-representation requests, mostly before the same trial judge. Referring to the lengthy record of psychiatric reports, the trial court noted that Edwards suffered from schizophrenia and concluded that, although it appeared he was competent to stand trial, he was not competent to defend himself at trial. The court therefore denied Edwards' self-representation request. He was represented by appointed counsel at trial and convicted on two counts. Indiana's intermediate appellate court ordered a new trial, agreeing with Edwards that the trial court's refusal to permit him to represent himself deprived him of his constitutional right of self-representation under the Sixth Amendment and *Faretta* v. *California,* 422 U.S. 806. Although finding that the record provided substantial support for the trial court's ruling, the Indiana Supreme Court nonetheless affirmed the intermediate appellate court on the ground that *Faretta* and *Godinez* v. *Moran,* 509 U.S. 389, required the State to allow Edwards to represent himself.

Held: The Constitution does not forbid States from insisting upon representation by counsel for those competent enough to stand trial but who suffer from severe mental illness to the point where they are not competent to conduct trial proceedings by themselves. Pp. 4–13.

(a) This Court's precedents frame the question presented, but they do not answer it. *Dusky* v. *United States,* 362 U.S. 402, and *Drope* v. *Missouri,* 420 U.S. 162, 171, set forth the Constitution's "mental competence" standard forbidding the trial of an individual lacking a rational and factual understanding of the proceedings and sufficient ability to consult with his lawyer with a reasonable degree of rational understanding. But those cases did not consider the issue presented here, namely, the relation of that "mental competence" standard to the self-representation right. Similarly the Court's foundational "self-representation" case, *Faretta, supra*—which held that the Sixth and Fourteenth Amendments include a "constitutional right to proceed *without* counsel when" a criminal defendant "voluntarily and intelligently elects to do so," 422 U.S., at 807—does not answer the question as to the scope of the self-representation right. Finally, although *Godinez, supra,* presents a question closer to the one at issue in that it focused upon a borderline-competent defendant who had asked a state trial court to permit him to represent himself and to change his pleas from not guilty to guilty, *Godinez* provides no answer here because that defendant's ability to conduct a defense at trial was expressly not at issue in that case, see 509 U.S., at 399–400, and because the case's constitutional holding that a State may *permit* a gray-area defendant to represent himself does not tell a State whether it may *deny* such a defendant the right to represent himself at his trial. Pp. 4–8.

(b) Several considerations taken together lead the Court to conclude that the Constitution permits a State to limit a defendant's self-representation right by insisting upon trial counsel when the defendant lacks the mental competency to conduct his trial defense unless represented. First, the Court's precedent, while not answering the question, points slightly in that direction. By setting forth a standard that focuses directly upon a defendant's ability to consult with his lawyer, *Dusky* and *Drope* assume representation by counsel and emphasize counsel's importance, thus suggesting (though not holding) that choosing to forgo trial counsel presents a very different set of circumstances than the mental competency determination for a defendant to stand trial. Also, *Faretta* rested its self-representation conclusion in part on pre-existing state cases that are consistent with, and at least two of which expressly adopt, a competency limitation on the self-representation right. See 422 U.S., at 813, and n. 9. *Second, the nature of mental illness—which is not a unitary concept, but varies in degree, can vary over time, and interferes with an individual's functioning at different times in different ways*—cautions against using a single

competency standard to decide both whether a defendant who is represented can proceed to trial and whether a defendant who goes to trial must be permitted to represent himself. *Third, a self-representation right at trial will not "affirm the dignity" of a defendant who lacks the mental capacity to conduct his defense without the assistance of counsel, see McKaskle* v. *Wiggins,* 465 U.S. 168, 176–177, and *may undercut the most basic of the Constitution's criminal law objectives, providing a fair trial.* The trial judge—particularly one such as the judge in this case, who presided over one of Edwards' competency hearings and his two trials—will often prove best able to make more fine-tuned mental capacity decisions, tailored to the particular defendant's individualized circumstances. Pp. 8–12.

(c) Indiana's proposed standard, which would deny a criminal defendant the right to represent himself at trial if he cannot communicate coherently with the court or a jury, is rejected because this Court is uncertain as to how that standard would work in practice. The Court also declines Indiana's request to overrule *Faretta* because today's opinion may well remedy the unfair trial concerns previously leveled against the case. Pp. 12–13.

866 N. E. 2d 252, vacated and remanded.

Breyer, J., delivered the opinion of the Court, in which *Roberts, C. J.,* and *Stevens, Kennedy, Souter, Ginsburg,* and *Alito, JJ.,* joined. *Scalia, J.,* filed a dissenting opinion, in which *Thomas, J.,* joined.

Majority Opinion of the U.S. Supreme Court

Indiana, Petitioner v. Ahmad Edwards

On Writ of Certiorari to the Supreme Court of Indiana.
[June 19, 2008]

Justice Breyer delivered the opinion of the Court.

This case focuses upon a criminal defendant whom a state court found mentally competent to stand trial if represented by counsel but not mentally competent to conduct that trial himself. We must decide whether in these circumstances the Constitution forbids a State from insisting that the defendant proceed to trial with counsel, the State thereby denying the defendant the right to represent himself. See U.S. Const., Amdt. 6; *Faretta* v. *California,* 422 U.S. 806 (1975). We conclude that the Constitution does not forbid a State so to insist.

I

In July 1999 Ahmad Edwards, the respondent, tried to steal a pair of shoes from an Indiana department store. After he was

discovered, he drew a gun, fired at a store security officer, and wounded a bystander. He was caught and then charged with attempted murder, battery with a deadly weapon, criminal recklessness, and theft. His mental condition subsequently became the subject of three competency proceedings and two self-representation requests, mostly before the same trial judge:

1. *First Competency Hearing: August 2000.* Five months after Edwards' arrest, his court-appointed counsel asked for a psychiatric evaluation. After hearing psychiatrist and neuropsychologist witnesses (in February 2000 and again in August 2000), the court found Edwards incompetent to stand trial, App. 365a, and committed him to Logansport State Hospital for evaluation and treatment, see *id.,* at 48a–53a.
2. *Second Competency Hearing: March 2002.* Seven months after his commitment, doctors found that Edwards' condition had improved to the point where he could stand trial. *Id.,* at 63a–64a. Several months later, however, but still before trial, Edwards' counsel asked for another psychiatric evaluation. In March 2002, the judge held a

competency hearing, considered additional psychiatric evidence, and (in April) found that Edwards, while "suffer[ing] from mental illness," was "competent to assist his attorneys in his defense and stand trial for the charged crimes." *Id.*, at 114a.

3. *Third Competency Hearing: April 2003.* Seven months later but still before trial, Edwards' counsel sought yet another psychiatric evaluation of his client. And, in April 2003, the court held yet another competency hearing. Edwards' counsel presented further psychiatric and neuropsychological evidence showing that Edwards was suffering from serious thinking difficulties and delusions. A testifying psychiatrist reported that Edwards could understand the charges against him, but he was "unable to cooperate with his attorney in his defense because of his schizophrenic illness"; "[h]is delusions and his marked difficulties in thinking make it impossible for him to cooperate with his attorney." *Id.*, at 164a. In November 2003, the court concluded that Edwards was not then competent to stand trial and ordered his recommitment to the state hospital. *Id.*, at 206a–211a.

4. *First Self-Representation Request and First Trial: June 2005.* About eight months after his commitment, the hospital reported that Edwards' condition had again improved to the point that he had again become competent to stand trial. *Id.*, at 228a–236a. And almost one year after that Edwards' trial began. Just before trial, Edwards asked to represent himself. *Id.*, at 509a, 520a. He also asked for a continuance, which, he said, he needed in order to proceed *pro se. Id.*, at 519a–520a. The court refused the continuance. *Id.*, at 520a. Edwards then proceeded to trial represented by counsel. The jury convicted him of criminal recklessness and theft but failed to reach a verdict on the charges of attempted murder and battery.

5. *Second Self-Representation Request and Second Trial: December 2005.* The State decided to retry Edwards on the attempted murder and battery charges. Just before the retrial, Edwards again asked the court to permit him to represent himself. *Id.*, at 279a–282a. Referring to the lengthy record of psychiatric reports, the trial court noted that Edwards still suffered from schizophrenia and concluded that "[w]ith these findings, he's competent to stand trial but I'm not going to find he's competent to defend himself." *Id.*, at 527a. The court denied Edwards' self-representation request. Edwards was represented by appointed counsel at his retrial. The jury convicted Edwards on both of the remaining counts.

Edwards subsequently appealed to Indiana's intermediate appellate court. He argued that the trial court's refusal to permit him to represent himself at his retrial deprived him of his constitutional right of self-representation. U.S. Const., Amdt. 6; *Faretta, supra.* The court agreed and ordered a new trial. The matter then went to the Indiana Supreme Court. That court found that "[t]he record in this case presents a substantial basis to agree with the trial court," 866 N.E. 2d

252, 260 (2007), but it nonetheless affirmed the intermediate appellate court on the belief that this Court's precedents, namely, *Faretta*, 422 U.S. 806, and *Godinez* v. *Moran*, 509 U.S. 389 (1993), required the State to allow Edwards to represent himself. At Indiana's request, we agreed to consider whether the Constitution required the trial court to allow Edwards to represent himself at trial.

II

Our examination of this Court's precedents convinces us that those precedents frame the question presented, but they do not answer it. The two cases that set forth the Constitution's "mental competence" standard, *Dusky* v. *United States*, 362 U.S. 402 (1960) *(per curiam)*, and *Drope* v. *Missouri*, 420 U.S. 162 (1975), specify that the Constitution does not permit trial of an individual who lacks "mental competency." *Dusky* defines the competency standard as including both (1) "whether" the defendant has "a rational as well as factual understanding of the proceedings against him" and (2) whether the defendant "has sufficient present ability *to consult with his lawyer* with a reasonable degree of rational understanding." 362 U.S., at 402 (emphasis added; internal quotation marks omitted). *Drope* repeats that standard, stating that it "has long been accepted that a person whose mental condition is such that he lacks the capacity to understand the nature and object of the proceedings against him, *to consult with counsel, and to assist in preparing his defense* may not be subjected to a trial." 420 U.S., at 171 (emphasis added). Neither case considered the mental competency issue presented here, namely, the relation of the mental competence standard to the right of self-representation.

The Court's foundational "self-representation" case, *Faretta*, held that the Sixth and Fourteenth Amendments include a "constitutional right to proceed *without* counsel when" a criminal defendant "voluntarily and intelligently elects to do so." 422 U.S., at 807 (emphasis in original). The Court implied that right from: (1) a "nearly universal conviction," made manifest in state law, that "forcing a lawyer upon an unwilling defendant is contrary to his basic right to defend himself if he truly wants to do so," *id.*, at 817–818; (2) Sixth Amendment language granting rights to the "accused;" (3) Sixth Amendment structure indicating that the rights it sets forth, related to the "fair administration of American justice," are "persona[l]" to the accused, *id.*, at 818–821; (4) the absence of historical examples of *forced* representation, *id.*, at 821–832; and (5) " 'respect for the individual,' " *id.*, at 834 (quoting *Illinois* v. *Allen*, 397 U.S. 337, 350–351 (1970) (Brennan, J., concurring) (a knowing and intelligent waiver of counsel "must be honored out of 'that respect for the individual which is the lifeblood of the law' ")).

Faretta does not answer the question before us both because it did not consider the problem of mental competency (cf. 422 U.S., at 835 (Faretta was "literate, competent, and understanding")), and because *Faretta* itself and later cases have made clear that the right of self-representation is not absolute. See *Martinez* v. *Court of Appeal of Cal., Fourth*

Appellate Dist., 528 U.S. 152, 163 (2000) (no right of self-representation on direct appeal in a criminal case); *McKaskle* v. *Wiggins*, 465 U.S. 168, 178–179 (1984) (appointment of standby counsel over self-represented defendant's objection is permissible); *Faretta*, 422 U.S., at 835, n. 46 (no right "to abuse the dignity of the courtroom"); *ibid.* (no right to avoid compliance with "relevant rules of procedural and substantive law"); *id.*, at 834, n. 46 (no right to "engag[e] in serious and obstructionist misconduct," referring to *Illinois* v. *Allen*, supra). The question here concerns a mental-illness-related limitation on the scope of the self-representation right.

The sole case in which this Court considered mental competence and self-representation together, *Godinez, supra*, presents a question closer to that at issue here. The case focused upon a borderline-competent criminal defendant who had asked a state trial court to permit him to represent himself and to change his pleas from not guilty to guilty. The state trial court had found that the defendant met *Dusky*'s mental competence standard, that he "knowingly and intelligently" waived his right to assistance of counsel, and that he "freely and voluntarily" chose to plead guilty. 509 U.S., at 393 (internal quotation marks omitted). And the state trial court had consequently granted the defendant's self-representation and change-of-plea requests. See *id.*, at 392–393. A federal appeals court, however, had vacated the defendant's guilty pleas on the ground that the Constitution required the trial court to ask a further question, namely, whether the defendant was competent to waive his constitutional right to counsel. See *id.*, at 393–394. Competence to make that latter decision, the appeals court said, required the defendant to satisfy a higher mental competency standard than the standard set forth in *Dusky*. See 509 U.S., at 393–394. *Dusky*'s more general standard sought only to determine whether a defendant represented by counsel was competent to stand trial, not whether he was competent to waive his right to counsel. 509 U.S., at 394–395.

This Court, reversing the Court of Appeals, "reject[ed] the notion that competence to plead guilty or to waive the right to counsel must be measured by a standard that is higher than (or even different from) the *Dusky* standard." *Id.*, at 398. The decision to plead guilty, we said, "is no more complicated than the sum total of decisions that a [represented] defendant may be called upon to make during the course of a trial." *Ibid.* Hence "there is no reason to believe that the decision to waive counsel requires an appreciably higher level of mental functioning than the decision to waive other constitutional rights." *Id.*, at 399. And even assuming that self-representation might pose special trial-related difficulties, "the competence that is required of a defendant seeking to waive his right to counsel is the competence to *waive the right,* not the competence to represent himself." *Ibid.* (emphasis in original). For this reason, we concluded, "the defendant's 'technical legal knowledge' is 'not relevant' to the determination." *Id.*, at 400 (quoting *Faretta, supra*, at 836).

We concede that *Godinez* bears certain similarities with the present case. Both involve mental competence and self-representation. Both involve a defendant who wants to represent himself. Both involve a mental condition that falls in a gray area between *Dusky*'s minimal constitutional requirement that measures a defendant's ability to stand trial and a somewhat higher standard that measures mental fitness for another legal purpose.

We nonetheless conclude that *Godinez* does not answer the question before us now. In part that is because the Court of Appeals higher standard at issue in *Godinez* differs in a critical way from the higher standard at issue here. In *Godinez*, the higher standard sought to measure the defendant's ability to proceed on his own to enter a guilty plea; here the higher standard seeks to measure the defendant's ability to conduct trial proceedings. To put the matter more specifically, the *Godinez* defendant sought only to change his pleas to guilty, he did not seek to conduct trial proceedings, and his ability to conduct a defense at trial was expressly not at issue. Thus we emphasized in *Godinez* that we needed to consider only the defendant's "competence to *waive the right.*" 509 U.S., at 399 (emphasis in original). And we further emphasized that we need *not* consider the defendant's "technical legal knowledge" about how to proceed at trial. *Id.*, at 400 (internal quotation marks omitted). We found our holding consistent with this Court's earlier statement in *Massey* v. *Moore*, 348 U.S. 105, 108 (1954), that "[o]ne might not be insane in the sense of being incapable of standing trial and yet lack the capacity to stand trial without benefit of counsel." See *Godinez, supra*, at 399–400, n. 10 (quoting *Massey* and noting that it dealt with "a question that is quite different from the question presented" in *Godinez*). In this case, the very matters that we did not consider in *Godinez* are directly before us.

For another thing, *Godinez* involved a State that sought to *permit* a gray-area defendant to represent himself. *Godinez*'s constitutional holding is that a State may do so. But that holding simply does not tell a State whether it may *deny* a gray-area defendant the right to represent himself—the matter at issue here. One might argue that *Godinez*'s grant (to a State) of permission to allow a gray-area defendant self-representation must implicitly include permission to deny self-representation. Cf. 509 U.S., at 402 ("States are free to adopt competency standards that are more elaborate than the *Dusky* formulation"). Yet one could more forcefully argue that *Godinez* simply did not consider whether the Constitution *requires* self-representation by gray-area defendants even in circumstances where the State seeks to disallow it (the question here). The upshot is that, in our view, the question before us is an open one.

III

We now turn to the question presented. We assume that a criminal defendant has sufficient mental competence to stand trial (*i.e.*, the defendant meets *Dusky*'s standard) and that the defendant insists on representing himself during that trial. We ask whether the Constitution permits a State to limit that defendant's self-representation right by insisting upon representation by counsel at trial—on the ground that the defendant lacks the mental capacity to conduct his trial defense unless represented.

Several considerations taken together lead us to conclude that the answer to this question is yes. First, the Court's precedent, while not answering the question, points slightly in the direction of our affirmative answer. *Godinez*, as we have just said, simply leaves the question open. But the Court's "mental competency" cases set forth a standard that focuses directly upon a defendant's "present ability to consult with his lawyer," *Dusky*, 362 U.S., at 402 (internal quotation marks omitted); a "capacity . . . to consult with counsel," and an ability "to assist [counsel] in preparing his defense," *Drope*, 420 U.S., at 171. See *ibid.* ("It has long been accepted that a person whose mental condition is such that he lacks the capacity to understand the nature and object of the proceedings against him, *to consult with counsel*, and to assist in preparing his defense may not be subjected to a trial" (emphasis added)). These standards assume representation by counsel and emphasize the importance of counsel. They thus suggest (though do not hold) that an instance in which a defendant who would choose to forgo counsel at trial presents a very different set of circumstances, which in our view, calls for a different standard.

At the same time *Faretta*, the foundational self-representation case, rested its conclusion in part upon pre-existing state law set forth in cases all of which are consistent with, and at least two of which expressly adopt, a competency limitation on the self-representation right. See 422 U.S., at 813, and n. 9 (citing 16 state-court decisions and two secondary sources). See, *e.g., Cappetta v. State*, 204 So. 2d 913, 917–918 (Fla. App. 1967), rev'd on other grounds, 216 So. 2d 749 (Fla. 1968), cited in *Faretta, supra*, at 813, n. 9 (assuring a "mentally competent" defendant the right "to conduct his own defense" *provided that* "no unusual circumstances exist" such as, *e.g.,* "mental derangement" that "would . . . depriv[e]" the defendant "of a fair trial if allowed to conduct his own defense," 204 So. 2d, at 917–918); *id.,* at 918 (noting that "whether unusual circumstances are evident is a matter resting in the sound discretion granted to the trial judge"); *Allen v. Commonwealth*, 324 Mass. 558, 562–563, 87 N.E. 2d 192, 195 (1949) (noting "the assignment of counsel" was "necessary" where there was some "special circumstance" such as when the criminal defendant was "mentally defective").

Second, the nature of the problem before us cautions against the use of a single mental competency standard for deciding both (1) whether a defendant who is represented by counsel can proceed to trial and (2) whether a defendant who goes to trial must be permitted to represent himself. Mental illness itself is not a unitary concept. It varies in degree. It can vary over time. It interferes with an individual's functioning at different times in different ways. The history of this case (set forth in Part I, *supra*) illustrates the complexity of the problem. In certain instances an individual may well be able to satisfy *Dusky's* mental competence standard, for he will be able to work with counsel at trial, yet at the same time he may be unable to carry out the basic tasks needed to present his own

defense without the help of counsel. See, *e.g.,* N. Poythress, R. Bonnie, J. Monahan, R. Otto, & S. Hoge, Adjudicative Competence: The MacArthur Studies 103 (2002) ("Within each domain of adjudicative competence (competence to assist counsel; decisional competence) the data indicate that understanding, reasoning, and appreciation [of the charges against a defendant] are separable and somewhat independent aspects of functional legal ability"). See also *McKaskle*, 465 U.S., at 174 (describing trial tasks as including organization of defense, making motions, arguing points of law, participating in *voir dire*, questioning witnesses, and addressing the court and jury).

The American Psychiatric Association (APA) tells us (without dispute) in its *amicus* brief filed in support of neither party that "[d]isorganized thinking, deficits in sustaining attention and concentration, impaired expressive abilities, anxiety, and other common symptoms of severe mental illnesses can impair the defendant's ability to play the significantly expanded role required for self-representation even if he can play the lesser role of represented defendant." Brief for APA et al. as *Amici Curiae* 26. Motions and other documents that the defendant prepared in this case (one of which we include in the Appendix, *infra*) suggest to a layperson the common sense of this general conclusion.

Third, in our view, a right of self-representation at trial will not "affirm the dignity" of a defendant who lacks the mental capacity to conduct his defense without the assistance of counsel. *McKaskle, supra*, at 176–177 ("Dignity" and "autonomy" of individual underlie self-representation right). To the contrary, given that defendant's uncertain mental state, the spectacle that could well result from his self-representation at trial is at least as likely to prove humiliating as ennobling. Moreover, insofar as a defendant's lack of capacity threatens an improper conviction or sentence, self-representation in that exceptional context undercuts the most basic of the Constitution's criminal law objectives, providing a fair trial. As Justice Brennan put it, "[t]he Constitution would protect none of us if it prevented the courts from acting to preserve the very processes that the Constitution itself prescribes." *Allen*, 397 U.S., at 350 (concurring opinion). See *Martinez*, 528 U.S., at 162 ("Even at the trial level . . . the government's interest in ensuring the integrity and efficiency of the trial at times outweighs the defendant's interest in acting as his own lawyer"). See also *Sell* v. *United States*, 539 U.S. 166, 180 (2003) ("[T]he Government has a concomitant, constitutionally essential interest in assuring that the defendant's trial is a fair one").

Further, proceedings must not only be fair, they must "appear fair to all who observe them." *Wheat* v. *United States*, 486 U.S. 153, 160 (1988). An *amicus* brief reports one psychiatrist's reaction to having observed a patient (a patient who had satisfied *Dusky*) try to conduct his own defense: "[H]ow in the world can our legal system allow an insane man to defend himself?" Brief for Ohio et al. as *Amici Curiae* 24 (internal quotation marks omitted). See *Massey*, 348 U.S., at 108 ("No trial can be fair that leaves the defense to a man who is insane, unaided by counsel, and who by reason of his mental condition stands helpless and alone before the court"). The application of *Dusky*'s basic mental competence standard can help in part to avoid this result. But given the different capacities needed to proceed to trial without counsel, there is little reason to believe that *Dusky* alone is sufficient. At the same time, the trial judge, particularly one such as the trial judge in this case, who presided over one of Edwards' competency hearings and his two trials, will often prove best able to make more fine-tuned mental capacity decisions, tailored to the individualized circumstances of a particular defendant.

We consequently conclude that the Constitution permits judges to take realistic account of the particular defendant's mental capacities by asking whether a defendant who seeks to conduct his own defense at trial is mentally competent to do so. That is to say, the Constitution permits States to insist upon representation by counsel for those competent enough to stand trial under *Dusky* but who still suffer from severe mental illness to the point where they are not competent to conduct trial proceedings by themselves.

IV

Indiana has also asked us to adopt, as a measure of a defendant's ability to conduct a trial, a more specific standard that would "deny a criminal defendant the right to represent himself at trial where the defendant cannot communicate coherently with the court or a jury." Brief for Petitioner 20 (emphasis deleted). We are sufficiently uncertain, however, as to how that particular standard would work in practice to refrain from endorsing it as a federal constitutional standard here. We need not now, and we do not, adopt it.

Indiana has also asked us to overrule *Faretta*. We decline to do so. We recognize that judges have sometimes expressed concern that *Faretta*, contrary to its intent, has led to trials that are unfair. See *Martinez, supra*, at 164 (*Breyer, J.*, concurring) (noting practical concerns of trial judges). But recent empirical research suggests that such instances are not common. See, *e.g.*, Hashimoto, Defending the Right of Self-Representation: An Empirical Look at the Pro Se Felony

Defendant, 85 N.C.L. Rev. 423, 427, 447, 428 (2007) (noting that of the small number of defendants who chose to proceed *pro se*—"roughly 0.3% to 0.5%" of the total, state felony defendants in particular "appear to have achieved higher felony acquittal rates than their represented counterparts in that they were less likely to have been convicted of felonies"). At the same time, instances in which the trial's fairness is in doubt may well be concentrated in the 20 percent or so of self-representation cases where the mental competence of the defendant is also at issue. See *id.*, at 428 (about 20 percent of federal *pro se* felony defendants ordered to undergo competency evaluations). If so, today's opinion, assuring trial judges the authority to deal appropriately with cases in the latter category, may well alleviate those fair trial concerns.

For these reasons, the judgment of the Supreme Court of Indiana is vacated, and the case is remanded for further proceedings not inconsistent with this opinion.

So ordered.

Appendix

Excerpt from respondent's filing entitled " 'Defendant's Version of the Instant Offense,' " which he had attached to his presentence investigation report:

" 'The appointed motion of permissive intervention filed therein the court superior on, 6-26-01 caused a stay of action and apon it's expiration or thereafter three years the plan to establish a youth program to and for the coordination of aspects of law enforcement to prevent and reduce crime amoung young people in Indiana became a diplomatic act as under the Safe Streets Act of 1967, A omnibuc considerate agent: I membered clients within the public and others that at/production of the courts actions showcased causes. The costs of the stay (Trial Rule 60) has a derivative property that is: my knowledged events as not unexpended to contract the membered clients is the commission of finding a facilitie for this plan or project to become organization of administrative recommendations conditioned by governors.' " 866 N.E. 2d, at 258, n. 4 (alterations omitted).

Key Excerpts from the Dissenting Opinion

Indiana, Petitioner v. Ahmad Edwards

On Writ of Certiorari to the Supreme Court of Indiana.
[June 19, 2008]

Justice Scalia, with whom *Justice Thomas* joins, dissenting.

The Constitution guarantees a defendant who knowingly and voluntarily waives the right to counsel the right to proceed *pro se* at his trial. *Faretta* v. *California*, 422 U.S. 806 (1975). A

mentally ill defendant who knowingly and voluntarily elects to proceed *pro se* instead of through counsel receives a fair trial that comports with the Fourteenth Amendment. *Godinez* v. *Moran*, 509 U.S. 389 (1993). The Court today concludes that a State may nonetheless strip a mentally ill defendant of the right to represent himself when that would be fairer. In my view the Constitution does not permit a State to substitute its own perception of fairness for the defendant's right to make his own case before the jury—a specific right long understood as essential to a fair trial.

I

Ahmad Edwards suffers from schizophrenia, an illness that has manifested itself in different ways over time, depending on how and whether Edwards was treated as well as on other factors that appear harder to identify. In the years between 2000 and 2003—years in which Edwards was apparently not treated with the antipsychotic medications and other drugs that are commonly prescribed for his illness—Edwards was repeatedly declared incompetent to stand trial. Even during this period, however, his mental state seems to have fluctuated. For instance, one psychiatrist in March 2001 described Edwards in a competency report as "free of psychosis, depression, mania, and confusion," "alert, oriented, [and] appropriate," apparently "able to think clearly" and apparently "psychiatrically normal." App. 61a.

Edwards seems to have been treated with antipsychotic medication for the first time in 2004. He was found competent to stand trial the same year. The psychiatrist making the recommendation described Edwards' thought processes as "coherent" and wrote that he "communicate[d] very well," that his speech was "easy to understand," that he displayed "good communications skills, cooperative attitude, average intelligence, and good cognitive functioning," that he could "appraise the roles of the participants in the courtroom proceedings," and that he had the capacity to challenge prosecution witnesses realistically and to testify relevantly. *Id.*, at 232a–235a (report of Dr. Robert Sena).

Over the course of what became two separate criminal trials, Edwards sought to act as his own lawyer. He filed a number of incoherent written pleadings with the judge on which the Court places emphasis, but he also filed several intelligible pleadings, such as a motion to dismiss counsel, a motion to dismiss charges under the Indiana speedy trial provision, and a motion seeking a trial transcript.

Edwards made arguments in the courtroom that were more coherent than his written pleadings. In seeking to represent himself at his first trial, Edwards complained in detail that the attorney representing him had not spent adequate time preparing and was not sharing legal materials for use in his defense. The trial judge concluded that Edwards had knowingly and voluntarily waived his right to counsel and proceeded to quiz Edwards about matters of state law. Edwards correctly answered questions about the meaning of *voir dire* and how it operated, and described the basic framework for admitting videotape evidence to trial, though he was unable to answer other questions, including questions about the topics covered by state evidentiary rules that the judge identified only by number. He persisted in his request to represent himself, but the judge denied the request because Edwards acknowledged he would need a continuance. Represented by counsel, he was convicted of criminal recklessness and theft, but the jury deadlocked on charges of attempted murder and battery.

At his second trial, Edwards again asked the judge to be allowed to proceed *pro se*. He explained that he and his attorney disagreed about which defense to present to the attempted murder charge. Edwards' counsel favored lack of intent to kill; Edwards, self-defense. As the defendant put it: "My objection is me and my attorney actually had discussed a defense, I think prosecution had mentioned that, and we are in disagreement with it. He has a defense and I have a defense that I would like to represent or present to the Judge." *Id.*, at 523a.

The court again rejected Edwards' request to proceed *pro se*, and this time it did not have the justification that Edwards had sought a continuance. The court did not dispute that Edwards knowingly and intelligently waived his right to counsel, but stated it was "going to carve out a third exception" to the right of self-representation, and—without explaining precisely what abilities Edwards lacked—stated Edwards was "competent to stand trial but I'm not going to find he's competent to defend himself." *Id.*, at 527a. Edwards sought—by a request through counsel and by raising an objection in open court—to address the judge on the matter, but the judge refused, stating that the issue had already been decided. Edwards' court-appointed attorney pursued the defense the attorney judged best—lack of intent, not self-defense—and Edwards was convicted of both attempted murder and battery. The Supreme Court of Indiana held that he was entitled to a new trial because he had been denied the right to represent himself. The State of Indiana sought certiorari, which we granted. 552 U.S. ___ (2007).

II

A

The Constitution guarantees to every criminal defendant the "right to proceed *without* counsel when he voluntarily and intelligently elects to do so." *Faretta*, 422 U.S., at 807. The right reflects "a nearly universal conviction, on the part of our people as well as our courts, that forcing a lawyer upon an unwilling defendant is contrary to his basic right to defend himself if he truly wants to do so." *Id.*, at 817. *Faretta*'s discussion of the history of the right, *id.*, at 821–833, includes the observation that "[i]n the long history of British criminal jurisprudence, there was only one tribunal that ever adopted a practice of forcing counsel upon an unwilling defendant in a criminal proceeding. The tribunal was the Star Chamber," *id.*, at 821. *Faretta* described the right to proceed *pro se* as a premise of the Sixth Amendment, which confers the tools for a defense on the "accused," and describes the role of the attorney as one of "assistance." The right of self-representation could also be seen as a part of the traditional meaning of the Due Process Clause. See *Martinez* v. *Court of Appeal of Cal., Fourth Appellate Dist.*, 528 U.S. 152, 165 (2000) (*Scalia, J.*, concurring in judgment). Whichever provision provides its source, it means that a State simply may not force a lawyer upon a criminal defendant who wishes to conduct his own defense. *Faretta*, 422 U.S., at 807.

Exercising the right of self-representation requires waiving the right to counsel. A defendant may represent himself only when he " 'knowingly and intelligently' " waives the lawyer's assistance that is guaranteed by the Sixth Amendment. *Id.*, at 835. He must "be made aware of the dangers and disadvantages of self-representation," and the record must "establish that 'he knows what he is doing and his choice is made with eyes open.' " *Ibid.* (quoting *Adams* v. *United States ex rel. McCann*, 317 U.S. 269, 279 (1942)). This limitation maybe relevant to many mentally ill defendants, but there is no dispute that Edwards was not one of them. Edwards was warned extensively of the risks of proceeding *pro se*. The trial judge found that Edwards had "knowingly and voluntarily" waived his right to counsel at his first trial, App. 512a, and at his second trial the judge denied him the right to represent himself only by "carv[ing] out" a new "exception" to the right beyond the standard of knowing and voluntary waiver, *id.*, at 527a.

When a defendant appreciates the risks of forgoing counsel and chooses to do so voluntarily, the Constitution protects his ability to present his own defense even when that harms his case. In fact waiving counsel "usually" does so. *McKaskle* v. *Wiggins*, 465 U.S. 168, 177, n. 8 (1984); see also *Faretta*, 422 U.S., at 834. We have nonetheless said that the defendant's "choice must be honored out of 'that respect for the individual which is the lifeblood of the law.' " *Ibid.* What the Constitution requires is not that a State's case be subject to the most rigorous adversarial testing possible—after all, it permits a defendant to eliminate *all* adversarial testing by pleading guilty. What the Constitution requires is that a defendant be given the right to challenge the State's case against him using the arguments *he* sees fit.

In *Godinez*, 509 U.S. 389, we held that the Due Process Clause posed no barrier to permitting a defendant who suffered from mental illness both to waive his right to counsel and to plead guilty, so long as he was competent to stand trial and knowingly and voluntarily waived trial and the counsel right. *Id.*, at 391, 400. It was "never the rule at common law" that a defendant could be competent to stand trial and yet incompetent to either exercise or give up some of the rights provided for his defense. *Id.*, at 404 (*Kennedy*, J., concurring in part and concurring in judgment). We rejected the invitation to craft a higher competency standard for waiving counsel than for standing trial. That proposal, we said, was built on the "flawed premise" that a defendant's "competence to represent himself" was the relevant measure: "[T]he competence that is required of a defendant seeking to waive his right to counsel is the competence to *waive the right*, not the competence to represent himself." *Id.*, at 399. We grounded this on *Faretta*'s candid acknowledgment that the Sixth Amendment protected the defendant's right to conduct a defense to his disadvantage. 509 U.S. at 399–400.

B

The Court is correct that this case presents a variation on *Godinez:* It presents the question not whether another constitutional requirement (in *Godinez*, the proposed higher degree of competence required for a waiver) limits a defendant's constitutional right to elect self-representation, but whether a State's view of fairness (or of other values) permits it to strip the defendant of this right. But that makes the question before us an easier one. While one constitutional requirement must yield to another in case of conflict, nothing permits a State, because of *its* view of what is fair, to deny a constitutional protection. Although "the purpose of the rights set forth in [the Sixth] Amendment is to ensure a fair trial," it "does not follow that the rights can be disregarded so long as the trial is, on the whole, fair." *United States* v. *Gonzalez-Lopez*, 548 U.S. 140, 145 (2006). Thus, although the Confrontation Clause aims to produce fairness by ensuring the reliability of testimony, States may not provide for unconfronted testimony to be used at trial so long as it is reliable. *Crawford* v. *Washington*, 541 U.S. 36, 61 (2004). We have rejected an approach to individual liberties that " 'abstracts from the right to its purposes, and then eliminates the right.' " *Gonzalez-Lopez, supra*, at 145 (quoting *Maryland* v. *Craig*, 497 U.S. 836, 862 (1990) (*Scalia, J.*, dissenting)).

Until today, the right of self-representation has been accorded the same respect as other constitutional guarantees. The only circumstance in which we have permitted the State to deprive a defendant of this trial right is the one under which we have allowed the State to deny *other* such rights: when it is necessary to enable the trial to proceed in an orderly fashion. That overriding necessity, we have said, justifies forfeiture of even the Sixth Amendment right to be present at trial—if, after being threatened with removal, a defendant "insists on conducting himself in a manner so disorderly, disruptive, and disrespectful of the court that his trial cannot be carried on with him in the courtroom." *Illinois* v. *Allen*, 397 U.S. 337, 343 (1970). A *pro se* defendant may not "abuse the dignity of the courtroom," nor may he fail to "comply with relevant rules of procedural and substantive law," and a court may "terminate" the self-representation of a defendant who "deliberately engages in serious and obstructionist misconduct." *Faretta, supra*, at 834–835, n. 46. This ground for terminating self-representation is unavailable here, however, because Edwards was not even allowed to begin to represent himself, and because he was respectful and compliant and did not provide a basis to conclude a trial could not have gone forward had he been allowed to press his own claims.

Beyond this circumstance, we have never constrained the ability of a defendant to retain "actual control over the case he chooses to present to the jury"—what we have termed "the core of the *Faretta* right." *Wiggins, supra*, at 178. Thus, while *Faretta* recognized that the right of self-representation does not bar the court from appointing standby counsel, we explained in *Wiggins* that "[t]he *pro se* defendant must be allowed to control the organization and content of his own defense, to make motions, to argue points of law, to participate in *voir dire*, to question witnesses, and to address the court and the jury at appropriate points in the trial." 465 U.S., at 174. Furthermore, because "multiple voices 'for the defense'" could "confuse the message the defendant wishes to convey," *id.*, at 177, a standby attorney's participation would be barred when it would "destroy the jury's perception that the defendant is representing himself," *id.*, at 178.

As I have explained, I would not adopt an approach to the right of self-representation that we have squarely rejected for other rights—allowing courts to disregard the right when doing so serves the purposes for which the right was intended. But if I were to adopt such an approach, I would remain in dissent, because I believe the Court's assessment of the purposes of the right of self-representation is inaccurate to boot. While there is little doubt that preserving individual "'dignity'" (to which the Court refers), *ante*, at 11, is paramount among those purposes, there is equally little doubt that the loss of "dignity" the right is designed to prevent is *not* the defendant's making a fool of himself by presenting an amateurish or even incoherent defense. Rather, the dignity at issue is the supreme human dignity of being master of one's fate rather than a ward of the State—the dignity of individual choice. *Faretta* explained that the Sixth Amendment's counsel clause should not be invoked to impair "'the exercise of [the defendant's] free choice'" to dispense with the right, 422 U.S., at 815 (quoting *Adams*, 317 U.S., at 280); for "whatever else may be said of those who wrote the Bill of Rights, surely there can be no doubt that they understood the inestimable worth of free choice," 422 U.S., at 833–834. Nine years later, when we wrote in *Wiggins* that the self-representation right served the "dignity and autonomy of the accused," 465 U.S., at 177, we explained in no uncertain terms that this meant according every defendant the right to his say in court. In particular, we said that individual dignity and autonomy barred standby counsel from participating in a manner that would to "destroy the jury's perception that the defendant is representing himself," and meant that "the *pro se* defendant is entitled to preserve actual control over the case he chooses to present to the jury." *Id.*, at 178. In sum, if the Court is to honor the particular conception of "dignity" that underlies the self-representation right, it should respect the autonomy of the individual by honoring his choices knowingly and voluntarily made.

A further purpose that the Court finds is advanced by denial of the right of self-representation is the purpose of assuring that trials "appear fair to all who observe them." *Ante*, at 11. To my knowledge we have never denied a defendant a right simply on the ground that it would make his trial appear less "fair" to outside observers, and I would not inaugurate that principle here. But were I to do so, I would not apply it to deny a defendant the right to represent himself when he knowingly and voluntarily waives counsel. When Edwards stood to say that "I have a defense that I would like to repre-

sent or present to the Judge," App. 523a, it seems to me the epitome of both actual and apparent unfairness for the judge to say, I have heard "your desire to proceed by yourself and I've denied your request, so your attorney will speak for you from now on," *id.*, at 530a.

III

It may be that the Court permits a State to deprive mentally ill defendants of a historic component of a fair trial because it is suspicious of the constitutional footing of the right of self-representation itself. The right is not explicitly set forth in the text of the Sixth Amendment, and some Members of this Court have expressed skepticism about *Faretta*'s holding. See *Martinez, supra*, at 156–158 (questioning relevance of historical evidence underlying *Faretta*'s holding); 528 U.S., at 164 (*Breyer, J.*, concurring) (noting "judges closer to the firing line have sometimes expressed dismay about the practical consequences" of the right of self-representation).

While the Sixth Amendment makes no mention of the right to forgo counsel, it provides the defendant, and not his lawyer, the right to call witnesses in his defense and to confront witnesses against him, and counsel is permitted to assist in "*his* defence" (emphasis added). Our trial system, however, allows the attorney representing a defendant "full authority to manage the conduct of the trial"—an authority without which "[t]he adversary process could not function effectively." *Taylor* v. *Illinois*, 484 U.S. 400, 418 (1988); see also *Florida* v. *Nixon*, 543 U.S. 175, 187 (2004). We have held that "the client must accept the consequences of the lawyer's decision to forgo cross-examination, to decide not to put certain witnesses on the stand, or to decide not to disclose the identity of certain witnesses in advance of trial." *Taylor, supra*, at 418. Thus, in order for the defendant's right to call his own witnesses, to cross-examine witnesses, and to put on a defense to be anything more than "a tenuous and unacceptable legal fiction," a defendant must have consented to the representation of counsel. *Faretta, supra*, at 821. Otherwise, "the defense presented is not the defense guaranteed him by the Constitution, for in a very real sense, it is not *his* defense." *Ibid.*

The facts of this case illustrate this point with the utmost clarity. Edwards wished to take a self-defense case to the jury. His counsel preferred a defense that focused on lack of intent. Having been denied the right to conduct his own defense, Edwards was convicted without having had the opportunity to present to the jury the grounds he believed supported his innocence. I do not doubt that he likely would have been convicted anyway. But to hold that a defendant may be deprived of the right to make legal arguments for acquittal simply because a state-selected agent has made different arguments on his behalf is, as Justice Frankfurter wrote in *Adams, supra*, at 280, to "imprison a man in his privileges and call it the Constitution." In singling out mentally ill defendants for this treatment, the Court's opinion does not even have the questionable virtue of being politically correct. At a time when all society is trying to mainstream the mentally impaired, the

Court permits them to be deprived of a basic constitutional right—for their own good.

Today's holding is extraordinarily vague. The Court does not accept Indiana's position that self-representation can be denied " 'where the defendant cannot communicate coherently with the court or a jury,' " *ante*, at 12. It does not even hold that Edwards was properly denied his right to represent himself. It holds only that lack of mental competence can under some circumstances form a basis for denying the right to proceed *pro se*, *ante*, at 1. We will presumably give some meaning to this holding in the future, but the indeterminacy

makes a bad holding worse. Once the right of self-representation for the mentally ill is a sometime thing, trial judges will have every incentive to make their lives easier—to avoid the painful necessity of deciphering occasional pleadings of the sort contained in the Appendix to today's opinion—by appointing knowledgeable and literate counsel.

Because I think a defendant who is competent to stand trial, and who is capable of knowing and voluntary waiver of assistance of counsel, has a constitutional right to conduct his own defense, I respectfully dissent.

1

Syllabus

Where it is feasible, a syllabus (headnote) will NOTE: be released, as is being done in connection with this case, at the time the opinion is issued. The syllabus constitutes no part of the opinion of the Court but has been prepared by the Reporter of Decisions for the convenience of the reader. See *United States v. Detroit Timber & Lumber Co.*, 200 U. S. 321.

SUPREME COURT OF THE UNITED STATES

CITIZENS UNITED *v.* FEDERAL ELECTION COMMISSION

APPEAL FROM THE UNITED STATES DISTRICT COURT FOR THE DISTRICT OF COLUMBIA

Argued March 24, 2009—Reargued September 9, No. 08-205. 2009—Decided January 21, 2010

As amended by §203 of the Bipartisan Campaign Reform Act of 2002 (BCRA), federal law prohibits corporations and unions from using their general treasury funds to make independent expenditures for speech that is an "electioneering communication" or for speech that expressly advocates the election or defeat of a candidate. 2 U. S. C. §441b. An electioneering communication is "any broadcast, cable, or satellite communication" that "refers to a clearly identified candidate for Federal office" and is made within 30 days of a primary election, §434(f)(3)(A), and that is "publicly distributed," 11 CFR §100.29(a)(2), which in "the case of a candidate for nomination for President . . . means" that the communication "[c]an be received by 50,000 or more persons in a State where a primary election . . . is being held within 30 days," §100.29(b)(3)(ii). Corporations and unions may establish a political action committee (PAC) for express advocacy or electioneering communications purposes. 2 U. S. C. §441b(b)(2). In *McConnell* v. *Federal Election Comm'n*, 540 U. S. 93, this Court upheld limits on electioneering communications in a facial challenge, relying on the holding in *Austin* v. *Michigan Chamber of Commerce*, 494 U. S. 652, that political speech may be banned based on the speaker's corporate identity.

In January 2008, appellant Citizens United, a nonprofit corporation, released a documentary (hereinafter *Hillary*) critical of then-Senator Hillary Clinton, a candidate for her party's Presidential nomination. Anticipating that it would make *Hillary* available on cable television through video-on-demand within 30 days of primary elections, Citizens United produced television ads to run on broadcast and cable television. Concerned about possible civil and criminal penalties for violating §441b, it sought declaratory and injunctive relief, arguing that (1) §441b is unconstitutional as applied to *Hillary;* and (2) BCRA's disclaimer, disclosure, and reporting requirements, BCRA §§201 and 311, were unconstitutional as applied to *Hillary* and the ads. The District Court denied Citizens United a preliminary injunction and granted appellee Federal Election Commission (FEC) summary judgment.

2   CITIZENS UNITED *v.* FEDERAL ELECTION COMMISSION

Syllabus

Held:

1. Because the question whether §441b applies to *Hillary* cannot be resolved on other, narrower grounds without chilling political speech, this Court must consider the continuing effect of the speech suppression upheld in *Austin.* Pp. 5–20.

(a) Citizen United's narrower arguments—that *Hillary* is not an "electioneering communication" covered by §441b because it is not "publicly distributed" under 11 CFR §100.29(a)(2); that §441b may not be applied to *Hillary* under *Federal Election Comm'n* v. *Wisconsin Right to Life, Inc.,* 551 U. S. 449 *(WRTL),* which found §441b unconstitutional as applied to speech that was not "express advocacy or its functional equivalent," *id.,* at 481 (opinion of ROBERTS, C. J.), determining that a communication "is the functional equivalent of express advocacy only if [it] is susceptible of no reasonable interpretation other than as an appeal to vote for or against a specific candidate," *id.,* at 469–470; that §441b should be invalidated as applied to movies shown through video-on-demand because this delivery system has a lower risk of distorting the political process than do television ads; and that there should be an exception to §441b's ban for nonprofit corporate political speech funded overwhelming by individuals—are not sustainable under a fair reading of the statute. Pp. 5–12.

(b) Thus, this case cannot be resolved on a narrower ground without chilling political speech, speech that is central to the First Amendment's meaning and purpose. Citizens United did not waive this challenge to *Austin* when it stipulated to dismissing the facial challenge below, since (1) even if such a challenge could be waived, this Court may reconsider *Austin* and §441b's facial validity here because the District Court "passed upon" the issue, *Lebron* v. *National Railroad Passenger Corporation,* 513 U. S. 374; (2) throughout the litigation, Citizens United has asserted a claim that the FEC has violated its right to free speech; and (3) the parties cannot enter into a stipulation that prevents the Court from considering remedies necessary to resolve a claim that has been preserved. Because Citizen United's narrower arguments are not sustainable, this Court must, in an exercise of its judicial responsibility, consider §441b's facial validity. Any other course would prolong the substantial, nationwide chilling effect caused by §441b's corporate expenditure ban. This conclusion is further supported by the following: (1) the uncertainty caused by the Government's litigating position; (2) substantial time would be required to clarify §441b's application on the points raised by the Government's position in order to avoid any chilling effect caused by an improper interpretation; and (3) because speech itself is of primary importance to the integrity of the election process, any speech arguably within the reach of rules created for regulating political speech is chilled. The regulatory scheme at issue may not be a prior restraint in the strict sense. However, given its complexity and the deference courts show to administrative determinations, a speaker wishing to avoid criminal liability threats and the heavy costs of defending against FEC enforcement must ask a governmental agency for prior permission to speak. The restrictions thus function as the equivalent of a prior restraint, giving the FEC power analogous to the type of government practices that the First Amendment was drawn to prohibit. The ongoing chill on speech makes it necessary to invoke the earlier precedents that a statute that chills speech can and must be invalidated where its facial invalidity has been demonstrated. Pp. 12–20.

2. *Austin* is overruled, and thus provides no basis for allowing the Government to limit corporate independent expenditures. Hence, §441b's restrictions on such expenditures are invalid and cannot be applied to *Hillary.* Given this conclusion, the part of *McConnell* that upheld BCRA §203's extension of §441b's restrictions on independent corporate expenditures is also overruled. Pp. 20–51.

(a) Although the First Amendment provides that "Congress shall make no law . . . abridging the freedom of speech," §441b's prohibition on corporate independent expenditures is an outright ban on speech, backed by criminal sanctions. It is a ban notwithstanding the fact that a PAC created by a corporation can still speak, for a PAC is a separate association from the corporation. Because speech is an essential mechanism of democracy—it is the means to hold officials accountable to the people—political speech must prevail against laws that would suppress it by design or inadvertence. Laws burdening such speech are subject to strict scrutiny, which requires the Government to prove that the restriction "furthers a compelling interest and is narrowly tailored to achieve that interest." *WRTL,* 551 U. S., at 464. This language provides a sufficient framework for protecting the interests in this case. Premised on mistrust of governmental power, the First Amendment stands against attempts to disfavor certain subjects or viewpoints or to distinguish among different speakers, which may be a means to control content. The Government may also commit a constitutional wrong when by law it identifies certain preferred speakers. There is no basis for the proposition that, in the political speech context, the Government may impose restrictions on certain disfavored speakers. Both history and logic lead to this conclusion. Pp. 20–25.

Syllabus

(b) The Court has recognized that the First Amendment applies to corporations, *e.g., First Nat. Bank of Boston* v. *Bellotti*, 435 U. S. 765, and extended this protection to the context of political speech, see, *e.g., NAACP* v. *Button*, 371 U. S. 415. Addressing challenges to the Federal Election Campaign Act of 1971, the *Buckley* Court upheld limits on direct contributions to candidates, 18 U. S. C. §608(b), recognizing a governmental interest in preventing *quid pro quo* corruption. 424 U. S., at 25–26. However, the Court invalidated §608(e)'s expenditure ban, which applied to individuals, corporations, and unions, because it "fail[ed] to serve any substantial governmental interest in stemming the reality or appearance of corruption in the electoral process," *id.,* at 47–48. While *Buckley* did not consider a separate ban on corporate and union independent expenditures found in §610, had that provision been challenged in *Buckley*'s wake, it could not have been squared with the precedent's reasoning and analysis. The *Buckley* Court did not invoke the overbreadth doctrine to suggest that §608(e)'s expenditure ban would have been constitutional had it applied to corporations and unions but not individuals. Notwithstanding this precedent, Congress soon recodified §610's corporate and union expenditure ban at 2 U. S. C. §441b, the provision at issue. Less than two years after *Buckley, Bellotti* reaffirmed the First Amendment principle that the Government lacks the power to restrict political speech based on the speaker's corporate identity. 435 U.S., at 784–785. Thus the law stood until *Austin* upheld a corporate independent expenditure restriction, bypassing *Buckley* and *Bellotti* by recognizing a new governmental interest in preventing "the corrosive and distorting effects of immense aggregations of [corporate] wealth . . . that have little or no correlation to the public's support for the corporation's political ideas." 494 U. S., at 660. Pp. 25–32.

(c) This Court is confronted with conflicting lines of precedent: a pre- *Austin* line forbidding speech restrictions based on the speaker's corporate identity and a post-*Austin* line permitting them. Neither *Austin*'s antidistortion rationale nor the Government's other justifications support §441b's restrictions. Pp. 32–47.

(1) The First Amendment prohibits Congress from fining or jailing citizens, or associations of citizens, for engaging in political speech, but *Austin*'s antidistortion rationale would permit the Government to ban political speech because the speaker is an association with a corporate form. Political speech is "indispensable to decision-making in a democracy, and this is no less true because the speech comes from a corporation." *Bellotti, supra,* at 777 (footnote omitted). This protection is inconsistent with *Austin*'s rationale, which is meant to prevent corporations from obtaining " 'an unfair advantage in the political marketplace' " by using " 'resources amassed in the economic marketplace.' " 494 U. S., at 659. First Amendment protections do not depend on the speaker's "financial ability to engage in public discussion." *Buckley, supra,* at 49. These conclusions were reaffirmed when the Court invalidated a BCRA provision that increased the cap on contributions to one candidate if the opponent made certain expenditures from personal funds. *Davis* v. *Federal Election Comm'n,* 554 U. S. ___, ___. Distinguishing wealthy individuals from corporations based on the latter's special advantages of, *e.g.,* limited liability, does not suffice to allow laws prohibiting speech. It is irrelevant for First Amendment purposes that corporate funds may "have little or no correlation to the public's support for the corporation's political ideas." *Austin, supra,* at 660. All speakers, including individuals and the media, use money amassed from the economic marketplace to fund their speech, and the First Amendment protects the resulting speech. Under the antidistortion rationale, Congress could also ban political speech of media corporations. Although currently exempt from §441b, they accumulate wealth with the help of their corporate form, may have aggregations of wealth, and may express views "hav[ing] little or no correlation to the public's support" for those views. Differential treatment of media corporations and other corporations cannot be squared with the First Amendment, and there is no support for the view that the Amendment's original meaning would permit suppressing media corporations' political speech. *Austin* interferes with the "open marketplace" of ideas protected by the First Amendment. *New York State Bd. of Elections* v. *Lopez Torres,* 552 U. S. 196. Its censorship is vast in its reach, suppressing the speech of both for-profit and nonprofit, both small and large, corporations. Pp. 32–40.

(2) This reasoning also shows the invalidity of the Government's other arguments. It reasons that corporate political speech can be banned to prevent corruption or its appearance. The *Buckley* Court found this rationale "sufficiently important" to allow contribution limits but refused to extend that reasoning to expenditure limits, 424 U.S., at 25, and the Court does not do so here. While a single *Bellotti* footnote purported to leave the question open, 435 U. S., at 788, n. 26, this Court now concludes that independent expenditures, including those made by corporations, do not give rise to corruption or the appearance of corruption. That speakers may have influence over or access to elected officials does not mean that those officials are corrupt. And the appearance of influence or access will not cause the electorate to lose faith in this democracy. *Caperton* v. *A. T. Massey Coal Co.,* 556 U. S. ___, distinguished. Pp. 40–45.

4   CITIZENS UNITED v. FEDERAL ELECTION COMMISSION

Syllabus

(3) The Government's asserted interest in protecting shareholders from being compelled to fund corporate speech, like the antidistortion rationale, would allow the Government to ban political speech even of media corporations. The statute is under-inclusive; it only protects a dissenting shareholder's interests in certain media for 30 or 60 days before an election when such interests would be implicated in any media at any time. It is also overinclusive because it covers all corporations, including those with one shareholder. P. 46.

(4) Because §441b is not limited to corporations or associations created in for-eign countries or funded predominately by foreign shareholders, it would be over-broad even if the Court were to recognize a compelling governmental interest in limit-ing foreign influence over the Nation's political process. Pp. 46–47.

(d) The relevant factors in deciding whether to adhere to *stare decisis*, beyond workability—the precedent's antiquity, the reliance interests at stake, and whether the decision was well reasoned—counsel in favor of abandoning *Austin*, which itself con-travened the precedents of *Buckley* and *Bellotti*. As already explained, *Austin* was not well reasoned. It is also undermined by experience since its announcement. Political speech is so ingrained in this country's culture that speakers find ways around cam-paign finance laws. Rapid changes in technology—and the creative dynamic inherent in the concept of free expression—counsel against upholding a law that restricts polit-ical speech in certain media or by certain speakers. In addition, no serious reliance issues are at stake. Thus, due consideration leads to the conclusion that *Austin* should be overruled. The Court returns to the principle established in *Buckley* and *Bellotti* that the Government may not suppress political speech based on the speaker's corpo-rate identity. No sufficient governmental interest justifies limits on the political speech of nonprofit or for-profit corporations. Pp. 47–50.

3. BCRA §§201 and 311 are valid as applied to the ads for *Hillary* and to the movie itself. Pp. 50–57.

(a) Disclaimer and disclosure requirements may burden the ability to speak, but they "impose no ceiling on campaign-related activities," *Buckley*, 424 U. S., at 64, or " ' "prevent anyone from speaking," ' " *McConnell, supra*, at 201. The *Buckley* Court explained that disclosure can be justified by a governmental interest in providing "the electorate with information" about election-related spending sources. The *McConnell* Court applied this interest in rejecting facial challenges to §§201 and 311. 540 U. S., at 196. However, the Court acknowledged that as-applied challenges would be available if a group could show a " 'reasonable probability' " that disclosing its contributors' names would " 'subject them to threats, harassment, or reprisals from either Government officials or private parties.' " *Id.*, at 198. Pp. 50–52.

(b) The disclaimer and disclosure requirements are valid as applied to Citizens United's ads. They fall within BCRA's "electioneering communication" definition: They referred to then-Senator Clinton by name shortly before a primary and contained pejo-rative references to her candidacy. Section 311 disclaimers provide information to the electorate, *McConnell, supra*, at 196, and "insure that the voters are fully informed" about who is speaking, *Buckley, supra*, at 76. At the very least, they avoid confusion by making clear that the ads are not funded by a candidate or political party. Citizens United's arguments that §311 is underinclusive because it requires disclaimers for broadcast advertisements but not for print or Internet advertising and that §311 decreases the quantity and effectiveness of the group's speech were rejected in *McConnell.* This Court also rejects their contention that §201's disclosure requirements must be confined to speech that is the functional equivalent of express advocacy under *WRTL*'s test for restrictions on independent expenditures, 551 U. S., at 469–476 (opinion of ROBERTS, C.J.). Disclosure is the less-restrictive alternative to more comprehensive speech regulations. Such requirements have been upheld in *Buckley* and *McConnell.* Citizens United's argument that no informational interest justifies applying §201 to its ads is similar to the argument this Court rejected with regard to disclaimers. Citizens United finally claims that disclosure requirements can chill donations by exposing donors to retaliation, but offers no evidence that its members face the type of threats, harassment, or reprisals that might make §201 unconstitutional as applied. Pp. 52–55.

(c) For these same reasons, this Court affirms the application of the §§201 and 311 disclaimer and disclosure requirements to *Hillary.* Pp. 55–56.

Reversed in part, affirmed in part, and remanded.

KENNEDY, J., delivered the opinion of the Court, in which ROBERTS, C. J., and SCALIA and ALITO, JJ., joined, in which THOMAS, J., joined as to all but Part IV, and in which STEVENS, GINSBURG, BREYER, and SOTOMAYOR, JJ., joined as to Part IV. ROBERTS, C. J., filed a concur-ring opinion, in which ALITO, J., joined. SCALIA, J., filed a concurring opinion, in which ALITO, J., joined, and in which THOMAS, J., joined in part. STEVENS, J., filed an opinion concurring in part and dissenting in part, in which GINSBURG, BREYER, and SOTOMAYOR, JJ., joined. THOMAS, J., filed an opinion concurring in part and dissenting in part.

1

SUPREME COURT OF THE UNITED STATES

SALAZAR, SECRETARY OF THE INTERIOR, ET AL. *v.* BUONO

CERTIORARI TO THE UNITED STATES COURT OF APPEALS FOR THE NINTH CIRCUIT

Argued October 7, 2009—Decided April 28, No. 08–472. 2010

In 1934, members of the Veterans of Foreign Wars (VFW) placed a Latin cross on federal land in the Mojave National Preserve (Preserve) to honor American soldiers who died in World War I. Claiming to be offended by a religious symbol's presence on federal land, respondent Buono, a regular visitor to the Preserve, filed this suit alleging a violation of the First Amendment's Establishment Clause and seeking an injunction requiring the Government to remove the cross. In the litigation's first stage *(Buono I)*, the District Court found that Buono had standing to sue and, concluding that the presence of the cross on federal land conveyed an impression of governmental endorsement of religion, see *Lemon* v. *Kurtzman,* 403 U. S. 602, it granted Buono's requested injunctive relief (2002 injunction). The District Court did not consider whether the Government's actions regarding the cross had a secular purpose or caused entanglement with religion. While the Government's appeal was pending, Congress passed the Department of Defense Appropriations Act, 2004, §8121 (a) of which directed the Secretary of the Interior to transfer the cross and the land on which it stands to the VFW in exchange for privately owned land elsewhere in the Preserve (land-transfer statute). Affirming the District Court's judgment both as to standing and on the merits, the Ninth Circuit declined to address the statute's effect on Buono's suit or the statute's constitutionality *(Buono II)*. Because the Government did not seek review by this Court, the Court of Appeals' judgment became final. Buono then returned to the District Court seeking injunctive relief against the land transfer, either through enforcement or modification of the 2002 injunction. In 2005, that court rejected the Government's claim that the transfer was a bona fide attempt to comply with the injunction, concluding, instead, that it was actually an invalid attempt to keep the cross on display. The court granted Buono's motion to enforce the 2002 injunction; denied as moot his motion to amend it; and permanently enjoined the Government from implementing the land-transfer statute *(Buono III)*. The Ninth Circuit again affirmed, largely following the District Court's reasoning.

Held: The judgment is reversed, and the case is remanded.

502 F. 3d 1069 and 527 F. 3d 758, reversed and remanded.

JUSTICE KENNEDY, joined in full by THE CHIEF JUSTICE and in part by JUSTICE ALITO, concluded:
   1. Buono has standing to maintain this action. Whatever the validity of the Government's argument that Buono's asserted injury—offense at a religious symbol's presence on federal land—is not personal to him and so does not confer Article III standing, that argument is not available at this stage of the litigation. The District Court rejected the argument in *Buono I*, the Ninth Circuit affirmed in *Buono II*, and the Court of Appeals' judgment became final and unreviewable upon the expiration of the 90-day deadline for filing a certiorari petition, 28 U. S. C. §2101(c). Moreover, Buono had standing in *Buono III* to seek application of the injunction against the land-transfer statute. A party that obtains a judgment in its favor acquires a "judicially cognizable" interest in ensuring compliance with that judgment. See *Allen* v. *Wright*, 468 U. S. 737. Buono's entitlement to an injunction having been established in *Buono I* and *II*, he sought in *Buono III* to prevent the Government from frustrating or evading that injunction. His interests in doing so were sufficiently personal and concrete to support his standing, given the rights he obtained under the earlier decree against the same party as to the same cross and the same land. The Government's contention that Buono sought to extend, rather than to enforce, the 2002 injunction is not an argument about standing, but about the merits of the District Court's order. Pp. 7–9.
   2. The District Court erred in enjoining the Government from implementing the land-transfer statute on the premise that the relief was necessary to protect Buono's rights under the 2002 injunction. Pp. 9–18.
      (a) A court may order an injunction only after taking into account all the circumstances bearing on the need for prospective relief. See, *e.g., United States* v. *Swift & Co.,* 286 U. S. 106. Here, the District Court did not engage in the appropriate inquiry. The land-transfer statute was a substantial change in circumstances bearing on the propriety of the requested relief. By dismissing as illicit the motives of Congress in passing it, the

District Court took insufficient account of the context in which the statute was enacted and the reasons for its passage. Placement of the cross on federal land by private persons was not an attempt to set the state's *imprimatur* on a particular creed. Rather, the intent was simply to honor fallen soldiers. Moreover, the cross stood for nearly seven decades before the statute was enacted, by which time the cross and the cause it commemorated had become entwined in the public consciousness. The 2002 injunction thus presented the Government with a dilemma. It could not maintain the cross without violating the injunction, but it could not remove the cross without conveying disrespect for those the cross was seen as honoring. Deeming neither alternative satisfactory, Congress enacted the land-transfer statute. The statute embodied a legislative judgment that this dispute is best resolved through a framework and policy of accommodation. The statute should not have been dismissed as an evasion, for it brought about a change of law and a congressional statement of policy applicable to the case. Pp. 9–13.

(b) Where legislative action undermines the basis for previous relief, the relevant question is whether an ongoing exercise of the court's equitable authority is supported by the prior showing of illegality, judged against the claim that changed circumstances render prospective relief inappropriate. The District Court granted the 2002 injunction based solely on its conclusion that the presence of the cross on federal land conveyed an impression of governmental endorsement of religion, and the Ninth Circuit affirmed on the same grounds. Neither court considered whether the Government had acted based on an improper purpose. Given this sole reliance on perception, any further relief grounded on the injunction should have rested on the same basis. But the District Court used an injunction granted for one reason (perceived governmental endorsement) as the basis for enjoining conduct that was alleged to be objectionable for a different reason (an illicit governmental purpose). Ordering relief under such circumstances was improper. The court failed to consider whether the change in law and circumstances effected by the land-transfer statute had rendered the "reasonable observer" standard inappropriate to resolve the dispute. Nor did the court attempt to reassess *Buono I*'s findings in light of the accommodation policy embraced by Congress. Rather, it concentrated solely on the religious aspects of the cross, divorced from its background and context. Pp. 13–17.

(c) The same respect for a coordinate branch of Government that forbids striking down an Act of Congress except upon a clear showing of unconstitutionality, see, *e.g.,* *United States* v. *Morrison*, 529 U. S. 598, requires that a congressional command be given effect unless no legal alternative exists. Even if, contrary to the congressional judgment, the land transfer were thought an insufficient accommodation in light of the earlier endorsement finding, it was incumbent upon the District Court to consider less drastic relief than complete invalidation of the statute. See, *e.g., Ayotte* v. *Planned Parenthood of Northern New Eng.*, 546 U. S. 320. On remand, that court should conduct a proper inquiry into the continued necessity for injunctive relief in light of the statute. Pp. 17–18.

JUSTICE ALITO concluded that this case should not be remanded for the lower courts to decide whether implementation of the land-transfer statute would violate the District Court's injunction or the Establishment Clause. Rather, because the factual record has been sufficiently developed to permit resolution of these questions, he would decide them and hold that the statute may be implemented. The case's singular circumstances presented Congress with a delicate problem. Its solution was an approach designed to eliminate any perception of religious sponsorship stemming from the location of the cross on federally owned land, while avoiding the disturbing symbolism that some would associate with the destruction of this historic monument. The mechanism Congress selected is quite common in the West, a "land exchange," whereby ownership of the land on which the cross is located would be transferred to the VFW in exchange for another nearby parcel of equal value. The land transfer would not violate the District Court injunction, the obvious meaning of which was simply that the Government could not allow the cross to remain on *federal* land. Nor would the statute's implementation constitute an endorsement of religion in violation of the Establishment Clause. The so-called "endorsement test" views a challenged religious display through the eyes of a hypothetical reasonable observer aware of the history and all other pertinent facts relating to the display. Here, therefore, this observer would be familiar with the monument's origin and history and thereby appreciate that the transfer represents an effort by Congress to address a unique situation and to find a solution that best accommodates conflicting concerns. Finally, the statute was not enacted for the illicit purpose of embracing the monument's religious message but to commemorate the Nation's war dead and to avoid the disturbing symbolism that would have been created by the monument's destruction. Pp. 1–7.

JUSTICE SCALIA, joined by JUSTICE THOMAS, concluded that this Court need not—indeed, *cannot*—decide this case's merits because Buono lacks Article III standing to pursue the relief he seeks, which is not enforcement of the original injunction but expansion of it. By enjoining the Government from implementing the statute at issue, the District

SALAZAR ET AL. *v.* BUONO   3

Court's 2005 order went well beyond the original injunction's proscription of the cross's display on public property. Because Buono seeks new relief, he must show that he has standing to pursue that relief by demonstrating that blocking the land transfer will "redress or prevent an actual or imminently threatened injury to [him] caused by private or official violation of law." *Summers* v. *Earth Island Institute*, 555 U. S. ____, ____. He has failed, however, to allege any such injury. Even assuming that being offended by a religious display constitutes a cognizable injury, it is merely speculative whether the cross will remain in place, and in any event Buono has made clear, by admitting he has no objection to Christian symbols on private property, that *he* will not be offended. Neither district courts' discretion to expand injunctions they have issued nor this District Court's characterization of its 2005 order as merely enforcing the existing injunction makes any difference. If in fact a court awards new relief, it must have Article III jurisdiction to do so. Pp. 1–7.

KENNEDY, J., announced the judgment of the Court and delivered an opinion, in which ROBERTS, C. J., joined, and in which ALITO, J., joined in part. ROBERTS, C. J., filed a concurring opinion. ALITO, J., filed an opinion concurring in part and concurring in the judgment. SCALIA, J., filed an opinion concurring in the judgment, in which THOMAS, J., joined. STEVENS, J., filed a dissenting opinion, in which GINSBURG and SOTOMAYOR, JJ., joined. BREYER, J., filed a dissenting opinion.

Street Law, Inc. and The Supreme Court Historical Society present

Landmark Cases of the U.S. Supreme Court
Background Summary & Questions (•••)

When the Japanese bombed Pearl Harbor on December 7, 1941, destroying much of the American Pacific Fleet, the American military became concerned about the security of the mainland United States, particularly along the West Coast. The Japanese military had achieved significant and swift success throughout the Pacific. Many Americans turned their fear and outrage over the actions of the Japanese government on people of Japanese descent, both citizens and non-citizens, living lawfully in the United States.

At the time, approximately 112,000 people of Japanese descent lived on the West Coast; about 70,000 of these were American citizens. Many Japanese Americans had close cultural ties with their homeland, sending children home for schooling and even collecting tinfoil and money to send to Japan during its war with China. At the time, however, there was no proven case of espionage or sabotage on the part of Japanese or Japanese Americans in the United States.

Nonetheless, in February 1942, General DeWitt, the commanding officer of the Western Defense Command, recommended that "Japanese and other subversive persons" be evacuated from the Pacific Coast. He claimed,

The Japanese race is an enemy race and while many second and third generation Japanese born on United States soil, possessed of United States citizenship, have become 'Americanized,' the racial strains are undiluted. To con-

clude otherwise is to expect that children born of white parents on Japanese soil sever all racial affinity and become loyal Japanese subjects ready to fight and, if necessary, to die for Japan in a war against the nation of their parents.

He also said that there was "no ground for assuming that any Japanese, barred from assimilation by convention as he is, though born and raised in the United States, will not turn against this nation when the final test of loyalty comes."

President Franklin D. Roosevelt acted on this recommendation by signing Executive Order 9066. This authorized the Secretary of War or any designated commander, at their sole discretion, to limit and even prohibit some people from being in certain areas. Soon after the order was enacted, Congress sanctioned the executive order by passing a law that imposed penalties for those who violated the restrictions that evolved from the order. The ensuing restrictions on people of Japanese origin included curfews and forced removal to assembly and relocation centers much farther inland. Relocation to these centers was called internment. Most were required to live in barracks, many of which did not having running water or cooking facilities. They were only allowed to bring basic personal items. Thus, many suffered heavy financial losses when they were forced to quickly sell their homes, vehicles, and other belongings.

Fred Korematsu was an American-born citizen of Japanese descent who grew up in Oakland, California. He tried to serve in the United States military, but was rejected for poor health. He was able, however, to get a job in a shipyard. When Japanese internment began in California, Korematsu evaded the order and moved to a nearby town. He also had some facial surgery, changed his name and claimed to be Mexican-American. He was later arrested and convicted of violating Exclusion Order No. 34 issued by General DeWitt, which barred all persons of Japanese descent from the "military area" of San Leandro, California. There was no question at the time of conviction that Korematsu had been loyal to the United States and was not a threat to the war effort.

Korematsu challenged his conviction on the grounds that the relocation orders were beyond the powers of Congress, the military authorities and the President. He also asserted that to apply these orders only to those of Japanese ancestry amounted to constitutionally prohibited discrimination based on race. The government argued that the exclusion and internment of Japanese Americans was justified because it was necessary to the war effort. They said there was evidence that some Japanese Americans were involved in espionage, and argued that because there was no way to tell the loyal from the disloyal, all people of Japanese descent had to be treated as though they were disloyal.

The federal appeals court ruled in favor of the United States, and Korematsu's appeal brought the issue before the U.S. Supreme Court.

QUESTIONS TO CONSIDER

1. Look at a copy of the Constitution. Which part (Article and Section) describes the war power of the President? Which Article and Section describes the war powers of the Congress?

2. In your opinion, how convincing is General DeWitt's argument about the loyalty of the Japanese and Japanese Americans?

3. The United States was also at war with Germany and Italy. People of German and Italian descent were also interned, but in relatively fewer numbers than the Japanese. What do you think explains the differences in the ways they were treated?

4. In times of war, governments often must balance the needs of national security with the civil rights of its citizens. In your opinion, did the Japanese internment order find the right balance between these competing values? Explain your reasons.

Street Law, Inc. and The Supreme Court Historical Society present

Landmark Cases of the U.S. Supreme Court
Key Excerpts from the Majority Opinion

The decision was 6–3, and Mr. Justice Black delivered the opinion of the Court.

The petitioner, an American citizen of Japanese descent, was convicted in a federal district court for remaining in San Leandro, California, a "Military Area," contrary to Civilian Exclusion Order No. 34 of the Commanding General of the Western Command, U.S. Army, which directed that after May 9, 1942, all persons of Japanese ancestry should be excluded from that area. No question was raised as to petitioner's loyalty to the United States. The Circuit Court of Appeals affirmed, and the importance of the constitutional question involved caused us to grant certiorari.

It should be noted, to begin with, that all legal restrictions which curtail the civil rights of a single racial group are immediately suspect. That is not to say that all such restrictions are unconstitutional. It is to say that courts must subject them to the most rigid scrutiny. Pressing public necessity may sometimes justify the existence of such restrictions; racial antagonism never can.

***

Exclusion Order No. 34, which the petitioner knowingly and admittedly violated, was one of a number of military orders and proclamations, all of which were substantially based upon Executive Order No. 9066, 7 Fed. Reg. 1407. That order, issued after we were at war with Japan, declared that "the successful prosecution of the war requires every possible protection against espionage and against sabotage to national-defense material, national-defense premises, and national-defense utilities. . . ."

One of the series of orders and proclamations, a curfew order, which like the exclusion order here was promulgated pursuant to Executive Order 9066, subjected all persons of Japanese ancestry in prescribed West Coast military areas to remain in their residences from 8 p.m. to 6 a.m. As is the case with the exclusion order here, that prior curfew order was designed as a "protection against espionage and against sabotage." In Hirabayashi v. United States, we sustained a conviction obtained for violation of the curfew order . . . . We upheld the curfew order as an exercise of the power of the government to take steps necessary to prevent espionage and sabotage in an area threatened by Japanese attack.

In the light of the principles we announced in the Hirabayashi case, we are unable to conclude that it was beyond the war power of Congress and the Executive to exclude those of Japanese ancestry from the West Coast war area at the time they did. True, exclusion from the area in which one's home is located is a far greater deprivation than constant confinement to the home from 8 p.m. to 6 a.m. Nothing short of apprehension by the proper military authorities of the gravest imminent danger to the public safety can constitutionally justify either. But exclusion from a threatened area, no less than curfew, has a definite and close relationship to the prevention of espionage and sabotage. The military authorities, charged with the primary responsibility of defending our shores, concluded that curfew provided inadequate protection and ordered exclusion. They did so, as pointed out in our Hirabayashi opinion, in accordance with Congressional authority to the military to say who should, and who should not, remain in the threatened areas.

. . . Here, as in the Hirabayashi case, ". . . we cannot reject as unfounded the judgment of the military authorities and of Congress that there were disloyal members of that population, whose number and strength could not be precisely and quickly ascertained. We cannot say that the war-making branches of the Government did not have ground for believing that in a critical hour such persons could not readily be isolated and separately dealt with, and constituted a menace to the national defense and safety, which demanded that prompt and adequate measures be taken to guard against it."

Like curfew, exclusion of those of Japanese origin was deemed necessary because of the presence of an unascertained number of disloyal members of the group, most of whom we have no doubt were loyal to this country. It was because we could not reject the finding of the military authorities that it was impossible to bring about an immediate segregation of the disloyal from the loyal that we sustained the validity of the curfew order as applying to the whole group. In the instant case, temporary exclusion of the entire group was rested by the military on the same ground. The judgment that exclusion of the whole group was for the same reason a military imperative answers the contention that the exclusion was in the nature of group

punishment based on antagonism to those of Japanese origin. That there were members of the group who retained loyalties to Japan has been confirmed by investigations made subsequent to the exclusion. Approximately five thousand American citizens of Japanese ancestry refused to swear unqualified allegiance to the United States and to renounce allegiance to the Japanese Emperor, and several thousand evacuees requested repatriation to Japan.

We uphold the exclusion order as of the time it was made and when the petitioner violated it. In doing so, we are not unmindful of the hardships imposed by it upon a large group of American citizens. But hardships are part of war, and war is an aggregation of hardships. All citizens alike, both in and out of uniform, feel the impact of war in greater or lesser measure. Citizenship has its responsibilities as well as its privileges, and in time of war the burden is always heavier. Compulsory exclusion of large groups of citizens from their homes, except under circumstances of direst emergency and peril, is inconsistent with our basic governmental institutions. But when under conditions of modern warfare our shores are threatened by hostile forces, the power to protect must be commensurate with the threatened danger.

***

It is said that we are dealing here with the case of imprisonment of a citizen in a concentration camp solely because of his ancestry, without evidence or inquiry concerning his loyalty and good disposition towards the United States. Our task would be simple, our duty clear, were this a case involving the imprisonment of a loyal citizen in a concentration camp because of racial prejudice. Regardless of the true nature of the assembly and relocation centers—and we deem it unjustifiable to call them concentration camps with all the ugly connotations that term implies—we are dealing specifically with nothing but an exclusion order. To cast this case into outlines of racial prejudice, without reference to the real military dangers which were presented, merely confuses the issue. Korematsu was not excluded from the Military Area because of hostility to him or his race. He was excluded because we are at war with the Japanese Empire, because the properly constituted military authorities feared an invasion of our West Coast and felt constrained to take proper security measures, because they decided that the military urgency of the situation demanded that all citizens of Japanese ancestry be segregated from the West Coast temporarily, and, finally, because Congress, reposing its confidence in this time of war in our military leaders—as inevitably it must—determined that they should have the power to do just this. There was evidence of disloyalty on the part of some, the military authorities considered that the need for action was great, and time was short. We cannot—by availing ourselves of the calm perspective of hindsight—now say that at that time these actions were unjustified.

Affirmed.

QUESTIONS TO CONSIDER

1. How does the Court compare Korematsu's challenge to the relocation order to Hirabayashi's challenge to the curfew that was imposed on Japanese Americans?

2. The Court says that the military order is not based on racial prejudice but instead is based on legiti-mate military concerns. What are those military concerns?

3. Do you agree that racial prejudice does not play a role in the government's treatment of Japanese Americans during World War II? Give reasons to support your answer.

Street Law, Inc. and The Supreme Court Historical Society present

Landmark Cases of the U.S. Supreme Court
Key Excerpts from the Dissenting Opinion

Mr. Justice Murphy, dissenting:

This exclusion of "all persons of Japanese ancestry, both alien and non-alien," from the Pacific Coast area on a plea of military necessity in the absence of martial law ought not to be approved. Such exclusion goes over "the very brink of constitutional power" and falls into the ugly abyss of racism.

In dealing with matters relating to the prosecution and progress of a war, we must accord great respect and consid-eration to the judgments of the military authorities who are on the scene and who have full knowledge of the mili-tary facts . . .

At the same time, however, it is essential that there be definite limits to military discretion, especially where martial law has not been declared. Individuals must not be left impoverished of their constitutional rights on a plea of military necessity that has neither substance nor support . . .

. . . Being an obvious racial discrimination, the order deprives all those within its scope of the equal protection of the laws as guaranteed by the Fifth Amendment. It fur-ther deprives these individuals of their constitutional rights to live and work where they will, to establish a home where they choose and to move about freely. In excommunicating them without benefit of hearings, this order also deprives them of all their constitutional rights to procedural due process. Yet no reasonable relation to an "immediate, imminent, and impending" public danger is evident to support this racial restriction which is one of the most sweeping and complete deprivations of constitutional rights in the history of this nation in the absence of martial law.

. . . The main reasons relied upon by those responsible for the forced evacuation, therefore, do not prove a reason-able relation between the group characteristics of Japanese Americans and the dangers of invasion, sabotage and espi-onage. The reasons appear, instead, to be largely an accu-mulation of much of the misinformation, half-truths and insinuations that for years have been directed against Japanese Americans by people with racial and economic prejudices—the same people who have been among the foremost advocates of the evacuation. A military judgment based upon such racial and sociological considerations is not entitled to the great weight ordinarily given the judgments based upon strictly military considerations. Especially is this so when every charge relative to race, reli-gion, culture, geographical location, and legal and eco-nomic status has been substantially discredited by inde-pendent studies made by experts in these matters.

. . . No one denies, of course, that there were some dis-loyal persons of Japanese descent on the Pacific Coast who did all in their power to aid their ancestral land. Similar disloyal activities have been engaged in by many persons of German, Italian and even more pioneer stock in our coun-try. But to infer that examples of individual disloyalty prove group disloyalty and justify discriminatory action against the entire group is to deny that under our system of law individual guilt is the sole basis for deprivation of rights. Moreover, this inference, which is at the very heart of the evacuation orders, has been used in support of the abhorrent and despicable treatment of minority groups by the dictatorial tyrannies which this nation is now pledged to destroy. To give constitutional sanction to that inference in this case, however well-intentioned may have been the military command on the Pacific Coast, is to adopt one of the cruelest of the rationales used by our enemies to destroy the dignity of the individual and to encourage and open the door to discriminatory actions against other minority groups in the passions of tomorrow.

No adequate reason is given for the failure to treat these Japanese Americans on an individual basis by holding investigations and hearings to separate the loyal from the disloyal, as was done in the case of persons of German and Italian ancestry . . .

I dissent, therefore, from this legalization of racism. Racial discrimination in any form and in any degree has no justifiable part whatever in our democratic way of life. It is unattractive in any setting but it is utterly revolting among a free people who have embraced the principles set forth in the Constitution of the United States. All residents of this nation are kin in some way by blood or culture to a foreign land. Yet they are primarily and necessarily a part of the new and distinct civilization of the United States. They must accordingly be treated at all times as the heirs of the American experiment and as entitled to all the rights and freedoms guaranteed by the Constitution.

QUESTIONS TO CONSIDER

1. Why does Justice Murphy believe that the Court should not defer to the military decisions in this case?

2. What rights does Justice Murphy claim are affected by the evacuation order?

3. Justice Murphy acknowledges that there are some disloyal persons in the United States. How does he believe the government should treat such disloyalty?

4. Justice Murphy accuses the American government of engaging in the same type of racism and discrimination as the United States' World War II enemies. Research some of the discriminatory activities in which Germany, Italy, and Japan were engaged during World War II. Do you agree with Justice Murphy's comparison? Explain your answer.

CHAPTER 6

"Negligence is not actionable unless it involves the invasion of a legally protected interest, the violation of a right. Proof of negligence in the air, so to speak, will not do."

—Chief Judge Cardozo
Palsgraf v. Long Island Railroad Co., 248 N.Y. 339, 162 N.E. 99, 1928 N.Y. Lexis 1269 (1928)

Intentional Torts and Negligence

Chapter Objectives

After studying this chapter, you should be able to:

1. List and describe intentional torts against persons.
2. List and explain the elements necessary to prove negligence.
3. Describe special negligence doctrines.

4. Describe assumption of the risk and other defenses to a charge of negligence.
5. Describe and apply the doctrine of strict liability.

Chapter Contents

Introduction to Intentional Torts and Negligence

Tort is the French word for a "wrong." The law provides remedies to persons and businesses that are injured by the tortuous actions of others. Under tort law, an injured party can bring a *civil lawsuit* to seek compensation for a wrong done to the party or to the party's property. Many torts have their origin in common law. The courts and legislatures have extended tort law to reflect changes in modern society.

Tort damages are monetary damages that are sought from the offending party. They are intended to compensate the injured party for the injury suffered. Such injury may consist of past and future medical expenses, loss of wages, pain and suffering, mental distress, and other damages caused by the defendant's tortious conduct. If the victim of a tort dies, his or her beneficiaries can bring a *wrongful death action* to recover damages from the defendant. *Punitive damages*, which are awarded to punish the defendant, may be recovered in intentional tort and strict liability cases. Other remedies, such as injunctions, may be available, too.

This chapter discusses intentional torts, negligence, and defenses to tort actions.

Intentional Torts Against Persons

The law protects a person from unauthorized touching, restraint, or other contact. In addition, the law protects a person's reputation and privacy. Violations of these rights are actionable as torts. **Intentional torts** against persons are discussed in the paragraphs that follow.

Assault

Assault is (1) the threat of immediate harm or offensive contact or (2) any action that arouses reasonable apprehension of imminent harm. Actual physical contact is unnecessary. Threats of future harm are not actionable.

Examples

Suppose a 6-foot-5-inch, 250-pound person makes a fist and threatens to punch a 5-foot, 100-pound person. If the threatened person is afraid that he or she will be physically harmed, that person can sue the threatening person to recover damages for the assault. If the threatened person is a black-belt karate champion and laughs at the threat, there is no assault because the threat does not cause any apprehension.

Battery

Battery is unauthorized and harmful or offensive physical contact with another person that causes injury. Basically, the interest protected here is each person's reasonable sense of dignity and safety. Direct physical contact, such as intentionally hitting someone with a fist, is battery.

Indirect physical contact between the victim and the perpetrator is also battery, as long as injury results.

Examples

Throwing a rock, shooting an arrow or a bullet, knocking off a hat, pulling a chair out from under someone, and poisoning a drink are all instances of actionable battery. The victim need not be aware of the harmful or offensive contact (e.g., it may take place while the victim is asleep).

Assault and battery often occur together, although they do not have to (e.g., the perpetrator hits the victim on the back of the head without any warning).

Transferred Intent Doctrine   Sometimes a person acts with the intent to injure one person but actually injures another. The **transferred intent doctrine** applies to such situations. Under this doctrine, the law transfers the perpetrator's intent from the target to the actual victim of the act. The victim can then sue the defendant.

---

tort
A wrong. There are three categories of torts: (1) intentional torts, (2) unintentional torts (negligence), and (3) strict liability.

intentional tort
A category of torts that requires that the defendant possessed the intent to do the act that caused the plaintiff's injuries.

assault
(1) The threat of immediate harm or offensive contact or (2) any action that arouses reasonable apprehension of imminent harm. Actual physical contact is unnecessary.

battery
Unauthorized and harmful or offensive direct or indirect physical contact with another person that causes injury.

False Imprisonment

false imprisonment
The intentional confinement or restraint of another person without authority or justification and without that person's consent.

The intentional confinement or restraint of another person without authority or justification and without that person's consent constitutes **false imprisonment**. The victim may be restrained or confined by physical force, barriers, threats of physical harm, or the perpetrator's false assertion of legal authority (i.e., false arrest). A threat of future harm or moral pressure is not considered false imprisonment. The false imprisonment must be complete.

Examples

Locking one's doors in a house or automobile and not letting the other person leave is false imprisonment. Merely locking one door to a building when other exits are not locked is not false imprisonment. However, a person is not obliged to risk danger or an affront to his or her dignity by attempting to escape.

Shoplifting and Merchant Protection Statutes

merchant protection statutes
Statutes that allow merchants to stop, detain, and investigate suspected shoplifters without being held liable for false imprisonment if (1) there are reasonable grounds for the suspicion, (2) suspects are detained for only a reasonable time, and (3) investigations are conducted in a reasonable manner.

Shoplifting causes substantial losses to retail and other merchants each year. Oftentimes, suspected shoplifters are stopped by the store employees, and their suspected shoplifting is investigated. These stops sometimes lead to the merchant being sued for false imprisonment because the merchant detained the suspect.

Almost all states have enacted **merchant protection statutes**, also known as the **shopkeeper's privilege**. These statutes allow merchants to stop, detain, and investigate suspected shoplifters without being held liable for false imprisonment if:

1. There are *reasonable grounds* for the suspicion.
2. Suspects are detained for only a *reasonable time*.
3. Investigations are conducted in a *reasonable manner*.

Proving these elements is sometimes difficult. The following case applies the merchant's protection statute.

CASE 6.1
False Imprisonment

Wal-Mart Stores, Inc. v. Cockrell

61 S.W.3d 774, Web 2001 Tex. App. Lexis 7992 (2001)
Court of Appeals of Texas

"He made me feel like I was scum. That I had no say-so in the matter, that just made me feel like a little kid on the block, like the bully beating the kid up. . . ."

—Karl Cockrell

Facts

Karl Cockrell and his parents went to the layaway department at a Wal-Mart store. Cockrell stayed for about five minutes and decided to leave. As he was going out the front door, Raymond Navarro, a Wal-Mart loss-prevention officer, stopped him and requested that Cockrell follow him to the manager's office. Once in the office, Navarro told him to pull his pants down. Cockrell put his hands between his shorts and underwear, pulled them out, and shook them. Nothing fell out. Next Navarro told him to take off his shirt. Cockrell raised his shirt, revealing a large bandage which covered a surgical wound on the right side of his abdomen. Cockrell had recently had a liver transplant. Navarro asked him to take off the bandage, despite Cockrell's explanation that the bandage maintained a sterile environment around his surgical wound. On Navarro's insistence Cockrell took down the bandage, revealing the wound. Afterwards Navarro apologized and let Cockrell go. Cockrell sued Wal-Mart to recover damages for false imprisonment. Wal-Mart defended, alleging that the shopkeeper's privilege protected it from liability. The trial court found in favor of Cockrell and awarded Cockrell $300,000 for his mental anguish. Wal-Mart appealed.

Issue

Does the shopkeeper's privilege protect Wal-Mart from liability under the circumstances of the case?

Language of the Court

Neither Raymond Navarro nor any other store employee saw Cockrell steal merchandise. However Navarro claimed he had reasons to suspect Cockrell of shoplifting. He said that Cockrell was acting suspiciously, because he saw him in the women's department standing very close to a rack of clothes and looking around. Later he saw Cockrell looking around and walking slowly by the cigarette aisle and then "pass out of the store." We conclude that a rational jury could have found that Navarro did not "reasonably believe" a theft had occurred and therefore lacked authority to detain Cockrell.

The extent to which Wal-Mart searched Cockrell compels us to address the reasonable manner of the detention. Navarro's search was unreasonable in scope, because he had no probable cause to believe that Cockrell had hidden any merchandise under the bandage. Removal of the bandage compromised the sterile environment surrounding the wound.

Evidence of Cockrell's mental anguish comes largely from the following testimony: Counsel asked Cockrell to describe his demeanor when he took down his bandage in the manager's office. He stated that Navarro: "Made me feel like I was scum. That I had no say-so in the matter,

that just made me feel like a little kid on the block, like the bully beating the kid up and saying, 'Well, I didn't catch you with nothing; but I'm going to humiliate him, twist a knife a little bit more into them.'"

Cockrell testified that after Navarro let him go he was shaking, crying, nervous, scared, and looking around to make sure no one else was trying to stop him. Cockrell's parents saw him in the Wal-Mart store immediately after he was let go. They said he was upset, nervous, had tears in his eyes, and looked scared, pale, and badly shaken up. When he arrived at home he was crying, nervous, and still "pretty well shook up." His mother said that he stayed upset for a "long time" and would not go out of the house.

Decision

The court of appeals upheld the trial court's finding that Wal-Mart had falsely imprisoned Cockrell and had not proved the shopkeeper's privilege. The court of appeals upheld the trial court's judgment that awarded Cockrell $300,000 for mental anguish.

Case Questions

Critical Legal Thinking What is the tort of false imprisonment? Explain.

Business Ethics Did Navarro, the Wal-Mart employee, act responsibly in this case? Did Wal-Mart act ethically in denying liability in this case?

Contemporary Business What does the shopkeeper's privilege provide? What are the elements necessary to prove the shopkeeper's privilege? Do you think Wal-Mart had a good chance of proving the shopkeeper's privilege in this case?

Misappropriation of the Right to Publicity

Each person has the exclusive legal right to control and profit from the commercial use of his or her name and identity during his or her lifetime. This is a valuable right, particularly to well-known persons such as sports figures and movie stars. Any attempt by another person to appropriate a living person's name or identity for commercial purposes is actionable. The wrongdoer is liable for the **tort of misappropriation of the right to publicity** (also called the **tort of appropriation**).

In such cases, the plaintiff can (1) recover the unauthorized profits made by the offending party and (2) obtain an injunction preventing further unauthorized use of his or her name or identity. Many states provide that the right to publicity survives a person's death and may be enforced by the deceased's heirs.

tort of misappropriation of the right to publicity
An attempt by another person to appropriate a living person's name or identity for commercial purposes.

Example

Brad Pitt is a famous movie star. If an advertising agency places Brad Pitt's likeness (e.g., photo) on a billboard advertising a product without Brad Pitt's permission, it has engaged in the tort of misappropriation of the right to publicity. Brad Pitt could sue and recover the profits made by the offending party as well as obtain an injunction to prevent unauthorized use of his likeness by the offending party.

Invasion of the Right to Privacy

The law recognizes each person's right to live his or her life without being subjected to unwarranted and undesired publicity. A violation of this right constitutes the tort of **invasion of the right to privacy**. If a fact is public information, there is no claim to privacy. However, a fact that was once public (e.g., commission of a crime) may become private after the passage of time.

Examples

Secretly taking photos of another person with a cell phone camera in a men's or women's locker room would constitute invasion of the right to privacy. Reading someone else's mail, wiretapping someone's telephone, and reading someone else's e-mail without authorization to do so are also examples of invasion of the right to privacy.

Placing someone in a "false light" constitutes an invasion of privacy.

Example

Sending an objectionable telegram to a third party and signing another's name would place the purported sender in a false light in the eyes of the receiver.

Defamation of Character

A person's reputation is a valuable asset. Therefore, every person is protected from false statements made by others during his or her lifetime. This protection ends upon a person's death. The tort of **defamation of character** requires a plaintiff to prove that:

1. The defendant made an *untrue statement of fact* about the plaintiff.
2. The statement was intentionally or accidentally *published* to a third party. In this context, *publication* simply means that a third person heard or saw the untrue statement. It does not require appearance in newspapers, magazines, or books.

A false statement that appears in writing or other fixed medium is **libel**. The name for an oral defamatory statement is **slander**.

Examples

False statements that appear in a letter, newspaper, magazine, book, photograph, movie, video, and the like would be libel. Most courts hold that defamatory statements in radio and television broadcasts are considered libel because of the permanency of the media.

The publication of an untrue statement of fact is not the same as the publication of an *opinion*. The publication of opinions is usually not actionable. Because defamation is defined as an untrue statement of fact, truth is an absolute defense to a charge of defamation.

Examples

The statement "My lawyer is lousy" is an opinion and is not defamation. The statement "My lawyer has been disbarred from the practice of law," when she has not been disbarred, is an untrue statement of fact and is actionable as defamation.

Public Figures as Plaintiffs In *New York Times Co. v. Sullivan*,[1] the U.S. Supreme Court held that *public officials* cannot recover for defamation unless they can prove that the defendant acted with "actual malice." Actual malice means that the defendant made the false statement knowingly or with reckless disregard of its falsity. This requirement has since been extended to *public figure* plaintiffs such as movie stars, sports personalities, and other celebrities.

Disparagement or Trade Libel

Business firms rely on their reputation and the quality of their products and services to attract and keep customers. That is why state unfair-competition laws protect businesses from disparaging statements made by competitors or others. A disparaging statement is an untrue statement made by one person or business about the products, services, property, or reputation of another business.

---

defamation of character
False statement(s) made by one person about another. In court, the plaintiff must prove that (1) the defendant made an untrue statement of fact about the plaintiff and (2) the statement was intentionally or accidentally published to a third party.

libel
A false statement that appears in a letter, newspaper, magazine, book, photograph, movie, video, and so on.

slander
Oral defamation of character.

Hard cases make bad law.

Legal Maxim

All slander must still be strangled in its birth, or time will soon conspire to make it strong enough to overcome the truth.

Sir William D'Avenant

Contemporary Environment

Eminem's Rap Song Is Not Slander

"It is therefore this court's ultimate position that Eminem is entitled to summary disposition."

—Judge Servitto

Eminem is a famous hip-hop artist and rapper who won a Grammy award for his music in the movie *8-Mile* in which he starred. Eminem's lyrics often contain references to his personal experiences. In "Brain Damage," a song from his 1999 CD *The Slim Shady LP*, Eminem sang lyrics he had written about his childhood experiences with DeAngelo Bailey. The lyrics read in part:

Way before my baby daughter Hailey
I was harassed daily by this fat kid named D'Angelo
* Bailey . . .*
He banged my head against the urinal til he broke my
* nose . . .*
Soaked my clothes in blood, grabbed me and choked
* my throat*

DeAngelo Bailey sued Eminem for $1 million, alleging that the lyrics were untrue and slanderous. Eminem's mother publicly defended her son's account of the bullying by Bailey. Under questioning, Bailey admitted that when he was in the fourth grade, he was part of a group at school that did "bully type things" such as pushing Eminem down. Bailey described what was done to Eminem as "jokes, play games, you know, like we probably like—I mean this is kid stuff, so I'm saying."

Bailey also testified that he was present when his friends pushed Eminem and that he would personally bump into Eminem by throwing a "little shove." Bailey offered no evidence to refute Eminem's claims in his deposition that Bailey was bigger than him, shoved him into walls, called him names, took his orange juice, and knocked over his books.

After hearing all the evidence, trial judge Deborah Servitto granted summary disposition in favor of Eminem. She wrote in her opinion:

Mr. Bailey complains that his rap is trash
So he's seeking compensation in the form of cash.
Bailey thinks he's entitled to some money gain
Because Eminem used his name in vain.
The lyrics are stories no one would take as fact
They're an exaggeration of a childish act.
It is therefore this court's ultimate position
That Eminem is entitled to summary disposition.

On appeal, the court of appeals of Michigan upheld the trial court's decision. *DeAngelo Bailey v. Marshall Bruce Mathers, III a/k/a/ Eminem*, 2005 Mich.App. Lexis 930 (Court of Appeals of Michigan, 2005)

To prove **disparagement**, which is also called **trade libel**, **product disparagement**, and **slander of title**, the plaintiff must show that the defendant (1) made an untrue statement about the plaintiff's products, services, property, or business reputation; (2) published that untrue statement to a third party; (3) knew the statement was not true; and (4) made the statement maliciously (i.e., with intent to injure the plaintiff).

Intentional Misrepresentation (Fraud)

One of the most pervasive business torts is **intentional misrepresentation**. This tort is also known as **fraud** or **deceit**. It occurs when a wrongdoer deceives another person out of money, property, or something else of value. A person who has been injured by intentional misrepresentation can recover damages from the wrongdoer. Four elements are required to find fraud:

1. The wrongdoer made a false representation of material fact.
2. The wrongdoer had knowledge that the representation was false and intended to deceive the innocent party.
3. The innocent party justifiably relied on the misrepresentation.
4. The innocent party was injured.

Item 2, which is called **scienter**, includes situations in which the wrongdoer recklessly disregards the truth in making a representation that is false. Intent or recklessness can be inferred from the circumstances.

product disparagement
False statements about a competitor's products, services, property, or business reputation. Also known as *trade libel, product disparagement,* and *slander of title.*

intentional misrepresentation
The intentional defrauding of a person out of money, property, or something else of value. Also known as *fraud* or *deceit.*

He that's cheated twice by the same man, is an accomplice with the Cheater.

Thomas Fuller
Gnomologia (1732)

Intentional Infliction of Emotional Distress

In some situations, a victim may suffer mental or emotional distress without first being physically harmed. The *Restatement (Second) of Torts* provides that a person whose *extreme and outrageous* conduct intentionally or recklessly causes severe emotional distress to another is liable for that emotional distress.[2] This is called the tort of **intentional infliction of emotional distress**, or the **tort of outrage**.

The plaintiff must prove that the defendant's conduct was "so outrageous in character and so extreme in degree as to go beyond all possible bounds of decency, and to be regarded as atrocious and utterly intolerable in a civilized society."[3] The tort does not require any publication to a third party or physical contact between the plaintiff and defendant.

An indignity, an annoyance, rough language, or an occasional inconsiderate or unkind act does not constitute outrageous behavior. However, repeated annoyances or harassment coupled with threats are considered outrageous.

The mental distress suffered by the plaintiff must be severe. Many states require that this mental distress be manifested by some form of physical injury, discomfort, or illness, such as nausea, ulcers, headaches, or miscarriage. This requirement is intended to prevent false claims. Some states have abandoned this requirement.

Examples
Shame, humiliation, embarrassment, anger, fear, and worry constitute severe mental distress.

Malicious Prosecution

Businesses and individuals often believe they have a reason to sue someone to recover damages or other remedies. If the plaintiff has a legitimate reason to bring the lawsuit and does so, but the plaintiff does not win the lawsuit, he or she does not have to worry about being sued by the person whom he or she sued. But a losing plaintiff does have to worry about being sued by the defendant in a second lawsuit for **malicious prosecution** if certain elements are met. In a lawsuit for malicious prosecution, the original defendant sues the original plaintiff. In this second lawsuit, which is a *civil* action for damages, the original defendant is the plaintiff and the original plaintiff is the defendant. To succeed in a malicious prosecution lawsuit, the courts require the plaintiff to prove all of the following:

1. The plaintiff in the original lawsuit (now the defendant) instituted or was responsible for instituting the original lawsuit.
2. There was no *probable cause* for the first lawsuit (i.e., it was a frivolous lawsuit).
3. The plaintiff in the original action brought it with *malice*. (Caution: This is a very difficult element to prove.)
4. The original lawsuit was terminated in favor of the original defendant (now the plaintiff).
5. The current plaintiff suffered injury as a result of the original lawsuit.

The courts do not look favorably on malicious prosecution lawsuits because they feel such lawsuits inhibit the original plaintiff's incentive to sue.

Unintentional Torts (Negligence)

Under the doctrine of **unintentional tort**, commonly referred to as **negligence**, a person is liable for harm that is the *foreseeable consequence* of his or her actions. *Negligence* is defined as "the omission to do something which a reasonable man would do, or doing something which a prudent and reasonable man would not do."[4]

To be successful in a negligence lawsuit, the plaintiff must prove that (1) the defendant owed a *duty of care* to the plaintiff, (2) the defendant *breached* this duty of care, (3) the plaintiff suffered *injury*, (4) the defendant's negligent act *caused* the plaintiff's injury and (5) the defendant's negligent act was the proximate cause of the plaintiff's injuries. Each of these elements is discussed in the paragraphs that follow.

intentional infliction of emotional distress
A tort that says a person whose extreme and outrageous conduct intentionally or recklessly causes severe emotional distress to another person is liable for that emotional distress. Also known as the *tort of outrage*.

malicious prosecution
A lawsuit in which the original defendant sues the original plaintiff. In the second lawsuit, the defendant becomes the plaintiff and vice versa.

Negligence is the omission to do something which a reasonable man would do, or doing something which a prudent and reasonable man would not do.

B. Alderson Blyth v. Birmingham Waterworks Co. (1856)

unintentional tort
A doctrine that says a person is liable for harm that is the foreseeable consequence of his or her actions. Also known as *negligence*.

Concept Summary
Elements of Negligence

1. The defendant owed a *duty of care* to the plaintiff.

2. The defendant *breached this duty*.

3. The plaintiff suffered *injury*.

4. The defendant's negligent act was the *actual cause* (or *causation in fact*) of the plaintiff's injuries.

5. The defendant's negligent act was the *proximate cause* (or *legal cause*) of the plaintiff's injuries. The defendant is liable only for the *foreseeable* consequences of his or her negligent act.

Duty of Care

To determine whether a defendant is liable for negligence, it must first be ascertained whether the defendant owed a **duty of care** to the plaintiff. *Duty of care* refers to the obligation people owe each other—that is, the duty not to cause any unreasonable harm or risk of harm.

duty of care
The obligation people owe each other not to cause any unreasonable harm or risk of harm.

Examples

Each person owes a duty to drive his or her car carefully, not to push or shove on escalators, not to leave skateboards on the sidewalk, and the like. Businesses owe a duty to make safe products, not to cause accidents, and so on.

The courts decide whether a duty of care is owed in specific cases by applying a *reasonable person standard*. Under this test, the courts attempt to determine how an *objective, careful, and conscientious person would have acted in the same circumstances* and then measure the defendant's conduct against that standard. The defendant's subjective intent ("I did not mean to do it") is immaterial in assessing liability. Certain impairments do not affect the reasonable person standard.

Defendants with a particular expertise or competence are measured against a *reasonable professional standard*. This standard is applied in much the same way as the reasonable person standard.

No court has ever given, nor do we think ever can give, a definition of what constitutes a reasonable or an average man.

Lord Goddard C.J.R. v.
McCarthy
(1954)

Breach of Duty

Once a court finds that the defendant actually owed the plaintiff a duty of care, it must determine whether the defendant breached that duty. A **breach of the duty of care** is the failure to exercise care. In other words, it is the failure to act as a reasonable person would act. A breach of this duty may consist of an action.

breach of the duty of care
A failure to exercise care or to act as a reasonable person would act.

Example

Throwing a lit match on the ground in the forest and causing a fire is a breach of a duty of care.

A breach of duty may also consist of a failure to act when there is a duty to act.

Example

A firefighter who refuses to put out a fire when her safety is not at stake breaches her duty of care for failing to act when she has a duty to act.

Passersby are generally not expected to rescue others gratuitously to save them from harm. However, most states require certain relatives—parents to children, children to parents if the children are old enough—to try to save their relatives from harm.

In the following case, the court had to determine whether the defendant was liable for negligence.

Contemporary Environment

Ouch! McDonald's Coffee Is Too Hot!

McDonald's Corporation found itself embroiled in one of the most famous negligence cases of modern times. Many studies have shown that people care less about how good their coffee tastes than whether it is hot. So restaurants, coffee shops, and other sellers make their coffee hot. McDonald's, however, discovered that it was in hot water for making its coffee too hot.

Stella Liebeck, a 79-year-old resident of Albuquerque, New Mexico, visited a drive-through window of a McDonald's restaurant with her grandson Chris. Her grandson, the driver of the vehicle, placed the order for breakfast. When breakfast came at the drive-through window, Chris handed a hot cup of coffee to Stella. Because there were no cup holders in the vehicle, Chris pulled over so that Stella could put cream and sugar in her coffee. Stella took the lid off the coffee cup she held in her lap and the hot coffee spilled in her lap. The coffee spilled all over Stella, who suffered third-degree burns on her legs, thighs, groin, and buttocks. Stella was driven to the emergency room and was hospitalized for seven days. She required medical treatment and later returned to the hospital to have skin grafts. She suffered permanent scars from the incident.

Stella's medical costs were $11,000. Stella asked McDonald's to pay her $20,000 to settle the case, but McDonald's offered only $800. Stella refused this settlement and sued McDonald's in court for negligence for selling coffee that was too hot and for failing to warn her of the danger of the hot coffee it served. McDonald's went to trial.

At trial, McDonald's denied that it had been negligent and asserted that Stella's own negligence—opening a hot coffee cup on her lap—had caused her injuries. The jury heard evidence that McDonald's enforces a quality-control rule that requires its restaurants and franchises to serve coffee at 180 to 190 degrees Fahrenheit. Third-degree burns occur on skin in just two to five seconds when coffee is served at 185 degrees. Evidence at trial showed that McDonald's coffee temperature was 20 degrees hotter than coffee served by competing restaurant chains and approximately 40 to 50 degrees hotter than normal house-brewed coffee. Evidence also showed that McDonald's had received more than 700 prior complaints of people who had been scalded by McDonald's coffee, but McDonald's had failed to place a warning on its cups to alert patrons that the coffee it served would scald skin.

Based on this evidence, the jury turned its anger on McDonald's and concluded that McDonald's acted recklessly and awarded Stella $200,000 compensatory damages (reduced by $40,000 for her own negligence) and $2.7 million punitive damages. The trial court judge reduced the amount of punitive damages to $480,000, which was three times the amount of compensatory damages. McDonald's has not turned down the temperature of its coffee, but it does place warnings on its coffee cups. *Liebeck v. McDonald's Restaurants, P.T.S., Inc.* (New Mexico District Court, Bernalillo County, New Mexico, 1994)

CASE 6.2
Negligence

James v. Meow Media, Inc.

300 F.3d 683, Web 2002 U.S. App. Lexis 16185 (2002)
United States Court of Appeals for the Sixth Circuit

"Our inquiry is whether the deaths of James, Steger, and Hadley were the reasonably foreseeable result of the defendants' creation and distribution of their games, movie, and Internet sites."

—Judge Boggs

Facts

Michael Carneal was a 14-year-old freshman student at Heath High School in Paducah, Kentucky. Carneal regularly played the violent interactive video and computer games "Doom," "Quake," "Castle Wolfenstein," "Rampage," "Nightmare Creatures," "Mech Warrior," "Resident Evil," and "Final Fantasy." These games involved the player shooting virtual opponents with computer guns and other weapons. Carneal also watched videotaped movies, including one called *The Basketball Diaries*, in which a high-school-student protagonist dreams of killing his teacher and several of his fellow classmates. On December 1, 1997, Carneal took a .22-caliber pistol and five shotguns into the lobby of Heath High School and shot several of his fellow students, killing three and wounding many others. The three students killed were Jessica James, Kayce Steger, and Nicole Hadley.

The parents of the three dead children ("James") sued the producers and distributors of the violent video games and movies that Carneal had watched previous to the shooting. The parents sued to recover damages for wrongful death, alleging that the defendants were negligent in producing and distributing such games and movies to Carneal. The U.S. District Court applied Kentucky law and held that the defendants did not owe or breach a duty to the plaintiffs and therefore were not liable for negligence. The plaintiffs appealed.

Issue

Did the defendant video and movie producers and distributors owe a duty of care to the plaintiffs by selling and licensing violent video games and movies to Carneal, who killed the three children?

Language of the Court

Kentucky courts have held that the determination of whether a duty of care exists is whether the harm to the plaintiff resulting from the defendant's negligence was "foreseeable." Kentucky courts have struggled with the formless nature of this inquiry. Our inquiry is whether the deaths of James, Steger, and Hadley were the reasonably foreseeable result of the defendants' creation and distribution of their games, movie, and Internet sites.

It appears simply impossible to predict that these games, movie, and Internet sites would incite a young person to violence. We find that it is simply too far a leap from shooting characters on a video screen (an activity undertaken by millions) to shooting people in a classroom (an activity undertaken by a handful, at most) for Carneal's actions to have been reasonably foreseeable to the manufacturers of the media that Carneal played and viewed. Carneal's reaction was not a normal reaction. Indeed, Carneal is not a normal person. Individuals are generally entitled to assume that third parties will not commit intentional criminal acts.

Decision

The Court of Appeals held that the defendant video game and movie producers and distributors did not owe a duty of care to the plaintiffs by selling and licensing violent video games and movies to Carneal, who murdered the three children.

Case Questions

Critical Legal Thinking   How do the courts define *foreseeability*? Did the Court of Appeals use a narrow, middle, or broad interpretation of foreseeability in deciding this case? Explain.

Business Ethics   Do producers and distributors of video games and movies owe a duty of care to society not to produce and distribute violent games and movies?

Contemporary Business   What would have been the consequences for the video game and movie industries if the court had held in favor of the plaintiffs? Are any free speech issues involved in this case? Explain.

Injury to Plaintiff

Even though a defendant's negligent act may have breached a duty of care owed to the plaintiff, this breach is not actionable unless the plaintiff suffers **injury** or injury to his or her property. That is, the plaintiff must have suffered some injury before he or she can recover any damages.

The damages recoverable depend on the effect of the injury on the plaintiff's life or profession.

injury
A plaintiff's personal injury or damage to his or her property that enables him or her to recover monetary damages for the defendant's negligence.

Examples

Suppose that a man injures his hand when a train door malfunctions. The train company is found negligent. If the injured man is a star professional basketball player who makes $5 million per year, with an expected seven years of good playing time left, this plaintiff can recover multiple millions of dollars because he can no longer play professional basketball. If the injured man is a college professor with 15 years until retirement who is making only one-fortieth per year of what the basketball player makes, he can recover some money for his injuries. Because he makes a lot less per year than the professional basketball player and because he can continue working, albeit with more difficulty, the professor can recover much less for the same injury.

Actual Cause

A defendant's negligent act must be the **causation in fact**, or **actual cause**, of the plaintiff's injuries. The test is this: "But for" the defendant's conduct, would the accident have happened? If the defendant's act caused the plaintiff's injuries, there is causation in fact.

actual cause
The actual cause of negligence. A person who commits a negligent act is not liable unless actual cause can be proven. Also called *causation in fact.*

Examples

Suppose a corporation negligently pollutes the plaintiff's drinking water. The plaintiff dies of a heart attack unrelated to the polluted water. Although the corporation has acted negligently, it is not liable for the plaintiff's death. There were a negligent act and an injury, but there was no cause-and-effect relationship between them. If, instead, the plaintiff had died from the polluted drinking water, there would have been causation in fact, and the polluting corporation would have been liable.

If two (or more) persons are liable for negligently causing the plaintiff's injuries, both (or all) can be held liable to the plaintiff if each of their acts is a substantial factor in causing the plaintiff's injuries.

Proximate Cause

proximate cause
A point along a chain of events caused by a negligent party after which this party is no longer legally responsible for the consequences of his or her actions. Also called *legal cause.*

Under the law, a negligent party is not necessarily liable for all damages set in motion by his or her negligent act. Based on public policy, the law establishes a point along the damage chain after which the negligent party is no longer responsible for the consequences of his or her actions. This limitation on liability is referred to as **proximate cause**, or **legal cause**. The general test of proximate cause is *foreseeability*. A negligent party who is found to be the actual cause—but not the proximate cause—of the plaintiff's injuries is not liable to the plaintiff. Situations are examined on a case-by-case basis.

Special Negligence Doctrines

The courts have developed many *special negligence doctrines.* The most important of these are discussed in the paragraphs that follow.

Professional Malpractice

professional malpractice
The liability of a professional who breaches his or her duty of ordinary care.

Professionals, such as doctors, lawyers, architects, accountants, and others, owe a duty of ordinary care in providing their services. This duty is known as the *reasonable professional standard.* A professional who breaches this duty of care is liable for the injury his or her negligence causes. This liability is commonly referred to as **professional malpractice**.

Examples

A doctor who amputates a wrong leg is liable for *medical malpractice.* A lawyer who fails to file a document with the court on time, causing the client's case to be dismissed, is liable for *legal malpractice.* An accountant who fails to use reasonable care, knowledge, skill, and judgment in providing auditing and other accounting services to a client is liable for *accounting malpractice.*

Negligent Infliction of Emotional Distress

negligent infliction of emotional distress
A tort that permits a person to recover for emotional distress caused by the defendant's negligent conduct.

Some jurisdictions have extended the tort of emotional distress to include the **negligent infliction of emotional distress**.

Example

The most common example of negligent infliction of emotional distress involve bystanders who witness the injury or death of a loved one that is caused by another's negligent conduct. Under this tort, the bystander, even though not personally physically injured, can sue the negligent party for his or her own mental suffering.

Generally, to be successful in this type of case, the plaintiff must prove that (1) a close relative was killed or injured by the defendant, (2) the plaintiff suffered severe emotional

Landmark Law

Palsgraf v. The Long Island Railroad Company

"Negligence is not actionable unless it involves the invasion of a legally protected interest, the violation of a right. Proof of negligence in the air, so to speak, will not do."

—Justice Cardozo

The landmark case establishing the doctrine of proximate cause is **Palsgraf v. The Long Island Railroad Company,** a New York case decided in 1928. Helen Palsgraf was standing on a platform, waiting for a passenger train. The Long Island Railroad Company owned and operated the trains and employed the station guards. As a man carrying a package wrapped in a newspaper tried to board the moving train, railroad guards tried to help him. In doing so, the package was dislodged from the man's arm, fell to the railroad tracks, and exploded. The package contained hidden fireworks. The explosion shook the railroad platform, causing a scale located on the platform to fall on Helen Palsgraf, injuring her.

Palsgraf sued the railroad for negligence. Justice Cardozo eloquently addressed the issue of proximate cause:

The conduct of the defendant's guard, if a wrong in its relation to the holder of the package, was not a wrong in its relation to the plaintiff, standing far away. Relatively to her it was not negligence at all. Nothing in the situation gave notice that the falling package had in it the potency of peril to persons thus removed. Negligence is not actionable unless it involves the invasion of a legally protected interest, the violation of a right. Proof of negligence in the air, so to speak, will not do. In every instance, before negligence can be predicated on a given act, in back of the act must be sought and found a duty to the individual complaining, the observance of which would have averted or avoided the injury.

The argument for the plaintiff is built upon the shifting meanings of such words as "wrong" and

"wrongful," and shares their instability. What the plaintiff must show is "a wrong" to herself, i.e., a violation of her own right, and not merely a wrong to some one else, nor conduct "wrongful" because unsocial. The risk reasonably to be perceived defines the duty to be obeyed, and risk imports relation; it is risk to another or to others within the range of apprehension. Here, by concession, there was nothing in the situation to suggest to the most cautious mind that the parcel wrapped in newspaper would spread wreckage through the station. If the guard had thrown it down knowingly and willfully, he would not have threatened the plaintiff's safety, so far as appearances could warn him. His conduct would not have involved, even then, an unreasonable probability of invasion of her bodily security. Liability can be no greater where the act is inadvertent.

Negligence, like risk, is thus a term of relation. Negligence in the abstract, apart from things related, is surely not a tort, if indeed it is understandable at all. One who seeks redress at law does not make out a cause of action by showing without more that there has been damage to his person. If the harm was not willful, he must show that the act as to him had possibilities of danger so many and apparent as to entitle him to be protected against the doing of it though the harm was unintended.

Justice Cardozo denied Palsgraf's recovery, finding that the railroad company was not the proximate cause of her injuries. *Palsgraf v. The Long Island Railroad Company,* 248 N.Y. 339, 162 N.E. 99, **Web** 1928 N.Y. Lexis 1269 (Court of Appeals of New York, 1928)

---

distress, and (3) the plaintiff's mental distress resulted from a sensory and contemporaneous observance of the accident. Some states require that the plaintiff's mental distress be manifested by some physical injury; other states have eliminated this requirement.

Negligence per se

Statutes often establish duties owed by one person to another. The violation of a statute that proximately causes an injury is **negligence per se.** The plaintiff in such an action must prove that (1) a statute existed, (2) the statute was enacted to prevent the type of injury suffered, and (3) the plaintiff was within a class of persons meant to be protected by the statute.

negligence per se

A tort in which the violation of a statute or an ordinance constitutes the breach of the duty of care.

Example

Most cities have an ordinance that places the responsibility for fixing public sidewalks in residential areas on the homeowners whose homes front the sidewalks. A homeowner is

Automobiles, Las Vegas, Nevada. *Most automobile and other vehicle drivers drive safely and are not often involved in accidents. However, vehicular accidents are a primary cause of injury and death. In the United States there are more than 40,000 fatalities of passenger car and SUV occupants, pedestrians, and cyclists each year. More than 4,000 motor cycle fatalities also occur each year.*

liable if he or she fails to repair a damaged sidewalk in front of his or her home and a pedestrian trips and is injured because of the damage. The injured party does not have to prove that the homeowner owed the duty because the statute establishes that.

Res Ipsa Loquitur

If a defendant is in control of a situation in which a plaintiff has been injured and has superior knowledge of the circumstances surrounding the injury, the plaintiff might have difficulty proving the defendant's negligence. In such a situation, the law applies the doctrine of *res ipsa loquitur* (Latin for "the thing speaks for itself"). This doctrine raises a presumption of negligence and switches the burden to the defendant to prove that he or she was not negligent. *Res ipsa loquitur* applies in cases where the following elements are met:

1. The defendant had exclusive control of the instrumentality or situation that caused the plaintiff's injury.
2. The injury would not have ordinarily occurred but for someone's negligence.

res ipsa loquitur
A tort in which the presumption of negligence arises because (1) the defendant was in exclusive control of the situation and (2) the plaintiff would not have suffered injury but for someone's negligence. The burden switches to the defendant to prove that he or she was not negligent.

Examples
Haeran goes in for major surgery and is given anesthesia to put her to sleep during the operation. Sometime after the operation, it is discovered that a surgical instrument was left in Haeran during the operation. She suffers severe injury because of the left-in instrument. Haeran has no way to identify which doctor or nurse carelessly left the instrument in her body. In this case, the court can apply the doctrine of *res ipsa loquitur* and place the presumption of negligence on the defendants. Any defendant who can prove he or she did not leave the instrument in Haeran escapes liability; any defendant who does not disprove his or her negligence is liable. Other typical *res ipsa loquitur* cases involve commercial airplane crashes, falling elevators, and the like.

Good Samaritan Laws

Good Samaritan law
A statute that relieves medical professionals from liability for ordinary negligence when they stop and render aid to victims in emergency situations.

In the past, liability exposure made many doctors, nurses, and other medical professionals reluctant to stop and render aid to victims in emergency situations, such as highway accidents. Almost all states have enacted **Good Samaritan laws** that relieve medical professionals from liability for injury caused by their ordinary negligence in such circumstances. Good Samaritan laws protect medical professionals only from liability for their *ordinary* *negligence*, not for injuries caused by their gross negligence or reckless or intentional conduct. Most Good Samaritan laws protect licensed doctors, nurses, and laypersons who have been certified in CPR. Laypersons not trained in CPR are not generally protected by Good Samaritan statutes—that is, they are liable for injuries caused by their ordinary negligence in rendering aid.

Examples

Sam is injured in an automobile accident and is unconscious in his automobile alongside the road. Doctor Pamela Heathcoat, who is driving by the scene of the accident, stops, pulls Sam from the burning wreckage, and administers first aid. In doing so, Pamela negligently breaks Sam's shoulder. If Pamela's negligence is ordinary negligence, she is not liable to Sam because the Good Samaritan law protects her from liability; if Pamela was grossly negligent or reckless in administering aid to Sam, she is liable to him for the injuries she caused. It is a question of fact for the jury to decide whether a doctor's conduct was ordinary negligence or gross negligence or recklessness.

Defenses Against Negligence

A defendant in a negligence lawsuit may raise several defenses to the imposition of liability. These defenses are discussed in the following paragraphs.

Superseding or Intervening Event

Under negligence, a person is liable only for foreseeable events. Therefore, an original negligent party can raise a **superseding event** or an **intervening event** as a defense to liability.

Example

Assume that an avid golfer negligently hits a spectator with a golf ball, knocking the spectator unconscious. While lying on the ground, waiting for an ambulance to come, the spectator is struck by a bolt of lightning and killed. The golfer is liable for the injuries caused by the golf ball. He is not liable for the death of the spectator, however, because the lightning bolt was an unforeseen intervening event.

Assumption of the Risk

If a plaintiff knows of and voluntarily enters into or participates in a risky activity that results in injury, the law recognizes that the plaintiff assumed, or took on, the risk involved. Thus, the defendant can raise the defense of **assumption of the risk** against the plaintiff. This defense assumes that the plaintiff (1) had knowledge of the specific risk and (2) voluntarily assumed that risk.

Example

Under assumption of the risk, a race-car driver assumes the risk of being injured or killed in a crash.

In the following case, the court had to decide whether the plaintiff had assumed the risk.

Contributory Negligence

Sometimes a plaintiff is partially liable for causing his or her own injuries. Under the common law doctrine of **contributory negligence**, a plaintiff who is partially at fault for his or her own injury cannot recover against the negligent defendant. Many states follow this rule.

Example

Suppose a driver who is driving over the speed limit negligently hits and injures a pedestrian who is jaywalking. Suppose the jury finds that the driver is 80 percent responsible for the accident, and the jaywalker is 20 percent responsible. The pedestrian suffered $100,000 in injuries. Under the doctrine of contributory negligence, the pedestrian cannot recover any damages from the driver.

Every unjust decision is a reproach to the law or the judge who administers it. If the law should be in danger of doing injustice, then equity should be called in to remedy it. Equity was introduced to mitigate the rigour of the law.

Lord Denning
M.R. Re Vandervell's Trusts
(1974)

superseding or intervening event
An event for which a defendant is not responsible. The defendant is not liable for injuries caused by the superseding or intervening event.

assumption of the risk
A defense a defendant can use against a plaintiff who knowingly and voluntarily enters into or participates in a risky activity that results in injury.

contributory negligence
A doctrine that says a plaintiff who is partially at fault for his or her own injury cannot recover against the negligent defendant.

Lilya v. The Greater Gulf State Fair, Inc.

855 So.2d 1049, Web 2003 Ala. Lexis 57 (2003)
Supreme Court of Alabama

"Here, the only evidence of danger stemming from the mechanical bull ride is the most open and obvious characteristic of the ride: the possibility of falling off the mechanical bull."

—Judge Houston

Facts

The Greater Gulf State Fair, Inc., operated the Gulf State Fair in Mobile County, Alabama. One of the events at the fair was a mechanical bull ride for which participants paid money to ride the mechanical bull. A mechanical bull is a ride where the rider sits on a motorized device shaped like a real bull, and the ride simulates a real bull ride as the mechanical bull turns, twists, and bucks. The challenge is to stay on the bull and not be thrown off the bull. A large banner above the ride read "Rolling Thunder."

John Lilya and a friend watched as a rider was thrown from the mechanical bull. Lilya also watched as his friend paid and rode the bull and also was thrown off. Lilya then paid the $5 admission charge and signed a release agreement that stated:

> I acknowledge that riding a mechanical bull entails known and unanticipated risks which could result in physical or emotional injury, paralysis, death, or damage to myself, to property, or to third parties. I expressly agree and promise to accept and assume all of the risks existing in this activity. My participation in this activity is purely voluntary, and I elect to participate in spite of the risks.

Lilya boarded the mechanical bull and was immediately thrown off onto a soft pad underneath the bull. Lilya reboarded the bull for a second ride. The bull ride began again and became progressively faster, spinning and bucking to the left and right until Lilya fell off the bull. On the fall, Lilya landed on his head and shoulders, and he suffered a fractured neck. Lilya sued Gulf State Fair to recover damages for his severe injuries. The trial court granted summary judgment to Gulf State Fair, finding that Lilya had voluntarily assumed an open and obvious danger. Lilya appealed.

Issue

Was riding a mechanical bull an open and obvious danger for which Lilya had voluntarily assumed the risk when he rode the mechanical bull?

Language of the Court

As the landowner, Gulf State Fair would owe Lilya, its invitee, the duty to use reasonable care. The owner of premises has no duty to warn an invitee of open and obvious defects in the premises which the invitee is aware of or should be aware of in the exercise of reasonable care. Here, the only evidence of danger stemming from the mechanical bull ride is the most open and obvious characteristic of the ride: the possibility of falling off the mechanical bull. Lilya was aware that the two riders who had ridden the mechanical bull immediately before he rode it had fallen off. He noticed the thick floor mat, and he knew that the mat was there to protect riders when they fell. Also, he signed a release that explicitly stated that riding the mechanical bull involved inherent risks and that the risks included falling off or being thrown from the bull which could result in head, neck, and back injuries. Additionally, the very name of the ride—"Rolling Thunder"—hanging on a banner above the ride, gives a somewhat graphic indication of what is the very nature of bull riding: an extremely turbulent ride, the challenge of which is to hang on and not fall off. The entertainment value—and, indeed, the concept—of bull riding becomes meaningless without the inherent possibility of falling off. "Volenti non fit injuria" (a person who knowingly and voluntarily risks danger cannot recover for any resulting injury).

Decision

The supreme court of Alabama held that riding a mechanical bull and being thrown and injured by the bull is an open and obvious danger and that Lilya had voluntarily assumed the risk when he rode the bull and was thrown and injured. The supreme court affirmed the trial court's grant of summary judgment in favor of Gulf State Fair.

Case Questions

Critical Legal Thinking What does the doctrine of assumption of the risk provide? Do you think the doctrine of assumption of the risk should be recognized by the law? Explain.

Business Ethics Did Gulf State Fair act ethically by making money from such a dangerous activity as mechanical bull riding? Did Lilya act ethically in suing for damages?

Contemporary Business What public purpose does the defense of assumption of the risk serve? What would be the consequences if this defense were not available? Explain.

Last Clear Chance Rule   There is one major exception to the doctrine of contributory negligence: The defendant has a duty under the law to avoid the accident if at all possible. This rule is known as the *last clear chance rule*.

Example

A driver who sees a pedestrian walking across the street against a "Don't Walk" sign must avoid hitting him or her if possible. When deciding cases involving this rule, the courts consider the attentiveness of the parties and the amount of time each had to respond to the situation.

Comparative Negligence

The application of the doctrine of contributory negligence could reach an unfair result where a party only slightly at fault for his or her injuries could not recover from an otherwise negligent defendant. Many states have replaced the doctrine of contributory negligence with the doctrine of **comparative negligence**, also called **comparative fault**. Under this doctrine, damages are apportioned according to fault.

comparative negligence
A doctrine under which damages are apportioned according to fault.

Example

When the comparative negligence rule is applied to the previous example, the result is much fairer. The plaintiff-pedestrian, who was 20 percent at fault for causing his own injuries, can recover 80 percent of his damages (or $80,000) from the defendant-driver. This is an example of **pure comparative negligence**.

Several states have adopted **partial comparative negligence**, which provides that a plaintiff must be less than 50 percent responsible for causing his or her own injuries to recover under comparative negligence; otherwise, contributory negligence applies.

Strict Liability

Strict liability, another category of torts, is *liability without fault*. That is, a participant in a covered activity will be held liable for any injuries caused by the activity, even if he or she was not negligent. This doctrine holds that (1) there are certain activities that can place the public at risk of injury even if reasonable care is taken and (2) the public should have some means of compensation if such injury occurs.

strict liability
Liability without fault.

Strict liability was first imposed for **abnormally dangerous activities**, such as crop dusting, blasting, fumigation, burning of fields, storage of explosives, and the keeping of wild animals as pets.

District of Shinjuku in Tokyo, Japan. *Each country has developed its own civil law system. In Japan, for example, no class actions or contingency fee arrangements are allowed. Plaintiffs must pay their lawyers an upfront fee of up to eight percent of the damages sought, plus a nonrefundable filing fee to the court of one-half of one percent of the damages sought. No discovery is permitted. Even if the plaintiff wins the lawsuit, damage awards are low. Therefore, most legal disputes in Japan are decided by private arbitrators.*

Test Review Terms and Concepts

Abnormally dangerous activities
Actual cause (causation in fact)
Assault
Assumption of the risk
Battery
Breach of the duty of care
Comparative negligence (comparative fault)
Contributory negligence
Defamation of character
Disparagement (trade libel, product disparagement, or slander of title)
Duty of care
False imprisonment
Good Samaritan law
Injury
Intentional infliction of emotional distress (tort of outrage)

Intentional misrepresentation (fraud or deceit)
Intentional tort
Intervening event
Invasion of the right to privacy
Libel
Malicious prosecution
Merchant protection statute (shopkeeper's privilege)
Misappropriation of the right to publicity (tort of appropriation)
Negligence (unintentional tort)
Negligence per se
Negligent infliction of emotional distress

New York Times Co. v. Sullivan
Palsgraf v. The Long Island Railroad Company
Partial comparative negligence
Professional malpractice
Proximate cause (legal cause)
Pure comparative negligence
Res ipsa loquitur
Scienter
Slander
Strict liability
Superseding event
Tort
Tort of appropriation
Transferred intent doctrine

Case Problems

6.1 Intentional Tort: The Baltimore Orioles, a professional baseball team, visited Boston's Fenway Park to play the Boston Red Sox, another professional baseball team. Ross Grimsley was a pitcher for the visiting Baltimore club. During one period of the game, Grimsley was warming up in the bullpen, throwing pitches to a catcher. During this warm-up, Boston spectators in the stands heckled Grimsley. After Grimsley had completed warming up, Grimsley wound up as if he were going to throw the ball in his hand at the plate but then turned and threw the ball at one of the hecklers in the stand. The ball traveled at about 80 miles an hour, passed through a wire fence protecting the spectators, missed the heckler that Grimsley was aiming at, and hit another spectator, David Manning, Jr., causing injury. Manning sued Grimsley and the Baltimore Orioles. Are the defendants liable? *Manning v. Grimsley*, 643 F.2d 20, **Web** 1981 U.S. App. Lexis 19782 (United States Court of Appeals for the First Circuit)

6.2 Merchant Protection Statute: At about 7:30 P.M., Deborah A. Johnson entered a Kmart store located in Madison, Wisconsin, to purchase some diapers and several cans of motor oil. She took her small child along to enable her to purchase the correct size diapers, carrying the child in an infant seat that she had purchased at Kmart two or three weeks previously. A large Kmart price tag was still attached to the infant seat. Johnson purchased the diapers and oil and some children's clothes. She was in a hurry to leave because it was 8:00 P.M., her child's feeding time, and she hurried through the checkout lane. She paid for the diapers, the oil, and the clothing. Just after leaving the store, she heard someone ask her to stop. She turned around and saw a Kmart security officer. He showed her a badge and asked her to come back into the store, which she did. The man stated, "I have reason to believe that you have stolen this car seat." Johnson explained that she had purchased the seat previously. She demanded to see the manager, who was called to the scene. When Johnson pointed out that the seat had cat hairs, food crumbs, and milk stains on it, the man said, "I'm really sorry, there's been a terrible mistake. You can go." Johnson looked at the clock, which read 8:20 P.M., when she left. Johnson sued Kmart for false imprisonment. Is Kmart liable? *Johnson v. K-Mart Enterprises, Inc.*, 98 Wis.2d 533, 297 N.W.2d 74, **Web** 1980 Wisc.App. Lexis 3197 (Court of Appeals of Wisconsin)

6.3 Negligence: George Yanase was a paying guest at the Royal Lodge-Downtown Motel in San Diego, California. Yanase was a member of the Automobile Club of Southern California. The Auto Club publishes a "Tourbook" in which it lists hotels and motels and rates the quality of their services, including the cleanliness of rooms, quality of the restaurant, level of personal service, and the like. Yanase had selected the Royal from the Tourbook. On the night of his stay at the Royal, Yanase was shot in the parking lot adjacent to the motel and died as a result of his injuries. Yanase's widow sued the Auto Club for negligence. Is the Auto Club liable? *Yanase v. Automobile Club of Southern California*, 212 Cal.App.3d 468, 260 Cal.Rptr. 513, **Web** 1989 Cal.App. Lexis 746 (Court of Appeal of California)

6.4 Causation: W. L. Brown purchased a new large Chevrolet truck from Days Chevrolet. The truck had been manufactured by General Motors Corporation. One month later, an employee of Brown's was operating the truck when it ceased to function in rush-hour traffic on Interstate Highway 75 in the Atlanta suburbs. A defect within the alternator had caused a complete failure of the truck's electrical system. The defect was caused by General Motors's negligence in manufacturing the truck. When the alternator failed to operate, the truck came to rest in the right-hand lane of two north-bound lanes of freeway traffic. Because of the electrical failure, no blinking lights could be used to warn traffic of the danger. The driver, however, tried to motion traffic around the truck. Sometime later, when the freeway traffic had returned to normal, the large Chevrolet truck was still motionless on the freeway. At approximately 6:00 P.M., a panel truck approached the stalled truck in the right-hand lane of traffic at freeway speed. Immediately behind the panel truck, Mr. Davis, driving a Volkswagen fastback, was unable to see the stalled truck. At the last moment, the driver of the panel truck saw the stalled truck and swerved into another lane to avoid it. Mr. Davis drove his Volkswagen into the stalled truck at freeway speed, causing his death. Mr. Davis's wife brought a wrongful death action based on negligence against General Motors. Is there causation linking the negligence of the defendant to the fatal accident? *General Motors Corporation v. Davis*, 141 Ga.App. 495, 233 S.E.2d 825, **Web** 1977 Ga.App. Lexis 1961 (Court of Appeals of Georgia)

6.5 Negligence Per Se: Julius Ebanks set out from his home in East Elmhurst, Queens, New York, en route to his employment in the downtown district of Manhattan. When Ebanks reached Bowling Green subway station, he boarded an escalator owned and operated by the New York City Transit Authority. While the escalator was ascending, Ebanks's left foot became caught in a two-inch gap between the escalator step on which he was standing and the side wall of the escalator. Ebanks was unable to free himself. When he reached the top of the escalator, he was thrown to the ground, fracturing his hip and causing other serious injuries. The two-inch gap exceeded the three-eighths-inch standard required by the city's building code. Ebanks sued the Transit Authority to recover damages for his injuries. Who wins? *Ebanks v. New York City Transit Authority*, 70 N.Y.2d 621, 518 N.Y.S.2d 776, **Web** 1987 N.Y. Lexis 17294 (Court of Appeals of New York)

6.6 Emotional Distress: Gregory and Demetria James, brother and sister, were riding their bicycles north on 50th Street in Omaha, Nebraska. Spaulding Street intersects 50th Street. A garbage truck owned by Watts Trucking Service, Inc., and driven by its employee, John Milton Lieb, was backing up into the intersection of 50th and Spaulding streets. The truck backed into the intersection, through a stop sign, and hit and ran over Demetria, killing her. Gregory helplessly watched the entire accident but was not in danger himself. As a result of watching his sister's peril, Gregory suffered severe emotional distress. Gregory sued Watts and Lieb to recover damages for his emotional distress. Who wins? *James v. Watts Trucking Service, Inc.*, 221 Neb. 47, 375 N.W.2d 109, **Web** 1985 Neb. Lexis 1209 (Supreme Court of Nebraska)

6.7 Defense: The New York Yankees professional baseball team played the Chicago White Sox at Shea Stadium, New York. Elliot Maddox played center field for the Yankees that night. It had rained the day before, and the previous night's game had been canceled because of bad weather. On the evening of the game, the playing field was still wet, and Maddox commented on this fact several times to the club's manager but continued to play. In the ninth inning, when Maddox was attempting to field a ball in center field, he slipped on a wet spot, fell, and injured his right knee. Maddox sued the City of New York, which owned Shea Stadium; the Metropolitan Baseball Club, Inc., as lessee; the architect; the consulting engineer; and the American Baseball League. Maddox alleged that the parties were negligent in causing the field to be wet and that the injury ended his professional career. Who wins? *Maddox v. City of New York*, 66 N.Y.2d 270, 487 N.E.2d 553, 496 N.Y.S.2d 726, **Web** 1985 N.Y. Lexis 17254 (Court of Appeals of New York)

Business Ethics Cases

6.8 Business Ethics: Radio station KHJ was a successful Los Angeles broadcaster of rock music that commanded a 48 percent market share of the teenage audience in the Los Angeles area. KHJ was owned and operated by RKO General, Inc. KHJ inaugurated a promotion titled "The Super Summer Spectacular." As part of this promotion, KHJ had a disc jockey known as "The Real Don Steele" ride around the Los Angeles area in a conspicuous red automobile. Periodically KHJ would announce to its radio audience Steele's location. The first listener to thereafter locate Steele and answer a question received a cash prize and participated in a brief interview on the air with Steele. One KHJ broadcast identified Steele's next destination as Canoga Park. Robert Sentner, 17 years old, heard the broadcast and immediately drove to Canoga Park. Marsha Baime, 19 years old, also heard the broadcast and drove to Canoga Park. By the time Sentner and Baime located Steele, someone else had already claimed the prize. Without the knowledge of the other, Sentner and Baime each decided to follow Steele to the next destination and to be first to "find" him.

Steele proceeded onto the freeway. For the next few miles Sentner and Baime tried to jockey for position closest to the Steele vehicle, reaching speeds of up to 80 miles per hour. There is no evidence that the Steele vehicle exceeded the speed limit. When Steele left the freeway at the Westlake off ramp, Sentner and Baime tried to follow. In their attempts to do so, they knocked another vehicle, driven by Mr. Weirum, into the center divider of the freeway, where it overturned. Mr. Weirum died in the accident. Baime stopped to report the accident. Sentner, after pausing momentarily to relate the tragedy to a passing police officer, got back into his car, pursued and successfully located Steele, and collected the cash prize. The wife and children of Mr. Weirum brought a wrongful death negligence action against Sentner, Baime, and RKO General. Who wins? Did RKO General, Inc., act responsibly in this case? *Weirum v. RKO General, Inc.*, 15 Cal.3d 40, 539 P.2d 36, 123 Cal.Rptr. 468, **Web** 1975 Cal. Lexis 220 (Supreme Court of California)

6.9 Business Ethics: Guy Portee, a seven-year-old, resided with his mother in an apartment building in Newark, New Jersey. Edith and Nathan Jaffee owned and operated the building. One day, Guy became trapped in the building's elevator, between its outer door and the wall of the elevator shaft. When someone activated the elevator, the boy was dragged up to the third floor. Another child who saw the accident ran to seek help. Soon afterward, Renee Portee, the boy's mother, and

Newark Police Department officers arrived. The officers worked for hours, trying to release the boy, during which time the mother watched as her son moaned, cried out, and flailed his arms. The police contacted the Atlantic Elevator Company, which was responsible for the installation and maintenance of the elevator, and requested that the company send a mechanic to assist in the effort to free the boy. Apparently no one came. The boy suffered multiple bone fractures and massive internal hemorrhaging. He died while still trapped, his mother a helpless observer.

After her son's death, Renee became severely distressed and seriously self-destructive. Three years after the incident, she attempted to take her own life. She survived, and the wound was repaired by surgery, but thereafter she required considerable physical therapy. She had received extensive counseling and psychotherapy to help overcome the mental and emotional problems associated with her son's death. Renee sued the Jaffees and Atlantic to recover damages for her emotional distress. Who wins? Did either of the defendants act unethically in this case? *Portee v. Jaffee*, 84 N.J. 88, 417 A.2d 521, **Web** 1980 N.J. Lexis 1387 (Supreme Court of New Jersey)

Endnotes

1. 376 U.S. 254, 84 S.Ct. 710, 11 L.Ed.2d 686, Web 1964 U.S. Lexis 1655 (Supreme Court of the United States, 1964).

2. *Restatement (Second) of Torts*, Section 46.

3. *Restatement (Second) of Torts*, Section 46, Comment d.

4. Justice B. Anderson, *Blyth v. Birmingham Waterworks Co.*, 11 Exch. 781, 784 (1856).

Key Excerpts from the Majority Opinion

Andrea Collier, as Parent and Natural Guardian for Matthew Collier, an Infant, Appellant, v. Charles Zambito et al., Respondents

Court of Appeals State of New York 1 NY3d 444 (2004)

Background and Facts

Defendants Charles and Mary Zambito own a dog named Cecil. He is a mixed breed, beagle-collie-rottweiler. He is kept as a family pet and had never attacked anyone. Quite the contrary he was a pet for their children. The Zambitos had owned Cecil for seven months since he was a puppy. Although he had never attacked anyone, Cecil was kept in the kitchen, behind a gate, whenever visitors came to the house. On December 31, 1998, 12-year-old Matthew

Collier was one of a group of boys visiting the Zambitos'. He had been to the house on previous occasions and knew Cecil. This night as he was passing, Cecil barked and Mrs. Zambito put Cecil on a leash. When Matthew came out of the bathroom Mrs. Zambito told Matthew to let Cecil smell him so that Cecil would realize his scent and that he knew Matthew. Matthew put his hand out and instead of smelling him Cecil lunged at Matthew and bit his face. The Zambitos did not dispute the fact that Cecil bit Matthew. They did however contend that they had no knowledge that Cecil would bite anyone since he had never attacked anyone. Matthew's parents brought an action against the Zambitos.

Issue

Whether the Zambitos knew or should have known of the dog's dangerous propensities, and, if so whether defendant was negligent in initiating the contact between the plaintiff's son and Cecil.

In the Language of the Court

The evidence submitted by plaintiff was simply insufficient to raise an issue of fact as to whether Cecil had vicious propensities that were known, or should have been known, to defendants. Cecil was kept as a family pet, not as a guard dog. Although the dog was restricted to the kitchen area, uncontroverted deposition testimony indicated that he was confined only because he would bark when guests were at the house. There was no evidence that Cecil was confined because the owners feared he would do any harm to their visitors. There was no evidence that the dog's behavior was ever threatening or menacing. Indeed, the dog's actions—barking and running around—are consistent with normal canine behavior. Barking and running around are what dogs do.

Decision

The Court of Appeals affirmed the Appellate Division's ruling for the Zambitos. There was no evidence that Cecil actually had vicious propensities of the type that resulted in Matthew's injury.

CHAPTER 7

"A manufacturer is strictly liable in tort when an article he places on the market, knowing that it is to be used without inspection for defects, proves to have a defect that causes injury to a human being."

—Greenman v. Yuba Power Products, Inc.
59 Cal.2d 57, 27 Cal.Rptr. 697, 1963 Cal. Lexis 140 (1963)

Strict Liability and Product Liability

Chapter Objectives

After studying this chapter, you should be able to:

1. Describe and distinguish among the several legal theories of product liability.
2. Define the doctrine of *strict liability*.
3. Identify and describe defects in manufacture and design.
4. Identify and describe defects of failure to warn and in packaging.
5. Describe the damages recoverable in a product liability lawsuit.

Chapter Contents

Introduction to Strict Liability and Product Liability

If a product defect causes injury or death to purchasers, lessees, users, or bystanders, the injured party or the heirs of a deceased person may bring legal actions and recover damages under certain tort doctrines. These tort doctrines include negligence, misrepresentation, and the modern theory of strict liability. The liability of manufacturers, sellers, lessors, and others for injuries caused by defective products is commonly referred to as **product liability**. If a violation of strict liability has been found, the plaintiff may also recover punitive damages if the defendant's conduct has been reckless or intentional.

The various tort principles that permit injured parties to recover damages caused by defective products are discussed in this chapter.

product liability
The liability of manufacturers, sellers, and others for the injuries caused by defective products.

Negligence and Misrepresentation

Depending on the circumstances of the case, persons who are injured by defective products may be able to recover damages under the tort theories of *negligence* and *misrepresentation*. Both theories require the defendant to be *at fault* for causing the plaintiff's injuries. These theories are discussed in the paragraphs that follow.

Negligence

A person injured by a defective product may bring an action for **negligence** against the negligent party. To be successful, the plaintiff must prove that the defendant breached a duty of due care to the plaintiff and thereby caused the plaintiff's injuries. In other words, the plaintiff must prove that the defendant was at fault for causing his injuries.

Failure to exercise due care includes failing to assemble a product carefully, negligent product design, negligent inspection or testing of a product, negligent packaging, failure to warn of the dangerous propensities of a product, and such. It is important to note that in a negligence lawsuit, only a party who was actually negligent is liable to the plaintiff.

negligence
A tort related to defective products in which the defendant has breached a duty of due care and caused harm to the plaintiff.

Example
Assume that the purchaser of a motorcycle is injured in an accident. The accident occurred because a screw was missing from the motorcycle. How does the buyer prove who was negligent? Was it the manufacturer, which left the screw out during the assembly of the motorcycle? Was it the retailer, who negligently failed to discover the missing screw while preparing the motorcycle for sale? Was it the mechanic, who failed to replace the screw after repairing the motorcycle? Negligence remains a viable, yet difficult, theory on which to base a product liability action.

An injustice anywhere is an injustice everywhere.

Samuel Johnson

Misrepresentation

A buyer or lessee who is injured because a seller or lessor fraudulently misrepresented the quality of a product can sue the seller for the tort of **intentional misrepresentation**, or **fraud**. Recovery is limited to persons who were injured because they relied on the misrepresentation.

Intentional misrepresentation occurs when a seller or lessor either (1) affirmatively misrepresents the quality of a product or (2) conceals a defect in it. Because most reputable manufacturers, sellers, and lessors do not intentionally misrepresent the quality of their products, fraud is not often used as the basis for product liability actions.

intentional misrepresentation
A tort in which a seller or lessor fraudulently misrepresents the quality of a product and a buyer is injured thereby. Also known as *fraud*.

Strict Liability

In the landmark case *Greenman v. Yuba Power Products, Inc.*,[1] the California Supreme court adopted the **doctrine of strict liability in tort** as a basis for product liability actions. Most states have now adopted this doctrine as a basis for product liability actions. The doctrine of strict liability removes many of the difficulties for the plaintiff associated with other theories of product liability. This section examines the scope of the strict liability doctrine.

Liability Without Fault

strict liability

A tort doctrine that makes manufacturers, distributors, wholesalers, retailers, and others in the chain of distribution of a defective product liable for the damages caused by the defect, *irrespective of fault.*

Unlike negligence, strict liability does not require the injured person to prove that the defendant breached a duty of care. **Strict liability** is **liability without fault**. A seller can be found strictly liable even though he or she has exercised all possible care in the preparation and sale of his or her product. Strict liability may not be disclaimed.

The doctrine of strict liability applies to sellers and lessors of products who are engaged in the business of selling and leasing products. Casual sales and transactions by nonmerchants are not covered. Thus, a person who sells a defective product to a neighbor in a casual sale is not strictly liable if the product causes injury.

Strict liability applies only to products, not services. In hybrid transactions that involve both services and products, the dominant element of the transaction dictates whether strict liability applies. For example, in a medical operation that requires a blood transfusion, the operation would be the dominant element, and strict liability would not apply. Strict liability may not be disclaimed.

All in the Chain of Distribution Are Liable

chain of distribution

All manufacturers, distributors, wholesalers, retailers, lessors, and subcomponent manufacturers involved in a transaction.

All parties in the **chain of distribution** of a defective product are strictly liable for the injuries caused by that product. Thus, all manufacturers, distributors, wholesalers, retailers, lessors, and subcomponent manufacturers may be sued under the doctrine of strict liability in tort. This view is based on public policy. Lawmakers presume that sellers and lessors will

Landmark Law

Restatement of Torts Definition of Strict Liability

Restatement (Second) of Torts

The most widely recognized articulation of the doctrine of strict liability in tort is found in *Section 402A* of the *Restatement (Second) of Torts*, which provides:

1. One who sells any product in a defective condition unreasonably dangerous to the user or consumer or to his property is subject to liability for physical harm thereby caused to the ultimate user or consumer, or to his property, if
   a. the seller is engaged in the business of selling such a product, and
   b. it is expected to and does reach the user or consumer without substantial change in the condition in which it is sold.
2. The rule stated in Subsection (1) applies although
   a. the seller has exercised all possible care in the preparation and sale of his product, and
   b. the user or consumer has not bought the product from or entered into any contractual relation with the seller.

Restatement (Third) of Torts

In 1997, the American Law Institute (ALI) adopted the *Restatement (Third) of Torts: Product Liability*. This new *Restatement* includes the following definition of *defect*:

A product is defective when, at the time of sale or distribution, it contains manufacturing defect, is defective in design, or is defective because of inadequate instructions or warnings.

A product:
   a. contains a manufacturing defect when the product departs from its intended design even though all possible care was exercised in the preparation and marketing of the product;
   b. is defective in design when the foreseeable risks of harm posed by the product could have been reduced or avoided by the adoption of a reasonable alternative design by the seller or other distributor, or a predecessor in the commercial chain of distribution, and the omission of the alternative design renders the product not reasonably safe;
   c. is defective because of inadequate instructions or warnings when the foreseeable risks of harm posed by the product could have been reduced or avoided by the provision of reasonable instructions or warnings by the seller or other distributor, or a predecessor in the commercial chain of distribution, and the omission of the instructions or warnings renders the product not reasonably safe.

insure against the risk of a strict liability lawsuit and spread the cost to their consumers by raising the price of products.

Example

Suppose a subcomponent manufacturer produces a defective tire and sells it to a truck manufacturer. The truck manufacturer places the defective tire on one of its new-model trucks. The truck is distributed by a distributor to a retail dealer. Ultimately, the retail dealer sells the truck to a buyer. The defective tire causes an accident in which the buyer is injured. All the parties in the tire's chain of distribution can be sued by the injured party; in this case, the liable parties are the subcomponent manufacturer, the truck manufacturer, the distributor, and the retailer.

Exhibit 7.1 compares the doctrines of negligence and strict liability.

A defendant who has not been negligent but who is made to pay a strict liability judgment can bring a separate action against the negligent party in the chain of distribution to recover its losses.

Parties Who Can Recover for Strict Liability

Because strict liability is a tort doctrine, *privity of contract* between the plaintiff and the defendant is not required. In other words, the doctrine applies even if the injured party had

Nobody has a more sacred obligation to obey the law than those who make the law.

Sophocles

■ **EXHIBIT 7.1** Negligence and Strict Liability Compared

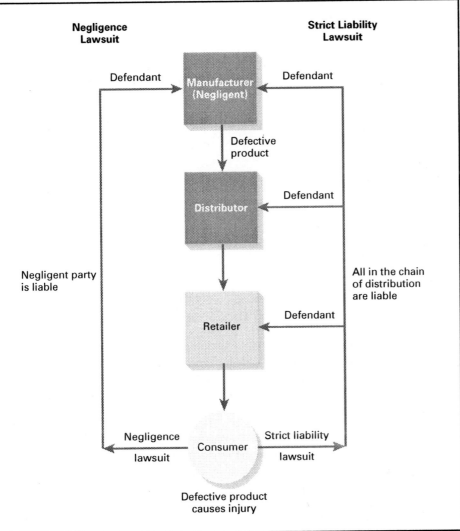

no contractual relations with the defendant. Thus, manufacturers, distributors, sellers, and lessors of a defective product are liable to the consumer who purchased the product and any user of the product. Users include the purchaser or lessee, family members, guests, employees, customers, and persons who passively enjoy the benefits of the product (e.g., passengers in automobiles).

The manufacturer, distributor, seller, and lessor of a defective product are also liable to third-party bystanders injured by the defective product. The courts have stated that bystanders who are injured by a defective product should be entitled to the same protection as a consumer or user. Bystanders and non-users do not even have the opportunity to inspect products for defects and to limit their purchases to articles manufactured by reputable manufacturers and sold by reputable retailers.

Damages Recoverable for Strict Liability

The damages recoverable in a strict liability action vary by jurisdiction. Damages for personal injuries are recoverable in all jurisdictions that have adopted the doctrine of strict liability, although some jurisdictions limit the dollar amount of the award. Property damage is recoverable in most jurisdictions, but economic loss (e.g., lost income) is recoverable in only a few jurisdictions.

Punitive damages, which are monetary damages awarded to punish the defendant, are generally allowed if the plaintiff can prove that the defendant either intentionally injured her or acted with reckless disregard for her safety.

Defective Product

To recover for strict liability, the injured party must first show that the product that caused the injury was somehow *defective*. (Remember that the injured party does not have to prove who caused the product to become defective.) Plaintiffs can allege multiple **product defects** in one lawsuit. A product can be found to be defective in many ways. The most common types of defects are:

product defect

Something wrong, inadequate, or improper in the manufacture, design, packaging, warning, or instructions about a product.

- Defect in manufacture
- Defect in design
- Failure to warn
- Defect in packaging
- Failure to provide adequate instructions

These defects are discussed in the following paragraphs.

Defect in Manufacture

defect in manufacture

A defect that occurs when a manufacturer fails to (1) properly assemble a product, (2) properly test a product, or (3) adequately check the quality of the product.

A **defect in manufacture** occurs when the manufacturer fails to (1) properly assemble a product, (2) properly test a product, or (3) adequately check the quality of a product.

Example

American Ladder Company designs, manufactures, and sells ladders. American Ladder Company manufactures a ladder, but a worker at the company fails to insert one of the screws that would support one of the steps of the ladder. The ladder is sold to Weingard Distributor, a wholesaler, which sells it to Reynolds Hardware Store, which sells the ladder to Heather, a consumer. When Heather is on the ladder painting her house, the step of the ladder breaks because of the missing screw, and Heather falls and is injured. The missing screw is an example of a defect in manufacture. Under the doctrine of strict liability, American Ladder Company, Weingard Distributor, and Reynolds Hardware Store are liable to Heather.

The following case is a classic example involving a defect in manufacture.

CASE 7.1
Defect in Manufacture

Shoshone Coca-Cola Bottling Company v. Dolinski

82 Nev. 439, 420 P.2d 855, Web 1966 Nev. Lexis 260 (1966) Supreme Court of Nevada

"In the case at hand, Shoshone contends that insufficient proof was offered to establish that the mouse was in the bottle of 'Squirt' when it left Shoshone's possession."

—Judge Thompson

Facts

Leo Dolinski purchased a bottle of Squirt, a soft drink, from a vending machine at a Sea and Ski plant, his place of employment. Dolinski opened the bottle and consumed part of its contents. He immediately became ill. Upon examination, it was found that the bottle contained the decomposed body of a mouse, mouse hair, and mouse feces. Dolinski visited a doctor and was given medicine to counteract nausea. Dolinski suffered physical and mental distress from consuming the decomposed mouse and thereafter possessed an aversion to soft drinks. The Shoshone Coca-Cola Bottling Company (Shoshone) had manufactured and distributed the Squirt bottle. Dolinski sued Shoshone, basing his lawsuit on the doctrine of strict liability. The state of Nevada had not previously recognized the doctrine of strict liability. However, the trial court adopted the doctrine of strict liability, and the jury returned a verdict in favor of the plaintiff. Shoshone appealed.

Issue

Should the state of Nevada judicially adopt the doctrine of strict liability? If so, was there a defect in the manufacture of the Squirt bottle that caused the plaintiff's injuries?

Language of the Court

In our view, public policy demands that one who places upon the market a bottled beverage in a condition dangerous for use must be held strictly liable to the ultimate user for injuries resulting from such use, although the seller has exercised all reasonable care.

Our acceptance of strict tort liability against the manufacturer and distributor of a bottled beverage does not mean that the plaintiff is relieved of the burden of proving a case. He must still establish that his injury was caused by a defect in the product and that such defect existed when the product left the hands of the defendant.

In the case at hand, Shoshone contends that insufficient proof was offered to establish that the mouse was in the bottle of "Squirt" when it left Shoshone's possession. The plaintiff offered the expert testimony of a toxicologist who examined the bottle and contents on the day the plaintiff drank from it. It was his opinion that the mouse "had been dead for a long time" and that the dark stains (mouse feces) that he found on the bottom of the bottle must have been there before the liquid was added. The jury apparently preferred the latter evidence that traced cause to the defendant.

Decision

The supreme court of Nevada adopted the doctrine of strict liability and held that the evidence supported the trial court's finding that there was a defect in manufacture. The supreme court affirmed the trial court's decision in favor of plaintiff Dolinski.

Case Questions

Critical Legal Thinking   Describe the doctrine of strict liability. How does it differ from negligence? Explain.

Business Ethics   Was it ethical for Shoshone to argue that it was not liable to Dolinski? Could this case have been "faked"?

Contemporary Business   Should all parties in the chain of distribution of a defective product—even parties that are not responsible for the defect—be held liable under the doctrine of strict liability? Or should liability be based only on fault?

Defect in Design

defect in design
A defect that occurs when a product is improperly designed.

A **defect in design** can support a strict liability action. Design defects that have supported strict liability awards include toys that are designed with removable parts that could be swallowed by children, machines and appliances designed without proper safeguards, and trucks and other vehicles designed without warning devices to let people know that the vehicle is backing up. A defect in design occurs when a product is designed incorrectly. In this case, not just one item but all of the defectively designed products can cause injury.

In evaluating the adequacy of a product's design, the courts apply a risk–utility analysis. This requires the court to consider the gravity of the danger posed by the design, the likelihood that injury will occur, the availability and cost of producing a safer alternative design, the social utility of the product, and other factors.

In the following case, the courts had to decide whether there was a design defect.

CASE 7.2
Design Defect

Higgins v. Intex Recreation Corporation

123 Wn.App. 821, 99 P.3d 421, Web 2004 Wash.App. Lexis 2424 (2004)
Court of Appeals of Washington

"Now, the ride down a snow-covered hill backward at 30 miles per hour may be a thrill. But it has very little social value when compared to the risk of severe injury."

—Judge Sweeney

Facts

Intex Recreation Corporation designed and sold the Extreme Sno-Tube II. This snow tube is ridden by a user down snow-covered hills and can reach speeds of 30 miles per hour. The snow tube has no steering device, and therefore a rider may end up spinning and going down a hill backward.

Dan Falkner bought an Extreme Sno-Tube II and used it sledding the same day. During Falkner's second run, the tube rotated him backward about one-quarter to one-third of the way down the hill. A group of parents, including Tom Higgins, stood near the bottom of the hill. Higgins saw seven-year-old Kyle Potter walking in the path of Falkner's speeding Sno-Tube. Higgins ran and grabbed Potter to save him from harm, but while he was doing so, the Sno-Tube hit Higgins and threw him into the air. Higgins landed on his forehead, which snapped his head back. The impact severed Higgins's spinal cord and left him quadriplegic.

Higgins sued Intex for damages based on strict liability. Evidence was introduced at trial that showed that the Sno-Tube could rotate while going downhill and that it had no guiding mechanism and no steering device. Evidence also showed that Intex made a Sno-Boggan that went just as fast but did not rotate because of ridges on the bottom of

the device. The jury found a design defect in the Sno-Tube and held Intex liable for 35 percent of Higgins's damages.

Issue

Was the Extreme Sno-Tube II defectively designed, thus supporting the judgment against Intex?

Language of the Court

There are two tests for determining whether a product is defective. The risk–utility test requires a showing that the likelihood and seriousness of harm outweigh the burden on the manufacturer to design a product that would have prevented that harm and would not have impaired the product's usefulness. The consumer-expectation test requires a showing that the product is more dangerous than the ordinary consumer would expect. This test focuses on the reasonable expectation of the consumer.

A plaintiff can satisfy its burden of proving an alternative design by showing that another product more safely serves the same function as the challenged product. There is evidence in this record from which a jury could conclude that the placement of ribs or ridges on the bottom of the Sno-Tube, like those used on Intex's Sno-Boggan, would keep the rider from facing downhill. The rider could then see obstacles and direct the tube. All this could be done without sacrificing speed. This is enough to prove an alternative safer design. Now, the ride down a snow-covered hill backward at 30 miles per hour may be a thrill. But it has very little social value when compared to the risk of severe injury. We do not think the Sno-Tube is a product that is necessary regardless of the risks involved to the user. We find ample evidence to support this verdict, applying the risk–utility test.

We next take up Intex's assertion that the tube was not unsafe to an extent beyond that which would be contemplated by the ordinary consumer. Again, we find ample evidence in this record to support the Higgins's assertion to the contrary. And a reasonable jury could easily infer that the average consumer may expect the Sno-Tube to rotate. But he or she might not expect that it would continue in a backward position. Here, the Sno-Tube is inexpensive. But so is Intex's Sno-Boggan. And the Sno-Boggan provides a fast ride but not a blind high-speed ride. A jury could then find that a reasonable consumer would expect that a snow sliding

product would not put him or her in a backward, high-speed slide. We find ample evidence in favor of the plaintiffs applying the consumer-expectation test.

Decision

The court of appeals held that the Sno-Tube was defectively designed and affirmed the judgment in favor of Higgins against Intex.

Case Questions

Critical Legal Thinking What is a design defect? Explain.

Business Ethics Should Intex have placed a ridge on the bottom of the Sno-Tube or equipped it with a steering device to make it safer? Would you have found for or against Intex in this case? Why or why not?

Contemporary Business What does the risk–utility test require? What does the consumer-expectation test require? How do these two tests differ?

Crashworthiness Doctrine

Often, when an automobile is involved in an accident, the driver or passengers are not injured by the blow itself. Instead, they are injured when their bodies strike something inside their own automobile (e.g., the dashboard, the steering wheel). This is commonly referred to as the "second collision." The courts have held that automobile manufacturers are under a duty to design automobiles to take into account the possibility of this second collision. This is called the **crashworthiness doctrine**. Failure to design an automobile to protect occupants from foreseeable dangers caused by a second collision subjects the manufacturer and dealer to strict liability.

crashworthiness doctrine
A doctrine that says automobile manufacturers are under a duty to design automobiles so they take into account the possibility of harm from a person's body striking something inside the automobile in the case of a car accident.

Failure to Warn

Certain products are inherently dangerous and cannot be made any safer and still accomplish the task for which they are designed. Many such products have risks and side effects caused by their use. Manufacturers and sellers owe a duty to warn consumers and users about the dangers of using these products. A proper and conspicuous warning placed on the product insulates the manufacturer and others in the chain of distribution from strict liability. **Failure to warn** of these dangerous propensities is a defect that will support a strict liability action.

failure to warn
A defect that occurs when a manufacturer does not place a warning on the packaging of products that could cause injury if the danger is unknown.

Example

The Universal Drug Corporation develops a new prescription drug that has tremendous success in preventing and treating a certain type of cancer. The drug, however, has a three percent probability of causing an increased risk of heart disease in patients who take the drug. The drug cannot be made any safer and still possess its cancer treatment effects. The Universal Drug Corporation owes a duty to warn potential users of its drug of these heart-related risks. If it failed to do so and a user suffered a heart attack because of using the drug, the Universal Drug Corporation would be held strictly liable for failure to warn.

In the following case, the court had to decide whether there was a failure to warn.

Bunch v. Hoffinger Industries, Inc.

123 Cal.App.4th 1278, 20 Cal.Rptr.3d 780, Web 2004 Cal.App. Lexis 1869 (2004)
Court of Appeal of California

"We find that the danger of diving into a shallow aboveground pool is not open and obvious to an 11 year old as a matter of law."

—Judge Raye

Facts

Joe and Loretta Frank, husband and wife, received a used frame for an aboveground swimming pool as a gift. The pool frame measured 33 feet long, 18 feet wide, and 4 feet deep. The Franks purchased a pool liner from McMasker Enterprises, Inc. (McMasker), a swimming pool supplier. Hoffinger Industries, Inc. (Hoffinger) manufactured the pool liner.

The Franks placed the pool in the yard of their house. Mr. Frank built a deck around the pool at the level of the pool frame and built a wooden bench on the deck next to the pool. Hoffinger did not place warning labels on their pool liners about the dangers of diving into the shallow pool. Instead, Hoffinger provided consumers with labels and instructions on how to place the labels on the pool liner. The warning label stated: "Caution—no diving—shallow water." The warning label was 0.75 inch wide and 5.25 inches long. The Franks testified that they affixed a warning label to the pool liner.

Leesa Bunch, 11 years old, and her brother Eric, 9 years old, were using the Franks' pool. Mrs. Frank told the children "not to dive" into the pool and went into the house. Leesa had watched the summer Olympics and tried to imitate the shallow racing dives of the Olympic swimmers. Leesa dove from the bench into the pool. Eric then saw Leesa curled up and floating in the pool, and he jumped in and dragged her to the edge of the pool. Leesa was rendered a quadriplegic by the dive.

Leesa Bunch sued McMasker and Hoffinger for strict liability for failure to adequately warn her of the danger of diving into the pool. Evidence at trial proved that during the past 17 years, there had been 47 prior incidents of persons becoming quadriplegic from diving into Hoffinger pools. McMasker settled with Leesa for $1 million. At trial, the jury found that Hoffinger had provided inadequate warnings of the dangers of diving into the pool and awarded Leesa $12,526,890 in damages plus costs. Hoffinger appealed.

Issue

Did Hoffinger adequately warn Leesa, an 11-year old girl, about the dangers of diving into a 4-foot-deep pool?

Language of the Court

We find that the danger of diving into a shallow aboveground pool is not open and obvious to an 11 year old as a matter of law. In the context of products liability actions, the plaintiff must prove that the defective products supplied by the defendant were a substantial factor in bringing about his or her injury. The court instructed that the jury must find "that the design of the warning system for the pool liner was a substantial factor in causing harm to the plaintiff." The court also instructed that the jury must find a "lack of sufficient warnings was a substantial factor in causing plaintiff's harm."

Bunch presented testimony by Ross Buck, Ph.D., a professor of communication sciences and psychology at the University of Connecticut. According to Buck, effective warnings "act as brakes to stop dangerous behaviors." Buck outlined the components of an effective persuasive warning: it must command attention, galvanize memory, evoke emotion, contain an explicit instruction, and show a consequence. This kind of warning is especially important for children under the age of 12. Dr. Buck testified that a young diver standing at the edge of an aboveground pool cannot necessarily judge the depth of the pool. Warnings act as "brakes to stop dangerous behaviors." Warnings to children between the ages of seven and 12 must be concrete and spell out the dangers and consequences of actions in order to be effective. Buck found the labels supplied with the Hoffinger pool liner neither adequate nor effective. The labels failed to spell out any consequences of diving into shallow water.

Dr. Johnson, another of Bunch's experts, testified that based on his experience and research, the risk of spinal paraplegia was not readily apparent to an 11 year old. Many people who dive into pools are unable to gauge the depth of the water. After reviewing the facts, Johnson opined that Bunch was attempting a shallow racing dive and was unaware of the possible consequences of that dive.

Given the testimony of Bunch and her two expert witnesses, we find sufficient evidence to support the conclusion that the lack of an adequate warning label was neither a negligible nor theoretical contribution to Bunch's injury. The evidence presented at trial revealed that the lack of a persuasive label outlining the consequences of diving into the pool was a substantial factor in causing the injury.

Decision

The court of appeal of California affirmed the trial court's finding that Hoffinger failed to adequately warn Leesa of the dangers of diving into the four-foot-deep pool. The

court of appeal upheld the monetary judgment in favor of Leesa against Hoffinger.

Case Questions

Critical Legal Thinking   Describe the doctrine of defect by failure to warn.

Business Ethics   Based upon the previous 47 cases in which users of Hoffinger pools were rendered quadriplegic, should the warning on the pool liner in this case have been stronger?

Contemporary Business   After the judgment of the trial court was issued, Hoffinger filed for bankruptcy. What are the consequences to Leesa of Hoffinger's filing for bankruptcy?

Food Counter. *Should sellers of foods that are not packaged but are easily tampered with be held liable if a consumer is injured by eating such tainted food?*

Defect in Packaging

Manufacturers owe a duty to design and provide safe packages for their products. This duty requires manufacturers to provide packages and containers that are tamperproof or that clearly indicate whether they have been tampered with. Certain manufacturers, such as drug manufacturers, owe a duty to place their products in containers that cannot be opened by children. A manufacturer's failure to meet this duty—a **defect in packaging**—subjects the manufacturer and others in the chain of distribution of the product to strict liability.

defect in packaging
A defect that occurs when a product has been placed in packaging that is insufficiently tamperproof.

Other Defects

Sellers are responsible to provide adequate instructions for the safe assembly and use of the products they sell. **Failure to provide adequate instructions** for the safe assembly and use of a product is a defect that subjects the manufacturer and others in the chain of distribution to strict liability.

failure to provide adequate instructions
A defect that occurs when a manufacturer does not provide detailed directions for safe assembly and use of a product.

Example

Mother buys her four-year-old daughter Lia a tricycle manufactured by Bicycle Corporation. The tricycle comes in a box with many parts that need to be assembled. The instructions for assembly are vague and hard to follow. Mother puts together the tricycle, using these instructions. The first time that Lia uses the tricycle, the handlebar becomes loose, and Lia's tricycle goes into the street, where she is hit and injured by an automobile. In this case, Mother could sue Bicycle Corporation on behalf of Lia for strict liability to recover damages for failing to provide adequate instructions.

Other defects that support a finding of product liability based on strict liability include inadequate testing of products, inadequate selection of component parts or materials, and improper certification of the safety of a product. The concept of "defect" is an expanding area of the law.

Punitive Damages

punitive damages
Monetary damages that are awarded to punish a defendant who either intentionally or recklessly injured the plaintiff.

In product liability cases, a court can award **punitive damages** if it finds that the defendant's conduct was committed with intent or with reckless disregard for human life. Punitive damages are meant to punish the defendant and to send a message to the defendant (and other companies) that such behavior will not be tolerated.

Defenses to Product Liability

Defendants in strict liability or negligence actions may raise several defenses to the imposition of liability. These defenses are discussed in the paragraphs that follow.

Generally Known Dangers

generally known dangers
A defense that acknowledges that certain products are inherently dangerous and are known to the general population to be so.

Certain products are inherently dangerous and are known to the general population to be so. Sellers are not strictly liable for failing to warn of **generally known dangers**.

Example
It is a known fact that guns shoot bullets. Manufacturers of guns do not have to place a warning on the barrel of a gun warning of this generally known danger.

Government Contractor Defense

government contractor defense
A defense that says a contractor who was provided specifications by the government is not liable for any defect in the product that occurs as a result of those specifications.

Many defense and other contractors manufacture products (e.g., rockets, airplanes) to government specification. Most jurisdictions recognize a **government contractor defense** to product liability actions. To establish this defense, a government contractor must prove that (1) the precise specifications for the product were provided by the government, (2) the product conformed to those specifications, and (3) the contractor warned the government of any known defects or dangers of the product.

Assumption of the Risk

Theoretically, the traditional doctrine of **assumption of the risk** is a defense to a product liability action. For this defense to apply, the defendant must prove that (1) the plaintiff knew and appreciated the risk and (2) the plaintiff voluntarily assumed the risk. In practice, the defense assumption of the risk is narrowly applied by the courts.

Misuse of the Product

Sometimes users are injured when they misuse a product. If a user brings a product liability action, the defendant-seller may be able to assert **misuse** as a defense. Whether the defense is effective depends on whether the misuse was foreseeable. The seller is relieved of product liability if the plaintiff has **abnormally misused** the product—that is, if there has been an **unforeseeable misuse** of the product. However, the seller is liable if there has been a **foreseeable misuse** of the product. This reasoning is intended to provide an incentive for manufacturers to design and manufacture safer products.

misuse
A defense that relieves a seller of product liability if the user *abnormally* misused the product. Products must be designed to protect against *foreseeable* misuse.

Correction of a Product Defect

A manufacturer that produces a defective product and later discovers said defect must (1) notify purchasers and users of the defect and (2) **correct the defect**. Most manufacturers faced with this situation recall the defective product and either repair the defect or replace the product.

The seller must make reasonable efforts to notify purchasers and users of the defect and the procedure to correct it. Reasonable efforts normally consist of sending letters to known purchasers and users and placing notices in newspapers and magazines of general circulation. If a user ignores such notice and fails to have the defect corrected, the seller may raise this as a defense against further liability with respect to the defect. Many courts have held that reasonable notice is effective even against users who did not see the notice.

Supervening Event

For a seller to be held strictly liable, the product it sells must reach the consumer or user "without substantial change" in its condition. Under the doctrine of **supervening event** or **intervening event**, the original seller is not liable if the product is materially altered or modified after it leaves the seller's possession and the alteration or modification causes an injury. A supervening or intervening event absolves all prior sellers in the chain of distribution from strict liability.

supervening event or intervening event
An alteration or a modification of a product by a party in the chain of distribution that absolves all prior sellers from strict liability.

Example

A manufacturer produces a safe piece of equipment. It sells the equipment to a distributor, which removes a safety guard from the equipment. The distributor sells it to a retailer, who sells it to a buyer. The buyer is injured because of the removal of the safety guard. The manufacturer can raise the defense of supervening event against the imposition of liability. However, the distributor and retailer are strictly liable for the buyer's injuries.

Statute of Limitation

Most states have **statutes of limitations** that require an injured person to bring an action within a certain number of years from the time that he or she was injured by a defective product. This limitation period varies from state to state. Failure to bring an action within the appropriate time relieves the defendant of liability.

In most jurisdictions, the statute of limitations does not begin to run until the plaintiff suffers an injury. This subjects sellers and lessors to exposure for an unspecified period of time because a defective product may not cause an injury for years, or even decades, after it was sold.

statute of limitations
A statute that requires an injured person to bring an action within a certain number of years from the time that he or she was injured by a defective product.

Statute of Repose

Some states have enacted **statutes of repose**, which limit the seller's liability to a certain number of years from the date when the product was first sold. The period of repose varies from state to state.

statute of repose
A statute that limits the seller's liability to a certain number of years from the date when the product was first sold.

Concept Summary
Statute of Limitation and Statute of Repose

Statute	Begins to Run
Statute of limitations	When the plaintiff suffers injury
Statute of repose	When the product is first sold

Contributory Negligence and Comparative Fault

Sometimes a person who is injured by a defective product is negligent and contributes to his or her own injuries. The defense of **contributory negligence** bars an injured plaintiff from recovering from the defendant in a negligence action. However, this doctrine generally does not bar recovery in strict liability actions.

Many states have held that the doctrine of **comparative fault** applies to strict liability actions. Under this doctrine, a plaintiff who is contributorily negligent for his or her injuries is responsible for a *proportional share* of the damages. In other words, the damages are apportioned between the plaintiff and the defendant.

Examples

An automobile manufacturer produces a car with a hidden defect, and a consumer purchases the car from an automobile dealer. The consumer is injured in an automobile accident in which the defect is found to be 75 percent responsible for the accident, and the consumer's reckless driving is found to be 25 percent responsible. The plaintiff suffers $1 million worth of injuries. Under the doctrine of *contributory negligence*, the plaintiff would recover nothing from the defendants. Under the doctrine of *comparative negligence*, the plaintiff would recover $750,000 from the defendants (75 percent of $1 million).

contributory negligence
A defense that says a person who is injured by a defective product but has been negligent and has contributed to his or her own injuries cannot recover from the defendant.

comparative fault
A doctrine that applies to strict liability actions that says a plaintiff who is contributorily negligent for his or her injuries is responsible for a proportional share of the damages.

Concept Summary
Contributory Negligence and Comparative Fault

Doctrine	Description
Contributory negligence	A person who is partially responsible for causing his or her own injuries may not recover anything from the manufacturer or seller of a defective product.
Comparative fault	A person who is partially responsible for causing his or her own injuries is responsible for a proportional share of the damages. The manufacturer or seller of the defective product is responsible for the remainder of the plaintiff's damages.

South Korean Currency. *Many countries have developed laws that permit lawsuits based on product defects. The Republic of Korea has enacted the Product Liability Act (PLA), which imposes strict liability on all parties along the chain of manufacture of a defective product, which would include the manufacturer of the product, an assembling manufacturer, and a manufacturer of defective component parts. Distributors, wholesalers, and the retailers that distribute defective products can be held liable if the manufacturer of the defective product cannot be found. Strict liability is imposed on importers of defective products.*

Test Review Terms and Concepts

Abnormal misuse (unforeseeable misuse)	Defect in packaging	Misuse of the product
Assumption of the risk	Doctrine of strict liability in tort	Negligence
Chain of distribution	Failure to provide adequate instructions	Product defect
Comparative fault	Failure to warn	Product liability
Contributory negligence	Foreseeable misuse	Punitive damages
Correction of a product defect	Generally known dangers	Statute of limitations
Crashworthiness doctrine	Government contractor defense	Statute of repose
Defect in design	*Greenman v. Yuba Power Products, Inc.*	Strict liability (liability without fault)
Defect in manufacture	Intentional misrepresentation (fraud)	Supervening event
	Intervening event	

Case Problems

7.1 Strict Liability: Jeppesen and Company produces charts that graphically display approach procedures for airplanes landing at airports. These charts are drafted from tabular data supplied by the Federal Aviation Administration (FAA), a federal agency of the U.S. government. By law, Jeppesen cannot construct charts that include information different from that supplied by the FAA. One day, the pilot of an airplane owned by World Airways was on descent to land at the Cold Bay, Alaska, airport. The pilot was using an instrument approach procedure chart published by Jeppesen. The airplane crashed into a mountain near Cold Bay, killing all six crew members and destroying the aircraft. Evidence showed that the FAA data did not include the mountain. The heirs of the deceased crew members and World Airways brought a strict liability action against Jeppesen. Does the doctrine of strict liability apply to this case? Is Jeppesen liable? *Brocklesby v. Jeppesen and Company*, 767 F.2d 1288, **Web** 1985 U.S. App. Lexis 21290 (United States Court of Appeals for the Ninth Circuit)

7.2 Failure to Warn: The Emerson Electric Co. manufactures and sells a product called the Weed Eater XR-90. The Weed Eater is a multipurpose weed-trimming and brush-cutting device. It consists of a handheld gasoline-powered engine connected to a long drive shaft, at the end of which can be attached various tools for cutting weeds and brush. One such attachment is a 10-inch circular saw blade capable of cutting through growth up to 2 inches in diameter. When this saw blade is attached to the Weed Eater, approximately 270 degrees of blade edge are exposed when in use. The owner's manual contained the following warning: "Keep children away. All people and pets should be kept at a safe distance from the work area, at least 30 feet, especially when using the blade." Donald Pearce, a 13-year-old boy, was helping his uncle clear an overgrown yard. The uncle was operating a Weed Eater XR-90 with the circular saw blade attachment. When Pearce stooped to pick up something off the ground about 6 to 10 feet behind and slightly to the left of where his uncle was operating the Weed Eater, the saw blade on the Weed Eater struck something near the ground. The

Weed Eater kicked back to the left and cut off Pearce's right arm to the elbow. Pearce, through his mother, Charlotte Karns, sued Emerson to recover damages under strict liability. Is Emerson liable? *Karns v. Emerson Electric Co.*, 817 F.2d 1452, **Web** 1987 U.S. App. Lexis 5608 (United States Court of Appeals for the Tenth Circuit)

7.3 Crashworthiness Doctrine: One night Verne Prior, while driving on U.S. 101 under the influence of alcohol and drugs at speeds of 65 to 85 miles per hour, crashed his automobile into the left rear of a Chevrolet station wagon stopped on the shoulder of the freeway because of a flat tire. Christine Smith was sitting in the passenger seat of the parked car when the accident occurred. In the crash, the Chevrolet station wagon was knocked into a gully, where its fuel tank ruptured. The vehicle caught fire, and Smith suffered severe burn injuries. The Chevrolet station wagon was manufactured by General Motors Corporation. Evidence showed that the fuel tank was located in a vulnerable position in the back of the station wagon, outside the crossbars of the frame. Evidence further showed that if the fuel tank had been located underneath the body of the station wagon, between the crossbars of the frame, it would have been well protected in the collision. Smith sued General Motors for strict liability. Is the Chevrolet station wagon a defective product? *Smith v. General Motors Corporation*, 42 Cal.App.3d 1, 116 Cal.Rptr. 575, **Web** 1974 Cal.App. Lexis 1199 (Court of Appeal of California)

7.4 Failure to Warn: Virginia Burke purchased a bottle of "Le Domaine" champagne that was manufactured by Almaden Vineyards, Inc. At home, she removed the wine seal from the top of the bottle but did not remove the plastic cork. She set the bottle on the counter, intending to serve it in a few minutes. Shortly thereafter, the plastic cork spontaneously ejected from the bottle, ricocheted off the wall, and struck Burke in the left lens of her eyeglasses, shattering the lens and driving pieces of glass into her eye. The champagne bottle did not contain any warning of this danger. Evidence showed that Almaden had previously been notified of the spontaneous ejection of the cork from its champagne bottles. Burke sued

Almaden to recover damages for strict liability. Is Almaden liable? *Burke v. Almaden Vineyards, Inc.*, 86 Cal.App.3d 768, 150 Cal.Rptr. 419, **Web** 1978 Cal.App. Lexis 2123 (Court of Appeal of California)

7.5 Assumption of Risk: Lillian Horn was driving her Chevrolet station wagon, which was designed and manufactured by General Motors Corporation, down Laurel Canyon Boulevard in Los Angeles, California. Horn swerved to avoid a collision when a car coming toward her crossed the center line and was coming at her. In doing so, her hand knocked the horn cap off the steering wheel, which exposed the area underneath the horn cap, including three sharp prongs that had held the horn cap to the steering wheel. A few seconds later, when her car hit an embankment, Horn's face was impaled on the three sharp exposed prongs, causing her severe facial injuries. Horn sued General Motors for strict liability. General Motors asserted the defense of assumption of the risk against Horn. Who wins? *Horn v. General Motors Corporation*, 17 Cal.3d 359, 551 P.2d 398, 131 Cal.Rptr. 78, **Web** 1976 Cal. Lexis 283 (Supreme Court of California)

7.6 Misuse: The Wilcox-Crittendon Company manufactured harnesses, saddles, bridles, leads, and other items commonly used for horses, cattle, and other ranch and farm animals. One such item was a stallion or cattle tie, a five-inch-long iron hook with a one-inch ring at one end. The tongue on the ring opened outward to allow the hook to be attached to a rope or another object. A purchasing agent for United Airlines, who was familiar with this type of hook because of his previous experience on a farm, purchased one of these hooks from Keystone Brothers, a harness and saddlery wares outlet located in San Francisco, California. Four years later Edward Dosier, an employee of United Airlines, was working to install a new grinding machine at a United Airlines maintenance plant. As part of the installation process, Dosier attached the hook to a 1,700-pound counterweight and raised the counterweight into the air. While the counterweight was suspended in the air, Dosier reached under the counterweight to retrieve a missing bolt. The hook broke, and the counterweight fell and crushed Dosier's arm. Dosier sued Wilcox-Crittendon for strict liability. Who wins? *Dosier v. Wilcox-Crittendon Company*, 45 Cal.App.3d 74, 119 Cal.Rptr. 135, **Web** 1975 Cal.App. Lexis 1665 (Court of Appeal of California).

Business Ethics Case

7.7 Business Ethics: Celestino Luque lived with his cousins Harry and Laura Dunn in Millbrae, California. The Dunns purchased a rotary lawn mower from Rhoads Hardware. The lawn mower was manufactured by Air Capital Manufacturing Company and was distributed by Garehime Corporation. Neighbors asked Luque to mow their lawn. While Luque was cutting the lawn, he noticed a small carton in the path of the lawn mower. Luque left the lawn mower in a stationary position with its motor running and walked around the side of the lawn mower to remove the carton. As he did so, he slipped on the wet grass and fell backward. Luque's left hand entered the unguarded hole of the lawn mower and was caught in its revolving blade, which turns at 175 miles per hour and 100 revolutions per second. Luque's hand was severely mangled and lacerated. The word *Caution* was printed above the unguarded hole on the lawn mower. Luque sued Rhoads Hardware, Air Capital, and Garehime Corporation for strict liability. The defendants argued that strict liability does not apply to *patent* (obvious) defects. Was it ethical for the defendants to argue that they were not liable for patent defects? Would patent defects ever be corrected if the defendants' contention was accepted by the court? Who wins? *Luque v. McLean, Trustee*, 8 Cal.3d 136, 501 P.2d 1163, 104 Cal.Rptr. 443, **Web** 1972 Cal. Lexis 245 (Supreme Court of California)

Endnote

1. 59 Cal.2d 57, 377 P.2d 897, 27 Cal.Rptr. 697, Web 1963 Cal. Lexis 140 (Supreme Court of California). For the complete opinion of this case, go to www.prenhall.com/cheeseman/.

CHAPTER 8

"It is better that ten guilty persons escape, than that one innocent suffer."

—Sir William Blackstone

Criminal Law and Cyber Crimes

Chapter Objectives

After studying this chapter, you should be able to:

1. List and describe the essential elements of a crime.
2. Describe criminal procedure, including arrest, indictment, arraignment, and the criminal trial.
3. Define major white-collar crimes, such as *embezzlement*, *bribery*, and *criminal fraud*.

4. List and describe laws involving domestic and international business crimes.
5. Explain the constitutional safeguards provided by the Fourth, Fifth, Sixth, and Eighth Amendments to the U.S. Constitution.

Chapter Contents

Introduction to Criminal Law and Cyber Crimes

For members of society to peacefully coexist and commerce to flourish, people and their property must be protected from injury by other members of society. Federal, state, and local governments' **criminal laws** are intended to afford this protection by providing an incentive for persons to act reasonably in society and imposing penalties on persons who violate them.

The United States has one of the most advanced and humane criminal law systems in the world. It differs from other criminal law systems in several respects. A person charged with a crime in the United States is *presumed innocent until proven guilty*. The *burden of proof* is on the government to prove that the accused is guilty of the crime charged. Further, the accused must be found guilty **beyond a reasonable doubt**. Conviction requires unanimous jury vote. Under many other legal systems, a person accused of a crime is presumed guilty unless the person can prove he or she is not. A person charged with a crime in the United States is also provided with substantial constitutional safeguards during the criminal justice process.

Many crimes are referred to as *white-collar crimes* because they are most often committed by business managers and employees. These crimes include fraud, bribery, and other such crimes. In addition, in the Information Age, many cyber crimes are committed using computers and the Internet.

This chapter discusses criminal procedure, white-collar crimes, business crimes, cyber crimes, and the constitutional safeguards afforded criminal defendants.

Definition of a Crime

crime
A violation of a statute for which the government imposes a punishment.

A **crime** is defined as any act done by an individual in violation of those duties that he or she owes to society and for the breach of which the law provides that the wrongdoer shall make amends to the public. Many activities have been considered crimes through the ages, whereas other crimes are of recent origin.

Penal Codes and Regulatory Statutes

penal code
A collection of criminal statutes.

regulatory statutes
Statutes such as environmental laws, securities laws, and antitrust laws that provide for criminal violations and penalties.

Statutes are the primary source of criminal law. Most states have adopted comprehensive **penal codes** that define in detail the activities considered to be crimes within their jurisdictions and the penalties that will be imposed for their commission. A comprehensive federal criminal code defines federal crimes.[1]

In addition, state and federal **regulatory statutes** often provide for criminal violations and penalties. The state and federal legislatures are continually adding to the list of crimes.

The penalty for committing a crime may consist of the imposition of a fine, imprisonment, both, or some other form of punishment (e.g., probation). Generally, imprisonment is imposed to (1) incapacitate the criminal so he or she will not harm others in society, (2) provide a means to rehabilitate the criminal, (3) deter others from similar conduct, and (4) inhibit personal retribution by the victim.

Parties to a Criminal Action

In a criminal lawsuit, the government (not a private party) is the **plaintiff**. The government is represented by a lawyer called the **prosecutor**. The accused, which is usually an individual or a business, is the **defendant**. The accused is represented by a **defense attorney**. Sometimes the accused will hire a private attorney to represent him if he can afford to do so. If the accused cannot afford a private defense lawyer, the government will provide one free of charge. This government defense attorney is often called a **public defender**. (See Exhibit 8.1.)

A crime is generally classified as a *felony*, *misdemeanor*, or *violation*.

■ **EXHIBIT 8.1** Parties and Attorneys Involved in a Criminal Case

Parties to a Criminal Lawsuit	
Government	**Person or Business**
(plaintiff)	(defendant)
Attorneys Representing the Parties	
Prosecutor	**Defense Attorney**
(government attorney)	(private attorney or public defender)

Law cannot persuade, where it cannot punish.

Thomas Fuller
Gnomologia (1732)

Felony

Felonies are the most serious kinds of crimes. Felonies include crimes that are *mala in se*—that is, inherently evil. Most crimes against persons (e.g., murder, rape) and certain business-related crimes (e.g., embezzlement, bribery) are felonies in most jurisdictions. Felonies are usually punishable by imprisonment. In some jurisdictions, certain felonies (e.g., first-degree murder) are punishable by death. Federal law[2] and some state laws require mandatory sentencing for specified crimes. Many statutes define different degrees of crimes (e.g., first-, second-, and third-degree murder). Each degree earns different penalties. Serious violations of regulatory statutes are also felonies.

felony
The most serious type of crime; inherently evil crime. Most crimes against persons and some business-related crimes are felonies.

Misdemeanor

Misdemeanors are less serious than felonies. They are crimes *mala prohibita*; that is, they are not inherently evil but are prohibited by society. Many crimes against property, such as robbery, burglary, and less serious violations of regulatory statutes, are included in this category. Misdemeanors carry lesser penalties than felonies. They are usually punishable by fines and/or imprisonment for one year or less.

misdemeanor
A less serious crime; not inherently evil but prohibited by society. Many crimes against property are misdemeanors.

Violation

Crimes such as traffic violations, jaywalking, and such are neither felonies nor misdemeanors. These crimes, which are called **violations**, are generally punishable by fines. Occasionally, a few days of imprisonment are imposed.

violation
A crime that is neither a felony nor a misdemeanor that is usually punishable by a fine.

Concept Summary
Classification of Crimes

Classification	Description
Felony	The most serious kinds of crimes. They are *mala in se* (inherently evil), and they are usually punishable by imprisonment.
Misdemeanor	Crimes that are less serious than felonies. They are *mala prohibita* (prohibited by society), and they are usually punishable by fine and/or imprisonment for less than one year.
Violation	Crimes that are neither felonies nor misdemeanors. Violations are generally punishable by a fine.

Intent Crimes

Most crimes require criminal intent to be proven before the accused can be found guilty of the defined crime. Two elements must be proven for a person to be found guilty of an intent crime: (1) criminal act (*actus reus*) and (2) criminal intent (*mens rea*).

actus reus
"Guilty act"–the actual performance of a criminal act.

Criminal Act (Actus Reus)   The defendant must have actually performed the prohibited act. The actual performance of the criminal act is called the **actus reus** (guilty act). Sometimes, the omission of an act can constitute the requisite *actus reus*.

Example
Killing someone without legal justification constitutes a criminal act (*actus reus*). This is because the law forbids persons from killing one another.

Example
If a taxpayer who is under a legal duty to file income tax returns and pay income taxes that are due the government fails to do so, there is the requisite criminal act (*actus reus*).

mens rea
"Evil intent"–the possession of the requisite state of mind to commit a prohibited act.

Criminal Intent (Mens Rea)   To be found guilty of an intent crime, the accused must be found to have possessed the requisite state of mind (i.e., specific or general intent) when the act was performed. This is called **mens rea** (evil intent). **Specific intent** is found where the accused purposefully, intentionally, or with knowledge commits a prohibited act. **General intent** is found where there is a showing of recklessness or a lesser degree of mental culpability. Individual criminal statutes state whether the crime requires a showing of specific or general intent. Juries may infer an accused's intent from the facts and circumstances of the case.

Merely thinking about committing a crime is not a crime because no action has been taken. Thus, merely thinking about killing someone or evading taxes and not actually doing so is not a crime.

Concept Summary
Elements of an Intent Crime

Element	Description
Actus reus	Guilty act.
Mens rea	Evil intent.

non-intent crime
A crime that imposes criminal liability without a finding of *mens rea* (intent).

The magnitude of a crime is proportionate to the magnitude of the injustice which prompts it. Hence, the smallest crimes may be actually the greatest.

Aristotle
The Rhetoric, Book 1, Chapter XIV

Non-Intent Crimes

Most states provide for certain **non-intent crimes**. The crime of **involuntary manslaughter** is often imposed for reckless or grossly negligent conduct.

Criminal Acts as the Basis for Tort Actions

An injured party may bring a *civil tort action* against a wrongdoer who has caused the party injury during the commission of a criminal act. Civil lawsuits are separate from the government's criminal action against the wrongdoer. In a civil lawsuit, the plaintiff usually wants to recover monetary damages from the wrongdoer. In many cases, a person injured by a criminal act will not sue the criminal to recover civil damages. This is because the criminal is often **judgment proof**—that is, the criminal does not have the money to pay a civil judgment.

Concept Summary
Civil and Criminal Law Compared

Issue	Civil Law	Criminal Law
Party who brings the action	The plaintiff	The government
Trial by jury	Yes, except actions for equity	Yes
Burden of proof	Preponderance of the evidence	Beyond a reasonable doubt
Jury vote	Judgment for plaintiff requires specific jury vote (e.g., 9 of 12 jurors)	Conviction requires unanimous jury vote
Sanctions and penalties	Monetary damages and equitable remedies (e.g., injunction, specific performance)	Imprisonment, capital punishment, fine, probation

Criminal Procedure

The procedure for initiating and maintaining a criminal action is quite detailed. It includes both pretrial procedures and the actual trial.

Arrest

Before the police can **arrest** a person for the commission of a crime, they usually must obtain an **arrest warrant** based on a showing of probable cause. The police go before a judge and present the evidence they have for arresting the suspect. If the judge finds that there is probable cause to issue the warrant, she will do so. The police will then use the arrest warrant to arrest the suspect. **Probable cause** is defined as the substantial likelihood that a person either committed or is about to commit a crime.

If there is no time for the police to obtain a warrant, the police may still arrest the suspect without obtaining an arrest warrant. Warrantless arrests are judged by the probable cause standard.

arrest warrant

A document for a person's detainment, based upon a showing of probable cause that the person committed a crime.

Examples
The police can make a warrantless arrest if they arrive during the commission of a crime, when a person is fleeing from the scene of a crime, or when it is likely that evidence will be destroyed.

Example
In *Atwater v. Lago Vista, Texas,*[3] the U.S. Supreme Court held that a police officer may make a warrantless arrest pursuant to a minor criminal offense. Gail Atwater was driving her pickup truck in Lago Vista, Texas, with her three-year-old son and five-year-old daughter in the front seat. None of them were wearing seat belts. Bart Turek, a Lago Vista police officer, observed the seat belt violation and pulled Atwater over. A friend of Atwater's arrived at the scene and took charge of the children. Turek handcuffed Atwater, placed her in his squad car, and drove her to the police station. Atwater was booked, her mug shot was taken, and she was placed in a jail cell for about one hour, until she was released on $310 bond. Atwater ultimately pleaded no contest to the misdemeanor seat belt offenses and paid a $50 fine. Atwater sued the City of Lago Vista and the police officer for compensatory and punitive damages for allegedly violating her Fourth Amendment right to be free from unreasonable seizure. The U.S. Supreme Court ruled against Atwater, finding that the Fourth Amendment permits police officers to make a warrantless arrest pursuant to a minor criminal offense.

After a person is arrested, he or she is taken to the police station to be booked. **Booking** is the administrative procedure for recording an arrest, fingerprinting the suspect, taking a photograph of the suspect (often called a "mug shot"), and so on.

Bail Bond. *When a person is arrested, a bail amount is usually set by the court. If the arrested person posts bail, either by paying the bail amount or by paying a bail bond company to post the bail, he or she can be released from prison until the date of trial. Bail will not be set if the alleged crime is heinous (e.g., murder) or if the arrestee is a flight risk who might not later show up for trial.*

Bail Bond

When a person is arrested, a **bail** amount is usually set. If the arrested person "posts" bail, he can be released from prison until the date of his trial. The arrested person can post the bail himself or pay a bail bonds person to post the bond. Bail will not be set if the crime is substantial (e.g., murder) or if the arrestee is a flight risk who might not later show up for trial.

Most arrestees (or their relatives or friend) pay a professional bail bonds person who operates a bail bonds business to post the bond. Bail bonds persons usually require payment of 10% of the bail in order to post bond. If the bail is set at $100,000, then the amount for payment of the bail bond is $10,000. The bail bonds person keeps this $10,000 payment. The bail bonds person guarantees the court that he will pay the court $100,000 if the arrestee does not show up for trial. If this happens, the bail bonds person will attempt to obtain the amount of the bond from the arrestee. Bail bonds persons often require collateral (e.g., title to an automobile, second mortgage on a house) before they issue a bail bond.

Indictment or Information

An accused person must be formally charged with a crime before he or she can be brought to trial. This is usually done through the issuance of a **grand jury indictment** or a **magistrate's information statement**.

Evidence of serious crimes, such as murder, is usually presented to a **grand jury**. Most grand juries comprise between 6 and 24 citizens who are charged with evaluating the evidence presented by the government. Grand jurors sit for a fixed period of time, such as one year. If the grand jury determines that there is sufficient evidence to hold the accused for trial, it issues an **indictment**. Note that the grand jury does not determine guilt. If an indictment is issued, the accused will be held for later trial.

For lesser crimes (e.g., burglary, shoplifting), the accused will be brought before a **magistrate** (judge). A magistrate who finds that there is enough evidence to hold the accused for trial will issue **information** statement.

The case against the accused is dismissed if neither an indictment nor information statement is issued.

indictment
The charge of having committed a crime (usually a felony), based on the judgment of a grand jury.
information
The charge of having committed a crime (usually a misdemeanor), based on the judgment of a judge (magistrate).

Arraignment

If an indictment or information is issued, the accused is brought before a court for an **arraignment** proceeding, during which the accused is (1) informed of the charges against him and (2) asked to enter a **plea**. The accused may plead **guilty** or **not guilty**.

Nolo Contendere   A party may also enter a plea of *nolo contendere*, whereby the accused agrees to the imposition of a penalty but does not admit guilt. The government has the option of accepting a *nolo contendere* plea or requiring the defendant to plead guilty or not guilty. If the government agrees to accept the *nolo contendere* plea, the accused and the government usually enter into a plea bargain in which the accused agrees to the imposition of a penalty but does not admit guilt. A *nolo contendere* plea cannot be used as evidence of liability against the accused at a subsequent civil trial. Corporate defendants often enter this plea.

Plea Bargaining

Sometimes the accused and the government enter into a **plea bargaining agreement**. The government engages in plea bargaining to save costs, avoid the risks of a trial, and prevent further overcrowding of the prisons. This type of arrangement allows the accused to admit to a lesser crime than charged. In return, the government agrees to impose a lesser penalty or sentence than might have been obtained had the case gone to trial. Over 90 percent of criminal cases are settled and do not go to trial.

The Criminal Trial

At a criminal trial, all jurors must *unanimously* agree before the accused is found *guilty* of the crime charged. If even one juror disagrees (i.e., has reasonable doubt) about the guilt of the accused, the accused cannot be found guilty of the crime charged. If all the jurors agree that the accused did not commit the crime, the accused is found *not guilty* of the crime charged. After trial, the following rules apply:

- If the defendant is found guilty, he or she may appeal.
- If the defendant is found not guilty, the government cannot appeal.
- If the jury cannot come to a **unanimous decision** about the defendant's guilt one way or the other, the jury is considered a **hung jury**. The government may choose to retry the case before a new judge and jury.

Common Crimes

Many **common crimes** are committed against persons and property. Some of the most important common crimes against persons and property are discussed in the following paragraphs.

Murder

Murder is defined as the unlawful killing of a human being by another with aforethought of malice. In most states there are several degrees of murder—such as **first-degree murder**, **second-degree murder**, **third-degree murder**—depending on the cicumstances of the case.

Felony Murder Rule

Sometimes a murder is committed during the commission of another crime even though the perpetrator did not originally intend to committ murder. Most states hold the perpetrator liable for the crime of murder in addition to the other crime. This is called the **felony murder rule**. The intent to commit the murder is inferred from the intent to commit the other crime. Many states also hold accomplices liable under this doctrine.

In the following case, the court found that the accused had committed murder.

---

arraignment
A hearing during which the accused is brought before a court and is (1) informed of the charges against him or her and (2) asked to enter a plea.

plea bargain
An agreement in which the accused admits to a lesser crime than charged. In return, the government agrees to impose a lesser sentence than might have been obtained had the case gone to trial.

There can be no equal justice where the kind of trial a man gets depends on the amount of money he has.

Justice Black
Griffin v. Illinois (1956)

hung jury
A jury that cannot come to a unanimous decision about the defendant's guilt. In the case of a hung jury, the government may choose to retry the case.

State of Ohio v. Wilson

2004 Ohio 2838, Web 2004 Ohio App. Lexis 2503 (2004) Court of Appeals of Ohio

"In determining whether a verdict is against the manifest weight of the evidence, the appellate court acts as a 'thirteenth juror.'"

—Judge Sadler

Facts

Gregory O. Wilson, who had been arguing earlier in the day with his girlfriend, Melissa Spear, approached a parked car within which Ms. Spear was seated, and poured gasoline from a beer bottle over her head. When Ms. Spear exited the car, Wilson ignited her with his cigarette lighter, setting her body on fire. As Ms. Spear became engulfed in flames, and while bystanders tried to assist her, Wilson walked away and down the street as if nothing had happened.

Paramedics arrived at the scene. One paramedic described Ms. Spear's burns as the worst he had ever seen. A witness described her after the fire as "totally black, no hair, laying there with her skin melted off of her, the flesh looked like was melted. She was black, looked up at me saying 'help me.'"

Ms. Spear was transported from the scene to the hospital. When she arrived, she had third-degree burns on her face, neck, trunk, arms, hands, and thighs. She was put in a medically induced coma and placed on a respirator. She remained in a coma for 45 days, during which time she underwent 10 surgeries that excised her burn wounds and placed synthetic skin dressing or skin grafts onto her wound sites. Ms. Spear was transferred to a rehabilitation facility. Upon her release from the rehabilitation facility, she received continual treatment and medicine for pain, infection, and depression. Nine months after the incident occurred, and five days before her 30th birthday, Ms. Spear's seven-year-old son found her lying dead in her bed.

The state of Ohio brought criminal charges against Wilson. He was convicted by a jury of aggravated murder and was sentenced to prison for 30 years to life. Mr. Wilson appealed his conviction.

Issue

Was there sufficient causation between Wilson's act of setting Ms. Spear on fire and Ms. Spear's death nine months later to warrant a conviction for murder?

Language of the Court

Wilson argues that the evidence was insufficient to support his conviction for aggravated murder, and that the verdict on this charge was against the manifest weight of the evidence. He contends that the state failed to prove the element of causation beyond a reasonable doubt. Specifically, appellant argues that the nine-month lapse of time between his act of setting Ms. Spear on fire and her eventual death render the verdict of guilty beyond a reasonable doubt on the aggravated murder charge unsupported by the manifest weight and sufficiency of the evidence.

An appellate court's function when reviewing the sufficiency of the evidence to support a criminal conviction is to examine the evidence admitted at trial to determine whether such evidence, if believed, would convince the average mind of the defendant's guilt beyond a reasonable doubt. In determining whether a verdict is against the manifest weight of the evidence, the appellate court acts as a "thirteenth juror." Under this standard of review, the appellate court weighs the evidence in order to determine whether the trier of fact clearly lost its way and created such a manifest miscarriage of justice that the conviction must be reversed and a new trial ordered.

A causal connection between the criminal agency and the cause of death is an essential element in a conviction for murder. Thus, the state must produce evidence to support each link in the chain of causation between the defendant's criminal act and the eventual death of the victim.

Proximate causation is the strongest if the victim dies immediately or shortly after being injured by the defendant. However, a defendant is not relieved of culpability for the natural consequences of inflicting serious wounds on another merely because the victim later died of complications brought on by the injury. The passing of nine months between appellant's act of setting Ms. Spear on fire and her eventual death does not, alone, render appellant's conviction for aggravated murder reversible. The evidence sufficiently demonstrates that the physical maladies that brought about the death of Ms. Spear were the natural, probable and foreseeable results of appellant's conduct. In short, there was sufficient evidence presented upon which the jury could have rationally concluded that appellant's act of setting Melissa Spear ablaze was the direct and proximate cause of both of the physical conditions that the coroner determined precipitated her death.

Decision

The court of appeals affirmed the trial court's conviction of Wilson of the crime of the murder of Ms. Spear. The court of appeals remanded the case to the trial court to permit Wilson to make a statement on his behalf prior to sentencing.

Case Questions

Critical Legal Thinking What is murder? Is it easy to define?

Business Ethics Do you think Wilson's legal argument on appeal was justified? Why or why not?

Contemporary Business If you were a juror in this case, would you have voted for the death penalty? Do you think the death penaly should be used or abolished? Why or why not?

Robbery

In common law, **robbery** is defined as the taking of personal property from another person or business by the use of fear or force. Robbery with a deadly weapon is generally considered aggravated robbery (or armed robbery) and carries a harsher penalty.

> **robbery**
> The taking of personal property from another person by the use of fear or force.

Examples

If a person threatens another person with the use of a gun unless the victim gives her purse to that person, this is the crime of robbery. If a person pick pockets somebody's wallet, it is not robbery because there has been no use of force or fear. This is a theft.

Burglary

In common law, **burglary** is defined as "breaking and entering a dwelling at night" with the intent to commit a felony. Modern penal codes have broadened this definition to include daytime thefts from homes, offices, commercial, and other buildings. In addition, the "breaking in" element has been abandoned by most modern definitions of burglary. Thus, unauthorized entering of a building through an unlocked door is sufficient. Aggravated burglary (or armed burglary) carries stiffer penalties.

> **burglary**
> The taking of personal property from another's home, office, or commercial or other type of building.

Larceny

In common law, **larceny** is defined as the wrongful and fraudulent taking of another person's personal property that is not robbery or burglary. Most personal property—including tangible property, trade secrets, computer programs, and other business property—is subject to larceny. Neither the use of force nor the entry of a building is required.

> **larceny**
> The taking of another's personal property other than from his or her person or building.

Examples

Stealing of automobiles and car stereos, pick pocketing, and such are larcenies. Some states distinguish between grand larceny and petit larceny. This distinction depends on the value of the property taken.

Theft

Some states have dropped the distinction among the crimes of robbery, burglary, and larceny. Instead, these states group these crimes under the general crime of **theft**. Most of these states distinguish between grand theft and petit theft. The distinction depends on the value of the property taken.

Receiving Stolen Property

receiving stolen property
To (1) knowingly receive stolen property and (2) intend to deprive the rightful owner of that property.

It is a crime for a person to (1) knowingly **receive stolen property** and (2) intend to deprive the rightful owner of that property. Knowledge and intent can be inferred from the circumstances. The stolen property can be any tangible property (e.g., personal property, money, negotiable instruments, stock certificates).

Arson

arson
The willful or malicious burning of a building.

In common law, **arson** is defined as the malicious or willful burning of the dwelling of another person. Modern penal codes have expanded this definition to include the burning of all types of private, commercial, and public buildings.

Examples
An owner of a motel burns down the motel to collect fire insurance proceeds. The owner is guilty of the crime of arson. In this case, the insurance company does not have to pay the proceeds of any insurance policy on the burned property to the arsonist-owner. On the other hand, if a third party arsonist burned down the motel without the knowledge or assistance of the owner, than the owner is entitled to recover the proceeds of any fire insurance he had on the property.

White-Collar Crime

Certain types of crimes, often referred to as **white-collar crimes**, are prone to being committed by businesspersons. These crimes usually involve cunning and deceit rather than physical force. Many of the most important white-collar crimes are discussed in the paragraphs that follow.

Forgery

forgery
The fraudulent making or alteration of a written document that affects the legal liability of another person.

The crime of **forgery** occurs if a written document is fraudulently made or altered and that change affects the legal liability of another person. Counterfeiting, falsifying public records, and materially altering legal documents are examples of forgery.

Example
Signing another person's signature to a check or changing the amount of a check without the owner's permission is forgery.

Note that signing another person's signature without intent to defraud is not forgery.

Example
Forgery has not been committed if one spouse signs the other spouse's payroll check for deposit in a joint checking or savings account at the bank.

Embezzlement

embezzlement
The fraudulent conversion of property by a person to whom that property was entrusted.

Unknown in common law, the crime of **embezzlement** is not a statutory crime. Embezzlement is the fraudulent conversion of property by a person to whom that property was entrusted. Typically, embezzlement is committed by an employer's employees, agents, or representatives (e.g., accountants, lawyers, trust officers, treasurers). Embezzlers often try to cover their tracks by preparing false books, records, or entries.

The key element here is that the stolen property was *entrusted* to the embezzler. This differs from robbery, burglary, and larceny, where property is taken by someone not entrusted with the property.

Examples
A bank entrusted a teller to take deposits from its customers and deposit them into the customers' accounts at the bank. Instead, the bank teller absconds with money. This is embezzlement. A lawyer who steals money from a trust fund that has been entrusted to him to administer commits the crime of embezzlement.

Landmark Law

Foreign Corrupt Practices Act

It is well known that the payment of bribes is pervasive in conducting international business. To prevent U.S. companies from engaging in this type of conduct, the U.S. Congress enacted the **Foreign Corrupt Practices Act (FCPA)** of 1977.[4] The FCPA makes it illegal for U.S. companies, or their officers, directors, agents, or employees, to bribe a foreign official, a foreign political party official, or a candidate for foreign political office. A bribe is illegal only where it is meant to influence the awarding of new business or the retention of a continuing business activity.

The FCPA imposes criminal liability where a person pays an illegal bribe himself or herself or supplies a payment to a third party or an agent, knowing that it will be used as a bribe. A firm can be fined up to $2 million, and an individual can be fined up to $100,000 and imprisoned for up to five years for violations of the FCPA.

There are two defenses. One excuses a firm or person charged with bribery under the FCPA if the firm or person can show that the payment was lawful under the written laws of that country. The other allows a defendant to show that a payment was a reasonable and bona fide expenditure related to the furtherance or execution of a contract. This latter exemption is difficult to interpret.

Some people argue that U.S. companies are placed at a disadvantage in international markets where commercial bribery is commonplace and firms from other countries are not hindered by laws similar to the FCPA.

Bribery

Bribery is one of the most prevalent forms of white-collar crime. A bribe can be money, property, favors, or anything else of value. The crime of commercial bribery entails the payment of bribes to private persons and businesses. This type of bribe is often referred to as a **kickback**, or **payoff**. Intent is a necessary element of this crime. The offeror of a bribe commits the crime of bribery when the bribe is tendered. The offeree is guilty of the crime of bribery when he or she accepts the bribe. The offeror can be found liable for the crime of bribery even if the person to whom the bribe is offered rejects the bribe.

bribery
A crime in which one person gives another person money, property, favors, or anything else of value for a favor in return. A bribe is often referred to as a *payoff* or *kickback*.

Example

Harriet Landers is the purchasing agent for the ABC Corporation and is in charge of purchasing equipment to be used by the corporation. Neal Brown, the sales representative of a company that makes equipment that can be used by the ABC Corporation, offers to pay her a 10% kickback if she buys equipment from him. She accepts the bribe and orders the equipment. Both parties are guilty of bribery.

In common law, the crime of bribery is defined as the giving or receiving of anything of value in corrupt payment for an "official act" by a public official. Public officials include legislators, judges, jurors, witnesses at trial, administrative agency personnel, and other government officials. Modern penal codes also make it a crime to bribe public officials. For example, a developer who is constructing an apartment building cannot pay the building inspector to overlook a building code violation.

Extortion

The crime of **extortion** involves the obtaining of property from another, with his or her consent, induced by wrongful use of actual or threatened force, violence, or fear. Extortion occurs when a person threatens to expose something about another person unless that other person gives money or property. The truth or falsity of the information is immaterial. Extortion of private persons is commonly referred to as **blackmail**. Extortion of public officials is called **extortion under color of official right**.

extortion
A threat to expose something about another person unless that other person gives money or property. Often referred to as *blackmail*.

Criminal Fraud

Obtaining title to property through deception or trickery constitutes the crime of **false pretenses**. This crime is commonly referred to as **criminal fraud** or **deceit**.

Example

Bob Anderson, a stockbroker, promises Mary Greenberg, a prospective investor, that he will use any money she invests to purchase interests in oil wells. Based on this promise, Ms. Greenberg decides to make the investment. Mr. Anderson never intended to invest the money. Instead, he used the money for his personal needs. This is criminal fraud.

Mail Fraud, Wire Fraud, and Internet Fraud   Federal law prohibits the use of mails or wires (e.g., telegraphs, telephone, the Internet) to defraud another person. These crimes are called **mail fraud**[5] and **wire fraud**,[6] respectively. The government often prosecutes a suspect under these statutes if there is insufficient evidence to prove the real crime that the criminal was attempting to commit or did commit. The maximum penalty for mail, wire, and Internet fraud is 20 years in prison.

In the following case, the Court found wire fraud and mail fraud.

CASE 8.2
Internet Fraud

United States of America v. Deppe

509 F.3d 54, Web 2007 U.S. App. Lexis 28562 (2007)
United States Court of Appeals for the First Circuit

"The circus impresario, P.T. Barnum, is famously reputed to have said that 'there's a sucker born every minute.'"

—Judge Selya

Facts

Michael R. Deppe, 21 years old, offered Rolex watches for sale over the Internet in exchange for funds wire-transferred directly to his bank account. He engaged in 27 transactions and snared approximately $115,000 in payments. But there was just one hitch: Deppe did not send a single customer a watch. Instead, he sent them packages that contained crumpled newspaper. Two weeks before a Super Bowl championship professional football game, Deppe and another person offered to sell over the Internet nonexistent tickets to the Super Bowl. This scheme netted nearly $263,000 for tickets that Deppe and his business partner did not possess.

A federal grand jury indicted Deppe of wire fraud and mail fraud, which are federal criminal violations. Deppe pled guilty regarding his Rolex fraud. The Super Bowl ticket scheme went to trial in U.S. District Court. The jury convicted Deppe, and the District Court judge sentenced Deppe to 78 months in jail. The court also fined Deppe

$520,375. Deppe appealed his sentence, arguing that his sentence should have been reduced because he accepted responsibility for his crimes.

Issue

Did the District Court err in not reducing Deppe's jail sentence?

Language of the Court

The circus impresario, P.T. Barnum, is famously reputed to have said that "there's a sucker born every minute." That droll commentary on the human condition, whether or not fairly attributed to Barnum, appears to be as insightful in cyber-commerce as in face-to-face business transactions. This conclusion is borne out by the case at hand, which involves an Internet fraud. In the appeal proper, we are asked to consider allegations of sentencing error. The overarching themes are those of chicanery and greed.

When a defendant proceeds to trial and puts the government to its proof, a credit for acceptance of responsibility normally will not be available. The district court concluded: "The defendant did not truthfully admit the conduct of the offensive conviction and did not truthfully admit and has falsely denied other relevant conduct." The court also spoke about the appellant's failure to accept full responsibility, the need for deterrence, and the unfortunate hallmarks of the appellant's crimes (cynicism, brazenness, greed, and deliberateness). The short of it is that the sentencing court provided a logical explanation for the 78-month sentence and—given the nature of the crimes committed and the characteristics of the criminal— that sentence represents a sensible punishment.

Decision

The U.S. Court of Appeals held that defendant Deppe did not deserve a sentence reduction. The Court of Appeals upheld the District Court's sentencing of Deppe to 78 months in prison.

Case Questions

Critical Legal Thinking   What is wire fraud? Explain. What is mail fraud? Explain.

Business Ethics   Did Deppe act ethically in using the Internet to perpetrate his frauds?

Contemporary Business   Does the Internet make it easier for crooks to commit fraud? Explain.

Money Laundering

When criminals make money from illegal activities, they are often faced with the problem of having large sums of money and no record of how this money was earned. This could easily tip the government off to their illegal activities. In order to "wash" the money and make it look as though it was earned legitimately, many criminals purchase legitimate businesses and run the money through those businesses to "clean" it before they receive the money. The legitimate business has "cooked" books, showing faked expenditures and receipts, in which the illegal money is buried. Restaurants, motels, and other cash businesses make excellent money laundries.

To address the problem of **money laundering**, the federal government enacted the **Money Laundering Control Act**.[7] This act makes it a crime to:

- Knowingly engage in a *monetary transaction* through a financial institution involving property from an unlawful activity worth more than $10,000.

Examples
Examples of monetary transactions through a financial institution are making deposits, making withdrawals, conducting transactions between accounts, or obtaining monetary instruments such as cashiers' checks, money orders, and travelers' checks from a bank or other financial institution for more than $10,000.

- Knowingly engage in a *financial transaction* involving the proceeds of an unlawful activity.

Examples
Examples of financial transactions involving the proceeds of an illegal activity include buying real estate, automobiles, personal property, intangible assets, or anything else of value with money obtained from illegal activities.

Thus, money laundering itself is now a federal crime. The money that is washed could have been made from illegal gambling operations, drug dealing, fraud, and other crimes, including white-collar crimes. Persons convicted of money laundering can be fined up to $500,000 or twice the value of the property involved, whichever is greater, and sentenced to up to 20 years in federal prison. In addition, violation of the act subjects any property involved in or traceable to the offense to forfeiture to the government.

Criminal Conspiracy

A **criminal conspiracy** occurs when two or more persons enter into an *agreement* to commit a crime. To be liable for a criminal conspiracy, a person must commit an *overt act* to

Money Laundering Control Act
A federal statute that makes it a crime to (1) knowingly engage in a *money transaction* through a financial institution involving property from an unlawful activity worth more than $10,000 and (2) knowingly engage in a *financial transaction* involving the proceeds of an unlawful activity.

criminal conspiracy
A crime in which two or more persons enter into an agreement to commit a crime and an overt act is taken to further the crime.

Ethics Spotlight

Identity Theft

The advent of the computer and the Internet has made one type of crime—identity theft—easier to commit. Identity theft was around long before the computer was invented, but the computer and the Internet have made it much easier for criminals to obtain the information they need to commit identity theft. In **Identity theft**—or **ID theft**—one person steals information about another person to pose as that person and take the innocent person's money or property or to purchase goods and services using the victim's credit information.

To commit ID theft, thieves must first obtain certain information about you. This could be your name, Social Security number, credit card numbers, bank account information, and other personal information. The **Federal Trade Commission (FTC)**, the federal administrative agency primarily charged with handling ID theft matters, lists the following methods thieves use to obtain your personal information:

- **Dumpster diving.** Thieves rummage through trash, looking for bills or other paper with your personal information on it.
- **Skimming.** Thieves steal credit and debit card numbers by using a special storage device when processing your card.
- **Phishing.** Thieves pretend to be financial institutions or companies and send spam or pop-up messages to you online to get you to reveal your personal information.
- **Changing your address.** Thieves divert your billing statements to another location by completing a change-of-address form.
- **Old-fashioned stealing.** Thieves steal wallets and purses; mail, including bank and credit card statements; preapproved credit offers; and new checks or tax information. They steal personnel records or bribe employees who have access to such records.
- **Pretexting.** Thieves use false pretenses to obtain your personal information from financial institutions, telephone companies, and other sources.

Credit card fraud is one of the crimes most commonly committed by identity thieves. A thief may open new credit card accounts in your name and purchase goods and services with these credit cards. Or the thief may change the billing address on your existing credit cards so that you no longer receive bills, and the thief then runs up charges on your account. Because your bills are now sent to a different address, it may be some time before you realize there's a problem. When the thief uses the cards and doesn't pay the bills, the delinquent accounts appear on your credit report.

A victim of identity theft often does not find out about the ID theft until a debt collection agency contacts the victim about overdue debts, when the victim applies for a car loan or a home mortgage and it is discovered when the bank or creditor conducts a credit check, or when the victim receives something in the mail about an apartment he never rented, a house he did not buy, or a job he never had.

DETER·DETECT·DEFEND

If you are a victim of ID theft, you could lose your money or property to the thieves. It is often impossible to trace the identity of the thieves or to recover your money or property if the thief is found. In addition, ID theft often destroys your credit rating and makes it difficult to obtain credit in the future.

If you are a victim of ID theft, there are several things you should do. You should file an **identity theft report** with the police, cancel certain credit cards, change bank accounts, change security and stock accounts, notify the credit reporting agencies of the items on your credit report that are not yours and that have been created by ID thieves, and have an extended fraud alert placed on your credit report so that credit agencies will notify you of questionable activity. In some cases of ID theft, the victim may not suffer much loss and may not have to do much work to repair his or her credit rating after the ID theft. In other cases, the victim may suffer substantial financial loss and have to spend thousands of dollars and countless hours trying to straighten out his or her credit history and financial life.

Business Ethics

Have you ever been a victim of identity theft? Do you know anyone who has been a victim of ID theft?

further the crime. The crime itself does not have to be committed, however. The government usually brings criminal conspiracy charges if (1) the defendants have been thwarted in their efforts to commit the substantive crime or (2) there is insufficient evidence to prove the substantive crime.

Example

Two securities brokers agree over the telephone to commit a securities fraud. They obtain a list of potential victims and prepare false financial statements necessary for the fraud. Because they entered into an agreement to commit a crime and took an overt act, the brokers are guilty of the crime of criminal conspiracy, even if they never carry out the securities fraud.

Corporate Criminal Liability

A *corporation* is a fictitious legal person that is granted legal existence by the state after certain requirements are met. A corporation cannot act on its own behalf. Instead, it must act through *agents*, such as managers, representatives, and employees.

The question of whether a corporation can be held criminally liable has intrigued legal scholars for some time. Originally, under the common law, it was generally held that corporations lacked the criminal mind (*mens rea*) to be held criminally liable. Modern courts, however, impose **corporate criminal liability**. These courts have held that corporations are criminally liable for the acts of their managers, agents, and employees. In any event,

corporate criminal liability
Criminal liability of corporations for actions of their officers, employees, or agents.

Racketeer Influenced and Corrupt Organizations Act (RICO)
A federal act that provides for both criminal and civil penalties for racketeering.

Landmark Law

Racketeer Influenced and Corrupt Organizations Act (RICO)

There are some frauds so well conducted that it would be stupidity not to be deceived by them.

—C. C. Colton, *Lacon, Volume 1 (1820)*

Organized crime has a pervasive influence on many parts of the U.S. economy. In 1980, Congress enacted the Organized Crime Control Act. The **Racketeer Influenced and Corrupt Organizations Act (RICO)** is part of this act.[8] Originally, RICO was intended to apply only to organized crime. However, the broad language of the RICO statute has been used against non–organized crime defendants as well. RICO, which provides for both criminal and civil penalties, is one of the most important laws affecting business today.

Criminal Rico

RICO makes it a federal crime to acquire or maintain an interest in, use income from, or conduct or participate in the affairs of an enterprise through a pattern of racketeering activity. An *enterprise* is defined as a corporation, a partnership, a sole proprietorship, another business or organization, or the government.

Racketeering activity consists of a number of specifically enumerated federal and state crimes, including such activities as gambling, arson, robbery, counterfeiting, and dealing in narcotics. Business-related crimes, such as bribery, embezzlement, mail fraud, and wire fraud, are also consid-

ered racketeering. To prove a *pattern of racketeering*, at least two of these acts must be committed by the defendant within a 10-year period. Commission of the same crime twice within this 10-year period constitutes **criminal RICO** as well.

Individual defendants found criminally liable for RICO violations can be fined, imprisoned for up to 20 years, or both. In addition, RICO provides for the *forfeiture* of any property or business interests (even interests in a legitimate business) that were gained because of RICO violations. This provision allows the government to recover investments made with monies derived from racketeering activities. The government may also seek civil penalties for RICO violations. These include injunctions, orders of dissolution, reorganization of business, and divestiture of the defendant's interest in an enterprise.

Civil Rico

Persons injured by a RICO violation can bring a private **civil RICO** action against the violator to recover for injury to business or property. A successful plaintiff may recover *treble damages* (three times actual loss) plus attorneys' fees.

because corporations cannot be put in prison, they are usually sanctioned with fines, loss of a license or franchise, and the like.

Corporate directors, officers, and employees are individually liable for crimes that they personally commit, whether for personal benefit or on behalf of the corporation. In addition, under certain circumstances, a corporate manager can be held criminally liable for the criminal activities of his or her subordinates. To be held criminally liable, the manager must have failed to supervise the subordinates appropriately. This is an evolving area of the law.

Protection Against Unreasonable Search and Seizure

In many criminal cases, the government relies on information obtained from searches of individuals and businesses. The **Fourth Amendment** to the U.S. Constitution protects persons and corporations from overzealous investigative activities by the government. It protects the rights of the people from **unreasonable search and seizure** by the government. It permits people to be secure in their persons, houses, papers, and effects.

Reasonable search and seizure by the government is lawful. **Search warrants** based on probable cause are necessary in most cases. Such a warrant specifically states the place and scope of the authorized search. General searches beyond the specified area are forbidden. *Warrantless searches* are permitted only (1) incident to arrest, (2) where evidence is in "plain view," or (3) where it is likely that evidence will be destroyed. Warrantless searches are judged by the probable cause standard.

Exclusionary Rule

Evidence obtained from an unreasonable search and seizure is considered tainted evidence ("fruit of a tainted tree"). Under the **exclusionary rule**, such evidence can generally be prohibited from introduction at a trial or an administrative proceeding against the person searched. However, this evidence is freely admissible against other persons. The U.S. Supreme Court created a *good faith exception* to the exclusionary rule.[9] This exception allows evidence otherwise obtained illegally to be introduced as evidence against the accused if the police officers who conducted the unreasonable search reasonably believed that they were acting pursuant to a lawful search warrant.

Case 8.3, on the following page, examines the reach of the Fourth Amendment's protection against unreasonable search and seizure.

Searches of Business Premises

Generally, the government does not have the right to search business premises without a search warrant.[10] Certain hazardous and regulated industries—such as sellers of firearms and liquor, coal mines, and the like—are subject to warrantless searches if proper statutory procedures are met.

Privilege Against Self-Incrimination

The **Fifth Amendment** to the U.S. Constitution provides that no person "shall be compelled in any criminal case to be a witness against himself." Thus, a person cannot be compelled to give testimony against himself or herself, although nontestimonial evidence (e.g., fingerprints, body fluids) may be required. A person who asserts this right is described as having "taken the Fifth." This protection applies to federal cases and is extended to state and local criminal cases through the Due Process Clause of the Fourteenth Amendment.

The protection against **self-incrimination** applies only to natural persons who are accused of crimes. Therefore, artificial persons (such as corporations and partnerships) cannot raise this protection against incriminating testimony.[11] Thus, business records of corporations and partnerships are not generally protected from disclosure, even if they incriminate individuals who work for the business. However, certain "private papers" of businesspersons (e.g., personal diaries) are protected from disclosure.

---

unreasonable search and seizure

Any search and seizure by the government that violates the Fourth Amendment.

search warrant

A warrant issued by a court that authorizes the police to search a designated place for specified contraband, articles, items, or documents. A search warrant must be based on probable cause.

exclusionary rule

A rule that says evidence obtained from an unreasonable search and seizure can generally be prohibited from introduction at a trial or an administrative proceeding against the person searched.

The criminal is to go free because the constable has blundered.

Chief Judge Cardozo
People v. Defore (1926)

self-incrimination

A person being a witness against himself or herself. The Fifth Amendment prevents self-incrimination in any criminal case.

U.S. Supreme Court
Kyllo v. United States

533 U.S. 27, 121 S.Ct. 2038, 150 L.Ed.2d 94, Web 2001 U.S. Lexis 4487 (2001)
Supreme Court of the United States

"At the very core of the Fourth Amendment stands the right of a man to retreat into his own home and there be free from unreasonable government intrusion."

—Justice Scalia

Facts

Government agents suspected that marijuana was being grown in the home of Danny Kyllo, which was part of a triplex building in Florence, Oregon. Indoor marijuana growth typically requires high-intensity lamps. In order to determine whether an amount of heat was emanating from Kyllo's home consistent with the use of such lamps, federal agents used a thermal imager to scan the triplex. Thermal imagers detect infrared radiation and produce images of the radiation. The scan of Kyllo's home, which was performed from an automobile on the street, showed that the roof over the garage and a side wall of Kyllo's home were "hot." The agents used this scanning evidence to obtain a search warrant authorizing a search of Kyllo's home. During the search, the agents found an indoor growing operation involving more than 100 marijuana plants.

Kyllo was indicted for manufacturing marijuana, a violation of federal criminal law. Kyllo moved to suppress the imaging evidence and the evidence it led to, arguing that it was an unreasonable search that violated the Fourth Amendment to the U.S. Constitution. The U.S. District Court disagreed with Kyllo and let the evidence be introduced and considered at trial. Kyllo then entered a conditional guilty plea and appealed the trial court's failure to suppress the challenged evidence to the U.S. Court of Appeals. The U.S. Court of Appeals affirmed the trial court's decision to admit the evidence. Kyllo appealed to the U.S. Supreme Court.

Issue

Is the use of a thermal-imaging device aimed at a private home from a public street to detect relative amounts of heat within the home a "search" within the meaning of the Fourth Amendment?

Language of the U.S. Supreme Court

At the very core of the Fourth Amendment stands the right of a man to retreat into his own home and there be free from unreasonable government intrusion. With few *exceptions, the question whether a warrantless search of a home is reasonable and hence constitutional must be answered no. The present case involves officers on a public street engaged in more than naked-eye surveillance of a home. The question we confront today is what limits there are upon this power of technology to shrink the realm of guaranteed privacy. We think that obtaining by sense-enhancing technology any information regarding the interior of the home that could not otherwise have been obtained without physical intrusion into a constitutionally protected area. This assures preservation of that degree of privacy against government that existed when the Fourth Amendment was adopted. On the basis of this criterion, the information obtained by the thermal imager in this case was the product of a search.*

Decision

The U.S. Supreme Court held that the use of a thermal-imaging device aimed at a private home from a public street to detect relative amounts of heat within the home is a "search" within the meaning of the Fourth Amendment. The Supreme Court reversed the decision of the U.S. Court of Appeals and remanded the case for further proceedings.

Case Questions

Critical Legal Thinking What does the Fourth Amendment's prohibition against unreasonable search and seizure provide? Explain.

Business Ethics Did the police act ethically in obtaining the evidence in this case? Did Kyllo act ethically in trying to suppress the evidence?

Contemporary Business Is selling illegal drugs a big business in this country? How can the government catch entrepreneurs such as Kyllo?

Web Exercise Go to **www.dailybreeze.com/ci_9009312** and read the ruling regarding searches of computers at the borders of the United States.

Miranda rights

Rights that a suspect must be informed of before being interrogated, so that the suspect will not unwittingly give up his or her Fifth Amendment right.

Miranda Rights

Most people have not read and memorized the provisions of the U.S. Constitution. The U.S. Supreme Court recognized this fact when it decided the landmark case *Miranda v. Arizona* in 1966.[12] In that case, the Supreme Court held that the Fifth Amendment privilege against self-incrimination is not useful unless a criminal suspect has knowledge of this right. Therefore, the Supreme Court required that the following warning—colloquially called the *Miranda* rights—be read to a criminal suspect before he or she is interrogated by the police or other government officials:

Miranda Rights

- You have the right to remain silent.

- Anything you say can and will be used against you in a court of law.

- You have the right to speak to an attorney and to have an attorney present during any questioning.

- If you cannot afford a lawyer, one will be provided for you at government expense.

Many police departments read an accused a more detailed version of the *Miranda* rights (see below). This is designed to cover all issues that a detainee might encounter while in police custody. A detainee may be asked to sign a statement acknowledging that the *Miranda* rights have been read to him or her.

Miranda Rights

- You have the right to remain silent and refuse to answer questions. Do you understand?

- Anything you do say may be used against you in a court of law. Do you understand?

- You have the right to consult an attorney before speaking to the police and to have an attorney present during questioning now or in the future. Do you understand?

- If you cannot afford an attorney, one will be appointed for you before any questioning if you wish. Do you understand?

- If you decide to answer questions now without an attorney present, you will still have the right to stop answering at any time until you talk to an attorney. Do you understand?

- Knowing and understanding your rights as I have explained them to you, are you willing to answer my questions without an attorney present?

Any statements or confessions obtained from a suspect prior to being read his or her *Miranda* rights can be excluded from evidence at trial. In 2000, the U.S. Supreme Court upheld *Miranda* in *Dickerson v. United States*.[13] In that opinion, Chief Justice Rehnquist stated, "We do not think there is justification for overruling *Miranda*. *Miranda* has become embedded in routine police practice to the point where the warnings have become part of our national culture."

Attorney–Client Privilege and Other Privileges

attorney–client privilege

A rule that says a client can tell his or her lawyer anything about the case without fear that the attorney will be called as a witness against the client.

To obtain a proper defense, an accused person must be able to tell his attorney facts about his case without fear that the attorney will be called as a witness against him. The **attorney–client privilege** is protected by the Fifth Amendment. Either the client or the attorney can raise this privilege. For the privilege to apply, the information must be told to the attorney in his or her capacity as an attorney, and not as a friend or neighbor or such.

The Fifth Amendment has also recognized the following privileges under which an accused may keep the following individuals from being witnesses against him:

- **Psychiatrist/psychologist–patient privilege** (so that the accused may tell the truth in order to seek help for his condition)
- **Priest/rabbi/minister/imam–penitent privilege** (so that the accused may tell the truth in order to repent, obtain help, and seek forgiveness for his deed)
- **Spouse–spouse privilege** (so that the family will remain together)
- **Parent–child privilege** (so that the family will remain together)

A spouse or child who is injured by a spouse or parent (e.g., domestic abuse) may testify against the accused. In addition, if the accused discloses that he is planning to commit a crime in the future (e.g., murder), the accused's lawyer; psychiatrist or psychologist; or priest, rabbi, minister, or imam is required to report this to the police or other relevant authorities.

The U.S. Supreme Court has held that there is no accountant–client privilege under federal law.[14] Thus, an accountant could be called as a witness in cases involving federal securities laws, federal mail or wire fraud, or other federal crimes. Nevertheless, approximately 20 states have enacted special statutes that create an **accountant–client privilege**. An accountant cannot be called as a witness against a client in a court action in a state where these statutes are in effect. Federal courts do not recognize these laws, however.

Immunity from Prosecution

On occasion, the government may want to obtain information from a suspect who has asserted his or her Fifth Amendment privilege against self-incrimination. The government can often achieve this by offering the suspect **immunity from prosecution**. Immunity from prosecution means that the government agrees not to use against a person granted immunity any evidence given by that person. Once immunity is granted, the suspect loses the right to assert his or her Fifth Amendment privilege.

Grants of immunity are often given when the government wants a suspect to give information that will lead to the prosecution of other, more important, criminal suspects. Partial grants of immunity are also available. A suspect must agree to a partial grant of immunity in order for it to occur.

In serious cases, the government can place a witness in a government protective program whereby after the trial the witness and her family are permanently moved to an undisclosed location, given a new identity, and provided monetary assistance. Such a witness is also usually protected prior to trial.

immunity from prosecution
The government's agreement not to use against a person granted immunity any evidence given by that person.

Other Constitutional Protections

Besides those already discussed in this chapter, there are many other provisions in the U.S. Constitution and its amendments that guarantee and protect certain other rights in the criminal process. Several of these additional rights are described in the paragraphs that follow.

Fifth Amendment Protection Against Double Jeopardy

The **Double Jeopardy Clause** of the Fifth Amendment protects persons from being tried twice for the same crime.

Example
If a state tries a suspect for the crime of murder, and the suspect is found not guilty, the state cannot bring another trial against the accused for the same crime. This is so even if more evidence later surfaces that would lead to conviction. The government is given the opportunity to bring its case against an accused once and cannot keep retrying the same case.

However, if the same criminal act involves several different crimes, the accused may be tried for each of the crimes separately without violating the Double Jeopardy Clause. If the same act violates the laws of two or more jurisdictions, each jurisdiction may try the accused.

Double Jeopardy Clause
A clause of the Fifth Amendment that protects persons from being tried twice for the same crime.

Example

Suppose an accused kills two people during a robbery. The accused may be tried for two murders and the robbery.

Example

If an accused kidnaps a person in one state and brings the victim across a state border into another state, the act violates the laws of two states and the federal government. Thus, three jurisdictions can prosecute the accused without violating the Double Jeopardy Clause.

If an accused is tried once and the jury reaches a *hung jury*—that is, the verdict is not unanimous for either guilty or not guilty—the government can retry the case against the accused without violating the Double Jeopardy Clause.

Sixth Amendment Right to a Public Jury Trial

The **Sixth Amendment** guarantees certain rights to criminal defendants. These rights are (1) to be tried by an impartial jury of the state or district in which the alleged crime was committed, (2) to confront (cross-examine) the witnesses against the accused, (3) to have the assistance of a lawyer, and (4) to have a speedy trial.[15]

Eighth Amendment Protection Against Cruel and Unusual Punishment

The **Eighth Amendment** protects criminal defendants from **cruel and unusual punishment**. For example, it prohibits the torture of criminals. However, this clause does not prohibit capital punishment.[16] The U.S. Supreme Court has held that in capital punishment cases, death by lethal injection is not cruel and unusual punishment.[17]

Test Review Terms and Concepts

Accountant–client privilege
Actus reus
Arraignment
Arrest
Arrest warrant
Arson
Attorney–client privilege
Bail
Beyond a reasonable doubt
Booking
Bribery
Burglary
Civil RICO
Common Crimes
Corporate criminal liability
Credit card fraud
Crime
Criminal conspiracy
Criminal fraud (false pretenses or deceit)
Criminal laws
Criminal RICO
Cruel and unusual punishment
Defendant
Defense attorney

Double Jeopardy Clause
Eighth Amendment
Embezzlement
Exclusionary rule
Extortion (blackmail)
Extortion under color of official right
Federal Trade Commission (FTC)
Felony
Felony murder rule
Fifth Amendment
First-degree murder
Foreign Corrupt Practices Act (FCPA)
Forgery
Fourth Amendment
General intent
Grand jury
Grand jury indictment
Guilty
Hung jury
Identity theft (ID theft)
Identity theft report
Immunity from prosecution
Indictment
Information
Internet fraud

Involuntary manslaughter
Judgment proof
Kickback (payoff)
Larceny
Magistrate
Magistrate's information statement
Mail fraud
Mala in se
Mala prohibita
Mens rea
Miranda rights
Misdemeanor
Money laundering
Money Laundering Control Act
Nolo contendere
Non-intent crime
Not guilty
Parent–child privilege
Penal code
Plaintiff
Plea
Plea bargaining agreement
Priest/rabbi/minister/imam–penitent privilege
Probable cause

Prosecutor
Psychiatrist/psychologist–patient
   privilege
Public defender
Racketeer Influenced and Corrupt
   Organizations Act (RICO)
Reasonable search and seizure
Receiving stolen property

Regulatory statutes
Robbery
Search warrant
Second-degree murder
Self-incrimination
Specific intent
Sixth Amendment
Spouse–spouse privilege

Theft
Third-degree murder
Unanimous decision
Unreasonable search and seizure
Violation
White-collar crime
Wire fraud

Case Problems

8.1 Criminal Liability of Corporations: Representatives of hotels, restaurants, hotel and restaurant supply companies, and other businesses located in Portland, Oregon, organized an association to attract conventions to their city. Members were asked to make contributions equal to one percent of their sales to finance the association. To aid collections, hotel members, including Hilton Hotels Corporation, agreed to give preferential treatment to suppliers who paid their assessments and to curtail purchases from those who did not. This agreement violated federal antitrust laws. The United States sued the members of the association, including Hilton Hotels, for the crime of violating federal antitrust laws. Can a corporation be held criminally liable for the acts of its representatives? If so, what criminal penalties can be assessed against the corporation? *United States v. Hilton Hotels Corp.*, 467 F.2d 1000, **Web** 1972 U.S. App. Lexis 7414 (United States Court of Appeals for the Ninth Circuit)

8.2 Forgery: Evidence showed that there was a burglary in which a checkbook belonging to Mary J. Harris, doing business as The Report Department, and a check encoder machine were stolen. Two of the checks from that checkbook were cashed at the Citizens & Southern National Bank branch office in Riverdale, Georgia, by Joseph Leon Foster, who was accompanied by a woman identified as Angela Foxworth. The bank teller who cashed the checks testified that the same man and woman cashed the checks on two different occasions at her drive-up window at the bank and that on both occasions, they were in the same car. Each time the teller wrote the license tag number of the car on the back of the check. The teller testified that both times, the checks and the driver's license used to identify the woman were passed to her by the man driving and that the man received the money from her. What crime has been committed? *Foster v. State of Georgia*, 193 Ga. App. 368, 387 S.E.2d 637, **Web** 1989 Ga.App. Lexis 1456 (Court of Appeals of Georgia)

8.3 Extortion: The victim (Mr. X) went to the premises at 42 Taylor Terrace in New Milford, Connecticut, where his daughter and her husband lived. Lisa Percoco, who was Gregory Erhardt's girlfriend, was at the residence. Mr. X and Percoco were in the bedroom, partially dressed, engaging in sexual activity, when Erhardt entered the room and photographed them. He then informed Mr. X that unless he pro-

cured $5,000 and placed it in a mailbox at a designated address by 8 P.M. that night, Erhardt would show the photographs to Mr. X's wife. Mr. X proceeded to make telephone arrangements for the procurement and placement of the money according to Erhardt's instructions. If the money were paid, what crime would have been committed? *State of Connecticut v. Erhardt*, 17 Conn.App. 359, 553 A.2d 188, **Web** 1989 Conn. App. Lexis 21 (Appellate Court of Connecticut)

8.4 Criminal Fraud: Miriam Marlowe's husband purchased a life insurance policy on his own life, naming his wife as the beneficiary. Three years later, after Marlowe's husband died in a swimming accident, Marlowe received payment on the life insurance policy. Marlowe later met John Walton, a friend of a friend. He convinced her and her representative that he had a friend who worked for the State Department and had access to gold in Brazil and that the gold could be purchased in Brazil for $100 an ounce and sold in the United States for $300 an ounce. Walton convinced Miriam to invest $25,000. Instead of investing the money in gold in Brazil, Walton opened an account at Tracy Collins Bank in the name of Jeffrey McIntyre Roberts and deposited Miriam's money in the account. He later withdrew the money in cash. What crime is Walton guilty of? *State of Utah v. Roberts*, 711 P.2d 235, **Web** 1985 Utah Lexis 872 (Supreme Court of Utah)

8.5 Bribery: The city of Peoria, Illinois, received federal funds from the Department of Housing and Urban Development (HUD) to be used for housing rehabilitation assistance. The city of Peoria designated United Neighborhoods, Inc. (UNI), a corporation, to administer the funds. Arthur Dixon was UNI's executive director, and James Lee Hinton was its housing rehabilitation coordinator. In these capacities, they were responsible for contracting with suppliers and tradespeople to provide the necessary goods and services to rehabilitate the houses. Evidence showed that Dixon and Hinton used their positions to extract 10 percent payments back on all contracts they awarded. What crime have they committed? *Dixon and Hinton v. United States*, 465 U.S. 482, 104 S.Ct. 1172, 79 L.Ed.2d 458, **Web** 1984 U.S. Lexis 35 (Supreme Court of the United States)

8.6 Administrative Search: Lee Stuart Paulson owned a liquor license for My House, a bar in San Francisco. The

California Department of Alcoholic Beverage Control is the administrative agency that regulates bars in that state. The California Business and Professions Code, which the department administers, prohibits "any kind of illegal activity on licensed premises." An anonymous informer tipped the department that narcotics sales were occurring on the premises of My House and that the narcotics were kept in a safe behind the bar on the premises. A special department investigator entered the bar during its hours of operation, identified himself, and informed Paulson that he was conducting an inspection. The investigator, who did not have a search warrant, opened the safe without seeking Paulson's consent. Twenty-two bundles of cocaine, totaling 5.5 grams, were found in the safe. Paulson was arrested. At his criminal trial, Paulson challenged the lawfulness of the search. Was the warrantless search of the safe a lawful search? *People v. Paulson*, 216 Cal.App.3d 1480, 265 Cal.Rptr. 579, **Web** 1990 Cal.App. Lexis 10 (Court of Appeal of California)

8.7 Search Warrant: The Center Art Galleries–Hawaii sells artwork. Approximately 20 percent of its business involves art by Salvador Dalí. The federal government, which suspected the center of fraudulently selling forged Dalí artwork, obtained identical search warrants for six locations controlled by the center. The warrants commanded the executing officer to seize items that were "evidence of violations of federal criminal law." The warrants did not describe the specific crimes suspected and did not stipulate that only items pertaining to the sale of Dalí's work could be seized. There was no evidence of any criminal activity unrelated to that artist. Are these search warrants valid? *Center Art Galleries–Hawaii, Inc. v. United States*, 875 F.2d 747, **Web** 1989 U.S. App. Lexis 6983 (United States Court of Appeals for the Ninth Circuit)

8.8 Privilege Against Self-Incrimination: John Doe is the owner of several sole proprietorship businesses. During the course of an investigation of corruption in awarding county and municipal contracts, a federal grand jury served several subpoenas on John Doe, demanding the production of certain business records. The subpoenas demanded the production of the following records: (1) general ledgers and journals, (2) invoices, (3) bank statements and canceled checks, (4) financial statements, (5) telephone company records, (6) safe deposit box records, and (7) copies of tax returns. John Doe filed a motion in federal court, seeking to quash the subpoenas, alleging that producing these business records would violate his Fifth Amendment privilege of not testifying against himself. Must John Doe disclose the records? *United States v. John Doe*, 465 U.S. 605, 104 S.Ct. 1237, 79 L.Ed.2d 552, **Web** 1984 U.S. Lexis 169 (Supreme Court of the United States)

Business Ethics Cases

8.9 Business Ethics: Leo Shaw, an attorney, entered into a partnership agreement with three other persons to build and operate an office building. From the outset, it was agreed that Shaw's role was to manage the operation of the building. Management of the property was Shaw's contribution to the partnership; the other three partners contributed the necessary capital. Ten years later, the other partners discovered that the loan on the building was in default and that foreclosure proceedings were imminent. Upon investigation, they discovered that Shaw had taken approximately $80,000 from the partnership's checking account. After heated discussions, Shaw repaid $13,000. When no further payment was forthcoming, a partner filed a civil suit against Shaw and notified the police. The state filed a criminal complaint against Shaw. Subsequently, Shaw repaid the remaining funds as part of a civil settlement. At his criminal trial, Shaw argued that the repayment of the money was a defense to the crime of embezzlement. Did Shaw act ethically in this case? Would your answer be different if Shaw had really only "borrowed" the money and had intended to return it? *People v. Shaw*, 10 Cal.App. 4th 969, 12 Cal.Rptr.2d 665, **Web** 1992 Cal.App. Lexis 1256 (Court of Appeal of California)

8.10 Business Ethics: Ronald V. Cloud purchased the Cal-Neva Lodge, a hotel and casino complex located in the Lake Tahoe area near the California–Nevada border, for $10 million. Cloud was a sophisticated 68-year-old entrepreneur who was experienced in buying and selling real estate and had real estate holdings valued at more than $65 million. He also had experience in banking and finance, having been the founder and chairman of Continental National Bank of Fresno. After two years of mounting operation losses, Cloud closed the Cal-Neva Lodge and actively began seeking a new buyer. Cloud met with Jon Perroton and orally agreed to transfer the lodge to Perroton for approximately $17 million. Perroton met with an executive of Hibernia Bank (Hibernia) to discuss a possible loan to finance the purchase of the lodge. Perroton made multiple false representations and presented false documents to obtain a $20 million loan from Hibernia. In particular, Perroton misrepresented the sale price for the lodge ($27.5 million) and stated that $7.5 million had already been paid to Cloud. An escrow account was opened with Transamerica Title Company (Transamerica).

Cloud and his attorney and Perroton met at Transamerica to sign mutual escrow instructions. Cloud reviewed the instructions and noticed that the sale price and down payment figures were incorrectly stated at $27.5 million and $7.5 million, respectively, and that the Hibernia loan was for $20 million, almost $3 million above what he knew to be the true sale price. Cloud signed the escrow instructions. Later, Cloud signed a settlement statement containing the same false figures and signed a grant deed to the property. The sale closed on January 23, 1985, with Hibernia making the $20 million loan to Perroton. Subsequently, when the loan went into default, Continental Insurance Company (Continental) paid Hibernia its loss of $7.5 million on the bank's blanket bond insurance policy. The United States sued Cloud for aiding and abetting a bank fraud in violation of federal law (18 U.S.C. Sections 2 and 1344). The jury convicted Cloud of the crime and ordered him to make restitution of $7.5 million to Continental. Cloud appealed. Did cloud act ethically in this case? Explain. Is Cloud guilty of aiding and abetting a bank fraud? *United States v. Cloud*, 872 F.2d 846, **Web** 1989 U.S. App. Lexis 4534 (United States Court of Appeals for the Ninth Circuit)

Endnotes

1. Title 18 of the U.S. Code contains the federal criminal code.
2. Sentencing Reform Act of 1984, 18 U.S.C. Section 3551 et seq.
3. 532 U.S. 318, 121 S.Ct. 1536, 149 L.Ed.2d 549, Web 2001 U.S. Lexis 3366 (Supreme Court of the United States, 2001).
4. 15 U.S.C. Section 78m.
5. 18 U.S.C. Section 1341.
6. 18 U.S.C. Section 1343.
7. 18 U.S.C. Section 1957.
8. 18 U.S.C. Sections 1961–1968.
9. *United States v. Leon*, 468 U.S. 897, 104 S.Ct. 3405, 82 L.Ed.2d 677, Web 1984 U.S. Lexis 153 (Supreme Court of the United States).
10. *Marshall v. Barlow's Inc.*, 436 U.S. 307, 98 S.Ct. 1816, 56 L.Ed.2d 305, Web 1978 U.S. Lexis 26 (Supreme Court of the United States).
11. *Bellis v. United States*, 417 U.S. 85, 94 S.Ct. 2.179, 40 L.Ed.2d 678, Web 1974 U.S. Lexis 58 (Supreme Court of the United States)
12. 384 U.S. 436, 86 S.Ct. 1602, 16 L.Ed.2d 694, Web 1966 U.S. Lexis 2817 (Supreme Court of the United States).
13. 530 U.S. 428, 120 S.Ct. 2326, 147 L.Ed.2d 405, Web 2000 U.S. Lexis 4305 (Supreme Court of the United States).
14. 409 U.S. 322, 93 S.Ct. 611, 34 L.Ed.2d 548, Web 1973 U.S. Lexis 23 (Supreme Court of the United States).
15. The Speedy Trial Act requires that a criminal defendant be brought to trial within 70 days after indictment [18 U.S.C. Section 316(c) (1)]. Continuances may be granted by the court to serve the "ends of justice."
16. *Baldwin v. Alabama*, 472 U.S. 372, 105 S.Ct. 2727, 86 L.Ed.2d 300, Web 1985 U.S. Lexis 106 (Supreme Court of the United States).
17. *Baze v. Rees*, 128 S.Ct. 1520, 170 L.Ed.2d 420, Web 2008 U.S. Lexis 3476 (Supreme Court of the United States, 2008).

Syllabus

NOTE: Where it is feasible, a syllabus (headnote) will be released, as is being done in connection with this case, at the time the opinion is issued. The syllabus constitutes no part of the opinion of the Court but has been prepared by the Reporter of Decisions for the convenience of the reader. See *United States* v. *Detroit Timber & Lumber Co.*, 200 U.S. 321, 337.

SUPREME COURT OF THE UNITED STATES

Syllabus

BRENDLIN *v.* CALIFORNIA

CERTIORARI TO THE SUPREME COURT OF CALIFORNIA

No. 06–8120. Argued April 23, 2007—Decided June 18, 2007

After officers stopped a car to check its registration without reason to believe it was being operated unlawfully, one of them recognized petitioner Brendlin, a passenger in the car. Upon verifying that Brendlin was a parole violator, the officers formally arrested him and searched him, the driver, and the car, finding, among other things, methamphetamine paraphernalia. Charged with possession and manufacture of that substance, Brendlin moved to suppress the evidence obtained in searching his person and the car, arguing that the officers lacked probable cause or reasonable suspicion to make the traffic stop, which was an unconstitutional seizure of his person. The trial court denied the motion, but the California Court of Appeal reversed, holding that Brendlin was seized by the traffic stop, which was unlawful. Reversing, the State Supreme Court held that suppression was unwarranted because a passenger is not seized as a constitutional matter absent additional circumstances that would indicate to a reasonable person that he was the subject of the officer's investigation or show of authority.

Held: When police make a traffic stop, a passenger in the car, like the driver, is seized for Fourth Amendment purposes and so may challenge the stop's constitutionality. Pp. 4–13.

   (a) A person is seized and thus entitled to challenge the government's action when officers, by physical force or a show of authority, terminate or restrain the person's freedom of movement through means intentionally applied. *Florida* v. *Bostick*, 501 U.S. 429, 434; *Brower* v. *County of Inyo*, 489 U.S. 598, 597. There is no seizure without that person's actual submission. See, *e.g.*, *California* v. *Hodari D.*, 499 U.S. 621, 626, n. 2. When police actions do not show an unambiguous intent to restrain or when an individual's submission takes the form of passive acquiescence, the test for telling when a seizure occurs is whether, in light of all the surrounding circumstances, a reasonable person would have believed he was not free to leave. *E.g., United States* v. *Mendenhall*, 446 U.S. 544, 554 (principal opinion). But when a person "has no desire to leave" for reasons unrelated to the police presence, the "coercive effect of the encounter" can be measured better by asking whether "a reasonable person would feel free to decline the officers' requests or otherwise terminate the encounter." *Bostick, supra*, at 435–436. Pp. 4–6.

   (b) Brendlin was seized because no reasonable person in his position when the car was stopped would have believed himself free to "terminate the encounter" between the police and himself. *Bostick, supra*, at 436. Any reasonable passenger would have understood the officers to be exercising control to the point that no one in the car was free to depart without police permission. A traffic stop necessarily curtails a passenger's travel just as much as it halts the driver, diverting both from the stream of traffic to the side of the road, and the police activity that normally amounts to intrusion on "privacy and personal security" does not normally (and did not here) distinguish between passenger and driver. *United States* v. *Martinez-Fuerte*, 428 U.S. 543, 554. An officer who orders a particular car to pull over acts with an implicit claim of right based on fault of some sort, and a sensible person would not expect the officer to allow people to come and go freely from the physical focal point of an investigation into faulty behavior or wrongdoing. If the likely wrongdoing is not the driving, the passenger will reasonably feel subject to suspicion owing to close association; but

2   BRENDLIN *v.* CALIFORNIA

Syllabus

even when the wrongdoing is only bad driving, the passenger will expect to be subject to some scrutiny, and his attempt to leave would be so obviously likely to prompt an objection from the officer that no passenger would feel free to leave in the first place. It is also reasonable for passengers to expect that an officer at the scene of a crime, arrest, or investigation will not let people move around in ways that could jeopardize his safety. See, *e.g., Maryland* v. *Wilson,* 519 U.S. 408, 414–415. The Court's conclusion comports with the views of all nine Federal Courts of Appeals, and nearly every state court, to have ruled on the question. Pp. 6–9.

(c) The State Supreme Court's contrary conclusion reflects three premises with which this Court respectfully disagrees. First, the view that the police only intended to investigate the car's driver and did not direct a show of authority toward Brendlin impermissibly shifts the issue from the intent of the police as objectively manifested to the motive of the police for taking the intentional action to stop the car. Applying the objective *Mendenhall* test resolves any ambiguity by showing that a reasonable passenger would understand that he was subject to the police display of authority. Second, the state court's assumption that Brendlin, as the passenger, had no ability to submit to the police show of authority because only the driver was in control of the moving car is unavailing. Brendlin had no effective way to signal submission while the car was moving, but once it came to a stop he could, and apparently did, submit by staying inside. Third, there is no basis for the state court's fear that adopting the rule this Court applies would encompass even those motorists whose movement has been impeded due to the traffic stop of another car. An occupant of a car who knows he is stuck in traffic because another car has been pulled over by police would not perceive the show of authority as directed at him or his car. Pp. 9–13.

(d) The state courts are left to consider in the first instance whether suppression turns on any other issue. P. 13.

38 Cal. 4th 1107, 136 P. 3d 845, vacated and remanded.

SOUTER, J., delivered the opinion for a unanimous Court.

Opinion of the Court

NOTICE: This opinion is subject to formal revision before publication in the preliminary print of the United States Reports. Readers are requested to notify the Reporter of Decisions, Supreme Court of the United States, Washington, D.C. 20543, of any typographical or other formal errors, in order that corrections may be made before the preliminary print goes to press.

SUPREME COURT OF THE UNITED STATES

___

No. 06–8120

___

BRUCE EDWARD BRENDLIN, PETITIONER v. CALIFORNIA

ON WRIT OF CERTIORARI TO THE SUPREME COURT OF CALIFORNIA

[June 18, 2007]

JUSTICE SOUTER delivered the opinion of the Court.

When a police officer makes a traffic stop, the driver of the car is seized within the meaning of the Fourth Amendment. The question in this case is whether the same is true of a passenger. We hold that a passenger is seized as well and so may challenge the constitutionality of the stop.

I

Early in the morning of November 27, 2001, Deputy Sheriff Robert Brokenbrough and his partner saw a parked Buick with expired registration tags. In his ensuing conversation with the police dispatcher, Brokenbrough learned that an application for renewal of registration was being processed. The officers saw the car again on the road, and this time Brokenbrough noticed its display of a temporary operating permit with the number "11," indicating it was legal to drive the car through November. App. 115. The officers decided to pull the Buick over to verify that the permit matched the vehicle, even though, as Brokenbrough admitted later, there was nothing unusual about the permit or the way it was affixed. Brokenbrough asked the driver, Karen Simeroth, for her license and saw a passenger in the front seat, petitioner Bruce Brendlin, whom he recognized as "one of the Brendlin brothers." *Id.*, at 65. He recalled that either Scott or Bruce Brendlin had dropped out of parole supervision and asked Brendlin to identify himself.[1] Brokenbrough returned to his cruiser, called for backup, and verified that Brendlin was a parole violator with an outstanding no-bail warrant for his arrest. While he was in the patrol car, Brokenbrough saw Brendlin briefly open and then close the passenger door of the Buick. Once reinforcements arrived, Brokenbrough went to the passenger side of the Buick, ordered him out of the car at gunpoint, and declared him under arrest. When the police searched Brendlin incident to arrest, they found an orange syringe cap on his person. A patdown search of Simeroth revealed syringes and a plastic bag of a green leafy substance, and she was also formally arrested. Officers then searched the car and found tubing, a scale, and other things used to produce methamphetamine.

Brendlin was charged with possession and manufacture of methamphetamine, and he moved to suppress the evidence obtained in the searches of his person and the car as fruits of an unconstitutional seizure, arguing that the officers lacked probable cause or reasonable suspicion to make the traffic stop. He did not assert that his Fourth Amendment rights were violated by the search of Simeroth's vehicle, cf. *Rakas v. Illinois*, 439 U.S. 128 (1978), but claimed only that the traffic stop was an unlawful seizure of his person. The trial court denied the suppression motion after finding that the stop was lawful and Brendlin was not seized until Brokenbrough ordered him out of the car and formally

___

[1] The parties dispute the accuracy of the transcript of the suppression hearing and disagree as to whether Brendlin gave his name or the false name "Bruce Brown." App. 115.

Opinion of the Court

arrested him. Brendlin pleaded guilty, subject to appeal on the suppression issue, and was sentenced to four years in prison.

The California Court of Appeal reversed the denial of the suppression motion, holding that Brendlin was seized by the traffic stop, which they held unlawful. 8 Cal. Rptr. 3d 882 (2004) (officially depublished). By a narrow majority, the Supreme Court of California reversed. The State Supreme Court noted California's concession that the officers had no reasonable basis to suspect unlawful operation of the car, 38 Cal. 4th 1107, 1114, 136 P. 3d 845, 848 (2006),[2] but still held suppression unwarranted because a passenger "is not seized as a constitutional matter in the absence of additional circumstances that would indicate to a reasonable person that he or she was the subject of the peace officer's investigation or show of authority," *id.*, at 1111, 136 P. 3d, at 846. The court reasoned that Brendlin was not seized by the traffic stop because Simeroth was its exclusive target, *id.*, at 1118, 136 P. 3d, at 851, that a passenger cannot submit to an officer's show of authority while the driver controls the car, *id.*, at 1118–1119, 135 P. 3d, at 851–852, and that once a car has been pulled off the road, a passenger "would feel free to depart or otherwise to conduct his or her affairs as though the police were not present," *id.*, at 1119, 136 P. 3d, at 852. In dissent, Justice Corrigan said that a traffic stop entails the seizure of a passenger even when the driver is the sole target of police investigation because a passenger is detained for the purpose of ensuring an officer's safety and would not feel free to leave the car without the officer's permission. *Id.*, at 1125,136 P. 3d, at 856.

We granted certiorari to decide whether a traffic stop subjects a passenger, as well as the driver, to Fourth Amendment seizure, 549 U.S. __ (2007). We now vacate.

II

A

A person is seized by the police and thus entitled to challenge the government's action under the Fourth Amendment when the officer, " 'by means of physical force or show of authority,' " terminates or restrains his freedom of movement, *Florida* v. *Bostick*, 501 U.S. 429, 434 (1991) (quoting *Terry* v. *Ohio*, 392 U.S. 1, 19, n. 16 (1968)), "*through means intentionally applied,*" *Brower* v. *County of Inyo*, 489 U.S. 593, 597 (1989) (emphasis in original). Thus, an "unintended person . . . [may be] the object of the detention," so long as the detention is "willful" and not merely the consequence of "an unknowing act." *Id.*, at 596; cf. *County of Sacramento* v. *Lewis*, 523 U.S. 833, 844 (1998) (no seizure where a police officer accidentally struck and killed a motorcycle passenger during a high-speed pursuit). A police officer may make a seizure by a show of authority and without the use of physical force, but there is no seizure without actual submission; otherwise, there is at most an attempted seizure, so far as the Fourth Amendment is concerned. See *California* v. *Hodari D.*, 499 U.S. 621, 626, n. 2 (1991); *Lewis, supra,* at 844, 845, n. 7.

When the actions of the police do not show an unambiguous intent to restrain or when an individual's submission to a show of governmental authority takes the form of passive acquiescence, there needs to be some test for telling when a seizure occurs in response to authority, and when it does not. The test was devised by Justice Stewart in *United States* v. *Mendenhall,* 446 U.S. 544 (1980), who wrote that a seizure occurs if "in view of all of the circumstances surrounding the incident, a reasonable person would have believed that he was not free to leave," *id.*, at 554 (principal opinion). Later on, the Court adopted Justice Stewart's touchstone, see, *e.g., Hodari D., supra,* at 627; *Michigan* v. *Chesternut*, 486 U.S. 567, 573 (1988); *INS* v. *Delgado*, 466 U.S. 210, 215 (1984), but added that when a person "has no desire to leave" for reasons unrelated to the police presence, the "coercive effect of the encounter" can be measured better by asking whether "a reasonable person would feel free to decline the officers' requests or otherwise terminate the encounter," *Bostick, supra,* at 435–436; see also *United States* v. *Drayton*, 536 U.S. 194, 202 (2002).

The law is settled that in Fourth Amendment terms a traffic stop entails a seizure of the driver "even though the purpose of the stop is limited and the resulting detention quite brief." *Delaware* v. *Prouse*, 440 U.S. 648, 653 (1979); see also *Whren* v. *United States*, 517 U.S. 806, 809–810 (1996). And although we have not, until today, squarely answered the question whether a passenger is also seized, we have said over and over in dicta that during a traffic stop an officer seizes everyone in the vehicle, not just the driver. See, *e.g., Prouse, supra,* at 653 ("[S]topping an automobile and detaining its occupants constitute a 'seizure' within the meaning of [the Fourth and Fourteenth] Amendments"); *Colorado* v. *Bannister*, 449 U.S. 1, 4, n. 3 (1980) (*per curiam*) ("There can be no question that the stopping of a vehicle and the detention of its occupants constitute a 'seizure' within the meaning of the Fourth Amendment"); *Berkemer* v. *McCarty*, 468 U.S. 420, 436–437 (1984) ("[W]e have long

---

[2] California conceded that the police officers lacked reasonable suspicion to justify the traffic stop because a " 'vehicle with an application for renewal of expired registration would be expected to have a temporary operating permit.' " 38 Cal. 4th, at 1114, 136 P. 3d, at 848 (quoting Brief for Respondent California in No. S123133 (Sup. Ct. Cal.), p. 24).

Opinion of the Court

acknowledged that stopping an automobile and detaining its occupants constitute a seizure" (internal quotation marks omitted)); *United States* v. *Hensley*, 469 U.S. 221, 226 (1985) ("[S]topping a car and detaining its occupants constitute a seizure"); *Whren, supra,* at 809–810 ("Temporary detention of individuals during the stop of an automobile by the police, even if only for a brief period and for a limited purpose, constitutes a 'seizure' of 'persons' within the meaning of [the Fourth Amendment]").

We have come closest to the question here in two cases dealing with unlawful seizure of a passenger, and neither time did we indicate any distinction between driver and passenger that would affect the Fourth Amendment analysis. *Delaware* v. *Prouse* considered grounds for stopping a car on the road and held that Prouse's suppression motion was properly granted. We spoke of the arresting officer's testimony that Prouse was in the back seat when the car was pulled over, see 440 U.S., at 650, n. 1, described Prouse as an occupant, not as the driver, and referred to the car's "occupants" as being seized, *id.,* at 653. Justification for stopping a car was the issue again in *Whren* v. *United States,* where we passed upon a Fourth Amendment challenge by two petitioners who moved to suppress drug evidence found during the course of a traffic stop. See 517 U.S., at 809. Both driver and passenger claimed to have been seized illegally when the police stopped the car; we agreed and held suppression unwarranted only because the stop rested on probable cause. *Id.,* at 809–810, 819.

B

The State concedes that the police had no adequate justification to pull the car over, see n. 2, *supra,* but argues that the passenger was not seized and thus cannot claim that the evidence was tainted by an unconstitutional stop. We resolve this question by asking whether a reasonable person in Brendlin's position when the car stopped would have believed himself free to "terminate the encounter" between the police and himself. *Bostick, supra,* at 436. We think that in these circumstances any reasonable passenger would have understood the police officers to be exercising control to the point that no one in the car was free to depart without police permission.

A traffic stop necessarily curtails the travel a passenger has chosen just as much as it halts the driver, diverting both from the stream of traffic to the side of the road, and the police activity that normally amounts to intrusion on "privacy and personal security" does not normally (and did not here) distinguish between passenger and driver. *United States* v. *Martinez-Fuerte,* 428 U.S. 543, 554 (1976). An officer who orders one particular car to pull over acts with an implicit claim of right based on fault of some sort, and a sensible person would not expect a police officer to allow people to come and go freely from the physical focal point of an investigation into faulty behavior or wrongdoing. If the likely wrongdoing is not the driving, the passenger will reasonably feel subject to suspicion owing to close association; but even when the wrongdoing is only bad driving, the passenger will expect to be subject to some scrutiny, and his attempt to leave the scene would be so obviously likely to prompt an objection from the officer that no passenger would feel free to leave in the first place. Cf. *Drayton, supra,* at 197–199, 203–204 (finding no seizure when police officers boarded a stationary bus and asked passengers for permission to search for drugs).[3]

It is also reasonable for passengers to expect that a police officer at the scene of a crime, arrest, or investigation will not let people move around in ways that could jeopardize his safety. In *Maryland* v. *Wilson,* 519 U.S. 408 (1997), we held that during a lawful traffic stop an officer may order a passenger out of the car as a precautionary measure, without reasonable suspicion that the passenger poses a safety risk. *Id.,* at 414–415; cf. *Pennsylvania* v. *Mimms,* 434 U.S. 106 (1977) (*per curiam*) (driver may be ordered out of the car as a matter of course). In fashioning this rule, we invoked our earlier statement that " '[t]he risk of harm to both the police and the occupants is minimized if the officers routinely exercise unquestioned command of the situation.' " *Wilson, supra,* at 414 (quoting *Michigan* v. *Summers,* 452 U.S. 692, 702–703 (1981)). What we have said in these opinions probably reflects a societal expectation of " 'unquestioned [police] command' " at odds with any notion that a passenger would feel free to leave, or to terminate the personal encounter any other way, without advance permission. *Wilson, supra,* at 414.[4]

---

[3] Of course, police may also stop a car solely to investigate a passenger's conduct. See, *e.g., United States* v. *Rodriguez-Diaz,* 161 F. Supp. 2d 627, 629, n. 1 (Md. 2001) (passenger's violation of local seatbelt law); *People* v. *Roth,* 85 P. 3d 571, 573 (Colo. App. 2003) (passenger's violation of littering ordinance). Accordingly, a passenger cannot assume, merely from the fact of a traffic stop, that the driver's conduct is the cause of the stop.

[4] Although the State Supreme Court inferred from Brendlin's decision to open and close the passenger door during the traffic stop that he was "awar[e] of the available options," 38 Cal. 4th 1107, 1120, 136 P. 3d 845, 852 (2006), this conduct could equally be taken to indicate that Brendlin felt compelled to remain inside the car. In any event, the test is not what Brendlin felt but what a reasonable passenger would have understood.

4   BRENDLIN *v.* CALIFORNIA

Opinion of the Court

Our conclusion comports with the views of all nine Federal Courts of Appeals, and nearly every state court, to have ruled on the question. See *United States* v. *Kimball*, 25 F. 3d 1, 5 (CA1 1994); *United States* v. *Mosley*, 454 F. 3d 249, 253 (CA3 2006); *United States* v. *Rusher*, 966 F. 2d 868, 874, n. 4 (CA4 1992); *United States* v. *Grant*, 349 F. 3d 192, 196 (CA5 2003); *United States* v. *Perez*, 440 F. 3d 363, 369 (CA6 2006); *United States* v. *Powell*, 929 F. 2d 1190, 1195 (CA7 1991); *United States* v. *Ameling*, 328 F. 3d 443, 446–447, n. 3 (CA8 2003); *United States* v. *Twilley*, 222 F. 3d 1092,1095 (CA9 2000); *United States* v. *Eylicio-Montoya*, 70 F. 3d 1158, 1163–1164 (CA10 1995); *State* v. *Bowers*, 334 Ark. 447, 451–452, 976 S.W. 2d 379, 381–882 (1998); *State* v. *Haworth*, 106 Idaho 405, 405–406, 679 P. 2d 1123, 1123–1124 (1984); *People* v. *Bunch*, 207 Ill. 2d 7, 13, 796 N.E. 2d 1024, 1029 (2003); *State* v. *Eis*, 348 N.W. 2d 224, 226 (Iowa 1984); *State* v. *Hodges*, 252 Kan. 989, 1002–1005, 851 P. 2d 352, 361–362 (1993); *State* v. *Carter*, 69 Ohio St. 3d 57, 63, 630 N.E. 2d 355, 360 (1994) (*per curiam*); *State* v. *Harris*, 206 Wis. 2d 243, 253–258, 557 N.W. 2d 245, 249–251 (1996). And the treatise writers share this prevailing judicial view that a passenger may bring a Fourth Amendment challenge to the legality of a traffic stop. See, *e.g.*, 6 W. LaFave, Search and Seizure §11.3(e), pp. 194, 195, and n. 277 (4th ed. 2004 and Supp. 2007) ("If either the stopping of the car, the length of the passenger's detention thereafter, or the passenger's removal from it are unreasonable in a Fourth Amendment sense, then surely the passenger has standing to object to those constitutional violations and to have suppressed any evidence found in the car which is their fruit" (footnote omitted)); 1 W. Ringel, Searches & Seizures, Arrests and Confessions §11:20, p. 11–98 (2d ed. 2007) ("[A] law enforcement officer's stop of an automobile results in a seizure of both the driver and the passenger").[5]

C

The contrary conclusion drawn by the Supreme Court of California, that seizure came only with formal arrest, reflects three premises as to which we respectfully disagree. First, the State Supreme Court reasoned that Brendlin was not seized by the stop because Deputy Sheriff Brokenbrough only intended to investigate Simeroth and did not direct a show of authority toward Brendlin. The court saw Brokenbrough's "flashing lights [as] directed at the driver," and pointed to the lack of record evidence that Brokenbrough "was even aware [Brendlin] was in the car prior to the vehicle stop." 38 Cal. 4th, at 1118, 136 P. 3d, at 851. But that view of the facts ignores the objective *Mendenhall* test of what a reasonable passenger would understand. To the extent that there is anything ambiguous in the show of force (was it fairly seen as directed only at the driver or at the car and its occupants?), the test resolves the ambiguity, and here it leads to the intuitive conclusion that all the occupants were subject to like control by the successful display of authority. The State Supreme Court's approach, on the contrary, shifts the issue from the intent of the police as objectively manifested to the motive of the police for taking the intentional action to stop the car, and we have repeatedly rejected attempts to introduce this kind of subjectivity into Fourth Amendment analysis. See, *e.g.*, *Whren*, 517 U.S., at 813 ("Subjective intentions play no role in ordinary, probable-cause Fourth Amendment analysis"); *Chesternut*, 486 U.S., at 575, n. 7 ("[T]he subjective intent of the officers is relevant to an assessment of the Fourth Amendment implications of police conduct only to the extent that that intent has been conveyed to the person confronted"); *Mendenhall*, 446 U.S., at 554, n. 6 (principal opinion) (disregarding a Government agent's subjective intent to detain Mendenhall); cf. *Rakas*, 439 U.S., at 132–135 (rejecting the "target theory" of Fourth Amendment standing, which would have allowed "any criminal defendant at whom a search was directed" to challenge the legality of the search (internal quotation marks omitted)).

California defends the State Supreme Court's ruling on this point by citing our cases holding that seizure requires a purposeful, deliberate act of detention. See Brief for Respondent 9–14. But *Chesternut, supra*, answers that argument. The intent that counts under the Fourth Amendment is the "intent [that] has been conveyed to the person confronted," *id.*, at 575, n. 7, and the criterion of willful restriction on freedom of movement is no invitation to look to subjective intent when determining who is seized. Our most recent cases are in accord on this point. In *Lewis*, 523 U.S. 833, we considered whether a seizure occurred when an officer accidentally ran over a passenger who had fallen off a motorcycle during a high-speed chase, and in holding

---

[5] Only two State Supreme Courts, other than California's, have stood against this tide of authority. See *People* v. *Jackson*, 39 P. 3d 1174, 1184–1186 (Colo. 2002) (en banc); *State* v. *Mendez*, 137 Wash. 2d 208, 222–223, 970 P. 2d 722, 729 (1999) (en banc).

Opinion of the Court

that no seizure took place, we stressed that the officer stopped Lewis's movement by accidentally crashing into him, not "through means intentionally applied." *Id.*, at 844 (emphasis deleted). We did not even consider, let alone emphasize, the possibility that the officer had meant to detain the driver only and not the passenger. Nor is *Brower*, 489 U.S. 593, to the contrary, where it was dispositive that "Brower was meant to be stopped by the physical obstacle of the roadblock—and that he was so stopped." *Id.*, at 599. California reads this language to suggest that for a specific occupant of the car to be seized he must be the motivating target of an officer's show of authority, see Brief for Respondent 12, as if the thrust of our observation were that Brower, and not someone else, was "meant to be stopped." But our point was not that Brower alone was the target but that officers detained him "through means intentionally applied"; if the car had had another occupant, it would have made sense to hold that he too had been seized when the car collided with the roadblock. Neither case, then, is at odds with our holding that the issue is whether a reasonable passenger would have perceived that the show of authority was at least partly directed at him, and that he was thus not free to ignore the police presence and go about his business.

Second, the Supreme Court of California assumed that Brendlin, "as the passenger, had no ability to submit to the deputy's show of authority" because only the driver was in control of the moving vehicle. 38 Cal. 4th, at 1118, 1119, 136 P. 3d, at 852. But what may amount to submission depends on what a person was doing before the show of authority: a fleeing man is not seized until he is physically overpowered, but one sitting in a chair may submit to authority by not getting up to run away. Here, Brendlin had no effective way to signal submission while the car was still moving on the roadway, but once it came to a stop he could, and apparently did, submit by staying inside.

Third, the State Supreme Court shied away from the rule we apply today for fear that it "would encompass even those motorists following the vehicle subject to the traffic stop who, by virtue of the original detention, are forced to slow down and perhaps even come to a halt in order to accommodate that vehicle's submission to police authority." *Id.*, at 1120, 136 P. 3d, at 853. But an occupant of a car who knows that he is stuck in traffic because another car has been pulled over (like the motorist who can't even make out why the road is suddenly clogged) would not perceive a show of authority as directed at him or his car. Such incidental restrictions on freedom of movement would not tend to affect an individual's "sense of security and privacy in traveling in an automobile." *Prouse*, 440 U.S., at 662. Nor would the consequential blockage call for a precautionary rule to avoid the kind of "arbitrary and oppressive interference by [law] enforcement officials with the privacy and personal security of individuals" that the Fourth Amendment was intended to limit. *Martinez-Fuerte*, 428 U.S., at 554.[6]

Indeed, the consequence to worry about would not flow from our conclusion, but from the rule that almost all courts have rejected. Holding that the passenger in a private car is not (without more) seized in a traffic stop would invite police officers to stop cars with passengers regardless of probable cause or reasonable suspicion of anything illegal.[7] The fact that evidence uncovered as a result of an arbitrary traffic stop would still be admissible against any passengers would be a powerful incentive to run the kind of "roving patrols" that would still violate the driver's Fourth Amendment right. See, *e.g.*, *Almeida-Sanchez* v. *United States*, 413 U.S. 266, 273 (1973) (stop and search by Border Patrol agents without a warrant or probable cause violated the Fourth Amendment); *Prouse, supra*, at 663 (police spot check of driver's license and registration without reasonable suspicion violated the Fourth Amendment).

---

[6] California claims that, under today's rule, "all taxi cab and bus passengers would be 'seized' under the Fourth Amendment when the cab or bus driver is pulled over by the police for running a red light." Brief for Respondent 23. But the relationship between driver and passenger is not the same in a common carrier as it is in a private vehicle, and the expectations of police officers and passengers differ accordingly. In those cases, as here, the crucial question would be whether a reasonable person in the passenger's position would feel free to take steps to terminate the encounter.

[7] Compare *Delaware* v. *Prouse*, 440 U.S. 648, 663 (1979) (requiring "at least articulable and reasonable suspicion" to support random investigative traffic stops), and *United States* v. *Brignoni-Ponce*, 422 U.S. 878, 880–884 (1975) (same), with *Whren* v. *United States*, 517, U.S. 808, 810 (1996) ("[T]he decision to stop an automobile is reasonable where the police have probable cause to believe that a traffic violation has occurred"), and *Atwater* v. *Lago Vista*, 532 U.S. 318, 354 (2001) ("If an officer has probable cause to believe that an individual has committed even a very minor criminal offense in his presence, he may, without violating the Fourth Amendment, arrest the offender").

Opinion of the Court

*   *   *

Brendlin was seized from the moment Simeroth's car came to a halt on the side of the road, and it was error to deny his suppression motion on the ground that seizure occurred only at the formal arrest. It will be for the state courts to consider in the first instance whether suppression turns on any other issue. The judgment of the Supreme Court of California is vacated, and the case is remanded for further proceedings not inconsistent with this opinion.

It is so ordered.

Key Excerpts from the Majority Opinion

ARIZONA v. GANT

Certiorari to the Supreme Court of Arizona

Argued October 7, 2008—Decided April 21, No. 07-542. 2009

Respondent Gant was arrested for driving on a suspended license, handcuffed, and locked in a patrol car before officers searched his car and found cocaine in a jacket pocket. The Arizona trial court denied his motion to suppress the evidence, and he was convicted of drug offenses. Reversing, the State Supreme Court distinguished *New York v. Belton*, 453 U.S. 454—which held that police may search the passenger compartment of a vehicle and any containers therein as a contemporaneous incident of a recent occupant's lawful arrest—on the ground that it concerned the scope of a search incident to arrest but did not answer the question whether officers may conduct such a search once the scene has been secured. Because *Chimel v. California*, 395 U.S. 752, requires that a search incident to arrest be justified by either the interest in officer safety or the interest in preserving evidence and the circumstances of Gant's arrest implicated neither of those interests, the State Supreme Court found the search unreasonable.

Held: Police may search the passenger compartment of a vehicle incident to a recent occupant's arrest only if it is reasonable to believe that the arrestee might access the vehicle at the time of the search or that the vehicle contains evidence of the offense of arrest. Pp. 5–18.

(a) Warrantless searches "are per se unreasonable," "subject only to a few specifically established and well-delineated exceptions." *Katz v. United States*, 389 U.S. 347, 357. The exception for a search incident to a lawful arrest applies only to "the area from within which [an arrestee] might gain possession of a weapon or destructible evidence." *Chimel*, 395 U.S., at 763. This Court applied that exception to the automobile context in *Belton*, the holding of which rested in large part on the assumption that articles inside a vehicle's passenger compartment are "generally . . . within 'the area into which an arrestee might reach.'" 453 U.S., at 460. Pp. 5–8.

(b) This Court rejects a broad reading of *Belton* that would permit a vehicle search incident to a recent occupant's arrest even if there were no possibility the arrestee could gain access to the vehicle at the time of the search. The safety and evidentiary justifications underlying Chimel's exception authorize a vehicle search only when there is a reasonable pos-

sibility of such access. Although it does not follow from *Chimel*, circumstances unique to the automobile context also justify a search incident to a lawful arrest when it is "reasonable to believe evidence relevant to the crime of arrest might be found in the vehicle." *Thornton v. United States*, 541 U.S. 615, 632 (Scalia, J., concurring in judgment). Neither *Chimel's* reaching-distance rule nor *Thornton's* allowance for evidentiary searches authorized the search in this case. In contrast to *Belton*, which involved a single officer confronted with four unsecured arrestees, five officers handcuffed and secured Gant and the two other suspects in separate patrol cars before the search began. Gant clearly could not have accessed his car at the time of the search. An evidentiary basis for the search was also lacking. Belton and Thornton were both arrested for drug offenses, but Gant was arrested for driving with a suspended license—an offense for which police could not reasonably expect to find evidence in Gant's car. Cf. *Knowles v. Iowa*, 525 U.S. 113, 118. The search in this case was therefore unreasonable. Pp. 8–11.

(c) This Court is unpersuaded by the State's argument that its expansive reading of *Belton* correctly balances law enforcement interests with an arrestee's limited privacy interest in his vehicle. The State seriously undervalues the privacy interests at stake, and it exaggerates both the clarity provided by a broad reading of *Belton* and its importance to law enforcement interests. A narrow reading of *Belton* and *Thornton*, together with this Court's other Fourth Amendment decisions, e.g., *Michigan v. Long*, 463 U.S. 103, and *United States v. Ross*, 456 U.S. 798, permit an officer to search a vehicle when safety or evidentiary concerns demand. Pp. 11–14.

(d) *Stare decisis* does not require adherence to a broad reading of *Belton*. The experience of the 28 years since *Belton* has shown that the generalization underpinning the broad reading of that decision is unfounded, and blind adherence to its faulty assumption would authorize myriad unconstitutional searches. Pp. 15–18.

216 Ariz. 1, 162 P. 3d 640, affirmed.

Stevens, J., delivered the opinion of the Court, in which *Scalia, Souter, Thomas,* and *Ginsburg, JJ.,* joined. *Scalia, J.,* filed a concurring opinion. *Breyer, J.,* filed a dissenting opinion. *Alito, J.,* filed a dissenting opinion, in which *Roberts, C. J.,* and *Kennedy, J.,* joined, and in which *Breyer, J.,* joined except as to Part II-E.

Key Excerpts from the Majority Opinion

MONTEJO v. LOUISIANA

Certiorari to the Supreme Court of Louisiana

Argued January 13, 2009—Decided May 26, No. 07-1529. 2009

At a preliminary hearing required by Louisiana law, petitioner Montejo was charged with first-degree murder, and the court ordered the appointment of counsel. Later that day, the police read Montejo his rights under *Miranda v. Arizona,* 384 U.S. 436, and he agreed to go along on a trip to locate the murder weapon. During the excursion, he wrote an inculpatory letter of apology to the victim's widow. Upon returning, he finally met his court-appointed attorney. At trial, his letter was admitted over defense objection, and he was convicted and sentenced to death. Affirming, the State Supreme Court rejected his claim that the letter should have been suppressed under the rule of *Michigan v. Jackson,* 475 U.S. 625, which forbids police to initiate interrogation of a criminal defendant once he has invoked his right to counsel at an arraignment or similar proceeding. The court reasoned that *Jackson's* prophylactic protection is not triggered unless the defendant has actually requested a lawyer or has otherwise asserted his Sixth Amendment right to counsel; and that, since Montejo stood mute at his hearing while the judge ordered the appointment of counsel, he had made no such request or assertion.

Held:

1. *Michigan v. Jackson* should be and now is overruled. Pp. 3–18.

(a) The State Supreme Court's interpretation of *Jackson* would lead to practical problems. Requiring an initial "invocation" of the right to counsel in order to trigger the *Jackson* presumption, as the court below did, might work in States that require an indigent defendant formally to request counsel before an appointment is made, but not in more than half the States, which appoint counsel without request from the defendant. Pp. 3–6.

(b) On the other hand, Montejo's solution is untenable as a theoretical and doctrinal matter. Eliminating the invocation requirement entirely would depart fundamentally from the rationale of Jackson, whose presumption was created by analogy to a similar prophylactic rule established in *Edwards v. Arizona,* 451 U.S. 477, to protect the Fifth Amendment-based *Miranda* right. Both *Edwards* and *Jackson* are meant to prevent police from badgering defendants into changing their minds about the right to counsel once they have invoked it, but a defendant who never asked for counsel has not yet made up his mind in the first instance. Pp. 6–13.

(c) *Stare decisis* does not require the Court to expand significantly the holding of a prior decision in order to cure its practical deficiencies. To the contrary, the fact that a decision has proved "unworkable" is a traditional ground for overruling it. *Payne v. Tennessee,* 501 U.S. 808, 827. Beyond workability, the relevant factors include the precedent's antiquity, the reliance interests at stake, and whether the decision was well reasoned. *Pearson v. Callahan,* 555 U.S. ___, ___. The first two cut in favor of jettisoning *Jackson:* the opinion is only two decades old, and eliminating it would not upset expectations, since any criminal defendant learned enough to order his affairs based on *Jackson's* rule would also be perfectly capable of interacting with the police on his own. As for the strength of *Jackson's* reasoning, when this Court creates a prophylactic rule to protect a constitutional right, the relevant "reasoning" is the weighing of the rule's benefits against its costs. Jackson's marginal benefits are dwarfed by its substantial costs. Even without *Jackson,* few badgering-induced waivers, if any, would be admitted at trial because the Court has taken substantial other, overlapping measures to exclude them. Under *Miranda,* any suspect subject to custodial interrogation must be advised of his right to have a lawyer present. 384 U.S., at 474. Under *Edwards,* once such a defendant "has invoked his [*Miranda*] right," interrogation must stop. 451 U.S., at 484. And under *Minnick v. Mississippi,* 498 U.S. 146, no subsequent interrogation may take place until counsel is present. *Id.,* at 153. These three layers of prophylaxis are sufficient. On the other side of the equation, the principal cost of applying *Jackson's* rule is that crimes can go unsolved and criminals unpunished when uncoerced confessions are excluded and when officers are deterred from even trying to obtain confessions. The Court concludes that the *Jackson* rule does not "pay its way," *United States v. Leon,* 468 U.S. 897, 907–908, n. 6, and thus the case should be overruled. Pp. 13–18.

2. Montejo should nonetheless be given an opportunity to contend that his letter of apology should have been suppressed under the *Edwards* rule. He understandably did not pursue an *Edwards* objection, because *Jackson* offered broader protections, but the decision here changes the legal landscape. Pp. 18–19.

06-1807 (La.), 974 So. 2d 1238, vacated and remanded.

Scalia, J., delivered the opinion of the Court, in which *Roberts, C. J.,* and *Kennedy, Thomas,* and *Alito, JJ.,* joined. *Alito, J.,* filed a concurring opinion, in which *Kennedy, J.,* joined. *Stevens, J.,* filed a dissenting opinion, in which *Souter* and *Ginsburg, JJ.,* joined, and in which *Breyer, J.,* joined, except for n. 5. *Breyer, J.,* filed a dissenting opinion.

SUPREME COURT OF THE UNITED STATES

Berghuis, Warden *v.* Thompkins

CERTIORARI TO THE UNITED STATES COURT OF APPEALS FOR THE SIXTH COURT

Argued March 1, 2010—Decided June 1, 2010 No. 08–1470.

After advising respondent Thompkins of his rights, in full compliance with *Miranda* v. *Arizona*, 384 U.S. 436, Detective Helgert and another Michigan officer interrogated him about a shooting in which one victim died. At no point did Thompkins say that he wanted to remain silent, that he did not want to talk with the police, or that he wanted an attorney. He was largely silent during the 3-hour interrogation, but near the end, he answered "yes" when asked if he prayed to God to forgive him for the shooting. He moved to suppress his statements, claiming that he had invoked his Fifth Amendment right to remain silent, that he had not waived that right, and that his inculpatory statements were involuntary. The trial court denied the motion. At trial on first-degree murder and other charges, the prosecution called Eric Purifoy, who drove the van in which Thompkins and a third accomplice were riding at the time of the shooting, and who had been convicted of firearm offenses but acquitted of murder and assault. Thompkins' defense was that Purifoy was the shooter. Purifoy testified that he did not see who fired the shots. During closing arguments, the prosecution suggested that Purifoy lied about not seeing the shooter and pondered whether Purifoy's jury had made the right decision. Defense counsel did not ask the court to instruct the jury that it could consider evidence of the outcome of Purifoy's trial only to assess his credibility, not to establish Thompkins' guilt. The jury found Thompkins guilty, and he was sentenced to life in prison without parole. In denying his motion for a new trial, the trial court rejected as nonprejudicial his ineffective-assistance-of-counsel claim for failure to request a limiting instruction about the outcome of Purifoy's trial. On appeal, the Michigan Court of Appeals rejected both Thompkins' *Miranda* and his ineffective-assistance claims. The Federal District Court denied his subsequent habeas request, reasoning that Thompkins did not invoke his right to remain silent and was not coerced into making statements during the interrogation, and that it was not unreasonable, for purposes of the Antiterrorism and Effective Death Penalty Act of 1996 (AEDPA), see 28 U. S. C. §2254(d)(1), for the State Court of Appeals to determine that he had waived his right to remain silent. The Sixth Circuit reversed, holding that the state court was unreasonable in finding an implied waiver of Thompkins' right to remain silent and in rejecting his ineffective-assistance-of-counsel claim.

Held:

   1. The state court's decision rejecting Thompkins' *Miranda* claim was correct under *de novo* review and therefore necessarily reasonable under AEDPA's more deferential standard of review. Pp. 7–17.

   (a) Thompkins' silence during the interrogation did not invoke his right to remain silent. A suspect's *Miranda* right to counsel must be invoked "unambiguously." *Davis* v. *United States*, 512 U.S. 452. If the accused makes an "ambiguous or equivocal" statement or no statement, the police are not required to end the interrogation, *ibid.*, or ask questions to clarify the accused's intent, *id.*, at 461–462. There is no principled reason to adopt different standards for determining when an accused has invoked the *Miranda* right to remain silent and the *Miranda* right to counsel at issue in *Davis*. Both protect the privilege against compulsory self-incrimination by requiring an interrogation to cease when either right is invoked. The unambiguous invocation requirement results in an objective inquiry that "avoid[s] difficulties of proof and . . . provide[s] guidance to officers" on how to proceed in the face of ambiguity. *Davis, supra*, at 458–459. Had Thompkins said that he wanted to remain silent or that he did not want to talk, he would have invoked his right to end the questioning. He did neither. Pp. 8–10.

   (b) Thompkins waived his right to remain silent when he knowingly and voluntarily made a statement to police. A waiver must be "the product of a free and deliberate choice rather than intimidation, coercion, or deception" and "made with a full awareness of both the nature of the right being abandoned and the consequences of the decision to abandon it." *Moran* v. *Burbine*, 475 U.S. 412. Such a waiver may be "implied" through a "defendant's silence, coupled with an understanding of his rights and a course of conduct indicating waiver." *North Carolina* v. *Butler*, 441 U.S. 369. If the State establishes that a *Miranda* warning was given and that it was understood by the accused, an accused's uncoerced statement establishes an implied waiver. The record here shows that Thompkins waived his right to remain silent. First, the lack of any contention that he did not understand his rights indicates that he knew what he gave up when he spoke. See *Burbine, supra,* at 421. Second, his answer to the question about God is a "course of conduct indicating waiver" of that right. *Butler, supra,* at 373. Had he wanted to remain silent, he could have said nothing in response or unambiguously invoked his *Miranda* rights, ending the interrogation. That he made a statement nearly three hours after receiving a *Miranda* warning does not overcome the fact that he engaged in a course of conduct indicating waiver. Third, there is no evidence that his statement was coerced. See *Burbine, supra,* at 421. He does not claim that police threatened or injured him or that he was fearful. The interrogation took place in a standard-sized room in the middle of the day, and there is no authority for the proposition that a 3-hour interrogation is inherently coercive. Cf. *Colorado* v. *Connelly,* 479 U.S. 157, n. 1. The fact that the question referred to religious beliefs also does not render his statement involuntary. *Id.,* at 170. Pp. 10–15.

   (c) Thompkins argues that, even if his answer to Helgert could constitute a waiver of his right to remain silent, the police were not allowed to question him until they first obtained a waiver. However, a rule requiring a waiver at the outset would be inconsistent with *Butler's* holding that courts can infer a waiver "from the actions and words of the person interrogated." 441 U. S., at 373. Any waiver, express or implied, may be contradicted by an invocation at any time, terminating further interrogation. When the suspect knows that *Miranda* rights can be invoked at any time, he or she can reassess his or her immediate and long-term interests as the interrogation progresses. After giving a *Miranda* warning, police may interrogate a suspect who has neither invoked nor waived *Miranda* rights. Thus, the police were not required to obtain a waiver of Thompkins' *Miranda* rights before interrogating him. Pp. 15–17.

   2. Even if his counsel provided ineffective assistance, Thompkins cannot show prejudice under a *de novo* review of this record. To establish ineffective assistance, a defendant "must show both deficient performance and prejudice." *Knowles* v. *Mirzayance,* 556 U. S. ____, ____. To establish prejudice, a "defendant must show that there is a reasonable probability that, but for counsel's unprofessional errors, the result of the proceeding would have been different," *Strickland* v. *Washington,* 466 U.S. 668, considering "the totality of the evidence before the judge or jury," *id.,* at 695. Here, the Sixth Circuit did not account for the other evidence presented against Thompkins. The state court rejected his claim that he was prejudiced by evidence of Purifoy's earlier conviction. Even if it used an incorrect legal standard, this Court need not determine whether AEDPA's deferential standard of review applies here, since Thompkins cannot show prejudice under *de novo* review, a more favorable standard for him. *De novo* review can be used in this case because a habeas petitioner will not be entitled to relief if his or her claim is rejected on *de novo* review. See §2254(a). Assuming that failure to request a limiting instruction here was deficient representation, Thompkins cannot show prejudice, for the record shows that it was not reasonably likely that such an instruction would have made any difference in light of other evidence of guilt. The surviving victim identified Thompkins as the shooter, and the identification was supported by a surveillance camera photograph. A friend testified that Thompkins confessed to him, and the details of that confession were corroborated by evidence that Thompkins stripped and abandoned the van after the shooting. The jury, moreover, was capable of assessing Purifoy's credibility, as it was instructed to do. Pp. 17–19.

547 F. 3d 572, reversed and remanded.

KENNEDY, J., delivered the opinion of the Court, in which ROBERTS, C. J., and SCALIA, THOMAS, and ALITO, JJ., joined. SOTOMAYOR, J., filed a dissenting opinion, in which STEVENS, GINSBURG, and BREYER, JJ., joined.

CHAPTER 9

"The movement of the progressive societies has hitherto been a movement from status to contract."

—Sir Henry Maine
Ancient Law, Chapter 5

Nature of Traditional and E-Contracts

Chapter Objectives

After studying this chapter, you should be able to:

1. Define *contract*.
2. List the elements necessary to form a valid contract.
3. Distinguish between bilateral and unilateral contracts.
4. Describe and distinguish between express and implied-in-fact contracts.
5. Describe and distinguish among valid, void, voidable, and unenforceable contracts.

Chapter Contents

Introduction to Nature of Traditional and E-Contracts

Contracts are the basis of many of our daily activities. They provide the means for individuals and businesses to sell and otherwise transfer property, services, and other rights. The purchase of goods, such as books and automobiles, is based on sales contracts; the hiring of employees is based on service contracts; the lease of an apartment is based on a rental contract; and the sale of goods and services over the Internet is based on electronic contracts. The list is almost endless. Without enforceable contracts, commerce would collapse.

Contracts are voluntarily entered into by parties. The terms of a contract become *private law* between the parties. One court has stated that "the contract between parties is the law between them and the courts are obliged to give legal effect to such contracts according to the true interests of the parties."[1]

Nevertheless, most contracts are performed without the aid of the court system. This is usually because the parties feel a moral duty to perform as promised. Although some contracts, such as illegal contracts, are not enforceable, most are **legally enforceable**.[2] This means that if a party fails to perform a contract, the other party may call upon the courts to enforce the contract.

This chapter introduces the study of **traditional law** and **e-contract law**. Such topics as the definition of *contract*, requirements for forming a contract, sources of contract law, and the various classifications of contracts are discussed.

legally enforceable contract
A contract in which if one party fails to perform as promised, the other party can use the court system to enforce the contract and recover damages or other remedy.

Definition of a Contract

A **contract** is an agreement that is enforceable by a court of law or equity. A simple and widely recognized definition of *contract* is provided by the *Restatement (Second) of Contracts*: "A contract is a promise or a set of promises for the breach of which the law gives a remedy or the performance of which the law in some way recognizes a duty."[3]

Parties to a Contract

Every contract involves at least two parties. The **offeror** is the party who makes an offer to enter into a contract. The **offeree** is the party to whom the offer is made (see Exhibit 9.1). In making an offer, the offeror promises to do—or to refrain from doing—something. The offeree then has the power to create a contract by accepting the offeror's offer. A contract is created if the offer is accepted. No contract is created if the offer is not accepted.

offeror
The party who makes an offer to enter into a contract.
offeree
The party to whom an offer to enter into a contract is made.

■ **EXHIBIT 9.1** Parties to a Contract

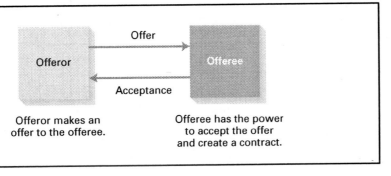

Offeror makes an offer to the offeree.   Offeree has the power to accept the offer and create a contract.

Contracts must not be the sports of an idle hour, mere matters of pleasantry and badinage, never intended by the parties to have any serious effect whatever.

Lord Stowell
Dalrymple v. Dalrymple (1811)

Elements of a Contract

For a contract to be enforceable, the following four basic requirements must be met:

1. **Agreement.**   To have an enforceable contract, there must be an **agreement** between the parties. This requires an **offer** by the offeror and an **acceptance** of the offer by the offeree. There must be mutual assent by the parties.
2. **Consideration.**   The promise must be supported by a bargained-for **consideration** that is legally sufficient. Money, personal property, real property, provision of services, and such qualify as consideration.
3. **Contractual capacity.**   The parties to a contract must have **contractual capacity** for the contract to be enforceable against them. Contracts cannot be enforced against parties who lacked contractual capacity when they entered into a contract.
4. **Lawful object.**   The object of the contract must be lawful. Most contracts have a **lawful object.** However, contracts that have an illegal object are void and will not be enforced.

Concept Summary
Elements of a Contract

1. Agreement

2. Consideration

3. Contractual capacity

4. Lawful object

Defenses to the Enforcement of a Contract

Two *defenses* may be raised to the enforcement of contracts:

1. **Genuineness of assent.**   The consent of the parties to create a contract must be **genuine.** If the consent is obtained by duress, undue influence, or fraud, there is no real consent.
2. **Writing and form.**   The law requires that certain contracts be in **writing** or in a certain **form.** Failure of such a contract to be in writing or to be in proper form may be raised against the enforcement of the contract.

   The requirements to form an enforceable contract and the defenses to the enforcement of contracts are discussed in this chapter and the following chapters on contract law.

Sources of Contract Law

There are several sources of contract law in the United States, including the *common law of contracts*, the *Uniform Commercial Code*, and the *Restatement (Second) of Contracts*. The following paragraphs explain these sources in more detail.

Common Law of Contracts

common law of contracts
Contract law developed primarily by state courts.

A major source of contract law is the **common law of contracts**, which developed from early court decisions that became precedent for later decisions. There is a limited federal common law of contracts that applies to contracts made by the federal government. The larger and more prevalent body of common law has been developed from state court decisions. Thus, although the general principles remain the same throughout the country, there is some variation from state to state.

The Restatement of the Law of Contracts

Uniform Commercial Code (UCC)
A comprehensive statutory scheme which includes laws that cover aspects of commercial transactions.

Restatement of the Law of Contracts
A compilation of model contract law principles drafted by legal scholars. The *Restatement* is not law.

In 1932, the American Law Institute, a group comprising law professors, judges, and lawyers, completed the **Restatement of the Law of Contracts.** The *Restatement* is a compilation of contract law principles, as agreed upon by the drafters. The *Restatement*, which

Contemporary Environment

The Evolution of the Modern Law of Contracts

The use of contracts originally developed in ancient times. The common law of contracts developed in England around the fifteenth century. U.S. contract law evolved from the English common law.

At first, the United States adopted a **laissez-faire** approach to the law of contracts. The central theme of this theory was *freedom of contract*. The parties (e.g., consumers, shopkeepers, farmers, traders) generally dealt with one another face-to-face, had equal knowledge and bargaining power, and had the opportunity to inspect goods prior to sale. Contract terms were openly negotiated. There was little, if any, government regulation of the right to contract. This "pure law," or **classical law of contracts** produced objective rules, which, in turn, produced certainty and predictability in the enforcement of contracts. It made sense until the Industrial Revolution.

The Industrial Revolution changed many of the underlying assumptions of pure contract law. For example, as large corporations developed and gained control of crucial resources, the traditional balance of parties' bargaining power shifted: Large corporations now had the most power. The chain of distribution for goods also changed because (1) buyers did not have to deal face-to-face with sellers and (2) there was not always an opportunity to inspect the goods prior to sale.

Eventually sellers began using **form contracts** that offered their goods to buyers on a take-it-or-leave-it basis.

That is, the consumer has no ability to negotiate the terms of the contract with the seller. The majority of contracts in this country today are form contracts.

Examples
Automobile sales contracts, automobile leases, mortgages, and sales contracts for consumer goods, credit card agreements, and software licenses usually use form contracts.

Although the phrase "freedom to contract" is often used, in many situations there is not an absolute ability of freedom of contract. Both federal and state governments have enacted statutes that regulate contracts. Many of these laws are intended to protect consumers, debtors, and others from unfair contracts. Today, under this modern law of contracts, there is substantial **government regulation** of the right to contract.

Examples
Federal labor laws protect the rights of workers to unionize and negotiate collective bargaining agreements with their employers. Consumer protection laws protect consumers from certain unscrupulous contracts. Equal opportunity in employment laws protect employees from contracts that attempt to discriminate against them based on race, sex, age, disability, and other protected categories. E-contracts are regulated by federal and state laws that govern transactions over the Internet.

Landmark Law

Uniform Commercial Code (UCC)

A major source of contract law is the **Uniform Commercial Code (UCC).** The UCC, which was first drafted by the National Conference of Commissioners on Uniform State Laws in 1952, has been amended several times. Its goal is to create a uniform system of commercial law among the 50 states. The provisions of the UCC normally take precedence over the common law of contracts. (The provisions of the UCC are discussed in other chapters in this book.)

The UCC is divided into nine main articles. Every state has adopted at least part of the UCC. In the area of contract law, two of the major provisions of the UCC are:

• **Article 2 (Sales). Article 2 (Sales)** prescribes a set of uniform rules for the creation and enforcement of con-

tracts for the sale of goods. These contracts are often referred to as **sales contracts.**

Examples
The sale of equipment, automobiles, computers, clothing, and such involve sales contracts subject to Article 2 of the UCC.

• **Article 2A (Leases). Article 2A (Leases)** prescribes a set of uniform rules for the creation and enforcement of contracts for the lease of goods. These contracts are referred to as **lease contracts**.

Examples
Leases of automobiles, leases of aircraft, and other leases involving goods are subject to Article 2A of the UCC.

is currently in its second edition, is cited in this book as the ***Restatement (Second) of Contracts***. Note that the *Restatement* is not law. However, lawyers and judges often refer to it for guidance in contract disputes because of its stature.

Objective Theory of Contracts

objective theory of contracts

A theory that says the intent to contract is judged by the reasonable person standard and not by the subjective intent of the parties.

The **objective theory of contracts** holds that the intent to enter into an express or implied-in-fact contract is judged by the **reasonable person standard**. Would a hypothetical reasonable person conclude that the parties intended to create a contract after considering (1) the words and conduct of the parties and (2) the surrounding circumstances? For example, no valid contract results from offers that are made in jest, anger, or undue excitement. Under the objective theory of contracts, the subjective intent of a party to enter into a contract is irrelevant.

E-Commerce

As we entered the twenty-first century, a new economic shift brought the United States and the rest of the world into the Information Age. Computer technology and the use of the Internet increased dramatically. A new form of commerce—**electronic commerce, or e-commerce**—is flourishing. All sorts of goods and services are now sold over the Internet. You can purchase automobiles and children's toys, participate in auctions, purchase airline tickets, make hotel reservations, and purchase other goods and services over the Internet.

Much of the new cyberspace economy is based on electronic contracts and the licensing of computer information. E-commerce created problems for forming **e-contracts** over the Internet, enforcing e-contracts, and providing consumer protection. In many situations, traditional contract rules apply to e-contracts. Many states have adopted rules that specifically regulate e-commerce transactions. The federal government has also enacted several laws that regulate e-contracts. Contract rules that apply to e-commerce will be discussed in this and the following chapters.

Uniform Computer Information Transactions Act (UCITA)

A model act that establishes uniform legal rules for the formation and enforcement of electronic contracts and licenses.

Classifications of Contracts

There are several types of contracts. Each differs somewhat in formation, enforcement, performance, and discharge. The different types of contracts are discussed in the following paragraphs.

Internet Law and Online Commerce

Uniform Computer Information Transactions Act (UCITA)

The National Conference of Commissioners on Uniform State Laws (a group of lawyers, judges, and legal scholars) drafted the **Uniform Computer Information Transactions Act (UCITA).**

The UCITA establishes uniform legal rules for the formation and enforcement of electronic contracts and licenses. The UCITA addresses most of the legal issues that are encountered while conducting e-commerce over the Internet.

The UCITA is a model act that does not become law until a state legislature adopts it as a statute for the state. Although most states have not adopted the UCITA, the UCITA has served as a model for states that have enacted their own statutes that govern e-commerce. Because of the need for uniformity of e-commerce rules, states are attempting to adopt uniform laws to govern the creation and enforcement of cyberspace contracts and licenses.

Bilateral and Unilateral Contracts

Contracts are either *bilateral* or *unilateral*, depending on what the offeree must do to accept the offeror's offer. A contract is **bilateral** if the offeror's promise is answered with the offeree's promise of acceptance. In other words, a bilateral contract is a "promise for a promise." This exchange of promises creates an enforceable contract. No act of performance is necessary to create a bilateral contract.

bilateral contract
A contract entered into by way of exchange of promises of the parties; "a promise for a promise."

Example

Mary, the owner of the Chic Dress Shop, says to Peter, a painter, "If you promise to paint my store by July 1, I will pay you $3,000." Peter says "I promise to do so." A *bilateral contract* was created at the moment Peter promised to paint the dress shop (a promise for a promise). If Peter fails to paint the shop, Mary can sue Peter and recover whatever damages result from his breach of contract. Similarly, Peter can sue Mary if she refuses to pay him after he has performed as promised.

A contract is **unilateral** if the offeror's offer can be accepted only by the performance of an act by the offeree. There is no contract until the offeree performs the requested act. An offer to create a unilateral contract cannot be accepted by a promise to perform. It is a "promise for an act."

unilateral contract
A contract in which the offeror's offer can be accepted only by the performance of an act by the offeree; a "promise for an act."

Example

Mary, the owner of the Chic Dress Shop, says to Peter, a painter, "If you paint my shop by July 1, I will pay you $3,000." This offer creates a *unilateral contract*. The offer can be accepted only by the painter's performance of the requested act. If Peter does not paint the shop by July 1, there has been no acceptance, and Mary cannot sue Peter for damages. If Peter paints the shop by July 1, Mary owes Peter $3,000. If Mary refuses to pay, Peter can sue Mary to collect payment.

The language of the offeror's promise must be carefully scrutinized to determine whether it is an offer to create a bilateral contract or an offer to create a unilateral contract. If there is any ambiguity as to which it is, it is presumed to be a bilateral contract.

Incomplete or Partial Performance   Problems can arise if the offeror in a unilateral contract attempts to revoke an offer after the offeree has begun performance. Generally, an offer to create a unilateral contract can be revoked by the offeror any time prior to the offeree's performance of the requested act. However, the offer cannot be revoked if the offeree has begun or has substantially completed performance.

Justice is the end of government. It is the end of civil society. It ever has been, and ever will be pursued, until it be obtained, or until liberty be lost in the pursuit.

James Madison
The Federalist No. 51 (1788)

Example

Suppose Alan Matthews tells Sherry Levine that he will pay her $5,000 if she finishes the Boston Marathon. Alan cannot revoke the offer once Sherry starts running the marathon.

A man must come into a court of equity with clean hands.

C.B. Eyre
Dering v. Earl of Winchelsea (1787)

Formal and Informal Contracts

Contracts may be classified as either *formal* or *informal*.

Formal contracts   **Formal contracts** are contracts that require a special form or method of creation. The *Restatement (Second) of Contracts* identifies the following types of formal contracts[4]:

formal contract
A contract that requires a special form or method of creation.

- **Negotiable instruments. Negotiable instruments,** which include checks, drafts, notes, and certificates of deposit, are special forms of contracts recognized by the UCC. They require a special form and language for their creation and must meet certain requirements for transfer.
- **Letters of credit.** A **letter of credit** is an agreement by the issuer of the letter to pay a sum of money upon the receipt of an invoice and other documents. Letters of credit are governed by the UCC.

- **Recognizance.** In a recognizance, a party acknowledges in court that he or she will pay a specified sum of money if a certain event occurs.
- **Contracts under seal.** This type of contract is one to which a seal (usually a wax seal) is attached. Although no state currently requires contracts to be under seal, a few states provide that no consideration is necessary if a contract is made under seal.

informal contract

A contract that is not formal. Valid informal contracts are fully enforceable and may be sued upon if breached.

Informal Contracts   All contracts that do not qualify as formal contracts are called **informal contracts** (or **simple contracts**). The term is a misnomer. Valid informal contracts (e.g., leases, sales contracts, service contracts) are fully enforceable and may be sued upon if breached. They are called informal contracts only because no special form or method is required for their creation. Thus, the parties to an informal contract can use any words they choose to express their contract. The majority of the contracts entered into by individuals and businesses are informal contracts.

Valid, Void, Voidable, and Unenforceable Contracts

Contract law places contracts in the following categories:

valid contract

A contract that meets all the essential elements to establish a contract; a contract that is enforceable by at least one of the parties.

void contract

A contract that has no legal effect; a nullity.

voidable contract

A contract in which one or both parties have the option to avoid their contractual obligations. If a contract is avoided, both parties are released from their contractual obligations.

unenforceable contract

A contract in which the essential elements to create a valid contract are met but there is some legal defense to the enforcement of the contract.

executed contract

A contract that has been fully performed on both sides; a completed contract.

executory contract

A contract that has not been fully performed by either or both sides.

1. **Valid contract.**   A **valid contract** meets all the essential elements to establish a contract. In other words, it (1) consists of an agreement between the parties, (2) is supported by legally sufficient consideration, (3) is between parties with contractual capacity, and (4) accomplished a lawful object. A valid contract is enforceable by at least one of the parties.
2. **Void contract.**   A **void contract** has no legal effect. It is as if no contract had ever been created. A contract to commit a crime is void. If a contract is void, neither party is obligated to perform the contract, and neither party can enforce the contract.
3. **Voidable contract.**   A **voidable contract** is a contract in which at least one party has the *option* to avoid his or her contractual obligations. If the contract is avoided, both parties are released from their obligations under the contract. If the party with the option chooses to ratify the contract, both parties must fully perform their obligations.

   With certain exceptions, contracts may be voided by minors; insane persons; intoxicated persons; persons acting under duress, undue influence, or fraud; and in cases involving mutual mistake.
4. **Unenforceable contract.**   With an **unenforceable contract**, there is some legal defense to the enforcement of the contract. If a contract is required to be in writing under the Statute of Frauds but is not, the contract is unenforceable. The parties may voluntarily perform a contract that is unenforceable.

Executed and Executory Contracts

A completed contract—that is, one that has been fully performed on both sides—is called an **executed contract**. A contract that has not been performed by both sides is called an **executory contract**. Contracts that have been fully performed by one side but not by the other are classified as executory contracts.

Examples

Suppose Elizabeth signs a contract to purchase a new BMW automobile from Ace Motors. She has not yet paid for the car and Ace Motors has not yet delivered the car to Elizabeth. This is an executory contract because the contract has not yet been performed. If Elizabeth has paid for the car but Ace Motors has not yet delivered the car to Elizabeth, there is an executory contract because Ace Motors has not performed the contract. If Elizabeth has paid for the car and Ace Motors has delivered the car to Elizabeth, the contract has been fully performed by both parties and is an executed contract.

Express and Implied Contracts

An **actual contract** may be either *express* or *implied-in-fact*.

Express Contract

An **express contract** is stated in oral or written words. Most personal and business contracts are express contracts. A contract that is oral or written is an express contract.

Examples

A written agreement to buy an automobile from a dealership is an express contract because it is in written words. An oral agreement to purchase a neighbor's bicycle is an express contract because it is in oral words.

Implied-in-Fact Contract

Implied-in-fact contracts are implied from the conduct of the parties. The following elements must be established to create an implied-in-fact contract:

1. The plaintiff provided property or services to the defendant.
2. The plaintiff expected to be paid by the defendant for the property or services and did not provide the property or services gratuitously.
3. The defendant was given an opportunity to reject the property or services provided by the plaintiff but failed to do so.

In the following case, the court had to decide whether the plaintiffs could sue a defendant for breach of an implied-in-fact contract.

express contract

An agreement that is expressed in written or oral words.

implied-in-fact contract

A contract in which agreement between parties has been inferred from their conduct.

CASE 9.1
Implied-in-Fact Contract

Wrench LLC v. Taco Bell Corporation

256 F.3d 446, Web 2001 U.S. App. Lexis 15097 (2001)
United States Court of Appeals for the Sixth Circuit

"The district court found that appellants produced sufficient evidence to create a genuine issue of material fact regarding whether an implied-in-fact contract existed between the parties."

—Judge Graham

Facts

Thomas Rinks and Joseph Shields created the "Psycho Chihuahua" cartoon character, which they promote, market, and license through their company, Wrench LLC. Psycho Chihuahua is a clever, feisty, cartoon character dog with an attitude, a self-confident, edgy, cool dog who knows what he wants and will not back down. Rinks and Shields attended a licensing trade show in New York City, where they were approached by two Taco Bell employees, Rudy Pollak, a vice president, and Ed Alfaro, a creative services manager. Taco Bell owns and operates a nationwide chain of fast-food Mexican restaurants. Pollak and Alfaro expressed interest in the Psycho Chihuahua character for Taco Bell advertisements because they thought his character would appeal to Taco Bell's core consumers, males aged 18 to 24. Pollak and Alfaro obtained some Psycho Chihuahua materials to take back with them to Taco Bell's headquarters.

Later, Alfaro contacted Rinks and asked him to create art boards combining Psycho Chihuahua with the Taco Bell name and image. Rinks and Shields prepared art boards and sent them to Alfaro, along with Psycho Chihuahua t-shirts, hats, and stickers. Alfaro showed these materials to Taco Bell's vice president of brand management as well as to Taco Bell's outside advertising agency. Alfaro tested the Psycho Chihuahua marketing concept with focus groups. Rinks suggested to Alfaro that instead of using the cartoon version of Psycho Chihuahua in its advertisements, Taco Bell should use a live Chihuahua dog manipulated by computer graphic imaging that had the personality of Psycho

Chihuahua and a love for Taco Bell food. Rinks and Shields gave a formal presentation of this concept to Taco Bell's marketing department. One idea presented by Rinks and Shields was a commercial in which a male Chihuahua dog passed by a female Chihuahua dog in order to get to Taco Bell food. Taco Bell did not enter into an express contract with Wrench LLC, Rinks, or Shields.

Just after Rinks' and Shields' presentation, Taco Bell hired a new outside advertising agency, Chiat/Day. Taco Bell gave Chiat/Day materials received from Rinks and Shields regarding Psycho Chihuahua. Three months later, Chiat/Day proposed using a Chihuahua in Taco Bell commercials. One commercial had a male Chihuahua passing up a female Chihuahua to get to a person seated on a bench eating Taco Bell food. Chiat/Day says that it conceived these ideas by itself. In July 1997, Taco Bell aired its first Chihuahua commercial in the United States, and it became an instant success and the basis of its advertising. Taco Bell paid nothing to Wrench LLC or to Rinks and Shields. Plaintiffs Wrench LLC, Rinks, and Shields sued defendant Taco Bell to recover damages for breach of an implied-in-fact contract. On this issue, the District Court agreed with the plaintiffs. The decision was appealed.

Issue
Did the plaintiffs Wrench LLC, Rinks, and Shields state a cause of action for the breach of an implied-in-fact contract?

Language of the Court
The district court found that appellants produced sufficient evidence to create a genuine issue of material fact regarding whether an implied-in-fact contract existed between the parties. On appeal, Taco Bell argues that this conclusion was erroneous, and asserts that the record contains no evidence of an enforceable contract. We agree with the district court's finding that appellants presented sufficient evidence to survive summary judgment on the question of whether an implied-in-fact contract existed under Michigan law.

Decision
The U.S. Court of Appeals held that the plaintiffs had stated a proper cause of action against defendant Taco Bell for breach of an implied-in-fact contract. The Court of Appeals remanded the case for trial.

Note: The U.S. Supreme Court denied review of the decision in this case. In 2003 a federal court jury ordered Taco Bell to pay $30 million to plaintiffs Thomas Rinks and Joseph Shields for stealing their idea for the Psycho Chihuahua commercials. Later, the court awarded an additional $11.8 million in prejudgment interest, bringing the total award to over $42 million.

Case Questions

Critical Legal Thinking   What does the doctrine of implied-in-fact contract provide? Explain.

Business Ethics   Did Taco Bell act ethically in this case? Did Chiat/Day act ethically in this case?

Contemporary Business   What is the purpose of recognizing implied-in-fact contracts? Do you think there was an implied-in-fact contract in this case? If so, what damages should have been awarded to the plaintiffs?

Web Exercise   Go to **http://transcripts.cnn.com/ TRANSCRIPTS/0306/05/se.03.html** to read about the jury awarding the plaintiffs $30 million. Go to **www .youtube.com/watch?v=B0oEw0IMLXI** for a video clip of Taco Bell's Chihuahua commercial.

Implied-in-Law Contract (Quasi-Contract)

quasi-contract (implied-in-law contract)

An equitable doctrine whereby a court may award monetary damages to a plaintiff for providing work or services to a defendant even though no actual contract existed. The doctrine is intended to prevent unjust enrichment and unjust detriment.

The equitable doctrine of **quasi-contract**, also called **implied-in-law contract**, allows a court to award monetary damages to a plaintiff for providing work or services to a defendant even though no actual contract existed between the parties. Recovery is generally based on the reasonable value of the services received by the defendant.

The doctrine of quasi-contract is intended to prevent **unjust enrichment** and **unjust detriment**. It does not apply where there is an enforceable contract between the parties. A quasi-contract is imposed where (1) one person confers a benefit on another, who retains the benefit, and (2) it would be unjust not to require that person to pay for the benefit received.

Example
Heather is driving her automobile when she is involved in a serious automobile accident in which she is knocked unconscious. She is rushed to Metropolitan Hospital, where the doctors and other staff perform the necessary medical procedures to save her life. Heather comes out of her coma, and after recovering is released from the hospital. Subsequently, Metropolitan Hospital sends Heather a bill for its services. The charges are reasonable.

Under the doctrine of quasi-contract, Heather is responsible for any charges that are not covered by her insurance coverage.

In the following case, the court found a quasi-contract.

CASE 9.2
Quasi-Contract

Powell v. Thompson-Powell

Web 2006 Del. C.P. Lexis 10 (2006) Court of Common Pleas of Delaware

"A contract implied in law permits recovery of that amount by which the defendant has benefited at the expense of the plaintiff in order to preclude unjust enrichment."

—Judge Trader

Facts

Samuel E. Powell, Jr., and Susan Thompson-Powell, husband and wife, borrowed $37,700 from Delaware Farm Credit and gave a mortgage to Delaware Farm Credit that pledged two pieces of real property as collateral for the loan. The first piece of property was 2.7 acres of land owned as marital property. Susan had inherited the other piece of property and owned it. Eight years later, Samuel Jr. and Susan defaulted on the mortgage. Samuel Jr. went to his father, Samuel E. Powell, Sr., and orally agreed that if his father would pay the mortgage and the back taxes, he would pay his father back. Samuel Sr. paid off the mortgage and the back taxes owed on the properties. Susan was not a party to this agreement.

Two years later, Samuel Jr. and Susan were divorced. The divorce court ordered that the 2.7 acres of marital real property be sold and the sale proceeds to be divided 50 percent to each party. When the property was sold, Samuel Jr. paid Samuel Sr. one-half of the monies he had previously borrowed from his father. Samuel Sr. sued Susan to recover the other half of the money. Susan defended, alleging that she was not a party to the contract between Samuel Jr. and Samuel Sr. and therefore was not bound by it. Samuel Sr. argued that Susan was liable to him for one-half of the money based on the doctrine of quasi-contract.

Issue

Is Susan liable for one-half the money borrowed by Samuel Jr. from Samuel Sr. under the doctrine of quasi-contract?

Language of the Court

The primary issue in this case is whether the plaintiff can recover from Susan Thompson-Powell on the theory of contract implied in law. A contract implied in law permits recovery of that amount by which the defendant has benefited at the expense of the plaintiff in order to preclude unjust enrichment. To claim restitution, the plaintiff must show that the defendant was unjustly enriched and secured a benefit that it would be unconscionable to allow her to retain.

The essential elements of a quasi-contract are a benefit conferred upon the defendant by the plaintiff, appreciation or realization of the benefit by the defendant, and acceptance and retention by the defendant of such benefit under such circumstances that it would be inequitable to retain without paying the value thereof.

In the case before me the plaintiff paid the mortgage of the son and daughter-in-law at a time when the bank was about to foreclose on the mortgage. If the property had been sold at a foreclosure sale, neither Samuel E. Powell, Jr. nor Susan Thompson-Powell would have received any benefit from the sale of the marital property. Additionally, payment of the mortgage protected Susan Thompson-Powell's inherited property. Thus, because of the plaintiff's acts in preserving the real estate from foreclosure Susan Thompson-Powell received a substantial benefit at the plaintiff's expense. Since the retention of the benefit in this case is unjust, she must repay her share of the money advanced by the plaintiff.

Decision

The court held that Samuel E. Powell, Sr., was entitled to recover from Susan Thompson-Powell one-half of the money advanced for her benefit.

Case Questions

Critical Legal Thinking   What does the doctrine of quasi-contract provide? Explain.

Business Ethics   Was it unethical for Susan Thompson-Powell to not pay back half of the money borrowed from Samuel E. Powell, Sr.?

Contemporary Business   What is the doctrine of quasi-contract designed to prevent? Explain.

Web Exercise   Go to **www.oscn.net/applications/oscn/ DeliverDocument.asp?CiteID=74212** to read a jury instruction on the issue of quasi-contract.

Concept Summary
Classifications of Contracts

Formation	
	1. **Bilateral contract.** A promise for a promise.
	2. **Unilateral contract.** A promise for an act.
	3. **Express contract.** A contract expressed in oral or written words.
	4. **Implied-in-fact contract.** A contract inferred from the conduct of the parties.
	5. **Quasi-contract.** A contract implied by law to prevent unjust enrichment.
	6. **Formal contract.** A contract that requires a special form or method of creation.
	7. **Informal contract.** A contract that requires no special form or method of creation.

Enforceability	
	1. **Valid contract.** A contract that meets all the essential elements of establishing a contract.
	2. **Void contract.** No contract exists.
	3. **Voidable contract.** A contract for which at least one party has the option of voiding the contract.
	4. **Unenforceable contract.** A contract that cannot be enforced because of a legal defense.

Performance	
	1. **Executed contract.** A contract that is fully performed on both sides.
	2. **Executory contract.** A contract that is not fully performed by one or both parties.

Equity

equity

A doctrine that permits judges to make decisions based on fairness, equality, moral rights, and natural law.

Recall that two separate courts developed in England: the courts of law and the Chancery Court (or courts of equity). The equity courts developed a set of maxims based on fairness, equality, moral rights, and natural law that were applied in settling disputes. **Equity** was resorted to when (1) an award of money damages "at law" would not be the proper remedy or (2) fairness required the application of equitable principles. Today, in most states of the United States, the courts of law and equity have been merged into one court. In an action "in equity," the judge decides the equitable issue; there is no right to a jury trial in an equitable action. The doctrine of equity is sometimes applied in contract cases.

India. *The economy of India is growing at over eight percent per year. This once-socialist-inspired country is becoming a major economic power. The second-largest country in the world—with over one billion in population—is transforming itself from an economy based on agriculture and handcrafted goods to an industrial and white-collar economy. Although per capita income remains low, sectors of the Indian economy—such as software engineering, telecommunications, biotechnology, and the provision of back office services—are growing rapidly. International contracts are necessary for India to conduct international trade.*

Ethics Spotlight

Equity Saves Contracting Party

"There is only minimal delay in giving notice, the harm to the lessor is slight, and the hardship to the lessee is severe."

—Judge Abbe

The courts usually interpret a valid contract as a solemn promise to perform. This view of the sanctity of a contract can cause an ethical conflict. Consider the following case.

A landlord leased a motel he owned to lessees for a 10-year period. The lessees had an option to extend the lease for an additional 10 years. To do so, they had to give written notice to the landlord three months before the first 10-year lease expired. The lease provided for forfeiture of all furniture, fixtures, and equipment installed by the lessees, free of any liens, upon termination of the lease.

For almost 10 years, the lessees devoted most of their assets and a great deal of their energy building up the business. During this time, they transformed a disheveled, unrated motel into a AAA three-star operation. With the landlord's knowledge, the lessees made extensive long-term improvements that greatly increased the value of both the property and the business. The landlord knew that the lessees had obtained long-term financing for the improvements that would extend well beyond the first 10-year term of the lease. The landlord also knew that the only source of income the lessees had to pay for these improvements was the income generated from the motel business. The lessees told the landlord orally in a conversation that they intended to extend the lease.

The lessees had instructed their accountant to exercise the option on time. Despite reminders from the lessees, the accountant failed to give the written notice within three months of the expiration of the lease. As soon as they discovered the mistake, the lessees personally delivered written notice of renewal of the option to the landlord, 13 days too late. The landlord rejected it as late and instituted a lawsuit for unlawful detainer to evict the lessees.

The trial and appellate courts held in favor of the lessees. They rejected the landlord's argument for strict adherence to the deadline for giving written notice of renewal of the lease. Instead, the courts granted **equitable relief** and permitted the late renewal notice. The court reasoned that "there is only minimal delay in giving notice, the harm to the lessor is slight, and the hardship to the lessee is severe." *Romasanta v. Mitton,* 189 Cal.App.3d 1026, 234 Cal.Rptr. 729, **Web** 1987 Cal.App. Lexis 1428 (Court of Appeal of California)

Business Ethics

Did the landlord act ethically in this case? Should the court have applied equity and saved the lessees from their mistake? Why or why not?

International Law

United Nations Convention on Contracts for the International Sale of Goods (CISG)

The **United Nations Convention on Contracts for the International Sale of Goods (CISG)** is a model act for international sales contracts. The CISG is the work of many countries and several international organizations. There are now approximately 70 signatory countries to the CISG. In adopting the CISG, the United Nations stated in its preamble:

PREAMBLE

The State Parties to this Convention,

Considering that the development of international trade on the basis of equality and mutual benefit is an important element in promoting friendly relations among States,

Being of the opinion that the adoption of uniform rules which govern contracts for the international sale of goods and take into account the different social, economic and legal systems would contribute to the removal of legal barriers in international trade and promote the development of international trade,

Have agreed as follows:

The text of the CISG follows the Preamble. The CISG provides legal rules that govern the formation, performance, and enforcement of international sales contracts entered into between international businesses. Many of its provisions are remarkably similar to those of the U.S. Uniform Commercial Code (UCC). The CISG incorporates rules from all the major legal systems. It has, accordingly, received widespread support from developed, developing, and Communist countries.

The CISG applies to contracts for the international sale of goods. The buyer and seller must have their places of business in different countries. In order for the CISG to apply to an international sales contract, either (1) both of the nations must be parties to the convention or (2) the contract may specify that the CISG controls. The contracting parties may agree to exclude (i.e., opt out of) or modify the application of the CISG.

Test Review Terms and Concepts

Acceptance
Actual contract
Agreement
Article 2 (Sales)
Article 2A (Leases)
Bilateral contract
Classical law of contracts
Common law of contracts
Consideration
Contract
Contractual capacity
E-contract
E-contract law
Electronic commerce (e-commerce)
Equitable relief
Equity
Executed contract
Executory contract
Express contract

Form contract
Formal contract
Genuineness of assent
Government regulation
Implied-in-fact contract
Implied-in-law contract
Informal contract (simple contract)
Laissez-faire
Lawful object
Lease contract
Legally enforceable
Letter of credit
Negotiable instrument
Objective theory of contracts
Offer
Offeree
Offeror
Quasi-contract (implied-in-law contract)

Reasonable person standard
Restatement of the Law of Contracts
Restatement (Second) of Contracts
Sales contract
Traditional law
Unenforceable contract
Uniform Commercial Code (UCC)
Uniform Computer Information Transactions Act (UCITA)
Unilateral contract
United Nations Convention on Contracts for the International Sale of Goods (CISG)
Unjust detriment
Unjust enrichment
Valid contract
Void contract
Voidable contract
Writing and form

Key Excerpts from the Majority Opinion

Lorraine Goldman, Respondent, v. White Plains Center for Nursing Care, LLC, et al., Appellants

11 NY 3d at 175

Background and Facts

On April 1, 1990, plaintiff Lorraine Goldman entered into a written employment agreement with nonparty The Nathan Miller Center for Nursing Care, Inc. (the Miller Center). The contract was for a term of two years as executive director of the Miller Center's two nursing homes. The contract specified the contract length and the manner in which the contract could be terminated. The contract specifies as follows:

"1. _Term of Employment_ . . .

"b. Subject to the terms of Section 6 hereof, the parties hereto agree to enter into good faith negotiations not less than nine (9) months prior to the end of the Employment Period with respect to renewal of this Agreement on mutually agreeable terms. . . ."
6. _Termination._ This Agreement may be terminated:

"a. By mutual agreement of the parties;

"b. By either party giving notice to the other at least six (6) months prior to the end of the Employment Period of its intention not to renew this Agreement in accordance with the notice provision of Section 9 . . .

"f. The Miller Center will, as of the effective date of termination or expiration of this Agreement, be released of any responsibility or obligation hereunder, except for payment of salary and benefits accrued to the effective date of such expiration or termination . . .

"9. _Notice._ Any notice hereunder will be in writing and shall be sent by certified mail, return receipt requested, to the parties at their addresses set [*2] forth below, or to such other addresses as the parties may from time to time fix in the same manner. . . ."

The employment agreement also provided, in section 8, that it constituted the entire agreement and understanding between the parties, that neither party would be bound by any condition, warranty or representation other than as expressly provided for therein, and that neither party could waive her or its rights thereunder unless in writing.

Goldman continued working for the Miller Center until January 19, 2005 when she was terminated. She never sought to renew her employment agreement as per the contract. After termination she brought an action against the Miller Center contending it breached the employment contract. Her contention was that even after the original written contract expired her contract was "impliedly renewed."

Issue

Did the plaintiffs continuation in employment after the contract expiration create an implied contract?

In the Language of the Court

In fact, plaintiff's argument contradicts the agreement's clear and unambiguous language that her term of employment was to be for a two-year period commencing April 1, 1990 unless it was terminated by mutual agreement or either party's notice of its intention not to renew. Plaintiff's argument, if we were to accept it, would also render meaningless the agreement's distinction between "termination" and "expiration," as well as the provision that renewal negotiations were to be begun no less than nine months prior to the end of the employment period. In addition, the court found that the language of the agreement dictated the duties of both parties: _the terms of an agreement are clear and unambiguous, its plain meaning should be enforced._

Decision

No implied contract was created. Goldman's employment ended after the first two year period expired. No negotiations for a new term were commenced as per the contract. The court held that her employment therafter constituted employment at will at the time she was discharged. Therefore her claim of breach of contract should have been dismissed.

Case Problems

9.1 Bilateral or Unilateral Contract: G. S. Adams, Jr., vice president of the Washington Bank & Trust Co., met with Bruce Bickham. An agreement was reached whereby Bickham agreed to do his personal and corporate banking business with the bank, and the bank agreed to loan Bickham money at 7½ percent interest per annum. Bickham would have 10 years to repay the loans. For the next two years, the bank made several loans to Bickham at 7½ percent interest. Adams then resigned from the bank. The bank notified Bickham that general economic changes made it necessary to charge a higher rate of interest on both outstanding and new loans. Bickham sued the bank for breach of contract. Was the contract a bilateral or a unilateral contract? Does Bickham win? *Bickham v. Washington Bank & Trust Company*, 515 So.2d 457, **Web** 1987 La.App. Lexis 10442 (Court of Appeal of Louisiana)

9.2 Implied-in-Fact Contract: For six years, Lee Marvin, an actor, lived with Michelle Marvin. They were not mar-ried. At the end of six years, Lee Marvin compelled Michelle Marvin to leave his household. He continued to support her for another year but thereafter refused to provide further support. During their time together, Lee Marvin earned substantial income and acquired property, including motion-picture rights worth over $1 million. Michelle Marvin brought an action against Lee Marvin, alleging that an implied-in-fact contract existed between them and that she was entitled to half of the property that they had acquired while living together. She claimed that she had given up a lucrative career as an entertainer and singer to be a full-time companion, homemaker, house-keeper, and cook. Can an implied-in-fact contract result from the conduct of unmarried persons who live together? *Marvin v. Marvin*, 18 Cal.3d 660, 557 P.2d 106, 134 Cal.Rptr. 815, **Web** 1976 Cal. Lexis 377 (Supreme Court of California)

Business Ethics Cases

9.3 Business Ethics: The Lewiston Lodge of Elks sponsored a golf tourna-ment at the Fairlawn Country Club in Poland, Maine. For promotional pur-poses, Marcel Motors, an automobile dealership, agreed to give any golfer who shot a hole-in-one a new Dodge auto-mobile. Fliers advertising the tournament were posted in the Elks Club and sent to potential participants. On the day of the tournament, the new Dodge automobile was parked near the clubhouse, with one of the posters conspicuously dis-played on the vehicle. Alphee Chenard, Jr., who had seen the promotional literature regarding the hole-in-one offer, registered for the tournament and paid the requisite entrance fee. While playing the 13th hole of the golf course, in the presence of the other members of his four-some, Chenard shot a hole-in-one. When Marcel Motors refused to tender the automobile, Chenard sued for breach of contract. Was the contract a bilateral or a unilateral con-tract? Does Chenard win? Was it ethical for Marcel Motors to refuse to give the automobile to Chenard? *Chenard v. Marcel Motors*, 387 A.2d 596, **Web** 1978 Me. Lexis 911 (Supreme Judicial Court of Maine)

9.4 Business Ethics: Loren Vranich, a doctor practicing under the corporate name Family Health Care, P.C., entered into a written employment contract to hire Dennis Winkel. The contract provided for an annual salary, insurance benefits, and other employment benefits. Another doctor, Dr. Quan, also practiced with Dr. Vranich. About nine months later, when Dr. Quan left the practice, Vranich and Winkel entered into an oral modification of their written contract whereby Winkel was to receive a higher salary and a profit-sharing bonus. During the next year, Winkel received the increased salary. However, a disagreement arose, and Winkel sued to recover the profit-sharing bonus. Under Montana law, a writ-ten contract can be altered only in writing or by an executed oral agreement. Dr. Vranich argued that the contract could not be enforced because it was not in writing. Does Winkel receive the profit-sharing bonus? Did Dr. Vranich act ethi-cally in raising the defense that the contract was not in writ-ing? *Winkel v. Family Health Care, P.C.*, 205 Mont. 40, 668 P.2d 208, **Web** 1983 Mont. Lexis 785 (Supreme Court of Montana)

Endnotes

1. *Rebstock v. Birthright Oil & Gas Co.*, 406 So.2d 636, Web 1981 La. App. Lexis 5242 (Court of Appeal of Louisiana).

2. *Restatement (Second) of Contracts*, Section 1.

3. *Restatement (Second) of Contracts*, Section 1.

4. Restatement (Second) of Contracts, Section 6.

CHAPTER 10

Agreement

"When I use a word," Humpty Dumpty said, in rather a scornful tone, "it means just what I choose it to mean—neither more nor less."

"The question is," said Alice, "whether you can make words mean so many different things."

"The question is," said Humpty Dumpty, "which is to be master—that's all."

—Lewis Carroll
Alice's Adventures in Wonderland (1865)

Chapter Objectives

After studying this chapter, you should be able to:

1. Define *agreement*, *offer*, and *acceptance*.
2. Describe the required terms of an offer and describe the terms that can be implied in an offer.
3. Describe special forms of offers, including Internet auctions.
4. Define *counteroffer* and describe the effects of a counteroffer.
5. Describe how offers are terminated by acts of the parties and the operation of law.

Chapter Contents

Introduction to Agreement

Contracts are voluntary agreements between the parties; that is, one party makes an offer that is accepted by the other party. Without **mutual assent**, there is no contract. Assent may be expressly evidenced by the oral or written words of the parties or implied from the conduct of the parties. This chapter discusses offer and acceptance.

Agreement

Agreement is the manifestation by two or more persons of the substance of a contract. It requires an *offer* and an *acceptance*. The process of reaching an agreement usually proceeds as follows. Prior to entering into a contract, the parties may engage in preliminary negotiations about price, time of performance, and such.

At some point during these negotiations, one party makes an *offer*. The person who makes the offer is called the **offeror**, and the person to whom the offer is made is called the **offeree**. The offer sets forth the terms under which the offeror is willing to enter into the contract. The offeree has the power to create an agreement by accepting the offer.

In the following case, the court applied the adage "A contract is a contract is a contract."

agreement
The manifestation by two or more persons of the substance of a contract.

offeror
The party who makes an offer.

offeree
The party to whom an offer has been made.

CASE 10.1
Contract

Marder v. Jennifer Lopez

450 F.3d 445, Web 2006 U.S. App. Lexis 14330 (2006)
United States Court of Appeals for the Ninth Circuit

"Though in hindsight the agreement appears to be unfair to Marder—she only received $2,300 in exchange for a release of all claims relating to a movie that grossed over $150 million. . . ."

—Judge Pregerson

Facts

The movie *Flashdance* tells a story of a woman construction worker who performs at night as an exotic dancer. She performs an innovative form of dancing that includes a chair dance. Her goal is to obtain formal dance training at a university. The movie is based on the life of Maureen Marder, a nightclub dancer. Paramount Pictures Corporation used information from Marder to create the screenplay for the movie. Paramount paid Marder $2,300, and Marder signed a general release contract that provided that Marder "releases and discharges Paramount Picture Corporation of and from each and every claim, demand, debt, liability, cost and expense of any kind or character which have risen or are based in whole or in part on any matters occurring at any time prior to the date of this Release." Marder also released Paramount from claims "arising out of or in any way connected with either directly or indirectly, any and all arrangements in connec-tion with the preparation of screenplay material and the production, filming and exploitation of *Flashdance*."

Paramount released the movie *Flashdance*, which grossed over $150 million in domestic box office receipts and is still shown on television and distributed through DVD rentals. Subsequently, Sony Music Entertainment paid Paramount for release of copyright and produced a music video for the Jennifer Lopez song "I'm Glad." The video featured Lopez's performance as a dancer and singer. Marder believed that the video contains re-creations of many well-known scenes from *Flashdance*.

Marder brought a lawsuit in U.S. District Court against Paramount, Sony, and Lopez. Marder sought a declaration that she had rights as a co-author of *Flashdance* and a co-owner with Paramount of the copyright to *Flashdance*. She sued Sony and Lopez for allegedly violating her copyright in *Flashdance*. The District Court dismissed Marder's claims against Paramount, Sony, and Lopez. Marder appealed.

Issue

Was the general release Marder signed an enforceable contract?

Language of the Court

The Release's language is exceptionally broad and we hold that it is fatal to each of Marder's claims against Paramount. Such a release of "each and every claim" covers all claims within the scope of the language. Accordingly, the law imputes to Marder an intention corresponding to the reasonable meaning of her words and acts. Here, Marder released a broad array of claims relating to any assistance she provided during the creation of a Hollywood movie. Thus, the only reasonable interpretation of the Release is that it encompasses the various copyright claims she asserts in the instant suit.

Though in hindsight the agreement appears to be unfair to Marder—she only received $2,300 in exchange for a release of all claims relating to a movie that grossed over $150 million—there is simply no evidence that her consent was obtained by fraud, deception, misrepresentation, duress, or undue influence.

We also affirm the district court's dismissal of claims against Sony and Lopez. As we held above, under the terms of the Release, Marder cannot sue Paramount to assert a co-ownership in Flashdance. It is therefore impossible for her to establish a prima facie case of copyright infringement against Sony and Lopez.

Decision

The U.S. Court of Appeals held that the general release Marder signed was an enforceable contract. The Court of Appeals affirmed the judgment of the District Court that dismissed Marder's complaint against Paramount, Sony, and Lopez.

Case Questions

Critical Legal Thinking What is an agreement? Explain.

Business Ethics Did Marder act ethically in bringing this lawsuit? Should Paramount have paid Marder more money after the movie *Flashdance* became a success?

Contemporary Business What does the adage "A contract is a contract is a contract" mean? Was it applied in this case?

Offer

offer

"The manifestation of willingness to enter into a bargain, so made as to justify another person in understanding that his assent to that bargain is invited and will conclude it." (Section 24 of the *Restatement (Second) of Contracts*)

Section 24 of the *Restatement (Second) of Contracts* defines an **offer** as "the manifestation of willingness to enter into a bargain, so made as to justify another person in understanding that his assent to that bargain is invited and will conclude it." The following three elements are required for an offer to be effective:

1. The offeror must *objectively intend* to be bound by the offer.
2. The terms of the offer must be definite or reasonably *certain*.
3. The offer must be *communicated* to the offeree.

The making of an offer is shown in Exhibit 10.1.

■ EXHIBIT 10.1 Offer

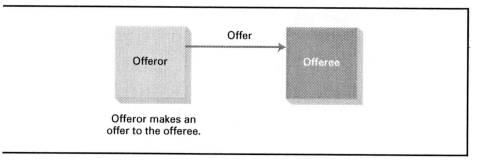

Offeror makes an offer to the offeree.

Objective Intent

The intent to enter into a contract is determined using the **objective theory of contracts**—that is, whether a reasonable person viewing the circumstances would conclude that the parties intended to be legally bound.

Example

The statement "I will buy your building for $2 million" is a valid offer because it indicates the offeror's present intent to contract.

Example

A statement such as "Are you interested in selling your building for $2 million?" is not an offer. It is an invitation to make an offer or an invitation to negotiate.

Offers that are made in jest, anger, or undue excitement do not include the necessary objective intent.

Example

The owner of Company A has lunch with the owner of Company B. In the course of their conversation, Company A's owner exclaims in frustration, "For $200, I'd sell the whole computer division!" An offer such as that cannot result in a valid contract.

objective theory of contracts

A theory that says the intent to contract is judged by the reasonable person standard and not by the subjective intent of the parties.

Express Terms

The terms of an offer must be clear enough for the offeree to be able to decide whether to accept or reject the terms of the offer. To be considered definite, an offer (and contract) generally must contain the following terms: (1) identification of the parties, (2) identification of the subject matter and quantity, (3) consideration to be paid, and (4) time of performance. Complex contracts usually state additional terms.

Most offers and contracts set forth express terms that identify the parties, the subject matter of the contract, the consideration to be paid by the parties, and the time of performance, as well as other terms of the offer and contract.

If the terms are indefinite, the courts usually cannot enforce the contract or determine an appropriate remedy for its breach. However, the law permits some terms to be implied.

A contract is a mutual promise.

William Paley
The Principles of Moral and Political Philosophy (1784)

Implied Terms

The common law of contracts required an exact specification of contract terms. If one essential term was omitted, the courts held that no contract had been made. This rule was inflexible.

The modern law of contracts is more lenient. The *Restatement (Second) of Contracts* merely requires that the terms of the offer be "reasonably certain."[1] Accordingly, the court can supply a missing term if a reasonable term can be implied.[2] The definition of *reasonable* depends on the circumstances. Terms that are supplied in this way are called **implied terms**.

Generally, time of performance can be implied. Price can be implied if there is a market or source from which to determine the price of the item or service (e.g., the "blue book" for an automobile price).

The parties or subject matter of the contract usually cannot be implied if an item or a service is unique or personal, such as the construction of a house or the performance of a professional sports contract.

implied term

A term in a contract that can reasonably be supplied by the courts.

Communication

An offer cannot be accepted if it is not communicated to the offeree by the offeror or a representative or an agent of the offeror.

All things obey fixed laws.

Lucretius (Titus Lucretius Carus)

Example

Mr. Jones, the CEO of Ace Corporation, wants to sell a manufacturing division to Baker Corporation. He puts the offer in writing, but he does not send it. Mr. Griswald, the CFO of Baker Corporation, visits Mr. Jones and sees the written offer lying on Jones's desk. Griswald tells his CEO about the offer. Because Mr. Jones never communicated the offer to Baker Corporation, there is no offer to be accepted.

Special Offers

There are several special types of offers. These include advertisements, rewards, and auctions. These special types of offers are discussed in the following paragraphs.

Advertisements

advertisement

An invitation to make an offer, or an actual offer.

As a general rule, **advertisements** for the sale of goods, even at specific prices, generally are treated as **invitations to make an offer**. This rule is intended to protect advertiser-sellers from the unwarranted breach of contract suits for nonperformance that would otherwise arise if the seller ran out of the advertised goods.

There is one exception to this rule: An advertisement is considered an offer if it is so definite or specific that it is apparent that the advertiser has the present intent to bind himself or herself to the terms of the advertisement.

Rewards

reward

An award given for performance of some service or attainment. To collect a reward, the offeree must (1) have knowledge of the reward offer prior to completing the requested act and (2) perform the requested act.

An offer to pay a **reward** (e.g., for the return of lost property or the capture of a criminal) is an offer to form a unilateral contract. To be entitled to collect the reward, the offeree must (1) have knowledge of the reward offer prior to completing the requested act and (2) perform the requested act.

Example

John Anderson accidentally leaves a briefcase containing $500,000 in negotiable bonds on a subway train. He places newspaper ads stating "$5,000 reward for return of briefcase left on a train in Manhattan on January 10, 2011, at approximately 10 A.M. Call 212-555-6789." Helen Smith, who is unaware of the offer, finds the briefcase. She reads the luggage tag containing Anderson's name, address, and telephone number, and she returns the briefcase to him. She is not entitled to the reward money because she did not know about it when she performed the requested act.

Auctions

auction with reserve

An auction in which the seller retains the right to refuse the highest bid and withdraw the goods from sale. Unless expressly stated otherwise, an auction is an auction with reserve.

auction without reserve

An auction in which the seller expressly gives up his or her right to withdraw the goods from sale and must accept the highest bid.

At an **auction**, the seller offers goods for sale through an auctioneer. Unless otherwise expressly stated, an auction is considered an **auction with reserve**—that is, it is an invitation to make an offer. The seller retains the right to refuse the highest bid and withdraw the goods from sale. A contract is formed only when the auctioneer strikes the gavel down or indicates acceptance by some other means. The bidder may withdraw his or her bid prior to that time.

If an auction is expressly announced to be an **auction without reserve**, the participants reverse the roles: The seller is the offeror, and the bidders are the offerees. The seller must accept the highest bid and cannot withdraw the goods from sale. However, if the auctioneer has set a minimum bid that it will accept, the auctioneer has to sell the item only if the highest bid is equal to or greater than the minimum bid.

In the following case, the court addressed the issue of an Internet auction.

Lim v. The.TV Corporation International

99 Cal.App.4th 684, 121 Cal.Rptr.2d 323, Web 2002 Cal. App. Lexis 4315 (2002)
Court of Appeal of California

"Defendant put the name 'Golf.tv' up for public auction, and plaintiff bid on that name and no other. That was an offer and acceptance, and formed a contract."

—Judge Epstein

Facts

The island nation of Tuvalu was awarded the top-level domain name "tv." Thus, Tuvalu controlled who could use domain names with the suffix "tv" on the Internet. For example, if a person named Jones acquired the suffix tv, her domain name on the Internet could be "jones.tv." Tuvalu hired The.TV Corporation International, a California corporation doing business under the name dotTV, to sell Internet names bearing the top-level domain name "tv." In April 2000, dotTV posted the name "golf.tv" for sale on its website, to be sold to the highest bidder. Je Ho Lim, a resident of South Korea, submitted the highest bid of $1,010 and authorized dotTV to charge his credit card for the amount of the bid. dotTV sent the following e-mail to Lim confirming the sale:

> DotTV—The New Frontier on the Internet
> E-Mail Invoice for Domain Registration
> NAME: Je Ho Lim
> Congratulations!
> You have won the auction for the following domain name:
> DOMAIN NAME: —golf
> SUBSCRIPTION LENGTH: 2 years, starts from activation date
> Amount (US$): $1,010 (first year registration fee)
> Please remember that the annual registration fee increases by 5 annually.
> You have the guaranteed right to renew the registration indefinitely.
> DotTV expects to charge your card and activate the registered domain name by May 15, 2000.
> See ya on the new frontier of the Internet!
> Lou Kerner CEO, dotTV Corporation www.TV

Shortly thereafter, dotTV sent another e-mail to Lim that stated "we have decided to release you from your bid" and that Lim should disregard the prior e-mail because of "an e-mail error that occurred." Later, dotTV publicly offered the domain name "golf.tv" with a beginning bid of $1 million. DotTV claimed that its original e-mail to Lim concerned a different domain name, "—golf," instead of "golf." Lim countered that characters such as two dashes ("—") are not recognized on the Internet and therefore the name "—golf" is an invalid domain name. When dotTV refused to transfer the domain name "golf.tv" to Lim, Lim sued dotTV for breach of contract. The trial court dismissed Lim's case against dotTV. Lim appealed.

Issue

Did Lim properly state a cause of action for breach of contract against dotTV?

Language of the Court

Defendant put the name "Golf.tv" up for public auction, and plaintiff bid on that name and no other. That was an offer and acceptance, and formed a contract. The distinction between "Golf.tv" and "—Golf.tv" comes from the acceptance e-mail sent by defendant. Certainly the hyphens preceding the name "golf" could not defeat the existence of an already formed contract. Defendant was accepting plaintiff's bid; it plainly was not making a counteroffer, particularly since, according to the pleading, the name "—Golf" did not "compute"; it did not qualify as a domain name. The e-mail must be read as an acknowledgment of plaintiff's winning bid and acceptance of the contract.

Decision

The court of appeal held that plaintiff Lim had properly pleaded a cause of action against defendant dotTV for breach of contract and reinstated Lim's case against dotTV.

Case Questions

Critical Legal Thinking What is the difference between an auction with reserve and an auction without reserve. Which type is presumed if there is no other statement to the contrary?

Business Ethics Did dotTV act ethically in this case? Why do you think that dotTV reneged on its e-mail confirmation to Lim?

Contemporary Business Are Internet domain names valuable? How do you register an Internet domain name?

Web Exercise Go to **www.golf.tv**. What types of goods or services are offered on this website? Think up an Internet domain name you would like to have. Go to the Network Solutions website, at **www.networksolutions.com**, and see if that name is available with the top-level domains .com, .org. or .net.

Concept Summary
Types of Auctions

Type	Does the seller offer the goods for sale
Auction with reserve	No. It is an invitation to make an offer. Because the bidder is the offeror, the seller (the offeree) may refuse to sell the goods. An auction is with reserve unless otherwise stated.
Auction without reserve	Yes. The seller is the offeror and must sell the goods to the highest bidder (the offeree). An auction is without reserve only if it is stipulated as such.

Termination of an Offer by Act of the Parties

An offer may be terminated by certain **acts of the parties**. The acts of the parties that terminate an offer are discussed in the following paragraphs.

Revocation of an Offer by the Offeror

revocation

Withdrawal of an offer by the offeror which terminates the offer.

Under the common law, an offeror may revoke (i.e., withdraw) an offer any time prior to its acceptance by the offeree. Generally, an offer can be so revoked even if the offeror promised to keep the offer open for a longer time. The **revocation** may be communicated to the offeree by the offeror or by a third party and made by (1) the offeror's express statement (e.g., "I hereby withdraw my offer") or (2) an act of the offeror that is inconsistent with the offer (e.g., selling the goods to another party). Most states provide that a revocation is not effective until it is actually received by the offeree or the offeree's agent.

Offers made to the public may be revoked by communicating the revocation by the same means used to make the offer.

Example

If a reward offer for a lost watch was published in two local newspapers each week for four weeks, notice of revocation must be published in the same newspapers for the same length of time. The revocation is effective against all offerees, even those who saw the reward offer but not the notice of revocation.

Contemporary Environment

Option Contract

An offeree can prevent the offeror from revoking his or her offer by paying the offeror compensation to keep the offer open for an agreed-upon period of time. This creates what is called an **option contract**. In other words, the offeror agrees not to sell the property to anyone except the offeree during the option period. An option contract is a contract in which the original offeree pays consideration (usually money) in return for the original offeror giving consideration (time of the option period). The death or incompetency of either party does not terminate an option contract unless the contract is for the performance of a personal service.

Example

Anne offers to sell a piece of real estate to Hal for $1 million. Hal wants time to investigate the property for possible environmental problems and to arrange financing if he decides to purchase the property, so he pays Anne $20,000 to keep her offer open to him for six months. At any time during the option period, Hal may exercise his option and pay Anne the $1 million purchase price. If Hal lets the option expire, however, Anne may keep the $20,000 and sell the property to someone else. Often option contracts are written so that if the original offeree purchases the property, the option amount is applied to the sale price.

Rejection of an Offer by the Offeree

An offer is terminated if the offeree **rejects** it. Any subsequent attempt by the offeree to accept the offer is ineffective and is construed as a new offer that the original offeror (now the offeree) is free to accept or reject. A rejection may be evidenced by the offeree's express words (oral or written) or conduct. Generally, a rejection is not effective until it is actually received by the offeror.

rejection
Express words or conduct by the offeree that rejects an offer. Rejection terminates the offer.

Example

Ji Eun, a sales manager at Apple Computer, Inc., offers to sell 4,000 iMac computers to Ted, the purchasing manager of General Motors Corporation, for $4,000,000. The offer is made on August 1. Ted telephones Ji Eun to say that he is not interested. This rejection terminates the offer. If Ted later decides that he wants to purchase the computers, an entirely new contract must be formed.

Counteroffer by the Offeree

A **counteroffer** by the offeree simultaneously terminates the offeror's offer and creates a new offer. Offerees' making of counteroffers is the norm in many industries. A counteroffer terminates the existing offer and puts a new offer into play. The previous offeree becomes the new offeror, and the previous offeror becomes the new offeree.

counteroffer
A response by an offeree that contains terms and conditions different from or in addition to those of the offer. A counteroffer terminates the previous offer.

Example

Fei says to Harold, "I will sell you my house for $700,000." Harold says, "I think $700,000 is too high; I will pay you $600,000." Harold has made a counteroffer. Fei's original offer is terminated, and Harold's counteroffer is a new offer that Fei is free to accept or reject.

Concept Summary
Termination of an Offer by Act of the Parties

Action	Description
Revocation	The offeror *revokes* (withdraws) the offer any time prior to its acceptance by the offeree.
Rejection	The offeree rejects the offer by his or her words or conduct.
Counteroffer	A counteroffer by the offeree creates a new offer and terminates the offeror's offer.

Termination of an Offer by Operation of Law

An offer can be terminated by **operation of law**. The ways that an offer can be terminated by operation of law are discussed in the following paragraphs.

Where law ends, there tyranny begins.

William Pitt, first Earl of Chatham
Case of Wilkes (speech)

Destruction of the Subject Matter

An offer terminates if the subject matter of the offer is destroyed through no fault of either party prior to the offer's acceptance.

Death or Incompetency of the Offeror or Offeree

Prior to acceptance of an offer, the death or incompetency of either the offeror or the offeree terminates an offer. Notice of the other party's death or incompetence is not a requirement.

Example

Suppose that on June 1, Shari offers to sell her house to Damian for $1,000,000, provided that Damian decides on or before June 15 that he will buy it. Shari dies on June 7, before Damian has made up his mind. The offer automatically terminates on June 7 when Shari dies.

Supervening Illegality

supervening illegality

The enactment of a statute, regulation, or court decision that makes the object of an offer illegal. This action terminates the offer.

If the object of an offer is made illegal prior to the acceptance of the offer, the offer terminates. This situation, which usually occurs when a statute is enacted or the decision of a court is announced that makes the object of the offer illegal, is called a **supervening illegality**.

Example

Suppose City Bank offers to loan ABC Corporation $5 million at an 18 percent interest rate. Prior to ABC's acceptance of the offer, the state legislature enacts a statute that sets a usury interest rate of 12 percent. City Bank's offer to ABC Corporation is automatically terminated when the usury statute became effective.

Lapse of Time

lapse of time

A stated time period after which an offer terminates. If no time is stated, an offer terminates after a reasonable time.

An offer expires at the **lapse of time** of an offer. An offer may state that it is effective only until a certain date. Unless otherwise stated, the time period begins to run when the offer is actually received by the offeree and terminates when the stated time period expires.

Example

If an offer states "This offer is good for 10 days," the offer expires at midnight of the 10th day after the offer was made. If an offer states "This offer must be accepted by January 1, 2012," the offer expires on midnight of January 1, 2012.

If no time is stated in the offer, the offer terminates after a "reasonable time" dictated by the circumstances. A reasonable time to accept an offer to purchase stock traded on a national stock exchange may be a few moments, but a reasonable time to accept an offer to purchase a house may be a week. Unless otherwise stated, an offer made face-to-face or during a telephone call usually expires when the conversation ends.

Concept Summary
Termination of an Offer by Operation of Law

Action	Description
Destruction of the subject matter	The subject matter of an offer is destroyed prior to acceptance through no fault of either party.
Death or incompetency	Prior to acceptance of an offer, either the offeror or the offeree dies or becomes incompetent.
Supervening illegality	Prior to the acceptance of an offer, the object of the offer is made illegal by statute, regulation, court decision, or other law.
Lapse of time	An offer terminates upon the expiration of a stated time in the offer. If no time is stated, the offer terminates after a "reasonable time."

Acceptance

acceptance

"A manifestation of assent by the offeree to the terms of the offer in a manner invited or required by the offer as measured by the objective theory of contracts." (Section 50 of the *Restatement (Second) of Contracts*)

Acceptance is "a manifestation of assent by the offeree to the terms of the offer in a manner invited or required by the offer as measured by the objective theory of contracts."[3] Recall that generally (1) unilateral contracts can be accepted only by the offeree's performance of the required act and (2) a bilateral contract can be accepted by an offeree who promises to perform (or, where permitted, by performance of) the requested act.

Who Can Accept an Offer?

Only the offeree has the legal power to accept an offer and create a contract. Third persons usually do not have the power to accept an offer. If an offer is made individually to two or more persons, each has the power to accept the offer. Once one of the offerees accepts the

■ EXHIBIT 10.2 Acceptance of an Offer

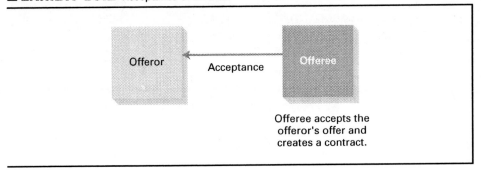

offer, it terminates as to the other offerees. An offer that is made to two or more persons jointly must be accepted jointly.

The acceptance of an offer is illustrated in Exhibit 10.2.

Unequivocal Acceptance

An offeree's acceptance must be **unequivocal**. For an acceptance to exist, the offeree must accept the terms as stated in the offer. This is called the **mirror image rule**.

mirror image rule
A rule which states that for an acceptance to exist, the offeree must accept the terms as stated in the offer.

Example
Abraham says to Caitlin, "I will sell you my iPhone for $300." Caitlin says, "Yes, I will buy your iPhone at that price." This is an unequivocal acceptance that creates a contract.

Usually, even a "grumbling acceptance" is a legal acceptance.

Example
Jordan offers to sell his computer to Taryn for $450. Taryn says "Okay, I'll take the computer, but I sure wish you would make me a better deal." This grumbling acceptance creates an enforceable contract because it was not a rejection or a counteroffer.

An equivocal response by the offeree does not create a contract.

Example
Halim offers to sell his iMac computer to Nicole for $400. Nicole says "I think I would like it, but I'm not sure." This is equivocation and does not amount to an acceptance.

In Case 10.3, on the following page, the court had to decide whether there had been an acceptance of the offer.

Silence as Acceptance

Silence usually is not considered acceptance, even if the offeror states that it is. This rule is intended to protect offerees from being legally bound to offers because they failed to respond. Nevertheless, silence *does* constitute acceptance in the following situations:

1. The offeree has indicated that silence means assent.

    Example "If you do not hear from me by Friday, ship the order."

2. The offeree signed an agreement indicating continuing acceptance of delivery until further notification.

    Example Book-of-the-month and CD-of-the-month club memberships are examples of such acceptances.

The law has outgrown its primitive stage of formalism when the precise word was the sovereign talisman, and every slip was fatal. It takes a broader view today. A promise may be lacking, and yet the whole writing may be "instinct with an obligation," imperfectly expressed.

Judge Cardozo
Wood v. Duff-Gordon (1917)

Montgomery v. English

902 So.2d 836, Web 2005 Fla.App. Lexis 4704 (2005)
Court of Appeal of Florida

"Florida employs the 'mirror image rule' with respect to contracts. Under this rule, in order for a contract to be formed, an acceptance of an offer must be absolute, unconditional, and identical with the terms of the offer."

—Judge Palmer

Facts

Norma English made an offer to purchase a house owned by Michael and Lourie Montgomery (Montgomery) for $272,000. English included in her offer a request to purchase several items of Montgomery's personal property, including paving stones and a fireplace screen. After Montgomery received English's offer, Montgomery made several changes to the offer, including (1) deleting certain items, including the paving stones and fireplace screen, from the personal property section of the offer; (2) deleting a provision regarding latent defects; (3) deleting a provision regarding building inspections; and (4) adding a specific "AS IS" rider. Montgomery signed their counteroffer and delivered it to English. English initialed most of Montgomery's changes except she did not initial the change that deleted the paving stones and fireplace screen —which were worth about $100—from the deal. Montgomery, relying on the "mirror image rule," notified English that she had not completely accepted their offer and that they were therefore withdrawing their offer to sell their house to English. That same day Montgomery signed a contract to sell their house to another buyer for $285,000. English sued Montgomery for specific performance of the contract. The trial court held in favor of English and ordered specific performance. Montgomery appealed.

Issue

Was an enforceable contract made between English and Montgomery?

Language of the Court

Montgomery argue that the trial court erred in denying their motion for summary judgment because the record demonstrated that there had been no meeting of the minds between the parties as to the essential terms of the con-
tract. We agree. Florida employs the "mirror image rule" with respect to contracts. Under this rule, in order for a contract to be formed, an acceptance of an offer must be absolute, unconditional, and identical with the terms of the offer. Applying the mirror image rule to these undisputed facts we hold that, as a matter of law, the parties failed to reach an agreement on the terms of the contract and, therefore, no enforceable contract was created.

Decision

The court of appeal held that because of the mirror image rule, no contract had been created between the parties. The court of appeal reversed the trial court's order of specific performance and remanded the case to the trial court, with instructions to enter summary judgment in favor of Montgomery.

Case Questions

Critical Legal Thinking What does the mirror image rule provide? Explain.

Business Ethics Did Montgomery act ethically when they backed out of selling the house? Did English act ethically by trying to force the sale of the house to her?

Contemporary Business Does the mirror image rule add certainty to contracting? Explain.

Web Exercise English appealed to the supreme court of Florida. Go to English's "Petitioner's Jurisdictional Brief" at **www.floridasupremecourt.org/clerk/briefs/2005/1001-1200/ 05-1186_JurisIni.pdf.** Scroll to the bottom of page 9 and read "II Strict Application of the 'Mirror Image Rule' Produces Harsh and Inequitable Results" on pages 9 and 10, and the "Conclusion" on page 10. The supreme court of Florida denied English's appeal to review the case.

3. Prior dealings between the parties indicate that silence means acceptance.

    Example A fish wholesaler who delivers 30 pounds of fish to a restaurant each Friday for several years and is paid for the fish can continue the deliveries with expectation of payment until notified otherwise by the restaurant.

4. The offeree takes the benefit of goods or services provided by the offeror even though the offeree (a) has an opportunity to reject the goods or services but fails to do so and (b) knows the offeror expects to be compensated.

    Example A homeowner who stands idly by and watches a painter whom she has not hired mistakenly paint her house owes the painter for the work.

Concept Summary
Offer and Acceptance

Type of Communication	Effective When
Offer	Received by offeree
Revocation of offer	Received by offeree
Rejection of offer	Received by offeror
Counteroffer	Received by offeror
Acceptance of offer in bilateral contract	Dispatched by offeree

Time of Acceptance

Under the common law of contracts, acceptance of a bilateral contract occurs when the offeree *dispatches* the acceptance by an authorized means of communication. This rule is called the **acceptance-upon-dispatch rule** or, more commonly, the **mailbox rule**. Under this rule, the acceptance is effective when it is dispatched, even if it is lost in transmission. If an offeree first dispatches a rejection and then sends an acceptance, the mailbox rule does not apply to the acceptance.[4]

The problem of lost acceptances can be minimized by expressly altering the mailbox rule. The offeror can do this by stating in the offer that acceptance is effective only upon actual receipt of the acceptance.

mailbox rule
A rule that states that an acceptance is effective when it is dispatched, even if it is lost in transmission. Also known as the *acceptance-upon-dispatch rule.*

Mailbox. *The mailbox rule provides that an acceptance is effective when it is dispatched.*

Mode of Acceptance

proper dispatch
The proper addressing, packaging, and posting of an acceptance.

An acceptance must be **properly dispatched**. The acceptance must be properly addressed, packaged in an appropriate envelope or container, and have prepaid postage or delivery charges. Under common law, if an acceptance is not properly dispatched, it is not effective until it is actually received by the offeror.

Generally, an offeree must accept an offer by an *authorized* means of communication. The offer can stipulate that acceptance must be by a specified means of communication (e.g., registered mail, telegram). Such stipulation is called **express authorization**. If the offeree uses an unauthorized means of communication to transmit the acceptance, the acceptance is not effective, even if it is received by the offeror within the allowed time period, because the means of communication was a condition of acceptance.

express authorization
A stipulation in an offer that says the acceptance must be by a specified means of communication.

implied authorization
A mode of acceptance that is implied from what is customary in similar transactions, usage of trade, or prior dealings between the parties.

Most offers do not expressly specify the means of communication required for acceptance. The common law recognizes certain implied means of communication. **Implied authorization** may be inferred from what is customary in similar transactions, usage of trade, or prior dealings between the parties. Section 30 of the *Restatement (Second) of Contracts* permits implied authorization "by any medium reasonable in the circumstances."

Test Review Terms and Concepts

Acceptance
Acceptance-upon-dispatch rule
   (mailbox rule)
Act of the parties
Advertisements
Agreement
Auction
Auction with reserve
Auction without reserve
Counteroffer

Express authorization
Implied authorization
Implied terms
Invitation to make an offer
Lapse of time
Mirror image rule
Mutual assent
Objective theory of contracts
Offer
Offeree

Offeror
Operation of law
Option contract
Properly dispatched
Rejection of an offer
Revocation of an offer
Reward
Supervening illegality
Unequivocal acceptance

Case Problems

10.1 Objective Theory of Contracts: While A.H. and Ida Zehmer, husband and wife, were drinking with W.O. Lucy, Mr. Zehmer made a written offer to sell a 471-acre farm the Zehmers owned to Lucy for $50,000. Zehmer contends that his offer was made in jest and that he only wanted to bluff Lucy into admitting that he did not have $50,000. Instead, Lucy appeared to take the offer seriously, offered $5 to bind the deal, and had Mrs. Zehmer sign it. When the Zehmers refused to perform the contract, Lucy brought this action to compel specific performance of the contract. Is the contract enforceable? *Lucy v. Zehmer* 196 Va. 493, 84 S.E.2d 516, **Web** 1954 Va. Lexis 244 (Supreme Court of Virginia)

10.2 Terms of a Contract: Ben Hunt and others operated a farm under the name S.B.H. Farms. Hunt went to McIlory Bank and Trust and requested a loan to build hog houses, buy livestock, and expand farming operations. The bank agreed to loan S.B.H. Farms $175,000, for which short-term promissory notes were signed by Hunt and the other owners of S.B.H. Farms. At that time, oral discussions were held with the bank

officer regarding long-term financing of S.B.H.'s farming operations; no dollar amount, interest rate, or repayment terms were discussed. When the owners of S.B.H. Farms defaulted on the promissory notes, the bank filed for foreclosure on the farm and other collateral. S.B.H. Farms counterclaimed for $750,000 damages, alleging that the bank breached its oral contract to provide long-term financing. Was there an oral contract for long-term financing? *Hunt v. McIlory Bank and Trust*, 2 Ark.App. 87, 616 S.W.2d 759, **Web** 1981 Ark.App. Lexis 716 (Court of Appeals of Arkansas)

10.3 Implied Terms: MacDonald Group, Ltd. (MacDonald), is the managing general partner of Fresno Fashion Square, a regional shopping mall in Fresno, California. The mall has several major anchor tenants and numerous smaller stores and shops, including Edmond's of Fresno, a jeweler. Edmond's signed a lease with MacDonald that provided that "there shall not be more than two jewelry stores" located in the mall. Nine years later, MacDonald sent Edmond's notice that it intended to expand the mall and lease space to other jewelers. The lease was silent as to the coverage of additional mall space. Edmond's sued MacDonald, arguing that the lease applied to mall additions. Who wins? *Edmond's of Fresno v. MacDonald Group, Ltd.*, 171 Cal.App.3d 598, 217 Cal.Rptr. 375, **Web** 1985 Cal.App. Lexis 2436 (Court of Appeal of California)

10.4 Implied Terms: Howard R. Wright hired John W. Cerdes to construct a home for him at a price of $43,150. The contract was silent regarding the time of completion. Construction was not completed after nine months. At that time, Wright obtained an injunction ordering Cerdes to stop work. Wright hired other contractors to complete the building. Cerdes sued Wright for breach of contract, claiming that he was due the contract price. How long should Cerdes have had to complete the house? *Cerdes v. Wright*, 408 So.2d 926, **Web** 1981 La.App. Lexis 5531 (Court of Appeal of Louisiana)

10.5 Reward: Rudy Turilli operated the Jesse James Museum in Stanton, Missouri. He contends that the man who was shot, killed, and buried as the notorious desperado Jesse James in 1882 was an impostor and that Jesse James lived for many years thereafter under the alias J. Frank Dalton and last lived with Turilli at his museum until the 1950s. Turilli appeared before a nationwide television audience and stated that he would pay $10,000 to anyone who could prove that his statements were wrong. After hearing this offer, Stella James, a relative of Jesse James, produced affidavits of persons related to and acquainted with the Jesse James family, constituting evidence that Jesse James was killed as alleged in song and legend on April 3, 1882. When Turilli refused to pay the reward, James sued for breach of contract. Who wins? *James v. Turilli*, 473 S.W.2d 757, **Web** 1971 Mo.App. Lexis 585 (Court of Appeals of Missouri)

10.6 Counteroffer: Glende Motor Company (Glende), an automobile dealership that sold new cars, leased premises from certain landlords. One day, fire destroyed part of the leased premises, and Glende restored the leasehold premises. The landlords received payment of insurance proceeds for the fire. Glende sued the landlords to recover the insurance proceeds. Ten days before the trial was to begin, the defendants jointly served on Glende a document titled "Offer to Compromise Before Trial," which was a settlement offer of $190,000. Glende agreed to the amount of the settlement but made it contingent upon the execution of a new lease. The next day, the defendants notified Glende that they were revoking the settlement offer. Glende thereafter tried to accept the original settlement offer. Has there been a settlement of the lawsuit? *Glende Motor Company v. Superior Court*, 159 Cal.App.3d 389, 205 Cal.Rptr. 682, **Web** 1984 Cal.App. Lexis 2435 (Court of Appeal of California)

10.7 Acceptance: Peter Andrus owned an apartment building that he had insured under a fire insurance policy sold by J. C. Durick Insurance (Durick). Two months prior to the expiration of the policy, Durick notified Andrus that the building should be insured for $48,000 (or 80 percent of the building's value), as required by the insurance company. Andrus replied that (1) he wanted insurance to match the amount of the outstanding mortgage on the building (i.e., $24,000) and (2) if Durick could not sell this insurance, he would go elsewhere. Durick sent a new insurance policy in the face amount of $48,000, with the notation that the policy was automatically accepted unless Andrus notified him to the contrary. Andrus did not reply. However, he did not pay the premiums on the policy. Durick sued Andrus to recover these premiums. Who wins? *J. C. Durick Insurance v. Andrus*, 139 Vt. 150, 424 A.2d 249, **Web** 1980 Vt. Lexis 1490 (Supreme Court of Vermont)

10.8 Mailbox Rule: William Jenkins and Nathalie Monk owned a building in Sacramento, California. They leased the building to Tuneup Masters for five years. The lease provided that Tuneup Masters could extend the lease for an additional five years if it gave written notice of its intention to do so by certified or registered mail at least six months prior to the expiration of the term of the lease.

Six months and three days before the expiration of the lease, Larry Selditz, vice president of Tuneup Masters, prepared a letter exercising the option, prepared and sealed an envelope with the letter in it, prepared U.S. Postal Service Form 3800, and affixed the certified mail sticker on the envelope, and had his secretary deliver the envelope to the Postal Service annex located on the ground floor of the office building. Postal personnel occupied the annex only between the hours of 9 and 10 A.M. At the end of each day, between 5 and 5:15 P.M., a postal employee picked up outgoing mail. The letter to the landlords was lost in the mail. The landlords thereafter refused to renew the lease and brought an unlawful detainer action against Tuneup Masters. Was the notice renewing the option effective? *Jenkins v. Tuneup Masters*, 190 Cal.App.3d 1, 235 Cal.Rptr. 214, **Web** 1987 Cal.App. Lexis 1475 (Court of Appeal of California)

Business Ethics Cases

10.9 Business Ethics: Kortney Dempsey took a cruise on a ship operated by Norwegian Cruise Line (Norwegian). In general, suits for personal injuries arising out of maritime torts are subject to a three-year statute of limitations. However, Congress permits this period to be reduced to one year by contract. The Norwegian passenger ticket limited the period to one year. Evidence showed that the cruise line ticket contained the notation "Important Notice" in a bright red box in the bottom-right corner of each of the first four pages of the ticket. The information in the box stated that certain pages of the ticket contain information that "affect[s] important legal rights." In addition, at the top of page 6 of the ticket, where the terms and conditions begin, it is stated in bold letters: "Passengers are advised to read the terms and conditions of the Passenger Ticket Contract set forth below." The clause at issue, which appears on page 8, clearly provides that suits must be brought within one year of injury. More than one year after Dempsey had taken the cruise (but within three years), she filed suit against Norwegian, seeking damages for an alleged injury suffered while on the cruise. Dempsey asserted that the one-year limitations period had not been reasonably communicated to her. Did Dempsey act ethically in suing when she did? Did Norwegian act ethically in reducing the limitations period to one year? Who wins the lawsuit? *Dempsey v. Norwegian Cruise Line*, 972 F.2d 998, **Web** 1992 U.S. App. Lexis 10939 (United States Court of Appeals for the Ninth Circuit)

10.10 Business Ethics: Genaro Munoz owned property that he leased to Goodwest Rubber Corporation (Goodwest) for five years. The lease granted Goodwest the option to buy the property at a fair market value. Goodwest sought to exercise the option to purchase the property and tendered $80,000 to Munoz. When Munoz rejected this offer, Goodwest filed suit, seeking specific performance of the option agreement. The court was presented with a single issue for review: Was a price designation of "fair market value" definite enough to support an action for specific performance? Do you think Munoz acted ethically in refusing to honor the option? Who wins? *Goodwest Rubber Corp. v. Munoz*, 170 Cal.App.3d 919, 216 Cal.Rptr. 604, **Web** 1985 Cal.App. Lexis 2288 (Court of Appeal of California)

Endnotes

1. Restatement (Second) of Contracts, Section 204.
2. Section 87(2) of the Restatement (Second) of Contracts states that an offer which the offeror should reasonably expect to induce action or forbearance of a substantial character on the part of the offeree before acceptance and which does induce such action or forbearance is binding as an option contract to the extent necessary to avoid injustice.
3. Restatement (Second) of Contracts, Section 50(1).
4. Restatement (Second) of Contracts, Section 40.

CHAPTER 11

"The law has outgrown its primitive stage of formalism when the precise word was the sovereign talisman, and every slip was fatal. It takes a broader view today. A promise may be lacking, and yet the whole writing may be "instinct with an obligation," imperfectly expressed."

—Justice Cardozo
Wood v. Duff-Gordon, 222 N.Y.88, 91 (1917)

Consideration and Promissory Estoppel

Chapter Objectives

After studying this chapter, you should be able to:

1. Define *consideration* and describe the requirements of consideration.
2. Define a *gift promise* and identify whether gift promises are enforceable.
3. Describe contracts that lack consideration, such as those involving illegal consideration, an illusory promise, a preexisting duty, or past consideration.
4. Define an accord and satisfaction of a disputed claim.
5. Define and apply the equitable doctrine of *promissory estoppel*.

Chapter Contents

Introduction to Consideration and Promissory Estoppel

To be enforceable, a contract must be supported by *consideration*, which is broadly defined as something of legal value. In general, this means that each side to a contract must give something of value for the contract to be enforceable. The consideration can consist of money, property, the provision of services, the forbearance of a right, or anything else of value. Most contracts are supported by consideration.

Contracts that are not supported by consideration are usually not enforceable. This means that a party who has not given consideration cannot enforce the contract. The parties may, however, voluntarily perform a contract that is lacking in consideration. If a contract that was lacking in consideration is performed by the parties, the parties cannot thereafter raise lack of consideration to undo the performed contract. *Promissory estoppel* is an equity doctrine that permits a court to order enforcement of a contract that lacks consideration.

This chapter discusses consideration, promises that lack consideration, and equity doctrines that permit promises that lack consideration to be enforced.

Consideration

consideration

Something of legal value given in exchange for a promise.

Consideration must be given before a contract can exist. **Consideration** is defined as something of legal value given in exchange for a promise. Consideration can come in many forms. The most common types consist of either a tangible payment (e.g., money, property) or the performance of an act (e.g., providing legal services). Less usual forms of consideration include the forbearance of a legal right (e.g., accepting an out-of-court settlement in exchange for dropping a lawsuit) and non-economic forms of consideration (e.g., refraining from "drinking, using tobacco, swearing, or playing cards or billiards for money"[1] for a specified time period).

Written contracts are presumed to be supported by consideration. This rebuttable presumption, however, may be overcome by sufficient evidence. A few states provide that contracts made under seal cannot be challenged for lack of consideration.

Requirements of Consideration

Consideration consists of two elements: (1) Something of legal value must be given (i.e., either a legal benefit must be received or legal detriment must be suffered) and (2) there must be a bargained-for exchange. Each of these is discussed in the paragraphs that follow:

legal value

Support for a contract when either (1) the promisee suffers a legal detriment or (2) the promisor receives a legal benefit.

bargained-for exchange

Exchange that parties engage in that leads to an enforceable contract.

1. **Legal value.**   Under the modern law of contracts, a contract is considered supported by **legal value** if (1) the promisee suffers a *legal detriment* or (2) the promisor receives a *legal benefit*.
2. **Bargained-for exchange.**   To be enforceable, a contract must arise from a **bargained-for exchange**. In most business contracts, the parties engage in such exchanges. The commercial setting in which business contracts are formed leads to this conclusion.

In the following case, the court had to decide whether there was consideration.

Gift Promise

gift promise

A promise that is unenforceable because it lacks consideration. Also known as a *gratuitous promise*.

Gift promises, also called **gratuitous promises**, are unenforceable because they lack consideration. To change a gift promise into an enforceable promise, the promisee must offer to do something in exchange—that is, in consideration—for the promise. Gift promises cause considerable trouble for persons who do not understand the importance of consideration.

CASE 11.1
Consideration

In the Matter of Wirth

14 A.D.3d 572, 789 N.Y.S.2d 69, Web 2005 N.Y.App. Div. Lexis 424 (2005)
Supreme Court of New York, Appellate Division

"The Pledge Agreement further stated: 'I acknowledge that Drexel's promise to use the amount pledged by me shall constitute full and adequate consideration for this pledge.'"

—Judge Schmidt

Facts

Raymond P. Wirth signed a pledge agreement which stated that in consideration of his interest in education, and "intending to be legally bound," he irrevocably pledged and promised to pay Drexel University the sum of $150,000. The pledge agreement provided that an endowed scholarship would be created in Wirth's name. Wirth died two months after signing the pledge but before any money had been paid to Drexel. When the estate of Wirth refused to honor the pledge, Drexel sued the estate to collect the $150,000. The estate alleged that the pledge was unenforceable because of lack of consideration. The surrogate court denied Drexel's motion for summary judgment and dismissed Drexel's claim against the estate. Drexel appealed.

Issue

Was the pledge agreement supported by consideration and therefore enforceable against the estate of Wirth?

Language of the Court

Pursuant to Pennsylvania's Uniform Written Obligations Act: "A written release or promise, hereafter made and signed by the person releasing or promising, shall not be invalid or unenforceable for lack of consideration, if the writing also contains an additional express statement, in any form or language, that the signer intends to be legally bound." Pursuant to this statute, the Pledge Agreement does not fail for lack of consideration, as the decedent expressly stated his intent to be legally bound by the pledge.

Moreover, even if we were to determine that the decedent, as promisor, anticipated consideration in return for his promise, there was no failure of consideration. The Pledge Agreement, which also was executed by representatives of Drexel, provided that the pledged sum "shall be used by" Drexel to create an endowed scholarship fund in the decedent's name, per the terms of the attached Letter

of Understanding. The Pledge Agreement further stated: "I acknowledge that Drexel's promise to use the amount pledged by me shall constitute full and adequate consideration for this pledge."

In our view, pursuant to the terms of the Pledge Agreement, Drexel provided sufficient consideration by expressly accepting the terms of the Pledge Agreement and by promising to establish the scholarship fund in the decedent's name. The fact that the decedent died before the initial gift was transferred into a special account set up by Drexel and therefore the scholarship fund was not yet implemented, did not negate the sufficiency of the promise as consideration to set up the fund.

Decision

The appellate court held that the pledge agreement was supported by consideration and was therefore enforceable against the estate of Wirth. The appellate court reversed the decision of the surrogate court and granted Drexel's motion for summary judgment against the estate of Wirth.

Case Questions

Critical Legal Thinking   What is consideration? What happens if there is lack of consideration supporting a promise? Explain.

Business Ethics   Was it ethical for the estate of Wirth to try to back out of the pledge agreement Wirth made before he died?

Contemporary Business   What special statute did Pennsylvania enact that solves the issue of lack of consideration in many contracts? Does such a statute take precedent over the common law contract rule of consideration? Explain.

Example

On May 1, Mrs. Colby promises to give her son $10,000 on June 1. When June 1 arrives Mrs. Colby refuses to pay the $10,000. The son cannot recover the $10,000 because it was a gift promise that lacked consideration. If, however, Mrs. Colby promises to pay her son $10,000 if he earns an "A" in his business law course and the son earns the "A," the contract is enforceable and the son can recover the $10,000.

A completed gift promise cannot be rescinded for lack of consideration.

Example

On May 1, Mr. Smith promises to give his granddaughter $10,000 on June 1. If on or before June 1 Mr. Smith actually gives the $10,000 to his granddaughter, it is a completed gift promise. Mr. Smith cannot thereafter recover the money from his granddaughter, even if the original promise lacked consideration.

The case that follows involves the issue of whether a giver can recover gifts that he made.

CASE 11.2
Gifts

Cooper v. Smith

800 N.E.2d 372, Web 2003 Ohio App. Lexis 5446 (2003)
Court of Appeals of Ohio

"Many gifts are made for reasons that sour with the passage of time. Unfortunately, gift law does not allow a donor to recover/revoke a gift simply because his or her reasons for giving it have soured."

—Judge Harsha

Facts

Lester Cooper suffered serious injuries that caused him to be hospitalized for an extended period of time. While he was hospitalized, Julie Smith, whom Cooper had met the year before, and Janet Smith, Julie's mother, made numerous trips to visit him. Although Julie was married to another man at the time, a romantic relationship developed between Cooper and Julie. While in the hospital, Cooper proposed marriage to Julie, and she accepted. Julie obtained a divorce from her husband. Cooper ultimately received an $180,000 settlement for his injuries.

After being released from the hospital, Cooper moved into Janet's house and lived with Janet and Julie. Over the next couple months, Cooper purchased a number of items for Julie, including a diamond engagement ring, a car, a computer, a tanning bed, and horses. On Julie's request, Cooper paid off Janet's car. Cooper also paid for various improvements to Janet's house, such as having a new furnace installed and having wood flooring laid in the kitchen. Several months later, the settlement money had run out, and Julie had not yet married Cooper. About six months later, Julie and Cooper had a disagreement, and

Cooper moved out of the house. Julie returned the engagement ring to Cooper. Cooper sued Julie and Janet to recover the gifts or the value of the gifts he had given them. The magistrate who heard the case dismissed Cooper's case, and the trial court affirmed the dismissal of the case. Cooper appealed.

Issue

Can Cooper recover the gifts or the value of the gifts he gave to Julie and Janet Smith?

Language of the Court

Unless the parties have agreed otherwise, the donor is entitled to recover the engagement ring (or its value) if the marriage does not occur, regardless of who ended the engagement. While we are willing to imply a condition concerning the engagement ring, we are unwilling to do so for other gifts given during the engagement period. Unlike the engagement ring, the other gifts have no symbolic meaning. Rather, they are merely "tokens of love and affection" which the donor bore for the donee. Many gifts are made for reasons that sour with the passage of time. Unfortunately, gift law does not allow a donor to recover/revoke a gift simply because his or her reasons for giving it have soured.

Generally, a completed gift is absolute and irrevocable. We believe the best approach is to treat gifts exchanged during the engagement period (excluding the engagement ring) as absolute and irrevocable gifts unless the donor has expressed intent that the gift be conditioned on the subsequent marriage. Cooper offered no evidence establishing that he gave the gifts on the express condition that they be returned to him if the engagement ended. Thus, the gifts are irrevocable gifts and Cooper is not entitled to their return.

Decision

The court of appeals held that the gifts made by Cooper to Julie (other than the engagement ring) and to Janet were irrevocable gifts that he could not recover simply because

his engagement with Julie ended. The court of appeals affirmed the judgment of the trial court, allowing Julie and Janet Smith to keep these gifts.

Case Questions

Critical Legal Thinking   Do you agree with the law that requires an engagement ring to be returned to the giver, no matter who breaks off the engagement? Explain.

Business Ethics   Did Julie and Janet Smith act ethically in keeping the gifts Cooper had given them? Did Cooper act ethically in trying to get the gifts back?

Contemporary Business   Why is there a different rule regarding the returning of engagement rings than for other gifts?

Web Exercise   Go to **www.nytimes.com/2006/03/05/ business/05goodie.html** to read about gifts to movie stars.

Contracts Lacking Consideration

Some contracts seem as though they are supported by consideration even though they are not. The contracts described in the following paragraphs fall into this category.

Illegal Consideration

A contract cannot be supported by a promise to refrain from doing an illegal act because that is **illegal consideration**. Contracts based on illegal consideration are void.

Example

The statement "I will burn your house down unless you agree to pay me $10,000," to which the homeowner agrees, is not an enforceable contract because the consideration given— not to burn down a house—is illegal consideration. Thus, the extortionist cannot enforce the contract against the homeowner.

Illusory Promise

If parties enter into a contract but one or both of the parties can choose not to perform their contractual obligations, the contract lacks consideration. Such promises, which are known as **illusory promises** (or **illusory contracts**), are unenforceable.

Example

A contract which provides that one of the parties has to perform only if he or she chooses to do so is an illusory contract.

Moral Obligation

Promises made out of a sense of **moral obligation**, or honor, are generally unenforceable on the grounds that they lack consideration. In other words, moral consideration is not treated as legal consideration. A minority of states hold that moral obligations are enforceable.

Preexisting Duty

A promise lacks consideration if a person promises to perform an act or do something he is already under an obligation to do. This is called a **preexisting duty**. The promise is unenforceable because no new consideration has been given.

illegal consideration
A promise to refrain from doing an illegal act. Such a promise will not support a contract.

illusory promise
A contract into which both parties enter but one or both of the parties can choose not to perform their contractual obligations. Thus, the contract lacks consideration. Also known as an illusory contract.

moral obligation
A sense of honor that prompts a person to make a promise. Promises made out of a sense of moral obligation lack consideration.

preexisting duty
Something a person is already under an obligation to do. A promise lacks consideration if a person promises to perform a preexisting duty.

There is grim irony in speaking of freedom of contract of those who, because of their economic necessities, give their service for less than is needful to keep body and soul together.

Harlan Fiske Stone
Morehead v. N.Y. ex rel. Tipaldo (1936)

Example

Many states have adopted statutes that prohibit police officers from demanding money for investigating and apprehending criminals or that prohibit fire fighters from demanding payment for fighting fires. If a person agrees to such a demand, she does not have to pay it because there was no new consideration; public servants are under a preexisting duty to perform their functions.

In the private sector, the preexisting duty rule often arises when one of the parties to an existing contract seeks to change the terms of the contract during the course of its performance. Such midstream changes are unenforceable: The parties have a preexisting duty to perform according to the original terms of the contract.

Sometimes a party to a contract runs into substantial *unforeseen difficulties* while performing his or her contractual duties. If the parties modify their contract to accommodate these unforeseen difficulties, the modification will be enforced even though it is not supported by new consideration.

Past Consideration

past consideration

A prior act or performance. Past consideration (e.g., prior acts) will not support a new contract. New consideration must be given.

Problems of **past consideration** often arise when a party promises to pay someone some money or other compensation for work done in the past. Past consideration is not consideration for a new promise; therefore, a promise based on past consideration is not enforceable.

Example

Felipe, who has worked in management for the Acme Corporation for 30 years, is retiring. The president of Acme says, "Because you were such a loyal employee, Acme will pay you a bonus of $100,000." Subsequently, the corporation refuses to pay the $100,000. Unfortunately for Felipe, he has already done the work for which he has been promised to be paid. The contract is unenforceable against Acme because it is based on past consideration.

In the following case, the court held that there was lack of consideration and there was fraud, and it refused to enforce the contract.

CASE 11.3
Lack of Consideration

West America Housing Corporation v. Pearson

2007 WY 184, 171 P.3d 539, Web 2007 Wyo. Lexis 196 (2007)
Supreme Court of Wyoming

"The district court stated on the record that he found Joelson's testimony to be wildly unbelievable and likely perjury."

—Justice Hill

Facts

Donald Pearson was 80 years of age and living in an assisted living facility. Jeanne Joelson, whom Pearson knew, convinced Pearson to purchase the Wrangler Road Property, to pay $75,755 as the down payment, and to borrow $279,200 from a lender who retained a mortgage on the property. Joelson told Pearson that she, Bobbie Charles Craver, and West America Housing Corporation (WAHC), which was

owned by Joelson, Craver, and Sheena Shoopman, Joelson's daughter, would pay the mortgage payments on the property.

WAHC made the mortgage payments and paid the insurance and property taxes on the property for approximately four years. Joelson then asked Pearson to deed the property to Larry Oltman, Joelson's brother, which Joelson claimed Pearson did. There was a quitclaim deed with Pearson's signature on it that transferred the property to

Oltman. The deed transferred ownership of the property to Oltman and indicated that Pearson had received $75,755 "in hand paid" as consideration for the transaction. Oltman subsequently deeded the property to WAHC.

Pearson sued Joelson, Craver, Shoopman, and WAHC, alleging that the transfer of the property from Pearson to Oltman lacked consideration and therefore was a voidable transfer. Pearson also alleged that the transfer of the property from Oltman to WAHC was a fraudulent transfer that was void. Pearson testified that he did not complete or sign the deed transferring the property to Oltman and that he did not receive the consideration indicated on the deed. Joelson testified that she paid Pearson $75,755 in cash that she brought to Pearson in a shoebox at the time of the sale to Oltman. However, Joelson could not produce any withdrawal slip from a bank or any other evidence of the source of the cash. The district court quieted title to the property to Pearson. Joelson, Craver, Shoopman, and WAHC appealed.

Issue

Did the transfer of the Wrangler Road Property from Pearson to Oltman lack consideration and was the transfer of the property from Oltman to WAHC a fraudulent transfer?

Language of the Court

The district court stated on the record that he found Joelson's testimony to be wildly unbelievable and likely perjury. The evidence is at best equivocal that Pearson actually signed the quitclaim deed to Oltman. The only evidence to support the element of consideration was Joelson's "wildly unbelievable" tale of delivering the consideration to Pearson on an unknown date, in the form of cash in a shoe box, for which she obtained no receipt. It was not plain error for the district court to conclude that the deed at issue was void for lack of consideration, despite the language on the face of the deed. It flows virtually without need for discussion that the succeeding deeds were also void. The district court's findings are not clearly erroneous, and its application of the law is not in error.

Decision

The supreme court of Wyoming held that there was no consideration to support the transfer of the deed from Pearson to Oltman. The court also held that the transfer of the property from Oltman to the defendants was fraudulent. The supreme court upheld the district court's decision that quieted title to the property to Pearson.

Case Questions

Critical Legal Thinking   What is the result if lack of consideration for a contract is found? Do you think that there was lack of consideration in this case? Explain.

Business Ethics   Did Joelson act ethically in this case? Did Oltman act ethically in this case?

Contemporary Business   Do you think that there was fraud in this case? Why or why not? Do you think elderly people are often targets of fraud?

Web Exercise   Go to **www.fraud.org/elderfraud/hangup .htm.** Read the article "Five Steps to Help Seniors Targeted by Telemarketing Fraud."

Concept Summary
Promises Lacking Consideration

Type of Consideration	Description of Promise
Illegal consideration	Promise to refrain from doing an illegal act.
Illusory promise	Promise in which one or both parties can choose not to perform their obligation.
Moral obligation	Promise made out of a sense of moral obligation, honor, love, or affection. Some states enforce these types of contracts.
Preexisting duty	Promise based on the preexisting duty of the promisor to perform.
Past consideration	Promise based on the past performance of the promisee.

Settlement of Claims

The law promotes the voluntary settlement of disputed claims. Settlement saves judicial resources and serves the interests of the parties entering into the settlement.

In some situations, one of the parties to a contract believes that he or she did not receive what he or she was due. This party may attempt to reach a compromise with the other party (e.g., by paying less consideration than was provided for in the contract). If the two

Contemporary Environment

Special Business Contracts

Generally, the courts tolerate a greater degree of uncertainty as to the issue of consideration in business contracts than in personal contracts, under the premise that sophisticated parties know how to protect themselves when negotiating contracts. The law imposes an obligation of good faith on the performance of the parties to requirements and output contracts.

The following paragraphs describe special types of business contracts that allow a greater-than-usual degree of uncertainty concerning consideration.

Output Contract

In an **output contract**, the seller agrees to sell all of its production to a single buyer. Output contracts serve the legitimate business purposes of (1) assuring the seller of a purchaser for all its output and (2) assuring the buyer of a source of supply for the goods it needs.

Example

Organic Foods Inc. is a company that operates farms that produce organically grown grains and vegetables. Urban Food Markets is a grocery store chain that sells organically grown foods. Urban Food Markets contracts with Organic Foods Inc. to purchase all the organic foods grown by Organic Foods Inc. this year. This is an example of an output contract: Organic Foods Inc. must sell all of its output to Urban Foods Market.

Requirements Contract

A **requirements contract** is one in which a buyer contracts to purchase all of its requirements for an item from one seller. Such contracts serve the legitimate business purposes

of (1) assuring the buyer of a uniform source of supply and (2) providing the seller with reduced selling costs.

Example

The Goodyear Tire & Rubber Company manufactures tires that are used on automobiles. Ford Motor Company manufactures automobiles on which it must place tires before the automobiles can be sold. Assume Ford Motor Company enters into a contract with Goodyear Tire & Rubber Company to purchase all of the tires it will need this year from Goodyear. This is an example of a requirements contract: Ford Motor Company has agreed to purchase all of the tires it will need from Goodyear. Goodyear may sell tires to other purchasers, however.

Best-Efforts Contract

A **best-efforts contract** is a contract that contains a clause that requires one or both of the parties to use their *best efforts* to achieve the objective of the contract. The courts generally have held that the imposition of the best-efforts duty provides sufficient consideration to make a contract enforceable.

Example

Real estate listing contracts often require a real estate broker to use his or her best efforts to find a buyer for the listed real estate. Contracts often require underwriters to use their best efforts to sell securities on behalf of their corporate clients. Both of these contracts would be enforceable. Of course, a party can sue another company for failing to use its promised best efforts.

accord
An agreement whereby the parties agree to accept something different in satisfaction of the original contract.

satisfaction
The performance of an accord.

parties agree to a compromise, a settlement of the claim has been reached. The settlement agreement is called an **accord**. If the accord is performed, it is called a **satisfaction**. This type of settlement is called an **accord and satisfaction** or a **compromise**. If the accord is not satisfied, the other party can sue to enforce either the accord or the original contract.

Example

A contract stipulated that the cost of a computer and software system that keeps track of inventory, accounts receivable, and so on is $300,000. After it is installed, the computer system does not perform as promised. To settle the dispute, the parties agree that $200,000 is to be paid as full and final payment for the computer. This accord is enforceable even though no new consideration is given because reasonable persons would disagree as to the worth of the computer system that was actually installed.

promissory estoppel
An equitable doctrine that prevents the withdrawal of a promise by a promisor if it will adversely affect a promisee who has adjusted his or her position in justifiable reliance on the promise.

Equity: Promissory Estoppel

The courts have developed the equitable doctrine of **promissory estoppel** or (**detrimental reliance**) to avoid injustice. This doctrine is a broad policy-based doctrine. It is used to provide a remedy to a person who has relied on another person's promise when that person

Courthouse, Santa Barbara, California. *This courthouse in Santa Barbara, California, was built in 1929 and is patterned after a Spanish–Moorish palace. The court hears cases, including cases to enforce contracts. To be enforceable, a contract must be supported by consideration. If a contract is lacking consideration, the court will not enforce the contract. However, an exception to this rule is that a court can enforce a contract that is otherwise lacking consideration, using the equitable doctrine of promissory estoppel.*

withdraws his or her promise and is not subject to a breach of contract action because one of the two elements contract requirements (i.e., agreement or consideration) is lacking.

The doctrine of promissory estoppel *estops* (prevents) the promisor from revoking his or her promise. Therefore, the person who has *detrimentally relied* on the promise for performance may sue the promisor for performance or other remedy the court feels is fair to award in the circumstances.

For the doctrine of promissory estoppel to be applied, the following elements must be shown:

• The promisor made a promise.
• The promisor should have reasonably expected to induce the promisee to reply on the promise.
• The promisee actually relied on the promise and engaged in an action or forbearance of a right of a definite and substantial nature.
• Injustice would be caused if the promise were not enforced.

Example

XYZ Construction Company, a general contractor, requests bids from subcontractors for work to be done on a hospital building that XYZ plans to submit a bid to build. Bert Plumbing Company, a plumbing subcontractor, submits the lowest bid for the plumbing work, and XYZ incorporates Bert's low bid in its own bid for the general contract. Based on all of the subcontractor's bids, XYZ submits the lowest overall bid to build the hospital and is awarded the contract. Bert Plumbing plans to withdraw its bid. However, the doctrine of promissory estoppel prevents Bert from withdrawing its bid. Since XYZ has been awarded the contract to build the hospital based partially upon Bert's plumbing subcontractor bid, XYZ can enforce Bert's promise to perform under the doctrine of promissory estoppel. Allowing Bert to withdraw its bid would cause injustice.

Now equity is no part of the law, but a moral virtue, which qualifies, moderates, and reforms the rigor, hardness, and edge of the law, and is a universal truth.

Lord Cowper
Dudley v. Dudley (1705)

Test Review Terms and Concepts

Accord
Accord and satisfaction (compromise)
Bargained-for exchange
Best-efforts contract
Consideration
Gift promise (gratuitous promise)

Illegal consideration
Illusory promise (illusory contract)
Legal value
Moral obligation
Output contract
Past consideration

Preexisting duty
Promissory estoppel (detrimental reliance)
Requirements contract
Satisfaction

Case Problems

11.1 Consideration: Clyde and Betty Penley were married. Eighteen years later, Clyde operated an automotive tire business, and Betty owned an interest in a Kentucky Fried Chicken (KFC) franchise. That year, when Betty became ill, she requested that Clyde begin spending additional time at the KFC franchise to ensure its continued operation. Subsequently, Betty agreed that if Clyde would devote full time to the KFC franchise, they would operate the business as a joint enterprise, share equally in the ownership of its assets, and divide its returns equally. Pursuant to this agreement, Clyde terminated his tire business and devoted his full time to the KFC franchise. Twelve years later, Betty abandoned Clyde and denied him any rights in the KFC franchise. Clyde sued to enforce the agreement with Betty. Is the agreement enforceable? *Penley v. Penley*, 314 N.C. 1, 332 S.E.2d 51, **Web** 1985 N.C. Lexis 1706 (Supreme Court of North Carolina)

11.2 Forbearance to Sue: When John W. Frasier died, he left a will that devised certain of his community and separate property to his wife, Lena, and their three children. These devises were more valuable to Lena than just her interest in the community property that she would otherwise have received without the will. The devises to her, however, were conditioned upon the filing of a waiver by Lena of her interest in the community property, and if she failed to file the waiver, she would then receive only her interest in the community property and nothing more. Lena hired her brother, D.L. Carter, an attorney, to represent her. Carter failed to file the waiver on Lena's behalf, thus preventing her from taking the devises under the will. Instead, she received her interest in the community property, which was $19,358 less than she would have received under the will. Carter sent Lena the following letter:

> This is to advise and confirm our agreement—that in the event the J. W. Frasier estate case now on appeal is not terminated so that you will receive settlement equal to your share of the estate as you would have done if your waiver had been filed in the estate in proper time, I will make up any balance to you in payments as suits my convenience and will pay interest on your loss at 6 percent.

The appeal was decided against Lena. When she tried to enforce the contract against Carter, he alleged that the contract was not enforceable because it was not supported by valid consideration. Who wins? *Frasier v. Carter*, 92 Idaho 79, 437 P.2d 32, **Web** 1968 Ida. Lexis 249 (Supreme Court of Idaho)

11.3 Past Consideration: A. J. Whitmire and R. Lee Whitmire were brothers. R. Lee Whitmire married Lillie Mae Whitmire. For 4 years, A. J. performed various services for his brother and sister-in-law. During this time, R. Lee and Lillie Mae purchased some land. Fifteen years later, in the presence of Lillie Mae, R. Lee told A. J., "When we're gone, this land is yours" At that time, A. J. had not done any work for R. Lee or Lillie Mae for 16 years, and none was expected or provided in the future. Thirty years later, after both R. Lee and Lillie Mae had died, A. J. filed a claim with the estate of Lillie Mae, seeking specific performance of the earlier promise to give him the land. Does A. J. get the property? *Whitmire v. Watkins*, 245 Ga. 713, 267 S.E.2d 6, **Web** 1980 Ga. Lexis 908 (Supreme Court of Georgia)

11.4 Preexisting Duty: Robert Chuckrow Construction Company (Chuckrow) was employed as the general contractor to build a Kinney Shoe Store. Chuckrow employed Ralph Gough to perform the carpentry work on the store. The contract with Gough stipulated that he was to provide all labor, materials, tools, equipment, scaffolding, and other items necessary to complete the carpentry work. Gough's employees erected 38 trusses at the job site. The next day, 32 of the trusses fell off the building. The reason for the trusses having fallen was unexplained, and evidence showed that it was not due to Chuckrow's fault or a deficiency in the building plans. Chuckrow told Gough that he would pay him to reerect the trusses and continue work. When the job was complete, Chuckrow paid Gough the original contract price but refused to pay him for the additional cost of reerecting the trusses. Gough sued Chuckrow for this expense. Can Gough recover? *Robert Chuckrow Construction Company v. Gough*, 117 Ga. App. 140, 159 S.E.2d 469, **Web** 1968 Ga.App. Lexis 1007 (Court of Appeals of Georgia)

11.5 Illegal Consideration: In 1972, Marna Balin was involved in two automobile accidents in which she suffered severe injuries. She hired Norman H. Kallen, an attorney, to represent her. Kallen filed lawsuits on behalf of Balin, seeking damages for her injuries. Kallen repeatedly urged Balin to settle the lawsuits for $25,000. In late 1974, when she became disappointed with Kallen's representation, she retained another attorney, Samuel P. Delug, and instructed him to obtain her legal files from Kallen. The California Rules of Professional Conduct for attorneys provide that an attorney may not retain a client's files [Rule 2-111 (A)(2)]. However, Kallen refused to release the files until Delug agreed to give Kallen 40 percent of the attorneys' fees recovered in the case. The cases were ultimately settled for $810,000, resulting in attorneys' fees of $324,000. When Delug refused to pay Kallen 40 percent of these fees, Kallen sued Delug. Was the fee-splitting agreement between Kallen and Delug supported by legal consideration? *Kallen v. Delug*, 157 Cal.App.3d 940, 203 Cal.Rptr. 879, **Web** 1984 Cal.App. Lexis 2257 (California Court of Appeal)

11.6 Promissory Estoppel: Nalley's, Inc. (Nalley's), was a major food distributor with its home office in the state of Washington. Jacob Aronowicz and Samuel Duncan approached Nalley's about the possibility of its manufacturing a line of sliced meat products to be distributed by Nalley's. When Nalley's showed considerable interest, Aronowicz and Duncan incorporated as Major Food Products, Inc. (Major). Meetings to discuss the proposal continued at length with Charles Gardiner, a vice president and general manager of the Los Angeles division of Nalley's. Gardiner delivered a letter to Major, agreeing to become the exclusive Los Angeles and Orange Country distributor for Major's products, but he stated in the letter "that should we determine your product line is not representative or is not compatible with our operation we are free to terminate our agreement within 30 days." Nalley's was to distribute the full production of products produced by Major.

Based on Gardiner's assurances, Major leased a plant, modified the plant to its specifications, purchased and installed equipment, signed contracts to obtain meat to be processed, and hired personnel. Both Aronowicz and Duncan resigned from their positions at other meat processing companies to devote full time to the project. Financing was completed when Aronowicz and Duncan used their personal fortunes to purchase the stock of Major. Gardiner and other representatives of Nalley's visited Major's plant and expressed satisfaction with the premises. Major obtained the necessary government approvals regarding health standards and immediately achieved full production. Because Nalley's was to pick up the finished products at Major's plant, Nalley's drivers visited Major's plant to acquaint themselves with its operations.

Gardiner sent the final proposal regarding the Nalley's–Major relationship to Nalley's home office for final approval. One week later, Nalley's home office in Washington made a decision not to distribute Major's products. Nalley's refused to give any reason to Major for its decision. No final agreement was ever executed between the parties. Immediate efforts by Major to secure other distribution for its products proved unsuccessful. Further, because Major owned no trucks itself and had no sales organization, it could not distribute the products itself. In less than six months, Major had failed, and Aronowicz's and Duncan's stock in Major was worthless. Major, Aronowicz, and Duncan sued Nalley's for damages under the doctrine of promissory estoppel. Do they win? *Aronowicz v. Nalley's. Inc.*, 30 Cal.App.3d 27, 106 Cal.Rptr. 424, **Web** 1972 Cal.App. Lexis 667 (Court of Appeal of California)

Business Ethics Cases

11.7 Business Ethics: Ocean Dunes of Hutchinson Island Development Corporation (Ocean Dunes) was a developer of condominium units. Prior to the construction, Albert and Helen Colangelo entered into a purchase agreement to buy one of the units and paid a deposit to Ocean Dunes. A provision in the purchase agreement provided that:

> If Developer shall default in the performance of its obligations pursuant to this agreement, Purchaser's only remedy shall be to terminate this agreement, whereupon the Deposit shall be refunded to Purchaser and all rights and obligations thereunder shall thereupon become null and void.

The purchase agreement provided that if the buyer defaulted, the developer could retain the buyer's deposit or sue the buyer for damages and any other legal or equitable rem-

edy. When Ocean Dunes refused to sell the unit to the Colangelos, they sued, seeking a decree of specific performance to require Ocean Dunes to sell them the unit. Ocean Dunes alleged that the above-quoted provision prevented the plaintiffs from seeking any legal or equitable remedy. Was the defendant's duty under the contract illusory? Was it ethical for Ocean Dunes to place the provision at issue in the contract? *Ocean Dunes of Hutchinson Island Development Corporation v. Colangelo*, 463 So.2d 437, **Web** 1985 Fla.App. Lexis 12298 (Court of Appeal of Florida)

11.8 Business Ethics: Red Owl Stores, Inc., a Minnesota corporation with its home office at Hopkins, Minnesota, owned and operated grocery supermarkets and granted franchises to franchisees to also operate such stores. Joseph Hoffman, who operated a bakery with his wife in Wautoma, Wisconsin, was interested in obtaining a Red Owl franchise to operate a grocery store in Wisconsin. Hoffman contacted a representative of

Red Owl and had numerous conversations regarding this proposal. Ten months later, Mr. Lukowitz became Red Owl's representative for the territory comprising upper Michigan and most of Wisconsin. Hoffman mentioned to Lukowitz that he had the capital to invest, and Lukowitz assured him that it would be sufficient to open a Red Owl franchise.

To gain experience in the grocery store business, and upon the advice of Lukowitz and other Red Owl representatives, Hoffman bought a small grocery store in Wautoma. After three months of operating this store, a Red Owl representative came in and took inventory, checked operations, and found that the store was operating at a profit. Lukowitz advised Hoffman to sell the store to his manager and assured Hoffman that Red Owl would find a larger store for him elsewhere. Although Hoffman was reluctant to sell at that time because it meant losing the summer tourist business, he sold on the assurance that he would be operating a Red Owl store at a new location by the fall. Again, Lukowitz assured Hoffman that the capital he had was sufficient to open a Red Owl franchise.

Red Owl had selected a site in Chilton, Wisconsin, for the proposed store. On Red Owl's insistence, Hoffman obtained an option to purchase the site. Hoffman and his wife rented a house in Chilton. Hoffman met with Lukowitz, who assured him, "Everything is ready to go. Get your money together and we are set." Lukowitz told Hoffman that he must sell his bakery business and building in Wautoma and that this was the only "hitch" in the entire plan. Hoffman sold his bakery building but retained the equipment to be used in the proposed Red Owl store. During the next two months, Red Owl prepared various financial projections for the proposed site. Hoffman met with Lukowitz and the credit manager for Red Owl, who demanded that Hoffman have more capital to invest in the store. Hoffman contacted his father-in-law, who agreed to provide the additional money. A week later, Red Owl sent Hoffman a telegram, demanding that he have more capital to invest. When Hoffman could not raise the additional money, the transaction fell through. Hoffman did not purchase the store site in Chilton and forfeited the option payment. The parties had never entered into a final agreement regarding the franchise.

Hoffman sued Red Owl under the doctrine of promissory estoppel, seeking damages for the money lost on the option payment on the Chilton property and the lease payments on the house in Chilton. Did the representatives of Red Owl Stores, Inc., act ethically in this case? Should the equitable doctrine of promissory estoppel apply in this case? *Hoffman v. Red Owl Stores, Inc.*, 26 Wis.2d 683, 133 N.W.2d 267, **Web** 1965 Wisc. Lexis 1026 (Supreme Court of Wisconsin)

Endnote

1. *Hamer v. Sidwa*, 124 N.Y. 538, 27 N.E. 256, **Web** 1891 N.Y. Lexis 1396 (Court of Appeal of New York).

CHAPTER 12

An unconscionable contract is one which no man in his senses, not under delusion, would make, on the one hand, and which no fair and honest man would accept on the other.

—Hume v. United States
132 U.S. 406, 10 S.Ct. 134, 1889 U.S. Lexis 1888 (1889)

Capacity and Legality

Chapter Objectives

After studying this chapter, you should be able to:

1. Define and describe the infancy doctrine.
2. Define *legal insanity* and *intoxication* and explain how they affect contractual capacity.
3. Identify illegal contracts that are contrary to statutes and those that violate public policy.
4. Describe covenants not to compete and exculpatory clauses and identify when they are lawful.
5. Define *unconscionable contract* and determine when such contracts are unlawful.

Chapter Contents

Introduction to Capacity and Legality

Generally, the law presumes that the parties to a contract have the requisite **contractual capacity** to enter into the contract. Certain persons do not have this capacity, however, including minors, insane persons, and intoxicated persons. The common law of contracts and many state statutes protect persons who lack contractual capacity from having contracts enforced against them. The party asserting incapacity or his or her guardian, conservator, or other legal representative bears the burden of proof.

An essential element for the formation of a contract is that the object of the contract be lawful. A contract to perform an illegal act is called an *illegal contract*. Illegal contracts are void. That is, they cannot be enforced by either party to the contract. The term *illegal contract* is a misnomer, however, because no contract exists if the object of the contract is illegal. In addition, courts hold that *unconscionable contracts* are unenforceable. An unconscionable contract is one that is so oppressive or manifestly unfair that it would be unjust to enforce it.

Capacity to contract and the lawfulness of contracts are discussed in this chapter.

Minors

minor
A person who has not reached the age of majority.

Minors do not always have the maturity, experience, or sophistication needed to enter into contracts with adults. Common law defines minors as females under the age of 18 and males under the age of 21. In addition, many states have enacted statutes that specify the **age of majority**. The most prevalent age of majority is 18 years of age for both males and females. Any age below the statutory age of majority is called the **period of minority**.

Infancy Doctrine

infancy doctrine
A doctrine that allows minors to disaffirm (cancel) most contracts they have entered into with adults.

To protect minors, the law recognizes the **infancy doctrine**, which gives minors the right to *disaffirm* (or *cancel*) most contracts they have entered into with adults. This right is based on public policy which reasons that minors should be protected from the unscrupulous behavior of adults. In most states, the infancy doctrine is an objective standard. If a person's age is below the age of majority, the court will not inquire into his or her knowledge, experience, or sophistication. Generally, contracts for the necessaries of life, which we discuss later in this chapter, are exempt from the scope of this doctrine.

Under the infancy doctrine, a minor has the option of choosing whether to enforce a contract (i.e., the contract is **voidable** by a minor). The adult party is bound to the minor's decision. If both parties to a contract are minors, both parties have the right to disaffirm the contract.

If performance of the contract favors the minor, the minor will probably enforce the contract. Otherwise, he or she will probably disaffirm the contract. A minor may not affirm one part of a contract and disaffirm another part.

Disaffirmance

disaffirmance
The act of a minor to rescind a contract under the infancy doctrine. Disaffirmance may be done orally, in writing, or by the minor's conduct.

A minor can expressly **disaffirm** a contract orally, in writing, or through his or her conduct. No special formalities are required. The contract may be disaffirmed at any time prior to the person's reaching the age of majority plus a "reasonable time." The designation of a reasonable time is determined on a case-by-case basis.

Minor's Duty of Restoration

If a minor's contract is executory and neither party has performed, the minor can simply disaffirm the contract: There is nothing to recover because neither party has given the other party anything of value. If the parties have exchanged consideration and partially or fully performed the contract by the time the minor disaffirms the contract, however, the issue becomes one of what consideration or restitution must be made. The following rules apply:

• **Minor's duty of restoration.** Generally, a minor is obligated only to return the goods or property he or she has received from the adult in the condition it is in at the time of disaffirmance (subject to several exceptions, discussed later in this chapter), even if the item has been consumed, lost, or destroyed or has depreciated in value by the time of disaffirmance. This rule, called the **minor's duty of restoration**, is based on the rationale that if a minor had to place the adult in status quo ante upon disaffirmance of a contract, there would be no incentive for an adult not to deal with a minor.

- **Competent party's duty of restitution.** If a minor has transferred consideration—money, property, or other valuables—to a competent party before disaffirming the contract, that party must place the minor in status quo ante. That is, the minor must be restored to the same position he or she was in before the minor entered into the contract. This restoration is usually done by returning the consideration to the minor. If the consideration has been sold or has depreciated in value, the competent party must pay the minor the cash equivalent. This action is called the **competent party's duty of restitution**.

Most states provide that the minor must put the adult in status quo ante upon disaffirmance of the contract if the minor's intentional, reckless, or grossly negligent conduct caused the loss of value to the adult's property. This rule is called the **minor's duty of restitution**.

On occasion, minors might misrepresent their age to adults when entering into contracts. Most state laws provide that minors who misrepresent their age must place the adult in status quo ante if they disaffirm the contract.

Ratification

If a minor does not disaffirm a contract either during the period of minority or within a reasonable time after reaching the age of majority, the contract is considered ratified (accepted). Hence, the minor (who is now an adult) is bound by the contract; the right to disaffirm the contract is lost. Note that any attempt by a minor to ratify a contract while still a minor can be disaffirmed just as the original contract can be disaffirmed.

The **ratification**, which relates back to the inception of the contract, can be by express oral or written words or implied from the minor's conduct (e.g., after reaching the age of majority, the minor remains silent regarding the contract).

Parents' Liability for Their Children's Contracts

Generally, parents owe a legal duty to provide food, clothing, shelter, and other necessaries of life for their minor children. Parents are liable for their children's contracts for necessaries of life if they have not adequately provided such items.

The parental duty of support terminates if a minor becomes *emancipated*. **Emancipation** occurs when a minor voluntarily leaves home and lives apart from his or her parents. The courts consider factors such as getting married, setting up a separate household, or joining the military in determining whether a minor is emancipated. Each situation is examined on its merits.

Necessaries of Life

Minors are obligated to pay for the **necessaries of life** that they contract for. Otherwise, many adults would refuse to sell these items to them. There is no standard definition of what is a necessary of life. The minor's age, lifestyle, and status in life influence what is considered necessary.

Examples
Items such as food, clothing, shelter, and medical services are generally understood to be necessities of life.

Examples
Goods and services such as automobiles, tools of trade, education, and vocational training have also been found to be necessaries of life in some situations.

The seller's recovery is based on the equitable doctrine of **quasi-contract** rather than on the contract itself. Under this theory, the minor is obligated only to pay the reasonable value of the goods or services received. Reasonable value is determined on a case-by-case basis.

minor's duty of restoration
A rule which states that a minor is obligated only to return the goods or property he or she has received from the adult in the condition it is in at the time of disaffirmance.

competent party's duty of restitution
A rule which states that if a minor has transferred money, property, or other valuables to the competent party before disaffirming the contract, that party must place the minor in status quo ante.

The right of a minor to disaffirm his contract is based upon sound public policy to protect the minor from his own improvidence and the overreaching of adults.

Justice Sullivan
Star Chevrolet v. Green (1985)

ratification
The act of a minor after the minor has reached the age of majority by which he or she accepts a contract entered into when he or she was a minor.

emancipation
The act or process of a minor voluntarily leaving home and living apart from his or her parents.

necessaries of life
Food, clothing, shelter, medical care, and other items considered necessary to the maintenance of life. Minors must pay the reasonable value of necessaries of life for which they contract.

Contemporary Environment

Special Types of Minors' Contracts

Based on public policy, many states have enacted statutes that make certain specified contracts enforceable against minors—that is, minors cannot assert the infancy doctrine against enforcement for these contracts. These usually include contracts for:

- Medical, surgical, and pregnancy care
- Psychological counseling
- Health insurance
- Life insurance
- The performance of duties related to stock and bond transfers, bank accounts, and the like

- Educational loan agreements
- Contracts to support children
- Contracts to enlist in the military
- Artistic, sports, and entertainment contracts that have been entered into with the approval of the court.

Many statutes mandate that a certain portion of the wages and fees earned by a minor (e.g., 50 percent) based on an artistic, sports, or entertainment contract be put in trust until the minor reaches the age of majority.

Mentally Incompetent Persons

Mental incapacity may arise because of mental illness, brain damage, mental retardation, senility, and the like. The law protects people suffering from substantial mental incapacity from enforcement of contracts against them because such persons may not understand the consequences of their actions in entering into a contract.

To be relieved of his or her duties under a contract, a person must have been legally insane at the time of entering into the contract. This state is called **legal insanity**. Most states use the *objective cognitive "understanding" test* to determine legal insanity. Under this test, the person's mental incapacity must render that person incapable of understanding or comprehending the nature of the transaction. Mere weakness of intellect, slight psychological or emotional problems, or delusions does not constitute legal insanity.

The law has developed two standards concerning contracts of mentally incompetent persons: (1) adjudged insane and (2) insane but not adjudged insane.

legal insanity
A state of contractual incapacity, as determined by law.

Adjudged Insane

In certain cases, a relative, a loved one, or another interested party may institute a legal action to have someone declared legally (i.e., adjudged) insane. If after hearing the evidence at a formal judicial or administrative hearing the person is **adjudged insane**, the court will make that person a ward of the court and appoint a guardian to act on that person's behalf. Any contract entered into by a person who has been adjudged insane is **void**. That is, no contract exists. The court-appointed guardian is the only one who has the legal authority to enter into contracts on behalf of the person.

adjudged insane
Declared legally insane by a proper court or administrative agency. A contract entered into by a person adjudged insane is *void*.

Insane but Not Adjudged Insane

If no formal ruling has been made about a person's sanity but the person suffers from a mental impairment that makes him or her legally insane—that is, the person is **insane but not adjudged insane**—any contract entered into by this person is voidable by the insane person. Unless the other party does not have contractual capacity, he or she does not have the option to void the contract.

Some people have alternating periods of sanity and insanity. Any contracts made by such persons during a lucid interval are enforceable. Contracts made while the person was not legally sane can be disaffirmed.

A person who has dealt with an insane person must place that insane person in status quo ante if the contract is either void or voided by the insane person. Most states hold that a

insane but not adjudged insane
Being insane but not having been adjudged insane by a court or an administrative agency. A contract entered into by such person is generally *voidable*. Some states hold that such a contract is void.

party who did not know he or she was dealing with an insane person must be placed in status quo ante upon avoidance of the contract. Insane persons are liable in *quasi-contract* to pay the reasonable value for the necessaries of life they receive.

Insanity vitiates all acts.

Sir John Nicholl
Countess of Portsmouth v. Earl of Portsmouth (1828)

Concept Summary
Disaffirmance of Contracts Based on Legal Insanity

Type of Legal Insanity	Disaffirmance Rule
Adjudged insane	Contract is void. Neither party can enforce the contract.
Insane but not adjudged insane	Contract is voidable by the insane person; the competent party cannot void the contract.

Intoxicated Persons

Most states provide that contracts entered into by certain **intoxicated persons** are voidable by those persons. The intoxication may occur because of alcohol or drugs. The contract is not voidable by the other party if that party had contractual capacity.

Under the majority rule, the contract is voidable only if the person was so intoxicated when the contract was entered into that he or she was incapable of understanding or comprehending the nature of the transaction. In most states, this rule holds even if the intoxication was self-induced. Some states allow the person to disaffirm the contract only if the person was forced to become intoxicated or did so unknowingly.

The amount of alcohol or drugs that must be consumed for a person to be considered legally intoxicated to disaffirm contracts varies from case to case. The factors that are considered include the user's physical characteristics and his or her ability to "hold" intoxicants.

A person who disaffirms a contract based on intoxication generally must be returned to the status quo ante. In turn, the intoxicated person generally must return the consideration received under the contract to the other party and make restitution that returns the other party to status quo ante. After becoming sober, an intoxicated person can ratify the contracts he or she entered into while intoxicated. Intoxicated persons are liable in *quasi-contract* to pay the reasonable value for necessaries they receive.

intoxicated person
A person who is under contractual incapacity because of ingestion of alcohol or drugs to the point of incompetence.

Men intoxicated are sometimes stunned into sobriety.

Lord Mansfield
R. v. Wilkes (1770)

Legality

One requirement to have an enforceable contract is that the object of the contract must be lawful. Most contracts that individuals and businesses enter into are **lawful contracts** that are enforceable. These include contracts for the sale of goods, services, real property, and intangible rights; the lease of goods; property leases; licenses; and other contracts.

Some contracts have illegal objects. A contract with an illegal object is *void* and therefore unenforceable. These contracts are called **illegal contracts**. The following paragraphs discuss various illegal contracts.

illegal contract
A contract that has an illegal object. Such contracts are *void*.

Contracts Contrary to Statutes

Both federal and state legislatures have enacted statutes that prohibit certain types of conduct. Contracts to perform activities that are prohibited by statute are illegal contracts.

Examples
An agreement between two companies to engage in price fixing in violation of federal antitrust statutes is illegal and therefore void. Thus, neither company to this illegal contract can enforce the contract against the other company.

Usury Laws

usury law

A law that sets an upper limit on the interest rate that can be charged on certain types of loans.

State **usury laws** set an upper limit on the annual interest rate that can be charged on certain types of loans. The limits vary from state to state. Lenders who charge a higher rate than the state limit are guilty of usury. These laws are intended to protect unsophisticated borrowers from loan sharks and others who charge exorbitant rates of interest.

Most states provide criminal and civil penalties for making usurious loans. Some states require lenders to remit the difference between the interest rate charged on the loan and the usury rate to the borrower. Other states prohibit lenders from collecting any interest on the loan. Still other states provide that a usurious loan is a void contract, permitting the borrower not to have to pay the interest or the principal of the loan to the lender.

Most usury laws exempt certain types of lenders and loan transactions involving legitimate business transactions from the reach of the law. These exemptions usually include loans made by banks and other financial institutions, loans above a certain dollar amount, and loans made to corporations and other businesses.

Contracts to Commit Crimes

Contracts to commit criminal acts are void. If the object of a contract becomes illegal after the contract is entered into because the government has enacted a statute that makes it unlawful, the parties are discharged from the contract. The contract is not an illegal contract unless the parties agree to go forward and complete it.

In the following case, the court had to determine whether a contract was illegal.

CASE 12.1
Illegal Contract

Parente v. Pirozzoli

87 Conn.App. 235, 866 A.2d 629, Web 2005 Conn.App. Lexis 25 (2005)
Appellate Court of Connecticut

"Thus, in the case of a contract whose inherent purpose is to violate the law, if both parties thereto are *in pari delicto*, the law will leave them where it finds them."

—Judge Lavery

Facts

Andrew Parente had a criminal record. He and Mario Pirozzoli, Jr., formed a partnership to open and operate the Speak Easy Café in Berlin, Connecticut, which was a bar that would serve alcohol. The owners were required to obtain a liquor license from the state of Connecticut before operating the bar. Because the state of Connecticut usually would not issue a liquor license to anyone with a criminal record, it was agreed that Pirozzoli would form a corporation called Centerfolds, Inc., to own the bar, sign the real estate lease for the bar in his name, and file for the liquor license in his name only. Pirozzoli did all of these things. Parente and Pirozzoli signed a partnership agreement that acknowledged that Parente was an equal partner in the business. The state of

Connecticut granted the liquor license, and the bar opened for business. Parente and Pirozzoli shared the profits of the bar.

Six years later, Pirozzoli terminated the partnership and kept the business. Parente sued Pirozzoli for breach of the partnership agreement to recover the value of his alleged share of the business. Pirozzoli defended, arguing that the partnership agreement was an illegal contract that should not be enforced against him. The trial court held that the partnership agreement had been breached and awarded Parente $138,000 in damages. Pirozzoli appealed.

Issue

Was the partnership agreement an illegal contract that was void and unenforceable by the court?

Language of the Court

Here, the partnership agreement was not offensive on its face, but had an illegal, ulterior purpose, namely, to evade the strictures of the liquor control laws. Because the partnership agreement was made to facilitate, foster, or support patently illegal activity, we conclude that it is illegal as against public policy and, consequently, that the court's enforcement of it was improper.

Although the end result of holding the partnership agreement illegal may be to allow Pirozzoli a windfall at Parente's expense, this result is common and necessary in many cases in which contracts are deemed unenforceable on the grounds of furthering overriding policies. It is in order to effectuate an underlying public policy, rather than sanction a party seeking to enforce an illegal contract, that courts refuse to lend assistance to those who have contributed to the illegality that taints the contract. Thus, in the case of a contract whose inherent purpose is to violate the law, if both parties thereto are in pari delicto, the law will leave them where it finds them. Knowing that they will receive no help from the courts and must trust completely to each other's good faith, the parties are less likely to enter an illegal arrangement in the first place.

Decision

The appellate court held that the partnership agreement between Parente and Pirozzoli was an illegal contract that was void and unenforceable. The appellate court reversed the judgment of the trial court, found that Pirozzoli was not liable to Parente, and held that Pirozzoli could keep the $138,000 windfall.

Case Questions

Critical Legal Thinking   What is an illegal contract? Explain.

Business Ethics   Did Parente act ethically in this case? Was it honorable for Pirozzoli to argue that his partnership agreement with Parente was an illegal contract?

Contemporary Business   What is the result of a court finding that a contract is illegal? Explain. Was it fair for Pirozzoli to receive the windfall in this case?

Gambling Statutes

All states either prohibit or regulate gambling, wagering, lotteries, and games of chance via **gambling statutes**. States provide various criminal and civil penalties for illegal gambling. There are many exceptions to wagering laws. Many states have enacted statutes that permit games of chance under a certain dollar amount, bingo games, lotteries conducted by religious and charitable organizations, and the like. Many states also permit and regulate horse racing, harness racing, dog racing, and state-operated lotteries.

gambling statutes
Statutes that make certain forms of gambling illegal.

Effect of Illegality

Because illegal contracts are void, the parties cannot sue for nonperformance. Further, if an illegal contract is executed, the court will generally leave the parties where it finds them.

Certain situations are exempt from the general rule of the effect of finding an illegal contract. If an exception applies, the innocent party may use the court system to sue for damages or to recover consideration paid under the illegal contract. Persons who can assert an exception are:

effect of illegality
A doctrine which states that the courts will refuse to enforce or rescind an illegal contract and will leave the parties where it finds them.

- Innocent persons who were justifiably ignorant of the law or fact that made the contract illegal.

  Example
  A person who purchases insurance from an unlicensed insurance company may recover insurance benefits from the unlicensed company.

- Persons who were induced to enter into an illegal contract by fraud, duress, or undue influence.

  Example
  A shop owner who pays $5,000 "protection money" to a mobster so that his store will not be burned down by the mobster can recover the $5,000.

Ethics Spotlight

Illegal Gambling Contract

"The trial court could not have compelled Ryno to honor his wager by delivering the BMW to Tyra. However, Ryno did deliver the BMW to Tyra and the facts incident to that delivery are sufficient to establish a transfer by gift of the BMW from Ryno to Tyra."

—Judge Farris

R. D. Ryno, Jr., owned Bavarian Motors, an automobile dealership in Fort Worth, Texas. One day, Lee Tyra discussed purchasing a BMW M-1 from Ryno for $125,000. Ryno then suggested a double-or-nothing coin flip, to which Tyra agreed. If the Ryno won the coin flip, Tyra would have to pay $250,000 for the car; if Tyra won the coin flip, he would get the car for free. The coin was flipped, and Tyra won the coin flip. Ryno said, "It's yours," and handed Tyra the keys, title, and possession to the car. Tyra drove away in the BMW. A lawsuit ensued as to the ownership of the car.

The court held that when Tyra won the coin toss and Ryno voluntarily gave the keys, title, and possession of the BMW to Tyra, this was a performed illegal gambling contract. There was sufficient evidence to find that Ryno intended to transfer to Tyra his ownership interest in the BMW at the time he delivered the documents, keys, and possession of the automobile to Tyra. The court left the parties where it found them: Tyra had the keys, title, and possession of the BMW; Ryno did not have either the car or payment for the car.

Note: If, when Tyra won the coin toss, Ryno had refused to give the BMW to Tyra, the result of this case would have been different. Tyra could not have compelled Ryno to honor his wager. This is because courts will not enforce an executory illegal gambling contract. The court would again have left the parties where it found them: Ryno would have had ownership and possession of the car and refused to honor the wager; Tyra would have won the coin toss but could not obtain the car from Ryno. *Ryno v. Tyra*, 752 S.W.2d 148, **Web** 1988 Tex. App. Lexis 1646 (Court of Appeals of Texas)

Business Ethics

Did Ryno act ethically in this case? Did Tyra act ethically in this case? Should the court have lent its help to Ryno to recover the BMW from Tyra? Why or why not?

- Persons who entered into an illegal contract who withdraw before the illegal act is performed.

Example

If the president of New Toy Corporation pays $10,000 to an employee of Old Toy Corporation to steal a trade secret from his employer but reconsiders and tells the employee not to do it before he has done it, the New Toy Corporation may recover the $10,000.

> **in pari delicto**
>
> A situation in which both parties are equally at fault in an illegal contract.
>
> **contract contrary to public policy**
>
> A contract that has a negative impact on society or that interferes with the public's safety and welfare.
>
> **immoral contract**
>
> A contract whose objective is the commission of an act that is society considers immoral.

- Persons who were less at fault than the other party for entering into the illegal contract. At common law, parties to an illegal contract were considered *in pari delicto* (in equal fault). Some states have changed this rule and permit the less-at-fault party to recover restitution of the consideration they paid under an illegal contract from the more-at-fault party.

Contracts Contrary to Public Policy

Certain contracts are illegal because they are **contrary to public policy**. Such contracts are void. Although *public policy* eludes precise definition, the courts have held contracts to be contrary to public policy if they have a negative impact on society or interfere with the public's safety and welfare.

Immoral contracts—that is, contracts whose objective is the commission of an act that society considers immoral—may be found to be against public policy. Judges are not free to

Kewadin Casino, Michigan. *This sign advertises an Indian gaming casino operated in the Upper Peninsula of Michigan. In 1988, Congress enacted the **Indian Gaming Regulatory Act (IGRA)**[1] that established the framework for permitting and regulating Indian gaming. There are more than 400 Indian gaming establishments in the country operated by more than 200 federally recognized tribes. Federal law permits Indian casino gambling only if the state permits such gambling. The Kewadin Casino in Brevort Township, Michigan, is operated by the Sault Ste. Marie Tribe of Chippewa Indians.*

define morality based on their individual views. Instead, they must look to the practices and beliefs of society when defining immoral conduct.

Example

A contract that is based on sexual favors is an immoral contract and void as against public policy.

Special Business Contracts

The issue of the lawfulness of contracts applies to several special business contracts. These include contracts that restrain trade; contracts to provide services that require a government license, exculpatory clauses, and covenants not to compete. These contracts are discussed in the following paragraphs.

Contract in Restraint of Trade

The general economic policy of this country favors competition. At common law, **contracts in restraint of trade**—that is, contracts that unreasonably restrain trade—are held to be unlawful.

contract in restraint of trade
A contract that unreasonably restrains trade.

Example

It would be an illegal restraint of trade for Toyota, General Motors, and Ford Motor to agree to fix the prices of the automobiles they sell. Their contract would be void and could not be enforced by any of the parties against the other parties.

Licensing Statute

All states have **licensing statutes** that require members of certain professions and occupations to be licensed by the state in which they practice. Lawyers, doctors, real estate agents, insurance agents, certified public accountants, teachers, contractors, hairdressers, and such are among them. In most instances, a license is granted to a person who demonstrates that

licensing statute
A statute that requires a person or business to obtain a license from the government prior to engaging in a specified occupation or activity.

Ethics Spotlight

Murder, She Wrote

Ellen and Richard Alvin Flood, who were married, lived in a mobile home in Louisiana. Richard worked as a maintenance man, and Ellen was employed at an insurance agency. Ellen was unhappy with her marriage. Ellen took out a life insurance policy on the life of her husband and named herself as beneficiary. The policy was issued by Fidelity & Guaranty Life Insurance Company (Fidelity).

Thereafter, Richard became unexpectedly ill. He was taken to the hospital, where his condition improved. After a visit at the hospital from his wife, however, Richard died. Ellen was criminally charged with the murder of her husband by poisoning. Evidence showed that six medicine bottles at the couple's home, including Tylenol and paregoric bottles, contained arsenic. The court found that Ellen had fed Richard ice cubes laced with arsenic at the hospital. Ellen was tried and convicted of the murder of her husband.

Subsequently, Ellen, as the beneficiary of Richard's life insurance policy, requested Fidelity to pay her the benefits. Fidelity refused to pay the benefits and returned all premiums paid on the policy. A lawsuit followed. Does Fidelity have to pay Ellen the life insurance proceeds for Richard's death?

The court held that Fidelity did not have to pay Ellen the life insurance proceeds from her husband Richard's death because a beneficiary named in a life insurance policy is not entitled to the proceeds of the insurance if the beneficiary kills the insured. The enforcement of such a contract would violate public policy. The court stated, "Louisiana follows the majority rule that holds, as a matter of public policy, that a beneficiary named in a life insurance policy is not entitled to the proceeds of the insurance if the beneficiary feloniously kills the insured." *Flood v. Fidelity & Guaranty Life Insurance Company*, 394 So.2d 1311, **Web** 1981 La.App. Lexis 3538 (Court of Appeal of Louisiana)

Business Ethics
Did Ellen Flood act ethically by trying to recover the life insurance proceeds from her husband's death? What would be the consequences if persons could recover insurance proceeds for losses caused by their illegal activities, such as murder?

---

he or she has the proper schooling, experience, and moral character required by the relevant statute. Sometimes, a written examination is also required.

Problems arise if an unlicensed person tries to collect payment for services provided to another under a contract. Some statutes expressly provide that unlicensed persons cannot enforce contracts to provide these services. If the statute is silent on the point, enforcement depends on whether it is a *regulatory statute* or a *revenue-raising statute*:

regulatory statute

A licensing statute enacted to protect the public.

- **Regulatory statute.** Licensing statutes enacted to protect the public are called **regulatory statutes**. Generally, unlicensed persons cannot recover payment for services that a regulatory statute requires a licensed person to provide.

    Example
    State law provides that legal services can be provided only by lawyers who have graduated from law school and passed the appropriate bar exam. Nevertheless, suppose Marie, a first-year law student, agrees to draft a will for Randy for a $350 fee. Because Marie is not licensed to provide legal services, she has violated a regulatory statute. She cannot enforce the contract and recover payment from Randy. Randy, even though receiving services by having his will drafted, does not have to pay Marie $350.

revenue-raising statute

A licensing statute with the primary purpose of raising revenue for the government.

- **Revenue-raising statute.** Licensing statutes enacted to raise money for the government are called **revenue-raising statutes**. A person who provides services pursuant to a contract without the appropriate license required by such a statute can enforce the contract and recover payment for services rendered.

    Example
    A state licensing statute requires licensed attorneys to pay an annual $500 renewal fee without requiring continuing education or other new qualifications. If a lawyer provides legal services but has not paid the annual licensing fee, the lawyer can still recover for her services.

Exculpatory Clause

An **exculpatory clause** (also called a **release of liability clause**) is a contractual provision that relieves one (or both) of the parties to a contract from tort liability. An exculpatory clause can relieve a party of liability for ordinary negligence. It cannot be used in a situation involving willful conduct, intentional torts, fraud, recklessness, or gross negligence. Exculpatory clauses are often found in leases, sales contracts, sporting event ticket stubs, parking lot tickets, service contracts, and the like. Such clauses do not have to be reciprocal (i.e., one party may be relieved of tort liability, whereas the other party is not).

exculpatory clause
A contractual provision that relieves one (or both) of the parties to a contract from tort liability for ordinary negligence. Also known as a *release of liability clause*.

Example

Jim Jackson voluntarily enrolled in a parachute jump course and signed a contract containing an exculpatory clause that relieved the parachute center of liability. After receiving proper instruction, he jumped from an airplane. Unfortunately, Jim was injured when he could not steer his parachute toward the target area. He sued the parachute center for damages. Here, the court would usually enforce the exculpatory clause, reasoning that parachute jumping was a voluntary choice and did not involve an essential service.

Exculpatory clauses that either affect the public interest or result from superior bargaining power are usually found to be void as against public policy. Although the outcome varies with the circumstances of the case, the greater the degree to which the party serves the general public, the greater the chance that the exculpatory clause will be struck down as illegal. The courts will consider such factors as the type of activity involved; the relative bargaining power, knowledge, experience, and sophistication of the parties; and other relevant factors.

Covenant Not to Compete

Entrepreneurs and others often buy and sell businesses. The sale of a business includes its "goodwill," or reputation. To protect this goodwill after the sale, the seller often enters into an agreement with the buyer not to engage in a similar business or occupation within a specified geographic area for a specified period of time following the sale. This agreement is called a **covenant not to compete**, or a **noncompete clause**.

covenant not to compete
A contract which provides that a seller of a business or an employee will not engage in a similar business or occupation within a specified geographical area for a specified time following the sale of the business or termination of employment. Also called a *noncompete clause*.

Employers often do not want an employee who resigns or is terminated to work in a position that competes with the employer for a certain length of time after the employee is gone from the employer. Employers often require an employee, usually before he or she is hired, to sign a noncompete clause, agreeing not to work for another employer or for themselves in a position that would compete with their prior employer for a certain period of time after the employee has left or been terminated by the employer.

Covenants not to compete that are *ancillary* to a legitimate sale of a business or employment contract are lawful if they are reasonable in three aspects: (1) the line of business protected, (2) the geographic area protected, and (3) the duration of the restriction. A covenant that is found to be unreasonable is not enforceable as written. The reasonableness of covenants not to compete is examined on a case-by-case basis. If a covenant not to compete is unreasonable, the courts may either refuse to enforce it or change it so that it is reasonable. Usually, the courts choose the first option.

Examples

Stacy is a certified public accountant (CPA) with a lucrative accounting practice in Providence, Rhode Island. Her business includes a substantial amount of goodwill with her clients. Stacy sells her accounting practice to Gregory. When she sells her practice to Gregory, Stacy agrees not to open another accounting practice in the state of Rhode Island for a 20-year period. This covenant not to compete is reasonable in the line of business protected but is unreasonable in geographic scope and duration. It will not be enforced by the courts as written. The covenant not to compete would be reasonable and enforceable if it prohibited Stacy only from practicing as a CPA in the city of Providence for 3 years.

Unconscionable Contracts

The general rule of freedom of contract holds that if the object of a contract is lawful and the other elements for the formation of a contract are met, the courts will enforce a contract according to its terms. Although it is generally presumed that parties are capable of protecting their own interests when contracting, it is a fact of life that dominant parties sometimes take advantage of weaker parties.

In addition, many contracts that consumers sign are **contracts of adhesion**—that is, they are preprinted forms whose terms the consumer cannot negotiate and which they must sign in order to obtain a product or service. Most adhesion contracts are lawful even though there is a disparity in power of contracting.

Examples

Automobile sales contracts and leases, mortgages, and apartment leases are usually contracts of adhesion.

However, when a contract is so oppressive or manifestly unfair as to be unjust, the law has developed the equity doctrine of unconscionability to prevent the enforcement of such contracts. The doctrine of unconscionability is based on public policy. A contract found to be unconscionable under this doctrine is called an **unconscionable contract**.

The courts are given substantial discretion in determining whether a contract or contract clause is unconscionable. There is no single definition of *unconscionability*. This doctrine may not be used merely to save a contracting party from a bad bargain.

Elements of Unconscionability

The following elements must be shown to prove that a contract or a clause in a contract is unconscionable:

- The parties possessed severely unequal bargaining power.
- The dominant party unreasonably used its unequal bargaining power to obtain oppressive or manifestly unfair contract terms.
- The adhering party had no reasonable alternative.

Unconscionable contracts are sometimes found where there is a consumer contract that takes advantage of uneducated, poor, or elderly people who have been persuaded to enter into an unfair contract. This often involves door-to-door sales and sales over the telephone. If the court finds that a contract or contract clause is unconscionable, it may (1) refuse to enforce the contract, (2) refuse to enforce the unconscionable clause but enforce the remainder of the contract, or (3) limit the applicability of any unconscionable clause so as to avoid any unconscionable result. The appropriate remedy depends on the facts and circumstances of each case. Note that because unconscionability is a matter of law, the judge may opt to decide the case without a jury trial.

Example

Suppose a door-to-door salesperson sells a poor family a freezer full of meat and other foods for $3,000, with monthly payments for 60 months at 20 percent interest. If the actual cost of the freezer and the food is $1,000, this contract could be found to be unconscionable. The court could either find the entire contract unenforceable or rewrite the contract so that it has reasonable terms.

In the following case, the court found a contract clause to be unconscionable.

unconscionable contract
A contract that courts refuse to enforce in part or at all because it is so oppressive or manifestly unfair as to be unjust.

A good judge decides fairly, preferring equity to strict law.

Legal maxim

CASE 12.2
Unconscionable Contract

Muhammad, on Her Own Behalf and All Others Similarly Situated v. County Bank of Rehoboth Beach

189 N.J. 1, 912 A.2d 88, Web 2006 N.J. Lexis 1154 (2006)
Supreme Court of New Jersey

"By permitting claimants to band together, class actions equalize adversaries and provide a procedure to remedy a wrong that might otherwise go unredressed."

—Judge LaVecchia

Facts

Jaliyah Muhammad was a part-time student at Berkeley College in Paramus, New Jersey. Muhammad obtained a short-term single advance, unsecured loan of $200 from County Bank of Rehoboth Beach (County Bank). County Bank charged a finance charge of $60 for the loan. The loan rate was 608.33 percent. The loan was due in 21 days. Muhammad obtained two similar loans from County Bank.

To obtain the loans, Muhammad had to complete and sign three pages of standard form contracts. These loan documents contained an agreement that all disputes regarding the loan were subject to arbitration and could not be brought in court and that the borrower could not bring, join, or participate in class actions as to any disputes regarding the loans. The agreement to arbitrate and the agreement not to bring, join, or participate in class actions were conspicuously stated in capital letters in the loan documents.

Muhammad filed a class action lawsuit in New Jersey superior court against County Bank, alleging that County Bank charged illegal rates of interest, in violation of New Jersey law. Muhammad sought restitution, damages, penalties, and costs from County Bank. Muhammad argued that the arbitration agreement was unconscionable based on the class action waiver. County Bank made a motion to compel arbitration. The trial court and the appellate court held that Muhammad's claims were subject to arbitration. Muhammad appealed.

Issue

Was the class action waiver in the arbitration agreement unconscionable?

Language of the Court

It is well settled that courts may refuse to enforce contracts that are unconscionable. The unconscionability issue in this matter centers on access to class-action proceeding in the arbitral setting. By permitting claimants to band together, class actions equalize adversaries and provide a procedure to remedy a wrong that might otherwise go unredressed. If each victim were remitted to an individual suit, the remedy would be illusory, for the individual loss may be too small to warrant a suit. A class-action proceeding can aid

the efficient administration of justice by avoiding the expense, in both time and money, of relitigating similar claims. In sum, the class-action mechanism is recognized to be valuable to litigants, to the courts, and to the public interest.

We hold, therefore, that the presence of the class-action waiver in Muhammad's consumer arbitration agreement renders that agreement unconscionable. As a matter of generally applicable state contract law, it was unconscionable for County Bank to deprive Muhammad of the mechanism of a class-wide action, whether in arbitration or in court litigation. Finally, although we find that the class-arbitration waivers in Muhammad's arbitration agreements are unconscionable, we find that the waivers are severable. Once the waivers are removed, the remainder of the arbitration agreement is enforceable.

Decision

The supreme court of New Jersey held that the class action waiver clause in County Bank's arbitration agreement was unconscionable. The court further held that this clause could be severed from the arbitration clause and that Muhammad's class action would be heard by an arbitration panel.

Case Questions

Critical Legal Thinking What is a contract of adhesion? Have you ever signed one? What is an unconscionable contract? Explain.

Business Ethics Did County Bank act ethically in placing the class action waiver in its loan documents? Why do you think County Bank included the class action waiver clause in its loan documents?

Contemporary Business Were the terms of the loans—the interest rate and finance charge—for County Bank's loans unconscionable?

Web Exercise Go to **www.bankrate.com/brm/news/cc/20020320a.asp** to read about credit card interest rates.

China. *Since 1976, Chinese leaders have opened the country to economic reform. Since taking over the island of Macau from the Portuguese in 1999, China has made Macau into one of the world's premiere gambling centers. Gambling revenues from Macau's casinos now exceed those of Las Vegas casinos. The Sands Macau, Wynn Macau, Venetian Macau, and MGM Grand Macau have opened on the island.*

Test Review Terms and Concepts

Adjudged insane
Age of majority
Competent party's duty of restitution
Contract contrary to public policy
Contract in restraint of trade
Contract of adhesion
Contractual capacity
Covenant not to compete (noncompete clause)
Disaffirm
Effect of illegality
Emancipation
Exculpatory clause (release of liability clause)

Gambling statute
Illegal contract
Immoral contract
Indian Gaming Regulatory Act (IGRA)
Infancy doctrine
In pari delicto
Insane but not adjudged insane
Intoxicated person
Lawful contract
Legal insanity
Licensing statute
Minor

Minor's duty of restitution
Minor's duty of restoration
Necessaries of life
Period of minority
Quasi-contract
Ratification
Regulatory statute
Revenue-raising statute
Unconscionable contract
Usury law
Void
Voidable contract

Case Problems

12.1 Infancy Doctrine: James Halbman, Jr., a minor, entered into a contract to purchase an Oldsmobile from Michael Lemke. Halbman paid $1,000 cash and agreed to make weekly payments until the full purchase price was paid. Five weeks later, a connecting rod on the vehicle's engine broke, and Halbman took the car to a garage, where it was repaired at a cost of $637.40. Halbman refused to pay for the repairs, disaffirmed the contract with Lemke, and notified Lemke where the car was located. When Lemke refused to pick up the car and pay the repair bill, the garage legally satisfied its garageman's lien by removing the vehicle's engine. It then towed the car to Halbman's residence. Halbman notified Lemke to remove the car, but Lemke refused to do so. The car was subsequently vandalized, making it worthless and unsalvageable. Halbman sued to disaffirm the contract and recover the consideration from Lemke. Lemke argued that Halbman must make full restitution. Who is correct? *Halbman v. Lemke*, 99 Wis.2d 241, 298 N.W.2d 562, **Web** 1980 Wisc. Lexis 2825 (Supreme Court of Wisconsin)

12.2 Ratification: Charles Edwards Smith, a minor, purchased an automobile from Bobby Floars Toyota (Toyota). Smith executed a security agreement to finance part of the balance due on the purchase price, agreeing to pay off the balance in 30 monthly installments. Smith turned 18, which was the age of majority in his state. Smith made 10 monthly payments after turning 18. He then decided to disaffirm the contract and stopped making the payments. Smith claims that he may disaffirm the contract entered into when he was a minor. Toyota argues that Smith has ratified the contract since attaining the age of majority. Who is correct? *Bobby Floars Toyota, Inc. v. Smith*, 48 N.C.App. 580, 269 S.E.2d 320, **Web** 1980 N.C.App. Lexis 3263 (Court of Appeals of North Carolina)

12.3 Adjudged Insane: Manzelle Johnson, who had been adjudicated insane, executed a quitclaim and warranty deed conveying real estate she owned to her guardian, Obbie Neal. Neal subsequently conveyed the real estate to James R. Beavers by warranty deed. Charles L. Weatherly, Johnson's present guardian, brought this action, seeking a decree of the court that title to the real estate be restored to Johnson because of her inability to contract. Should Johnson be allowed to void the contract? *Beavers v. Weatherly*, 250 Ga. 546, 299 S.E.2d 730, **Web** 1983 Ga. Lexis 581 (Supreme Court of Georgia)

12.4 Intoxication: Betty Galloway, an alcoholic, signed a settlement agreement upon her divorce from her husband, Henry Galloway. Henry, in Betty's absence in court, stated that she had lucid intervals from her alcoholism, had been sober for two months, and was lucid when she signed the settlement agreement. Betty moved to vacate the settlement agreement, after she had retained present legal counsel. Four months later, Betty was declared incompetent to handle her person and her affairs, and a guardian and conservator was appointed. Betty, through her guardian, sued to have the settlement agreement voided. Who wins? *Galloway v. Galloway*, 281 N.W.2d 804, **Web** 1979 N.D. Lexis 279 (Supreme Court of North Dakota)

12.5 Licensing Statute: The state of Hawaii requires a person who wants to practice architecture to meet certain educational requirements and to pass a written examination before being granted a license to practice. After receiving the license, an architect must pay an annual license fee of $15. Ben Lee Wilson satisfied the initial requirements and was granted an architecture license. Four years later, Wilson failed to renew his license by paying the required annual fee. Wilson contracted with Kealakekua Ranch, Ltd., and Gentry Hawaii (defendants) to provide architectural services for the Kealakekua Ranch Center project. Wilson provided $33,994 of architectural services to the defendants. The defendants refused to pay this fee because Wilson did not have an architectural license. Wilson sued to collect his fees. Who wins? *Wilson v. Kealakekua Ranch, Ltd., and Gentry Hawaii*, 57 Haw. 124, 551 P.2d 525, **Web** 1976 Haw. Lexis 119 (Supreme Court of Hawaii)

12.6 Covenant Not to Compete: Gerry Morris owned a silk screening and lettering shop in Tucson, Arizona. Morris entered into a contract to sell the business to Alfred and Connie Gann. The contract contained the following covenant not to compete: "Seller agrees not to enter into silk screening or lettering shop business within Tucson and a 100-mile radius of Tucson, for a period of ten (10) years from the date of this agreement and will not compete in any manner whatsoever with buyers, and seller further agrees that he will refer all business contracts to buyers." Morris opened a silk screening and lettering business in competition with the Ganns and in violation of the noncompete clause. The Ganns brought this action against Morris for breach of contract and to enforce the covenant not to compete. Is the covenant not to compete valid and enforceable in this case? *Gann v. Morris*, 122 Ariz. 517, 596 P.2d 43, **Web** 1979 Ariz.App. Lexis 487 (Court of Appeals of Arizona)

12.7 Exculpatory Clause: Grady Perkins owned the Raleigh Institute of Cosmetology (Institute), and Ray Monk and Rovetta Allen were employed as instructors there. The school trained students to do hair styling and coloring, cosmetology, and other beauty services. The students received practical training by providing services to members of the public under the supervision of the instructors. Francis I. Alston went to Institute to have her hair colored and styled by a student who was under the supervision of Monk and Allen. Before receiving any services, Alston signed a written release form that released Institute and its employees from liability for their negligence. While coloring Alston's hair, the student negligently used a chemical that caused Alston's hair to fall out. Alston sued Institute, Perkins, Monk, and Allen for damages. The defendants asserted that the release form signed by Alston barred her suit. Is the exculpatory clause valid? *Alston v. Monk*, 92 N.C.App.59, 373 S.E.2d 463, **Web** 1988 N.C. App. Lexis 987 (Court of Appeals of North Carolina)

12.8 Exculpatory Clause: Wilbur Spaulding owned and operated the Jacksonville racetrack at the Morgan Country Fairgrounds, where automobile races were held. Lawrence P. Koch was a flagman at the raceway. One day when Koch arrived at the pit shack at the raceway, he was handed a clipboard on which was a track release and waiver of liability form that released the racetrack from liability for negligence. Koch signed the form and took up his position as flagman. During the first race, the last car on the track lost control and slid off the end of the track, striking Koch. Koch suffered a broken leg and other injuries and was unable to work for 14 months. Koch sued Spaulding for damages for negligence. Spaulding asserted that the release form signed by Koch barred his suit. Is the exculpatory clause valid against Koch? *Koch v. Spaulding*, 174 Ill.App.3d 692, 529 N.E.2d 19, **Web** 1988 Ill. App. Lexis 1427 (Appellate Court of Illinois)

Business Ethics Cases

12.9 Business Ethics: Joe Plumlee owned and operated an ambulance company. He alleged that the law firm Paddock, Loveless & Roach agreed to pay him an up-front fee and a percentage of the law firm's fees generated from personal injury case referrals. When the law firm did not pay Plumlee, he sued to recover damages for breach of contract. Texas law prohibits lawyers from sharing fees with laypersons [Tex. Penal Code Section 38.12; supreme court of Texas]. A disciplinary rule also forbids such activity [State Bar Rules Art. X, Section 9]. The law firm asserted that the contract could not be enforced because it would be an illegal contract. Who wins? Did Plumlee act ethically in this case? If the contract existed, did the lawyers act ethically? *Plumlee v. Paddock, Loveless, and Roach*, 832 S.W.2d 757, **Web** 1992 Tex.App. Lexis 1544 (Court of Appeals of Texas)

12.10 Business Ethics: Richard Zientara was friends with Chester and Bernice Kaszuba. All three were residents of Indiana. Bernice, who was employed in an Illinois tavern where Illinois state lottery tickets were sold, had previously obtained lottery tickets for Zientara because Indiana did not have a state lottery. One day, Zientara requested that Kaszuba purchase an Illinois lottery ticket for him. He gave Kaszuba the money for the ticket and the numbers 6–15–16–23–24–37. Kaszuba purchased the ticket, but when it turned out to be the winning combination worth $1,696,800, she refused to give the ticket to Zientara and unsuccessfully tried to collect the money. Zientara filed suit against Kaszuba in Indiana, claiming the ticket and proceeds thereof. Was the contract legal? Did the Kaszubas act ethically in this case? *Kaszuba v. Zientara*, 506 N.E.2d 1, **Web** 1987 Ind. Lexis 874 (Supreme Court of Indiana)

Endnote

1. 25 U.S.C. Section 2701 et seq.

CHAPTER 13

"Freedom of contract begins where equality of bargaining power begins."

—Oliver Wendell Holmes, Jr.
June 4, 1928

Genuineness of Assent and Undue Influence

Chapter Objectives

After studying this chapter, you should be able to:

1. Explain genuineness of assent.
2. Explain how mutual mistake of fact excuses performance.
3. Describe intentional misrepresentation (fraud).
4. Describe duress.
5. Define *equitable doctrine of undue influence.*

Chapter Contents

Introduction to Genuineness of Assent and Undue Influence

Voluntary *assent* by the parties is necessary to create an enforceable contract. Assent is determined by the relevant facts surrounding the negotiation and formation of a contract. Assent may be manifested in any manner sufficient to show agreement, including express words or conduct of the parties.

A contract may not be enforced if the assent of one or both of the parties to the contract was not genuine or real. *Genuine assent* may be missing because a party entered into a contract based on mistake, fraudulent misrepresentation, or duress. A court may permit the rescission of a contract based on the equitable doctrine of *undue influence*. Problems concerning **genuineness of assent** are discussed in this chapter.

genuineness of assent
The requirement that a party's assent to a contract be genuine.

Mistake

A **mistake** occurs where one or both of the parties to a contract have an erroneous belief about the subject matter, value, or some other aspect of the contract. Mistakes may be either *unilateral* or *mutual*. The law permits **rescission** of some contracts made in mistake.

rescission
An action to undo a contract.

Unilateral Mistake

Unilateral mistakes occur when only one party is mistaken about a material fact regarding the subject matter of the contract. In most cases of unilateral mistake, the mistaken party will not be permitted to rescind the contract. The contract will be enforced on its terms.

There are three types of situations in which a contract may not be enforced due to a unilateral mistake:

unilateral mistake
A mistake in which only one party is mistaken about a material fact regarding the subject matter of a contract.

1. One party makes a unilateral mistake of fact, and the other party knew (or should have known) that a mistake was made.
2. A unilateral mistake occurs because of a clerical or mathematical error that is not the result of gross negligence.
3. The mistake is so serious that enforcing the contract would be unconscionable.[1]

Example

Suppose Trent wants to purchase a new car from the showroom floor. He looks at several models. Although he decides to purchase a car with a sunroof, he does not tell the salesperson about his preference. The model named in the contract he signs does not have this feature, although he believes it does. Trent's unilateral mistake will not relieve him of his contractual obligation to purchase the car.

Words are chameleons, which reflect the color of their environment.

Justice L. Hand
Commissioner v. National Carbide Co. (1948)

In Case 13.1, on the following page, the court had to decide whether to allow a party to rescind a contract because of the party's unilateral mistake.

Mutual Mistake of Fact

A party may rescind a contract if there has been a **mutual mistake of a past or existing material fact**.[2] A **material fact** is a fact that is important to the subject matter of a contract. An ambiguity in a contract may constitute a mutual mistake of a material fact. An ambiguity occurs where a word or term in the contract is susceptible to more than one logical interpretation. If there has been a mutual mistake, the contract may be rescinded on the grounds that no contract has been formed because there has been no "meeting of the minds" between the parties.

mutual mistake of fact
A mistake made by both parties concerning a material fact that is important to the subject matter of a contract.

Example

In the celebrated case *Raffles v. Wichelhaus*,[3] which has become better known as the case of the good ship *Peerless*, the parties agreed on a sale of cotton that was to be delivered from Bombay by the ship. There were two ships named *Peerless*, however, and each party, in agreeing to the sale, was referring to a different ship. Because the sailing time of the two

CASE 13.1
Unilateral Mistake

Wells Fargo Credit Corporation v. Martin

650 So.2d 531, Web 1992 Fla.App. Lexis 9927 (1992)
Court of Appeal of Florida

"We accept the trial court's conclusion that the amount of the sale was grossly inadequate. This inadequacy, however, occurred due to an avoidable, unilateral mistake by an agent of Wells Fargo."

—Judge Altenbernd

Facts

Wells Fargo Credit Corporation (Wells Fargo) obtained a judgment of foreclosure on a house owned by Mr. and Mrs. Clevenger. The total indebtedness stated in the judgment was $207,141. The foreclosure sale was scheduled for 11:00 A.M. July 12, 1991, at the west front door of the Hillsborough County Courthouse.

Wells Fargo was represented by a paralegal, who had attended more than 1,000 similar sales. Wells Fargo's handwritten instruction sheet informed the paralegal to make one bid at $115,000, the tax-appraised value of the property. Because the first "1" in the number was close to the "$," the paralegal misread the bid instruction as $15,000 and opened the bidding at that amount.

Harley Martin, who was attending his first judicial sale, bid $20,000. The county clerk gave ample time for another bid and then announced, "$20,000 going once, $20,000 going twice, sold to Harley. . . ." The paralegal screamed, "Stop, I'm sorry. I made a mistake!" The certificate of sale was issued to Martin. Wells Fargo filed suit to set aside the judicial sale based on its unilateral mistake. The trial court held for Martin. Wells Fargo appealed.

Issue

Does Wells Fargo's unilateral mistake constitute grounds for setting aside the judicial sale?

Language of the Court

We accept the trial court's conclusion that the amount of the sale was grossly inadequate. This inadequacy, however,

occurred due to an avoidable, unilateral mistake by an agent of Wells Fargo. As between Wells Fargo and a good faith purchaser at the judicial sale, the trial court had the discretion to place the risk of this mistake upon Wells Fargo.

Thus, we affirm the trial court's orders denying relief to Wells Fargo. We are certain that this result seems harsh to Wells Fargo. Nevertheless, Mr. Martin's bid was accepted when the clerk announced "sold." Without ruling that a unilateral mistake by the complaining party could never justify relief, we hold that the trial court had the discretion under these facts to make Wells Fargo suffer the loss.

Decision

The appellate court held that Wells Fargo's unilateral mistake did not entitle it to relief from the judicial sale.

Case Questions

Critical Legal Thinking   What is a unilateral mistake? Explain.

Business Ethics   Did Martin act ethically in trying to enforce the judicial sale after being informed of the mistake? What would you have done in similar circumstances?

Contemporary Business   Should a contract be allowed to be rescinded because of a unilateral mistake? What would be the danger if the assertion of unilateral mistakes could undo contracts?

ships was materially different, neither party was willing to agree to shipment by the other *Peerless*. The court ruled that there was no binding contract because each party had a different ship in mind when the contract was formed.

Mutual Mistake of Value

A **mutual mistake of value** exists if both parties know the object of the contract but are mistaken as to its value. Here, the contract remains enforceable by either party because the identity of the subject matter of the contract is not at issue. If the rule were different, almost all contracts could later be rescinded by the party who got the "worst" of the deal.

Example

Helen cleans her attic and finds a red and green silkscreen painting of a tomato soup can. She has no use for the painting, so she offers to sell it to Qian for $100. Qian, who thinks that the painting is "cute," accepts the offer and pays Helen $100. It is later discovered that the painting is worth $2 million because it was painted by the famous American pop artist Andy Warhol. Neither party knew this at the time of contracting. It is a mistake of value. Helen cannot recover the painting.

Fraud

A misrepresentation occurs when an assertion is made that is not in accord with the facts.[4] An intentional misrepresentation occurs when one person consciously decides to induce another person to rely and act on a misrepresentation. Intentional misrepresentation is commonly referred to as **fraudulent misrepresentation**, or **fraud**. When fraudulent misrepresentation is used to induce another to enter into a contract, the innocent party's assent to the contract is not genuine, and the contract is voidable by the innocent party.[5] The innocent party can either rescind the contract and obtain restitution or enforce the contract and sue for contract damages.

Proving Fraud

To prove fraud, the following elements must be shown:

- The wrongdoer made a false representation of material fact.
- The wrongdoer intended to deceive the innocent party.
- The innocent party justifiably relied on the misrepresentation.
- The innocent party was injured.

Each of these elements is discussed in the following paragraphs.

Material Misrepresentation of Fact A **misrepresentation** may occur by words (oral or written) or by the conduct of a party. To be actionable as fraud, the misrepresentation must be of a past or existing *material fact*. This means that the misrepresentation must have been a significant factor in inducing the innocent party to enter into the contract. It does not have to have been the sole factor. Statements of opinion or predictions about the future generally do not form the basis for fraud.

Intent to Deceive To prove fraud, the person making the misrepresentation must have either had knowledge that the representation was false or made it without sufficient knowledge of the truth. This is called **scienter** ("**guilty mind**"). The misrepresentation must have been made with the **intent to deceive** the innocent party. Intent can be inferred from the circumstances.

Reliance on the Misrepresentation A misrepresentation is not actionable unless the innocent party to whom the misrepresentation was directed acted on it. Further, an innocent party who acts in **reliance on a misrepresentation** must justify his or her reliance. Justifiable reliance is generally found unless the innocent party knew that the misrepresentation was false or was so extravagant as to be obviously false.

Injury to the Innocent Party   To recover damages, the innocent party must prove that the fraud caused him or her economic **injury**. The measure of damages is the difference between the value of the property as represented and the actual value of the property. This measure of damages gives the innocent party the "benefit of the bargain." In the alternative, the buyer can rescind the contract and recover the purchase price.

Individuals must be on guard in their commercial and personal dealings not to be taken by fraud. Basically, something sounding "too good to be true" is a signal that the situation might be fraudulent. Although the law permits a victim of fraud to rescind the contract and recover damages from the wrongdoer, often the wrongdoer cannot be found or the money has been spent.

Fraud in the Inception

Fraud in the inception, or **fraud in the factum**, occurs if a person is deceived as to the nature of his or her act and does not know what he or she is signing. Contracts involving fraud in the inception are void rather than just voidable.

fraud in the inception
Fraud that occurs if a person is deceived as to the nature of his or her act and does not know what he or she is signing. Also known as fraud in the factum.

Example
Heather brings her professor a grade card to sign. The professor signs the grade card on the front without reading the grade card. On the front, however, are contract terms that transfer all of the professor's property to Heather. Here, there is fraud in the inception. The contract is void.

Fraud in the Inducement

Many fraud cases concern **fraud in the inducement**. Here, the innocent party knows what he or she is signing or doing but has been fraudulently induced to enter into the contract. Such contracts are voidable by the innocent party.

fraud in the inducement
Fraud that occurs when the party knows what he or she is signing but has been fraudulently induced to enter into the contract.

Example
Lyle tells Candice that he is forming a partnership to invest in drilling for oil in an oil field and invites her to invest in this venture. In reality, though, there is no oil field, and Lyle intends to use whatever money he receives from Candice for his personal expenses. Candice relies on Lyle's statements and invests $30,000 with Lyle. Lyle absconds with Candice's $30,000 investment. Here, there has been fraud in the inducement. Candice has been induced to give Lyle $30,000 based on Lyle's misrepresentation of fact. Candice can rescind the contract and recover the money from Lyle, if she can find him and locate his money or property.

Fraud by Concealment

Fraud by concealment occurs when one party takes specific action to conceal a material fact from another party.[6]

fraud by concealment
Fraud that occurs when one party takes specific action to conceal a material fact from another party.

Example
Steel Inc. contracts to buy used manufacturing equipment from United Inc. United Inc. does not show Steel Inc. the repair invoices for repairs to the equipment even though Steel Inc. has asked to see all of the repair invoices for the equipment. Relying on the knowledge that the equipment is in good condition and has never had been repaired, Steel Inc. purchases the equipment from United Inc. If Steel Inc. subsequently discovers that a significant repair record has been concealed by United Inc., Steel Inc. can sue United Inc. for fraud by concealment.

Silence as Misrepresentation

Generally, neither party to a contract owes a duty to disclose all the facts to the other party. Ordinarily, such **silence** is not a misrepresentation unless (1) nondisclosure would cause bodily injury or death, (2) there is a fiduciary relationship (i.e., a relationship of trust and confidence) between the contracting parties, or (3) federal and state statutes require disclosure. The *Restatement (Second) of Contracts* specifies a broader duty of disclosure: Nondisclosure is a misrepresentation if it would constitute a failure to act in "good faith."[7]

Misrepresentation of Law

Usually, a **misrepresentation of law** is not actionable as fraud. The innocent party cannot generally rescind the contract because each party to a contract is assumed to know the law that applies to the transaction, either through his or her own investigation or by hiring a lawyer. There is one major exception to this rule: The misrepresentation will be allowed as grounds for rescission of the contract if one party to the contract is a professional who should know what the law is and intentionally misrepresents the law to a less sophisticated contracting party.[8]

Innocent Misrepresentation

innocent misrepresentation

Fraud that occurs when a person makes a statement of fact that he or she honestly and reasonably believes to be true even though it is not.

An **innocent misrepresentation** occurs when a person makes a statement of fact that he or she honestly and reasonably believes to be true even though it is not. Innocent misrepresentation is not fraud. If an innocent misrepresentation has been made, the aggrieved party may rescind the contract but may not sue for damages. Often, innocent misrepresentation is treated as a mutual mistake.

In the following case, the court found fraud and awarded punitive damages.

CASE 13.2
Fraud

Krysa v. Payne

176 S.W.3d 150, Web 2005 Mo.App. Lexis 1680 (2005)
Court of Appeals of Missouri

"Punitive damages differ from compensatory damages in that compensatory damages are intended to redress the concrete loss that the plaintiff has suffered by reason of the defendant's wrongful conduct, while the well-established purpose of punitive damages is to inflict punishment and to serve as an example and a deterrent to similar conduct."

—Judge Ellis

Facts

Frank and Shelly Krysa were shopping for a truck to pull their 18-foot trailer. During the course of their search, they visited Payne's Car Company, a used car dealership owned by Emmett Payne. Kemp Crane, a used car salesman, showed the Krysas around the car lot. The Krysas saw an F-350 truck that they were interested in purchasing. Crane told the Krysas that the truck would tow their trailer, that the truck would make it to 400,000 miles, and that it was "a one-owner trade-in." The Krysas took the truck for a test drive and decided to purchase the truck. The Krysas, who had to borrow some of the money from Mrs. Krysas's mother, paid for the truck and took possession.

Later that day, the Krysas noticed that the power locks did not work on the truck. A few days later, the truck took three hours to start. The heater was not working. Mr. Krysa tried to fix some problems and noticed that the radiator was smashed up, the radiator cap did not have a seal, and the thermostat was missing. Mr. Krysa noticed broken glass on the floor underneath the front seats and that the driver's side window had been replaced. Shortly thereafter, Mr. Krysa attempted to tow his trailer, but within 2 miles, he had his foot to the floor trying to get the truck to pull the trailer. A large amount of smoke was pouring out of the back of the truck. Mr. Krysa also noticed that the truck was consuming a lot of oil. Mr. Krysa obtained a

CARFAX report for the truck, which showed that the truck had had 13 prior owners. Evidence proved that the truck was actually two halves of different trucks that had been welded together. An automobile expert told the Krysas not to drive the truck because it was unsafe.

Mr. Krysa went back to the dealership to return the truck and get his money back. Payne told Krysa that he would credit the purchase price of the truck toward the purchase of one of the other vehicles on the lot but that he would not give Krysa his money back. Krysa could not find another vehicle on Payne's used car lot that would suit his needs. The Krysas sued Payne for fraudulent nondisclosure and fraudulent misrepresentation, and they sought to recover compensatory and punitive damages. The jury returned a verdict for the Krysas and awarded them $18,449 in compensatory damages and $500,000 in punitive damages. Payne appealed the award of punitive damages.

Issue

Did Payne engage in fraudulent nondisclosure, fraudulent misrepresentation, and reckless disregard for the safety of the Krysas and the public to support the award of $500,000 in punitive damages?

Language of the Court

Punitive damages differ from compensatory damages in that compensatory damages are intended to redress the concrete loss that the plaintiff has suffered by reason of the defendant's wrongful conduct, while the well-established purpose of punitive damages is to inflict punishment and to serve as an example and a deterrent to similar conduct. While the damage actually sustained by the Krysas was relatively small and was economic in nature, the record clearly supports a finding that Payne acted indifferently to or in reckless disregard of the safety of the Krysas in selling them a vehicle that he knew or should have known was not safe to drive and that the potential harm to the Krysas was much greater than the harm that was actually incurred.

The evidence also supported a finding that the harm sustained by Krysas was the result of intentional malice, trickery, or deceit, and was not merely an accident. Payne had a significant amount of work done to the vehicle to make it appear to be in good shape. This included, among numerous other repairs, straightening both the bed and cab of the truck. Payne's salesman, Crane, lied to the Krysas on several occasions about the condition of the truck, its origin, and its capabilities. This evidence, in

addition to other evidence previously described, sufficiently established that Payne affirmatively misrepresented the condition of the F-350 to the Krysas in an attempt to trick them into buying the vehicle.

In sum, while the harm actually sustained by the Krysas in this case was economic as opposed to physical, Payne's conduct did pose a significant risk to the physical welfare of Respondents and evinced an indifference to or reckless disregard of the health or safety of Krysas and the general public as well. Furthermore, the conduct was consistent with Payne's regular business practices and was not an isolated incident, involved acts of intentional trickery and deceit, and targeted victims that were financially vulnerable. Thus, in society's eyes, viewing the totality of the circumstances, Payne's conduct can only be seen as exhibiting a very high degree of reprehensibility.

Payne contends that the ratio between the actual damages awarded, $18,449.53, and the punitive award, $500,000, is grossly excessive, in that the ratio of punitive to actual damages is approximately 27:1. The initial problem with Payne's argument is that it fails to consider the evidence of the potential harm that could have been sustained by the Krysas. In this case, given the relatively small amount of actual damages awarded, the egregious nature of Payne's acts, Payne's open refusal to alter his behavior, and the magnitude of the potential harm that could have been sustained had the structural problems with the truck not been discovered by the Krysas's expert, the ratio of the punitive to actual damages does not, in and of itself, offend due process.

Decision

The court of appeals found that Payne's fraudulent concealment, fraudulent misrepresentation, and reckless disregard for the safety of the Krysas and the public justified the award of $500,000 of punitive damages to the Krysas.

Case Questions

Critical Legal Thinking   What is fraudulent concealment? What is fraudulent misrepresentation?

Business Ethics   Did Payne, the used car dealer, act ethically in this case? Should punitive damages have been awarded in this case? Why or why not?

Contemporary Business   Do you have any apprehension about purchasing a car from a used car dealership? Why or why not?

Concept Summary
Types of Misrepresentation

Type of Misrepresentation	Legal Party May: Consequences—Innocent for	
	Sue for Damages	Rescind Contract
Fraud in the inception	Yes	Yes
Fraud in the inducement	Yes	Yes
Fraud by concealment	Yes	Yes
Silence as misrepresentation	Yes	Yes
Misrepresentation of law	Usually no	Usually no
Innocent misrepresentation	No	Yes

Duress

duress

A situation in which one party threatens to do a wrongful act unless the other party enters into a contract.

Duress occurs when one party threatens to do some wrongful act unless the other party enters into a contract. If a party to a contract has been forced into making the contract, the assent is not voluntary. Such a contract is not enforceable against the innocent party. If someone threatens to physically harm another person unless that person signs a contract, this is *physical duress*. If the victim of the duress signs the contract, it cannot be enforced against the victim.

The threat to commit extortion unless someone enters into a contract constitutes duress. So does a threat to bring (or not drop) a criminal lawsuit. Such threats are duress even if the criminal lawsuit is well founded.[9] A threat to bring (or not drop) a civil lawsuit, however, does not constitute duress unless such a suit is frivolous or brought in bad faith.

Equity: Undue Influence

undue influence

A situation in which one person takes advantage of another person's mental, emotional, or physical weakness and unduly persuades that person to enter into a contract; the persuasion by the wrongdoer must overcome the free will of the innocent party.

The courts may permit the rescission of a contract based on the equitable doctrine of **undue influence**. Undue influence occurs when one person (the **dominant party**) takes advantage of another person's mental, emotional, or physical weakness and unduly persuades that person (the **servient party**) to enter into a contract. The persuasion by the wrongdoer must overcome the free will of the innocent party. A contract that is entered into because of undue influence is voidable by the innocent party.[10]

The following elements must be shown to prove undue influence:

- A fiduciary or confidential relationship must have existed between the parties.
- The dominant party must have unduly used his or her influence to persuade the servient party to enter into a contract.

If there is a confidential relationship between persons—such as a lawyer and a client, a doctor and a patient, a psychiatrist and a patient—any contract made by the servient party that benefits the dominant party is presumed to be entered into under undue influence. This rebuttable presumption can be overcome through proper evidence.

The meaning of words varies according to the circumstances of and concerning which they are used.

Justice Blackburn
Allgood v. Blake (1873)

Example

Mr. Johnson, 70 years old, has a stroke and is partially paralyzed. He is required to use a wheelchair, and he needs constant nursing care. Prior to his stroke, Mr. Johnson had executed a will, leaving his property upon his death equally to his four grandchildren. Edward, a licensed nurse, is hired to care for Mr. Johnson on a daily basis, and Mr. Johnson relies on Edward's care. Edward works for Mr. Johnson for 2 years before Mr. Johnson passes away.

Mongolia. *In Mongolia, many contracts are oral agreements where a person's word is as good as a bond. In countries where the nomadic form of living is prevalent, herders graze their animals on land owned by the government. Mongolia is a country where a large proportion of the country's residents still live the nomadic lifestyle. They have little access to lawyers or courts, so contract disputes are settled by members of the nomadic society.*

It is later discovered that Mr. Johnson had executed a written contract with Edward three months before he died, deeding a valuable piece of real estate to Edward. If it is shown that Edward has used his dominant and fiduciary position to unduly influence Mr. Johnson to enter into this contract, then the contract is invalid. If no undue influence is shown, the contract with Edward is valid, and Edward will receive the property deeded to him by Mr. Johnson.

Test Review Terms and Concepts

Dominant party
Duress
Fraud by concealment
Fraud in the inception (fraud in the factum)
Fraud in the inducement
Fraudulent misrepresentation (fraud)
Genuineness of assent
Injury to the innocent party

Innocent misrepresentation
Intent to deceive
Material fact
Material misrepresentation of fact
Misrepresentation of law
Mistake
Mutual mistake of a past or existing material fact

Mutual mistake of value
Reliance on a misrepresentation
Rescission
Scienter ("guilty mind")
Servient party
Silence as misrepresentation
Undue influence
Unilateral mistake

Case Problems

13.1 Unilateral Mistake: Mrs. Chaney died, leaving a house in Annapolis, Maryland. The representative of her estate listed the property for sale with a real estate broker, stating that the property was approximately 15,650 square feet. Drs. Steele and Faust made an offer of $300,000 for the property, which was accepted by the estate. A contract for the sale of the property was signed by all the parties. When a subsequent survey (done before the deed was transferred) showed that the property had an area of 22,047 square feet, the estate requested the buyers to pay more money for the property.

When the estate refused to transfer the property to the buyers, they sued for specific performance. Can the estate rescind the contract? *Steele v. Goettee*, 313 Md. 11, 542 A.2d 847, **Web** 1988 Md. Lexis 91 (Court of Appeals of Maryland)

13.2 Unilateral Mistake: The County of Contra Costa, California, held a tax sale in which it offered for sale a vacant piece of property located in the city of El Cerrito. Richard J. Schultz, a carpenter, saw the notice of the pending tax sale and was interested in purchasing the lot to build a house.

Prior to attending the tax sale, Schultz visited and measured the parcel, examined the neighborhood and found the houses there to be "very nice," and had a title search done that turned up no liens or judgments against the property. Schultz did not, however, check with the city zoning department regarding the zoning of the property.

Schultz attended the tax sale and, after spirited bidding, won with a bid of $9,100 and received a deed to the property. Within one week of the purchase, Schultz discovered that the city's zoning laws prevented building a residence on the lot. In essence, the lot was worthless. Schultz sued to rescind the contract. Can the contract be rescinded? *Schultz v. County of Contra Costa, California*, 157 Cal.App.3d 242, 203 Cal.Rptr. 760, **Web** 1984 Cal.App. Lexis 2198 (Court of Appeal of California)

13.3 Mutual Mistake: Ron Boskett, a part-time coin dealer, purchased a dime purportedly minted in 1916 at the Denver Mint; he paid nearly $450. The fact that the "D" on the coin signified Denver mintage made the coin rare and valuable. Boskett sold the coin to Beachcomber Coins, Inc. (Beachcomber), a retail coin dealer, for $500. A principal of Beachcomber examined the coin for 15 to 45 minutes prior to its purchase. Soon thereafter, Beachcomber received an offer of $700 for the coin, subject to certification of its genuineness by the American Numismatic Society. When this organization labeled the coin counterfeit, Beachcomber sued Boskett to rescind the purchase of the coin. Can Beachcomber rescind the contract? *Beachcomber Coins, Inc. v. Boskett*, 166 N.J. Super. 442, 400 A.2d 78, **Web** 1979 N.J. Super Lexis 659 (Superior Court of New Jersey)

13.4 Fraud: Robert McClure owned a vehicle salvage and rebuilding business. He listed the business for sale and had a brochure printed that described the business and stated that the business grossed $581,117 and netted $142,727 the prior year. Fred H. Campbell saw the brochure and inquired about buying the business. Campbell hired a CPA to review McClure's business records and tax returns, but the CPA could not reconcile them with the income claimed for the business in the brochure. When Campbell asked McClure about the discrepancy, McClure stated that the business records did—and tax returns did not—accurately reflect the cash flow or profits of the business because it was such a high-cash operation, with much of the cash not being reported to the Internal Revenue Service on tax returns. McClure signed a warranty which stated that the true income of the business was as represented in the brochure.

Campbell bought the business based on McClure's representations. However, the business, although operated in substantially the same manner as when owned by McClure, failed to yield a net income similar to that warranted by McClure. Evidence showed that McClure's representations were substantially overstated. Campbell sued McClure for damages for fraud. Who wins? *Campbell v. McClure*, 182 Cal.App.3d 806, 227 Cal.Rptr. 450, **Web** 1986 Cal. App.Lexis 1751 (Court of Appeal of California)

13.5 Fraud: James L. "Skip" Deupree, a developer, was building a development of townhouses called Point South in Destin, Florida. All the townhouses in the development were to have individual boat slips. Sam and Louise Butner, husband and wife, bought one of the townhouses. The sales contract between Deupree and the Butners provided that a boat slip would be built and was included in the price of the townhouse. The contract stated that permission from the Florida Department of Natural Resources (DNR) had to be obtained to build the boat slips. It is undisputed that a boat slip adds substantially to the value of the property and that the Butners relied on the fact that the townhouse would have a boat slip.

Prior to the sale of the townhouse to the Butners, the DNR had informed Deupree that it objected to the plan to build the boat slips and that permission to build them would probably not be forthcoming. Deupree did not tell the Butners this information but instead stated that there would be "no problem" getting permission from the state to build the boat slips. The Butners purchased the townhouse. When the DNR would not approve the building of the boat slips for the Butners' townhouse, they sued for damages for fraud. Who wins? *Deupree v. Butner*, 522 So.2d 242, **Web** 1988 Ala. Lexis 55 (Supreme Court of Alabama)

13.6 Innocent Misrepresentation: W. F. Yost, who owned the Red Barn Barbecue Restaurant (Red Barn), listed it for sale. Richard and Evelyn Ramano of Rieve Enterprises, Inc. (Rieve), were interested in buying the restaurant. After visiting and conducting a visual inspection of the premises, Rieve entered into a contract to purchase the assets and equipment of Red Barn, as well as the five-year lease of, and option to buy, the land and the building. Prior to the sale, the restaurant had been cited for certain health violations that Yost had corrected. In the contract of sale, Yost warranted that "the premises will pass all inspections" to conduct the business.

Rieve took possession immediately after the sale and operated the restaurant. After two weeks, when the Board of Health conducted a routine inspection, it cited 52 health code violations and thereupon closed the restaurant. Rieve sued to rescind the purchase agreement. Evidence established that Yost's misrepresentations were innocently made. Can Rieve rescind the contract? *Yost v. Rieve Enterprises, Inc.*, 461 So.2d 178, **Web** 1984 Fla.App. Lexis 16490 (Court of Appeals of Florida)

13.7 Duress: Judith and Donald Eckstein were married and had two daughters. Years later, Judith left the marital abode in the parties' jointly owned Volkswagen van with only the clothes on her back. She did not take the children, who were six and eight years old at the time. She had no funds, and the husband promptly closed the couple's bank account. The wife was unemployed. Shortly after she left, the husband discovered her whereabouts and the location of the van and seized and secreted the van. The husband refused the wife's request to visit or communicate with her children and refused to give her clothing. He told her that she could see the children and take her clothes only if she signed a separation agreement prepared by his lawyer. The wife contacted Legal Aid but was advised that she did not qualify for assistance.

The wife was directed to go to her husband's lawyer's office. A copy of a separation agreement was given to her to read. The separation agreement provided that the wife (1) give custody of the children to her husband, (2) deed her interest in their jointly owned house to the husband, (3) assign her interest in a jointly owned new Chevrolet van to her husband, and (4) waive alimony, support, maintenance, court costs, attorneys' fees, and any right to inheritance in her husband's estate. By the agreement, she was to receive $1,100 cash, her clothes, the Volkswagen van, and any furniture she desired. The wife testified that her husband told her over an interoffice phone in the lawyer's office that if she did not sign the separation agreement, he would get her for desertion, that she would never see her children again, and that she would get nothing—neither her clothes nor the van—unless she signed the agreement. The wife signed the separation agreement. Immediately thereafter, her clothes were surrendered to her, and she was given $1,100 cash and the keys to the Volkswagen van. The husband filed for divorce. The wife filed an answer seeking to rescind the separation agreement. Can she rescind the separation agreement? *Eckstein v. Eckstein*, 38 Md.App. 506, 379 A.2d 757, **Web** 1978 Md.App. Lexis 324. (Court of Special Appeals of Maryland)

13.8 Undue Influence: Conrad Schaneman, Sr., had eight sons and five daughters. He owned an 80-acre farm in the Scotts Bluff area of Nebraska. Conrad was born in Russia and could not read or write English. All of his children had frequent contact with Conrad and helped with his needs. Subsequently, however, his eldest son, Lawrence, advised the other children that he would henceforth manage his father's business affairs. After much urging by Lawrence, Conrad deeded the farm to Lawrence for $23,500. Evidence showed that at the time of the sale, the reasonable fair market value of the farm was between $145,000 and $160,000.

At the time of the conveyance, Conrad was over 80 years old, had deteriorated in health, suffered from heart problems and diabetes, had high and uncontrollable blood sugar levels, weighed almost 300 pounds, had difficulty breathing, could not walk more than 15 feet, and had to have a jackhoist lift him in and out of the bathtub. He was for all purposes an invalid, relying on Lawrence for most of his personal needs, transportation, banking, and other business matters. After Conrad died, the conservators of the estate brought an action to cancel the deed transferring the farm to Lawrence. Can the conservators cancel the deed? *Schaneman v. Schaneman*, 206 Neb. 113, 291 N.W.2d 412, **Web** 1980 Neb. Lexis 823 (Supreme Court of Nebraska)

Business Ethics Cases

13.9 Business Ethics: The First Baptist Church of Moultrie, Georgia, invited bids for the construction of a music, education, and recreation building. The bids were to be accompanied by a bid bond of five percent of the bid amount. Barber Contracting Company (Barber Contracting) submitted a bid in the amount of $1,860,000. A bid bond in the amount of five percent of the bid—$93,000—was issued by The American Insurance Company. The bids were opened by the church, and Barber Contracting was the lowest bid.

On the next day, Albert W. Barber, the president of Barber Contracting, informed the church that his company's bid was in error and should have been $143,120 higher. The error was caused in totaling the material costs on Barber Contracting's estimate worksheets. The church had not been provided these worksheets. Barber Contracting sent a letter to the church, stating that it was withdrawing its bid. The next day, the church sent a construction contract to Barber Contracting, containing the original bid amount. When Barber Contracting refused to sign the contract and refused to do the work for the original contract price, the church signed a contract with the second-lowest bidder, H & H Construction and Supply Company, Inc., to complete the work for

$1,919,272. The church sued Barber Contracting and The American Insurance Company, seeking to recover the amount of the bid bond. Who wins? Did Barber act ethically in trying to get out of the contract? Did the church act ethically in trying to enforce Barber's bid? *First Baptist Church of Moultrie v. Barber Contracting Co.*, 189 Ga.App. 804, 377 S.E.2d 717, **Web** 1989 Ga.App. Lexis 25 (Court of Appeals of Georgia)

13.10 Business Ethics: Lockheed Missiles & Space Company, Inc. (Lockheed), sent out a request to potential subcontractors, seeking bids for the manufacture of 124 ballast cans for the Trident II nuclear submarines it was building for the U.S. Navy. In February 1989, Lockheed received eight bids, including one from Sulzer Bingham Pumps, Inc. (Sulzer). Sulzer was the lowest bidder, at $6,544,055. The next lowest bid was $10,176,670, and the bids ranged up to $17,766,327. Lockheed itself estimated that the job would cost at least $8.5 million. Lockheed's employees were shocked by Sulzer's bid and thought it was surprisingly low.

Lockheed then inspected Sulzer's Portland facility to evaluate Sulzer's technical capabilities. The inspection revealed that Sulzer would have to make many modifications to its existing facility in order to complete the contract.

Lockheed did not reveal its findings to Sulzer. In addition, it never notified Sulzer that its bid was significantly lower than the next lowest bid and lower than Lockheed's own estimate of the cost of the job as well. Finally, Sulzer was never told that Lockheed suspected that the contract could not be completed at the bid price.

Lockheed accepted Sulzer's bid, and Sulzer started work. Nine months later, Sulzer revised its estimate of the cost of the job and asked Lockheed for an additional $2,110,000 in compensation. When Lockheed rejected this request, Sulzer sued Lockheed, asking the court to either increase the price of the contract to $8,645,000 or, alternatively, to rescind its bid. Did Lockheed act ethically in this case by not notifying Sulzer of the suspected mistake? Did Sulzer act ethically by trying to get out of the contract because of its own economic misjudgments? Legally, who wins? *Sulzer Bingham Pumps, Inc. v. Lockheed Missiles & Space Company, Inc.*, 947 F.2d 1362, **Web** 1991 U.S. App. Lexis 24966 (United States Court of Appeals for the Ninth Circuit)

Endnotes

1. *Restatement (Second) of Contracts*, Section 153.
2. *Restatement (Second) of Contracts*, Section 152.
3. 59 Eng. Rep. 375 (1864).
4. *Restatement (Second) of Contracts*, Section 159.
5. *Restatement (Second) of Contracts*, Sections 163 and 164.
6. *Restatement (Second) of Contracts*, Section 160.
7. *Restatement (Second) of Contracts*, Section 161.
8. *Restatement (Second) of Contracts*, Section 170.
9. *Restatement (Second) of Contracts*, Section 177.
10. *Restatement (Second) of Contracts*, Section 176.

CHAPTER 14

"A verbal contract isn't worth the paper it's written on."
—Samuel Goldwyn

Statute of Frauds and Equitable Exceptions

Chapter Objectives

After studying this chapter, you should be able to:

1. List the contracts that must be in writing under the Statute of Frauds.
2. Explain the effect of noncompliance with the Statute of Frauds.
3. Describe how the Statute of Frauds is applicable to the sale of goods.
4. Describe the formality of the writing of contracts and the parol evidence rule.
5. Apply the equity doctrines of *part performance* and *promissory estoppel*.

Chapter Contents

- **Introduction to Statute of Frauds and Equitable Exceptions**

- **Statute of Frauds**
  Case 14.1 · *Sawyer v. Mills*
  Case 14.2 · *Page v. Gulf Coast Motors*

- **Equity: Part Performance**
  Ethics Spotlight · *Equity: Part Performance*

- **Formality of the Writing**

- **Parol Evidence Rule**

- **Equity: Promissory Estoppel**

Introduction to Statute of Frauds and Equitable Exceptions

Certain types of contracts must be in writing pursuant to the Statute of Frauds. Other issues regarding the form of a contract may arise, such as the form of signature that is required on a written contract, whether a contract can be created by the integration of several documents, whether any previous oral or written agreements between the parties can be given effect, and how contract language should be interpreted. Also, there are several equitable exceptions to the Statute of Frauds—namely the part performance exception and the doctrine of promissory estoppel.

Issues regarding the Statute of Frauds, the formality of the writing of contracts and equitable doctrines that allow exceptions to the Statute of Frauds are discussed in this chapter.

Statute of Frauds

In 1677, the English Parliament enacted a statute called "An Act for the Prevention of Frauds and Perjuries." This act required that certain types of contracts had to be in writing and signed by the party against whom enforcement was sought. Today, every U.S. state has enacted a **Statute of Frauds** that requires certain types of contracts to be in *writing*. This statute is intended to ensure that the terms of important contracts are not forgotten, misunderstood, or fabricated. One court stated about the Statute of Frauds, "It is the purpose of the Statute of Frauds to suppress fraud, i.e., cooked-up claims of agreement, sometimes fathered by wish, sometimes imagined in the light of subsequent events, and sometimes simply conjured up."[1]

Writing Requirement

Although the statutes vary slightly from state to state, most states require the following types of contracts to be in writing.[2]

- Contracts involving interests in real property
- Contracts that by their own terms cannot possibly be performed within one year
- Collateral contracts in which a person promises to answer for the debt or duty of another
- Promises made in consideration of marriage
- Contracts for the sale of goods for $500 or more
- Contracts for the lease of goods with payments of $1,000 or more
- Real estate agents' contracts
- Agents' contracts where the underlying contract must be in writing
- Promises to write a will
- Contracts to pay debts barred by the statute of limitations or discharged in bankruptcy
- Contracts to pay compensation for services rendered in negotiating the purchase of a business
- Finder's fee contracts

Generally, an **executory contract** that is not in writing even though the Statute of Frauds requires it to be is unenforceable by either party. The Statute of Frauds is usually raised by one party as a defense to the enforcement of the contract by the other party.

If an oral contract that should have been in writing under the Statute of Frauds is already executed, neither party can seek to **rescind** the contract on the ground of noncompliance with the Statute of Frauds. That is, the contract may be voluntarily performed by the parties.

Generally, contracts listed in the Statute of Frauds must be in writing to be enforceable. There are several equity exceptions to this rule. The contracts that must be in writing pursuant to the Statute of Frauds and the exceptions to this rule are discussed in the following paragraphs.

Statute of Frauds

A state statute that requires certain types of contracts to be in writing.

Statute of Frauds: That unfortunate statute, the misguided application of which has been the cause of so many frauds.

Bacon, Viscount
Morgan v. Worthington (1878)

Don't get it right, just get it written.

James Thurber

Contracts Involving Interests in Real Property

Under the Statute of Frauds, any contract that transfers an ownership interest in **real property** must be in writing to be enforceable. Real property includes the land itself, buildings, trees, soil, minerals, timber, plants, crops, fixtures, and things permanently affixed to the land or buildings. Certain items of personal property that are permanently affixed to the real property are fixtures that become part of the real property.

real property
The land itself, as well as buildings, trees, soil, minerals, timber, plants, crops, fixtures and other things permanently affixed to the land or buildings.

Example

Built-in cabinets in a house are *fixtures* that become part of the real property.

Other contracts that transfer an ownership interest in land must be in writing under the Statute of Frauds. These interests include the following:

- **Mortgages.** Borrowers often give a lender an interest in real property as security for the repayment of a loan. This action must be done through the use of a written **mortgage** or **deed of trust**.

mortgage
An interest in real property given to a lender as security for the repayment of a loan.

Example

Ida purchases a house for $1 million. She pays $400,000 toward the payment of the house and borrows $600,000 of the purchase price from CityBank. CityBank requires that the house be collateral for the loan and takes a mortgage on the house. Here, the mortgage between Ida and CityBank must be in writing to be enforceable.

- **Leases.** A **lease** is the transfer of the right to use real property for a specified period of time. Most Statutes of Frauds require leases for a term over one year to be in writing.
- **Life estates.** On some occasions, a person is given a **life estate** in real property. In other words, the person has an interest in the real property for the person's lifetime, and the interest will be transferred to another party on that person's death. A life estate is an ownership interest that must be in writing under the Statute of Frauds.
- **Easements.** An **easement** is a given or required right to use another person's land without owning or leasing it. Easements may be either express or implied. Express easements must be in writing to be enforceable, while implied easements need not be written.

lease
The transfer of the right to use real property for a specified period of time.

life estate
An interest in real property for a person's lifetime; upon that person's death, the interest will be transferred to another party.

easement
A right to use someone else's land without owning or leasing it.

One-Year Rule

According to the Statute of Frauds, an executory contract that cannot be performed by its own terms within one year of its formation must be in writing.[3] This **one-year rule** is intended to prevent disputes about contract terms that may otherwise occur toward the end of a long-term contract. If the performance of the contract is possible within the one-year period, the contract may be oral.

The extension of an oral contract might cause the contract to violate the Statute of Frauds if the original term and the extension period exceed one year.

one-year rule
A rule which states that an executory contract that cannot be performed by its own terms within one year of its formation must be in writing.

Example

Frederick, the owner of a store, hires Anna as the store manager for 6 months. Assume that after 3 months Frederick and Anna agree to extend the contract for an additional 11 months. At the time of the extension, the contract would be for 14 months (the 3 left on the original contract plus 11 months added by the extension). The modification would have to be in writing because it exceeds the one-year rule.

In the following case, the court held that the one-year rule prohibited the enforcement of an oral contract.

Guaranty Contract

A **guaranty contract** occurs when one person agrees to answer for the debts or duties of another person. Guaranty contracts are required to be in writing under the Statute of Frauds.[4]

guaranty contract
A promise in which one person agrees to answer for the debts or duties of another person. It is a contract between the guarantor and the original creditor.

Sawyer v. Mills

Web 2007 Ky.App. Lexis 92 Court of Appeals of Kentucky (2007)

"The end result may not seem 'fair' to Sawyer. The Statute of Frauds, by its own terms, can be considered 'harsh' in that it will bar oral agreements between parties under certain conditions. This is simply the nature of the beast."

—Trial Court Judge Ishmael

Facts

Barbara Lucinda Sawyer worked as a paralegal for Melbourne Mills, Jr., an attorney at a law firm. Sawyer proposed that Mills and the law firm become engaged in class action lawsuits. Mills agreed to pay Sawyer an unspecified bonus when "the ship comes in." After Sawyer's assistance and persistence, the law firm became involved in class action litigation—primarily the Fen-Phen class action litigation. After the law firm received millions of dollars in fees from the Fen-Phen class action lawsuits, Sawyer and her husband Steve met with Mills to discuss Sawyers' bonus. Mills orally agreed to pay Sawyer $1,065,000 as a bonus to be paid in monthly installments over 107 months. Sawyer secretly tape recorded the conversation. Mills later refused to sign a written contract conveying the terms of the oral agreement.

After Mills had paid $165,000, he quit making further payments. Sawyer sued Mills to collect the remaining $900,000. Mills defended, arguing that the oral contract exceeded one year and was therefore unenforceable because it was not in writing, as required by the Statute of Frauds. The jury ruled in favor of Sawyer. Mills made a motion to the trial court judge to refuse to enforce the oral contract against him. The trial court heard and decided the motion.

Language of the Court

Sawyer produced no writing signed by Mills consistent with the oral discussions of the parties. Sawyer argues that the "writing" requirement of the Statute of Frauds has been satisfied in this case because of the cassette tape which was played to the jury and which surreptitiously recorded the discussions between Sawyer, her husband, and Mills, taken together with the several checks written by Mills and signed by him totaling $165,000. The Court cannot accept this argument. First of all, the cassette tape recording is not a "writing signed by the party to be charged" as required by the Statute of Frauds. The checks signed by

Mills are, at best, evidence confirming the agreement of the parties, i.e., that the total amount of the bonus would be paid out in monthly installments of $10,000 on the first of each month for 107 months. These checks, at best, merely confirm the oral agreement of the parties.

The Court is aware of the apparent harshness of this ruling. The trial jury found, and the Court heard Mills state on the tape recording, that he agreed to make monthly payments to Sawyer which would eventually total over One Million Dollars. Honoring that oral agreement would be the "moral" and "right" thing for Mills to do. However, this Court is obligated by Oath of Office and Kentucky law, to consider cases based on the facts presented and the applicable law. The end result may not seem "fair" to Sawyer. The Statute of Frauds, by its own terms, can be considered "harsh" in that it will bar oral agreements between parties under certain conditions. This is simply the nature of the beast.

Decision

The trial court held that the Statute of Frauds required the bonus agreement between Sawyer and Mills to be in writing to be enforceable. Because the oral agreement exceeded one year, it did not meet the requirements of the Statute of Frauds and is therefore unenforceable. The court of appeals of Kentucky affirmed the trial court's decision.

Case Questions

Critical Legal Thinking   What does the one-year rule provide? Explain.

Business Ethics   Should Mills do the "moral" and "right" thing and pay the remainder of the money to Sawyer?

Contemporary Business   Does the adage "Get it in writing!" mean anymore to you now that you have read this case?

■ EXHIBIT 14.1 Guaranty Contract

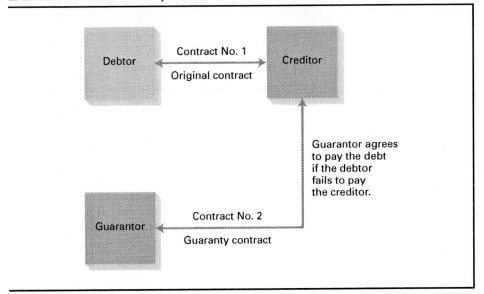

In a guaranty situation, there are at least three parties and two contracts (see Exhibit 14.1). The *first contract*, which is known as the **original contract**, or **primary contract**, is between the debtor and the creditor. It does not have to be in writing (unless another provision of the Statute of Frauds requires it to be). The *second contract*, called the *guaranty contract*, is between the person who agrees to pay the debt if the primary debtor does not (i.e., the **guarantor**) and the original creditor. The guarantor's liability is secondary because it does not arise unless the party primarily liable fails to perform.

guarantor
A person who agrees to pay a debt if the primary debtor does not.

Example

Wei, a recent college graduate, offers to purchase a new automobile on credit from a Mercedes-Benz automobile dealership. Because Wei does not have a credit history, the dealer will agree to sell the car to her only if there is a guarantor. If Wei's father signs a written guaranty contract, he becomes responsible for any payments his daughter fails to make. If Wei's father only orally guaranteed Wei's contract, he would not be bound to the guaranty because it was oral.

The "Main Purpose" Exception   If the main purpose of a transaction and an oral collateral contract is to provide pecuniary (i.e., financial) benefit to the guarantor, the collateral contract is treated like an original contract and does not have to be in writing to be enforced.[5] This exception is called the **main purpose exception**, or **leading object exception**, to the Statute of Frauds. This exception is intended to ensure that the primary benefactor of the original contract (i.e., the guarantor) is answerable for the debt or duty.

main purpose exception
An exception to the Statute of Frauds which states that if the main purpose of a transaction and an oral collateral contract is to provide pecuniary benefit to the guarantor, the collateral contract does not have to be in writing to be enforced. Also known as the *leading object exception.*

Example

Ethel is president and sole shareholder of Computer Corporation, Inc. Assume that (1) the corporation borrows $100,000 from CityBank for working capital, and (2) Ethel orally guarantees to repay the loan if the corporation fails to pay it. CityBank can enforce the oral guaranty contract against Ethel if the corporation does not meet its obligation because the main purpose of the loan was to benefit her as the sole shareholder of the corporation.

In the following case, the court refused to enforce an oral guaranty contract.

Page v. Gulf Coast Motors

903 So.2d 148, Web 2004 Ala. Civ. App. Lexis 982 (2004)
Court of Civil Appeal of Alabama

"A promise to pay the debt of another is barred by the Statute of Frauds unless it is in writing."

—Judge Murdock

Facts

Glenn A. Page (Glenn) had a long-term friendship with Jerry Sellers, an owner of Gulf Coast Motors. Glenn began borrowing money from Gulf Coast Motors on a recurring basis during a two-year period. The loan process was informal: Gulf Coast Motors set up a ledger account and recorded each loan made to Glenn, and Glenn would sign the ledger "I agree to pay Jerry Sellers as above." At various times, Glenn would make small payments toward his account, but he would thereafter borrow more money. At the times the loans were made, Glenn was not working and had no assets in his own name. There was no evidence as to what Glenn used the loan proceeds for, but evidence showed that he had a gambling problem.

Sellers testified that toward the end of the two-year period of making loans to Glenn, he telephoned Mary R. Page, Glenn's wife, and Mary orally guaranteed to repay Glenn's loans. Mary had significant assets of her own. Mary denied that she had promised to pay any of Glenn's debt, and she denied that Sellers had asked her to pay Glenn's debt. Gulf Coast Motors sued Glenn and Mary to recover payment for the unpaid loans. The trial court entered judgment in the amount of $23,020 in favor of Gulf Coast Motors. Mary appealed.

Issue

Was Mary's alleged oral promise to guarantee her husband's debts an enforceable guaranty contract?

Language of the Court

A promise to pay the debt of another is barred by the Statute of Frauds unless it is in writing. It is not disputed that Mary did not sign a note, guaranty, or any other writing promising to pay any part of Glenn's debts. Therefore, if the purported agreement to pay Glenn's debt is within the Statute of Frauds, Mary is not liable even if the trial court found Seller's testimony to be credible. Mary's alleged oral promises are not enforceable under the Statute of Frauds. We conclude that Mary's alleged promises to guaranty or repay Glenn's debts were within the Statute of Frauds and, therefore, were not enforceable.

Decision

The court of civil appeals held that Mary's alleged oral promises to guarantee her husband's debts were not in writing, as required by the Statute of Frauds. The court remanded the case to the trial court to enter judgment in Mary's favor.

Case Questions

Critical Legal Thinking   What is a guaranty contract? Explain.

Business Ethics   Did Glenn act ethically in this case? Would Mary have acted unethically if she had actually orally guaranteed to repay her husband's debts and then raised the Statute of Frauds to prevent enforcement of the oral promises?

Contemporary Business   Are guaranty contracts often used in business? Can you think of a situation in which a guaranty contract would be required?

Contract for the Sale of Goods

Section 2-201(1) of the Uniform Commercial Code (UCC) is the basic Statute of Frauds provision for **sales contracts**. It states that contracts for the sale of goods costing *$500 or more* must be in writing to be enforceable. If the contract price of an original sales contract is below $500, it does not have to be in writing under the **UCC Statute of Frauds**. However, if a modification of the sales contract increases the sales price to $500 or more, the *modification* has to be in writing to be enforceable.

Example

Echo enters into an oral contract to sell James her used car for $10,000, with the delivery date to be May 1. When May 1 comes and James tenders $10,000 to Echo, Echo refuses to sell her car to James. The contract will not be enforced against Echo because it was an oral contract for the sale of goods costing $500 or more, and it should have been in writing.

The most recent revision to UCC 2-201 requires that contracts for the sale of goods costing *$5,000 or more* must be in writing to be enforceable. A state must adopt this amendment for it to become effective.

UCC Statute of Frauds Section 2-201(1)
A section of the Uniform Commercial Code which states that sales contracts for the sale of goods costing $500 or more must be in writing.

To break an oral agreement which is not legally binding is morally wrong.

Bava Metzi'a
The Talmud

Contract for the Lease of Goods

Section 2A-201(1) of the Uniform Commercial Code (UCC) is the Statute of Frauds provision that applies to the lease of goods. It states that **lease contracts** involving payments of $1,000 or more must be in writing. If a lease payment of an original lease contract is below $1,000, it does not have to be in writing under the UCC Statute of Frauds. However, if a modification of the lease contract increases the lease payment to $1,000 or more, the *modification* has to be in writing to be enforceable.

UCC Statute of Frauds Section 2A-201(1)
A section of the Uniform Commercial Code which states that lease contracts involving payments of $1,000 or more must be in writing.

Agents' Contracts

Many state Statutes of Frauds require that **agents' contracts** to sell real property covered by the Statute of Frauds be in writing to be enforceable. The requirement is often referred to as the **equal dignity rule**.

Example

Barney hires Cynthia, a licensed real estate broker, to sell his house. Because a contract to sell real estate must be in writing pursuant to the Statute of Frauds, the equal dignity rule requires that the real estate agents' contract be in writing as well. Some state Statutes of Frauds expressly state that the real estate broker and agents' contracts must be in writing.

equal dignity rule
A rule which says that agents' contracts to sell property covered by the Statute of Frauds must be in writing to be enforceable.

Promises Made in Consideration of Marriage

Under the Statute of Frauds, a unilateral promise to pay money or property in consideration for a promise to marry must be in writing.

Example

A **prenuptial agreement**, which is a contract entered into by parties prior to marriage that defines their ownership rights in each other's property, must be in writing.

Equity: Part Performance

If an oral contract for the sale of land or transfer of another interest in real property has been partially performed, it may not be possible to return the parties to their *status quo*. To solve this problem, the courts have developed the equitable doctrine of **part performance**. This doctrine allows the court to order such an oral contract to be specifically performed if performance is necessary to avoid injustice. For this performance exception to apply, most courts require that the purchaser either pay part of the purchase price and take possession of the property or make valuable improvements on the property.

part performance
An equitable doctrine that allows the court to order an oral contract for the sale of land or transfer of another interest in real property to be specifically performed if it has been partially performed and performance is necessary to avoid injustice.

Ethics Spotlight

Equity: Part Performance

"The doctrine of part performance by the purchaser is a well-recognized exception to the Statute of Frauds as applied to contracts for the sale of real property."

—Judge Kline, P. J.

Arlene and Donald Warner inherited a home at 101 Molimo Street in San Francisco. The Warners obtained a $170,000 loan on the property. Donald Warner and Kenneth Sutton were friends. Donald Warner proposed that Sutton and his wife purchase the residence. His proposal included a $15,000 down payment toward the purchase price of $185,000. The Suttons were to pay all the mortgage payments and real estate taxes on the property for five years, and at any time during the five-year period, they could purchase the house. All this was agreed to orally.

The Suttons paid the down payment and cash payments equal to the monthly mortgage to the Warners. The Suttons paid the annual property taxes on the house. The Suttons also made improvements to the property. Four and one-half years later, the Warners reneged on the oral sales/option agreement. At that time, the house had risen in value to between $250,000 and $320,000. The Suttons sued for specific performance of the sales agreement. The Warners defended, alleging that the oral promise to sell real estate had to be in writing under the Statute of Frauds and was therefore unenforceable.

The trial court applied the equitable doctrine of part performance and ordered the Warners to specifically perform the oral contract. The court of appeal, which agreed, stated:

> The doctrine of part performance by the purchaser is a well-recognized exception to the Statute of Frauds as applied to contracts for the sale of real property. The actions taken by the Suttons in reliance upon the oral agreement, when considered together with the Warners' admission that there was an oral agreement of some duration, satisfy the elements of the part performance doctrine.

The court of appeal held that the equitable doctrine of part performance made the oral contract for the sale of real property in this case enforceable. *Sutton v. Warner*, 12 Cal.App.4th 415, 15 Cal.Rptr.2d 632, **Web** 1993 Cal.App. Lexis 22 (Court of Appeal of California)

Business Ethics

What does the equitable doctrine of part performance provide? Did the Statute of Frauds give the Warners a justifiable reason not to go through with the deal?

Formality of the Writing

Most of the disputes in the world arise from words.

Lord Mansfield, C. J.
Morgan v. Jones (1773)

Some written commercial contracts are long, detailed documents that have been negotiated by the parties and drafted and reviewed by their lawyers. Others are preprinted forms with blanks that can be filled in to fit the facts of a particular situation.

A written contract does not, however, have to be either drafted by a lawyer or formally typed to be legally binding. Generally, the law only requires a writing containing the essential terms of the parties' agreement. Thus, any writing—including letters, telegrams, invoices, sales receipts, checks, and handwritten agreements written on scraps of paper—can be an enforceable contract under this rule.

Required Signature

The Statute of Frauds and the UCC require a written contract, whatever its form, to be signed *by the party against whom enforcement is sought*. The signature of the person who is enforcing the contract is not necessary. Thus, a written contract may be enforceable against one party but not the other party.

Generally, the signature may appear anywhere on the writing. In addition, it does not have to be a person's full legal name. The person's last name, first name, nickname, initials, seal, stamp, engraving, or other symbol or mark (e.g., an *X*) that indicates the person's intent can be binding. The signature may be affixed by an authorized agent.

If a signature is suspected of being forged, the victim can hire handwriting experts and use modern technology to prove it is not his or her signature.

Integration of Several Writings

Both the common law of contracts and the UCC permit several writings to be **integrated** to form a single written contract. That is, the entire writing does not have to appear in one document to be an enforceable contract.

Integration may be by an *express reference* in one document that refers to and incorporates another document within it. This procedure is called **incorporation by reference**. Thus, what may often look like a simple one-page contract may actually be hundreds of pages long when all of the documents incorporated by reference are considered.

Example
Credit card contracts often incorporate by express reference such documents as the master agreement between the issuer and cardholders, subsequent amendments to the agreement, and such.

Several documents may be integrated to form a single written contract if they are somehow physically attached to each other to indicate a party's intent to show integration. Attaching several documents together with a staple, paper clip, or some other means may indicate integration. Placing several documents in the same container (e.g., an envelope) may also indicate integration. Such an action is called *implied integration*.

Interpreting Contract Words and Terms

When contracts are at issue in a lawsuit, courts are often called upon to interpret the meaning of certain contract words or terms. The parties to a contract may define the words and terms used in their contract. Many written contracts contain a detailed definition section—usually called a **glossary**—that defines many of the words and terms used in the contract.

If the parties have not defined the words and terms of a contract, the courts apply the following **standards of interpretation**:

- *Ordinary* words are given their usual meaning according to the dictionary.
- *Technical words* are given their technical meaning, unless a different meaning is clearly intended.
- *Specific terms* are presumed to qualify *general terms*. For example, if a provision in a contract refers to the subject matter as "corn," but a later provision refers to the subject matter as "feed corn" for cattle, this specific term qualifies the general term.
- If both parties are members of the same trade or profession, words will be given their meaning as used in the trade (i.e., *usage of trade*). If the parties do not want trade usage to apply, the contract must indicate that.
- Where a preprinted form contract is used, *typed words* in a contract prevail over *preprinted words*. *Handwritten words* prevail over both preprinted and typed words.
- If there is an ambiguity in a contract, the ambiguity will be resolved against the party who drafted the contract.

Parol Evidence Rule

By the time a contract is reduced to writing, the parties usually have engaged in prior or contemporaneous discussions and negotiations or exchanged prior writings. Any oral or written words outside the *four corners* of the written contract are called **parol evidence**. *Parol* means "word."

The **parol evidence rule** was originally developed by courts as part of the common law of contracts. The UCC has adopted the parol evidence rule for sales and lease contracts.[6] The parol evidence rule states that if a written contract is a complete and final statement of the parties' agreement (i.e., a **complete integration**), any prior or contemporaneous oral or

---

integration of several writings
The combination of several writings to form a single contract.

incorporation by reference
Integration made by express reference in one document that refers to and incorporates another document within it.

Counsel Randle Jackson: In the book of nature, my lords, it is written—
—Lord Ellenborough: Will you have the goodness to mention the page, sir, if you please?

Lord Campbell
Lives of the Chief Justices (1857)

parol evidence
Any oral or written words outside the four corners of a written contract.

parol evidence rule
A rule that says if a written contract is a complete and final statement of the parties' agreement, any prior or contemporaneous oral or written statements that alter, contradict, or are in addition to the terms of the written contract are inadmissible in court regarding a dispute over the contract. There are several exceptions to this rule.

written statements that alter, contradict, or are in addition to the terms of the written contract are inadmissible in any court proceeding concerning the contract.[7] In other words, a completely integrated contract is viewed as the best evidence of the terms of the parties' agreement.

Merger, or Integration, Clause

merger clause
A clause in a contract that stipulates that it is a complete integration and the exclusive expression of the parties' agreement. Also known as an *integration clause*.

The parties to a written contract may include a clause stipulating that the contract is a complete integration and the exclusive expression of their agreement and that parol evidence may not be introduced to explain, alter, contradict, or add to the terms of the contract. This type of clause, called a **merger clause**, or an **integration clause**, expressly reiterates the parol evidence rule.

Exceptions to the Parol Evidence Rule

There are several major exceptions to the parol evidence rule. Parol evidence may be admitted in court if it:

The meaning of words varies according to the circumstances of and concerning which they are used.

Justice Blackburn
Allgood v. Blake (1873)

- Shows that a contract is void or voidable (e.g., evidence that the contract was induced by fraud, misrepresentation, duress, undue influence, or mistake).
- Explains ambiguous language.
- Concerns *a prior course of dealing or course of performance* between the parties or a *usage of trade*.[8]
- *Fills in the gaps* in a contract (e.g., if a price term or time of performance term is omitted from a written contract, the court can hear parol evidence to imply the reasonable price or time of performance under the contract).
- Corrects an obvious clerical or typographical error. The court can *reform* the contract to reflect the correction.

Equity: Promissory Estoppel

promissory estoppel
An equitable doctrine that permits enforcement of oral contracts that should have been in writing. It is applied to avoid injustice. Also known as *equitable estoppel*.

The doctrine of **promissory estoppel**, or **equitable estoppel**, is another equitable exception to the strict application of the Statute of Frauds. The version of promissory estoppel in the *Restatement (Second) of Contracts* provides that if parties enter into an oral contract that should be in writing under the Statute of Frauds, the oral promise is enforceable against the promisor if three conditions are met: (1) The promise induces action or forbearance of action by another, (2) the reliance on the oral promise was foreseeable, and (3) injustice can be avoided only by enforcing the oral promise.[9] Where this doctrine applies, the promisor is *estopped* (*prevented*) from raising the Statute of Frauds as a defense to the enforcement of the oral contract.

Impression Made by an Eighteenth-Century Chinese Civil Service Seal. *In China, Vietnam, Japan, and other countries of Asia, individuals often follow the age-old tradition of using a stamp as their signature. Government organizations and businesses have to use stamps on contracts and other documents of official business. The stamp is a character or set of characters carved onto one end of a cylinder-shaped piece—made out of ivory, jade, agate, gold, animal's horn, wood, or plastic. The owner places the end bearing the characters in ink and then applies this end to the document to be signed, leaving an ink imprint that serves as the owner's signature. The ink is red—thus the saying "red head" document. In China it is called a chop, in Japan it is called a hanko, and in Vietnam it is called a seal. These seals are registered with the government. Younger persons in these countries are increasingly using hand-applied signatures instead of traditional seals.*

Test Review Terms and Concepts

Agents' contract
Complete integration
Easement
Equal dignity rule
Executory contract
Glossary
Guarantor
Guaranty contract
Incorporation by reference
Integration of several writings
Lease
Lease contract
Life estate

Main purpose exception (leading object exception)
Merger clause (integration clause)
Mortgage (deed of trust)
One-year rule
Original contract (primary contract)
Parol evidence
Parol evidence rule
Part performance
Prenuptial agreement
Promissory estoppel (equitable estoppel)

Real property
Rescission
Sales contract
Section 2-201(1) of the Uniform Commercial Code (UCC)
Section 2A-201(1) of the Uniform Commercial Code (UCC)
Standards of interpretation
Statute of Frauds
UCC Statute of Frauds

Case Problems

14.1 Statute of Frauds: Fritz Hoffman and Fritz Frey contracted the Sun Valley Company (Company) about purchasing a 1.64-acre piece of property known as the "Ruud Mountain Property," located in Sun Valley, Idaho, from Company. Mr. Conger, a representative of Company, was authorized to sell the property, subject to the approval of the executive committee of Company. Conger reached an agreement on the telephone with Hoffman and Frey, whereby they would purchase the property for $90,000, payable at 30 percent down, with the balance to be payable quarterly at an annual interest rate of 9.25 percent. The next day, Hoffman sent Conger a letter confirming the conversation.

The executive committee of Company approved the sale. Sun Valley Realty prepared the deed of trust, note, seller's closing statement, and other loan documents. However, before the documents were executed by either side, Sun Valley Company sold all its assets, including the Ruud Mountain property, to another purchaser. When the new owner refused to sell the Ruud Mountain lot to Hoffman and Frey, they brought this action for specific performance of the oral contract. Who wins? *Hoffman v. Sun Valley Company*, 102 Idaho 187, 628 P.2d 218, **Web** 1981 Ida. Lexis 320 (Supreme Court of Idaho)

14.2 Real Property: Robert Briggs and his wife purchased a home located at 167 Lower Orchard Drive, Levittown, Pennsylvania. They made a down payment and borrowed the balance on a 30-year mortgage. Six years later, when Mr. and Mrs. Briggs were behind on their mortgage payments, they entered into an oral contract to sell the house to Winfield and Emma Sackett if the Sacketts would pay the three months' arrearages on the loan and agree to make the future payments on the mortgage. Mrs. Briggs and Mrs. Sackett were sisters. The Sacketts paid the arrearages, moved into the house, and continued to live there. Fifteen years later, Robert

Briggs filed an action to void the oral contract as in violation of the Statute of Frauds and evict the Sacketts from the house. Who wins? *Briggs v. Sackett*, 275 Pa. Super. 13, 418 A.2d 586, **Web** 1980 Pa.Super. Lexis 2034 (Superior Court of Pennsylvania)

14.3 One-Year Contract: Robert S. Ohanian was vice president of sales for the West Region of Avis Rent a Car System, Inc. (Avis). Officers of Avis testified that Ohanian's performance in the West Region was excellent, and, in a depressed economic period, Ohanian's West Region stood out as the one region that was growing and profitable. In the fall of 1980, when Avis's Northeast Region was doing badly, the president of Avis asked Ohanian to take over that region. Ohanian was reluctant to do so because he and his family liked living in San Francisco, and he had developed a good team in the West Region, was secure in his position, and feared the politics of the Northeast Region. Ohanian agreed to the transfer only after the general manager of Avis orally told him "unless you screw up badly, there is no way you are going to get fired— you will never get hurt here in this company." Ohanian did a commendable job in the Northeast Region. Approximately one year later, at the age of 47, Ohanian was fired without cause by Avis. Ohanian sued Avis for breach of the oral lifetime contract. Avis asserted the Statute of Frauds against this claim. Who wins? *Ohanian v. Avis Rent a Car System, Inc.*, 779 F.2d 101, **Web** 1985 U.S. App. Lexis 25456 (United States Court of Appeals for the Second Circuit)

14.4 Guaranty Contract: David Brown met with Stan Steele, a loan officer with the Bank of Idaho (now First Interstate Bank) to discuss borrowing money from the bank to start a new business. After learning that he did not qualify for the loan on the basis of his own financial strength, Brown told Steele that his former employers, James and Donna West of California, might be willing to guarantee the payment of the loan. Steele talked to Mr. West, who orally stated on the telephone that he would personally guarantee the loan to Brown. Based on this guaranty, the bank loaned Brown the money. The bank sent a written guarantee to Mr. and Mrs. West for their signatures, but it was never returned to the bank. When Brown defaulted on the loan, the bank filed suit against the Wests to recover on their guaranty contract. Are the Wests liable? *First Interstate Bank of Idaho, N.A. v. West*, 107 Idaho 851, 693 P.2d 1053, **Web** 1984 Ida. Lexis 600 (Supreme Court of Idaho)

14.5 Guaranty Contract: Six persons, including Benjamin Rosenbloom and Alfred Feiler, were members of the board of directors of the Togs Corporation. A bank agreed to loan the corporation $250,000 if the members of the board would personally guarantee the payment of the loan. Feiler objected to signing the guaranty to the bank because of other pending personal financial negotiations that the contingent liability of the guaranty might adversely affect. Feiler agreed with Rosenbloom and the other board members that if they were held personally liable on the guaranty, he would pay his one-sixth share of that amount to them directly. Rosenbloom and the other members of the board signed the personal guaranty with the bank, and the bank made the loan to the corporation. When the corporation defaulted on the loan, the five guarantors had to pay the loan amount to the bank. When they attempted to collect a one-sixth share from Feiler, he refused to pay, alleging that his oral promise had to be in writing under the Statute of Frauds. Does Feiler have to pay the one-sixth share to the other board members? *Feiler v. Rosenbloom*, 46 Md.App. 297, 416 A.2d 1345, **Web** 1980 Md.App. Lexis 328 (Court of Special Appeals of Maryland)

14.6 Agent's Contract: Paul L. McGirr operated an Enco service station in Los Angeles that sold approximately 25,000 to 35,000 gallons of gasoline a month. McGirr telephoned Gulf Oil Corporation (Gulf) regarding an advertisement for dealers. McGirr met with Theodore Marks, an area representative of Gulf, to discuss the possibility of McGirr's operating a Gulf service station. McGirr asked Marks if Gulf had any good, high-producing units available. Marks replied that he had a station at the corner of Figueroa and Avenue 26 that sold about 200,000 gallons of gasoline a month. Marks told McGirr that this station would not be available for about 90 days because Gulf had to terminate the arrangement with the current operator of the station. Marks told McGirr that he could have the Figueroa station only if he also took a "dog" station on Garvey Avenue. Marks agreed to take this station only if he also was assured he would get the Figueroa station. Marks assured him he would. When McGirr asked Marks for this assurance in writing, Marks stated that he did not have to put it in writing because he was the "kingpin in his territory." So they shook hands on the deal.

McGirr terminated his arrangement with Enco and moved to the Garvey Avenue station. He signed a written lease for the Garvey station, which was signed by Max Reed, Gulf's regional sales manager. Under the Statute of Frauds, the lease for a service station must be in writing. Nothing in writing was ever signed by the parties regarding the Figueroa station. A few months later, Marks was transferred to a different territory, and Gulf refused to lease the Figueroa station to McGirr. McGirr sued Marks and Gulf for breach of an oral contract. Is Marks or Gulf liable? *McGirr v. Gulf Oil Corporation*, 41 Cal.App. 3d 246, 115 Cal.Rptr. 902, **Web** 1974 Cal.App. Lexis 783 (Court of Appeal of California)

14.7 Promissory Estoppel: The Atlantic Wholesale Co., Inc. (Atlantic), located in Florence, South Carolina, was in the business of buying and selling gold and silver for customers' accounts. Gary A. Solondz, a New York resident, became a customer of Atlantic and thereafter made several purchases through Atlantic. One day, Solondz telephoned Atlantic and received a quotation on silver bullion. Solondz then bought 300 ounces of silver for a total price of $12,978. Atlantic immediately contracted United Precious Metals in Minneapolis and purchased the silver for Solondz. The silver was shipped to Atlantic, which paid for it.

Atlantic placed the silver in its vault while it waited for payment from Solondz. When Atlantic telephoned Solondz about payment, he told Atlantic to continue to hold the silver in its vault until he decided whether to sell it. Meanwhile, the price of silver had fallen substantially and continued to fall. When Solondz refused to pay for the silver, Atlantic sold it for $4,650, sustaining a loss of $8,328. When Atlantic sued Solondz to recover this loss, Solondz asserted that the Statute of Frauds prevented enforcement of his oral promise to buy the silver. Does the doctrine of promissory estoppel prevent the application of the Statute of Frauds in this case? *Atlantic Wholesale Co., Inc. v. Solondz*, 283 S.C. 36, 320 S.E.2d 720, **Web** 1984 S.C. App. Lexis 555 (Court of Appeals of South Carolina)

14.8 Sufficiency of a Writing: Irving Levin and Harold Lipton owned the San Diego Clippers Basketball Club, a professional basketball franchise. Levin and Lipton met with Philip Knight to discuss the sale of the Clippers to Knight. After the meeting, they all initialed a three-page handwritten memorandum that Levin had drafted during the meeting. The memorandum outlined the major terms of their discussion, including subject matter, price, and the parties to the agreement. Levin and Lipton forwarded to Knight a letter and proposed sale agreement. Two days later, Knight informed Levin that he had decided not to purchase the Clippers. Levin and Lipton sued Knight for breach of contract. Knight argued in defense that the handwritten memorandum was not enforceable because it did not satisfy the Statute of Frauds. Is he correct? *Levin v. Knight*, 865 F.2d 1271, **Web** 1989 U.S. App. Lexis 458 (United States Court of Appeals for the Ninth Circuit)

Business Ethics Cases

14.9 Business Ethics: American Broadcasting Company Merchandising, Inc., a subsidiary of American Broadcasting Company, Inc. (collectively, ABC), entered into a written contract with model Cheryl Tiegs, whereby ABC would pay Tiegs $400,000 per year for the right to be the exclusive agent to license the merchandising of goods under her name. When ABC was unsuccessful in attracting licensing arrangements for Tiegs, a representative of ABC contacted Paul Sklar, who had previous experience in marketing apparel and licensing labels. Sklar enlisted the help of Mark Blye, and together they introduced ABC and Tiegs to Sears, Roebuck and Company (Sears). This introduction led to an agreement between Sears, ABC, and Tiegs, whereby Sears marketed a line of "Cheryl Tiegs" female apparel through Sears department stores and catalog sales. Blye and Sklar sued ABC for a finder's fee for introducing ABC and Tiegs to Sears. Because there was no express written or oral contract between ABC and Blye and Sklar, they alleged that there was an implied-in-fact contract between the parties. Section 5-701(a)(10) of the New York Statute of Frauds requires a finder's fee contract of the type in this case to be in writing. Who wins? Did ABC act ethically in this case? *Blye v. American Broadcasting Company Merchandising, Inc.*, 102 A.D.2d 297, 476 N.Y.S.2d 874, **Web** 1984 N.Y. App. Div. Lexis 18341 (Supreme Court of New York)

14.10 Business Ethics: Adolfo Mozzetti, who owned a construction company, orally promised his son, Remo, that if Remo would manage the family business for their mutual benefit and would take care of him for the rest of his life, he would leave the family home to Remo. Section 2714 of the Delaware Code requires contracts for the transfer of land to be in writing. Section 2715 of the Delaware Code requires testamentary transfers of real property to be in writing. Remo performed as requested: He managed the family business and took care of his father until the father died. When the father died, his will devised the family home to his daughter, Lucia M. Shepard. Remo brought an action to enforce his father's oral promise that the home belonged to him. The daughter argued that the will should be upheld. Who wins? Did the daughter act ethically in trying to defeat the father's promise to leave the property to the son? Did the son act ethically in trying to defeat his father's will? *Shepard v. Mozzetti*, 545 A.2d 621, **Web** 1988 Del. Lexis 217 (Supreme Court of Delaware)

Endnotes

1. *Elias v. George Sahely & Co.*, 1983 App. Cas. (P.C.) 646, 655.
2. *Restatement (Second) of Contracts*, Section 110.
3. *Restatement (Second) of Contracts*, Section 130.
4. *Restatement (Second) of Contracts*, Section 112.
5. *Restatement (Second) of Contracts*, Section 116.
6. UCC Section 2-202 and UCC Section 2A-202.
7. *Restatement (Second) of Contracts*, Section 213.
8. UCC Sections 1-205, 2-202, and 2-208.
9. *Restatement (Second) of Contracts*, Section 139.

CHAPTER 15

"An honest man's word is as good as his bond."
—Don Quixote

Third-Party Rights and Discharge

Chapter Objectives

After studying this chapter, you should be able to:

1. Describe assignment of contract rights and what contract rights are assignable.
2. Define *intended beneficiary* and describe this person's rights under a contract.
3. Define *covenant*.
4. Distinguish between conditions precedent, conditions subsequent, and concurrent conditions.
5. Explain when the performance of a contract is excused because of objective impossibility or commercial impracticability.

Chapter Contents

Introduction to Third-Party Rights and Discharge

The parties to a contract are said to be in **privity of contract**. Contracting parties have a legal obligation to perform the duties specified in their contract. A party's duty of performance may be discharged by agreement of the parties, excuse of performance, or operation of law. If one party fails to perform as promised, the other party may enforce the contract and sue for breach.

With two exceptions, third parties do not acquire any rights under other people's contracts. The exceptions are (1) *assignees* to whom rights are subsequently transferred and (2) *intended third-party beneficiaries* to whom the contracting parties intended to give rights under the contract at the time of contracting.

This chapter discusses the rights of third parties under a contract, conditions to performance, and ways of discharging the duty of performance.

privity of contract
The state of two specified parties being in a contract.

Assignment of a Right

In many cases, the parties to a contract can transfer their rights under the contract to other parties. The transfer of contractual rights is called an **assignment of rights** or just an **assignment**.

assignment
The transfer of contractual rights by an obligee to another party.

Form of Assignment

A party who owes a duty of performance is called the **obligor**. A party who is owed a right under a contract is called the **obligee**. An obligee who transfers the right to receive performance is called an **assignor**. The party to whom the right has been transferred is called the **assignee**. The assignee can assign the right to yet another person (called a **subsequent assignee**, or **subassignee**). Exhibit 15.1 illustrates these relationships.

Generally, no formalities are required for a valid assignment of rights. Although the assignor often uses the word *assign*, other words or terms, such as *sell, transfer, convey,* and *give*, are sufficient to indicate intent to transfer a contract right.

assignor
An obligee who transfers a right.

assignee
A party to whom a right has been transferred.

Example

A retail clothing store purchases $5,000 worth of goods on credit from a manufacturer. Payment is due in 120 days. If the manufacturer needs cash before the 120-day period

EXHIBIT 15.1 Assignment of a Right

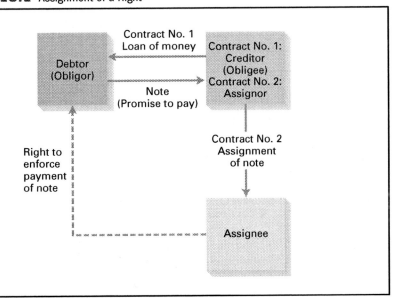

expires, the manufacturer (assignor) can sell its right to collect the money to another party (assignee) for some price, let's say $4,000. If the retail store is given proper notice of the assignment, it must pay $5,000 to the assignee when the 120-day period is reached.

In the United States, public policy favors a free flow of commerce. Hence, most contract rights are assignable, including sales contracts and contracts for the payment of money. The following paragraphs discuss types of contracts that present special problems for assignment.

Personal Service Contract

Contracts for the provision of personal services are generally not assignable.[1]

Example

If Angie Warhol, a famous artist, contracts to paint Jay-Z's portrait, Angie cannot assign this contract to another artist and send that artist to do the painting without the prior approval of Jay-Z. Jay-Z can reject this assignment and refuse to have his painting done by any artist except Angie Warhol.

The parties may agree that a **personal service contract** may be assigned.

Example

Professional athletes often sign contracts with professional teams which provide that their personal service contract can be assigned.

Assignment of a Future Right

Usually, a person cannot assign a currently nonexistent right that he or she expects to have in the future (i.e., a **future right**).

Example

Henrietta, an heiress worth millions of dollars, signs a will, leaving all her property to her granddaughter Brittany. Brittany has only an expected future right, and not a current right, to the money. Brittany cannot lawfully assign her expected future right to receive her inheritance. The assignment would be invalid.

Contract Where an Assignment Would Materially Alter the Risk

A contract cannot be assigned if the assignment would materially alter the risk or duties of the obligor.

Example

Laura, who has a safe driving record, purchases automobile insurance from an insurance company. Laura cannot assign her rights to be insured to another driver because the assignment would materially alter the risk and duties of the insurance company.

Assignment of Legal Action

The right to sue another party for a violation of personal rights cannot usually be assigned.

Example

Donald is severely injured by Alice in an automobile accident caused by Alice's negligence. Donald can sue Alice for the tort of negligence to recover monetary damages for his injuries. Donald's right to sue Alice is a personal right that cannot be assigned to another person.

A legal right that arises out of a breach of contract may be assigned.

Example

Andrea borrows $10,000 from Country Bank with an 8% interest rate. The loan is to be repaid in equal monthly installments over a five-year period. If Andrea defaults on the loan, Country Bank may sue Andrea to collect the unpaid amount of the loan. Instead,

If a man will improvidently bind himself up by a voluntary deed, and not reserve a liberty to himself by a power of revocation, this court will not loose the fetters he hath put upon himself, but he must lie down under his own folly.

Lord Chancellor Lord
Nottingham
Villers v. Beaumont (1682)

Country Bank may sell (assign) its legal right to a collection agency to recover the money Andrea still owes on the loan. In this case, Country Bank is the assignor, and the collection agency is the assignee.

Effect of an Assignment of a Right

Where there has been a valid assignment of rights, the assignee "stands in the shoes of the assignor." That is, the assignor is entitled to performance from the obligor. The unconditional assignment of a contract right extinguishes all the assignor's rights, including the right to sue the obligor directly for nonperformance.[2] An assignee takes no better rights under the contract than the assignor had.

Example

If the assignor has a right to receive $10,000 from a debtor, the right to receive this $10,000 is all that the assignor can assign to the assignee.

An obligor can assert any defense he or she had against the assignor or the assignee. An obligor can raise the defenses of fraud, duress, undue influence, minority, insanity, illegality of the contract, mutual mistake, or payment by worthless check of the assignor, against enforcement of the contract by the assignee. The obligor can also raise any personal defenses (e.g., participation in the assignor's fraudulent scheme) he or she may have directly against the assignee.

Notice of Assignment

When an assignor makes an assignment of a right under a contract, the assignee is under a duty to notify the obligor that (1) the assignment has been made and (2) performance must be rendered to the assignee. If the assignee fails to provide **notice of assignment** to the obligor, the obligor may continue to render performance to the assignor, who no longer has a right to it. The assignee cannot sue the obligor to recover payment because the obligor has performed according to the original contract. The assignee's only course of action is to sue the assignor for damages.

The result changes if the obligor is notified of the assignment but continues to render performance to the assignor. In such situations, the assignee can sue the obligor and recover payment. The obligor will then have to pay twice: once wrongfully to the assignor and then rightfully to the assignee. The obligor's only recourse is to sue the assignor for damages.

Anti-Assignment Clause

Some contracts contain an **anti-assignment clause** that prohibits the assignment of rights under the contract. Such clauses may be used if the obligor does not want to deal with or render performance to an unknown third party. Anti-assignment clauses are usually given effect.

Approval Clause

Some contracts contain an **approval clause**. Such clauses require that the obligor approve any assignment of a contract. Where there is an approval clause, many states prohibit the obligor from unreasonably withholding approval.

Delegation of a Duty

Unless otherwise agreed, the parties to a contract can generally transfer the performance of their duties under the contract to other parties. This transfer is called the **delegation of a duty**, or just **delegation**.

An obligor who transfers his or her duty is called a **delegator**. The party to whom the duty is transferred is the **delegatee**. The party to whom the duty is owed is the *obligee*. Generally, no special words or formalities are required to create a delegation of duties. Exhibit 15.2 illustrates the parties to a delegation of a duty.

Make fair agreements and stick to them.

Confucius

That what is agreed to be done, must be considered as done.

Lord Chancellor Lord Hardwicke
Guidot v. Guidot (1745)

anti-assignment clause
A clause that prohibits the assignment of rights under the contract.

delegation of duties
A transfer of contractual duties by an obligor to another party for performance.

delegator
An obligor who has transferred his or her duty.

delegatee
A party to whom a duty has been transferred.

Ethics Spotlight

Successive Assignment of the Same Right

An obligee (the party who is owed performance, money, a right, or another thing of value) has the right to assign a contract right or a benefit to another party. If the obligee fraudulently or mistakenly makes successive assignments of the same right to a number of assignees, which assignee has the legal right to the assigned right? To answer this question, the following rules apply:

American Rule (New York Rule)

The **American rule** (or **New York Rule**) provides that the first assignment *in time* prevails, regardless of notice. Most states follow this rule.

English Rule

The **English rule** provides that the first assignee to *give notice* to the obligor (the person who owes the performance, money, duty, or other thing of value) prevails.

Possession of Tangible Token Rule

The **possession of tangible token rule** provides that under either the American or English rule, if the assignor makes successive assignments of a contract right that is represented by a tangible token, such as a stock certificate or a savings account passbook, the first assignee who receives delivery of the tangible token prevails over subsequent assignees.

Business Ethics

Why does an assignor attempt to assign a contract right more than once? How can a first assignee protect his rights?

■ **EXHIBIT 15.2** Delegation of a Duty

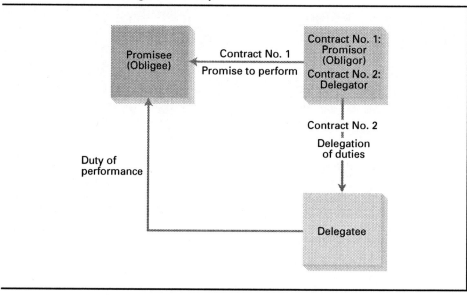

Duties That Can and Cannot Be Delegated

If an obligee has a substantial interest in having an obligor perform the acts required by a contract, these duties cannot be transferred.[3] This restriction includes obligations under the following types of contracts:

1. Personal service contracts calling for the exercise of personal skills, discretion, or expertise

   Example If P Diddy is hired to give a concert on a college campus, the Dixie Chicks cannot appear in his place.

"If there's no meaning in it," said the King, "that saves a world of trouble, you know, we needn't try to find any."

Lewis Carroll
Alice in Wonderland, Chapter 12

Morocco. *The negotiation and enforcement of contracts differs in various cultures of the world.*

2. Contracts whose performance would materially vary if the obligor's duties were delegated

   Example If a person hires an experienced surgeon to perform a complex surgery, a recent medical school graduate cannot be substituted to perform the operation.

   Often, contracts are entered into with companies or firms rather than with individuals. In such cases, a firm may designate any of its qualified employees to perform the contract.

   Example If a client retains a firm of lawyers to represent her, the firm can **delegate** the duties under the contract to any qualified member of the firm.

Effect of Delegation of Duties

Where a valid delegation of duties contains the term *assumption* or other similar language, there is an **assumption of duties** by the delegatee. Here, the obligee can sue the delegatee and recover damages for nonperformance or negligent performance by the delegatee. In addition, the delegator remains legally liable for the performance of the contract. Thus, if the delegatee does not perform properly, the obligee can sue the obligor-delegator for any resulting damages caused by the delegatee's nonperformance or negligent conduct.

assumption of duties
A situation in which a delegation of duties contains the term *assumption, I assume the duties,* or other similar language. In such a case, the delegatee is legally liable to the obligee for nonperformance.

Anti-Delegation Clause

The parties to a contract can include an **anti-delegation clause** indicating that the duties cannot be delegated. Anti-delegation clauses are usually enforced. Some courts, however, have held that duties that are totally impersonal in nature—such as the payment of money—can be delegated despite such clauses.

anti-delegation clause
A clause that prohibits the delegation of duties under the contract.

Assignment and Delegation

An **assignment and delegation** occurs when there is a transfer of both rights and duties under a contract. If the transfer of a contract to a third party contains only language of assignment, the modern view holds that there is corresponding delegation of the duties of the contract.[4]

Third-Party Beneficiary

Third parties sometimes claim rights under others' contracts; these parties are called **third-party beneficiaries**. Such third parties are either *intended* or *incidental beneficiaries*. Each of these designations is discussed here.

Intended Beneficiary

When parties enter into a contract, they can agree that the performance of one of the parties should be rendered to or directly benefit a third party. Under such circumstances, the third party is called an **intended third-party beneficiary**. An intended third-party beneficiary can enforce the contract against the party who promised to render performance.[5]

Examples

The beneficiary may be expressly named in a contract from which he or she is to benefit ("I leave my property to my son Ben") or may be identified by another means ("I leave my property to all my children, equally").

Intended third-party beneficiaries may be classified as either *donee* or *creditor* beneficiaries. These terms are defined in the following paragraphs. The *Restatement (Second) of Contracts* and many state statutes have dropped this distinction, however, and now refer to both collectively as *intended beneficiaries*.[6]

Donee Beneficiary   The first type of intended beneficiary is the *donee beneficiary*. When a person enters into a contract with the intent to confer a benefit or gift on an intended third party, the contract is called a **donee beneficiary contract**. The three persons involved in such a contract are:

1. The **promisee** (the contracting party who directs that the benefit be conferred on another)
2. The **promisor** (the contracting party who agrees to confer performance for the benefit of the third person)
3. The **donee beneficiary** (the third person on whom the benefit is to be conferred)

If the promisor fails to perform the contract, the donee beneficiary can sue the promisor directly.

Example

Nina goes to Life Insurance Company and purchases a $2 million life insurance policy on her life. Nina names her husband John as the beneficiary of the life insurance policy—that is, he is to be paid the $2 million if Nina dies. John is an intended beneficiary of the Nina–Life Insurance Company contract. Nina makes the necessary premium payments to Life Insurance Company. She dies in an automobile accident. Life Insurance Company does not pay the $2 million life insurance benefits to John. John, as an intended beneficiary, can sue Life Insurance Company to recover the life insurance benefits. Here, John has rights as an intended third-party beneficiary to enforce the Nina–Life Insurance Company contract. (See Exhibit 15.3.)

■ **EXHIBIT 15.3** Donee Beneficiary Contract

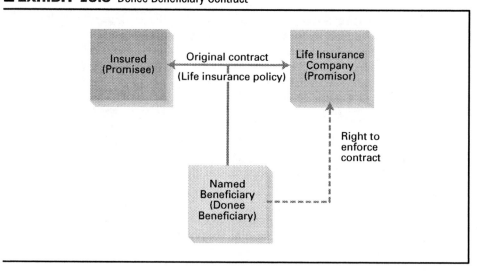

---

intended third-party beneficiary
A third party who is not in privity of contract but who has rights under the contract and can enforce the contract against the promisor.

donee beneficiary contract
A contract entered into with the intent to confer a benefit or gift on an intended third party.

donee beneficiary
A third party on whom a benefit is to be conferred.

He who derives the advantage ought to sustain the burden.

Legal maxim

Creditor Beneficiary The second type of intended beneficiary is the *creditor beneficiary.* A **creditor beneficiary contract** usually arises in the following situation:

1. A debtor (promisor) borrows money from a creditor (promisee) to purchase some item.
2. The debtor signs an agreement to pay the creditor the amount of the loan plus interest.
3. The debtor sells the item to another party before the loan is paid.
4. The new buyer (new promisor) promises the original debtor (new promisee) that he will pay the remainder of the loan amount to the original creditor.

The original creditor is now the creditor beneficiary of this second contract.[7] The parties to the second contract are the original debtor (promisee of the second contract) and the new party (promisor of the second contract). The original creditor is the **creditor beneficiary** of the second contract. (See Exhibit 15.4.)

If the new debtor (promisor) fails to perform according to the second contract, the creditor beneficiary may either (1) enforce the original contract against the original debtor-promisor or (2) enforce the new contract against the new debtor-promisor. However, the creditor can collect only once.

Example

Big Hotels obtains a loan from City Bank to build an addition to a hotel it owns in Atlanta, Georgia. The parties sign a promissory note requiring Big Hotels (promisor) to pay off the loan in equal monthly installments over a period of 10 years to City Bank (promisee). With six years left before the loan would be paid, Big Hotels sells the hotel to Palace Hotels, another chain of hotels. Palace Hotels (new promisor) agrees with Big Hotels (new promisee) to complete the payments due to City Bank on the loan. If Palace Hotels fails to pay the loan, City Bank has two options: It can sue Big Hotels on the original promissory note to recover the unpaid loan amount, or it can use its status as a creditor beneficiary to sue and recover the unpaid loan amount from Palace Hotels.

Incidental Beneficiary

In many instances, the parties to a contract unintentionally benefit a third party when a contract is performed. In such situations, the third party is referred to as an **incidental beneficiary**. An incidental beneficiary has no rights to enforce or sue under other people's contracts.

---

creditor beneficiary contract
A contract that arises in the following situation: (1) a debtor borrows money, (2) the debtor signs an agreement to pay back the money plus interest, (3) the debtor sells the item to a third party before the loan is paid off, and (4) the third party promises the debtor that he or she will pay the remainder of the loan to the creditor.

creditor beneficiary
An original creditor who becomes a beneficiary under the debtor's new contract with another party.

incidental beneficiary
A party who is unintentionally benefited by other people's contracts.

■ **EXHIBIT 15.4** Creditor Beneficiary Contract

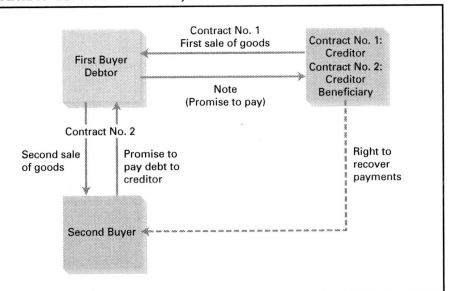

Example

Heather owns a house on Residential Street. Her house, which is somewhat older, needs a new exterior coat of paint. Her neighbor John owns the house next door. If Heather has her house painted, John will benefit by having a nicer-looking house next door that may actually raise housing values on the street. Heather contracts with George, a painting contractor, to paint her house. George breaches the contract and does not paint Heather's house. Although John may have benefitted if Heather's house had been painted, he is merely an incidental beneficiary to the Heather–George contract and has no cause of action to sue George for not painting Heather's house. Heather, of course, can sue George for breach of contract.

Generally, the public and taxpayers are only incidental beneficiaries to contracts entered into by the government on their behalf. As such, they acquire no right to enforce government contracts or to sue parties who breach these contracts.

Covenant

covenant

An unconditional promise to perform.

In contracts, parties make certain promises to each other. A **covenant** is an *unconditional* promise to perform. Nonperformance of a covenant is a breach of contract that gives the other party the right to sue. The majority of provisions in contracts are covenants.

Example

Seed Company borrows $400,000 from Rural Bank and signs a promissory note to repay the $400,000 plus 10 percent interest in one year. This promise is a covenant. That is, it is an unconditional promise to perform.

Conditions

condition

A qualification of a promise that becomes a covenant if it is met. There are three types of conditions: conditions precedent, conditions subsequent, and concurrent conditions.

Some contract provisions are conditions rather than covenants. A **conditional promise** (or qualified promise) is not as definite as a covenant. The promisor's duty to perform or not perform arises only if the **condition** does or does not occur.[8] It becomes a covenant if the condition is met, however.

Generally, contractual language such as *if, on condition that, provided that, when, after,* and *as soon as* indicates a condition. A single contract may contain numerous conditions that trigger or excuse performance.

There are three primary types of conditions: *conditions precedent, conditions subsequent,* and *concurrent conditions.* Each of these are discussed in the following paragraphs.

Condition Precedent

condition precedent

A condition that requires the occurrence of an event before a party is obligated to perform a duty under a contract.

If a contract requires the occurrence (or nonoccurrence) of an event *before* a party is obligated to perform a contractual duty, this is a **condition precedent**. The happening (or nonhappening) of the event triggers the contract or duty of performance. If the event does not occur, no duty to perform the contract arises because there is a failure of condition.

Condition Precedent Based on Satisfaction   Some contracts reserve the right to a party to pay for services provided by the other only if the services meet the first party's "satisfaction." The courts have developed two tests—the *personal satisfaction test* and the *reasonable person test*—to determine whether this special form of condition precedent has been met:

personal satisfaction test

A subjective test that applies to contracts involving personal taste and comfort.

1. **Personal satisfaction test.**   The **personal satisfaction test** is a *subjective* test that applies if the performance involves personal taste and comfort (e.g., contracts for interior decorating, contracts for tailoring clothes). The only requirement is that the person given the right to reject the contract acts in good faith.

   Example Gretchen employs an artist to paint her daughter's portrait. The contract provides that Gretchen does not have to accept and pay for the portrait unless she is personally satisfied with it. This is a condition precedent based upon the personal sat-

Contemporary Environment

"Time Is of the Essence"

Generally, there is a breach of contract if a contract is not performed when due. Nevertheless, if the other party is not jeopardized by the delay, most courts treat the delay as a minor breach and give the nonperforming party additional time to perform.

Conversely, if a contract expressly provides that **"time is of the essence"** or similar language, performance by the stated time is an express condition. There is a breach of contract if the contracting party does not perform by the stated date.

---

isfaction test. Gretchen rejects the painting because she personally dislikes it. This rejection is lawful because it is based on the personal satisfaction test.

2. **Reasonable person test.**   The **reasonable person test** is an *objective* test that is used to judge contracts involving mechanical fitness and most commercial contracts. Most contracts that require the work to meet the satisfaction of a third person (e.g., engineer, architect) are judged by this standard.

Example E-Commerce Company hires Einstein to install a state-of-the-art Internet webpage ordering system that will handle its order entry and record-keeping functions. Einstein installs a state-of-the-art Internet webpage ordering system that meets current industry standards. E-Commerce Company rejects the contract as not meeting its personal satisfaction. This is a breach of contract because the personal satisfaction test does not apply to this contract. Instead, the objective reasonable person test applies, and a reasonable e-commerce company in the same situation would have accepted the system.

> **reasonable person test**
> An objective test that applies to commercial contracts and contracts involving mechanical fitness.

Condition Subsequent

A **condition subsequent** exists when there is a condition in a contract which provides that the occurrence or nonoccurrence of a specific event automatically excuses the performance of an existing duty to perform. That is, failure to meet the condition subsequent relieves the other party from obligation under the contract.

Note that the *Restatement (Second) of Contracts* eliminates the distinction between conditions precedent and conditions subsequent. Both are referred to as "conditions."9

> *Freedom of contracts begins where equality of bargaining power begins.*
>
> Oliver Wendell Holmes, Jr.
> (1928)

> **condition subsequent**
> A condition whose occurrence or nonoccurrence of a specific event automatically excuses the performance of an existing contractual duty to perform.

Concurrent Conditions

Concurrent conditions arise when the parties to a contract agree to render performance simultaneously—that is, when each party's absolute duty to perform is conditioned on the other party's absolute duty to perform.

> **concurrent condition**
> A condition that exists when the parties to a contract must render performance simultaneously; each party's absolute duty to perform is conditioned on the other party's absolute duty to perform.

Example

A contract by Samantha's Club to purchase goods from Kid's Toys Inc. provides that payment is due upon delivery of the goods. In other words, Samantha's Club's duty to pay and Kid's Toys Inc.'s duty to deliver the goods are concurrent conditions. Recovery of damages is available if one party fails to respond to the other party's performance.

Implied Condition

Any of the previous types of conditions may be further classified as either express or implied conditions. An *express condition* exists if the parties expressly agree on it. An **implied-in-fact-condition** is one that can be implied from the circumstances surrounding a contract and the parties' conduct.

> **implied-in-fact condition**
> A condition that can be implied from the circumstances surrounding a contract and the parties' conduct.

Example

A contract in which a buyer agrees to purchase grain from a farmer implies that there are proper street access to the delivery site, proper unloading facilities, and the like.

Concept Summary
Types of Conditions

Type of Condition	Description
Condition precedent	A specified event must occur or not occur before a party is obligated to perform contractual duties.
Condition subsequent	The occurrence or nonoccurrence of a specified event excuses the performance of an existing contractual duty to perform.
Concurrent condition	The parties to a contract are obligated to render performance simultaneously. Each party's duty to perform is conditioned on the other party's duty to perform.
Implied condition	An implied-in-fact condition is implied from the circumstances surrounding a contract and the parties' conduct.

Discharge of Performance

A party's duty to perform under a contract may be discharged by *mutual agreement* of the parties, by *impossibility of performance*, or by *operation of law*. These methods of discharge are discussed in the paragraphs that follow.

Men keep agreements when it is to the advantage of neither to break them.

Solon

Discharge by Agreement

In many situations, the parties to a contract mutually decide to **discharge** their contractual duties. The parties can do so by *mutual rescission, substituted contract, novation*, and *accord and satisfaction*. The different types of mutual agreement are discussed in the following paragraphs:

Mutual Rescission   If a contract is wholly or partially executory on both sides, the parties can agree to rescind (i.e., cancel) the contract. **Mutual rescission** requires parties to enter into a second agreement that expressly terminates the first one.

Unilateral rescission of a contract by one of the parties without the other party's consent is not effective. Unilateral rescission of a contract constitutes a breach of that contract.

Substituted Contract   The parties to a contract may enter into a new contract that revokes and discharges an existing contract. The new contract is called a **substituted contract**.

If one of the parties fails to perform his or her duties under a substituted contract, the nonbreaching party can sue to enforce its terms against the breaching party. The prior contract cannot be enforced against the breaching party because it has been discharged.

novation agreement
An agreement that substitutes a new party for one of the original contracting parties and relieves the exiting party of liability on the contract. Also known as simply a *novation*.

Novation   A **novation agreement** (commonly called **novation**) substitutes a third party for one of the original contracting parties. The new substituted party is obligated to perform the contract. All three parties must agree to the substitution. In a novation, the exiting party is relieved of liability on the contract.

accord and satisfaction
The settlement of a contract dispute.

Accord and Satisfaction   The parties to a contract may agree to settle a contract dispute by an **accord and satisfaction**. The agreement whereby the parties agree to accept something different in satisfaction of the original contract is called an *accord*.[10] The performance of an accord is called a *satisfaction*.

An accord does not discharge the original contract. It only suspends it until the accord is performed. Satisfaction of the accord discharges both the original contract and the accord. If an accord is not satisfied when it is due, the aggrieved party may enforce either the accord or the original contract.

impossibility of performance
Nonperformance that is excused if a contract becomes impossible to perform. It must be objective impossibility, not subjective.

Discharge by Impossibility

Under certain circumstances, the nonperformance of contractual duties is excused—that is, discharged—because of *impossibility of performance*. **Impossibility of performance** (or

objective impossibility) occurs if a contract becomes impossible to perform.[11] The impossibility must be objective impossibility ("it cannot be done") rather than subjective impossibility ("I cannot do it"). The following types of objective impossibility excuse nonperformance:

• The death or incapacity of the promisor prior to the performance of a personal service contract[12]

Example

If a professional athlete dies prior to or during a contract period, his or her contract with the team is discharged.

• The destruction of the subject matter of a contract prior to performance[13]

Example

If a building is destroyed by fire, the lessees are discharged from further performance unless otherwise provided in the lease.

• A supervening illegality that makes performance of the contract illegal[14]

Example

An art dealer contracts to purchase native art found in a foreign country. The contract is discharged if the foreign country enacts a law forbidding native art from being exported from the country before the contract is performed.

In the following case, the court had to decide whether impossibility existed that excused performance.

CASE 15.1
Impossibility of Performance

Parker v. Arthur Murray, Inc.

295 N.E.2d 487, Web 1973 Ill.App. Lexis 2760 (1973)
Appellate Court of Illinois

"Although neither party to a contract should be relieved from performance on the ground that good business judgment was lacking, a court will not place upon language a ridiculous construction."

—Judge Stamos

Facts

Ryland S. Parker, a 37-year-old college-educated bachelor, went to the Arthur Murray Studios (Arthur Murray) in Oak Park, Illinois, to redeem a certificate entitling him to three free dancing lessons. At that time, he lived alone in a one-room attic apartment. During the free lessons, the instructor told Parker that he had "exceptional potential to be a fine and accomplished dancer." Parker thereupon signed a contract for more lessons. Parker attended lessons regularly and was praised and encouraged by his instructors despite his lack of progress. Contract extensions and new contracts for additional instructional hours were executed, which Parker prepaid. Each written contract contained the bold-type words "NONCANCELABLE CONTRACT." Two years after having started to take dancing lessons, Parker was severely injured in an automobile accident, rendering him incapable of continuing his dancing lessons. At that time, he had contracted for a total of 2,734 hours of dance lessons, for which he had prepaid $24,812. When Arthur Murray refused to refund any of the money, Parker sued to rescind the outstanding contracts. The trial courts held in favor of Parker and ordered Arthur Murray to return the prepaid contract payments. Arthur Murray appealed.

Issue

Does the doctrine of impossibility excuse Parker's performance of the personal service contracts?

Language of the Court

Plaintiff was granted rescission on the grounds of impossibility of performance. Defendants do not deny that the doctrine of impossibility of performance is generally applicable to the case at bar. Rather they assert that certain contract provisions bring the case within the Restatement's limitation that the doctrine is inapplicable if "the contract indicates a contrary intention." It is contended that such bold-type phrases as "NON-CANCELLABLE CONTRACT," NON-CANCELLABLE NEGOTIABLE CONTRACT," and "I UNDERSTAND THAT NO REFUNDS WILL BE MADE UNDER THE TERMS OF THIS CONTRACT" manifest the parties' mutual intent to waive their respective rights to invoke the doctrine of impossibility.

This is a construction that we find unacceptable. Courts engage in the construction and interpretation of contracts with the sole aim of determining the intention of the parties. We need rely on no construction aids to conclude that plaintiff never contemplated that by signing a contract with such terms as "NON-CANCELLABLE" and "NO REFUNDS," he was waiving a remedy expressly recognized by Illinois courts. Although neither party to a contract should be relieved from performance on the ground that good business judgment was lacking, a court will not place upon language a ridiculous con-

struction. We conclude that plaintiff did not waive his right to assert the doctrine of impossibility.

Suffice it to say that overwhelming evidence supported plaintiff's contention that he was incapable of continuing his lessons.

Decision

The appellate court held that the doctrine of impossibility of performance excused Parker's performance of the personal service contracts. The appellate court affirmed the trial court's judgment that ordered Arthur Murray to return the prepaid contract payments.

Case Questions

Critical Legal Thinking   What does the doctrine of impossibility of performance provide? Explain.

Business Ethics   Did Arthur Murray act ethically in not returning Parker's money? Did Arthur Murray act ethically by allowing Parker to sign up for and prepay for over 2,700 hours of dance lessons?

Contemporary Business   Should the doctrine of impossibility excuse parties from performance of their contracts? Why or why not?

Force Majeure Clause

force majeure clause
A clause in a contract in which the parties specify certain events that will excuse nonperformance.

The parties may agree in a contract that certain events will excuse nonperformance of the contract. These clauses are called *force majeure* **clauses**.

Example

A *force majeure* clause usually excuses nonperformance caused by natural disasters such as floods, tornadoes, earthquakes, and such. Modern clauses also often excuse performance due to labor strikes, shortages of raw materials, and the like.

Commercial Impracticability

commercial impracticability
Nonperformance that is excused if an extreme or unexpected development or expense makes it impractical for the promisor to perform.

Many states recognize the doctrine of **commercial impracticability** as an excuse for nonperformance of contracts. Commercial impracticability excuses performance if an unforeseeable event makes it impractical for the promisor to perform. This doctrine has not yet been fully developed by the courts. It is examined on a case-by-case basis.

Example

A utility company enters into a contract to purchase uranium for its nuclear-powered generator from a uranium supplier at a fixed price of $1 million per year for five years. Suppose a new uranium cartel is formed worldwide, and the supplier must pay $5 million for uranium to supply the utility with each year's supply. It is not impossible for the supplier to satisfy the contract: The supplier can purchase the uranium for $5 million and resell it to the utility company for $1 million (losing $4 million per year). However, in this situation, the court would likely allow the supplier to rescind its contract with the utility based on commercial impracticability.

Statute of Limitations

Certain legal rules discharge parties from performing contractual duties. Every state has a **statute of limitations** that applies to contract actions. Although the time periods vary from state to state, the usual period for bringing a lawsuit for breach of contract is one to five years. The UCC provides that a cause of action based on a breach of sales or lease contract must be brought within four years after the cause of action accrues.[15]

statute of limitations
A statute that establishes the time period during which a lawsuit must be brought; if the lawsuit is not brought within this period, the injured party loses the right to sue.

Bankruptcy

Bankruptcy, which is governed by federal law, is a means of allocating the debtor's nonexempt property to satisfy his or her debts. Debtors may also reorganize in bankruptcy. In most cases, the debtor's assets are insufficient to pay all the creditors' claims. In this case, the debtor receives a **discharge** of the unpaid debts. The debtor is then relieved of legal liability to pay the discharged debts.

Test Review Terms and Concepts

Accord and satisfaction
American rule (New York Rule)
Anti-assignment clause
Anti-delegation clause
Approval clause
Assignee
Assignment and delegation
Assignment of future right
Assignment of right (assignment)
Assignor
Assumption of duties
Commercial impracticability
Concurrent condition
Condition
Condition precedent
Condition subsequent
Conditional promise
Covenant

Creditor beneficiary
Creditor beneficiary contract
Delegate
Delegatee
Delegation of a duty (delegation)
Delegator
Discharge by agreement
Discharge in bankruptcy
Donee beneficiary
Donee beneficiary contract
English rule
Force majeure clause
Implied-in-fact-condition
Impossibility of performance (objective impossibility)
Incidental beneficiary
Intended third-party beneficiary

Mutual rescission
Notice of assignment
Novation agreement (novation)
Obligee
Obligor
Personal satisfaction test
Personal service contract
Possession of tangible token rule
Privity of contract
Promisee
Promisor
Reasonable person test
Statute of limitation
Subsequent assignee (subassignee)
Substituted contract
Third-party beneficiary
"Time is of the essence"

Case Problems

15.1 Third-Party Beneficiary: Eugene H. Emmick hired L. S. Hamm, an attorney, to draft his will. The will named Robert Lucas and others (Lucas) as beneficiaries. When Emmick died, it was discovered that the will was improperly drafted, violated state law, and was therefore ineffective. Emmick's estate was transferred pursuant to the state's intestate laws. Lucas did not receive the $75,000 he would have otherwise received had the will been valid. Lucas sued Hamm for breach of the Emmick–Hamm contract to recover what he would have received under the will. Who wins? *Lucas v. Hamm*, 56 Cal.2d 583, 364 P.2d 685, 15 Cal.Rptr. 821, **Web** 1961 Cal. Lexis 321 (Supreme Court of California)

15.2 Third-Party Beneficiary: Angelo Boussiacos hired Demetrios Sofias, a general contractor, to build a restaurant for him. Boussiacos entered into a loan agreement with Bank of America (B of A) whereby B of A would provide the construction financing to build the restaurant. The loan agreement provided that loan funds would be periodically disbursed by B of A to Boussiacos at different stages of construction, as requested by Boussiacos. Problems arose in the progress of the construction. When Boussiacos did not pay Sofias for certain work that had been done, Sofias sued B of A for breach of contract to collect payment directly from B of A. Can Sofias maintain the lawsuit against B of A? *Sofias v.*

Bank of America, 172 Cal.App.3d 583, 218 Cal.Rptr. 388, **Web** 1985 Cal.App. Lexis 2545 (Court of Appeal of California)

15.3 Assignment: William John Cunningham, a professional basketball player, entered into a contract with Southern Sports Corporation, which owned the Carolina Cougars, a professional basketball team. The contract provided that Cunningham was to play basketball for the Cougars for a three-year period. The contract contained a provision that it could not be assigned to any other professional basketball franchise without Cunningham's approval. Subsequently, Southern Sports Corporation sold its assets, including its franchise and Cunningham's contract, to the Munchak Corporation (Munchak). There was no change in the location of the Cougars after the purchase. When Cunningham refused to play for the new owners, Munchak sued to enforce Cunningham's contract. Is Cunningham's contract assignable to the new owner? *Munchak Corporation v. Cunningham*, 457 F.2d 721, **Web** 1972 U.S. App. Lexis 10272 (United States Court of Appeals for the Fourth Circuit)

15.4 Assignment: Berlinger Foods Corporation (Berlinger), pursuant to an oral contract, became a distributor for Häagen-Dazs ice cream. Over the next decade, both parties flourished as the marketing of high-quality, high-priced ice cream took hold. Berlinger successfully promoted the sale of Häagen-Dazs to supermarket chains and other retailers in the Baltimore–Washington, DC, area. Ten years later, the Pillsbury Company acquired Häagen-Dazs. Pillsbury adhered to the oral distribution agreement and retained Berlinger as a distributor for Häagen-Dazs ice cream. Two years later, Berlinger entered into a contract and sold its assets to Dreyers, a manufacturer of premium ice cream that competed with Häagen-Dazs. Dreyers ice cream had previously been sold primarily in the western part of the United States. Dreyers attempted to expand its market to the east by choosing to purchase Berlinger as a means to obtain distribution in the mid-Atlantic region. When Pillsbury learned of the sale, it advised Berlinger that its distributorship for Häagen-Dazs was terminated. Berlinger, which wanted to remain a distributor for Häagen-Dazs, sued Pillsbury for breach of contract, alleging that the oral distribution agreement with Häagen-Dazs and Pillsbury was properly assigned to Dreyers. Who wins? *Berlinger Foods Corporation v. The Pillsbury Company*, 633 F.Supp. 557, **Web** 1986 U.S. Dist. Lexis 26431 (United States District Court for the District of Maryland)

15.5 Anti-Assignment Clause: The city of Vancouver, Washington, contracted with B & B Contracting Corporation (B & B) to construct a well pump at a city-owned water station. The contract contained the following anti-assignment clause: "The contractor shall not assign this contract or any part thereof, or any moneys due or to become due thereunder." The work was not completed on time, and the city withheld $6,510 as liquidated damages from the contract price. B & B

assigned the claim to this money to Portland Electric and Plumbing Company (PEPCo). PEPCo, as the assignee, filed suit against the City of Vancouver, alleging that the city had breached its contract with B & B by wrongfully refusing to pay $6,510 to B & B. Can PEPCo maintain the lawsuit against the City of Vancouver? *Portland Electric and Plumbing Company v. City of Vancouver*, 29 Wn.App. 292, 627 P.2d 1350, **Web** 1981 Wash.App. Lexis 2295 (Court of Appeals of Washington)

15.6 Delegation of Duties: C.W. Milford owned a registered Quarterhorse named Hired Chico. Milford sold the horse to Norman Stewart. Recognizing that Hired Chico was a good stud, Milford included the following provision in the written contract that was signed by both parties: "I, C.W. Milford, reserve 2 breedings each year on Hired Chico registration #403692 for the life of this stud horse regardless of whom the horse may be sold to." The agreement was filed with the County Court Clerk of Shelby County, Texas. Stewart later sold Hired Chico to Sam McKinnie. Prior to purchasing the horse, McKinnie read the Milford–Stewart contract and testified that he understood the terms of the contract. When McKinnie refused to grant Milford the stud services of Hired Chico, Milford sued McKinnie for breach of contract. Who wins? *McKinnie v. Milford*, 597 S.W.2d 953, **Web** 1980 Tex.App. Lexis 3345 (Court of Appeals of Texas)

15.7 Condition: Shumann Investments, Inc. (Shumann), hired Pace Construction Corporation (Pace), a general contractor, to build "Outlet World of Pasco Country." In turn, Pace hired OBS Company, Inc. (OBS), a subcontractor, to perform the framing, drywall, insulation, and stucco work on the project. The contract between Pace and OBS stipulated: "Final payment shall not become due unless and until the following conditions precedent to final payment have been satisfied . . . (c) receipt of final payment for subcontractor's work by contractor from owner." When Shumann refused to pay Pace, Pace refused to pay OBS. OBS sued Pace to recover payment. Who wins? *Pace Construction Corporation v. OBS Company, Inc.*, 531 So.2d 737, **Web** 1988 Fla.App. Lexis 4020 (Court of Appeal of Florida)

15.8 Excuse of Condition: Maco, Inc. (Maco), a roofing contractor, hired Brian Barrows as a salesperson. Barrows was assigned a geographical territory and was responsible for securing contracts for Maco within his territory. The employment contract provided that Barrows was to receive a 26 percent commission on the net profits from roofing contracts that he obtained. The contract contained the following provision: "To qualify for payment of the commission, the salesperson must sell and supervise the job; the job must be completed and paid for; and the salesperson must have been in the continuous employment of Maco, Inc., during the aforementioned period." Barrows obtained a $129,603 contract with the Board of Education of Cook County for Maco to make repairs to the roof of the Hoover School in Evanston, Illinois. During the course of the work, Barrows visited the site more than 60 times. Before the work was completed, Maco fired Barrows. Later, Maco refused to pay Barrows the commission when the project was completed and paid for. Barrows sued Maco to recover the commission. Who wins? *Barrows v. Maco, Inc.*, 94 Ill.App.3d 959, 419 N.E.2d 634, **Web** 1981 Ill. App. Lexis 2371 (Appellate Court of Illinois)

Business Ethics Cases

15.9 Business Ethics: Pabagold, Inc. (Pabagold), a manufacturer and distributor of suntan lotions, hired Mediasmith, an advertising agency, to develop an advertising campaign for Pabagold's Hawaiian Gold Pabatan suntan lotion. In the contract, Pabagold authorized Mediasmith to enter into agreements with third parties to place Pabagold advertisements for the campaign and to make payments to these third parties for the Pabagold account. Pabagold agreed to pay Mediasmith for its services and to reimburse it for expenses incurred on behalf of Pabagold. The Pabagold–Mediasmith contract provided for arbitration of any dispute arising under the contract.

Mediasmith entered into a contract with Outdoor Services, Inc. (Outdoor Services), an outdoor advertising company, to place Pabagold ads on billboards owned by Outdoor Services. Outdoor Services provided the agreed-upon work and billed Mediasmith $8,545 for its services. Mediasmith requested payment of this amount from Pabagold so it could pay Outdoor Services. When Pabagold refused to pay, Outdoor Services filed a demand for arbitration, as provided in the Pabagold–Mediasmith contract. Pabagold defended, asserting that Outdoor Services could not try to recover the money because it was not in privity of contract with Pabagold.

Did Pabagold act ethically in refusing to pay Outdoor Services? From an ethical perspective, does it matter that Outdoor Services and Pabagold were not in privity of contract? Who wins? *Outdoor Services, Inc. v. Pabagold, Inc.*, 185 Cal.App.3d 676, 230 Cal.Rptr. 73, **Web** 1986 Cal.App. Lexis 2030 (Court of Appeal of California)

15.10 Business Ethics: Indiana Tri-City Plaza Bowl (Tri-City) leased a building from Charles H. Glueck for use as a bowling alley. The lease provided that Glueck was to provide adequate paved parking for the building. The lease gave Tri-City the right to approve the plans for the construction and paving of the parking lot. When Glueck submitted paving plans to Tri-City, it rejected the plans and withheld its approval. Tri-City argued that the plans were required to meet its personal satisfaction before it had to approve them. Evidence showed that the plans were commercially reasonable in the circumstances. A lawsuit was filed between Tri-City and Glueck. Who wins? Was it ethical for Tri-City to reject the plans? *Indiana Tri-City Plaza Bowl, Inc. v. Estate of Glueck*, 422 N.E.2d 670, **Web** 1981 Ind.App. Lexis 1506 (Court of Appeals of Indiana)

Endnotes

1. *Restatement (Second) of Contracts*, Sections 311 and 318.
2. *Restatement (Second) of Contracts*, Section 317.
3. *Restatement (Second) of Contracts*, Section 318(2).
4. *Restatement (Second) of Contracts*, Section 328.
5. *Restatement (Second) of Contracts*, Section 302.
6. *Restatement (Second) of Contracts*, Section 302(1)(b).
7. *Restatement (Second) of Contracts*, Section 302(1)(a).
8. *The Restatement (Second) of Contracts*, Section 224, defines *condition* as "an event, not certain to occur, which must occur, unless its nonperformance is excused, before performance under a contract is due."
9. *Restatement (Second) of Contracts*, Section 224.
10. *Restatement (Second) of Contracts*, Section 281.
11. *Restatement (Second) of Contracts*, Section 261.
12. *Restatement (Second) of Contracts*, Section 262.
13. *Restatement (Second) of Contracts*, Section 263.
14. *Restatement (Second) of Contracts*, Section 264.
15. UCC Section 2-725 and UCC Section 2A-506.

CHAPTER 16

"Contracts must not be sports of an idle hour, mere matters of pleasantry and badinage, never intended by the parties to have any serious effect whatsoever."

—Lord Stowell
Dalrymple v. Dalrymple, 2 Hag. Con. 54, at 105 (1811)

Remedies for Breach of Traditional and E-Contracts

Chapter Objectives

After studying this chapter, you should be able to:

1. Describe complete, substantial, and inferior performance of contractual duties.
2. Describe compensatory, consequential, and nominal damages awarded for the breach of traditional and e-contracts.
3. Explain rescission and restitution.
4. Define the equitable remedies of specific performance, reformation, and injunction.
5. Describe torts associated with contracts.

Chapter Contents

- **Introduction to Remedies for Breach of Traditional and E-Contracts**

- **Performance and Breach**

- **Monetary Damages**
  Ethics Spotlight · *Liquidated Damages at Trump World Tower*

- **Rescission and Restitution**
  Case 16.1 · *Hickman v. Bates*

- **Equitable Remedies**
  Case 16.2 · *Alba v. Kaufmann*

- **Torts Associated with Contracts**
  Ethics Spotlight · *Bad Faith Tort*

Introduction to Remedies for Breach of Traditional and E-Contracts

There are three levels of performance of a contract: *complete*, *substantial*, and *inferior*. Complete (or strict) performance by a party discharges that party's duties under the contract. Substantial performance constitutes a minor breach of the contract. Inferior performance constitutes a material breach that impairs or destroys the essence of the contract. Various remedies may be obtained by a nonbreaching party if a **breach of contract** occurs— that is, if a contracting party fails to perform an absolute duty owed under a contract.[1]

The most common remedy for a breach of contract is an award of *monetary damages*, often called the "law remedy." If a monetary award does not provide adequate relief, however, the court may order any one of several *equitable remedies*, including specific performance, reformation, and injunction. Equitable remedies are based on the concept of fairness.

This chapter discusses breach of contract and the remedies available to the nonbreaching party.

breach of contract
A contracting party's failure to perform an absolute duty owed under a contract.

Performance and Breach

If a contractual duty has not been discharged (i.e., terminated) or excused (i.e., relieved of legal liability), the contracting party owes an absolute duty (i.e., covenant) to perform the duty. As mentioned in the chapter introduction, there are three types of performance of a contract: (1) *complete performance*, (2) *substantial performance* (or minor breach), and (3) *inferior performance* (or material breach). These concepts are discussed in the following paragraphs.

Men keep their agreements when it is an advantage to both parties not to break them.

Solon
(c. 600 B.C.)

Complete Performance

Most contracts are discharged by the **complete performance**, or **strict performance**, of the contracting parties. Complete performance occurs when a party to a contract renders performance exactly as required by the contract. A fully performed contract is called an **executed contract**.

Tender of performance also discharges a party's contractual obligations. **Tender** is an unconditional and absolute offer by a contracting party to perform his or her obligations under the contract.

complete performance
A situation in which a party to a contract renders performance exactly as required by the contract. Complete performance discharges that party's obligations under the contract.

tender of performance
An unconditional and absolute offer by a contracting party to perform his or her obligations under a contract. Also known as *tender*.

Example

Ashley, who owns a women's retail store, contracts to purchase high-fashion blue jeans from a manufacturer for $75,000. At the time of performance, Ashley tenders the $75,000. Ashley has performed her obligation under the contract once she tenders the $75,000 to the manufacturer. The manufacturer fails to deliver the blue jeans. There is no completed contract, and Ashley can sue the manufacturer for breach of contract.

Substantial Performance: Minor Breach

Substantial performance occurs when there has been a **minor breach** of contract. In other words, it occurs when a party to a contract renders performance that deviates slightly from complete performance. The nonbreaching party may try to convince the breaching party to elevate his or her performance to complete performance. If the breaching party does not correct the breach, the nonbreaching party can sue to recover *damages* by (1) deducting the cost to repair the defect from the contract price and remitting the balance to the breaching party or (2) suing the breaching party to recover the cost to repair the defect if the breaching party has already been paid (see Exhibit 16.1).

substantial performance
Performance by a contracting party that deviates only slightly from complete performance.

minor breach
A breach that occurs when a party renders substantial performance of his or her contractual duties.

Examples

Donald Trump contracts with Big Apple Construction Co. to have Big Apple construct an office building for $100 million. The architectural plans call for installation of three-ply windows in the building. Big Apple constructs the building exactly to plan except that it

No cause of action arises from a bare promise.

Legal maxim

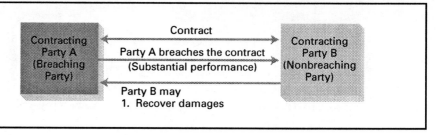

■ EXHIBIT 16.1 Remedy Where There Has Been Substantial Performance (Minor Breach)

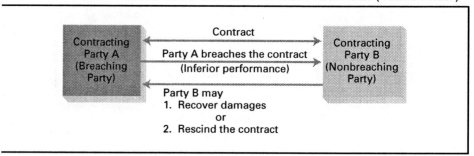

■ EXHIBIT 16.2 Remedies Where There Has Been Inferior Performance (Material Breach)

installs two-ply windows. There has been substantial performance. It would cost $5 million to install the correct windows. If Big Apple agrees to replace the windows and does so, its performance is elevated to complete performance, and Trump must pay the entire contract price. However, if Trump has to hire someone else to replace the windows, he may deduct this cost of repair of $5 million from the contract price of $100 million and remit the difference of $95 million to Big Apple.

Inferior Performance: Material Breach

A **material breach** of a contract occurs when a party renders **inferior performance** of his or her contractual obligations that impairs or destroys the essence of the contract. There is no clear line between a minor breach and a material breach. A determination is made on a case-by-case basis.

Where there has been a material breach of contract, the nonbreaching party may *rescind* the contract and seek restitution of any compensation paid under the contract to the breaching party. The nonbreaching party is discharged from any further performance under the contract.[2] Alternatively, the nonbreaching party may treat the contract as being in effect and sue the breaching party to recover *damages* (see Exhibit 16.2).

Example

A university contracts with a general contractor to build a new three-story classroom building with classroom space for 1,000 students. The contract price is $100 million. However, the completed building cannot support more than 500 students because the contractor used inferior materials. The defect cannot be repaired without rebuilding the entire structure. Because this is a material breach, the university may rescind the contract, recover any money that it has paid to the contractor, and require the contractor to remove the building. The university is discharged of any obligations under the contract and is free to employ another contractor to rebuild the building. However, the building does meet building codes so that it can be used as an administration building of the university. Thus, as an alternative remedy, the university could accept the building as an administration building, which has a value of $20 million. The university would owe this amount—$20 million—to the contractor.

material breach
A breach that occurs when a party renders inferior performance of his or her contractual duties.

inferior performance
A situation in which a party fails to perform express or implied contractual obligations and impairs or destroys the essence of a contract.

Concept Summary
Types of Performance

Type of Performance	Legal Consequence
Complete performance	The contract is discharged.
Substantial performance (minor breach)	The nonbreaching party may recover damages caused by the breach.
Inferior performance (material breach)	The nonbreaching party may either (1) rescind the contract and recover restitution or (2) affirm the contract and recover damages.

Anticipatory Breach

Anticipatory breach (or **anticipatory repudiation**) of contract occurs when a contracting party informs the other party in advance that he or she will not perform his or her contractual duties when due. This type of material breach can be expressly stated or implied from the conduct of the repudiator. Where there is an anticipatory repudiation, the nonbreaching party's obligations under the contract are discharged immediately. The nonbreaching party also has the right to sue the repudiating party when the anticipatory breach occurs; there is no need to wait until performance is due.[3]

anticipatory breach
A breach that occurs when one contracting party informs the other that he or she will not perform his or her contractual duties when due.

Monetary Damages

A nonbreaching party may recover **monetary damages** from a breaching party. Monetary damages are available whether the breach was minor or material. Several types of monetary damages may be awarded. These include *compensatory, consequential, liquidated,* and *nominal damages.*

monetary damages
An award of money.

Compensatory Damages

Compensatory damages are intended to compensate a nonbreaching party for the loss of the bargain. In other words, they place the nonbreaching party in the same position as if the contract had been fully performed by restoring the "benefit of the bargain."

compensatory damages
An award of money intended to compensate a nonbreaching party for the loss of the bargain. Compensatory damages place the nonbreaching party in the same position as if the contract had been fully performed by restoring the "benefit of the bargain."

Examples
Lederle Laboratories enters into a written contract to employ Wei as a chief operations officer (COO) of the company for three years, at a salary of $20,000 per month. After one year at work, Lederle informs Wei that her employment is terminated. This is a material breach of the contract. If Wei is unable to find a comparable job, Wei can sue Lederle Laboratories and recover $480,000 (24 months × $20,000) as compensatory damages. If after six months Wei finds a comparable job that pays $20,000 per month, Wei can recover $360,000 from Lederle (18 months × $20,000) as compensatory damages. In these examples, the damages awarded to Wei place her in the same situation as if her contract with Lederle had been performed.

The amount of compensatory damages that will be awarded for breach of contract depends on the type of contract involved and which party breached the contract. The award of compensatory damages in some special types of contracts is discussed in the following paragraphs.

Sale of a Good Compensatory damages for a breach of a sales contract involving goods are governed by the Uniform Commercial Code (UCC). The usual measure of damages for a breach of a sales contract is the difference between the contract price and the market price of the goods at the time and place the goods were to be delivered.[4]

It is a vain thing to imagine a right without a remedy; for want of right and want of remedy are reciprocal.

Lord Chief Justice Holt
Ashby v. White (1703)

Example

Revlon, Inc., contracts to buy a piece of equipment from Greenway Supply Co. for $80,000. Greenway does not deliver the equipment to Revlon when it is required to do so. Revlon purchases the equipment from another vendor but has to pay $100,000 because the current market price for the equipment has risen. Revlon can recover $20,000 from Greenway—the difference between the market price paid ($100,000) and the contract price ($80,000)—in compensatory damages.

Construction Contract   A construction contract arises when the owner of real property contracts to have a contractor build a structure or do other construction work. The compensatory damages recoverable for a breach of a construction contract vary with the stage of completion of the project when the breach occurs.

A contractor may recover the profits he or she would have made on the contract if the owner breaches the construction contract before construction begins.

Example

RXZ Corporation contracts to have Ace Construction Company build a factory building for $1,200,000. It will cost Ace $800,000 in materials and labor to build the factory for RXZ. If RXZ Corporation breaches the contract before construction begins, Ace can recover $400,000 in "lost profits" from RXZ as compensatory damages.

Example

Entel Corporation contracts to have the Beta Construction Company build a factory building for Entel for $1,200,000. It will cost Beta Construction Company $800,000 to construct the building. Thus, Beta Corporation will make $400,000 profit on the contract. Beta begins construction and has spent $300,000 on materials and labor before Entel breaches the contract by terminating Beta. Here, Beta can recover $700,000, which is comprised of $400,000 lost profits ($1,200,000 − $800,000) plus $300,000 expended on materials and labor. The $700,000 of compensatory damages will make Beta Construction Company "whole."

If the builder breaches a construction contract, either before or during construction, the owner can recover the increased cost above the contract price that he or she has to pay to have the work completed by another contractor.

Example

Ethenol Corporation contracts to have the Sherry Construction Company build a factory building for Ethenol for $1,200,000. Just before Sherry Construction Company is to begin work, it breaches the contract by withdrawing from the project. Ethenol seeks new bids, and the lowest bid to construct the building is $1,700,000. Here, Ethenol can recover $500,000 in compensatory damages from Sherry Construction Company (the $1,700,000 new contract price − $1,200,000 Sherry Construction's original price).

Employment Contract   An employee whose employer breaches an employment contract can recover lost wages or salary as compensatory damages. If the employee breaches the contract, the employer can recover the costs to hire a new employee plus any increase in salary paid to the replacement.

Mitigation of Damages

If a contract has been breached, the law places a duty on the innocent nonbreaching party to make reasonable efforts to **mitigate** (i.e., avoid or reduce) the resulting damages. The extent of mitigation required depends on the type of contract involved.

If an employer breaches an employment contract, the employee owes a duty to mitigate damages by trying to find substitute employment. The employee is only required to accept

Every unjust decision is a reproach to the law or the judge who administers it. If the law should be in danger of doing injustice, then equity should be called in to remedy it. Equity was introduced to mitigate the rigor of the law.

Lord Denning, Master
of the Rolls
Re: Vandervell's Trusts (1974)

mitigation

A nonbreaching party's legal duty to avoid or reduce damages caused by a breach of contract.

comparable employment. The courts consider such factors as compensation, rank, status, job description, and geographical location in determining the comparability of jobs.

Consequential Damages

A nonbreaching party can sometimes recover **consequential damages**, or **special damages**, from the breaching party. Consequential damages are **foreseeable damages** that arise from circumstances outside a contract. To be liable for consequential damages, the breaching party must know or have reason to know that the breach will cause special damages to the other party.

Example

W-Mart, a major retailer, contracts with Maytell, a major manufacturer of toys, to purchase 1,000,000 of the new "G.I. Barby Dolls" produced by Maytell at $20 per doll. W-Mart plans to sell these dolls in its stores nationwide at $50 per doll, and Maytell is aware that W-Mart intends to resell the dolls. The popularity of Barby Dolls guarantees that all the dolls purchased by W-Mart will be sold. If Maytell breaches this contract and fails to deliver the dolls to W-Mart, W-Mart cannot purchase the dolls elsewhere because Maytell holds the copyright and trademark on the doll. Therefore, W-Mart can recover the lost profits on each lost sale as consequential damages from Maytell—that is, the difference between the would-be sales price of the dolls ($50) and the purchase price of each doll ($20), or $30 lost profit per doll. In total, W-Mart can recover $30 million in consequential damages from Maytell ($50 − $20 = $30 × 1,000,000).

Liquidated Damages

Under certain circumstances, the parties to a contract may agree in advance to the amount of damages payable upon a breach of contract. These damages are called **liquidated damages**. To be lawful, the actual damages must be difficult or impracticable to determine, and the liquidated amount must be reasonable in the circumstances.[5] An enforceable liquidated damages clause is an exclusive remedy, even if actual damages are later determined to be different.

A liquidated damages clause is considered a **penalty** if actual damages are clearly determinable in advance or if the liquidated damages are excessive or unconscionable. If a liquidated damages clause is found to be a penalty, it is unenforceable. The nonbreaching party may then recover actual damages.

Nominal Damages

A nonbreaching party can sue a breaching party to a contract for nominal damages even if no financial loss resulted from the breach. **Nominal damages** are usually awarded in a small amount, such as $1. Cases involving nominal damages are usually brought on principle. Most courts disfavor nominal damages lawsuits because they use valuable court time and resources.

Example

Mary enters into an employment contract with Microhard Corporation. It is a three-year contract, and Mary is to be paid $100,000 per year. After Mary works for one year, Microhard Corporation fires Mary. The next day, Mary finds a better position at Microsoft Corporation, in the same city, paying $125,000 per year on a two-year contract. Mary has suffered no monetary damages but could bring a civil lawsuit against Microhard Corporation because of its breach and recover nominal damages ($1).

---

consequential damages
Foreseeable damages that arise from circumstances outside a contract. To be liable for these damages, the breaching party must know or have reason to know that the breach will cause special damages to the other party.

The very definition of a good award is that it gives dissatisfaction to both parties.

Sir Thomas Plumer, Master of the Rolls
Goodman v. Sayers (1820)

liquidated damages
Damages that parties to a contract agree in advance should be paid if the contract is breached.

nominal damages
Damages awarded when the nonbreaching party sues the breaching party even though no financial loss has resulted from the breach. Nominal damages are usually $1 or some other small amount.

Ethics Spotlight

Liquidated Damages at Trump World Tower

"In his affidavit Donald Trump stated that he sought 25% down payments from preconstruction purchasers at the Trump World Tower because of the substantial length of time between contract signing and closing, and because of the obvious associated risks."

—Judge Mazzarelli

The Trump World Tower is a luxury condominium building constructed at 845 United Nations Plaza in Manhattan, New York. Donald Trump is managing general partner of the building, which is New York City's highest residential building. 845 UN Limited Partnership (845 UN) began selling condominiums at the building before the building was constructed. The condominium offering plan required a nonrefundable down payment of 25 percent of the purchase price. The purchase contract provided that if a purchaser defaulted and did not complete the purchase, 845 UN could keep the 25 percent down payment as liquidated damages.

Cem Uzan and Hakan Uzan, brothers and Turkish billionaires, each contracted to purchase two condominium units on the top floors of the building. Cem and Hakan were both represented by attorneys. Over the course of two years, while the building was being constructed, the brothers paid the 25 percent nonrefundable down payment of $8 million. On September 11, 2001, before the building was complete, terrorists attacked New York City by flying two planes into the World Trade Center, the city's two tallest buildings, murdering thousands of people. Cem and Hakan sent letters to 845 UN, rescinding their purchase agreements because of the terrorist attack that occurred on September 11.

That day, 845 UN sent Cem and Hakan default letters, notifying them that they had 30 days to cure their default. Upon the expiration of the cure period, 845 UN terminated the four purchase agreements and kept the 25 percent down payments on the four condominiums as liquidated damages. Cem and Hakan sued 845 UN, alleging that the 25 percent nonrefundable down payment liquidated damages clause was an unenforceable and unconscionable penalty and that the money should be returned to them. 845 UN defended, arguing that the 25 percent nonrefundable down payment was an enforceable liquidated damages clause. The issue for the court was: Is the 25 percent nonrefundable down payment an enforceable liquidated damages clause, or is it an unconscionable and unenforceable penalty?

The supreme court of New York, appellate division, sided with 845 UN and held that Cem and Hakan had breached their contract with 845 UN and that 845 UN was entitled to keep the 25 percent down payment as liquidated damages. The court stated:

It is clear that plaintiffs are not entitled to a return of any portion of their down payment. Here the 25% down payment was a specifically negotiated element of the contracts. There is no question that this was an arm's length transaction. The parties were sophisticated businesspeople, represented by counsel, who spent two months at the bargaining table before executing the amended purchase agreements. The detailed provision concerning the nonrefundable deposit was integral to the transaction. Clearly, plaintiffs were fully aware of and accepted the requirement of a nonrefundable 25% down payment for these luxury preconstruction condominiums. If plaintiffs were dissatisfied with the 25% nonrefundable down payment provision in the purchase agreements, the time to have voiced objection was at the bargaining table.

The appellate court held that the 25 percent nonrefundable down payment was an enforceable liquidated damages clause and not an unconscionable penalty. The appellate court, as a matter of law, granted 845 UN's motion for summary judgment, allowing 845 UN to keep Cem and Hakan's down payments and dismissed their complaint. *Uzan v. 845 UN Limited Partnership,* 10 A.D.3d 230, 778 N.Y.S.2d 171, **Web** 2004 N.Y.App. Div. Lexis 8362 (Supreme Court of New York, Appellate Division)

Business Ethics

Should sophisticated businesspersons be held to their bargains? Was it ethical for Cem and Hakan to try to back out of the purchase agreements and get their money back? Was it ethical for Donald Trump and 845 UN not to pay Cem and Hakan their money back?

Concept Summary

Types of Monetary Damages

Type of Damage	Description
Compensatory	Damages that compensate a nonbreaching party for the loss of a bargain. It places the nonbreaching party in the same position as if the contract had been fully performed.
Consequential	Damages that compensate a nonbreaching party for foreseeable special damages that arise from circumstance outside a contract. The breaching party must have known or should have known that these damages would result from the breach.
Liquidated	An agreement by the parties in advance that sets the amount of damages recoverable in case of breach. These damages are lawful if they do not cause a penalty.
Nominal	Damages awarded against the breaching party even though the nonbreaching party has suffered no financial loss because of the breach. A small amount (e.g., $1) is usually awarded.

Enforcement of Remedies

If a nonbreaching party brings a successful lawsuit against a breaching party to a contract, the court will enter a **judgment** in his or her favor. This judgment must then be collected. If the breaching party refuses to pay the judgment, the court may:

- **Issue a writ of attachment.** A **writ of attachment** orders the sheriff or other government officer to seize property in the possession of the breaching party that he or she owns and to sell the property at auction to satisfy the judgment.
- **Issue a writ of garnishment.** A **writ of garnishment** orders that wages, bank accounts, or other property of the breaching party that is in the hands of third parties be paid over to the nonbreaching party to satisfy the judgment. Federal and state laws limit the amount of the breaching party's wages or salary that can be garnished.

Rescission and Restitution

Rescission is an action to undo a contract. It is available where there has been a material breach of contract, fraud, duress, undue influence, or mistake. Generally, to rescind a contract, the parties must make **restitution** of the consideration they received under the contract.[6] Restitution consists of returning the goods, property, money, or other consideration received from the other party. If possible, the actual goods or property must be returned. If the goods or property have been consumed or are otherwise unavailable, restitution must be made by conveying a cash equivalent. The rescinding party must give adequate notice of the rescission to the breaching party. Rescission and restitution restore the parties to the positions they occupied prior to the contract.

Example

Pralene's Store contracts to purchase $1,000,000 of goods from a clothing manufacturer. Pralene's pays $100,000 as a down payment, and the first $200,000 of goods are delivered. The goods are materially defective, and the defect cannot be cured. This breach is a material breach. Pralene's can rescind the contract. Pralene's is entitled to receive its $100,000 down payment back from the manufacturer, and the manufacturer is entitled to receive the goods back from Pralene's.

In the following case, the court had to decide whether to order the rescission of a contract.

writ of attachment
An order of the court that enables a government officer to seize property of the breaching party and sell it at auction to satisfy a judgment.

writ of garnishment
An order of the court that orders that wages, bank accounts, or other property of the breaching party held by third persons be paid to the nonbreaching party to satisfy a judgment.

rescission
An action to rescind (undo) a contract. Rescission is available if there has been a material breach of contract, fraud, duress, undue influence, or mistake.

restitution
The return of goods or property received from the other party to rescind a contract. If the actual goods or property are not available, a cash equivalent must be made.

Hickman v. Bates

889 So.2d 1249, Web 2004 La.App. Lexis 3076 (2004)
Court of Appeal of Louisiana

"The Court finds that Keith's failure to inform his young, limited, first cousin was intentional and was done to obtain an advantage over her. That is, of divesting her interest in 45 acres in Bienville Parish and 236 acres in Madison Parish for a pittance."

—Judge Caraway

Facts

Patricia Dianne Hickman inherited one-half interests to two pieces of real property when her mother died. One of the properties, in Bienville Parish, Louisiana, contained 45 acres of woodland. The second property, in Madison Parish, Louisiana, contained approximately 236 acres of land and a house. Patricia was 20 years old and had a mental condition that required medication. Patricia, who lived separately from her parents, received a telephone call from her father, Joe Hickman, to come and visit him. Joe was ill with cancer and lived with his sister Christine Bates and her husband, who are parents of Keith Bates, Patricia's first cousin.

The day after Patricia arrived, Joe informed Patricia that an important concern of his was for her to sell her interests in the two pieces of property to Keith Bates and his wife Sheila (the Bates). Joe expressed his doubts that Patricia would be able to maintain the properties and his interest in keeping the property in the family. Patricia agreed to sell the properties to the Bates for $500. Patricia signed legal documents that had been drawn by an attorney prior to her arrival.

Subsequently, through a friend, Patricia sued the Bates to rescind the contracts that sold her interest in the two pieces of property to them, alleging fraud. Expert testimony at trial valued the Madison Parish property at $259,000 and the Bienville Parish property at $20,700. The trial court found fraud and rescinded the contracts. The trial court did not, however, award Patricia attorneys' fees. Both sides appealed.

Issue

Should the sales contracts be rescinded because of fraud, and should Patricia be awarded attorneys' fees?

Language of the Court

A contract is formed by the consent of the parties. However, consent may be vitiated by error, fraud, or duress. Fraud is a misrepresentation or a suppression of the truth made with the intention either to obtain an unjust advantage for one party or to cause a loss or inconvenience to the other. Fraud need only be proven by a preponderance of the evidence and may be established by circumstantial evidence. In its very thorough and well-reasoned oral ruling, the trial court made the following findings of fact concerning its determination of fraud:

> *The court finds that Patricia's intellectual abilities are limited, both from her lack of education and from her mental condition that requires medicine. Considering her situation, her youth, she was then 20 years old, and her limited abilities, as well as her lack of prior knowledge of the purpose of the visit, and her father's illness, and the fact that she trusted her father and her cousin, the Court finds that Keith had a responsibility to make sure Patricia was informed fully about the transactions and make sure that she understood everything she was doing and the import of everything she was doing, including the fact that she would own nothing, and including the price considerations involved before she signed those documents. The Court finds that Keith's failure to inform his young, limited, first cousin was intentional and was done to obtain an advantage over her. That is, of divesting her interest in 45 acres in Bienville Parish and 236 acres in Madison Parish for a pittance.*

> *We can discern no manifest error in these determinations. Accordingly, we find that the trial court committed no error in rescinding the sales on the ground of fraud.*

Decision

The court of appeal affirmed the trial court's finding of fraud and its judgment rescinding the sales contracts by which Patricia sold her interests in the two properties to the Bates. The court of appeal reversed the trial court's denial of an award of attorneys' fees to Patricia and awarded $12,000 in attorneys' fees to Patricia.

Case Questions

Critical Legal Thinking Describe the rescission of a contract. When can a contract be rescinded? Explain.

Business Ethics Did Patricia's father, Joe Hickman, and her first cousin, Keith Bates, act ethically in this case? Did Patricia need the court's help in this case?

Contemporary Business Describe a fraud. Do you think people take advantage of their relatives very often?

Equitable Remedies

Equitable remedies are available if there has been a breach of contract that cannot be adequately compensated through a legal remedy. They are also available to prevent unjust enrichment. The most common equitable remedies are *specific performance*, *reformation*, and *injunction*, discussed in the following paragraphs.

Specific Performance

An award of **specific performance** orders the breaching party to perform the acts promised in a contract. The courts have the discretion to award this remedy if the subject matter of the contract is unique.[7] Specific performance is available to enforce land contracts because every piece of real property is considered to be unique. Works of art, antiques, and items of sentimental value, rare coins, stamps, heirlooms, and such also fit the requirement for uniqueness. Most other personal property does not.

Specific performance of personal service contracts is not granted because the courts would find it difficult or impracticable to supervise or monitor performance of such a contract.

The court had to decide whether to issue an order of specific performance in the following case.

specific performance
A remedy that orders the breaching party to perform the acts promised in the contract. Specific performance is usually awarded in cases in which the subject matter is unique, such as in contracts involving land, heirlooms, and paintings.

CASE 16.2
Specific Performance

Alba v. Kaufmann

27 A.D.3d 816, 810 N.Y.S.2d 539, Web 2006 N.Y.App. Div. Lexis 2321 (2006)
Supreme Court of New York, Appellate Division

"The case law reveals that the equitable remedy of specific performance is routinely awarded in contract actions involving real property, on the premise that each parcel of real property is unique."

—Judge Crew

Facts

Jean-Claude Kaufmann owned approximately 37 acres of real property located in the town of Stephentown, Rensselaer County, New York. The property is located in a wooded area and is improved with a nineteenth-century farmhouse. Kaufmann and his spouse, Christine Cacace, reside in New York City and use the property as a weekend or vacation home. After Kaufmann and Cacace lost their jobs, their financial situation prompted Kaufmann to list the property for sale for $350,000.

Richard Alba and his spouse (Albas) looked at the property and offered Kaufmann the full asking price. The parties executed a contract for sale, and the Albas paid a deposit, obtained a mortgage commitment, and procured a satisfactory home inspection and title insurance. A date for closing the transaction was set. Prior to closing, Cacace sent the Albas an e-mail, indicating that she and Kaufmann had "a change of heart" and no longer wished to go forward

with the sale. Albas sent a reply e-mail, stating their intent to go forward with the scheduled closing. Cacace responded with another e-mail, informing the Albas that she had multiple sclerosis and alleging that the "remorse and dread" over the impending sale was making her ill. When Kaufmann refused to close, the Albas sued, seeking specific performance, and moved for summary judgment. The supreme court denied the motion. The Albas appealed.

Issue

Was an order of specific performance of the real estate contract warranted in this case?

Language of the Court

In order to establish their entitlement to summary judgment, the Albas were required to demonstrate that they substantially performed their contractual obligations and were ready, willing and able to fulfill their remaining obligations, that Kaufmann was able but unwilling to convey the property and that there is no adequate remedy at law. The Albas plainly discharged that burden here. In short, the record demonstrates that the Albas were ready, willing and able to close and, but for Kaufmann's admitted refusal to do so, would have consummated the transaction.

As to the remedy the Albas seek, the case law reveals that the equitable remedy of specific performance is routinely awarded in contract actions involving real property, on the premise that each parcel of real property is unique. Moreover, volitional unwillingness, as distinguished from good faith inability, to meet contractual obligations furnishes neither a ground for cancellation of the contract nor a defense against its specific performance.

Even accepting, for purposes of this discussion, that the alleged exacerbation of Cacace's symptoms is both genuine and causally related to the proposed sale of property, as she is not a party to the contract, her connection to the transaction is simply too attenuated for Kaufmann to claim undue hardship. Simply put, permitting a defendant to raise an undue hardship defense under the circumstances present here would place a nearly impossible *burden upon potential purchasers of real property namely, to ascertain whether any of the signatories' relatives had any potential objection to the sale in question.*

Decision

The appellate court reversed the supreme court's denial of Alba's motion for summary judgment. The appellate court, as a matter of law, granted the Albas' motion for summary judgment and ordered Kaufmann to specifically perform the real estate contract.

Case Questions

Critical Legal Thinking   What does the doctrine of specific performance provide? Explain.

Business Ethics   Was it ethical for Kaufman to try to back out of the contract? Once the Albas were aware of Cacace's health problems, should they have withdrawn their contract?

Contemporary Business   Should a seller be permitted to cancel a contract for the sale of real estate because he or she has "seller's remorse"?

Reformation

reformation

An equitable doctrine that permits the court to rewrite a contract to express the parties' true intentions.

Reformation is an equitable doctrine that permits the court to rewrite a contract to express the parties' true intentions. Reformation is usually available to correct clerical errors in contracts. For example, suppose a clerical error is made during the typing of a contract, and both parties sign the contract without discovering the error. If a dispute later arises, the court can reform the contract to correct the clerical error to read as the parties originally intended.

Injunction

injunction

A court order that prohibits a person from doing a certain act.

An **injunction** is a court order that prohibits a person from doing a certain act. To obtain an injunction, the requesting party must show that he or she will suffer irreparable injury if the injunction is not issued.

Concept Summary
Types of Equitable Remedies

Type of Equitable Remedy	Description
Specific performance	A court orders the breaching party to perform the acts promised in the contract. The subject matter of the contract must be unique.
Reformation	A court rewrites a contract to express the parties' true intentions. This remedy is usually used to correct clerical errors.
Injunction	A court prohibits a party from doing a certain act. Injunctions are available in contract actions only in limited circumstances.

Torts Associated with Contracts

The recovery for breach of contract is usually limited to contract damages. A party who can prove a contract-related **tort**, however, may also recover tort damages. Tort damages include compensation for personal injury, pain and suffering, emotional distress, and possibly punitive damages.

Generally, punitive damages are not recoverable for breach of contract. They are recoverable, however, for certain tortious conduct that may be associated with the non-performance of a contract.

The major torts associated with contracts are *intentional interference with contractual relations* and *breach of the implied covenant of good faith and fair dealing*. These torts are discussed in the following paragraphs.

Intentional Interference with Contractual Relations

A party to a contract may sue any third person who intentionally interferes with the contract and causes that party injury. The third party does not have to have acted with malice or bad faith. This tort, which is known as the tort of **intentional interference with contractual relations**, usually arises when a third party induces a contracting party to breach a contract with another party. The following elements must be shown:

1. A valid, enforceable contract between the contracting parties
2. Third-party knowledge of this contract
3. Third-party inducement to breach the contract

A third party can contract with the breaching party without becoming liable for this tort if a contracting party has already breached the contract and thus the third party cannot be held to have induced a breach of the other parties' contract.

intentional interference with contractual relations
A tort that arises when a third party induces a contracting party to breach the contract with another party.

Breach of the Implied Covenant of Good Faith and Fair Dealing

Several states have held that a **covenant of good faith and fair dealing** is implied in certain types of contracts. Under this covenant, the parties to a contract are not only held to the express terms of the contract but are also required to act in "good faith" and deal fairly in all respects in obtaining the objective of the contract. A breach of this implied covenant is a tort for which tort damages are recoverable. This tort, which is sometimes referred to as the **tort of bad faith**, is an evolving area of the law.

covenant of good faith and fair dealing
An implied covenant under which the parties to a contract not only are held to the express terms of the contract but are also required to act in "good faith" and deal fairly in all respects in obtaining the objective of the contract.

Ethics Spotlight

Bad Faith Tort

"Where an insurer is pursued for its refusal to settle a claim, 'bad faith' lies in an insurer's failure to give at least equal consideration to the insured's interests when the insurer arrives at a decision on whether to settle the claim."

—Judge Clyde L. Kuehn

On Halloween Day, Christine Narvaez drove her automobile onto the parking lot of a busy supermarket. Narvaez had her two-year-old grandchild with her. The youngster was riding, unconstrained, in a booster seat. Narvaez saw a friend and decided to stop for a brief chat. She parked the car and exited the car, leaving the keys in the ignition and the motor running. The youngster crawled behind the wheel, slipped the car into gear, and set it in motion. The car struck Marguerite O'Neill, a woman in her 80s, pinned her between the Narvaez car and another car and slowly crushed the woman's trapped body.

O'Neill was pried loose and airlifted to a hospital trauma center. O'Neill suffered a crushed hip, a broken arm, and four cracked ribs, and she lost more than 40 percent of her blood supply as a result of internal bleeding. She spent one month in the hospital intensive care unit and had to be placed in a nursing home and was deprived of the ability to live independently.

Narvaez carried the $20,000 minimum amount of liability insurance allowed by law. She was insured by Gallant Insurance Company. O'Neill's medical bills totaled $105,000. O'Neill sued Narvaez and her insurance company, Gallant. O'Neill's attorney demanded the policy limit of $20,000 from Gallant in settlement of O'Neill's claim and offered a complete release from liability for Narvaez. Three Gallant insurance adjusters, its claims manager, and the lawyer of the law firm representing Gallant for the case all stated to John Moss, Gallant's executive vice president, that Gallant should accept the settlement offer. Moss rejected their advice and refused to settle the case.

One year later, on the eve of trial, Moss offered to settle for the $20,000 policy limit, but O'Neill then refused. The case went to trial, and the jury returned a verdict against Narvaez of $731,063. Gallant paid $20,000 of this amount, closed its file, and left Narvaez liable for the $711,063 excess judgment. To settle her debt to O'Neill, Narvaez assigned her claims against Gallant to O'Neill. O'Neill then sued Gallant for a bad faith tort for breaching the implied covenant of good faith and fair dealing that Gallant owed to Narvaez to settle the case. The jury found Gallant liable for a bad faith tort and awarded O'Neill $710,063 ($1,000 short of the judgment in the first trial) in actual damages and $2.3 million in punitive damages. The appellate court agreed. The court stated:

> Where an insurer is pursued for its refusal to settle a claim, "bad faith" lies in an insurer's failure to give at least equal consideration to the insured's interests when the insurer arrives at a decision on whether to settle the claim. The jury's finding of bad faith was not against the manifest weight of the evidence. We must side with O'Neill and against Gallant on the extent to which the evidence established the existence of reprehensible conduct on the part of Narvaez's insurance provider.

The appellate court held that Gallant was liable for a bad faith tort and upheld the trial court's judgment, awarding O'Neill $710,063 in actual damages and $2.3 million in punitive damages. *O'Neill v. Gallant Insurance Company*, 769 N.E.2d 100, **Web** 2002 Ill.App. Lexis 311 (Appellate Court of Illinois)

Business Ethics

Did Gallant act ethically in this case? Will the implied covenant of good faith and fair dealing make insurance companies act more ethically toward their customers?

Test Review Terms and Concepts

Anticipatory breach (anticipatory repudiation)

Breach of contract

Compensatory damages

Complete performance (strict performance)

Consequential damages (special damages or foreseeable damages)

Covenant of good faith and fair dealing

Equitable remedies

Executed contract

Inferior performance

Injunction

Intentional interference with contractual relations

Judgment

Liquidated damages

Material breach

Minor breach

Mitigation of damages

Monetary damages

Nominal damages

Penalty

Reformation

Rescission

Restitution

Specific performance

Substantial performance

Tender of performance (tender)

Tort

Tort of bad faith

Writ of attachment

Writ of garnishment

Case Problems

16.1 Performance: Louis Haeuser, who owned several small warehouses, contracted with Wallace C. Drennen, Inc. (Drennen), to construct a road to the warehouses. The contract price was $42,324. After Drennen completed the work, some cracks appeared in the road, causing improper drainage. In addition, "birdbaths" that accumulated water appeared in the road. When Haeuser refused to pay, Drennen sued to recover the full contract price. Haeuser filed a cross complaint to recover the cost of repairing the road. Who wins? *Wallace C. Drennen, Inc. v. Haeuser*, 402 So.2d 771, **Web** 1981 La. App. Lexis 4453 (Court of Appeal of Louisiana)

16.2 Anticipatory Repudiation: Muhammad Ali (Ali), a professional heavyweight boxer, successfully defended his heavyweight boxing championship of the world by defeating Ken Norton. Shortly after the fight, Ali held a press conference and, as he had done on several occasions before, announced his retirement from boxing. At that time, Ali had beaten every challenger except Duane Bobick, whom he had not yet fought. Subsequently, Madison Square Garden Boxing, Inc. (MSGB), a fight promoter, offered Ali $2.5 million if he would fight Bobick. Ali agreed, stating, "We are back in business again." MSGB and Ali signed a fighters' agreement, and MSGB paid Ali a $125,000 advance payment. The fight was to take place in Madison Square Garden. Three months before the fight was to take place, Ali told MSGB that he was retiring from boxing and would not fight Bobick in February. Must MSGB wait until the date performance is due to sue Ali for breach of contract? *Madison Square Garden Boxing, Inc. v. Muhammad Ali*, 430 F.Supp. 679, **Web** 1977 U.S. Dist. Lexis 16101 (United States District Court for the Northern District of Illinois)

16.3 Damages: Hawaiian Telephone Company entered into a contract with Microform Data Systems, Inc. (Microform), for Microform to provide a computerized assistance system that would handle 15,000 calls per hour with a one-second response time and with a "nonstop" feature to allow automatic recovery from any component failure. The contract called for installation of the host computer no later than mid-February of the next year. Microform was not able to meet the initial installation date, and at that time, it was determined that Microform was at least nine months away from providing a system that met contract specifications. Hawaiian Telephone canceled the contract and sued Microform for damages. Did Microform materially breach the contract? Can Hawaiian Telephone recover damages? *Hawaiian Telephone Co. v. Microform Data Systems Inc.*, 829 F.2d 919, **Web** 1987 U.S. App. Lexis 13425 (United States Court of Appeals for the Ninth Circuit)

16.4 Damages: Raquel Welch was a movie actress who appeared in about 30 films over a 15-year period. She was considered a sex symbol, and her only serious dramatic role was as a roller derby queen in *Kansas City Bomber*. During that time period, Michael Phillips and David Ward developed a film package based on the John Steinbeck novella *Cannery Row*. Metro-Goldwyn-Mayer Film Company (MGM) accepted to produce the project and entered into a contract with Welch to play the leading female character, a prostitute named Suzy. At 40 years of age, Welch relished the chance to direct her career toward more serious roles. Welch was to receive $250,000 from MGM, with payment being divided into weekly increments during filming. Filming began, but three weeks later, MGM fired Welch and replaced her with another actress, Debra Winger. Welch sued MGM to recover the balance of $194,444 that remained unpaid under the contract. Who wins? *Welch v. Metro-Goldwyn-Mayer Film Co.*, 207 Cal.App.3d 164, 254 Cal.Rptr. 645, **Web** 1988 Cal.App. Lexis 1202 (Court of Appeal of California)

16.5 Damages: Ptarmigan Investment Company (Ptarmigan), a partnership, entered into a contract with Gundersons, Inc. (Gundersons), a South Dakota corporation in the business of golf course construction. The contract provided that Gundersons would construct a golf course for Ptarmigan for a contract price of $1,294,129. Gundersons immediately started work and completed about one-third of the work by about three months later, when bad weather forced cessation of most work. Ptarmigan paid Gundersons for the work to that date. In the following spring, Ptarmigan ran out of funds and was unable to pay for the completion of the golf course. Gundersons sued Ptarmigan and its individual partners to recover the lost profits that it would have made on the remaining two-thirds of the contract. Can Gundersons recover these lost profits as damages? *Gundersons, Inc. v. Ptarmigan Investment Company*, 678 P.2d 1061, **Web** 1983 Colo.App. Lexis 1133 (Court of Appeals of Colorado)

16.6 Liquidated Damages: H. S. Perlin Company, Inc. (Perlin), and Morse Signal Devices of San Diego (Morse) entered into a contract whereby Morse agreed to provide burglar and fire alarm service to Perlin's coin and stamp store. Perlin paid $50 per month for this service. The contract contained a liquidated damages clause limiting Morse's liability to $250 for any losses incurred by Perlin based on Morse's failure of service. Six years after the burglary system was installed, a burglary occurred at Perlin's store. Before entering the store, the burglars cut a telephone line that ran from the burglar system in Perlin's store to Morse's central location. When the line was cut, a signal indicated the interruption of service at Morse's central station. Inexplicably, Morse took no further steps to investigate the interruption of service at Perlin's store. The burglars stole stamps and coins with a wholesale value of $958,000, and Perlin did not have insurance against this loss. Perlin sued Morse to recover damages. Is the liquidated damages clause enforceable? *H. S. Perlin Company, Inc. v. Morse Signal Devices of San Diego*, 209 Cal.App.3d 1289, 258 Cal.Rptr. 1, **Web** 1989 Cal.App. Lexis 400 (Court of Appeal of California)

16.7 Liquidated Damages: United Mechanical Contractors, Inc. (UMC), an employer, agreed to provide a pension plan for its unionized workers. UMC was to make monthly payments into a pension fund administered by the Idaho Plumbers and Pipefitters Health and Welfare Fund (Fund). Payments were due by the 15th of each month. The contract between UMC and Fund contained a liquidated damages clause which provided that if payments due from UMC were received later than the 20th of the month, liquidated damages of 20 percent of the required contribution would be assessed against UMC. In one month, Fund received UMC's payment on the 24th. Fund sued UMC to recover $9,245.23 in liquidated damages. Is the liquidated damages clause enforceable? *Idaho Plumbers and Pipefitters Health and Welfare Fund v. United Mechanical Contractors, Inc.*, 875 F.2d 212, **Web** 1989 U.S. App. Lexis 14528 (United States Court of Appeals for the Ninth Circuit)

16.8 Specific Performance: Liz Claiborne, Inc. (Claiborne), is a large maker of sportswear in the United States and a well-known name in fashion, with sales of over $1 billion per year.

Claiborne distributes its products through 9,000 retail outlets in the United States. Avon Products, Inc. (Avon), is a major producer of fragrances, toiletries, and cosmetics, with annual sales of more than $3 billion per year. Claiborne, which desired to promote its well-known name on perfumes and cosmetics, entered into a joint venture with Avon whereby Claiborne would make available its names, trademarks, and marketing experience and Avon would engage in the procurement and manufacture of the fragrances, toiletries, and cosmetics. The parties would equally share the financial requirements of the joint venture. During its first year of operation, the joint venture had sales of more than $16 million. In the second year, sales increased to $26 million, making it one of the fastest-growing fragrance and cosmetic lines in the country. One year later, Avon sought to "uncouple" the joint venture. Avon thereafter refused to procure and manufacture the line of fragrances and cosmetics for the joint venture. When Claiborne could not obtain the necessary fragrances and cosmetics from any other source for the fall/Christmas season, Claiborne sued Avon for breach of contract, seeking specific performance of the contract by Avon. Is specific performance an appropriate remedy in this case? *Liz Claiborne, Inc. v. Avon Products, Inc.*, 141 A.D.2d 329, 530 N.Y.S.2d 425, **Web** 1988 N.Y.App. Div. Lexis 6423 (Supreme Court of New York)

16.9 Injunction: Anita Baker, a then-unknown singer, signed a multiyear recording contract with Beverly Glen Music, Inc. (Beverly Glen). Baker recorded for Beverly Glen a record album that was moderately successful. After having some difficulties with Beverly Glen, Baker was offered a considerably more lucrative contract by Warner Communications, Inc. (Warner). Baker accepted the Warner offer and informed Beverly Glen that she would not complete their contract because she had entered into an agreement with Warner. Beverly Glen sued Baker and Warner, and it sought an injunction to prevent Baker from performing as a singer for Warner. Is an injunction an appropriate remedy in this case? *Beverly Glen Music, Inc. v. Warner Communications, Inc.*, 178 Cal.App.3d 1142, 224 Cal.Rptr. 260, **Web** 1986 Cal.App. Lexis 2729 (Court of Appeal of California)

16.10 Intentional Interference with Contractual Relations: Pacific Gas and Electric Company (PG & E) entered into a contract with Placer County Water Agency (Agency) to purchase hydroelectric power generated by Agency's Middle Fork American River Project. The contract was not terminable until 2013. As energy prices rose during the 1970s, the contract became extremely valuable to PG & E. The price PG & E paid for energy under the contract was much lower than the cost of energy from other sources. Ten year later, Bear Stearns & Company (Bear Stearns), an investment bank and securities underwriting firm, learned of Agency's power contract with PG & E. Bear Stearns offered to assist Agency in an effort to terminate the power contract with PG & E in exchange for a share of Agency's subsequent profits and the right to underwrite any new securities issued by Agency. Bear Stearns also agreed to pay the legal fees incurred by Agency in litigation concerning the attempt to get out of the PG & E contract. Who wins and why? *Pacific Gas and Electric Company v. Bear Stearns & Company*, 50 Cal.3d 1118, 791 P.2d 587, 270 Cal.Rptr. 1, **Web** 1990 Cal. Lexis 2119 (Supreme Court of California)

Business Ethics Cases

16.11 Business Ethics: Walgreen Company began operating a pharmacy in the Southgate Mall in Milwaukee when the mall opened. It had a lease for a 30-year term that contained an exclusivity clause in which the landlord, Sara Creek Property Company (Sara Creek), promised not to lease space in the mall to anyone else who wanted to operate a pharmacy or a store containing a pharmacy. With 11 years left on the Walgreen–Sara Creek lease, after its anchor tenant went broke, Sara Creek informed Walgreen that it intended to lease the anchor tenant space to Phar-Mor Corporation. Phar-Mor, a "deep discount" chain, would occupy 100,000 square feet, of which 12,000 square feet would be occupied by a pharmacy the same size as Walgreen's. The entrances to the two stores would be within a few hundred feet of each other. Walgreen sued Sara Creek for breach of contract and sought a permanent injunction against Sara Creek's leasing the anchor premises to Phar-Mor. Do the facts of this case justify the issuance of a permanent injunction? Did Sara Creek act ethically in not living up to the contract with Walgreen? *Walgreen Co. v. Sara Creek Property Co.*, 966 F.2d 273, **Web** 1992 U.S. App. Lexis 14847 (United States Court of Appeals for the Seventh Circuit)

16.12 Business Ethics: Rosina Crisci owned an apartment building in which Mrs. DiMare was a tenant. One day while DiMare was descending a wooden staircase on the outside of the apartment building, she fell through the staircase and was left hanging 15 feet above the ground until she was rescued. Crisci had a $10,000 liability insurance policy on the building from the Security Insurance Company (Security) of New Haven, Connecticut. DiMare sued Crisci and Security for $400,000 for physical injuries and psychosis suffered from the fall. Prior to trial, DiMare agreed to take $10,000 in settlement of the case. Security refused this settlement offer. DiMare reduced her settlement offer to $9,000, of which Crisci offered to pay $2,500. Security again refused to settle the case. The case proceeded to trial, and the jury awarded DiMare and her husband $110,000. Security paid $10,000, pursuant to the insurance contract, and Crisci had to pay the difference. Crisci, a widow of 70 years of age, had to sell her assets, became dependent on her relatives, declined in physical health, and suffered from hysteria and suicide attempts. Crisci sued Security for tort damages for breach of the implied covenant of good faith and fair dealing. Did Security act in bad faith? *Crisci v. Security Insurance Company of New Haven, Connecticut*, 66 Cal.App.2d 425, 426 P.2d 173, 58 Cal.Rptr. 13, **Web** 1967 Cal. Lexis 313 (Supreme Court of California)

Endnotes

1. *Restatement (Second) of Contracts*, Section 235(2).
2. *Restatement (Second) of Contracts*, Section 241.
3. *Restatement (Second) of Contracts*, Section 253; UCC Section 2-610.
4. UCC Sections 2-708 and 2-713.
5. *Restatement (Second) of Contracts*, Section 356(1).
6. *Restatement (Second) of Contracts*, Section 370.
7. *Restatement (Second) of Contracts*, Section 359.

CHAPTER 17

*"Without that sense of security which property gives,
the land would still be uncultivated."*

—Francois Quesnay
Maximes, IV

Real Property

Chapter Objectives

After studying this chapter, you should be able to:

1. List and describe the different types of real property.
2. Describe the different types of freehold estates and future interests in real property.
3. Identify the different types of concurrent ownership of real property.

4. Explain how ownership interests in real property can be transferred.
5. Describe the zoning laws.

Chapter Contents

Introduction to Real Property

Property and ownership rights in *real property* play an important part in the society and economy of the United States. Individuals and families own houses, farmers and ranchers own farmland and ranches, and businesses own commercial and office buildings. The concept of real property is concerned with the legal rights to the property rather than the physical attributes of the tangible land. Thus, real property includes some items of personal property that are affixed to real property (e.g., fixtures) and other rights (e.g., minerals, air).

Although the United States has the most advanced private property system in the world, the ownership and possession of real estate are not free from government regulation. Pursuant to constitutional authority, federal, state, and local governments have enacted myriad laws that regulate the ownership, possession, lease, and use of real property. These laws include zoning laws, and the like.

This chapter covers the law concerning the ownership and transfer of real property.

Real Property

Property is usually classified as either real or personal property. **Real property** is immovable or attached to immovable land or buildings, whereas personal property is movable. The various types of real property are described in the following paragraphs.

Land and Buildings

Land is the most common form of real property. A landowner usually purchases the **surface rights** to the land—that is, the right to occupy the land. The owner may use, enjoy, and develop the property as he or she sees fit, subject to any applicable government regulation.

Buildings constructed on land are real property. Houses, apartment buildings, manufacturing plants, and office buildings constructed on land are real property. Such things as radio towers and bridges are usually considered real property as well.

Subsurface Rights

The owner of land possesses **subsurface rights**, or **mineral rights**, to the earth located beneath the surface of the land. These rights can be very valuable. Gold, uranium, oil, or natural gas may lie beneath the surface of the land. Theoretically, mineral rights extend to the center of the earth. In reality, mines and oil wells usually extend only several miles into the earth. Subsurface rights may be sold separately from surface rights.

Plant Life and Vegetation

Plant life and vegetation growing on the surface of land are considered real property. Such vegetation includes both natural plant life (e.g., trees) and cultivated plant life (e.g., crops). When land is sold, any plant life growing on the land is included, unless the parties agree otherwise. Plant life that is severed from the land is considered personal property.

Fixtures

Certain personal property is so closely associated with real property that it becomes part of the realty. Such items are called **fixtures**. Kitchen cabinets, carpet, and doorknobs are fixtures, but throw rugs and furniture are personal property. Unless otherwise provided, if a building is sold, the fixtures are included in the sale. If the sale agreement is silent as to whether an item is a fixture, the courts make their determination on the basis of whether the item can be removed without causing substantial damage to the realty.

Estates in Land

A person's ownership right in real property is called an **estate in land** (or **estate**). An estate is defined as the bundle of *legal rights* that the owner has to possess, use, and enjoy the

real property
The land itself as well as buildings, trees, soil, minerals, timber, plants, and other things permanently affixed to the land.

Good fences make good neighbors.

Robert Frost
"Mending Wall" (1914)

subsurface rights
Rights to the earth located beneath the surface of the land.

fixtures
Goods that are affixed to real estate so as to become part thereof.

estate
Ownership rights in real property; the bundle of legal rights that the owner has to possess, use, and enjoy the property.

Contemporary Environment

Air Rights

Common law provided that the owners of real property owned that property from the center of the earth to the heavens. This rule has been eroded by modern legal restrictions such as land use regulation laws, environmental protection laws, and air navigation requirements. Even today, however, the owners of land may sell or lease air space parcels above their land.

An **air space parcel** is the air space above the surface of the earth of an owner's real property. Air space parcels are valuable property rights, particularly in densely populated metropolitan areas, where building property is scarce.

Examples

Railroads have made money by leasing or selling air rights over their railroad tracks. For example, the Grand Central Terminal in New York City sold air rights over its railroad property for the construction of the PanAm Building (now MetLife Building) next to Grand Central Terminal. Many other developments have been built in air space parcels in New York City.

Owners of highways—including states and cities—often sell or lease **air rights** over the highways.

Example

Many fast food restaurants and gasoline stations are located on air rights over freeways. In addition, air rights are often developed so that historic buildings can be preserved. This is often accomplished by the city premitting a developer to purchase air rights above the historic building in exchange for preserving the historic building.

Owners of air rights, and parties who want to build on those air rights, will continue to come up with unique solutions to meet building needs.

---

property. The type of estate that an owner possesses is determined from the deed, will, lease, or other document that transferred the ownership rights to him or her.

Freehold Estate

freehold estate

An estate in which the owner has a present possessory interest in the real property.

A **freehold estate** is an estate in which the owner has a *present possessory interest* in the real property; that is, the owner may use and enjoy the property as he or she sees fit, subject to any applicable government regulation or private restraint. There are three types of freehold estates: two *estates in fee—fee simple absolute (or fee simple)* and *fee simple defeasible (or qualified fee)—*and *life estate.* These are discussed in the following paragraphs.

fee simple absolute

A type of ownership of real property that grants the owner the fullest bundle of legal rights that a person can hold in real property. Also known as *fee simple.*

Fee Simple Absolute (or Fee Simple)   A **fee simple absolute** (or **fee simple**) is an estate in fee that is the highest form of ownership of real property because it grants the owner the fullest bundle of legal rights that a person can hold in real property. It is the type of ownership most people connect with "owning" real property. A fee simple owner has the right to exclusively possess and use his or her property to the extent that the owner has not transferred any interest in the property (e.g., by lease).

If a person owns real property in fee simple, his or her ownership:

- Is infinite in duration (fee)
- Has no limitation on inheritability (simple)
- Does not end upon the occurrence of any event (absolute)

fee simple defeasible

A type of ownership of real property that grants the owner all the incidents of a fee simple absolute except that it may be taken away if a specified condition occurs or does not occur. Also known as *qualified fee.*

Fee Simple Defeasible (or Qualified Fee)   A **fee simple defeasible** (or **qualified fee**) grants the owner all the incidents of a fee simple absolute except that it may be taken away if a specified *condition* occurs or does not occur.

Example

A conveyance of property to a church "as long as the land is used as a church or for church purposes" creates a qualified fee. The church has all the rights of a fee simple absolute owner except that its ownership rights are terminated if the property is no longer used for church purposes.

Life Estate   A **life estate** is an interest in real property that lasts for the life of a specified person, usually the grantee. For example, a conveyance of real property "to Anna for her life" creates a life estate. A life estate may also be measured by the life of a third party, which is called *estate pour autre vie* (e.g., "To Anna for the life of Benjamin"). A life estate may be defeasible (e.g., "To John for his life but only if he continues to occupy this residence").

Upon the death of the named person, the life estate terminates, and the property reverts to the grantor or the grantor's estate or another designated person.

life estate
An interest in real property for a person's lifetime; upon that person's death, the interest is transferred to another party.

Concept Summary
Freehold Estates

Estate	Description
Fee simple absolute	Is the highest form of ownership of real property. Ownership (1) is infinite in duration, (2) has no limitation on inheritability, and (3) does not end upon the occurrence or nonoccurrence of an event.
Fee simple defeasible	Grants the owner all the incidents of a fee simple absolute except that it may be taken away if a specified condition occurs or does not occur.
Life estate	Is an interest in property that lasts for the life of a specified person. A life estate terminates upon the death of the named person and reverts back to the grantor or his or her estate or other designated person.

Concurrent Ownership

Two or more persons may own a piece of real property. This is called **co-ownership**, or **concurrent ownership**. The following forms of co-ownership are recognized: *joint tenancy, tenancy in common, tenancy by the entirety, community property, condominiums*, and *cooperatives*.

co-ownership
A situation in which two or more persons own a piece of real property. Also called *concurrent ownership*.

Joint Tenancy

To create a joint tenancy, words that clearly show a person's intent to create a joint tenancy must be used. Language such as "Marsha Leest and James Leest, as joint tenants" is usually sufficient. The most distinguished feature of a **joint tenancy** is the co-owners' **right of survivorship**. This means that upon the death of one of the **co-owners** (or **joint tenants**), the deceased person's interest in the property automatically passes to the surviving joint tenant or joint tenants. Any contrary provision in the deceased's will is ineffective. Each joint tenant has a right to sell or transfer his or her interest in the property, but such conveyance terminates the joint tenancy. The parties then become tenants in common.

joint tenancy
A form of co-ownership that includes the right of survivorship.

Example
ZiYi, Heathcliff, Manuel, and Mohammad own a large commercial building as joint tenants. They are joint tenants with the right to survivorship. Heathcliff executes a will that leaves all of his property to his alma mater university. Heathcliff dies. The surviving joint tenants—ZiYi, Manuel, and Mohammad—and not the university—acquire Heathcliff's ownership interest in the building. ZiYi, Manuel, and Mohammad are now joint tenants with a one-third interest in the building.

Example
ZiYi, Heathcliff, Manuel, and Mohammad own a large commercial building as joint tenants. They are joint tenants with the right to survivorship. ZiYi sells her one-quarter interest in the building to Wolfgang. At that time, the joint tenancy is broken, and the four owners—Wolfgang, Heathcliff, Manuel, and Mohammad—become tenants in common, with no right of survivorship. Wolfgang executes a will that leaves all of his property to his alma mater university. Wolfgang dies. Because the owners are not joint tenants, but are instead tenants in common, Wolfgang's quarter interest in the building goes to the university. The university is now a tenant in common with Heathcliff, Manuel, and Mohammad.

tenancy in common
A form of co-ownership in which the interest of a surviving tenant in common passes to the deceased tenant's estate and not to the co-tenants.

tenancy by the entirety
A form of co-ownership of real property that can be used only by married couples.

community property
A form of ownership in which each spouse owns an equal one-half share of the income of both spouses and the assets acquired during the marriage.

Property is an instrument of humanity. Humanity is not an instrument of property.

Woodrow Wilson
Speech (1912)

Tenancy in Common

In a **tenancy in common**, the interests of a surviving tenant in common pass to the deceased tenant's estate and not to the co-tenants. A tenancy in common may be created by express words (e.g., "Ian Cespedes and Joy Park, as tenants in common"). Unless otherwise agreed, a tenant in common can sell, give, devise, or otherwise transfer his or her interest in the property without the consent of the other co-owners.

Example

Lopez, who is one of four tenants in common who own a piece of property, has a will that leaves all his property to his granddaughter. When Lopez dies, the granddaughter receives his interest in the tenancy in common, and the granddaughter becomes a tenant in common with the other three owners.

Tenancy by the Entirety

Tenancy by the entirety is a form of co-ownership of real property that can be used only by married couples. This type of tenancy must be created by express words (e.g., "Harold Jones and Maude Jones, husband and wife, as tenants by the entirety"). A surviving spouse has the right of survivorship. Tenancy by the entirety is distinguished from joint tenancy in that neither spouse may sell or transfer his or her interest in the property without the other spouse's consent. Only about half of the states recognize tenancy by the entirety.

Contemporary Environment

Community Property

Nine states—Arizona, California, Idaho, Louisiana, Nevada, New Mexico, Texas, Washington, and Wisconsin—recognize a form of co-ownership known as **community property**. This method of co-ownership applies only to married couples. It is based on the notion that a husband and wife should share equally in the fruits of the marital partnership. Under these laws, each spouse owns an equal one-half share of the *income* both spouses earned during the marriage and one-half of the *assets acquired by this income during the marriage,* regardless of who earns the income. Property that is acquired through gift or inheritance either before or during marriage remains **separate property**. Interest payments, dividends, and appreciation of separate property received or accrued during marriage is also separate property.

When a spouse dies, the surviving spouse automatically receives one-half the community property. The other half passes to the heirs of the deceased spouse, as directed by will or by state intestate statute if there is no will. During the marriage, neither spouse can sell, transfer, or gift community property without the consent of the other spouse. Upon a divorce, each spouse has a right to one-half the community property.

The location of the real property determines whether community property law applies. If a married couple who lives in a non-community property state purchases real property located in a community property state, community property laws apply to that property.

Example

Elma is a successful brain surgeon who makes $500,000 income per year. She meets and marries Brad, a struggling actor who makes $10,000 per year. When Elma gets married, she owns $1 million of real estate and $2 million in securities, which she retains as her separate property. Brad has no separate property when he and Elma are married. After three years, Elma and Brad get a divorce. Assume that Elma has made $500,000 and Brad has made $10,000 each of the three years of their marriage, their living expenses were $110,000 per year, and they have $1,200,000 of earned income saved in a bank account. During the marriage, Elma's real estate has increased in value to $1.5 million, and her securities have increased in value to $3 million. Upon divorce, Elma receives her $1.5 million in real estate and $3 million in securities as her separate property. If they live in a state that recognizes community property, Elma and Brad each receive $600,000 from the community property bank account.

Concept Summary
Concurrent Ownership

Form of Ownership Interest	Right of Survivorship	Tenant May Unilaterally Transfer His or Her
Joint tenancy	Yes, deceased tenant's interest automatically passes to co-tenants.	Yes, tenant may transfer his or her interest without the consent of co-tenants. Transfer severs joint tenancy.
Tenancy in common	No, deceased tenant's interest passes to his or her estate.	Yes, tenant may transfer his or her interest without the consent of co-tenants. Transfer does not sever tenancy in common.
Tenancy by the entirety	Yes, deceased tenant's interest automatically passes to his or her spouse.	No, neither spouse may transfer his or her interest without the other spouse's consent.
Community property	Yes, when a spouse dies, the surviving spouse automatically receives one-half of the community property. The other half passes to the heirs of the deceased spouse, as directed by a valid will or by state intestate statute if there is no will.	No, neither spouse may transfer his or her interest without the other spouse's consent.

Condominium

Condominiums are a common form of ownership in multiple-dwelling buildings. Purchasers of a condominium (1) have title to their individual units and (2) own the common areas (e.g., hallways, elevators, parking areas, recreational facilities) as tenants in common with the other owners. Owners may sell or mortgage their units without the permission of the other owners. Owners are assessed monthly fees for the maintenance of common areas. In addition to being used for dwelling units, the condominium form of ownership is often used for office buildings, boat docks, and such.

condominium
A common form of ownership in a multiple-dwelling building where the purchaser has title to the individual unit and owns the common areas as a tenant in common with the other condominium owners.

Cooperative

A **cooperative** is a form of co-ownership of a multiple-dwelling building in which a corporation owns the building, and the residents own shares in the corporation. Each cooperative owner leases a unit in the building from the corporation under a renewable, long-term, proprietary lease. Individual residents may not secure loans for the units they occupy. The corporation can borrow money on a blanket mortgage, and each shareholder is jointly and severally liable on the loan. Usually, cooperative owners may not sell their shares or sublease their units without the approval of the other owners.

cooperative
A form of co-ownership of a multiple-dwelling building in which a corporation owns the building and the residents own shares in the corporation.

Future Interests

A person may be given the right to possess property in the *future* rather than in the present. This right is called a **future interest**. The two forms of future interests are *reversion* and *remainder*.

future interest
The interest that a grantor retains for him- or herself or a third party.

Reversion

A **reversion** is a right of possession that returns to the grantor after the expiration of a limited or contingent estate. Reversions do not have to be expressly stated because they arise automatically by law.

reversion
A right of possession that returns to the grantor after the expiration of a limited or contingent estate.

Example

Edgar, an owner of real property, conveys his property "to Harriet Lawson for life." The grantor, Edgar, has retained a reversion in the property. That is, when Harriet dies, the property reverts to Edgar or, if he is not living, to his estate.

Remainder

remainder

A right of possession that returns to a third party upon the expiration of a limited or contingent estate.

If the right of possession returns to a *third party* upon the expiration of a limited or contingent estate, it is called a **remainder**. The person who is entitled to the future interest is called a **remainder beneficiary**.

Example

Janice, an owner of real property, conveys her property "to Joe Jackson for life, remainder to Meredith Smith." This creates a vested remainder, with Meredith being the remainder beneficiary. The only contingency to Meredith's possessory interest is Joe's death. When Joe dies, Meredith obtains ownership to the property or, if she is not living, it goes to her estate.

Concept Summary
Future Interests

Future Interest	Description
Reversion	Right to possession of real property returns to the grantor after the expiration of a limited or contingent estate.
Remainder	Right to possession of real property goes to a third person upon the expiration of a limited or contingent estate.

Transfer of Ownership of Real Property

Ownership of real property can be transferred from one person to another. Title to real property can be transferred by sale; tax sale; gift, will, or inheritance; and adverse possession. The different methods of transfer provide different degrees of protection to the transferee.

Sale of Real Estate

sale

The passing of title from a seller to a buyer for a price. Also called a *conveyance*.

A **sale**, or **conveyance**, is the most common method for transferring ownership rights in real property. An owner may offer his or her real estate for sale either by himself or herself or by using a real estate broker. When a buyer has been located and the parties have negotiated the terms of the sale, a **real estate sales contract** is executed by the parties. The Statute of Frauds in most states requires this contract to be in writing.

deed

A writing that describes a person's ownership interest in a piece of real property.

The seller delivers a deed to the buyer, and the buyer pays the purchase price at the **closing**, or **settlement**. Unless otherwise agreed, it is implied that the seller is conveying fee simple absolute title to the buyer. If either party fails to perform, the other party may sue for breach of contract and obtain either monetary damages or specific performance.

grantor

The party who transfers an ownership interest in real property.

Deeds

grantee

The party to whom an interest in real property is transferred.

Deeds are used to convey real property by sale or gift. The seller or donor is called the **grantor**. The buyer or recipient is called the **grantee**. A deed may be used to transfer a fee simple absolute interest in real property or any lesser estate (e.g., life estate). State laws recognize different types of deeds that provide different degrees of protection to grantees. They are:

- A **warranty deed** (i.e., a deed in which the grantor warrants that he or she has clear title to the real property) contains the greatest number of warranties and provides the most protection to a grantee.
- A **quitclaim deed** (i.e., a deed in which the grantor transfers only whatever interest he or she has in the real property) provides the least amount of protection because only the grantor's interest is conveyed.

Recording Statutes

Every state has a **recording statute** which provides that copies of deeds and other documents concerning interests in real property (e.g., mortgages, liens, easements) may be filed in a government office, where they become public records, open to viewing by the public. Recording statutes are intended to prevent fraud and to establish certainty in the ownership and transfer of property. Instruments are usually filed in the **county recorder's office** of the county in which the property is located. A fee is charged to record an instrument.

Persons interested in purchasing property or lending on property should check these records to determine whether the grantor or borrower actually owns the property in question and whether any other parties (e.g., lienholders, mortgages, easement holders) have an interest in the property. The recordation of a deed is not required to pass title from the grantor to the grantee. Recording the deed gives **constructive notice** to the world of the owner's interest in the property.

recording statute
A state statute that requires a mortgage or deed of trust to be recorded in the county recorder's office of the county in which the real property is located.

Quiet Title Action

A party who is concerned about his or her ownership rights in a parcel of real property can bring a **quiet title action**, which is a lawsuit to have a court determine the extent of those rights. Public notice of the hearing must be given so that anyone claiming an interest in the property can appear and be heard. After the hearing, the judge declares who has title to the property; that is, the court "quiets title" by its decision.

quiet title action
An action brought by a party, seeking an order of the court declaring who has title to disputed property. The court "quiets title" by its decision.

Marketable Title

A grantor has the obligation to transfer **marketable title**, or **good title**, to the grantee. Marketable title means that the title is free from any encumbrances, defects of title, or other defects that are not disclosed but would affect the value of the property. The three most common ways of assuring marketable title are as follows:

marketable title
Title to real property that is free from any encumbrances or other defects that are not disclosed but would affect the value of the property. Also called *good title*.

1. **Attorney's opinion.** An attorney examines an **abstract of title** (i.e., a chronological history of the chain of title and encumbrances affecting the property) and renders an **opinion** concerning the status of the title. The attorney can be sued for any losses caused by his or her negligence in rendering the opinion.
2. **Torrens system.** The **Torrens system** is a method of determining title to real property in a judicial proceeding at which everyone claiming an interest in the property can appear and be heard. After the evidence is heard, the court issues a **certificate of title** to the person who is determined to be the rightful owner.
3. **Title insurance.** The best way for a grantee to be sure that he or she has obtained marketable title is to purchase **title insurance** from an insurance company. The title insurer must reimburse the insured for any losses caused by undiscovered defects in title. Each time a property is transferred or refinanced, a new title insurance policy must be obtained.

Tax Sale

If an owner of real property fails to pay property taxes, the government can obtain a lien on the property for the amount of the taxes. If the taxes remain unpaid for a statutory period

tax sale
A method of transferring property ownership that involves a lien on property for unpaid property taxes. If the lien remains unpaid after a certain amount of time, a tax sale is held to satisfy the lien.

The right of property enables an industrious man to reap where he has sown.

Anonymous

adverse possession
A situation in which a person who wrongfully possesses someone else's real property obtains title to that property if certain statutory requirements are met.

The disseisor must unfurl his flag on the land, and keep it flying, so that the owner may see, if he will, that an enemy has invaded his domains, and planted the standard of conquest.

Judge Ellington
Johnson v. Asfaw and Tanus
(2005)

of time, the government can sell the property at a **tax sale** to satisfy the lien. Any excess proceeds are paid to the taxpayer. The buyer receives title to the property. Many states provide a **period of redemption** after a tax sale during which the taxpayer can redeem the property by paying the unpaid taxes and penalties. In these states, the buyer at a tax sale does not receive title to the property until the period of redemption has passed.

Gift, Will, or Inheritance

Ownership of real property can be transferred by **gift**. The gift is made when the deed to the property is delivered by the donor to the donee or to a third party to hold for the donee. No consideration is necessary.

Example

A grandfather wants to give his farm to his granddaughter. To do so, he only has to execute a deed and give the deed to her or to someone to hold for her, such as her parents.

Real property can also be transferred by **will**.

Example

A person may leave a piece of real estate to his best friend by will when he dies. This transfer does not require the transfer of a deed during the testator's lifetime. A deed will be issued to the beneficiary when the will is probated. If a person dies without a valid will, his or her property is distributed to the heirs pursuant to the applicable state interstate statute.

Adverse Possession

In most states, a person who wrongfully possesses someone else's real property obtains title to that property if certain statutory requirements are met. This is called **adverse possession**. Property owned by federal and state governments is not subject to adverse possession.

Under the doctrine of adverse possession, the transfer of the property is involuntary and does not require the delivery of a deed. To obtain title under adverse possession, the wrongful possession must be:

- **For a statutorily prescribed period of time.** In most states, this period is between 10 and 20 years.
- **Open, visible, and notorious.** The adverse possessor must occupy the property so as to put the owner on notice of the possession.
- **Actual and exclusive.** The adverse possessor must physically occupy the premises. The planting of crops, grazing of animals, or building of a structure on the land constitutes physical occupancy.
- **Continuous and peaceful.** The occupancy must be continuous and uninterrupted for the required statutory period. Any break in normal occupancy terminates the adverse possession. This means that the adverse possessor may leave the property to go to work, to the store, on a vacation, and such. The adverse possessor cannot take the property by force from an owner.
- **Hostile and adverse.** The possessor must occupy the property without the express or implied permission of the owner. Thus, a lessee cannot claim title to property under adverse possession.

If the elements of adverse possession are met, the adverse possessor acquires clear title to the land. However, title is acquired only as to the property actually possessed and occupied during the statutory period, and not the entire tract.

Example

An adverse possessor who occupies 1 acre of a 200,000-acre ranch for the statutory period of time acquires title only to the 1 acre.

In the following case, the court had to decide whether the elements for adverse possession had been met.

Witt v. Miller

845 S.W.2d 665, Web 1993 Mo.App. Lexis 20 (1993)
Court of Appeals of Missouri

"Hostility does not imply animosity."

—Judge Gaertner

Facts

Edward and Mary Shaughnessey purchased a 16-acre tract in St. Louis County, Missouri. Subsequently, they subdivided 12 acres into 18 lots offered for sale and retained possession of the remaining 4-acre tract. Thirteen years later, Charles and Elaine Witt purchased lot 12, which is adjacent to the 4-acre tract. The Witts constructed and moved into a house on their lot. The next year, they cleared an area of land that ran the length of their property and extended 40 feet onto the 4-acre tract. The Witts constructed a pool and a deck, planted a garden, made a playground for their children, set up a dog run, and built a fence along the edge of the property line, which included the now-disputed property. Neither the Witts nor the Shaughnesseys realized that the Witts had encroached on the Shaughnesseys' property.

Twenty years later, the Shaughnesseys sold the 4-acre tract to Thomas and Rosanne Miller. When a survey showed the Witts' encroachment, the Millers demanded that the Witts remove the pool and cease using the property. When the Witts refused to do so, the Millers sued to quiet title. The Witts defended, arguing that they had obtained title to the disputed property through adverse possession. The trial court held that there was no adverse possession and ruled in favor of the Millers. The Witts appealed.

Issue

Have the elements for adverse possession been met?

Language of the Court

We address the element of "hostile possession." Hostility does not imply animosity. There is no substantial evidence to support the finding that plaintiffs' possession was not hostile. Plaintiffs testified that they intended to possess the disputed property as their own because they believed it was part of lot 12. That intent manifests itself in plaintiffs' actions which include clearing the area, maintaining the area, planting grass and a garden, erecting a fence, installing playground equipment and a dog run, and building an above ground pool with a deck.

The evidence established plaintiffs' claim to title of the disputed property under adverse possession. The trial court's decision was not supported by substantial evidence and erroneously declared the law.

Decision

The court of appeals held that the Witts had proven the necessary elements for adverse possession under state law. The Witts' occupation of the land was open and notorious, actual and exclusive, hostile and adverse, and continuous and peaceful, and it had occurred for over the statutory period of 10 years. The court of appeals reversed the decision of the trial court and issued an order quieting title to the disputed property in the Witts' favor.

Case Questions

Critical Legal Thinking What does the doctrine of adverse possession provide? What elements need to be proven?

Business Ethics Did the Witts act ethically in claiming title to someone else's land? Should they be allowed to benefit from their own mistake?

Contemporary Business What should owners of property do to protect themselves from adverse possession claims? Explain.

Nonpossessory Interests

nonpossessory interest
A situation in which a person holds an interest in another person's property without actually owning any part of the property.
easement
A given or required right to make limited use of someone else's land without owning or leasing it.

A person can own a **nonpossessory interest** in another's real estate. Three nonpossessory interests—*easement*, *license*, and *profit*—are discussed in the following paragraphs.

Easement

An **easement** is an interest in land that gives the holder the right to make limited use of another's property without taking anything from it. Typical easements are common driveways, party walls, and rights-of-way. Easements can be expressly created by *grant* (where an owner gives another party an easement across his or her property) or *reservation* (where an owner sells land that he or she owns but reserves an easement on the land). Easement can also be implied by (1) *implication*, where an owner subdivides a piece of property with a well, path, road, or other beneficial appurtenant that serves the entire parcel, or by (2) *necessity*—for example, where "landlocked" property has an implied easement across surrounding property to enter and exit the landlocked property. Easements can also be created by *prescription*—that is, by adverse possession.

There are two types of easements: *easements appurtenant* and *easements in gross*. These are described in the following paragraphs.

easement appurtenant
A situation created when the owner of one piece of land is given an easement over an adjacent piece of land.

Easements Appurtenant   An **easement appurtenant** is created when the owner of one piece of land is given an easement over an adjacent piece of land. The land over which the easement is granted is called the **servient estate**. The land that benefits from the easement is called the **dominant estate**. *Adjacent land* is defined as two estates that are in proximity to each other but that do not necessarily abut each other. An appurtenant easement runs with the land.

Example
If an owner sells the dominant estate, the new owner acquires the benefit of the easement. If an owner sells the servient estate, the buyer purchases the property subject to the easement.

easement in gross
An easement that authorizes a person who does not own adjacent land to use another's land.

Easements in Gross   An **easement in gross** authorizes a person who does not own adjacent land the right to use another person's land. An easement in gross is a personal right because it does not depend on the easement holder owning adjacent land. Thus, there is no dominant estate.

Examples
Easements in gross include those granted to run power, telephone, and cable television lines across an owner's property. Commercial easements in gross run with the land.

The easement holder owes a duty to maintain and repair the easement. The owner of the estate can use the property as long as doing so does not interfere with the easement.

Example
If a piece of property is subject to an easement for an underground pipeline, the owner of the property could graze cattle or plant crops on the land above the easement, subject to the easement holder's right to repair the pipeline.

In the following case, the court had to decide whether an implied easement had been created.

License

license
A document that grants a person the right to enter upon another's property for a specified and usually short period of time.

A **license** grants a person the right to enter upon another's property for a specified and usually short period of time. The person granting the license is called the **licensor;** the person receiving the license is called the **licensee**.

Example
A ticket to a movie theater or sporting event that grants the holder the right to enter the premises for the performance is a common license. A license does not transfer any inter-

CASE 17.2
Implied Easement

Walker v. Ayres

Web 1993 Del. Lexis 105 (1993)
Supreme Court of Delaware

"An implied easement was created by the severance which landlocked Bluff Point."

—Judge Moore

Facts

Elizabeth Star Ayres and Clara Louise Quillen owned in fee simple absolute a tract of land in Sussex County known as "Bluff Point." The tract was surrounded on three sides by Rehoboth Bay and was landlocked on the fourth side by land owned by Irvin C. Walker. At one time, the two tracts were held by a common owner. In 1878, Bluff Point was sold in fee simple absolute apart from the other holdings, thereby landlocking the parcel. A narrow dirt road, which traversed Walker's land, connected Bluff Point to a public road and was its only means of access to Bluff Point. Ayres and Quillen sought an easement to use this road, and Walker objected. This lawsuit ensued. The trial court granted an easement to Ayres and Quillen. Walker appealed.

Issue

Should Ayres and Quillen's estate be granted an easement against Walker's estate?

Language of the Court

Based upon our review of the record, we conclude that the factual findings of the trial court are clearly sustainable. There is ample evidence in the record to support the finding that the two tracts originated from the unified holdings of one owner, and that an implied ease-ment was created by the severance which landlocked Bluff Point. The record also sufficiently supports the finding that navigable access to Bluff Point was not feasible.

Decision

The supreme court of Delaware held that an implied easement had been created. The supreme court affirmed the trial court's judgment, granting Ayres and Quillen an easement to use the road that traversed Walker's property.

Case Questions

Critical Legal Thinking   What is an easement? Should easements be recognized by the law? Why or why not?

Business Ethics   Did Walker act ethically in denying the easement? Did Ayres and Quillen act ethically in seeking to use Walker's property?

Contemporary Business   Do easements across a person's property increase or decrease the value of their property? Does an easement increase or decrease the value of the easement holder's property?

est in the property. A license is a personal privilege that may be revoked by the licensor at any time.

Profit

A *profit-à-prendre* (or **profit**) gives the holder the right to remove something from another's real property.

Examples

Examples of profit are rights to remove gravel, minerals, grain, or timber from another person's property.

profit
A document that grants a person the right to remove something from another's real property. Also known as *profit-à-prendre*.

Concept Summary
Nonpossessory Interests

Nonpossessory Interest	Description
Easement appurtenant	Is an easement over a servient estate that benefits a dominant estate. The easement runs with the land.
Easement in gross	Is an easement that grants a person a right to use another's land. It is a personal right that does not run with the land.
License	Grants a person the right to enter upon another's real property for a specified event or time (e.g., for a concert).
Profit	Grants the holder the right to remove something from another's real property (e.g., timber, grain).

Zoning

zoning ordinances
Local laws that are adopted by municipalities and local governments to regulate land use within their boundaries.

Most counties and municipalities have enacted **zoning ordinances** to regulate land use. Zoning ordinances generally (1) establish use districts within the municipality (i.e., areas are generally designated residential, commercial, or industrial); (2) restrict the height, size, and location of buildings on a building site; and (3) establish aesthetic requirements or limitations for the exterior of buildings.

A **zoning commission** usually formulates zoning ordinances, conducts public hearings, and makes recommendations to the city council, which must vote to enact an ordinance. Once a zoning ordinance is enacted, the zoning ordinance commission enforces it. If landowners believe that a zoning ordinance is illegal or that it has been unlawfully applied to them or their property, they may institute a court proceeding, seeking judicial review of the ordinance or its application.

variance
An exception that permits a type of building or use in an area that would not otherwise be allowed by a zoning ordinance.

nonconforming uses
Uses and buildings that already exist in a zoned area that are permitted to continue even though they do not fit within new zoning ordinances.

An owner who wants to use his or her property for a use different from that permitted under a current zoning ordinance may seek relief from the ordinance by obtaining a **variance**. To obtain a variance, the landowner must prove that the ordinance causes an undue hardship by preventing him or her from making a reasonable return on the land as zoned. Variances are usually difficult to obtain.

Zoning laws act prospectively; that is, uses and buildings that already exist in the zoned area are permitted to continue even though they do not fit within new zoning ordinances. Such uses are called **nonconforming uses**. For example, if a new zoning ordinance is enacted, making an area a residential zone, an existing funeral parlor is a nonconforming use.

Test Review Terms and Concepts

Abstract of title	Co-ownership (concurrent ownership)	Future interest
Adverse possession	County recorder's office	Gift
Air rights	Deed	Grantee
Air space parcel	Dominant estate	Grantor
Attorney's opinion	Easement	Joint tenancy
Buildings	Easement appurtenant	Land
Certificate of title	Easement in gross	License
Closing (settlement)	Estate in land (estate)	Licensee
Community property	*Estate pour autre vie*	Licensor
Condominium	Fee simple absolute (fee simple)	Life estate
Constructive notice	Fee simple defeasible (qualified fee)	Marketable title (good title)
Cooperative	Fixtures	Nonconforming use
Co-owners (joint tenants)	Freehold estate	Nonpossessory interest

Period of redemption
Plant life and vegetation
Profit-à-prendre (profit)
Quiet title action
Quitclaim deed
Real estate sales contract
Real property
Recording statute
Remainder

Remainder beneficiary
Reversion
Right of survivorship
Sale (conveyance)
Separate property
Servient estate
Subsurface rights (mineral rights)
Surface rights
Tax sale

Tenancy by the entirety
Tenancy in common
Title insurance
Torrens system
Variance
Warranty deed
Will
Zoning commission
Zoning ordinance

Case Problems

17.1 Subsurface Rights: In 1883, Isaac McIlwee owned 100 acres of land in Valley Township, Guernsey Country, Ohio. In that year, he sold the property to Akron & Cambridge Coal Company (Akron & Cambridge) in fee simple but reserved in fee simple "the surface of all said lands" to himself. Over the years, the interests in the land were transferred to many different parties. One hundred years after McIlwee's transfer of an interest in the property to Akron & Cambridge, the Mid-Ohio Coal Company owned the rights originally transferred to Akron & Cambridge, and Peter and Irene Minnich owned the rights reserved by Isaac McIlwee in 1883. The Minniches claimed that they possessed subsurface rights to the property except for coal rights. Who wins? *Minnich v. Guernsey Savings and Loan Company*, 36 Ohio App.3d 54, 521 N.E.2d 489, **Web** 1987 OhioApp. Lexis 10497 (Court of Appeals of Ohio)

17.2 Life Estate and Remainder: Baudilio Bowles died testate. His will devised to his sister, Julianita B. Vigil, "one-half of any income, rents, or profits from any real property located in Bull Creek or Colonias, New Mexico." The will contained another clause that left to his children "my interest in any real property owned by me at the time of my death, located in Bull Creek and/or Colonias, San Miguel County." The property referred to in both devises was the same property. Julianita died before the will was probated. Her heirs claimed a one-half ownership interest in the real property. Bowles's children asserted that they owned all his property. Who wins? *In the Matter of the Estate of Bowles*, 107 N.M. 739, 764 P.2d 510, **Web** 1988 N.M.App. Lexis 93 (Court of Appeals of New Mexico)

17.3 Reversion: W.E. and Jennie Hutton conveyed land they owned to the Trustees of Schools of District Number One of the Town of Allison, Illinois (School District), by warranty deed "to be used for school purpose only; otherwise to revert to Grantor." The School District built a school on the site, commonly known as Hutton School. The Huttons conveyed the adjoining farmland and their reversionary interest in the school site to the Jacqmains, who in turn conveyed their interest to Herbert and Betty Mahrenholz. The 1.5-acre site sits in the middle of Mahrenhoz's farmland. Over 30 years after School District built the school, School District discontinued holding regular classes at Hutton School. Instead, it used the school building to warehouse and store miscellaneous school equipment, supplies, unused desks, and the like. Mahrenholz filed suit to quiet title to the school property to them. Who wins? *Mahrenholz v. County Board of School Trustees of Lawrence County*, 188 Ill.App.3d 260, 544 N.E.2d 128, **Web** 1989 Ill.App. Lexis 1445 (Appellate Court of Illinois)

17.4 Joint Tenancy: Verna M. Chappell owned a piece of real property. On June 16, 1965, Chappell transferred the property to herself and her niece, Bertha M. Stewart, as joint tenants. When Chappell died in 1981, Chappell's gross estate was set at $28,321, which included the value of the house. Claims, debts, and charges against the estate totaled $19,451, which included a $14,040 claim by Lorna M. Rembe for services provided as conservator. The probate assets available to pay the claims and debts came to only $1,571 if the real property went to Stewart as the joint tenant. Rembe sued, alleging that the value of the real property should be used to pay off Chappell's debts and claims. Who wins? *Rembe v. Stewart*, 387 N.W.2d 313, **Web** 1986 Iowa Sup. Lexis 1177 (Supreme Court of Iowa)

17.5 Tenancy by the Entirety: Charles Jetter Eichman and his wife, Cora Paton Eichman, were married on August 12, 1965. In 1968, they purchased a house in Tallahassee, Florida, taking title in their joint names as husband and wife, thus creating a tenancy by the entirety. In 1971, they separated, and Cora moved to Vancouver, Canada. Charles continued to live in the marital home in Florida. In January 1975, Cora filed a petition for divorce. On March 31, 1975, Charles struck Cora on the head with a pipe, causing injuries that rendered her incapable of managing herself or her affairs and bringing to an end the divorce proceeding. A guardian was appointed for her. Charles was convicted of attempted murder and was sentenced to prison for 10 years. Cora's guardian filed an action, seeking to partition the marital property located in Florida. Charles answered, alleging that an estate by the entirety is not subject to partition as long as the parties remain married. Who wins? *Eichman v. Paton*, 393 So.2d 655, **Web** 1981 Fla.App. Lexis 19454 (District Court of Appeal of Florida)

17.6 Community Property: Daniel T. Yu and his wife, Bernice, owned a house and two lots as community property. Yu entered into an agreement with Arch, Ltd. (Arch), whereby he agreed to exchange these properties for two office buildings owned by Arch. Yu signed the agreement, but his wife did not. At the date set for closing, Arch performed its obligations under the agreement, executed all documents, and was prepared to transfer title to its properties to Yu. Yu, however, refused to perform his obligations under the agreement. Evidence showed that the office buildings had decreased in value from $800,000 to $700,000 from the date of the agreement to the date set for closing. Arch sued Yu to recover damages for breach of contract. Who wins? *Arch, Ltd. v. Yu*, 108 N.M. 67, 766 P.2d 911, **Web** 1988 N.M. Lexis 330 (Supreme Court of New Mexico)

17.7 Easement in Gross: John L. Yutterman died, leaving one piece of property, located in Fort Smith, Arkansas, to his two sons and two daughters. Each child received approximately one-fourth of the property in fee simple. A 40-foot driveway divided the property. Concerning the driveway, Yutterman's will provided as follows: "Further, a specific condition of this will and of these devises is that the forty (40) foot driveway from Free Ferry Road, three hundred (300) feet Northward, shall be kept open for the common use of the devisees in this will." Subsequently, one of the daughters wanted to sell her property to a third party. If the third party purchases the property, will that party have an easement to use the driveway? *Merriman v. Yutterman*, 291 Ark. 207, 723 S.W.2d 823, **Web** 1987 Ark. Lexis 1934 (Supreme Court of Arkansas)

17.8 Adverse Possession: Joseph and Helen Naab purchased a tract of land in a subdivision of Williamstown, West Virginia. At the time of purchase, there were both a house and a small concrete garage on the property. Evidence showed that the garage had been erected sometime prior to 20 years earlier by one of the Naabs' predecessors in title. Two years after the Naabs bought their property, Roger and Cynthia Nolan pur-

chased a lot contiguous to that owned by the Naabs. The following year, the Nolans had their property surveyed. The survey indicated that one corner of the Naabs' garage encroached 1.22 feet onto the Nolans' property and the other corner encroached 0.91 feet over the property line. The Nolans requested that the Naabs remove the garage from their property. When the Naabs refused, a lawsuit ensued. Who wins? *Naab v. Nolan*, 174 W.Va. 390, 327 S.E.2d 151, **Web** 1985 W.Va. Lexis 476 (Supreme Court of Appeals of West Virginia)

17.9 Zoning: The city of Ladue is one of the wealthy suburban residential areas of metropolitan St. Louis. The homes in the city are considerably more expensive than those in surrounding areas and consist of homes of traditional design, such as colonial, French provincial, and English. The city set up an architectural board to approve plans for buildings that:

> Conform to certain minimum architectural standards of appearance and conformity with surrounding structures, and that unsightly, grotesque, and unsuitable structures, detrimental to the stability of value and the welfare of surrounding property, structures, and residents, and to the general welfare and happiness of the community, be avoided.

The owner of a lot in the city submitted a plan to build a house of ultramodern design. It was pyramid shaped, with a flat top and triangular-shaped windows and doors. Although the house plans met other city zoning ordinances and building codes, the architectural board rejected the owner's petition for a building permit, based on aesthetic reasons. The owner sued the city. Who wins? *State of Missouri v. Berkeley*, 458 S.W.2d 305, **Web** 1970 Mo. Lexis 902 (Supreme Court of Missouri)

Business Ethics Cases

17.10 Business Ethics: Victor and Phyllis Garber acquired a piece of real property by warranty deed. The deed was recorded. The property consisted of 80 acres enclosed by a fence that had been in place for over 50 years. The enclosed area was used to graze cattle and produce hay. Ten years after the Garbers acquired their property, William and Herbert Doenz acquired a piece of real property adjacent to the Garbers' and employed a surveyor to locate their land's boundaries. As a result of the survey, it was discovered that the shared fence was 20 to 30 feet inside the deed line on the Doenz property. The amount of property between the old fence and the deed line was 3.01 acres. The Doenzes removed the old fence and constructed a new fence along the deed line. The Garbers brought suit to quiet title. Did the Doenzes act ethically in removing the fence? Did the Garbers act ethically in claiming title to property that originally belonged with the adjacent property? Have the Garbers

acquired title to the property between the fence and the deed through adverse possession? *Doenz v. Garber*, 665 P.2d 932, **Web** 1983 Wyo. Lexis 339 (Supreme Court of Wyoming)

17.11 Business Ethics: The town of Hempstead, New Hampshire, enacted a zoning ordinance "in order to retain the beauty and countrified atmosphere of the town, and to promote health, safety, morals, order, convenience, peace, prosperity, and general welfare of its inhabitants." To preserve abutting property owners' views and light, the ordinance limits the homes in the town to one-and-one-half stories. In violation of the ordinance, John M. Alexander built a shell of a second story and a new roof on his house. After the town ordered him to halt construction and denied him permission to occupy the second floor, he applied for a variance. Should the variance be granted? Did John M. Alexander act ethically in this case? *Alexander v. Town of Hempstead*, 129 N.H. 278, 525 A.2d 276, **Web** 1987 N.H. Lexis 171 (Supreme Court of New Hampshire)

The Constitution of the United States of America

APPENDIX A

We the People of the United States, in Order to form a more perfect Union, establish Justice, insure domestic Tranquility, provide for the common defense, promote the general Welfare, and secure the Blessings of Liberty to ourselves and our Posterity, do ordain and establish this Constitution for the United States of America.

Article I

Section 1. All legislative Powers herein granted shall be vested in a Congress of the United States, which shall consist of a Senate and House of Representatives.

Section 2. The House of Representatives shall be composed of Members chosen every second Year by the People of the several states, and the Electors in each State shall have the Qualifications requisite for Electors of the most numerous Branch of the State Legislature.

No Person shall be a Representative who shall not have attained to the Age of twenty five Years, and been seven Years a Citizen of the United States, and who shall not, when elected, be an Inhabitant of that State in which he shall be chosen.

Representatives and direct Taxes shall be apportioned among the several states which may be included within this Union, according to their respective Numbers, which shall be determined by adding to the whole Number of free Persons, including those bound to Service for a Term of Years, and excluding Indians not taxed, three fifths of all other Persons. The actual Enumeration shall be made within three Years after the first Meeting of the Congress of the United States, and within every subsequent Term of ten Years, in such Manner as they shall by Law direct. The number of Representatives shall not exceed one for every thirty Thousand, but each State shall have at Least one Representative; and until such enumeration shall be made, the State of New Hamp-shire shall be entitled to chuse three, Massachusetts eight, Rhode Island and Providence Plantations one, Connecticut five, New York six, New Jersey four, Pennsylvania eight, Delaware one, Maryland six, Virginia ten, North Carolina five, South Carolina five, and Georgia three.

When vacancies happen in the Representation from any State, the Executive Authority thereof shall issue Writs of Election to fill such vacancies.

The House of Representatives shall chuse their Speaker and other Officers; and shall have the sole Power of Impeachment.

Section 3. The Senate of the United States shall be composed of two Senators from each State, chosen by the Legislature thereof, for six Years; and each Senator shall have one Vote.

Immediately after they shall be assembled in Consequence of the first Election, they shall be divided as equally as may be into three Classes. The Seats of the Senators of the first Class shall be vacated at the Expiration of the second Year, of the second Class at the Expiration of the fourth Year, and the third Class at the Expiration of the sixth Year, so that one third may be chosen every second Year; and if Vacancies happen by Resignation, or otherwise, during the Recess of the Legislature of any State, the Executive thereof may make temporary Appointments until the next meeting of the Legislature, which shall then fill such Vacancies.

No person shall be a Senator who shall not have attained to the Age of thirty Years, and been nine Years a Citizen of the United States, and who shall not, when elected, be an Inhabitant of that State for which he shall be chosen.

The Vice President of the United States shall be President of the Senate, but shall have no Vote, unless they be equally divided.

The Senate shall chuse their other Officers, and also a President pro tempore, in the Absence of the Vice President, or when he shall exercise the Office of President of the United States.

The Senate shall have the sole power to try all Impeachments. When sitting for that Purpose, they shall be an Oath or Affirmation. When the President of the United States is tried, the Chief Justice shall preside: And no Person shall be convicted without the Concurrence of two thirds of the Members present.

Judgment in Cases of Impeachment shall not extend further than to removal from Office, and disqualification to hold and enjoy any Office of honor, Trust or Profit under the United States: but the Party convicted shall nevertheless be liable and subject to Indictment, Trial, Judgment and Punishment, according to Law.

Section 4. The Times, Places and Manner of holding Elections for Senators and Representatives, shall be prescribed in each State by the Legislature thereof: but the Congress may at any time by Law make or alter such Regulations, except as to the Places of choosing Senators.

The Congress shall assemble at least once in every Year, and such Meeting shall be on the first Monday in December, unless they shall by Law appoint a different day.

Section 5. Each House shall be the Judge of the Elections, Returns and Qualifications of its own Members, and a

Majority of each shall constitute a Quorum to do Business; but a smaller Number may adjourn from day to day, and may be authorized to compel the Attendance of absent Members, in such Manner, and under such Penalties as each House may provide.

Each House may determine the Rules of its Proceedings, punish its Members for disorderly Behaviour, and, with the Concurrence of two thirds, expel a Member.

Each House shall keep a Journal of its Proceedings, and from time to time publish the same, excepting such Parts as may in their Judgment require Secrecy; and the Yeas and Nays of the Members of either House on any question shall, at the Desire of one fifth of those Present, be entered on the Journal.

Neither House, during the Session of Congress, shall, without the Consent of the other, adjourn for more than three days, nor to any other Place than that in which the two Houses shall be sitting.

Section 6. The Senators and Representatives shall receive a Compensation for their Services, to be ascertained by Law, and paid out of the Treasury of the United States. They shall in all Cases, except Treason, Felony and Breach of the Peace, be privileged from Arrest during their Attendance at the Session of their respective Houses, and in going to and returning from the same; and for any Speech or Debate in either House, they shall not be questioned in any other Place.

No Senator or Representative shall, during the Time for which he was elected, be appointed to any civil Office under the Authority of the United States, which shall have been created, or the Emoluments whereof shall have been encreased during such time; and no Person holding any Office under the United States, shall be a Member of either House during his Continuance in Office.

Section 7. All Bills for raising Revenue shall originate in the House of Representatives; but the Senate may propose or concur with Amendments as on other Bills.

Every Bill which shall have passed the House of Representatives and the Senate, shall, before it become a Law, be presented to the President of the United States; If he approve he shall sign it, but if not he shall return it, with his Objections to that House in which it shall have originated, who shall enter the Objections at large on their Journal, and proceed to reconsider it. If after such Reconsideration two thirds of that House shall agree to pass the Bill, it shall be sent, together with the Objections, to the other House, by which it shall likewise be reconsidered, and if approved by two thirds of that House, it shall become a Law. But in all such Cases the Votes of both Houses shall be determined by Yeas and Nays, and the Names of the Persons voting for and against the Bill shall be entered on the Journal of each House respectively. If any Bill shall not be returned by the President within ten Days (Sundays excepted) after it shall have been presented to him, the Same shall be a Law, in like Manner as if he had signed it, unless the Congress by their Adjournment prevent its Return, in which Case it shall not be a Law.

Every Order, Resolution, or Vote to which the Concurrence of the Senate and House of Representatives may be necessary (except on a question of Adjournment) shall be presented to the President of the United States; and before the Same shall take Effect, shall be approved by him, or being disapproved by him, shall be repassed by two thirds of the Senate and House of Representatives, according to the Rules and Limitations prescribed in the Case of a Bill.

Section 8. The Congress shall have Power to lay and collect Taxes, Duties, Imposts and Excises, to pay the Debts and provide for the common Defence and general Welfare of the United States; but all Duties, Imposts and Excises shall be uniform throughout the United States;

To borrow Money on the credit of the United States;

To regulate Commerce with foreign Nations, and among the several States, and with the Indian Tribes;

To establish an uniform Rule of Naturalization, and uniform Laws on the subject of Bankruptcies throughout the United States;

To coin Money, regulate the Value thereof, and of foreign Coin, and fix the Standard of Weights and Measures;

To provide for the Punishment of counterfeiting the Securities and current Coin of the United States;

To establish Post Offices and post Roads;

To promote the Progress of Science and useful Arts, by securing for limited Times to Authors and Inventors the exclusive Right to their respective Writings and Discoveries;

To constitute Tribunals inferior to the supreme Court;

To define and punish Piracies and Felonies committed on the high Seas, and Offenses against the Law of Nations;

To declare War, grant Letters of Marque and Reprisal, and make Rules concerning Captures on Land and Water;

To raise and support Armies, but no Appropriation of Money to that Use shall be for a longer Term than two Years;

To provide and maintain a Navy;

To make Rules for the Government and Regulation of the land and naval Forces;

To provide for calling forth the Militia to execute the Laws of the Union, suppress Insurrections and repel Invasions;

To provide for organizing, arming, and disciplining, the Militia, and for governing such Part of them as may be employed in the Service of the United States, reserving to the States respectively, the Appointment of the Officers, and the Authority of training the Militia according to the discipline prescribed by Congress;

To exercise exclusive Legislation in all Cases whatsoever, over such District (not exceeding ten Miles square) as may, by Cession of particular States, and the Acceptance of Congress, become the Seat of the Government of the United States, and to exercise like Authority over all Places purchased by the Consent of the Legislature of the State in which the Same shall be, for the Erection of Forts, Magazines, Arsenals, dock-Yards, and other needful Buildings;—And

To make all Laws which shall be necessary and proper for carrying into Execution the foregoing Powers, and all other Powers vested by this Constitution in the Government of the United States, or in any Department or Officer thereof.

Section 9. The Migration or Importation of such Persons as any of the States now existing shall think proper to admit, shall not be prohibited by the Congress prior to the Year one thousand eight hundred and eight, but a Tax or Duty may be imposed on such Importation, not exceeding ten dollars for each Person.

The Privilege of the Writ of Habeas Corpus shall not be suspended, unless when in Cases of Rebellion or Invasion the public Safety may require it.

No Bill of Attainder or ex post facto Law shall be passed.

No Capitation, or other direct, Tax shall be laid, unless in Proportion to the Census or Enumeration herein before directed to be taken.

No Tax or Duty shall be laid on Articles exported from any State.

No Preference shall be given by any Regulation of Commerce or Revenue to the Ports of one State over those of another; nor shall Vessels bound to, or from, one State, be obliged to enter, clear, or pay Duties in another.

No Money shall be drawn from the Treasury, but in Consequence of Appropriations made by Laws; and a regular Statement and Account of the Receipts and Expenditures of all public Money shall be published from time to time.

No Title of Nobility shall be granted by the United States: And no Person holding any Office of Profit or Trust under them, shall, without the Consent of the Congress, accept of any present, Emolument, Office, or Title, of any kind whatever, from any King, Prince, or foreign State.

Section 10. No State shall enter into any Treaty, Alliance, or Confederation; grant Letters of Marque and Reprisal; coin Money; emit Bills of Credit; make any Thing but gold and silver Coin a Tender in Payment of Debts; pass any Bill of Attainder, ex post facto Law, or Law impairing the Obligation of Contracts, or grant any Title of Nobility.

No State shall, without the Consent of the Congress, lay any Imposts or Duties on Imports or Exports, except what may be absolutely necessary for executing its inspection Laws: and the net Produce of all Duties and Imposts, laid by any State on Imports or Exports, shall be for the Use of the Treasury of the United States; and all such Laws shall be subject to the Revision and Control of the Congress.

No State shall, without the Consent of Congress, lay any Duty of Tonnage, keep Troops, or Ships of War in time of Peace, enter into any Agreement or Compact with another State, or with a foreign Power, or engage in War, unless actually invaded, or in such imminent Danger as will not admit of delay.

Article II

Section 1. The executive Power shall be vested in a President of the United States of America. He shall hold his Office during the Term of four Years, and, together with the Vice President, chosen for the same Term, be elected, as follows:

Each State shall appoint, in such Manner as the Legislature thereof may direct, a Number of Electors, equal to the whole Number of Senators and Representatives to which the State may be entitled in the Congress: but no Senator or Representative, or Person holding an Office of Trust or Profit under the United States, shall be appointed an Elector.

The Electors shall meet in their respective States, and vote by Ballot for two Persons, of whom one at least shall not be an Inhabitant of the same State with themselves. And they shall make a list of all the Persons voted for, and of the Number of Votes for each; which List they shall sign and certify, and transmit sealed to the Seat of the Government of the United States, directed to the President of the Senate. The President of the Senate shall, in the presence of the Senate and House of Representatives, open all the Certificates, and the Votes shall be counted. The Person having the greatest Number of Votes shall be the President, if such Number be a Majority of the whole Number of Electors appointed; and if there be more than one who have such Majority, and have an equal Number of Votes, then the House of Representatives shall immediately choose by Ballot one of them for President; and if no Person have a Majority, then from the five highest on the List the said House shall in like Manner choose the President. But in chusing the President, the Votes shall be taken by States, the Representation from each State having one Vote; A quorum for this Purpose shall consist of a Member or Members from two thirds of the States, and a Majority of all the States shall be necessary to a Choice. In every Case, after the Choice of the President, the Person having the greatest Number of Votes of the Electors shall be the Vice President. But if there should remain two or more who have equal Votes, the Senate shall chuse from them by Ballot the Vice President.

The Congress may determine the Time of Chusing the Electors, and the Day on which they shall give their Votes; which Day shall be the same throughout the United States.

No Person except a natural born Citizen, or a Citizen of the United States, at the time of the Adoption of this Constitution, shall be eligible to the Office of President; neither shall any Person be eligible to that Office who shall not have attained to the Age of thirty five Years, and been fourteen Years a Resident within the United States.

In Case of the Removal of the President from Office, or of his Death, Resignation, or Inability to discharge the Powers and Duties of the said Office, the Same shall devolve on the Vice President, and the Congress may by Law provide for the Case of Removal, Death, Resignation or Inability, both of the President and Vice President, declaring what Officer shall then act as President, and such Officer shall act accordingly, until the Disability be removed, or a President shall be elected.

The President shall, at stated Times, receive for his Services, a Compensation, which shall neither be encreased nor diminished during the Period for which he shall have been elected, and he shall not receive within that Period any other Emolument from the United States, or any of them.

Before he enter on the Execution of his Office, he shall take the following Oath or Affirmation:—"I do solemnly swear (or affirm) that I will faithfully execute the Office of President of the United States, and will to the best of my Ability, preserve, protect and defend the Constitution of the United States."

Section 2. The President shall be Commander in Chief of the Army and Navy of the United States, and of the Militia of the several States, when called into the actual Service of the United States; he may require the Opinion, in writing, of the principal Officer in each of the executive Departments, upon any Subject relating to the Duties of their respective Offices, and he shall have Power to grant Reprieves and Pardons for Offences against the United States, except in Cases of Impeachment.

He shall have Power, by and with the Advice and Consent of the Senate, to make Treaties, provided two thirds of the Senators present concur; and he shall nominate, and by and with the Advice and Consent of the Senate, shall appoint Ambassadors, other public Ministers and Consuls, Judges of the supreme Court, and all other Officers of the United States, whose Appointments are not herein otherwise provided for, and which shall be established by Law: but the Congress may by Law vest the Appointment of such inferior Officers, as they think proper, in the President alone, in the Courts of Law, or in the Heads of Departments.

The President shall have Power to fill up all Vacancies that may happen during the Recess of the Senate, by granting Commissions which shall expire at the End of their next Session.

Section 3. He shall from time to time give to the Congress Information of the State of the Union, and recommend to their Consideration such Measures as he shall judge necessary and expedient; he may, on extraordinary Occasions, convene both Houses, or either of them, and in Case of Disagreement between them, with Respect to the Time of Adjournment, he may adjourn them to such Time as he shall think proper; he shall receive Ambassadors and other public Ministers; he shall take Care that the Laws be faithfully executed, and shall Commission all the Officers of the United States.

Section 4. The President, Vice President and all civil Officers of the United States, shall be removed from Office on Impeachment for, and Conviction of, Treason, Bribery, or other high Crimes and Misdemeanors.

Article III

Section 1. The judicial Power of the United States, shall be vested in one supreme Court, and in such inferior Courts as the Congress may from time to time ordain and establish. The Judges, both of the supreme and inferior Courts, shall hold their Offices during good Behaviour, and shall, at Times, receive for their Services, a Compensation, which shall not be diminished during their Continuance in Office.

Section 2. The judicial Power shall extend to all Cases, in Law and Equity, arising under this Constitution, the Laws of the United States, and Treaties made, or which shall be made, under their Authority;—to all Cases affecting Ambassadors, other public Ministers and Consuls;—to all Cases of admiralty and maritime Jurisdiction;—to Controversies to which the United States shall be a Party;—to controversies between two or more States;—between a State and Citizens of another State;—between Citizens of different States;—between Citizens of the same State claiming Lands under Grants of different States, and between a State, or the Citizens thereof, and foreign States, Citizens or Subjects.

In all Cases affecting Ambassadors, other public Ministers and Consuls, and those in which a State shall be Party, the supreme Court shall have original Jurisdiction. In all the other Cases before mentioned, the supreme Court shall have appellate Jurisdiction, both as to Law and Fact, with such Exceptions, and under such Regulations as the Congress shall make.

The Trial of all Crimes, except in Cases of Impeachment, shall be by Jury; and such Trial shall be held in the State where the said Crimes shall have been committed; but when not committed within any State, the Trial shall be at such Place or Places as the Congress may by Law have directed.

Section 3. Treason against the United States, shall consist only in levying War against them, or in adhering to their Enemies, giving them Aid and Comfort. No Person shall be convicted of Treason unless on the Testimony of two Witnesses to the same overt Act, or on Confession in open Court.

The Congress shall have Power to declare the Punishment of Treason, but no Attainder of Treason shall work Corruption of Blood, or Forfeiture except during the Life of the Person attainted.

Article IV

Section 1. Full Faith and Credit shall be given in each State to the public Acts, Records, and judicial Proceedings of every other State. And the Congress may by general Laws prescribe the Manner in which such Arts, Records, and Proceedings shall be proved, and the Effect thereof.

Section 2. The Citizens of each State shall be entitled to all Privileges and Immunities of Citizens in the several States.

A person charged in any State with Treason, Felony, or other Crime, who shall flee from Justice, and be found in another State, shall on Demand of the executive Authority of the State from which he fled, be delivered up, to be removed to the State having Jurisdiction of the Crime.

No Person held to Service or Labour in one State, under the Laws thereof, escaping into another, shall, in Consequence of any Law or Regulation therein, be discharged from such Service or Labour, but shall be delivered up on Claim of the Party to whom such Service or Labour may be due.

Section 3. New States may be admitted by the Congress into this Union; but no new state shall be formed or erected within the Jurisdiction of any other State; nor any State be formed by the Junction of two or more States, or Parts of States, without the Consent of the Legislatures of the States concerned as well as of the Congress.

The Congress shall have Power to dispose of and make all needful Rules and Regulations respecting the Territory or other Property belonging to the United States; and nothing in this Constitution shall be so construed as to Prejudice any Claims of the United States, or of any particular State.

Section 4. The United States shall guarantee to every State in this Union a Republican Form of Government, and shall protect each of them against Invasion; and on Application of the Legislature, or of the Executive (when the Legislature cannot be convened) against domestic Violence.

Article V

The Congress, whenever two thirds of both Houses shall deem it necessary, shall propose Amendments to this Constitution, or, on the Application of the Legislatures of two thirds of the several States, shall call a Convention for proposing Amendments, which, in either Case, shall be valid to all Intents and Purposes, as Part of this Constitution, when ratified by the Legislatures of three fourths of the several States, or by Conventions in three fourths thereof, as the one or the other Mode of Ratification may be proposed by the Congress; Provided that no Amendment which may be made prior to the Year One thousand eight hundred and eight shall in any Manner affect the first and fourth Clauses in the Ninth Section of the first Article; and that no State, without its Consent, shall be deprived of its equal Suffrage in the Senate.

Article VI

All Debts contracted and Engagements entered into, before the Adoption of this Constitution, shall be as valid against the United States under this Constitution, as under the Confederation.

This Constitution, and the Laws of the United States which shall be made in Pursuance thereof; and all Treaties made, or which shall be made, under the Authority of the United States, shall be the supreme Law of the Land; and the Judges in every State shall be bound thereby, any Thing in the Constitution or Laws of any State to the Contrary notwithstanding.

The Senators and Representatives before mentioned, and the Members of the several State Legislatures, and all executive and judicial Officers, both of the United States and of the Several States, shall be bound by Oath or Affirmation, to support this Constitution; but no religious Test shall ever be required as a Qualification to any Office or public Trust under the United States.

Article VII

The Ratification of the Conventions of nine States, shall be sufficient for the Establishment of this Constitution between the States so ratifying the Same.

Amendment I [1791]

Congress shall make no law respecting an establishment of religion, or prohibiting the free exercise thereof; or abridging the freedom of speech, or the press; or the right of the people peaceably to assemble, and to petition the Government for a redress of grievances.

Amendment II [1791]

A well regulated Militia, being necessary to the security for a free State, the right of the people to keep and bear Arms, shall not be infringed.

Amendment III [1791]

No Soldier shall, in time of peace be quartered in any house, without the consent of the Owner, nor in time of war, but in a manner to be prescribed by law.

Amendment IV [1791]

The right of the people to be secure in their persons, houses, papers, and effects, against unreasonable searches and seizures, shall not be violated, and no Warrants shall issue, but upon probable cause, supported by Oath or Affirmation, and particularly describing the place to be searched, and the persons or things to be seized.

Amendment V [1791]

No person shall be held to answer for a capital, or otherwise infamous crime, unless on a presentment or indictment of a Grand Jury, except in cases arising in the land or naval forces, or in the Militia, when in actual service in time of War or public danger; nor shall any person be subject for the same offense to be twice put in jeopardy of life or limb; nor shall be compelled in any criminal case to be a witness against himself, nor be deprived of life, liberty, or property, without due process of law; nor shall private property be taken for public use, without just compensation.

Amendment VI [1791]

In all criminal prosecutions, the accused shall enjoy the right to a speedy and public trial, by an impartial jury of the State and district wherein the crime shall have been committed, which district shall have been previously ascertained by law, and to be informed of the nature and cause of the accusation; to be confronted with the Witnesses against him; to have compulsory process for obtaining witnesses in his favor, and to have the Assistance of counsel for his defence.

Amendment VII [1791]

In suits at common law, where the value in controversy shall exceed twenty dollars, the right of trial by jury shall be preserved, and no fact tried by a jury, shall be otherwise re-examined in any Court of the United States, than according to the rules of the common law.

Amendment VIII [1791]

Excessive bail shall not be required, nor excessive fines imposed, nor cruel and unusual punishments inflicted.

Amendment IX [1791]

The enumeration in the Constitution, of certain rights, shall not be construed to deny or disparage others retained by the people.

Amendment X [1791]

The powers not delegated to the United States by the Constitution, nor prohibited by it to the States, are reserved to the States respectively, or to the people.

Amendment XI [1798]

The judicial power of the United States shall not be construed to extend to any suit in law or equity, commenced or prosecuted against one of the United States by Citizens of another State, or by Citizens or Subjects of any Foreign State.

Amendment XII [1804]

The Electors shall meet in their respective states and vote by ballot for President and Vice-President, one of whom, at least, shall not be an inhabitant of the same state with themselves; they shall name in their ballots the person voted for as President, and in distinct ballots the person voted for as Vice-President, and they shall make distinct lists of all persons voted for as President, and of all persons voted for as Vice-President, and of the number of votes for each, which lists they shall sign and certify, and transmit sealed to the seat of the government of the United States, directed to the President of the Senate;—The President of the Senate shall, in the presence of the Senate and House of Representatives, open all the certificates and the votes shall then be counted;—The person having the greatest number of votes for President, shall be the President, if such number be a majority of the whole number of Electors appointed; and if no person have such majority, then from the persons having the highest numbers not exceeding three on the list of those voted for as President, the House of Representatives shall choose immediately, by ballot, the President. But in choosing the President, the votes shall be taken by states, the representation from each state having one vote; a quorum for this purpose shall consist of a member or members from two-thirds of the states, and a majority of all the states shall be necessary to a choice. And if the House of Representatives shall not choose a President whenever the right of choice shall devolve upon them, before the fourth day of March next following, then the Vice-President shall act as President, as in the case of the death or other constitutional disability of the President. The person having the greatest number of votes as Vice-President, shall be the Vice-President, if such number be a majority of the whole number of Electors appointed, and if no person have a majority, then from the two highest numbers on the list, the Senate shall choose the Vice-President; a quorum for the purpose shall consist of two-thirds of the whole number of Senators, and a majority of the whole number shall be necessary to a choice. But no person constitutionally ineligible to the office of President shall be eligible to that of the Vice-President of the United States.

Amendment XIII [1865]

Section 1. Neither slavery nor involuntary servitude, except as a punishment for crime whereof the party shall have been duly convicted, shall exist within the United States, or any place subject to their jurisdiction.

Section 2. Congress shall have power to enforce this article by appropriate legislation.

Amendment XIV [1868]

Section 1. All persons born or naturalized in the United States, and subject to the jurisdiction thereof, are citizens of the United States and of the State wherein they reside. No State shall make or enforce any law which shall abridge the privileges or immunities of citizens of the United States; nor shall any State deprive any person of life, liberty, or property, without due process of law; nor deny to any person within its jurisdiction the equal protection of the laws.

Section 2. Representatives shall be appointed among the several States according to their respective numbers, counting the whole number of persons in each State, excluding Indians not taxed. But when the right to vote at any election for the choice of electors for President and Vice President of the United States, Representatives in Congress, the Executive and Judicial officers of a State, or the members of the Legislature thereof, is denied to any of the male inhabitants of such State, being twenty-one years of age, and citizens of the United States, or in any way abridged, except for participation in rebellion, or other crime, the basis of representation therein shall be reduced in the proportion which the number of such male citizens shall bear to the whole number of male citizens twenty-one years of age in such State.

Section 3. No person shall be a Senator or Representative in Congress, or elector of President and Vice President, or hold any office, civil or military, under the United States, or under any State, who, having previously taken an oath, as a member of Congress, or as an officer of the United States, or as a member of any State legislature, or as an executive or judicial officer of any State, to support the Constitution of the United States, shall have engaged in insurrection or rebellion against the same, or given aid or comfort to the enemies thereof. But Congress may by a vote of two-thirds of each House, remove such disability.

Section 4. The validity of the public debt of the United States, authorized by law, including debts incurred for payment of pensions and bounties for services in suppressing insurrection or rebellion, shall not be questioned. But neither the United States nor any State shall assume or pay any debt or obligation incurred in aid of insurrection of rebellion against the United States, or any claim for the loss or emancipation of any slave; but all such debts, obligations and claims shall be held illegal and void.

Section 5. The Congress shall have power to enforce, by appropriate legislation, the provisions of this article.

Amendment XV [1870]

Section 1. The right of citizens of the United States to vote shall not be denied or abridged by the United States or by any State on account of race, color, or previous condition of servitude.

Section 2. The Congress shall have power to enforce this article by appropriate legislation.

Amendment XVI [1913]

The Congress shall have power to lay and collect taxes on incomes, from whatever source derived, without apportionment among the several States, and without regard to any census or enumeration.

Amendment XVII [1913]

The Senate of the United States shall be composed of two Senators from each State, elected by the people thereof, for six years; and each Senator shall have one vote. The electors in each State shall have the qualifications requisite for electors of the most numerous branch of the State legislatures.

When vacancies happen in the representation of any State in the Senate, the executive authority of each State shall issue writs of election to fill such vacancies; *Provided,* That the legislature of any State may empower the executive thereof to make temporary appointments until the people fill the vacancies by election as the legislature may direct.

This amendment shall not be so construed as to affect the election or term of any Senator chosen before it becomes valid as part of the Constitution.

Amendment XVIII [1919]

Section 1. After one year from the ratification of this article the manufacture, sale, or transportation of intoxicating liquors within, the importation thereof into, or the exportation thereof from the United States and all territory subject to the jurisdiction thereof for beverage purposes is hereby prohibited.

Section 2. The Congress and the several States shall have concurrent power to enforce this article by appropriate legislation.

Section 3. This article shall be inoperative unless it shall have been ratified as an amendment to the Constitution by the legislatures of the several States, as provided in the Constitution, within seven years from the date of the submission hereof to the States by the Congress.

Amendment XIX [1920]

The right of citizens of the United States to vote shall not be denied or abridged by the United States or by any State on account of sex.

Congress shall have power to enforce this article by appropriate legislation.

Amendment XX [1933]

Section 1. The terms of the President and Vice President shall end at noon on the 20th day of January, and the terms of Senators and Representatives at noon on the 3rd day of January, of the years in which such terms would have ended if this article had not been ratified; and the terms of their successors shall then begin.

Section 2. The Congress shall assemble at least once in every year, and such meeting shall begin at noon on the 3rd day of January, unless they shall by law appoint a different day.

Section 3. If, at the time fixed for the beginning of the term of the President, the President elect shall have died, the Vice President elect shall become President. If a President shall not have been chosen before the time fixed for the beginning of his term, or if the President elect shall have failed to qualify, then the Vice President elect shall act as President until a President shall have qualified; and the Congress may by law provide for the case wherein neither a President elect nor a Vice President elect shall have qualified, declaring who shall then act as President, or the manner in which one who is to act shall be selected, and such person shall act accordingly until a President or Vice President shall have qualified.

Section 4. The Congress may by law provide for the case of the death of any of the persons from whom the House of Representatives may choose a President whenever the right of choice shall have devolved upon them, and for the case of the death of any of the persons from whom the Senate may choose a Vice President whenever the right of choice shall have devolved upon them.

Section 5. Sections 1 and 2 shall take effect on the 15th day of October following the ratification of this article.

Section 6. This article shall be inoperative unless it shall have been ratified as an amendment to the Constitution by the legislatures of three-fourths of the several States within seven years from the date of its submission.

Amendment XXI [1933]

Section 1. The eighteenth article of amendment to the Constitution of the United States is hereby repealed.

Section 2. The transportation or importation into any State, Territory, or possession of the United States for delivery or use therein of intoxicating liquors, in violation of the laws thereof, is hereby prohibited.

Section 3. This article shall be inoperative unless it shall have been ratified as an amendment to the Constitution by conventions in the several States, as provided in the Constitution, within seven years from the date of the submission hereof to the States by the Congress.

Amendment XXII [1951]

Section 1. No person shall be elected to the office of the President more than twice, and no person who has held the office of President, or acted as President, for more than two years of a term to which some other person was elected President shall be elected to the office of the President more than once. But this Article shall not apply to any person holding the office of President when this article was proposed by the Congress, and shall not prevent any person who may be holding the office of President, or acting as President, during the term within which this Article becomes operative from holding the office of President, or acting as President during the remainder of such term.

Section 2. This article shall be inoperative unless it shall have been ratified as an amendment to the Constitution by the legislatures of three-fourths of the several States within seven years from the date of its submission to the States by the Congress.

Amendment XXIII [1961]

Section 1. The District constituting the seat of government of the United States shall appoint in such manner as the Congress may direct:

A number of electors of President and Vice President equal to the whole number of Senators and Representatives in Congress to which the District would be entitled if it were a State, but in no event more than the least populous State; they shall be in addition to those appointed by the States, but they shall be considered, for the purposes of the election of President and Vice President, to be electors appointed by a State; and they shall meet in the District and perform such duties as provided by the twelfth article of amendment.

Section 2. The Congress shall have power to enforce this article by appropriate legislation.

Amendment XXIV [1964]

Section 1. The right of citizens of the United States to vote in any primary or other election for President or Vice President, for electors for President or Vice President, or for Senator or Representative in Congress, shall not be denied or abridged by the United States or any State by reason of failure to pay any poll tax or other tax.

Section 2. The Congress shall have power to enforce this article by appropriate legislation.

Amendment XXV [1967]

Section 1. In case of the removal of the President from office or of his death or resignation, the Vice President shall become President.

Section 2. Whenever there is a vacancy in the office of the Vice President, the President shall nominate a Vice President who shall take office upon confirmation by a majority vote of both Houses of Congress.

Section 3. Whenever the President transmits to the President pro tempore of the Senate and the Speaker of the House of Representatives his written declaration that he is unable to discharge the powers and duties of his office, and until he transmits to them a written declaration to the contrary, such powers and duties shall be discharged by the Vice President as Acting President.

Section 4. Whenever the Vice President and a majority of either the principal officers of the executive departments or of such other body as Congress may by law provide, transmit to the President pro tempore of the Senate and the Speaker of the House of Representatives their written declaration that the President is unable to discharge the powers and duties of his office, the Vice President shall immediately assume the powers and duties of the office as Acting President.

Thereafter, when the President transmits to the President pro tempore of the Senate and the Speaker of the House of Representatives his written declaration that no inability exists, he shall resume the powers and duties of his office unless the Vice President and a majority of either the principal officers of the executive department or of such other body as Congress may by law provide, transmit within four days to the President pro tempore of the Senate and the Speaker of the House of Representatives their written declaration that the President is unable to discharge the powers and duties of his office. Thereupon Congress shall decide the issue, assembling within forty-eight hours for that purpose if not in session. If the Congress, within twenty-one days after receipt of the latter written declaration, or, if Congress is not in session, within twenty-one days after Congress is required to assemble, determines by two-thirds vote of both Houses that the President shall continue to discharge the same as Acting President; otherwise, the President shall resume the powers and duties of his office.

Amendment XXVI [1971]

Section 1. The right of citizens of the United States, who are 18 years of age or older, to vote, shall not be denied or abridged by the United States or any State on account of age.

Section 2. The Congress shall have the power to enforce this article by appropriate legislation.

Amendment XXVII [1992]

No law, varying the compensation for the services of the Senators and Representatives, shall take effect, until an election of Representatives shall have intervened.

Spanish Equivalents for Important Legal Terms in English

Abandoned property: bienes abandonados
Acceptance: aceptacion; consentimiento; acuerdo
Acceptor: aceptante
Accession: toma de posesion; aumento
Accession accomodation indorser: avalista de savor
Accommodation party: firmante de favor
Accord: acuerdo; convenio; arregio
Accord and satisfaction: transaccion elecutada
Act of state doctrine: doctrina de acto e gobierno
Administrative law: derecho administrativo
Administrative process: procedimiento o metodo administrativo
Administrator: administrador (-a)
Adverse possession: posesion de hecho susceptible de proscripcion adquisitiva
Affirmative action: accion afirmativa
Affirmative defense: defensa afirmativa
After-acquired property: bienes adquiridos con posterioridad a un hecho dada
Agency: mandato; agencia
Agent: mandatorio; agente; representante
Agreement: convenio; acuerdo; contrato
Alien corporation: empress extranjera
Allonge: hojas adicionales de endosos
Answer: contestacion de la demande; alegato
Anticipatory repudiation: anuncio previo de las partes de su imposibilidad de cumplir con el contrato
Appeal: apelacion; recurso de apelacion
Appellate jurisdiction: jurisdiccion de apelaciones
Appraisal right: derecho de valuacion
Arbitration: arbitraje
Arson: incendio intencional
Articles of partnership: contrato social
Artisan's lien: derecho de retencion que ejerce al artesano
Assault: asalto; ataque; agresion
Assignment of rights: transmision; transferencia; cesion
Assumption of risk: no resarcimiento por exposicion voluntaria al peligro
Attachment: auto judicial que autoriza el embargo; embargo

Bailee: depositario
Bailment: deposito; constitucion en deposito
Bailor: depositante
Bankruptcy trustee: fideicomisario de insolvencia
Battery: agresion; fisica
Bearer: portador; tenedor
Bearer instrument: documento at portador
Bequest or legacy: legado (de bienes muebles)
Bilateral contract: contrato bilateral
Bill of lading: conocimiento de embarque; carta de porte
Bill of Rights: declaracion de derechos
Binder: poliza de seguro provisoria; recibo de pago a cuenta del precio
Blank indorsement: enclose, en blanco
Blue sky laws: leyes reguladoras del comercio bursatil
Bond: titulo de credito; garantfa; caucion
Bond indenture: contrato de emision de bonos; contrato del amprestito
Breach of contract: incumplimiento de contrato
Brief: escrito; resumen; informe
Burglary: violacion de domicilio
Business judgment rule: regla de juicio comercial
Business tort: agravio comercial
Case law: ley de casos; derecho casufstico
Cashier's check: cheque de caja
Causation in fact: causalidad en realidad
Cease-and-desist order: orden para cesar y desistir
Certificate of deposit: certificado de deposito
Certified check: cheque certificado
Charitable trust: fideicomiso para fines beneficos
Chattel: bien mueble
Check: cheque
Chose in action: derecho inmaterial; derecho de accion
Civil law: derecho civil
Close corporation: sociedad de un solo accionista o de un grupo restringido de accionistas
Closed shop: taller agremiado (emplea solamente a miembros de un gremio)
Closing argument: argumento al final

Codicil: codicilo

Collateral: guarantfa; bien objeto de la guarantia real

Comity: cortesfa; cortesfa entre naciones

Commercial paper: instrumentos negociables; documentos a valores commerciales

Common law: derecho consuetudinario; derecho comun; ley comun

Common stock: action ordinaria

Comparative negligence: negligencia comparada

Compensatory damages: danos y perjuicios reales o compensatorios

Concurrent conditions: condiciones concurrentes

Concurrent jurisdiction: competencia concurrente de varios tribunales para entender en una misma causa

Concurring opinion: opinion concurrente

Condition: condicion

Condition precedent: condicion suspensiva

Condition subsequent: condicion resolutoria

Confiscation: confiscation

Confusion: confusion; fusion

Conglomerate merger: fusiors de firmas que operan en distintos mercados

Consent decree: acuerdo entre las partes aprobado por un tribunal

Consequential damages: danos y perjuicios indirectos

Consideration: consideration; motivo; contraprestacion

Consolidation: consolidation

Constructive delivery: entrega simbolica

Constructive trust: fideicomiso creado por aplicacion de la ley

Consumer protection law: ley para proteger el consumidor

Contract: contrato

Contract under seal: contrato formal o sellado

Contributory negligence: negligencia de la parte actora

Conversion: usurpation; conversion de valores

Copyright: derecho de autor

Corporation: sociedad anomina; corporation; persona juridica

Co-sureties: cogarantes

Counterclaim: reconvention; contrademanda

Counteroffer: contraoferta

Course of dealing: torso de transacciones

Course of performance: curso de cumplimiento

Covenant: pacto; garantia; contrato

Covenant not to sue: pacto or contrato a no demandar

Covenant of quiet enjoyment: garantia del use y goce pacifico del inmueble

Creditors' composition agreement: concordato preventivo

Crime: crimen; delito; contravention

Criminal law: derecho penal

Cross-examination: contrainterrogatorio

Cure: cura; cuidado; derecho de remediar un vicio contractual

Customs receipts: recibos de derechos aduaneros

Damages: danos; indemnizacion por danos y perjuicios

Debit card: tarjeta de de bito

Debtor: deudor

Debt securities: seguridades de deuda

Deceptive advertising: publicidad engafiosa

Deed: escritura; titulo; acta translativa de domino

Defamation: difamacion

Delegation of duties: delegation de obligaciones

Demand deposit: deposito a la vista

Depositions: declaration de un testigo fuera del tribunal

Devise: legado; deposition testamentaria (bienes inmuebles)

Direct examination: interrogatorio directo; primer interrogatorio

Directed verdict: veredicto segun orden del juez y sin participacion activa del jurado

Disaffirmance: repudiation; renuncia; anulacion

Discharge: descargo; liberation; cumplimiento

Disclosed principal: mandante revelado

Discovery: descubrimiento; production de la prueba

Dissenting opinion: opinion disidente

Dissolution: disolucion; termination

Diversity of citizenship: competencia de los tribunales federales para entender en causas cuyas partes intervinientes son cuidadanos de distintos estados

Divestiture: extincion premature de derechos reales

Dividend: dividendo

Docket: orden del dia; lista de causas pendientes

Domestic corporation: sociedad local

Draft: orden de pago; letrade cambio

Drawee: girado; beneficiario

Drawer: librador

Duress: coaccion; violencia

Easement: servidumbre

Embezzlement: desfalco; malversacion

Eminent domain: poder de expropiacion

Employment discrimination: discrimination en el empleo

Entrepreneur: empresario

Environmental law: ley ambiental

Equal dignity rule: regla de dignidad egual

Equity security: tipo de participacion en una sociedad

Estate: propiedad; patrimonio; derecho

Estop: impedir; prevenir

Ethical issue: cuestion etica

Exclusive jurisdiction: competencia exclusiva

Exculpatory clause: clausula eximente

Executed contract: contrato ejecutado

Execution: ejecucion; cumplimiento

Executor: albacea

Executory contract: contrato atin no completamente consumado

Executory interest: derecho futuro

Express contract: contrato expreso

Expropriation: expropriation

Federal question: caso federal

Fee simple: pleno dominio; dominio absoluto

Fee simple absolute: dominio absoluta

Fee simple defeasible: dominio sujeta una condicion resolutoria

Felony: crimen; delito grave

Fictitious payee: beneficiario ficticio

Fiduciary: fiduciaro
Firm offer: oferta en firme
Fixture: inmueble por destino, incorporation a anexacion
Floating lien: gravamen continuado
Foreign corporation: sociedad extranjera; U.S. sociedad constitu otro estado
Forgery: (also; falsification)
Formal contract: contrato formal
Franchise: privilegio; franquicia concesion
Franchisee: persona que *recibe* una concesion
Franchisor: persona que, vende concesionario
est: bien futuro
ent: embargo de derechos
artner: socio comanditario
warranty deed: escritura tiva de domino con garantia de nacion asa Mortis: donacion por causa e *er vivos*: donacion entre vivos
Faith: buena fe
Faith purchaser: comprador de fe jet: tenedor por contraprestacion *der in*
due course: tenedor legitimo
Holographic will: testamento olografico mestead exemption laws: leyes que ptuan las casas de familia, de ucion por duedas generates
Horizontal merger: fusion horizontal
Identification: identification
Implied-in-fact contract: contrato implicito en realidad
Implied warranty: guarantia implicita
Implied warranty of merchantability: garantia implicita de vendibilidad
Impossibility of performance: reposibilidad de cumplir un contrato
Imposter: imposter
Incidental beneficiary: beneficiario incidental; beneficiario secundario
Incidental damages: danos incidentales
Indictment: auto de acusacion; acusacion
Indorsee: endorsatario
Indorsement: endoso
Indorser: endosante
Informal contract: contrato no formal; contrato verbal
Information: acusacion hecha por el ministerio publico
Injunction: mandamiento; orden de no innovar
Innkeeper's lien: derecho de retention que ejerce el posadero
Installment contract: contrato de pago en cuotas
Insurable interest: interes asegurable
Intended beneficiary: beneficiario destinado
Intentional tort: agravio; cuasidelito intentional
International law: derecho internacional
Interrogatories: preguntas escritas sometidas por una parte a la otra o a un testigo
Inter vivos **trust:** fideicomiso entre vivos
Intestacy laws: Leyes de la condition de morir intestado
Intestate: intestado
Investment company: compania de inversiones

Issue: emision
Joint tenancy: derechos conjuntos en un bien inmueble en favor del beneficiario sobreviviente
Judgment n.o.v: juicio no obstante veredicto
Judgment rate of interest: interes de juicio
Judicial process: acto de procedimiento; proceso juridico
Judicial review: revision judicial
Jurisdiction: jurisdiction
Larceny: robo; hurto
Law: derecho; ley; jurisprudencia
Lease: contrato de location; contrato de alquiler
Leasehold estate: bienes forales
Legal rate of interest: interes legal
Legatee: legatario
Letter of credit: carta de credito
Levy: embargo; comiso
Libel: libelo; difamacion escrita
Life estate: usufructo
Limited partner: comanditario
Limited partnership: sociedad en comandita
Liquidation: liquidation; realization
Lost property: objetos perdidos
Majority opinion: opinion de la mayoria
Maker: persona que realiza u ordena; librador
Mechanic's lien: gravamen de constructor
Mediation: mediation; intervention
Merger: fusion
Mirror image rule: fallo de reflejo
Misdemeanor: infraction; contravention
Mislaid property: bienes extraviados
Mitigation of damages: reduction de danos
Mortgage: hypoteca
Motion to dismiss: exception parentoria
Mutual fund: fondo mutual
Negotiable instrument: instrumento negociable
Negotiation: negotiation
Nominal damages: danos y perjuicios nominates
Novation: novacion
Nuncupative will: testamento nuncupativo
Objective theory of contracts: teoria objetiva de contratos
Offer: oferta
Offeree: persona que recibe una oferta
Offeror: oferente
Order instrument: instrumento o documento a la orden
Original jurisdiction: jurisdiction de primera instancia
Output contract: contrato de production
Parol evidence rule: regla relativa a la prueba oral
Partially disclosed principal: mandante revelado en parte
Partnership: sociedad colectiva; asociacion; asociacion de participation
Past consideration: causa o contraprestacion anterior
Patent: patente; privilegio
Pattern or practice: muestra o practica
Payee: beneficiario de un pago
Penalty: pena; penalidad
Per capita: por cabeza

Perfection: perfecion
Performance: cumplimiento; ejecucion
Personal defenses: excepciones personales
Personal property: bienes muebles
Per stirpes: por estirpe
Plea bargaining: regateo por un alegato
Pleadings: alegatos
Pledge: prenda
Police powers: poders de policia y de prevention del crimen
Policy: poliza
Positive law: derecho positivo; ley positiva
Possibility of reverter: posibilidad de reversion
Precedent: precedente
Preemptive right: derecho de prelacion
Preferred stock: acciones preferidas
Premium: recompensa; prima
Presentment warranty: garantia de presentation
Price discrimination: discrimination en los precios
Principal: mandante; principal
Privity: nexo jurldico
Privity of contract: relacion contractual
Probable cause: causa probable
Probate: verificacion; verificacion del testamento
Probate court: tribunal de sucesiones y tutelas
Proceeds: resultados; ingresos
Profit: beneficio; utilidad; lucro
Promise: promesa
Promisee: beneficiario de una promesa
Promisor: promtente
Promissory estoppel: impedimento promisorio
Promissory note: pagare; nota de pago
Promoter: promotor; fundador
Proximate cause: causa inmediata o proxima
Proxy: apoderado; poder
Punitive, or exemplary, damages: danos y perjuicios punitivos o ejemplares
Qualified indorsement: endoso con reservas
Quasi contract: contrato tacito o implicito
Quitclaim deed: acto de transferencia de una propiedad por finiquito, pero sin ninguna garantia sobre la validez del titulo transferido
Ratification: ratification
Real property: bienes inmuebles
Reasonable doubt: duda razonable
Rebuttal: refutacion
Recognizance: promesa; compromiso; reconocimiento
Recording statutes: leyes estatales sobre registros oficiales
Redress: reporacion
Reformation: rectificacion; reforma; correction
Rejoinder: duplica; contrarreplica
Release: liberation; renuncia a un derecho
Remainder: sustitution; reversion
Remedy: recurso; remedio; reparation
Replevin: accion reivindicatoria; reivindicacion
Reply: replica
Requirements contract: contrato de suministro

Rescission: rescision
Res judicata: cosa juzgada; res judicata
Respondeat superior: responsabilidad del mandante o del maestro
Restitution: restitution
Restrictive indorsement: endoso restrictivo
Resulting trust: fideicomiso implicito
Reversion: reversion; sustitucion
Revocation: revocation; derogation
Right of contribution: derecho de contribution
Right of reimbursement: derecho de reembolso
Right of subrogation: derecho de subrogation
Right-to-work law: ley de libertad de trabajo
Robbery: robo
Rule 10b-5: Regla 10b-5
Sale: yenta; contrato de compreventa
Sale on approval: yenta a ensayo; yenta sujeta a la aprobacion del comprador
Sale or return: yenta con derecho de devolution
Sales contract: contrato de compraventa; boleto de compraventa
Satisfaction: satisfaction; pago *Scienter*, a sabiendas
S corporation: S corporation
Secured party: acreedor garantizado
Secured transaction: transaction garantizada
Securities: volares; titulos; seguridades
Security agreement: convenio de seguridad
Security interest: interes en un bien dado en garantfa que permite a quien lo detenta venderlo en caso de incumplimiento
Service mark: marca de identificacion de servicios
Shareholder's derivative suit: accion judicial entablada por un accionista en nombre de la sociedad
Signature: firma; rubrica
Slander: difamacion oral; calumnia
Sovereign immunity: immunidad soberana
Special indorsement: endoso especial; endoso a la orden de una person en particular
Specific performance: ejecucion precisa, segun los terminos del contrato
Spendthrift trust: fideicomiso para prodigos
Stale check: cheque vencido
Stare decisis: acatar las decisiones, observar los precedentes
Statutory law: derecho estatutario; derecho legislado; derecho escrito
Stock: acciones
Stock warrant: certificado, para la compra de acciones
Stop-payment order: orden de suspension del pago de un cheque dada por el librador del mismo
Strict liability: responsabilidad unconditional
Summary judgment: fallo sumario
Tangible property: bienes corporeos
Tenancy at will: inguilino por tiempo indeterminado (segun la voluntad del propietario)
Tenancy by sufferance: posesion por tolerancia
Tenancy by the entirety: location conyugal conjunta
Tenancy for years: inguilino por un termino fijo

Tenancy in common: specie de copropiedad indivisa

Tender: oferta de pago; oferta de ejecucior

Testamentary trust: fideicomiso testamentario

Testator: testador (-a)

Third party beneficiary contract: contrato para el beneficio del tercero-beneficiario

Tort: agravio; cuasi-delito

Totten trust: fideicomiso creado por u deposito bancario

Trade acceptance: letra de cambio aceptada

Trade name: nombre comercial; razon social

Trademark: marca registrada

Traveler's check: cheque del viajero

Trespass to land: ingreso no authoriza a las tierras de otro

Trespass to personal property: violac de los derechos posesorios de un *terc* con respecto a bienes muebles

Trust: fideicomiso; trust

Ultra vires: ultra vires; fuera de facultad (de una sociedad anonim)

Unanimous opinion: opinion unam

Unconscionable contract or clause: contrato leonino; clausula leonine

Underwriter: subscriptor; asegura

Unenforceable contract: contrato se puede hacer cumplir usufructo

APPENDIX C

Supplemental Articles and Materials

An Ethics Lesson for Business Schools

By Robert Prentice

AUSTIN, Tex. When Joseph Wharton established the nation's first business school at the University of Pennsylvania in 1881, he made business law one of five basic business school disciplines. More than a century later, the study of business law has given way to the study of business ethics.

But business students do not need to study business ethics so much as they need to study business law. The scandals at Enron, WorldCom and ImClone did not occur because executives were not conversant with the difference between teleological and deontological approaches to resolving ethical questions. It goes without saying that these scandals involved serious ethical lapses. But they also involved serious violations of business laws. They occurred, at least in part, because their participants had an insufficient knowledge of, appreciation for and, yes, fear of the law. Business schools have played a role in this disaster.

Because today businesses face far more complicated rules and regulations than they did a century ago, the need for managers to have a realistic appreciation of the legal environment in which they operate is more important than ever. Some business schools still have strong business law programs, but most have spent much of the last three decades reducing, marginalizing and often eliminating their business law faculty as other disciplines grew in stature and popularity.

Consequently, in many business schools most students get their only look at the legal environment in which they will operate from faculty who view the law as an impediment. Finance professors have told me that insider trading rules and financial disclosure requirements simply undermine the efficiency of the markets. Accounting professors have explained to me that rules limiting the ability of accounting firms to provide internal auditing services to a client (and thereby prepare the same books that they later purport to audit independently) are pointless, because accountants would never risk their reputation by acting

improperly. (Many accounting professors still believe this, but they are quieter in the aftermath of Enron.) No wonder many business professors impart to their students an impression that the law exists simply to be manipulated or evaded.

At several leading business schools, many of the faculty that teach business law no longer even have law degrees: economists and political scientists offer policy courses that focus on lobbying. Indeed, much finance and economics research and teaching is built on the silly (though occasionally useful) assumption that man is a rational maximizer of his own utilities—and that these utilities can be measured financially. Not only is this unrealistic but, as the law professor Charles Pouncy has noted, it also encourages the view that any business strategy or activity that does not maximize monetary reward is suspect. This is the message that business schools tend to send—and companies like Enron tend to follow.

With the help of well-intentioned donors, several business schools have established business ethics centers. Unfortunately, research shows that it is very difficult to teach ethical values to undergraduates, harder still to teach them to M.B.A. students and all but impossible to get through to those enrolled in executive M.B.A. courses. If they didn't get a sense of right and wrong from their families or their faith, it's unlikely a business school professor can instill one.

Ethics courses can't help those who are truly well-intentioned find their way through ethical dilemmas where the law gives no clear answer. But even these people will founder when they go to work for companies that value results over honesty; at such firms, acting ethically is always difficult.

There has never been a more crucial time to emphasize law in a business curriculum. Too many people forget that capitalism was saved from its own excesses by the securities laws passed in the 1930's. Recent scholarship shows that countries with strong judicial systems administering rigorous

Robert Prentice teaches business law at the McCombs School of Business at the University of Texas at Austin.

323

financial laws enable companies to raise money more quickly and facilitate more efficient stock markets. Legitimate companies want laws that require accurate financial disclosure and rules that punish fraudulent firms.

Centers for the study of business ethics are necessary to represent the ideals to which we aspire. But most business students will always view business ethics as hortatory rather than mandatory, as extra credit rather than required.

Instead, business law professors should explain to students that legal requirements are not optional. Such requirements enable our free-enterprise system to function—and disobedience carries a personal as well as a societal cost. My colleagues and I must tell this story more forcefully than we have in the past. But to do so we need a more prominent forum in the business schools of America.

Constitutional Rights That May Surprise You

Steven Pressman

If you're an American, you probably have rights under two constitutions. And in some cases, the rights your state constitution gives you may be more valuable than your federal rights.

Ask most Americans what they know about their constitutional rights, and chances are they'll mention the First Amendment promise of free speech. Or they'll think about "taking the Fifth" to avoid incriminating themselves.

But there are 50 other constitutions in this country, many of which give citizens of particular states a dazzling array of individual rights that are nowhere to be found in our precious national charter.

From Hawaii to Maine, each state in the union has its own constitution. A quick glance at some of these gives some colorful examples of how they depart from the U.S. Constitution.

New York guarantees its citizens a state-run lottery game. Tennesseans enjoy a right to sail on the Mississippi River. Residents of California and Rhode Island have a constitutional right to fish.

Only the citizens of New Hampshire, however, are guaranteed the "right of revolution."

Obviously some of these constitutional nuggets—rooted in the unique historical, cultural, or geographical traditions of particular states—have little relevance to modern society. In recent years, however, on increasing number of lawyers and legal scholars, taking a keener look at state constitutions have discovered—along with state court judges—that the U.S. Constitution is not always the last word on individual rights.

The Sharing of Power

State courts have handed down hundreds of rulings expanding individual rights beyond those spelled out by federal court judges interpreting the federal Constitution. State courts have dealt with such controversial legal matters as abortion rights, drug testing and other privacy issues, the rights of criminal defendants and environmental disputes.

Together these rulings add up to the "new judicial federalism." It sounds a little dry, but the term aptly describes one of the unique features of life in the United States—political power that is shared between the federal government and the individual states.

Consider abortion. Although the Supreme Court of the United States, in *Roe v. Wade*, declared abortions legal, it has since upheld congressional legislation to prevent poor women from using federal Medicaid funds to pay for the procedure. But in 1981 the California Supreme Court struck down similar state legislation. The reasoning a woman's right to an abortion is protected by privacy rights guaranteed in the California Constitution as well as the U.S. Constitution. The Massachusetts and New Jersey supreme courts have reached similar conclusions.

What about the growing debate over whether public and private workers can be required to take drug or lie-detector tests as a condition of employment? In October 1987, the Texas Supreme Court struck down the use of polygraph tests for employees of the state mental health department. The justices said that state agencies had the right to evaluate the performance of their employees, but that subjecting them to lie-detector tests went too far under the Texas constitutional right to privacy. New York and California courts have prohibited both urinalysis and polygraph tests as violating similar state constitutional rights.

The Fundamental Principle

The national Constitution sets the minimum levels of individual rights for everyone in the United States. But the states are perfectly free to expand individual rights above that floor.

"There's something very troubling about the fact that in an airplane age, as we fly from one state to another our rights change," says Ronald K. L. Collins, visiting professor of law at The American University in Washington, D.C., and a leading expert on state constitutional law. "But ours isn't a nationalist regime. It's a federalist regime. So it has a schizophrenic quality about it."

Steven Pressman is a free-lance writer in Washington. D.C.

As early as 1859, the Wisconsin Supreme Court decided that poor criminal defendants were entitled to a lawyer even if they could not afford one. Tennessee reached the same conclusion in 1951. But it was 1963 before the Supreme Court in *Gideon v. Wainright* applied the same logic throughout the country.

Women's groups have long been frustrated over the failure to add the Equal Rights Amendment (ERA) to the U.S. Constitution. But 18 states already have their own constitutional versions of the ERA; Wyoming's dates back to 1889.

Still, over the years, state constitutions largely remained in the shadows—ignored by law school professors, practicing lawyers, and even state court judges. "I practiced law for nearly 15 years before I even realized there was a state constitution," says Colorado Attorney General Duane Woodard. Oregon Supreme Court Justice Hans Linde offers a reason why state constitutions are often ignored: they have, he says, "all the literary quality of the Yellow Pages."

During the 1950s and 1960s state constitutions were overshadowed when the Supreme Court of the United States launched a legal revolution by issuing a stream of decisions greatly expanding individual rights. From the outlawing of school segregation and the expansion of voting rights to ordering broad protections for criminal defendants, the Court blazed new trails in federal constitutional law.

The tide began to shift after President Nixon selected Warren E. Burger as the new Chief Justice and Nixon's more conservative appointees began taking their place on the federal bench. "There's no question but that in its initial form, state constitutional law was a clear reaction to the opinions of the Burger Court," says Kenneth Gornley, a St. Louis lawyer who has studied the application of state constitutions to criminal cases.

During the last three years, state supreme courts have handed down more than 250 decisions relying on their own constitutions to protect individual rights. That compares to about 50 such rulings from 1950 to 1965.

State v. Federal

Some state courts have used their own constitutions to completely reject Supreme Court decisions. That happened in New York and Mississippi after the Supreme Court in 1984 limited the "exclusionary rule," which prohibits the admission of illegally-seized evidence in a criminal trial. The New York Court of Appeal said the purpose of the exclusionary rule—preventing illegal police behavior—would be "completely frustrated" by the Supreme Court decision.

Some prominent federal judges have encouraged the use of state constitutions to protect individual rights. Supreme Court justice William J. Brennan, Jr., has described this trend as "probably the most important development in constitutional jurisprudence today." Conservative as well as liberal groups have taken advantage of state constitutions. "It's a strange combination of bedfellows when you have the National Rifle Association (NRA) waltzing hand-in-hand with the American Civil Liberties Union (ACLU)," says Collins.

To bolster its steadfast opposition to gun control laws, the NRA has long relied on the second amendment to the U.S. Constitution, which protects the right "to keep and bear arms." The true meaning of the second amendment has never been fully explored by the Supreme Court, but some 40 state constitutions guarantee the right to bear arms, according to NRA lawyer Robert Dowlut. More than half give a specific right to possess arms for "personal defense."

The Oregon Supreme Court, for instance, ruled in 1984 that a statute outlawing the possession of switchblades and billy clubs violated the state constitution. The justices concluded that the drafters of the Oregon Constitution "intended that the private citizen . . . have the right to possess certain arms for the defense of person and property."

Idaho undoubtedly goes the furthest on the issue of guns: its constitution prohibits any licensing or registration of firearms or ammunition and also bans the confiscation of any weapons, except for those used to commit a felony.

A Changing Document

Unlike the U.S. Constitution, state constitutions are usually easy to amend. As a result, they are often barometers of public opinion. The Massachusetts Constitution, first drafted in 1780, has since been amended over 100 times. Louisiana has had 11 different constitutions.

Voters in Oregon have see-sawed on the death penalty. In 1981, the state supreme court declared that death sentences

The Right to a Remedy

The Connecticut Constitution is typical of many others when it states: "All courts shall be open, and every person, for an injury done to him in his person, property or reputation, shall have remedy by due course of law."

In plain English, that means everyone in Connecticut has a constitutional right to demand compensation for a wrong suffered.

The legal right to a remedy has been traced to the Magna Carta, the document that limited the powers of England's King John in 1215.

When the framers of the U.S. Constitution assembled more than 200 years ago, however, they did not include the guarantee in the Bill of Rights. At least two states—North Carolina and Virginia—asked that it be added, to no avail.

That has left state constitutions to pick up the slack. Courts in some states have upheld laws spelling out caps on verdicts. Others have invalidated statutory restrictions.

The Supreme Court has stayed out of the controversy. Peter J. Galie, a political science professor at Canistus College in Buffalo, says that means state courts have "both an opportunity and obligation . . . to play an important role in protecting economic rights."

violated the state constitutional ban against cruel, unusual, or vindictive punishments. Three years later, voters passed a constitutional amendment specifically exempting death sentences from that category of punishments.

After the Florida state supreme court had decided some criminal cases more liberally than the U.S. Supreme Court, voters in 1982 approved a constitutional amendment requiring state courts to conform to Supreme Court rulings in illegal-evidence cases. The vote caught the attention of Chief Justice Burger, who encouraged voters in other states to tow liberal state court judges into line.

Some legal observers warn against too much reliance on state constitutions subject to the shifting whims of the public. But others respond that constitutions ought to reflect the changing values of the citizens of a state. "The whole purpose of having states is to have citizens disagree about what

is fundamentally right," says Bruce Fein, a legal scholar at the Heritage Foundation in Washington, D.C.

Despite the growing prominence of state constitutions, most lawyers still rely heavily on the U.S. Constitution. Burt Neubome, former national legal director for the ACLU who now teaches at New York University School of Law, says the reason is that lawyers are far more familiar with federal constitutional law.

But Collins also blames legal educators. "The reason more state courts don't render state constitutional opinions is because litigators aren't raising the issues," he says. "And litigators aren't raising them because law schools aren't."

Lawyers may be courting danger, however. Oregon's Justice Linde bluntly warns that a lawyer who fails to adequately research a case involving state constitutional issues "is skating on the edge of malpractice."

Why Lawyers Lie

If the O.J. Simpson case has taught anything, it's that finding out the truth isn't always the highest priority in a criminal trial. Winning is. That's the way the system is built.

By Floyd Abrams

As the O.J. Simpson case has transfixed the public, it has also taught it. Not only have the attorneys in the case been on constant public display, but other lawyers have served as television commentators, explaining, critiquing and judging the performance of their colleagues. Never before has so wide a swath of the public been subjected to such detailed, thought-by-thought analysis of how real lawyers think and what they do.

It is not always an attractive portrait, even to lawyers themselves. Viewed through my own prism of almost 35 years of practice, the Simpson case raises broad questions about just what it is our society asks lawyers to do, and the rather breathtakingly amoral way in which they do it.

Consider first the rules that govern the conduct of lawyers. They are not quite given James Bond's license to kill. But as lawyers, they have a license that requires them to defend their clients whether they are guilty or not; their responsibility is to attack those who have accused them, whatever the truth of those accusations. Regardless of whether Simpson committed the murders of which he is accused, it is Robert Shapiro's *job* as Simpson's lawyer to attack the validity of the DNA rests, in impugn the credibility of the police and, if useful and at all plausible, to attack the character of Simpson's former wife whom he is accused of murdering. Only lawyers are expected to do such things.

Lawyers are not asked to do justice. They participate in what everyone hopes is a system of justice, a system that seeks justice by asking lawyers on both sides to represent their clients zealously. Lawyers are the legal embodiment of—the spokesmen for—those clients. Subject only to the constraints of criminal law (a lawyer may not break open a mailbox as the Paul Newman character did in the movie "The Verdict") and the canons of legal ethics (a lawyer may not plant a spy within the camp of opposing counsel as the James Mason character did in the same movie), a lawyer is supposed to do whatever can be done to defend and vindicate the client's position in a case.

Those are wide, extraordinarily wide, boundaries. Within them, lawyers for rapists and murderers have accused their clients' victims of being responsible for their plight. Lawyers for warring husbands and wives have dropped the equivalent of tactical nuclear weapons on families, destroying all within range—children included.

All, all for clients. Prosecutors are at least in theory, supposed to be governed by somewhat different standards. Although no less zealous than defense counsel, they are supposed to indict only those they think guilty and to understand that, as the Supreme Court put it 60 years ago, the interest of the government "in a criminal prosecution is not that it shall win a case, but that justice shall be done." It is not always so. Certainly the potentially prejudicial comments of the Los Angeles District Attorney, Gil Garcetti, on "This Week With David Brinkley" suggesting that Simpson might well admit to the killings of which he is accused—and proffer some form of Menendez brothers-like psychological defense—offered little basis for thinking so.

Public statements of prosecutors and defense counsel alike must be viewed with the greatest skepticism. The Robert Shapiro who asserted, in one of his unending series

---

Floyd Abrams, a partner in the New York law firm of Cahill Gordon & Reindel, tries cases and argues appeals in constitutional law.

of interviews, that Simpson was innocent was not the Shapiro one might have met before he was retained by Simpson. He is now Simpson's Shapiro, Simpson's representative, sometimes Simpson's flack. Whatever he says is said for Simpson's benefit, not because it is true.

So with Alan M. Dershowitz, when he was representing Mike Tyson. The frequent public assertions by Dershowitz of Tyson's innocence after he began to represent him were not those of the Bill of Rights protecting Harvard Law School Professor Alan Dershowitz. The Tyson-defending Dershowitz was, in the end, little more than a better-spoken Tyson, Tyson in Harvard garb. That does not make what Dershowitz said of Tyson untrue. It does not mean that he did not mean what he said. But we should take care not to get our Dershowitzes confused.

So with all of us. Shortly after I argued before the Supreme Court representing a deathrow inmate in Parchman, Miss., I received a call from a newspaper in the small town in which the defendant had been tried, convicted and sentenced to death. "I know you only sought to persuade the Supreme Court to set aside the death sentence in the case," the reporter observed. "What I'd like to ask you is whether you believe he committed the crime."

I paused. It was true that I had only argued that the death sentence imposed upon my client was unconstitutional, a sentence the Supreme Court later set aside. It was also true that my client continued to deny his guilt. And it was true that I had never reached for myself any definitive conclusion as to his guilt.

But I was his lawyer. Silence might be taken as assent to his guilt. Even a "no comment" must have sounded as if I did not believe him innocent. Without a gulp, I answered, "I believe he is not guilty."

I did what I think a lawyer was supposed to do. Whether my client was guilty or not, whether I suspected he was guilty or not, I was obliged to defend him. But you are not obliged to believe me when I do so.

Nor should you take too seriously many of the published and broadcast reactions to the Simpson case of lawyers who represent criminal defendants. Their personal posturing aside, they often confuse what might be useful for his defense with what might serve justice. When the fact was first revealed that Simpson had been interviewed for three hours by the police days before his arrest, for example, defense counsel around the country expressed shock. "It was horrendous," said Harland Braun, a Los Angeles defense counsel. "It really hems in tremendously what Bob Shapiro can do, in terms of strategy."

In terms of defense strategy, Braun is undoubtedly correct. A defendant who says one thing to the police may have difficulty persuading a jury of something else. A defendant who lies to the police about some things may not be viewed as credible by a jury when he swears to something else—his innocence, for example.

But wait a minute. Is this really a bad thing? From society's point of view, if not that of a potential defendant is it anything but admirable when someone voluntarily speaks to the police about a crime of which he has knowledge? The individual interviewed may provide useful information which can aid the police in apprehending a criminal. He may demonstrate to the police his own innocence. He may inadvertently but justifiably incriminate himself. He may even confess.

If he does, and if the confession is true, we—if not his lawyer—should be pleased. As Justice Antonin Scalia of the Supreme Court observed in a 1990 dissenting opinion, "the procedural protections of the Constitution protect the guilty as well as the innocent, but it is not their objective to set the guilty free. . . . We should, then, rejoice at an honest confession, rather than pity the 'poor fool' who has made it."

Recall now the most telling part of Braun's statement that the Simpson statement to the police might "hem in" what his counsel could later argue. Translate the statement into plainer English. Because Simpson has told one story to the police, if he tells another at his trial, he does so at his peril.

Or say it even more directly. Because Simpson has either told some truths or some lies to the police—or some of both—his lawyer cannot be as creative, as fertile in framing a defense. Is the public really supposed to feel sorry about that?

Lawyers are trained to think that way. Most people, when confronted with a problem, gather whatever information they can and reason toward an answer. Lawyers start with the answer—their clients' answer—and then search for evidence to support it. So, inexorably, their reasoning veers toward Braun's: if I am to argue that Simpson cannot be proven guilty, I must either maintain that he was not at the scene of the crime; or that if he was there, he either did not stab the two inconveniently dead victims or that if he did, he did so in self-defense, or that if he did kill them, there was some legally sanctioned psychological reason for doing so. All are possibilities. Anything Simpson said to the police limits my options. Isn't it awful?

The problem with all this is not its lack of logic; it is perfectly logical. It simply has nothing to do with truth. While it is not the role of Simpson's lawyer to take any step that might result in his conviction, Shapiro is not a novelist, free to create an entirely fictional world into which Simpson comes and goes—or came and went.

And so for the rest of us. Some arguments are not only implausible; they are impossible. Some scenarios are not only untrue; they could not have been true. It may be that society should ask both more and less of lawyers. More willingness to say to clients that there are some arguments that lawyers will not make, less willingness to counsel lawful conduct that is morally odious. More willingness of lawyers to view themselves as part of a system of law, less willingness to view themselves as the alter egos of their clients.

Judges need to rethink their roles as well. There are times, as Rudolph J. Gerber, an Arizona appellate judge, has observed, when "judicial spectatorship" at lawyers' antics

A Simplified Organization of the Federal Court System

amounts "to indefensible patience when righteous anger would be appropriate." A little more anger directed at lawyers when they misbehave might go a long way.

Attorneys have frequently played valiant roles, defending the innocent, prosecuting the guilty, vindicating principle, settling disputes that should never have been litigated in the first place. They must continue to play those roles. But it is time to ask whether it really leads to justice to have a system in which many lawyers spend far more time avoiding truth than finding it. And it is never too late to ask whether we can continue to justify creating a sort of legal game in which the players lose sight of why they started playing in the first place and the spectators forget that what they are watching was not supposed to be a sport at all.

The Bill of Rights

AMENDMENT I
Congress shall make no law respecting an establishment of religion, or prohibiting the free exercise thereof; or abridging the freedom of speech, or of the press, or the right of the people peaceably to assemble, and to petition the Government for a redress of grievances.

AMENDMENT II
A well regulated Militia, being necessary to the security of a free State, the right of the people to keep and bear Arms, shall not be infringed.

AMENDMENT III
No Soldier shall, in time of peace be quartered in any house, without the consent of the Owner, nor in time of war, but in a manner to be prescribed by law.

AMENDMENT IV
The right of the people to be secure in their persons, houses, papers, and effects, against unreasonable searches and seizures, shall not be violated, and no Warrants shall issue, but upon probable cause, supported by Oath or affirmation, and particularly describing the place to be searched, and the persons or things to be seized.

AMENDMENT V
No person shall be held to answer for a capital, or other wise infamous crime, unless on a presentment or indictment of a Grand Jury, except in crimes arising in the land or naval forces, or in the Militia, when in actual service in time of War or public danger; nor shall any person be subject for the same offence to be twice put in jeopardy of life or limb; nor shall be compelled in any criminal case to be a witness against himself, nor be deprived of life, liberty, or property, without due process of law; nor shall private property be taken for public use, without just compensation.

AMENDMENT VI
In all criminal prosecutions, the accused shall enjoy the right to a speedy and public trial, by an impartial jury of the State and district wherein the crime shall have been committed, which district shall have been previously ascertained by law, and to be informed of the nature and cause of the accusation: to be confronted with the witnesses against him; to have compulsory process for obtaining witnesses in his favor, and to have the Assistance of Counsel for his defense.

AMENDMENT VII
In suits at common law, where the value in controversy shall exceed twenty dollars, the right of trial by jury shall be preserved and no fact tried by a jury shall be otherwise reexamined in any Court of the United States, than according to the rules of the common law.

AMENDMENT VIII
Excessive bail shall not be required, nor excessive fines imposed, nor cruel and unusual punishments inflicted.

AMENDMENT IX
The enumeration in the Constitution, of certain rights, shall not be construed to deny or disparage others retained by the people.

AMENDMENT X
The powers not delegated to the United States by the Constitution, nor prohibited by it to the States, are reserved to the States respectively, or to the people.

A Rape Defendant with No Identity, but a DNA Profile

By Bill Dedman

Unusual Legal Strategy

Law Catches Up to Science—Charges
Are Hedge Against Statute of Limitations

CHICAGO, Oct. 6—In an unusual legal strategy that stretches the law to match the developing science of DNA, a prosecutor in Wisconsin has filed rape and kidnapping charges against a defendant who has no name. John Doe is known only by his DNA code, extracted from semen samples from three rapes and tested after six years in a police property room.

"We know that one person raped these three women," said the prosecutor, Norman Gahn, assistant district attorney for Milwaukee County. "We just don't know who that person is. We will catch him."

The prosecutor's strategy is an effort to keep the six-year time limit for bringing charges from running out. A warrant must identify a person to be arrested, and this one names "John Doe, unknown male with matching deoxyribonucleic acid profile." Every month, an F.B.I. computer will compare the description of John Doe's DNA with thousands of new genetic samples from around the country.

"John Doe" is typically used in a warrant when the accused is known by an alias or by a physical description. The Milwaukee case is unusual in that it describes the suspect by only DNA information.

The case raises several questions about the gaps between science and law. Can a person be identified on a warrant by only a DNA code, or is a more traditional identification required, like a name or a physical description? Is the legal concept of a statute of limitations relevant in an age of DNA testing? Legal experts said the case had merit but would be challenged.

The case also reveals the promise and limitations of the national DNA databank, one year old this month, which, much like a national finger-print databank, was intended to allow investigators to share in the DNA information collected by state and municipal law-enforcement agencies.

The Federal Bureau of Investigation says the databank had helped solve 583 cases, including one involving a serial rapist in Washington, D.C., who turned out to also be a serial rapist in Florida. Police routinely collect DNA evidence not only in rape cases but also from saliva on beer cans left by a burglar, from sweat on a baseball bat used in a beating and from blood on a bullet that passed through a suspect.

But only 18 of the states are booked into the databank, the Combined DNA Index System, or Codis, while the rest are working on the technology and the financing. The databank is far smaller than the F.B.I.'s fingerprint bank. Much of the DNA evidence that is collected never makes its way into the databank.

For example, about 180,000 boxes of evidence, known as rape kits, sit unexamined on shelves in police departments across the nation, according to a survey of police agencies for the National Commission for the Future of DNA Evidence. These flat, rectangular boxes include blood vials, swabs of semen, locks of hair and fingernail scrapings—evidence collected from rape victims.

New York City alone has 12,000 unexamined rape kits and is trying to reduce the backlog by contracting with private laboratories. It has stopped destroying untested kits after five years, but other police departments continue the practice.

"We have the technology to solve these crimes, and we're not doing it," said Christopher Asplen, executive director of the DNA commission, which commissioned the survey.

Many police departments still use DNA evidence the way they have used fingerprints and tire tracks, to determine whether a suspect committed the crime. But the DNA databank makes the evidence useful for matching cases to convicted offenders, or to other cases in which a suspect may be known.

Cities vary widely in the use of DNA testing.

In Cleveland, "We only do DNA testing when there's an identifiable suspect," said Lieut. Edward Thiery, a spokesman for the Police Department.

In Chicago, "We now submit every sample for testing, but we still have a backlog of untested samples," said Pat Camden, a Police Department spokesman.

In Los Angeles, the Police Department buys a 40-foot refrigerated trailer truck every six months. Just to hold DNA evidence.

"The Los Angeles Police Department, right now, if you didn't have a suspect in custody and a court date, that thing is not going to get analyzed, whatever it is," Maria Foster, detective supervisor, told the DNA Commission.

The three DNA samples that uncovered a serial rapist in Milwaukee were collected in 1993. In each case, a man grabbed a woman from behind, told her that he had a knife, took her to a quiet place, raped her and then demanded money, the police said. After each woman reported the crime, vaginal and cervical swabs of semen were collected at a hospital.

The samples sat in the police evidence room, along with 2,300 other unexamined rape kits, for almost six years. To test them all would have swamped the state crime laboratory.

So Detective Lori Gaglione and her colleagues in Milwaukee's Sensitive Crimes Unit narrowed down the 2,300 cases to 53 based on such factors as the availability of victims and witnesses.

From the 53 samples that were tested, one case matched a convicted rapist in Minnesota. Another matched a convicted rapist elsewhere in Wisconsin, allowing charges to be filed only eight hours before the statute of limitations expired. And the three samples from 1993 matched each other. The other 47 remain in the national databank.

Using genetics to stymie the statute of limitations.

The Wisconsin state law, as in other states, requires that a warrant identify the accused. If the name is not known, the law allows identification "by any description by which the person to be arrested can be identified with reasonable certainty."

"My argument is going to be that genetic code goes well beyond reasonable certainty," said Mr. Gahn, who is a member of the Federal DNA Commission. "We're pushing the envelope as far as we can. It does something for the victim of the sexual assault, to know that someone cares and to know that we're out there working on the case."

The forensic science supervisor in the Wisconsin State Crime Laboratory, Dirk Janssen, said the probability of randomly selecting an unrelated individual who would have a DNA profile matching the three samples would be about 1 in 7.25 billion—more than the world's population—In the United States Caucasian population, and 1 in 1.98 billion in the African-American population.

Such a John Doe warrant based on DNA evidence has been used at least one other time, in Kansas in 1991. No one was arrested, so the issue has not been tested.

The warrant, which was signed by a judge last month, appeared to have merit, said Myram Raeder, a professor of law at Southwestern University in Los Angeles and the former head of the criminal section of the American Bar Association.

"It's clearly novel and therefore courts are really going to have to struggle with the intention of the statute and whether the clear meaning of the statute would cover this," Professor Raeder said.

In Wisconsin, as in most states, only people convicted of sexual offenses are required to give samples for DNA testing. The Legislature is close to expanding that to all felony offenses, as Alabama and Virginia have done. The Legislature is also considering eliminating the statute of limitations in cases of rape.

Someday, prosecutors hope, a man will leave a cigarette behind at another rape. Or cut himself on broken glass at a burglary. His saliva or blood will be tested, its DNA catalogued and entered in the F.B.I. databank.

And he will be charged with raping and kidnapping a woman in Milwaukee on Nov. 9, 1993.

Other Voices

Borough of Manhattan Community College Business Management Department

By Jerry Frug

Why Courts Are Always Making Law

Most judges hate to admit that they make social and political choices. It's time to get the truth out in the open.

A new movement that seeks to change the way people think about law has emerged in the past decade. Called critical legal studies, it goes to the core of the controversy over judicial activism. These days conservatives often criticize judges for trying to make law rather than simply apply it. Those involved in the new movement deny that it's possible simply to apply the law. They insist that whenever judges make legal decisions they choose among alternative possible results. Making such a choice requires courts to select among different sets of values and ways to organize society.

In some contexts, the political nature of judicial decision-making is obvious to everyone. The debate over the constitutional status of abortion, for example, is plainly connected with the current political struggle between those who support the right to life and those who are pro-choice. In deciding the constitutional issue, the Supreme Court cannot avoid choosing one of these positions over the other.

Another example is the current controversy over the definition of racial discrimination in the job market. Employment discrimination can be defined narrowly to prohibit only employer action that is intentionally motivated by racial bias, but it also can be defined broadly to prohibit any systematic exclusion of blacks or other minorities from parts of the job market, whether or not the exclusion is intentional. The choice between these positions is a political one and any choice the courts make involves judicial activism. Either judicial result would be an intervention in social life.

What is not so obvious is that even an interpretation of the rules of contract and property law involves a political choice. With corporate legal expenses mounting and litigation a national pastime, understanding what this means for the world of everyday business has significance far beyond the classroom.

CONSIDER in some depth, for example, the legal issues raised by employment-at-will contracts. Most American workers—including many executives—have employment contracts that don't specify how long their jobs will last or the reasons for which they might be fired. The extent of their job security depends on how these contracts are interpreted.

Many nonlawyers expect the law to have a ready answer to this kind of issue. They think that law is a cut-and-dried body of rules that lawyers either know or can easily look up. Many people seem to think, for example, that because employees can quit their jobs at any time, they can also be fired at any time for any reason.

Lawyers these days, in fact, rarely offer such a definitive description of the law. The difficulty in specifying the precise legal status of employees-at-will illustrates why. Over the past 25 years, courts have carved a number of exceptions into the freewheeling notion that employees can be fired for any reason. Employers have been held liable, for example, for attempting to fire employees who refused to perjure themselves before a legislative hearing, who blew the whistle about illegal conduct by their employers, and who filed workers' compensation claims. One way to sum up these recent cases is to say that employees can now recover damages from their employer if they are fired for reasons that undermine an important public policy.

But what counts as such a policy? One court has decided that it does not violate an important public policy to fire an employee for reporting to company (rather than public) officials that his supervisor is taking bribes. Another court has

---

Jerry Frug, 49, is a professor at Harvard law school, specializing in legal theory, contracts, and local government law, about which he has written a casebook.

decided that it does not violate an important public policy to fire an employee who refused to reduce staffing in a hospital's intensive care unit on the grounds that it would endanger patients lives. On the other hand, a third court has decided that firing an employee for refusing to date her foreman did violate "the best interest of the economic system or the public good." No wonder there's confusion about the law.

For decades legal scholars have devoted a vast amount of energy trying to make sense of conflicting decisions such as these. Over the past ten years, an increasing number of them have argued that the conflicts can best be understood in political terms. Called critical legal scholars—or simply "crits"—they contend that the decisions conflict with one another because they are based on different, and controversial, moral and political ideals. Lawyers cannot give a simple answer to a question, the crits say, because the legal system, like our society at large cannot reconcile the contradictory instincts people feel when they confront social problems. Rather than deciding which of these conflicting instincts to honor, the law embraces them all.

LOOKING AT the employment-at-will issue in this way points up something important about the judicial activism many conservatives find so abhorrent. The courts' acceptance for many years of the extensive employer power over employees reflected the conventional conservative idea that employers are entitled to run their business as they see fit. The more recent decisions limiting employers' power, by contrast have been justified by conventional legal arguments emphasizing the unfairness of arbitrary employer power over employees and the inefficiencies that result when people work under the threat of losing their jobs without adequate justification. Conservatives often treat these recent decisions as classic instances of liberal judges making law rather than following it.

But the conservative interpretation of employment-at-will itself became part of the law only through judicial activism. The conservative version of employment-at-will was first articulated by courts only in the late 19th century, and it replaced an earlier rule providing that employment contracts that were silent as to the length of the term of employment were presumed to last for a year. Modern courts have changed existing law no more than did the 19th century courts in their own time.

Some legal experts are currently seeking to create an even more extensive limitation of employer power. They have suggested, for example, that in the absence of an agreement to the contrary, all employees are entitled to at least some defensible explanation before they can be dismissed from their jobs. Others have argued that employees ought at least to have adequate notice before they can be fired. One way to implement this requirement would be to reintroduce the presumption that employment contracts are meant to last for a year. It is important to recognize that both these interpretations of employment-at-will are as legally defensible today as the earlier positions were when adopted.

By understanding law in terms of its creative nature, future lawyers and judges can learn to take responsibility for the positions they adopt.

There is, in short, no neutral basis on which to choose the proper legal interpretation of employment-at-will. Each interpretation represents a political choice about the proper nature of the employment relationship in the United States. None can be justified by reference to statute. Congress or state legislatures could decide the issue, but they haven't. Yet choosing among these different positions is of great significance to the American work force. According to one study, as many as one million employees-at-will are fired in the U.S. each year, and more than 150,000 of them would not have lost their jobs had the law required that they could be fired only for good cause.

Crits contend that it obscures the nature of a judicial decision when course and commentators present the legal issue as if it were an objective, or even relatively objective, matter of legal reasoning rather than a political choice. This does not mean that crits think that legal decision-making is simply subjective—that judges decide cases in any way they want.

Judges, the crits point out, go to great lengths to deny, even to themselves, the extent to which they make law rather than simply apply it. They consider employer power over employees not a matter of choice but a natural and necessary implication of modern workplace organization. They discount the influence of their moral and political views on their decisions by treating their own understanding of the employment relationship as common sense. They think of themselves as constrained by their professional role and by their understanding of legal precedent. For reasons such as these, they are very unlikely to experience their decision-making as a personal political decision. The political choices involved in selecting legal rules, in other words, are largely made unselfconsciously.

Those who are engaged in critical legal studies have employed a wide variety of methods—such as feminist theory, literary theory, political theory, and social theory—to expose the nature of the choices being made and to subject them to debate. Judges, the crits say, can learn to recognize the contestable nature of their own views of the world—and can learn to transform them—only if they become aware of the limits and political implications of their own imagination. A critical analysis of law is designed to identify these limits and implications and to describe the alternative moral and political values, also embraced by the legal system, that permit legal problems to be solved in alternative ways.

NOT SURPRISINGLY, the introduction of this kind of critical approach into American law schools has been controversial. Some scholars fear that teaching law students the political and moral basis of legal argument will engender cynicism about law and legal institutions and, as a result will undermine belief in the rule of law. But law students, like many others in our society, are already for too cynical about the legal system. The task of legal education is to overcome this cynicism, and that can't be done by relying on the fantasy that law is—or could be made to be—objective. A more promising approach, the crits suggest is to demonstrate the stakes involved in the selection of legal rules. By understanding law in terms of its controversial and creative nature, future lawyers and judges can become aware of and learn to take responsibility for the positions they adopt on matters of social policy.

Moreover, the American people generally can begin to understand that legal solutions to social problems are always provisional and contestable, never natural of necessary. Those who benefit by an existing legal rule are entitled to their privileged position only justifiable.

'I Was Certain, but I Was Wrong'

By Jennifer Thompson

In 1984 I was a 22-year-old college student with a grade point average of 4.0, and I really wanted to do something with my life. One night someone broke into my apartment, put a knife to my throat and raped me.

During my ordeal, some of my determination took an urgent new direction. I studied every single detail on the rapist's face. I looked at his hairline; I looked for scars, for tattoos, for anything that would help me identify him. When and if I survived the attack, I was going to make sure that he was put in prison and he was going to rot.

When I went to the police department later that day, I worked on a composite sketch to the very best of my ability. I looked through hundreds of noses and eyes and eyebrows and hairlines and nostrils and lips. Several days later, looking at a series of police photos. I identified my attacker. I knew this was the man. I was completely confident. I was sure.

I picked the same man in a lineup. Again, I was sure. I knew it, I had picked the right guy, and he was going to go to jail. If there was the possibility of a death sentence, I wanted him to die. I wanted to flip the switch.

When the case went to trial in 1986, I stood up on the stand, put my hand on the Bible and swore to tell the truth. Based on my testimony, Ronald Junior Cotton was sentenced to prison for life. It was the happiest day of my life because I could begin to put it all behind me.

In 1987, the case was retried because an appellate court had overturned Ronald Cotton's conviction. During a pre-trial hearing, I learned that another man had supposedly claimed to be my attacker and was bragging about it in the same prison wing where Ronald Cotton was being held. This man, Bobby Poole, was brought into court, and I was asked, "Ms. Thompson, have you ever seen this man?"

I answered: "I have never seen him in my life. I have no idea who he is."

Ronald Cotton was sentenced again to two life sentences. Ronald Cotton was never going to see light; he was never going to get out; he was never going to hurt another woman; he was never going to rape another woman.

In 1995, 11 years after I had first identified Ronald Cotton, I was asked to provide a blood sample so that DNA tests could be run on evidence from the rape. I agreed because I knew that Ronald Cotton had raped me and DNA was only going to confirm that. The test would allow me to move on once and for all.

I will never forget the day I learned about the DNA results. I was standing in my kitchen when the detective and the district attorney visited. They were good and decent people who were trying to do their jobs—as I had done mine, as anyone would try to do the right thing. They told me "Ronald Cotton didn't rape you. It was Bobby Poole."

The man I was so sure I had never seen in my life was the man who was inches from my throat, who raped me, who hurt me, who took my spirit away, who robbed me of my soul. And the man I had identified so emphatically on so many occasions was absolutely innocent.

Ronald Cotton was released from prison after serving 11 years. Bobby Poole pleaded guilty to raping me.

Ronald Cotton and I are the same age, so I knew what he had missed during those 11 years. My life had gone on. I had gotten married. I had graduated from college. I worked. I was a parent. Ronald Cotton hadn't gotten to do any of that.

Mr. Cotton and I have now crossed the boundaries of both the terrible way we came together and our racial difference (he is black and I am white) and have become friends. Although he is now moving on with his own life, I live with constant anguish that my profound mistake cost him so dearly. I cannot begin to imagine what would have happened had my mistaken identification occurred in a capital case.

Today there is a man in Texas named Gary Graham who is about to be executed because one witness is confident that Mr. Graham is the killer she saw from 30 to 40 feet away. This woman saw the murderer for only a fraction of the time that I saw the man who raped me. Several other witnesses contradict her, but the jury that convicted Mr. Graham never heard any of the conflicting testimony.

Jennifer Thompson is a homemaker in North Carolina and does volunteer work with abused children.

If anything good can come out of what Ronald Cotton suffered because of my limitations as a human being, let it be an awareness of the fact that eyewitnesses can and do make mistakes. I have now had occasion to study this subject a bit, and I have come to realize that eyewitness error has been recognized as the leading cause of wrongful convictions. One witness is not enough, especially when her story is contradicted by other good people.

Last week, I traveled to Houston to beg Gov. George W. Bush and his parole board not to execute Gary Graham based on this kind of evidence. I have never before spoken out on behalf of any inmate. I stood with a group of 11 men and women who had been convicted based on mistaken eyewitness testimony, only to be exonerated later by DNA or other evidence.

With them, I urged the Texas officials to grant Gary Graham a new trial, so that the eyewitnesses who are so sure that he is innocent can at long last be heard.

I know that there is an eyewitness who is absolutely positive she saw Gary Graham commit murder. But she cannot possibly be any more positive than I was about Ronald Cotton. What if she is dead wrong?

Regina v. Dudley and Stephens

(1) Case Title

[1884[L.R.. Q.B. 61   (Citation)
Lord Coleridge. C.J.   (Judge)

On July 5, 1884. . . . Thomas Dudley and Edward [sic] Stephens, with one Brooks. . . English seaman, and the deceased also an English boy between seventeen and eighteen years of age . . . . were cast away in a storm on the high seas 1,600 miles from the Cape of Good Hope. And were compelled to put into an open boat belonging to the said yacht. That in this boat they had no supply of water and no supply of food, except two 1 lb. Tins of turnips. . . [and a small turtle which they caught. That on the twelfth day the remains of the turtle were entirely consumed, and for the next eight days they had nothing to eat. That they had no fresh water. . . That the boat was drifting on the ocean, and was probably more than 1,000 miles away from land. That on the eighteenth day. When they had been seven days without food and five without water. The prisoners spoke to Brooks as to what should be done if no succour came. And suggested that someone be sacrificed to save the rest, but Brooks dissented, and the boy to whom they were understood to refer. Was not consulted. That on the 24th day of July. The day before the act now in question, the prisoner Dudley proposed to Stephens and Brooks that lots should be cast who should be put to death to save the rest, but Brooks refused to consent. And it was not put to the boy. . . Dudley proposed that if there was no vessel in sight by the morrow morning the boy should be killed. That next day, the 25th of July. No vessel appearing. . . . the prisoner Stephens agreed to the act, but Brooks dissented from it. That the boy was then lying at the bottom of the boat quite helpless and extremely weakened by famine and by drinking sea water, and unable to make any resistance, nor did he ever assent to his being killed. . . that Dudley. With the assent of Stephens, went to the boy, and telling him that his time was come. Put a knife into his throat and killed him then and there; that the three men fed upon the body on the boy. . . that on the fourth day after the act had been committed the boat was picked up by the passing vessel, and the prisoners rescued. . . That they were carried to the port of Falmouth, and committed for trial at Exeter. That if the men had not fed upon the body of the boy they would probably not have survived to be picked up and rescued, but would within the four days have died of famine. . . That at the time of the act in question there was no sail in sight, nor any reasonable prospect of relief. That under these circumstance there appeared to the prisoners every probability that unless they then fed or very soon fed upon the boy or one of themselves they would die of starvation. That there was no appreciable chance of saving life except by killing someone for the others to eat. . . [if] upon the whole matter the Court shall be of opinion that the killing Richard Parker be felony and murder as alleged in the indictment. . . [This case differs from killing done] in the service of. . . [the] Sovereign and in the defense of. . . [the] country. Now it is admitted that the deliberate killing of this unoffending and unresisting boy was clearly murder, unless the killing can be justified by some well-recognized excuse admitted by the law. It is further admitted that there was in this case no such excuse, unless the killing was justified by what has been called "necessity." But the temptation to the act which existed here was not what the law has ever called necessity. Not is this to be regretted. Though law and morality are not the same, the many things may be immoral which are not necessarily illegal, yet the absolute divorce of law from morality would be of fatal consequences; and such divorce would follow if the temptation to murder in this case were to be held by law an absolute defense of murder in this case, is not so. . .

It must not be supposed that in refusing to admit temptation to be an excuse for crime it is forgotten how terrible the temptation was; how awful the suffering; how hard in such trials to keep the judgment and the conduct pure. We are often compelled to set up standards we cannot reach ourselves. . . . A man has no right to . . . allow compassion for the criminal to change or weaken in any manner the legal definition of the crime. It is therefore our duty to declare that the prisoners' act in this case was willful murder. That

the facts as stated in the verdict are no legal justification of the homicide; and to say that in or unanimous opinion the prisoners are upon this special verdict guilty of murder.

What to Do When Stopped by the Police

A Community/Citizen Guide

Foreword

The basic materials in this pamphlet were prepared by Police and Community Enterprises—Project PACE. The National Black Police Association, an umbrella organization representing more than 35,000 dedicated African American police officers nationally, stands for unity, justice, and peace. The NBPA exists to help prod law enforcement agencies to be sensitive to the needs and concerns of minorities, women and the poor. We hope this pamphlet will be helpful. We urge, however, that you do not rely on it as a legal advisor. But we hope the information presented here will keep you from having to go to jail.

It Could Happen to You

What is your name?
Where do you live?
Have you got any identification?

These are very simple questions which can be easily answered by almost everyone. But when a police officer is involved, it can cause a lot of problems both for the officer and for YOU. Most of the time, there is a reason for the officer to question you—even if it may not seem so at the time. The officer may be investigating a complaint in the neighborhood, or following up on a radio call concerning a crime committed in the area. For one reason or another, you may be the individual the police suspect. You may have knowledge that will help in the investigation, or the officer may think that you are experiencing some kind of trouble.

Sometimes the manner in which the police question you may involve not respecting YOUR RIGHTS. Sometimes you may overreact to the questions and create an even more serious situation. We will attempt to explain your rights, what to remember, and what to expect when an officer starts asking you a lot of questions . . . it could save you from answering a lot more unnecessarily.

If You Are Stopped by the Police in Your Car

If you are driving a vehicle, the police can ask you to pull over at any time. The best thing to do in this situation is to pull over and follow the directions of the officer. You will probably be asked to produce your driver's license and registration of the vehicle. This you must do if asked. If you are

stopped at night, turn on your dome light and show the officer that nothing is wrong. It is best to do nothing which may give reason to search further. Having your lights on and keeping your hands on the steering wheel will usually put the officer's mind at ease.

Chances are that the officer is going to write out a ticket for a traffic violation. Of course, you may start to explain at this point but you should limit your comments. Be careful how you protest. A simple traffic violation may start costing you a fortune in fines for other violations. If you think that the ticket is incorrect, then carry your protest to Traffic Court.

If You Are Stopped by the Police on the Street

Most of the problems you may encounter with the police can be avoided. Remember, they think they have reason (probable cause) to stop you and ask questions. At this time, you should stop, collect your thoughts and remain calm. Whether or not you are arrested, may just depend on how calm and prepared you are at this time.

There are many factors that the police may take into consideration when observing you. Every situation is different and the officer may consider the following factors:

1. When you are running and a crime has been reported in the area.
2. If you are hanging around with people under police investigation.
3. You are near an area where crime has just been reported.
4. You are in an area which the police believe to be abandoned or unoccupied.
5. You are acting in a manner which appears to be suspicious.
6. The police believe you are in possession of stolen property.
7. When stopped while walking or driving your car, you refuse to answer police questions, give false, evasive or contradictory information.
8. You have been identified to the police by someone else.
9. When you use derogatory or offensive language . . . you may be saying the wrong thing at the wrong time.

While these things are taken into consideration when questioning you, the police MUST STILL RESPECT YOUR RIGHTS TO NOT ANSWER QUESTIONS THAT SOUND ACCUSATORY.

If the Police Come Knocking at Your Door

If the police knock at your door, you do not have to let them in unless there is a signed warrant. If it is proper on its face, you must step aside and let them into your home. If it is an *arrest warrant*, look at the name on the warrant to make certain they have the right person. If it is a search warrant, make sure the address is correct and note what is specifically listed on the warrant to be searched for in your home. If the police *do not have a warrant*, you do not have to let them in unless they insist. Perhaps you can settle this matter at the door. If they do insist, over your objections, then be careful to:

First, ask for a police badge.

Second, ask the purpose of entering your home.

Third, let them in only after they insist.

Fourth, if you object, make sure that the police know that you do not consent to any search of your home.

Fifth, remember badge numbers, officer's faces, and the time of day. Write this information down.

The police are not required to give you a receipt for property they intend to book as evidence such as stolen goods, guns, etc. However, when property is taken from your home, ask the police for a receipt. The police may also search without a warrant whenever arresting an individual. They may search the individual under arrest, the area near the arrest, and the room where the arrest was made if inside the home. They may also search after consent is given. Police may also search when there is an emergency (for example, someone screaming for help inside your home), or when chasing you or someone else into your home.

Remember

1. If the police have stopped you, they believe there is reason to do so.
2. It is best to be calm and identify yourself.
3. In many situations, you can talk your way INTO jail as well as talk yourself out of jail. By yelling or threatening an officer, the BEST you can do is get yourself arrested . . . and who needs that.

National Black Police Association
3251 Mt. Pleasant Street, N.W.
Second Floor Washington, D.C. 20010-2103
(202) 986-2070
FAX (202) 986-04103

New York Hazing Law

January 20, 2005

Introduced by Sens. LITTLE, BALBONI, BONACIC, FARLEY, JOHNSON, LAVALLE, MARCELLINO, MARCHI, MAZIARZ, McGEE, PADAVAN, RATH, SALAND, SKELOS, WINNER, WRIGHT—read twice and ordered printed, and when printed to be committed to the Committee on Codes.

AN ACT to amend the penal law, in relation to increasing the penalties for hazing

THE PEOPLE OF THE STATE OF NEW YORK, REPRESENTED IN SENATE AND ASSEMBLY, DO ENACT AS FOLLOWS:

Section 1. Section 120.16 of the penal law, as amended by chapter 86 of the laws of 1988, is amended to read as follows: S 120.16 Hazing in the first degree.

A person is guilty of hazing in the first degree when, in the course of another person's initiation into or affiliation with any organization, he OR SHE intentionally or recklessly engages in conduct which creates a substantial risk of SERIOUS physical injury OR DEATH to such other person or a third person and thereby causes such SERIOUS injury OR DEATH TO SUCH PERSON OR TO A THIRD PERSON.

Hazing in the first degree is a class {A misdemeanor} D FELONY.

S 2. Section 120.17 of the penal law, as added by chapter 86 of the laws of 1988, is amended to read as follows: S 120.17 Hazing in the second degree.

A person is guilty of hazing in the second degree when, in the course of another person's initiation or affiliation with any organization, he OR SHE intentionally or recklessly engages in conduct which creates a substantial risk of physical injury to such other person or a third person AND THEREBY CAUSES SUCH INJURY.

Hazing in the second degree is a {violation} CLASS E FELONY.

S 3. The penal law is amended by adding a new section 120.18 to read as follows:

S 120.18 HAZING IN THE THIRD DEGREE.

EXPLANATION—Matter in ITALICS (underscored) is new; matter in brackets { } is old law to be omitted.

LBD04463-01-5
191S. 719

A PERSON IS GUILTY OF HAZING IN THE THIRD DEGREE WHEN, IN THE COURSE OF ANOTHER PERSON'S INITIATION OR AFFILIATION WITH ANY ORGANIZATION, HE OR SHE INTENTIONALLY OR RECK- LESSLY ENGAGES IN CONDUCT WHICH CREATES A SUBSTANTIAL RISK OF PHYSICAL INJURY TO SUCH OTHER PERSON OR A THIRD PERSON. HAZING IN THE THIRD DEGREE IS A CLASS A MISDEMEANOR.

S 4. This act shall take effect on the first of November next succeeding the date on which it shall have become a law.

Hazing in Black Fraternities

Dr. John A. Williams
Executive Director, Center for the Study of Pan-Hellenic Issues

If you wanted to make a case for hazing in Black fraternities, you have lots of buttons you can push to make a new member accept being "made right" as the phrase goes. You can appeal to his manhood, by reminding him that "only the strong survive." You can appeal to his sense of racial pride by reminding him that the pressures he is expected to endure from "the brothers" is nothing compared to what the "real world" will put on him. And if you wanted to appeal to his spiritual being, you could challenge him with Scriptures such as Psalms 66:10-12:

> *"For Thou hast tested us O Lord; Thou hast tried us as silver is tried. Thou didst bring us into the net, Thou didst lay affliction on our loins, Thou didst let men ride over our heads. We have gone through fire and through water; Yet Thou hast brought us forth to a spacious place"*

If you wanted to make a case for hazing, these are but a few of the options you have to convince a pledgee to accept what they are being asked to endure before "crossing the sands" to come into the frat. But there are some questions you have to ask yourself if you have any sense of history and any sense of racial pride. How do you explain to him that after slavery is abolished for over a hundred years, a pledge should submit to being treated worse by his "brothers" than his ancestors were by their "masters"? How do you justify beating a brother into submission with boards, belts, fists and other instruments to teach him that he is becoming a "man" by allowing himself to be punished like a child?

There is much we do in Black fraternities that we attempt to justify by saying "it's a Black thing, you wouldn't understand." But in the final analysis, even the Blackest of us still don't understand why it is necessary to haze a prospective member in the name of "making him right."

If we want a brother to be smarter and tougher so he can succeed "in the real world" then why don't we make sure he gets to class on time, refreshed instead of exhausted from all-night pledge sessions? Have we given in to the racist views of our oppressors who only judge a Black man's manhood by the stripes he can endure from the whip and not by the mental prowess he can display in the classroom? Or is that just being soft?

Hank Nuwer, the author of "*Broken Pledges*" and "*The Wrongs of Passage*" has said that hazing is for cowards. I prefer the term punks. If we in Black fraternities reject that notion, then why do we deny our participation when "all hell breaks loose" and someone is injured? Why did Michael Davis' murderers lie and say he had been injured playing football when they had slapped, hit and body-slammed him into unconsciousness? Their failure to step up and be Black men when their behavior was questioned cost Kappa Alpha Psi fraternity $2.25 million dollars in 1997. And yet that is what it is be Black men? I don't think so!

When Joseph Snell was driven to near suicide by the brothers of Omega Psi Phi at the University of Maryland in 1993 after he had been beaten with hammers, whips, brushes and broken pieces of furniture, he landed in the hospital. Joseph's crime was that he wasn't "Black enough" so some idiot decided to place a space heater next to his face to make him darker. That display cost their fraternity nearly $400,000 in damages. All in the name of "making a brother right"!

We all know that undergraduate members of Black fraternities have pretty much ignored the no-pledge policy for new member intake. Underground pledging has replaced a system designed to eliminate hazing and reduce the liability pledging and/or hazing places on Black fraternities. No one wants to be a paper brother. No one wants to let someone "skate" into the frat. No one wants to be accused of being "soft," and so the madness continues.

If this is what it takes to be a Black man, then why not be a real man when the "accident" happens. Don't run around looking for some story for the other brothers to memorize.

Don't hide behind the shield because you know others in the frat "have your back." Pick up the phone . . . no better yet, get in your car and go to his mother's house and tell her. *"I just broke your son's ribs, bloodied his lip, crushed his skull and kicked his Black a-- until he collapsed in the basement. He was trying to skate into the frat, you know? And we wasn't having any of that. But you know something? He went out like a true brother! He took it like a man!"*

Stop and Frisk Cases in Connecticut and New York

By: Christopher Reinhart, Research Attorney

You asked about cases in Connecticut and New York defining the power of police to stop and frisk people.

Attached is a copy of the New York statute and more information on New York case law.

Summary

The basis for stop and frisk cases is the U.S. Supreme Court's decision in *Terry v. Ohio* (392 U.S. 1 (1968)). In that case, the Court ruled that an officer who observes unusual conduct that leads him to reasonably believe, based on his experience, that criminal activity may occur and that the person may be armed and dangerous can conduct a limited search of the person's outer clothing for weapons. The purpose of the search is to protect the officer and others in the area.

The Connecticut Supreme Court stated that the federal and state constitutions allow a police officer to briefly detain a person for an investigation if the officer has a reasonable and articulable suspicion that the individual has committed or is about to commit a crime. If the officer reasonably believes that the person might be armed and dangerous, the officer can conduct a pat down search strictly limited to the search for weapons. The officer cannot conduct a general exploratory search for evidence of criminal activity. A pat-down search justified in its inception can become unconstitutional if it is more intrusive than necessary to protect the officer (*State v. Trine*, 236 Conn. 216 (1996)).

In New York, a statute sets the standard for a stop and frisk. Under the law, a police officer can stop a person in public if he reasonably suspects that the person is committing, has committed, or is about to commit a felony or misdemeanor. The officer then can conduct a search for deadly weapons or other instruments that could cause serious physical injury if he reasonably suspects he is in danger of physical injury (NY Crim. Pro. Law § 140.50).

The standard appears to be the same in both states. And the cases in Connecticut and New York are similar. Courts in both states look at the facts of a specific case. The courts consider all of the information available to the police officer and require something more than a hunch or speculation.

The section below describes case law in Connecticut and New York and two recent U.S. Supreme Court rulings.

Connecticut

Under the Connecticut cases, whether a police officer has a reasonable and articulable suspicion is an objective test that focuses on the state of mind of the officer and what a reasonable person with the information known to the officer would believe. A hunch or speculation is not enough. There must be specific facts and rational inferences that reasonably warrant the intrusion (*State v. Trine*, 236 Conn. 216 (1996)). One function of the stop is to maintain the status quo for a brief period while the police investigate a suspected crime.

In a recent case, the Connecticut Supreme Court ruled that a person's presence in a high-crime area at odd hours did not justify stopping him for questioning. In this case, the defendant pulled his car into a vacant lot of a social club that had closed for the evening. The area recently experienced a dramatic increase in criminal activity and people often parked there before engaging in drug dealing and prostitution. The police arrested the defendant for driving under the influence. The court ruled that the detention and arrest violated the state constitution because the police officer did not have a reasonable and articulable suspicion to stop the defendant since his decision was based only on the location and time of day (*State v. Donahue*, 251 Conn. 636 (1999)).

Below is a list of cases that demonstrate circumstances when a stop and frisk is proper.

1. A person's presence in a high crime area, his attempt to conceal himself from the officers, and his refusal to follow the officers' directions supported the decision to pat-down the individual (*State v. Gregory*, 56 Conn. App. 47 (1999)).
2. The police had a reasonable suspicion to stop a person when he began to flee before the police attempted to stop him, he was a known burglar observed in someone's yard at 1:30 a.m., and he was seen carrying items and fleeing into another back yard (*State v. Groomes*, 232 Conn. 455 (1995)).

3. An officer's hunch that the person committed or was about to commit a crime did not justify an investigative stop when it was based on recognizing an individual as someone recently arrested for burglary, he was present at night in a neighborhood where burglaries had occurred, and he was carrying a duffel bag and wearing a winter jacket on a warm night in August (*State v. Oquendo,* 223 Conn. 635 (1992)).

4. Police were justified in frisking a person for weapons when he ran, then stopped, and reached into his waistband (*State v. Mierez,* 24 Conn. App. 543 (1991)).

In addition, the Connecticut Supreme Court ruled that what an officer detects during a lawful pat-down search could provide probable cause to believe that an object is non-threatening contraband. The court stated that after a lawful pat down, any further intrusion must be based on an independent justification—either a warrant or an exception to the warrant requirement. The information from the pat down can trigger an exception to the warrant requirement (*State v. Trine,* 236 Conn. 216 (1996)). In this case, the court found that once the officer had probable cause to believe that the defendant was committing a felony in his presence, he had authority to arrest the person without a warrant.

New York

Under the New York statute, the courts use an objective test of whether a person of reasonable caution with the facts available at the time of the encounter would believe the officer's actions warranted. A frisk is unreasonable if there are no objective factors. Absolute certainty is not required (NY Jur.2d Crim.Law §450-459).

A hunch or gut reaction is not enough (*People v. Sobotker,* 43 NY2d 559 (1978)). Evasive or erratic behavior often justifies a frisk. A suspect's negative answers only justify an inquiry but false or inconsistent responses justify a belief that criminal activity is occurring. Flight alone without other information does not give an officer a reasonable suspicion. Pursuing someone who flees after an approach for an investigative inquiry is justified only when there is reasonable suspicion that the person committed or was about to commit a crime. The person's location is a factor along with other objective factors to determine reasonable suspicion of criminal activity (NY Jur.2d Crim.Law §450-459).

The scope of the search must reasonably relate to the circumstances. Police can conduct a limited search for weapons of the suspect's outer clothing for their protection and other in the area. Police can search a bag that a suspect is carrying (*People v. Weeks,* 524 NYS2d 844 (1988, 2d Dept).

Below is a list of cases that demonstrate circumstances when a stop and frisk is proper.

1. A stop and frisk was not proper when the person was suspected only of possessing an open container of alcohol with intent to drink in public (*People v. Bothwell,* 671 NYS2d 595 (Sup.Ct. 1998)).

2. Waistband bulges are a sign of a weapon that can warrant a stop and frisk (*People v. Wright,* 678 NYS2d 17 (App.Div. 1st Dept 1998)).

3. A pocket bulge that is not indefinable does not justify a frisk because it could be caused by an innocuous item (*People v. De Bour,* 386 NYS2d 375 (1976)).

4. Police did not have a reasonable suspicion that a person possessed a gun when his actions were innocuous, there were no threatening gestures, and no bulges or weapons observed (*People v. Powell,* 667 NYS2d 725 (App. Div. 1st Dep't 1998)).

5. Police had a reasonable belief that a suspect might be armed and could conduct a pat-down search when the suspect refused to answer questions, was severely agitated, nervous, and shaking uncontrollably (*People v. Nichols,* 672 NYS2d 326 (App.Div. 1st Dep't 1998)).

6. An officer who began a lawful inquiry could frisk the suspect after he failed to remove his hands from his pockets after repeated requests (*People v. Perez,* 638 NYS2d 441 (1996, 1st Dept)).

7. After receiving a report of a person with a firearm, an officer could pat down the outer clothing of a person who fit the report's description and location (*People v. Salaman,* 71 NYS2d 869 (1988)).

8. A search is improper when the description of a suspect is too general but it could justify stopping and questioning the person (*People v. Robinson,* 507 NYS2d 268 (1986, 2d Dept)).

Recent U.S. Supreme Court Cases

The U.S. Supreme Court recently ruled that, at least in some circumstances, police can stop and question someone who runs at the sight of a police officer. In this case, a man ran from an area known for narcotics trafficking after seeing the police. The police tracked him down and, after searching him, discovered he was illegally carrying a gun. The Court ruled that the stop was proper because the police had a "reasonable, articulable suspicion" that criminal activity was occurring and could conduct a brief, investigatory stop. Relevant factors included the person's location in a high crime area, his nervous behavior, and his unprovoked flight (*Illinois v. Wardlow,* No. 98-1036 (January 12, 2000))

In its most recent stop and frisk decision, the Court ruled that an anonymous tip that a person is carrying a gun is not enough on its own to justify a stop and frisk of the person. In this case, an anonymous caller stated that a young black male wearing a plaid shirt at a bus stop was carrying a gun. The officer saw three black men at the bus stop and he frisked the person wearing a plaid shirt. The Court stated that the frisk was improper because the officer's suspicion came from an unknown caller at an unknown location rather than from the officer's observations. The tip lacked sufficient reliability and the officer could not test the informant's credibility. The officer also did not have a reason to suspect the three people of illegal conduct and did not see a gun or any unusual movements (*Florida v. J.L.*, No. 98-1993 (March 28, 2000)). The Court distinguished this case from other situations where tips are corroborated and have sufficient reliability or are from known informant whose reputations can be assessed.

Fourth Amendment Supreme Court Cases
Stop and Frisk

Terry v. Ohio (Stop and Frisk)
392 U.S. 1, 88 S.Ct. 1968,
20 L.Ed.2d 889 (1968)

A police officer witnessed three men pacing in front of a jewelry store and suspected that a robbery was being planned. He approached the men and identified himself, then performed frisks of defendants Chilton and Terry and discovered illegal concealed weapons. Defendants were convicted and appealed, claiming that the frisk violated their Fourth Amendment right against unlawful searches and seizures.

The Supreme Court upheld the conviction, finding that when a law enforcement officer has "reasonable grounds" for suspecting that a criminal suspect may be armed, he may pat down the outer layer of the suspect's clothing for weapons. The ruling held that the Fourth Amendment protection against unreasonable searches and seizures is not violated when a pat-down is performed based on reasonable suspicion for the purpose of ensuring officer safety.

What you should know about stop and frisk law:

The Court's ruling in *Terry v. Ohio* has been understood to validate the practice of frisking (or patting down) suspects for weapons under diverse circumstances. Generally, law enforcement officers will perform frisks at their discretion, regardless of the "reasonable suspicion" standard established by the Terry ruling. Thus, it is not uncommon for frisks to be conducted for investigatory purposes where no actual evidence of a threat to officer safety exists.

Due to the prevalence of police frisks it is important for citizens to understand the rationale behind police authority to pat down suspects, and the limitations the Court has placed on that authority:

1. After initiating contact, police officers may pat down criminal suspects for weapons in order to provide for their safety and that of the public. This police practice is rarely, if ever, a violation of your constitutional rights.
2. If you are frisked, any hard objects the officer detects can be removed from your pockets and inspected.
3. You can be charged for possession of illegal weapons discovered through a lawful pat down.
4. Indicate that you do not consent to a full search of your person. Your proximity to the officer creates a limited window of opportunity in which to assert your rights. If you do not wish to be searched following the pat down, verbally indicate your refusal to be searched as soon as possible in order to avoid any misunderstandings.
5. ***Police CANNOT conduct frisks for the purpose of discovering evidence other than weapons. The Supreme Court has ruled that suspicious items other than weapons retain their Fourth Amendment protection during a frisk. This means that if a police officer claims that objects in your pocket feel like drugs, the objects cannot be further investigated without your consent.

Investigatory Stops and Detentions

Florida v. Bostick
501 U.S. 429, 111 S. Ct. 2382,
115 L.Ed.2d 389 (1991)

Defendant Bostick boarded a bus from Miami to Atlanta. At a stopover in Ft. Lauderdale, the bus was boarded by two uniformed narcotics officers who were performing a routine inspection of the bus. Without reasonable suspicion, the officers approached Bostick in his seat and requested to see his ticket and identification. Finding nothing out of the ordinary, the officers proceeded to request consent to search his luggage. Bostick reportedly consented, at which point the officers performed a search and discovered cocaine. Bostick was subsequently convicted, and appealed claiming that due to his apparent inability to leave the bus, the encounter constituted an unlawful seizure, the evidence obtained through which must be suppressed. The Supreme Court upheld Bostick's conviction, finding that the practice of contacting citizens on buses in this fashion did not constitute an unlawful seizure under the Fourth Amendment. The Court's ruling rejected Bostick's claim that because the officers were armed and positioned such that he could not leave his seat or the bus, the encounter was a seizure. Since it was never directly communicated to the defendant that he was not free to leave, the Court concluded that the police officers' actions did not violate the Fourth Amendment. So long as nature of the officers' contact with the defendant is held constitutionally valid, his consent to be searched and the resultant evidence are held valid as well.

What you should know about investigatory stops and detentions:

Florida v. Bostick is a clear example of law enforcement officers' systematic reliance on the tendency of citizens to overestimate police authority. Moreover, the Supreme Court's ruling in this case indicates a willingness to accommodate manipulative law enforcement practices in order to prevent the Constitution's provisions from interfering with the arrest of drug suspects. So long as the police and the courts cooperate in using the ignorance of suspects as a tool through which to obtain convictions, it is extremely important for citizens to know their rights.

In the context of investigatory stops and detentions, here are a few important principles that should be remembered:

1. Police may stop you for any reason, but are not entitled to any information other than your identification.
2. Police may not detain you without reasonable suspicion.
3. Police may not search you without either probable cause or your consent. Don't consent to warrantless searches!
4. Police will often try to trick you into thinking you can't leave. Ask if you are free to go.

An investigatory stop is a particularly difficult encounter for the citizen, because police officers are experienced at controlling the situation. It is an important reality, however, that it is actually the citizen who technically controls all police encounters until evidence emerges to justify police intrusion into the citizen's privacy or freedom of movement.

**Remember that your refusal to be searched cannot be legally interpreted as evidence that you may be involved in a crime. Police cannot detain you only because you refused a search.

Consent Searches

Schneckloth v. Bustamonte
412 U.S. 218, 93 S.Ct. 2041,
36 L.Ed.2d 854 (1973)

Officer James Rand stopped a car with six occupants and received consent from the driver to search the vehicle. It was determined that the officer did not pressure the driver into consenting. In the back seat he found three checks which had been stolen from a car wash. Defendant Robert Bustamonte challenged his arrest, arguing that while he had consented voluntarily, he had not been informed of his right not to consent to the search.

In *Schneckloth v. Bustamonte*, the Supreme Court ruled that consent is valid as long as it is voluntarily given. The ruling held that police may not use threats or coercion to obtain consent, but that they need not inform suspects of their right not to consent to a search. In reaching this decision, the Court rejected the stricter "waiver test," which holds that suspects must be fully informed of their Fourth Amendment right against unreasonable searches and seizures before they can give valid consent.

What you should know about consent searches:

As demonstrated by the Court in the Schneckloth ruling, the police are under no obligation to inform citizens of their Fourth Amendment rights when requesting to perform a search. This means it is up to the individual to understand and exercise their right not to be searched. Some states require that police obtain the citizen's signature on a waiver form before conducting the search, however in most places police merely need to obtain the citizen's permission verbally. This can be a tricky situation because police will sometimes interpret a broad range of statements or actions as implied consent. Here's what you should remember about police search requests:

1. According to the Fourth Amendment, you cannot be searched without a warrant or probable cause, unless you consent. Don't consent to warrantless searches.
2. The officer cannot "make things easier" for you if you consent. Consenting makes it easier for the officer to arrest you.
3. If you consent to a search, any evidence found can be used against you in court.
4. If you don't consent to a search and the officer searches you anyway, your lawyer can get the evidence thrown out in court.
5. You cannot get in trouble or become a criminal suspect for refusing to be searched.
6. The officer cannot detain you unless he has reasonable suspicion to believe you are involved in something illegal.

Source URL:
http://www.flexyourrights.org/fourth_amendment_supreme_court_cases

What To Do If You're Stopped By The Police

KEEP THIS CARD HANDY! IF YOU HAVE A POLICE ENCOUNTER, YOU CAN PROTECT YOURSELF.

NYCLU
NEW YORK CIVIL LIBERTIES UNION

www.nyclu.org

What To Do If You're Stopped By The Police

We all recognize the need for effective law enforcement, but we should also understand our own rights and responsibilities — especially in our interactions with the police.

This card tells you what to do if you are stopped, arrested, or injured in your encounter with the police, and how to file a complaint.

Produced by the New York Civil Liberties Union and American Civil Liberties Union.

NYCLU
NEW YORK CIVIL LIBERTIES UNION

125 Broad Street
New York, NY 10004
212.607.3300
Fax 212.607.3318
www.nyclu.org

WHAT TO DO IF YOU'RE STOPPED BY THE POLICE

- **Stay calm and in control** of your words, body language and emotions.

- **Don't get into an argument** with the police.

- Never bad-mouth a police officer.

- Remember, **anything you say or do** can be used against you.

- **Keep your hands** where the police can see them.

- **Don't run. Don't touch** any police officer.

- **Don't resist** even if you believe you are innocent.

- **Don't complain** at the scene or tell the police they're wrong or that you're going to file a complaint.

- **Do not make any statements** regarding the incident.

- **Ask for a lawyer** immediately if you are arrested.

- Remember **officers' badge and patrol** car numbers.

- **Write down everything** you remember ASAP.

- Try to find **witnesses** and their names and phone numbers.

- If you are injured, **take photos of the injuries** as soon as possible, but make sure **you get medical attention first.**

342

If You Have A Police Encounter, You Can Protect Yourself.

1. What you say to the police is always important. What you say can and will be used against you, and it can give the police an excuse to arrest you, especially if you bad-mouth a police officer.

2. You don't have to consent to a search of yourself, your car or your house. If you **do** consent to a search, it can affect your rights later in court. If the police say they have a search warrant, **ask to see it**. If they don't, use the phrase **"I do not consent to this search."**

3. Do not interfere with or obstruct the police — you can be arrested for it.

IF YOU ARE STOPPED FOR QUESTIONING:

1. Police may stop and detain you only if there is reasonable suspicion that you committed, are committing or are about to commit a crime.

2. You can ask if you are under arrest or free to leave. If you are arrested, you have a right to know why.

3. Police can't lawfully require that you identify yourself or produce ID if they don't reasonably suspect you of a crime. But **use your judgment** — refusal could lead to your arrest even if unjustified.

4. If police reasonably suspect you pose a danger to them or others, they may pat down your outer clothing. Don't physically resist, but say you don't consent to the search. If an officer asks you to empty your pockets before he pats you down — even if he says you won't get in trouble — decline to do so. Use the phrase **"I do not consent to this search."**

5. Don't bad-mouth a police officer or run away, even if you believe what is happening is unreasonable. That could lead to your arrest.

IF YOU ARE STOPPED IN YOUR CAR:

1. Upon request, show the police your driver's license, registration and proof of insurance. In certain cases, your car can be searched without a warrant. To protect yourself later, you should state that you **do not consent to a search**. It is not lawful for police to arrest you simply for refusing to consent to a search.

2. If you're given a ticket, you should sign it; otherwise you can be arrested. You can always fight the case in court later.

3. If you're suspected of drunk driving (DWI) you will be asked to take a breath-alcohol and coordination test. If you fail the tests, or if you refuse to take them, you will be arrested, your driver's license may be suspended and your car may be taken away.

IF POLICE COME TO YOUR HOME:

1. The police can enter your home without permission if they have a warrant or if it is an emergency situation. If the police say they have a warrant, ask to see it. They must show it to you when they are able to do so safely.

2. If you are arrested in your home or office, the police can search you and the area immediately surrounding you or where evidence of criminal activity is in plain view.

IF YOU ARE ARRESTED OR TAKEN TO A POLICE STATION:

1. You have the right to remain silent and to talk to a lawyer before you talk to the police. **Don't tell the police anything except your name and address.** Don't give any explanations, excuses or stories. You can make your defense later, in court, based on what you and your lawyer decide is best.

2. If you have a lawyer, ask to see your lawyer immediately. If you can't afford a lawyer, you have a right to a free one once your case goes to court. You can ask the police how to contact a lawyer. **Don't say anything without a lawyer.**

3. Within a reasonable time after your arrest or booking, you should ask the police to contact a family member or friend. If you are permitted to make a phone call, anything you say at the precinct may be recorded or listened to. Be very careful. Never talk about the facts of your case over the telephone.

4. Do not make any decisions in your case until you have talked with a lawyer.

To File A Police Misconduct Complaint:
Contact the Civilian Complaint Review Board by calling **311** or by visiting **www.nyc.gov/html/ccrb.**

New York Minorities More Likely to Be Frisked

By Al Baker
May 12, 2012

Blacks and Latinos were nine times as likely as whites to be stopped by the police in New York City in 2009, but, once stopped, were no more likely to be arrested.

The more than 575,000 stops of people in the city, a record number of what are known in police parlance as "stop and frisks," yielded 762 guns.

Of the reasons listed by the police for conducting the stops, one of those least commonly cited was the claim that the person fit the description of a suspect. The most common reason listed by the police was a category known as "furtive movements."

Under Commissioner Raymond W. Kelly, the New York Police Department's use of such street stops has more than quintupled, fueling not only an intense debate about the effectiveness and propriety of the tactic, but also litigation intended to force the department to reveal more information about the encounters.

The Center for Constitutional Rights, which got the data on stop and frisks after it first sued the city over the issue after the 1999 killing of Amadou Diallo, said its analysis of the 2009 data showed again what it argued was the racially driven use of the tactic against minorities and its relatively modest achievements in fighting crime.

The center, a nonprofit civil and human rights organization financed by donors and foundations, and other critics of the tactic like to note that a gun buyback program conducted by the police at several Bronx churches one day in January yielded 1,186 guns.

Police officials, for their part, vigorously praise the stop-and-frisk policy as a cornerstone of their efforts to suppress crime. The stops led to 34,000 arrests and the seizing of more than 6,000 weapons other than guns, according to the center's analysis.

The police officials argue that the widespread use of the tactic has forced criminals to keep their guns at home and allowed the department to bank thousands of names in a database for detectives to mine in fighting future crimes.

Besides better reporting, the surge in the number of stops, they said, is also a byproduct of flooding high-crime areas with more officers, a strategy for a force with a shrinking headcount.

"These are not unconstitutional," Paul J. Browne, the Police Department's chief spokesman, said of the stops. "We are saving lives, and we are preventing crime."

According to the analysis of the 2009 raw data by the Center for Constitutional Rights, nearly 490,000 blacks and Latinos were stopped by the police on the streets last year, compared with 53,000 whites.

But once stopped, the arrest rates were virtually the same. Whites were arrested in slightly more than 6 percent of the stops, blacks in slightly fewer than 6 percent. About 1.7 percent of whites who were stopped were found to have a weapon, while 1.1 percent of blacks were found with one.

Given that, some experts who have studied stop-and-frisk data over the last several years say that what prompts an officer's suspicion for a stop, and the discretion used, are important.

In examining the stated reasons for the stops, as checked off by police officers on department forms, the center found that about 15 percent of the stops last year cited "fits a relevant description." Officers can check off more than one reason, but in nearly half the stops, the category called "furtive movements" was cited. Nearly 30 percent of stops cited a category called "casing a victim or location"; nearly 19 percent cited a catchall category of "other."

"These stats suggest that racial disparities in who gets stopped has more to do with officer bias and discretion than with crime rates, which is what the Police Department argues," said Darius Charney, a lawyer with the Center for Constitutional Rights.

Mr. Browne, the department spokesman, said stop-and-frisk data was "examined in great detail," in 2007 by the RAND Corporation, "which found no racial profiling." He said the stops mirrored crime—that while a large percentage of the stops involved blacks, an even larger percentage of violent crimes involved suspects described as black by their victims.

The work by the Center for Constitutional Rights is the latest in a series of examinations of the police tactic defined by a Supreme Court decision from decades ago, Terry v. Ohio, which permitted officers to detain someone briefly based on "reasonable suspicion," a threshold lower than the probable cause necessary for a formal arrest.

The issue exploded in New York after Mr. Diallo's killing, when those who protested the shooting contended there was a pattern of racial profiling in stop and frisks. A study in 1999 by Eliot Spitzer, then the state's attorney general, found that blacks and Hispanics were disproportionately stopped in relation to their involvement in crime and their share of the city's population.

In 2001, the city enacted a law requiring the police to provide quarterly reports about the raw data to the City Council and settled a lawsuit, also brought by the constitutional rights group, requiring that plaintiffs be given more valuable raw data.

Reporting by the police has recently become more regular. On April 30, Mr. Browne said that in 2010 there were 149,299 stops through March 31, about 13 percent fewer than in the first quarter of 2009. So far, he said, the stops yielded 186 guns.

As the numbers come out, analysts and academics pore over them to gauge effectiveness.

In March, researchers from the Center on Race, Crime and Justice at John Jay College of Criminal Justice said that more data and "increased public discussion of this controversial policing practice" were essential.

"If the public does not have access to the data, in a format that allows the experts to identify important trends, then it harms the public discourse," said Donna Lieberman, the executive director of the New York Civil Liberties Union, which successfully sued to get the raw data. "And that is precisely the situation that we are in."

Particularly vexing to Jeffrey A. Fagan, a professor of law at Columbia University who studied the issue for Mr. Spitzer, is that few can say what happens once the "11 or 12 percent" of street stops that lead to an arrest or summons get to court.

"Are these cases that stand up?" he said. "Do they result in convictions?"

Professor Fagan said it was impossible to tell what dent in crime the tactic had made. Christopher T. Dunn of the civil liberties group said there was no proof it had. Crime has gone down steadily since 1991, but, he said, "stop and frisk exploded in 2004."

But Heather Mac Donald, a research fellow at the Manhattan Institute who has spoken to police officials about the tactic, said there was no question it had an effect on crime. She said that great disparities existed in who committed crime in New York and that the police fought crime where it was highest, in mostly minority neighborhoods.

"Where are they supposed to go?" she asked.

Ms. Mac Donald echoed Mr. Browne, who said the police were confident the tactic was stopping crime before it occurred.

Mr. Browne took issue with the constitutional rights group's conclusions about the numbers of arrests or gun seizures the street stops yield, saying, "762 guns can do a lot of damage." He said taking guns from people in the street was different from accepting their surrender from "moms and grandmothers."

And he laid out the logic of the stops: More police are sent to higher crime areas, where criminals and victims live; more suspicious activity is associated with that crime, so there are more opportunities for officers to observe suspicious behavior as a result.

John A. Eterno, a former city police captain who worked to computerize the department's stop-and-frisk data before he retired in 2004, said the tactic could be effective in pushing down crime. But Dr. Eterno, now an associate dean of criminal justice at Molloy College, said retired commanders had spoken of the pressures to reflect their use of stop and frisk in CompStat, the department's computerized crime-tracking system.

"My take is that this has become more like a 'throw a wide net and see what you can find' kind of thing," he said. "I don't see it as targeted enforcement, especially when you see numbers that we are talking about."

The Center for Constitutional Rights also studied post-stop outcomes.

It found that officers frisked more people in 2009 than a year earlier but that the rate of frisks for blacks and Latinos was much higher than it was for whites. It found that the police used force in 24 percent of stops—drawing a weapon, say, or throwing people to the ground. The police used force in 19 percent of the stops involving whites but in 27 percent of stops against Latinos and in 25 percent of those involving blacks.

Mr. Charney of the Center for Constitutional Rights said the disparities in the use of force, compared with the numbers of arrests and summonses and of weapons and contraband seized, was something that "the police have not really explained to the public."

Research Tools

Prepared by Moyee Huei-Lambert MLS

Statutes & Legislative History

http://thomas.loc.gov/—THOMAS: Legislative Information on the Internet

http://uscode.house.gov/search/criteria.shtml—U.S. Code Online

http://www.gpoaccess.gov/plaws/index.html—U.S. Public & Private Laws

Federal Legislative Information

http://www.house.gov/—House homepage

http://www.senate.gov/—Senate homepage

Information About Congress and How to Contact Its Members

http://www.congress.org/congressorg/home/

http://www.votesmart.org/

Federal Executive Information

http://www.whitehouse.gov/

http://www.lib.lsu.edu/gov/index.html—Weekly Compilation of Presidential Documents

http://www.gpoaccess.gov/fr/index.html

http://www.fedworld.gov/

http://www.uscourts.gov/

http://www.law.emory.edu/index.php?id=2997/

http://www.fjc.gov/history/home.nsf

U.S. Supreme Court

http://www.supremecourtus.gov/

http://supreme.lp.findlaw.com/supreme_court/resources.html

http://www.findlaw.com/casecode/supreme.html

http://www.lexisone.com/caselaw/freecaselaw

Other Federal Court Decisions

http://supct.law.cornell.edu/supct/index.html

http://www.law.cornell.edu/usca/search/

http://www.law.cornell.edu/federal/opinions.html

http://www.findlaw.com/10fedgov/judicial/district_courts.html

Federal Courts in New York

http://www.ca2.uscourts.gov/

http://www.nyed.uscourts.gov/

http://www.nynd.uscourts.gov/

http://www1.nysd.uscourts.gov/index.php

http://www.nywd.uscourts.gov/mambo/

Forms & Contracts

http://forms.lp.findlaw.com/

Miscellaneous Government Web Sites & Documents

http://www.ojp.usdoj.gov/bjs/

Glossary

abandoned property Property that an owner has discarded with the intent to relinquish his or her rights in it and mislaid or lost property that the owner has given up any further attempts to locate.

abatement A doctrine that says if the property a testator leaves is not sufficient to satisfy all the beneficiaries named in a will and there are both general and residuary bequests, the residuary bequest is abated first (i.e., paid last).

abusive filing A Chapter 7 filing that is found to be an abuse of Chapter 7 liquidation bankruptcy. In such a case, the court can dismiss the case or convert the case to a Chapter 13 or Chapter 11 proceeding, with the debtor's consent.

acceptance "A manifestation of assent by the offeree to the terms of the offer in a manner invited or required by the offer as measured by the objective theory of contracts." (Section 50 of the Restatement (Second) of Contracts. An act that occurs when a buyer or lessee takes any of the following actions after a reasonable opportunity to inspect the goods: (1) signifies to the seller or lessor in or by conduct that the goods are conforming or that the buyer or lessee will take or retain the goods despite their nonconformity or (2) fails to effectively reject the goods within a reasonable time after their delivery or tender by the seller or lessor. Acceptance also occurs if a buyer acts inconsistently with the seller's ownership rights in the goods.

acceptance method A method whereby the court confirms a plan of reorganization if the creditors accept the plan and if other requirements are met.

accession An increase in the value of personal property because it is added to or improved by natural or manufactured means.

accommodation A shipment that is offered to a buyer as a replacement for the original shipment when the original shipment cannot be filled.

accord An agreement whereby the parties agree to accept something different in satisfaction of the original contract.

accord and satisfaction The settlement of a contract dispute.

accountant–client privilege A state statute which provides that an accountant cannot be called as a witness against a client in a court action.

act of monopolizing An act that is required for there to be a violation of Section 2 of the Sherman Act. Possession of monopoly power without such act does not violate Section 2.

act of state doctrine A doctrine which states that judges of one country cannot question the validity of an act committed by another country within that other country's borders. It is based on the principle that a country has absolute authority over what transpires with-in its own territory.

action for an accounting A formal judicial proceeding in which the court is authorized to (1) review the partnership and the partners' transactions and (2) award each partner his or her share of the partnership assets.

actual cause The actual cause of negligence. A person who commits a negligent act is not liable unless actual cause can be proven. Also called causation in fact.

actus reus "Guilty act"—the actual performance of a criminal act.

ademption A principle that says if a testator leaves a specific devise of property to a beneficiary, but the property is no longer in the estate when the testator dies, the beneficiary receives nothing.

adequate assurance of performance Adequate assurance of performance from the other party if there is an indication that the contract will be breached by that party.

adjudged insane Declared legally insane by a proper court or administrative agency. A contract entered into by a person adjudged insane is void.

administrative agencies Agencies (such as the Securities and Exchange Commission and the Federal Trade Commission) that the legislative and executive branches of federal and state governments are empowered to establish.

administrative dissolution Involuntary dissolution of a corporation that is ordered by the secretary of state if a corporation has failed to comply with certain procedures required by law.

administrative law judge (ALJ) A judge who presides over administrative proceedings and decides questions of law and fact concerning a case. A federal act that establishes certain administrative procedures that federal administrative

administrative law Substantive and procedural law that governs the operation of administrative agencies.

Administrative Procedure Act (APA) Agencies must follow in conducting their affairs.

administrative subpoena An order that directs the subject of the subpoena to disclose the requested information.

adoption A situation in which a person becomes the legal parent of a child who is not his or her biological child.

adverse possession A situation in which a person who wrongfully possesses someone else's real property obtains title to that property if certain statutory requirements are met.

advertisement An invitation to make an offer, or an actual offer.

affirmative action A policy which provides that certain job preferences will be given to minority or other protected-class applicants when an employer makes an employment decision.

AFL-CIO The 1955 combination of the AFL and the CIO.

Age Discrimination in Employment Act (ADEA) of 1967 A federal statute that prohibits age discrimination practices against employees who are 40 and older.

agency The principal–agent relationship; the fiduciary relationship "which results from the manifestation of consent by one person to another that the other shall act in his behalf and subject to his control, and consent by the other so to act" [Restatement (Second) of Agency].

agency adoption An adoption that occurs when a person adopts a child from a social service organization of a state.

agency by ratification An agency that occurs when (1) a person misrepresents him- or herself as another's agent when in fact he or she is not and (2) the purported principal ratifies the unauthorized act.

agency coupled with an interest A special type of agency that is created for the agent's benefit and that the principal cannot revoke.

agency law The large body of common law that governs agency; a mixture of contract law and tort law.

agency shop A workplace where an employee does not have to join the union but must pay a fee equal to the union dues.

agent A party who agrees to act on behalf of another. A person who has been authorized to sign a negotiable instrument on behalf of another person.

agent's duty of loyalty   A fiduciary duty owed by an agent not to act adversely to the interests of the principal.

agreement of conversion   A document that states the terms for converting an existing business to an LLC.

agreement   The manifestation by two or more persons of the substance of a contract.

air pollution   Pollution caused by factories, homes, vehicles, and the like that affects the air.

alien corporation   A corporation that is incorporated in another country.

allonge   A separate piece of paper attached to an instrument on which an indorsement is written.

altered check   A check that has been altered without authorization and thus modifies the legal obligation of a party.

alternative dispute resolution (ADR)   Methods of resolving disputes other than litigation.

American Inventors Protection Act   A federal statute that permits an inventor to file a provisional application with the U.S. Patent and Trademark Office three months before the filing of a final patent application, among other provisions.

Americans with Disabilities Act (ADA)   A federal statute that imposes obligations on employers and providers of public transportation, telecommunications, and public accommodations to accommodate individuals with disabilities.

annual financial statement   A statement provided to shareholders that contains a balance sheet, an income statement, and a statement of changes in shareholder equity.

annual shareholders' meeting   A meeting of the shareholders of a corporation that must be held by the corporation to elect directors and to vote on other matters.

annulment   An order of the court which declares that a marriage did not exist.

answer   The defendant's written response to a plaintiff's complaint that is filed with the court and served on the plaintiff.

anti-assignment clause   A clause that prohibits the assignment of rights under the contract.

antideficiency statute   A statute that prohibits deficiency judgments regarding certain types of mortgages, such as those on residential property.

anti-delegation clause   A clause that prohibits the delegation of duties under the contract.

antitakeover statutes   Statutes enacted by a state legislature that protect against the hostile takeover of corporations incorporated in or doing business in the state.

anticipatory breach   A breach that occurs when one contracting party informs the other that he or she will not perform his or her contractual duties when due.

anticipatory repudiation   The repudiation of a sales or lease contract by one of the parties prior to the date set for performance.

antifraud provision   Section 14(a) of the Securities Exchange Act of 1934, which prohibits misrepresentations or omissions of a material fact in the proxy materials.

antitrust laws   A series of laws enacted to limit anticompetitive behavior in almost all industries, businesses, and professions operating in the United States.

apparent agency   Agency that arises when a franchisor creates the appearance that a franchisee is its agent when in fact an actual agency does not exist. Agency that arises when a principal creates the appearance of an agency that in actuality does not exist.

appeal   The act of asking an appellate court to overturn a decision after the trial court's final judgment has been entered.

appellant   The appealing party in an appeal. Also known as the petitioner.

appellee   The responding party in an appeal. Also known as the respondent.

arbitration   A form of ADR in which the parties choose an impartial third party to hear and decide the dispute.

arbitration clause   A clause in a contract that requires disputes arising out of the contract to be submitted to arbitration.

arraignment   A hearing during which the accused is brought before a court and is (1) informed of the charges against him or her and (2) asked to enter a plea.

arrest warrant   A document for a person's detainment, based upon a showing of probable cause that the person committed a crime.

arson   The willful or malicious burning of a building.

Article 2 (Sales)   An article of the UCC that governs sale of goods.

Article 2A (Leases)   An article of the UCC that governs leases of goods.

Article 3 of the UCC   A model code that establishes rules for the creation of, transfer of, enforcement of, and liability on negotiable instruments.

Article 3 of the UCC   An article of the UCC that sets forth the requirements for negotiable instruments, including checks.

Article 4 of the UCC   An article of the UCC that establishes the rules and principles that regulate bank deposit and collection procedures.

Article 4A of the UCC   An article of the UCC that establishes rules regulating the creation and collection of and liability for wire transfers.

articles of incorporation   The basic governing documents of a corporation. It must be filed with the secretary of state of the state of incorporation. Also known as a corporate charter.

articles of organization   The formal documents that must be filed at the secretary of state's office of the state of organization of an LLC to form the LLC.

assault   (1) The threat of immediate harm or offensive contact or (2) any action that arouses reasonable apprehension of imminent harm. Actual physical contact is unnecessary.

assignee   A party to whom a right has been transferred. A party to whom rights are transferred under a lease. A transferee in an assignment situation.

assignment   A transfer by a tenant of his or her rights under a lease to another. The transfer of contractual rights by an obligee to another party. The transfer of rights under a contract.

assignor   A party who transfers rights under a lease. A transferor in an assignment situation. An obligee who transfers a right.

assumption of duties   A situation in which a delegation of duties contains the term assumption, I assume the duties, or other similar language. In such a case, the delegatee is legally liable to the obligee for nonperformance.

assumption of the risk   A defense a defendant can use against a plaintiff who knowingly and voluntarily enters into or participates in a risky activity that results in injury.

attestation   The action of a will being witnessed by two or three objective and competent people.

attorney–client privilege   A rule that says a client can tell his or her lawyer anything about the case without fear that the attorney will be called as a witness against the client.

at-will LLC   An LLC that has no specified term of duration.

auction with reserve   An auction in which the seller retains the right to refuse the highest bid and withdraw the goods from sale. Unless expressly stated otherwise, an auction is an auction with reserve.

auction without reserve   An auction in which the seller expressly gives up his or her right to withdraw the goods from sale and must accept the highest bid.

audit   A verification of a company's books and records pursuant to federal securities laws, state laws, and stock exchange rules that must be performed by an independent CPA.

auditor's opinion An opinion of an auditor about how fairly the financial statements of the client company represent the company's financial position, results of operations, and change in financial position.

authorized shares The number of shares provided for in the articles of incorporation.

automatic stay The suspension of certain legal actions by creditors against a debtor or the debtor's property.

automobile liability insurance Automobile insurance that covers damages that the insured causes to third parties.

backward vertical merger A vertical merger in which the customer acquires the supplier.

bailee A holder of goods who is not a seller or a buyer (e.g., warehouse, common carrier).

bailment A transaction in which an owner transfers his or her personal property to another to be held, stored, delivered, or for some other purpose. Title to the property does not transfer.

bailment at will A bailment without a fixed term; can be terminated at any time by either party.

bailment for a fixed term A bailment that terminates at the end of the term or sooner, by mutual consent of the parties.

bailment for the sole benefit of the bailee A gratuitous bailment that benefits only the bailee. The bailee owes a duty of utmost care to protect the bailed property.

bailment for the sole benefit of the bailor A gratuitous bailment that benefits only the bailor. The bailee owes only a duty of slight care to protect the bailed property.

bailor The owner of property in a bailment.

bait and switch A type of deceptive advertising that occurs when a seller advertises the availability of a low-cost discounted item but then pressures the buyer into purchasing more expensive merchandise.

bank check A certified check or a cashier's check, the payment for which a bank is solely or primarily liable.

Bankruptcy Abuse Prevention and Consumer Protection Act of 2005 A federal act that substantially amended federal bankruptcy law. This act makes it more difficult for debtors to file for bankruptcy and have their unpaid debts discharged.

Bankruptcy Code The name given to federal bankruptcy law, as amended.

bankruptcy courts Special federal courts that hear and decide bankruptcy cases.

bankruptcy estate The debtor's property and earnings that comprise the estate of a bankruptcy proceeding.

Bankruptcy Reform Act of 1978 A federal act that substantially changed federal bankruptcy law. The act made it easier for debtors to file for bankruptcy and have their unpaid debts discharged. This act was considered debtor friendly.

bargained-for exchange Exchange that parties engage in that leads to an enforceable contract.

battery Unauthorized and harmful or offensive direct or indirect physical contact with another person that causes injury.

bearer paper An instrument that is negotiated by delivery; indorsement is not necessary.

beneficiary A person or an organization designated in a will to receive all or a portion of the testator's property at the time of the testator's death. A person who is to receive life insurance proceeds when the insured dies.

bequest A gift of personal property by will. Also known as a legacy.

bilateral contract A contract entered into by way of exchange of promises of the parties; "a promise for a promise."

Bill of Rights The first 10 amendments to the Constitution, which were added to the U.S. Constitution in 1791.

blank indorsement An indorsement that does not specify a particular indorsee. It creates bearer paper.

board of directors A panel of decision makers who are elected by the shareholders.

bona fide occupational qualification (BFOQ) A true job qualification. Employment discrimination based on a protected class (other than race or color) is lawful if it is job related and a business necessity. This exception is narrowly interpreted by the courts.

bond A long-term debt security that is secured by some form of collateral.

breach Failure of a party to perform an obligation in a sales or lease contract.

breach of contract A contracting party's failure to perform an absolute duty owed under a contract.

breach of the duty of care A failure to exercise care or to act as a reasonable person would act.

bribery A crime in which one person gives another person money, property, favors, or anything else of value for a favor in return. A bribe is often referred to as a *payoff* or *kickback*.

building codes State and local statutes that impose specific standards on property owners to maintain and repair leased premises. Also called housing codes.

burglary The taking of personal property from another's home, office, or commercial or other type of building.

business interruption insurance Insurance that reimburses a business for loss of revenue incurred when the business has been damaged or destroyed by fire or some other peril.

business judgment rule A rule that protects the decisions of a board of directors that acts on an informed basis, in good faith, and in the honest belief that the action taken was in the best interests of the corporation and its shareholders. A rule that says directors and officers are not liable to the corporation or its shareholders for honest mistakes of judgment.

buy-and-sell agreement An agreement that requires selling shareholders to sell their shares to the other shareholders or to the corporation at the price specified in the agreement.

buyer in the ordinary course of business A person who in good faith and without knowledge that the sale violates the ownership or security interests of a third party buys goods in the ordinary course of business from a person in the business of selling goods of that kind. A buyer in the ordinary course of business takes the goods free of any third-party security interest in the goods.

buyer's or lessee's cancellation A buyer or lessee has the right to cancel a sales or lease contract if the seller or lessor fails to deliver conforming goods or repudiates the contract or if the buyer or lessee rightfully rejects the goods or justifiably revokes acceptance of the goods.

bylaws A detailed set of rules adopted by the board of directors after a corporation is incorporated that contains provisions for managing the business and the affairs of the corporation.

cancellation The termination of a contract by a contracting party upon the material breach of the contract by the other party.

cashier's check A check issued by a bank for which the customer has paid the bank the amount of the check and a fee. The bank guarantees payment of the check.

certificate of deposit (CD) A two-party negotiable instrument that is a special form of note created when a depositor deposits money at a financial institution in exchange for the institution's promise to pay back the amount of the deposit plus an agreed-upon rate of interest upon the expiration of a set time period agreed upon by the parties.

certification A process in which the accepting bank writes or stamps the word certified on an ordinary check of an account holder and sets aside funds from that account to pay the check.

certified check A type of check for which a bank agrees in advance (certifies) to accept the check when it is presented for payment.

chain of distribution All manufacturers, distributors, wholesalers, retailers, lessors, and subcomponent manufacturers involved in a transaction.

check A distinct form of draft drawn on a financial institution and payable on demand. An order by a drawer to a drawee bank to pay a specified sum of money from the drawer's checking account to the named payee (or holder).

checks and balances A system built into the U.S. Constitution to prevent any one of the three branches of the government from becoming too powerful.

choice-of-law clause A contract provision that designates a certain state's law or country's law that will be applied in any dispute concerning nonperformance of the contract.

C.O.D. shipment A type of shipment contract in which the buyer agrees to pay the shipper cash upon the delivery of the goods.

collateral Security against repayment of a note that lenders sometimes require; can be a car, a house, or other property.

collecting bank The depository bank and other banks in the collection process (other than the payer bank).

Commerce Clause A clause of the U.S. Constitution that grants Congress the power "to regulate commerce with foreign nations, and among the several states, and with Indian tribes."

commercial impracticability Nonperformance that is excused if an extreme or unexpected development or expense makes it impractical for the promisor to perform.

commercial speech Speech used by businesses, such as advertising. It is subject to time, place, and manner restrictions.

commercial wire transfer An electronic transfer of funds from one party to another party. Also known as a wholesale wire transfer.

common law Law developed by judges who issued their opinions when deciding a case. The principles announced in these cases became precedent for later judges deciding similar cases.

common law of contracts Contract law developed primarily by state courts.

comparative fault A doctrine that applies to strict liability actions that says a plaintiff who is contributorily negligent for his or her injuries is responsible for a proportional share of the damages.

comparative negligence A doctrine under which damages are apportioned according to fault.

compensatory damages An award of money intended to compensate a non-breaching party for the loss of the bargain. Compensatory damages place the non-breaching party in the same position as if the contract had been fully performed by restoring the "benefit of the bargain." Damages that are generally equal to the difference between the value of the goods as warranted and the actual value of the goods accepted at the time and place of acceptance.

competent party's duty of restitution A rule which states that if a minor has transferred money, property, or other valuables to the competent party before disaffirming the contract, that party must place the minor in status quo.

complaint The document a plaintiff files with the court and serves on the defendant to initiate a lawsuit.

complete performance A situation in which a party to a contract renders performance exactly as required by the contract. Complete performance discharges that party's obligations under the contract.

conciliation A form of ADR in which the parties use a third party to help them resolve their dispute.

concurrent condition A condition that exists when the parties to a contract must render performance simultaneously; each party's absolute duty to perform is conditioned on the other party's absolute duty to perform.

concurrent jurisdiction Jurisdiction shared by two or more courts.

condition A qualification of a promise that becomes a covenant if it is met. There are three types of conditions: conditions precedent, conditions subsequent, and concurrent conditions.

condition precedent A condition that requires the occurrence of an event before a party is obligated to perform a duty under a contract.

condition subsequent A condition whose occurrence or nonoccurrence of a specific event automatically excuses the performance of an existing contractual duty to perform.

consequential damages Foreseeable damages that arise from circumstances outside a contract. To be liable for these damages, the breaching party must know or have reason to know that the breach will cause special damages to the other party.

consideration Something of legal value given in exchange for a promise.

consignment An arrangement in which a seller (the consignor) delivers goods to a buyer (the consignee) to sell.

conspicuous A requirement that warranty disclaimers be noticeable to the reasonable person.

consolidation The act of a court to combine two or more separate lawsuits into one lawsuit.

Constitution of the United States of America The supreme law of the United States.

consumer expectation test A test to determine merchantability based on what the average consumer would expect to find in food products.

Consumer Leasing Act (CLA) An amendment to the TILA that extends the TILA's coverage to lease terms in consumer leases.

contract contrary to public policy A contract that has a negative impact on society or that interferes with the public's safety and welfare.

contract in restraint of trade A contract that unreasonably restrains trade.

contributory negligence A defense that says a person who is injured by a defective product but has been negligent and has contributed to his or her own injuries cannot recover from the defendant. A doctrine that says a plaintiff who is partially at fault for his or her own injury cannot recover against the negligent defendant.

copyright infringement An infringement that occurs when a party copies a substantial and material part of a plaintiff's copyrighted work without permission. A copyright holder may recover damages and other remedies against the infringer.

Copyright Revision Act A federal statute that (1) establishes the requirements for obtaining a copyright and (2) protects copyrighted works from infringement.

corporate criminal liability Criminal liability of corporations for actions of their officers, employees, or agents.

counteroffer A response by an offeree that contains terms and conditions different from or in addition to those of the offer. A counteroffer terminates the previous offer.

Court of Appeals for the Federal Circuit A U.S. Court of Appeals in Washington, DC, that has special appellate jurisdiction to review the decisions of the Court of Federal Claims, the Patent and Trademark Office, and the Court of International Trade.

covenant An unconditional promise to perform.

covenant not to compete A contract which provides that a seller of a business or an employee will not engage in a similar business or occupation within a specified geographical area for a specified time following the sale of the business or termination of employment. Also called a noncompete clause.

covenant of good faith and fair dealing An implied covenant under which the parties to a contract not only are held to the express terms of the contract but are also required to act in "good faith" and deal fairly in all respects in obtaining the objective of the contract.

cover A licensee's right to engage in a commercially reasonable substitute transaction after the licensor has breached the contract.

crashworthiness doctrine A doctrine that says automobile manufacturers are under a duty to design automobiles so they take into account the possibility of harm from a person's body striking something inside the automobile in the case of a car accident.

credit report Information about a person's credit history that can be secured from a credit bureau reporting company.

creditor The lender in a credit transaction.

creditor beneficiary An original creditor who becomes a beneficiary under the debtor's new contract with another party.

creditor beneficiary contract A contract that arises in the following situation: (1) a debtor borrows money, (2) the debtor signs an agreement to pay back the money plus interest, (3) the debtor sells the item to a third party before the loan is paid off, and (4) the third party promises the debtor that he or she will pay the remainder of the loan to the creditor.

creditor–debtor relationship A relationship that is created when a customer deposits money into the bank; the customer is the creditor, and the bank is the debtor.

crime A violation of a statute for which the government imposes a punishment.

criminal conspiracy A crime in which two or more persons enter into an agreement to commit a crime and an overt act is taken to further the crime.

criminal fraud A crime that involves obtaining title to property through deception or trickery. Also known as *false pretenses* or *deceit*.

cure An opportunity to repair or replace defective or nonconforming goods.

damages Damages a buyer or lessee recovers from a seller or lessor who fails to deliver the goods or repudiates the contract. Damages are measured as the difference between the contract price (or original rent) and the market price (or rent) at the time the buyer or lessee learned of the breach.

debenture A long-term unsecured debt instrument that is based on a corporation's general credit standing.

debt securities Securities that establish a debtor–creditor relationship in which the corporation borrows money from the investor to whom a debt security is issued.

debtor The borrower in a credit transaction.

debtor-in-possession A debtor who is left in place to operate the business during the reorganization proceeding.

decree of divorce A court order that terminates a marriage.

deductible clause A clause in an insurance policy which provides that insurance proceeds are payable only after the insured has paid a specified amount toward the damage or loss.

deed A writing that describes a person's ownership interest in a piece of real property.

deed of trust An instrument that gives a creditor a security interest in the debtor's property that is pledged as collateral.

defamation of character False statement(s) made by one person about another. In court, the plaintiff must prove that (1) the defendant made an untrue statement of fact about the plaintiff and (2) the statement was intentionally or accidentally published to a third party.

defect in design A defect that occurs when a product is improperly designed.

defect in manufacture A defect that occurs when a manufacturer fails to (1) properly assemble a product, (2) properly test a product, or (3) adequately check the quality of the product.

defect in packaging A defect that occurs when a product has been placed in packaging that is insufficiently tamperproof.

deferred posting rule A rule that allows banks to fix an afternoon hour of 2:00 p.m. or later as a cutoff hour for the purpose of processing items.

deficiency judgment A judgment of a court that permits a secured lender to recover other property or income from a defaulting debtor if the collateral is insufficient to repay the unpaid loan.

delegatee A party to whom a duty has been transferred.

delegation doctrine A doctrine that says when an administrative agency is created, it is delegated certain powers; the agency can use only those legislative, judicial, and executive powers that are delegated to it.

delegation of duties A transfer of contractual duties by an obligor to another party for performance.

delegator An obligor who has transferred his or her duty.

demand instrument An instrument payable on demand.

demand note A note payable on demand.

deponent A party who gives his or her deposition.

deposition Oral testimony given by a party or witness prior to trial. The testimony is given under oath and is transcribed.

depository bank The bank where the payee or holder has an account.

derivative lawsuit A lawsuit a shareholder brings against an offending party on behalf of a corporation when the corporation fails to bring the lawsuit.

destination contract A contract that requires the seller to deliver the goods either to the buyer's place of business or to another destination specified in the sales contract. A sales contract that requires the seller to deliver the goods to the buyer's place of business or another specified destination. The seller bears the risk of loss during transportation.

devise A gift of real estate by will.

Digital Millennium Copyright Act (DMCA) A federal statute that prohibits unauthorized access to copyrighted digital works by circumventing encryption technology or the manufacture and distribution of technologies designed for the purpose of circumventing encryption protection of digital works.

direct price discrimination Price discrimination in which (1) the defendant sold commodities of like grade and quality, (2) to two or more purchasers at different prices at approximately the same time, and (3) the plaintiff suffered injury because of the price discrimination.

directors' and officers' liability insurance Insurance that protects directors and officers of a corporation from liability for actions taken on behalf of the corporation.

disability insurance Insurance that provides a monthly income to an insured who is disabled and cannot work.

disaffirmance The act of a minor to rescind a contract under the infancy doctrine. Disaffirmance may be done orally, in writing, or by the minor's conduct.

discharge A court order that relieves a debtor of the legal liability to pay his or her debts that were not paid in the bankruptcy proceeding.

discovery A legal process during which each party engages in various activities to discover facts of the case from the other party and witnesses prior to trial.

dishonored instrument An instrument that is presented for payment and payment is refused.

disparate-impact discrimination A form of discrimination that occurs when an employer discriminates against an entire protected class. An example would be discrimination in which a racially neutral employment practice or rule causes an adverse impact on a protected class.

disparate-treatment discrimination A form of discrimination that occurs when an employer discriminates against a specific individual because of his or her race, color, national origin, sex, or religion.

dissenting shareholder appraisal rights The rights of shareholders who object to a proposed merger, share exchange, or sale or lease of all or substantially all of the property of a corporation to have their shares valued by the court and receive cash payment of this value from the corporation.

dissolution The change in the relation of the partners caused by any partner ceasing to be associated in the carrying on of the business [UPA Section 29].

distinctive Being unique and fabricated.

distributional interest A member's ownership interest in an LLC that entitles the member to receive distributions of money and property from the LLC.

diversity of citizenship A means for bringing a lawsuit in federal court that involves a nonfederal question if the parties are (1) citizens of different states or (2) a citizen of a state and a citizen or subject of a foreign country.

dividend A distribution of profits of the corporation to shareholders.

dividend preference The right to receive a fixed dividend at stipulated periods during the year (e.g., quarterly).

division of markets A restraint of trade in which competitors agree that each will serve only a designated portion of the market.

divorce An order of the court that terminates a marriage.

doctrine of sovereign immunity A doctrine which states that countries are granted immunity from suits in courts of other countries.

document of title An actual piece of paper, such as a warehouse receipt or bill of lading, that is required in some transactions of pickup and delivery.

domain name A unique name that identifies an individual's or company's website.

domestic corporation A corporation in the state in which it was formed.

domestic limited partnership A limited partnership in the state in which it was formed.

donee A person who receives a gift.

donee beneficiary A third party on whom a benefit is to be conferred.

donee beneficiary contract A contract entered into with the intent to confer a benefit or gift on an intended third party.

donor A person who gives a gift.

double Jeopardy Clause A clause of the Fifth Amendment that protects persons from being tried twice for the same crime.

draft A three-party instrument that is an unconditional written order by one party that orders a second party to pay money to a third party.

drawee of a check The bank where a check drawer has his or her account. The party who must pay the money stated in a draft. Also called the acceptor of a draft.

drawer of a check The checking account holder and writer of a check.

drawer of a draft The party who writes an order for a draft.

dual-purpose mission An errand or another act that a principal requests of an agent while the agent is on his or her own personal business.

due diligence defense A defense to a Section 11 action that, if proven, makes the defendant not liable.

Due Process Clause A clause which provides that no person shall be deprived of "life, liberty, or property" without due process of the law.

duress A situation in which one party threatens to do a wrongful act unless the other party enters into a contract.

duty of care A duty of corporate directors and officers to use care and diligence when acting on behalf of the corporation. A duty owed by a member of a member-managed LLC and a manager of a manager-managed LLC not to engage in (1) a known violation of law, (2) intentional conduct, (3) reckless conduct, or (4) grossly negligent conduct that injures the LLC. The obligation partners owe to use the same level of care and skill that a reasonable person in the same position would use in the same circumstances. A breach of the duty of care is negligence. The obligation people owe each other not to cause any unreasonable harm or risk of harm.

duty of loyalty A duty owed by a member of a member-managed LLC and a manager of a manager-managed LLC to be honest in his or her dealings with the LLC and to not act adversely to the interests of the LLC. A duty that a partner owes not to act adversely to the interests of the partnership. A duty that directors and officers have not to act adversely to the interests of the corporation

and to subordinate their personal interests to those of the corporation and its shareholders.

duty of obedience A duty that directors and officers of a corporation have to act within the authority conferred upon them by state corporation statutes, the articles of incorporation, the corporate bylaws, and the resolutions adopted by the board of directors. A duty that requires partners to adhere to the provisions of the partnership agreement and the decisions of the partnership.

duty to account A duty that an agent owes to maintain an accurate accounting of all transactions undertaken on the principal's behalf. Also known as the duty of accountability.

duty to compensate A duty that a principal owes to pay an agreed-upon amount to the agent either upon the completion of the agency or at some other mutually agreeable time.

duty to inform A duty a partner owes to inform his or her co-partners of all information he or she possesses that is relevant to the affairs of the partnership.

duty to perform An agent's duty to a principal that includes (1) performing the lawful duties expressed in the contract and (2) meeting the standards of reasonable care, skill, and diligence implicit in all contracts.

easement A given or required right to make limited use of someone else's land without owning or leasing it.

easement appurtenant A situation created when the owner of one piece of land is given an easement over an adjacent piece of land.

easement in gross An easement that authorizes a person who does not own adjacent land to use another's land.

e-commerce The sale of goods and services by computer over the Internet.

effect of illegality A doctrine which states that the courts will refuse to enforce or rescind an illegal contract and will leave the parties where it finds them.

electronic funds transfer system (EFTS) Computer and electronic technology that makes it possible for banks to offer electronic payment and collection systems to bank customers. E-banking and e-money consists of: (1) Automated teller machines (ATMs); (2) Point-of-sale terminals; (3) Direct deposit and withdrawal; (4) Online banking; and (5) Debit cards.

electronic mail (e-mail) Electronic written communication between individuals using computers connected to the Internet.

e-mail and web contracts Contracts that are entered into by e-mail and over the World Wide Web.

emancipation A minor's act of legally separating from his or her parents and providing for himself or herself.

embezzlement The fraudulent conversion of property by a person to whom that property was entrusted.

eminent domain The government's power to take private property for public use, provided that just compensation is paid to the private property holder.

Employee Retirement Income Security Act (ERISA) A federal act designed to prevent fraud and other abuses associated with private pension funds.

employer lockout An act of an employer to prevent employees from entering the work premises when the employer reasonably anticipates a strike.

employer–employee relationship A relationship that results when an employer hires an employee to perform some task or service but the employee has not been authorized to enter into contracts on behalf of his employer.

Endangered Species Act A federal statute that protects endangered and threatened species of wildlife.

engagement A formal entrance into a contract between a client and an accountant.

entrepreneur A person who forms and operates a new business either by him- or herself or with others.

enumerated powers Certain powers delegated to the federal government by the states.

environmental impact statement (EIS) A document that must be prepared for any proposed legislation or major federal action that significantly affects the quality of the human environment.

Environmental Protection Agency (EPA) A federal administrative agency created by Congress to coordinate the implementation and enforcement of the federal environmental protection laws.

Equal Access to Justice Act A federal act that protects persons from harassment by federal administrative agencies.

Equal Credit Opportunity Act (ECOA) A federal statute that prohibits discrimination in the extension of credit based on sex, marital status, race, color, national origin, religion, age, or receipt of income from public assistance programs.

equal dignity rule A rule which says that agents' contracts to sell property covered by the Statute of Frauds must be in writing to be enforceable.

Equal Employment Opportunity Commission (EEOC) The federal administrative agency that is responsible for enforcing most federal antidiscrimination laws.

equal opportunity in employment The right of all employees and job applicants (1) to be treated without discrimination and (2) to be able to sue employers if they are discriminated against.

Equal Pay Act A federal statute that protects both sexes from pay discrimination based on sex. It extends to jobs that require equal skill, equal effort, equal responsibility, and similar working conditions.

Equal Protection Clause A clause which provides that a state cannot "deny to any person within its jurisdiction the equal protection of the laws."

equitable distribution A law used by many states where the court orders a fair distribution of marital property to the divorcing spouses.

equity A doctrine that permits judges to make decisions based on fairness, equality, moral rights, and natural law.

equity securities Representation of ownership rights to a corporation. Also called stocks.

Establishment Clause A clause to the First Amendment that prohibits the government from either establishing a state religion or promoting one religion over another.

estate Ownership rights in real property; the bundle of legal rights that the owner has to possess, use, and enjoy the property.

estray statute A statute that permits a finder of mislaid or lost property to clear title to the property if certain prescribed legal formalities are met.

ethical fundamentalism A theory of ethics that says a person looks to an outside source for ethical rules or commands.

ethical relativism A moral theory which holds that individuals must decide what is ethical based on their own feelings about what is right and wrong.

ethics A set of moral principles or values that governs the conduct of an individual or a group.

European Union A regional international organization that comprises many countries of western and eastern Europe and was created to promote peace and security as well as economic, social, and cultural development.

exclusionary rule A rule that says evidence obtained from an unreasonable search and seizure can generally be prohibited from introduction at a trial or an administrative proceeding against the person searched.

exclusive agency contract A contract a principal and agent enter into that says the principal cannot employ any agent other than the exclusive agent.

exclusive jurisdiction Jurisdiction held by only one court.

exclusive license A license that grants the licensee exclusive rights to use informational rights for a specified duration.

exculpatory clause A contractual provision that relieves one (or both) of the parties to a contract from tort liability for ordinary negligence. Also known as a release of liability clause.

executed contract A contract that has been fully performed on both sides; a completed contract.

executive branch The part of the U.S. government that enforces the federal law; it consists of the president and vice president.

executive order An order issued by a member of the executive branch of the government.

executive power Power that administrative agencies are granted, such as the investigation and prosecution of possible violations of statutes, administrative rules, and administrative orders.

executory contract A contract that has not been fully performed by either or both sides.

executory contract or unexpired lease A contract or lease that has not been fully performed. With the bankruptcy court's approval, a debtor may reject executory contracts and unexpired leases in bankruptcy.

exempt property Property that may be retained by the debtor pursuant to federal or state law that does not become part of the bankruptcy estate.

express agency An agency that occurs when a principal and an agent expressly agree to enter into an agency agreement with each other.

express authorization A stipulation in an offer that says the acceptance must be by a specified means of communication.

express contract An agreement that is expressed in written or oral words.

express powers Powers given to a corporation by (1) the U.S. Constitution, (2) state constitutions, (3) federal statutes, (4) state statues, (5) articles of incorporation, (6) bylaws, and (7) resolutions of the board of directors.

express trust A trust created voluntarily by a settlor.

express warranty A warranty that is created when a seller or lessor makes an affirmation that the goods he or she is selling or leasing meet certain standards of quality, description, performance, or condition.

extortion   A threat to expose something about another person unless that other person gives money or property. Often referred to as blackmail.

failure to provide adequate instructions   A defect that occurs when a manufacturer does not provide detailed directions for safe assembly and use of a product.

failure to warn   A defect that occurs when a manufacturer does not place a warning on the packaging of products that could cause injury if the danger is unknown.

Fair Credit and Charge Card Disclosure Act   An amendment to the TILA that requires disclosure of certain credit terms on credit card and charge card solicitations and applications.

Fair Credit Reporting Act (FCRA)   An amendment to the TILA that protects a consumer who is the subject of a credit report by setting out guidelines for credit bureaus.

Fair Debt Collection Practices Act (FDCPA)   A federal act that protects consumer-debtors from abusive, deceptive, and unfair practices used by debt collectors.

Fair Housing Act   A federal statute that makes it unlawful for a party to refuse to rent or sell a dwelling to any person because of his or her race, color, national origin, sex, or religion.

Fair Labor Standards Act (FLSA)   A federal act enacted in 1938 to protect workers. It prohibits child labor and spells out minimum wage and overtime pay requirements.

fair price rule   A rule that says any increase in price paid for shares tendered must be offered to all shareholders, even those who have previously tendered their shares.

fair use doctrine   A doctrine that permits certain limited use of a copyright by someone other than the copyright holder without the permission of the copyright holder.

false imprisonment   The intentional confinement or restraint of another person without authority or justification and without that person's consent.

Family and Medical Leave Act (FMLA)   A federal act that guarantees workers up to 12 weeks of unpaid leave in a 12-month period to attend to family and medical emergencies and other specified situations.

family farmer   An individual, a corporation, or a partnership that engages in farming operations and meets the requirements for filing for a Chapter 12 proceeding.

family fisherman   An individual, a corporation, or a partnership that engages in commercial fishing operations and meets the requirements for filing for a Chapter 12 proceeding.

federal administrative agencies   Administrative agencies that are created by the executive or legislative branch of federal government.

Federal Arbitration Act (FAA)   A federal statute that provides for the enforcement of most arbitration agreements.

Federal Dilution Act   A federal statute that protects famous marks from dilution, erosion, blurring, or tarnishing.

Federal Patent Statute   A federal statute that establishes the requirements for obtaining a patent and protects patented inventions from infringement.

federal question case   A case arising under the U.S. Constitution, treaties, or federal statutes and regulations.

Federal Reserve System   A system of 12 regional Federal Reserve banks that assist other banks in the collection of checks.

Federal Trade Commission (FTC)   A federal administrative agency empowered to enforce the Federal Trade Commission Act and other federal consumer protection statutes.

Federal Unemployment Tax Act (FUTA)   A federal act that requires employers to pay unemployment taxes; unemployment compensation is paid to workers who are temporarily unemployed.

federalism   The U.S. form of government, in which the federal government and the 50 state governments share powers.

fee simple absolute   A type of ownership of real property that grants the owner the fullest bundle of legal rights that a person can hold in real property. Also known as fee simple.

fee simple defeasible   A type of ownership of real property that grants the owner all the incidents of a fee simple absolute except that it may be taken away if a specified condition occurs or does not occur. Also known as qualified fee.

felony   The most serious type of crime; inherently evil crime. Most crimes against persons and some business-related crimes are felonies.

fiduciary duties   The duties of obedience, care, and loyalty owed by directors and officers to their corporation and its shareholders.

final settlement   A situation in which a payer bank (1) pays a check in cash, (2) settles for a check without having a right to revoke the settlement, or (3) fails to dishonor a check within certain statutory time periods.

finance lease   A three-party transaction consisting of a lessor, a lessee, and a supplier.

fixed amount of money   A requirement that a negotiable instrument contain a promise or an order to pay a fixed amount of money.

fixed amount requirement   A requirement of a negotiable instrument that ensures that the value of the instrument can be determined with certainty.

fixtures   Goods that are affixed to real estate so as to become part thereof.

Food and Drug Administration (FDA)   The federal administrative agency that administers and enforces the federal Food, Drug, and Cosmetic Act and other federal consumer protection laws.

Food, Drug, and Cosmetic Act (FDCA)   A federal statute that provides the basis for the regulation of much of the testing, manufacture, distribution, and sale of foods, drugs, cosmetics, and medicinal products.

force majeure **clause**   A clause in a contract in which the parties specify certain events that will excuse nonperformance.

foreclosure sale   A legal procedure by which a secured creditor causes the judicial sale of the secured real estate to pay a defaulted loan.

Foreign Commerce Clause   A clause of the U.S. Constitution that vests Congress with the power "to regulate commerce with foreign nations."

foreign corporation   A corporation in any state or jurisdiction other than the one in which it was formed.

foreign limited partnership   A limited partnership in all other states besides the one in which it was formed.

Foreign Sovereign Immunities Act (FSIA)   An act that exclusively governs suits against foreign nations that are brought in federal or state courts in the United States. It codifies the principle of qualified, or restricted, immunity.

foreign substance test   A test to determine merchantability based on foreign objects found in food.

foreseeability standard   A rule which says that an accountant is liable for negligence to third parties who are foreseeable users of the client's financial statements. It provides the broadest standard for holding accountants liable to third parties for negligence.

forged indorsement   The forged signature of a payee or holder on a negotiable instrument.

forged instrument   A check with a forged drawer's signature on it.

forgery   The fraudulent making or alteration of a written document that affects the legal liability of another person.

formal contract   A contract that requires a special form or method of creation.

forum-selection clause A contract provision that designates a certain court to hear any dispute concerning nonperformance of the contract.

forward vertical merger A vertical merger in which the supplier acquires the customer.

Fourteenth Amendment An amendment added to the U.S. Constitution in 1868 that contains the Due Process, Equal Protection, and Privileges and Immunities clauses.

franchise An arrangement that is established when one party (the franchisor) licenses another party (the franchisee) to use the franchisor's trade name, trademarks, commercial symbols, patents, copyrights, and other property in the distribution and selling of goods and services.

franchise agreement An agreement that a franchisor and franchisee enter into that sets forth the terms and conditions of a franchise.

fraud by concealment Fraud that occurs when one party takes specific action to conceal a material fact from another party.

fraud in the inception Fraud that occurs if a person is deceived as to the nature of his or her act and does not know what he or she is signing. Also known as fraud in the factum.

fraud in the inducement Fraud that occurs when the party knows what he or she is signing but has been fraudulently induced to enter into the contract.

fraudulent misrepresentation An event that occurs when one person consciously decides to induce another person to rely and act on a misrepresentation. Also called fraud.

fraudulent transfer A transfer of a debtor's property or an obligation incurred by a debtor within two years of the filing of a petition, where (1) the debtor had actual intent to hinder, delay, or defraud a creditor or (2) the debtor received less than a reasonable equivalent in value, and the debtor was insolvent or unable to pay at the time the transfer was made or the obligation was incurred.

Free Exercise Clause A clause to the First Amendment that prohibits the government from interfering with the free exercise of religion in the United States.

Freedom of Information Act A federal act that gives the public access to documents in the possession of federal administrative agencies. There are many exceptions to disclosure.

freedom of speech The right to engage in oral, written, and symbolic speech protected by the First Amendment.

freehold estate An estate in which the owner has a present possessory interest in the real property.

fresh start The goal of federal bankruptcy law, to grant a debtor relief from some of his or her burdensome debts, while protecting creditors by requiring the debtor to pay more of his or her debts than would otherwise have been required prior to the 2005 act.

frolic and detour A situation in which an agent does something during the course of his or her employment to further his or her own interests rather than the principal's.

FTC franchise rule A rule set out by the FTC that requires franchisors to make full presale disclosures to prospective franchisees.

FTC notice A statement required by the FTC to appear in at least 12-point boldface type on the cover of a franchisor's required disclosure statement to prospective franchisees.

fully disclosed agency An agency in which a contracting third party knows (1) that the agent is acting for a principal and (2) the identity of the principal.

future goods Goods not yet in existence (e.g., ungrown crops, unborn stock animals).

future interest The interest that a grantor retains for him- or herself or a third party.

gambling statutes Statutes that make certain forms of gambling illegal.

gap-filling rule A rule that says an open term can be "read into" a contract.

general duty A duty that an employer has to provide a work environment free from recognized hazards that are causing or are likely to cause death or serious physical harm to employees.

general gift A gift that does not identify the specific property from which the gift is to be made.

general partners Partners in a limited partnership who invest capital, manage the business, and are personally liable for partnership debts. Persons liable for the debts and obligations of a general partnership. Also known simply as partners.

general partnership An association of two or more persons to carry on as co-owners of a business for profit [UPA Section 6(1)]. Also known as an ordinary partnership.

general-jurisdiction trial court A court that hears cases of a general nature that are not within the jurisdiction of limited-jurisdiction trial courts. Testimony and evidence at trial are recorded and stored for future reference.

generally accepted accounting principles (GAAPs) Standards for the preparation and presentation of financial statements.

generally accepted auditing standards (GAASs) Standards for the methods and procedures that must be used to conduct audits.

generally known dangers A defense that acknowledges that certain products are inherently dangerous and are known to the general population to be so.

generic name A term for a mark that has become a common term for a product line or type of service and therefore has lost its trademark protection.

genuineness of assent The requirement that a party's assent to a contract be genuine.

gift The voluntary transfer of title to property without payment of consideration by the donee. To be a valid gift, three elements must be shown: (1) donative intent, (2) delivery, and (3) acceptance.

gift causa mortis A gift that is made in contemplation of death.

gift inter vivos A gift made during a person's lifetime that is an irrevocable present transfer of ownership.

gift promise A promise that is unenforceable because it lacks consideration. Also known as a gratuitous promise.

good faith Honesty in fact in the conduct or transaction concerned. The good faith test is subjective.

good faith purchaser for value A person to whom good title can be transferred from a person with voidable title. The real owner cannot reclaim goods from a good faith purchaser for value.

good faith subsequent lessee A person to whom a lease interest can be transferred from a person with voidable title. The real owner cannot reclaim the goods from the subsequent lessee until the lease expires.

Good Samaritan law A statute that relieves medical professionals from liability for ordinary negligence when they stop and render aid to victims in emergency situations.

goods Tangible things that are movable at the time of their identification to a contract.

government contractor defense A defense that says a contractor who was provided specifications by the government is not liable for any defect in the product that occurs as a result of those specifications.

Government in the Sunshine Act A federal act that opens most federal administrative agency meetings to the public.

grantee The party to whom an interest in real property is transferred.

grantor The party who transfers an ownership interest in real property. A person who creates a living trust. Also called a *trustor*.

greenmail The purchase by a target corporation of its stock from an actual or perceived tender offeror at a premium.

group boycott A restraint of trade in which two or more competitors at one level of distribution agree not to deal with others at another level of distribution. Also known as refusal to deal.

guarantee of collection A form of accommodation in which the accommodation party guarantees collection of a negotiable instrument; the accommodation party is secondarily liable on the instrument.

guarantee of payment A form of accommodation in which the accommodation party guarantees payment of a negotiable instrument; the accommodation party is primarily liable accommodation party. A party who signs an instrument and lends his or her name (and credit) to another party to the instrument.

guarantor A person who agrees to pay a debt if the primary debtor does not.

guaranty arrangement An arrangement in which a third party promises to be secondarily liable for the payment of another's debt.

guaranty contract A promise in which one person agrees to answer for the debts or duties of another person. It is a contract between the guarantor and the original creditor.

Hart-Scott-Rodino Antitrust Improvement Act An act that requires certain firms to notify the FTC and the Justice Department in advance of a proposed merger. Unless the government challenges a proposed merger within 30 days, the merger may proceed.

hazardous waste Hazardous waste that may cause or significantly contribute to an increase in mortality or serious illness or pose a hazard to human health or the environment if improperly managed.

health care directive (health care proxy) A document in which the maker names someone to be his or her health care agent to make all health care decisions in accordance with his or her wishes, as outlined in the living will.

health insurance Insurance that is purchased to help cover the costs of medical treatment, surgery, or hospital care.

heir The receiver of property under intestacy statutes.

holder A person who is in possession of a negotiable instrument that is drawn, issued, or indorsed to him or his order, or to bearer, or in blank.

holder in due course (HDC) A holder who takes a negotiable instrument for value, in good faith, and without notice that it is defective or overdue.

holographic will A will that is entirely handwritten and signed by the testator.

homeowners' policy A comprehensive insurance policy that includes coverage for the risks covered by a fire insurance policy as well as personal liability insurance.

homestead exemption Equity in a debtor's home that the debtor is permitted to retain.

honor To pay a drawer's properly drawn check.

horizontal merger A merger between two or more companies that compete in the same business and geographical market.

horizontal restraint of trade A restraint of trade that occurs when two or more competitors at the same level of distribution enter into a contract, combination, or conspiracy to restrain trade.

hung jury A jury that cannot come to a unanimous decision about the defendant's guilt. In the case of a hung jury, the government may choose to retry the case.

identification of goods Distinguishing the goods named in a contract from the seller's or lessor's other goods.

illegal consideration A promise to refrain from doing an illegal act. Such a promise will not support a contract.

illegal contract A contract that has an illegal object. Such contracts are void.

illusory promise A contract into which both parties enter but one or both of the parties can choose not to perform their contractual obligations. Thus, the contract lacks consideration. Also known as an illusory contract.

immoral contract A contract whose objective is the commission of an act that is society considers immoral.

immunity from prosecution The government's agreement not to use against a person granted immunity any evidence given by that person.

impairment of right of recourse A situation in which certain parties (holders, indorsers, accommodation parties) are discharged from liability on an instrument if the holder (1) releases an obligor from liability or (2) surrenders collateral without the consent of the parties who would benefit by it.

implied authorization A mode of acceptance that is implied from what is customary in similar transactions, usage of trade, or prior dealings between the parties.

implied exemptions Exemptions from antitrust laws that are implied by the federal courts.

implied term A term in a contract that can reasonably be supplied by the courts.

implied warranties Certain warranties that the law implies on transferors of negotiable instruments. There are two types of implied warranties: transfer and presentment warranties.

implied warranty of authority A warranty of an agent who enters into a contract on behalf of another party that he or she has the authority to do so.

implied warranty of fitness for a particular purpose A warranty that arises where a seller or lessor warrants that the goods will meet the buyer's or lessee's expressed needs.

implied warranty of fitness for human consumption A warranty that applies to food or drink consumed on or off the premises of restaurants, grocery stores, fast-food outlets, and vending machines.

implied warranty of habitability A warranty that provides that leased premises must be fit, safe, and suitable for ordinary residential use.

implied warranty of merchantability Unless properly disclosed, a warranty that is implied that sold or leased goods are fit for the ordinary purpose for which they are sold or leased, as well as other assurances.

implied-in-fact condition A condition that can be implied from the circumstances surrounding a contract and the parties' conduct.

implied-in-fact contract A contract in which agreement between parties has been inferred from their conduct.

impossibility of performance Nonperformance that is excused if a contract becomes impossible to perform. It must be objective impossibility, not subjective.

imputed knowledge Information that is learned by an agent that is attributed to the principal.

in pari delicto A situation in which both parties are equally at fault in an illegal contract.

in personam jurisdiction Jurisdiction over the parties to a lawsuit.

in rem jurisdiction Jurisdiction to hear a case because of jurisdiction over the property of the lawsuit.

inaccessibility exception A rule that permits employees and union officials to engage in union solicitation on company property if the employees are beyond reach of reasonable union efforts to communicate with them.

incidental damages Reasonable expenses incurred in stopping delivery, transportation charges, storage charges, sales commissions, and so on.

income beneficiary of a living trust A person who receives the income from a living trust during his or her life. This is usually the grantor.

income beneficiary of a trust A person or an entity to be paid income from a trust.

incontestability clause A clause that prevents insurers from contesting statements made by insureds in applications for insurance after the passage of a stipulated number of years.

incorporator The person or persons, partnerships, or corporations that are responsible for incorporation of a corporation.

indemnification The right of a partner to be reimbursed for expenditures incurred on behalf of the partnership.

indenture agreement A contract between a corporation and a holder that contains the terms of a debt security.

independent adoption An adoption that occurs when there is a private arrangement between biological and adoptive parents of a child.

independent contractor "A person who contracts with another to do something for him who is not controlled by the other nor subject to the other's right to control with respect to his physical conduct in the performance of the undertaking" [Restatement (Second) of Agency]. A person or business that is not an employee but is employed by a principal to perform a certain task on behalf of the principal.

indictment The charge of having committed a crime (usually a felony), based on the judgment of a grand jury.

indirect price discrimination A form of price discrimination (e.g., favorable credit terms) that is less readily apparent than direct forms of price discrimination.

indorsee A person to whom a negotiable instrument is indorsed.

indorsee of a check A party to whom a check is indorsed.

indorsement The signature (and other directions) written by or on behalf of the holder somewhere on an instrument.

indorsement for deposit or collection An indorsement that makes the indorsee the indorser's collecting agent (e.g., "for deposit only").

indorsement of a check A payee's signing of the back of a check in order to turn it over to another party.

indorser A person who indorses a negotiable instrument.

indorser of a check A payee who indorses a check to another party.

infancy doctrine A doctrine that allows minors to disaffirm (cancel) most contracts they have entered into with adults.

informal contract A contract that is not formal. Valid informal contracts are fully enforceable and may be sued upon if breached.

information The charge of having committed a crime (usually a misdemeanor), based on the judgment of a judge (magistrate).

injunction A court order that prohibits a person from doing a certain act.

injury A plaintiff's personal injury or damage to his or her property that enables him or her to recover monetary damages for the defendant's negligence.

innkeepers' statutes State statutes that limit an innkeeper's common law liability. An innkeeper can avoid liability for loss caused to a guest's property if (1) a safe is provided in which the guest's valuable property may be kept and (2) the guest is notified of this fact.

innocent misrepresentation Fraud that occurs when a person makes a statement of fact that he or she honestly and reasonably believes to be true even though it is not.

insane but not adjudged insane Being insane but not having been adjudged insane by a court or an administrative agency. A contract entered into by such person is generally voidable. Some states hold that such a contract is void.

Insecticide, Fungicide, and Rodenticide Act A federal statute that requires pesticides, herbicides, fungicides, and rodenticides to be registered with the EPA; the EPA may deny, suspend, or cancel registration.

inside director A member of the board of directors who is also an officer of the corporation.

insider trading A situation in which an insider makes a profit by personally purchasing shares of the corporation prior to public release of favorable information or by selling shares of the corporation prior to the public disclosure of unfavorable information.

Insider Trading Sanctions Act A federal statute that permits the SEC to obtain a civil penalty of up to three times the illegal benefits received from insider trading.

installment contract A contract that requires or authorizes goods to be delivered and accepted in separate lots.

insurable interest A requirement that a person who purchases insurance have a personal interest in the insured item or person.

insurance A means for persons and businesses to protect themselves against the risk of loss.

insurance policy An insurance contract.

insured A party who pays a premium to a particular insurance company for insurance coverage.

insurer An insurance company that underwrites insurance coverage.

intangible property Rights that cannot be reduced to physical form, such as stock certificates, certificates of deposit, bonds, and copyrights.

integration of several writings The combination of several writings to form a single contract.

intellectual property rights Patents, copyrights, trademarks, and trade secrets. Federal and state laws protect intellectual property rights from misappropriation and infringement.

intended third-party beneficiary A third party who is not in privity of contract but who has rights under the contract and can enforce the contract against the promisor.

intentional infliction of emotional distress A tort that says a person whose extreme and outrageous conduct intentionally or recklessly causes severe emotional distress to another person is liable for that emotional distress. Also known as the tort of outrage.

intentional interference with contractual relations A tort that arises when a third party induces a contracting party to breach the contract with another party.

intentional misrepresentation A deceit in which an agent makes an untrue statement that he or she knows is not true. A tort in which a seller or lessor fraudulently misrepresents the quality of a product and a buyer is injured thereby. The intentional defrauding of a person out of money, property, or something else of value. Also known as fraud or deceit. Also known as *fraud* or *deceipt*.

intentional tort A category of torts that requires that the defendant possessed the intent to do the act that caused the plaintiff's injuries.

inter vivos **trust** A trust that is created while the settlor is alive.

intermediary bank A bank in the collection process that is not the depository bank or the payer bank.

intermediate appellate court An intermediate court that hears appeals from trial courts.

intermediate scrutiny test A test that is applied to classifications based on protected classes other than race (e.g., sex, age).

International Court of Justice (ICJ) The judicial branch of the United Nations that is located in The Hague, the Netherlands. Also called the World Court.

international law Law that governs affairs between nations and that regulates transactions between individuals and businesses of different countries.

internet A collection of millions of computers that provide a network of electronic connections between the computers.

interpretive rule A rule issued by an administrative agency that interprets existing statutory language.

interrogatories Written questions submitted by one party to another party. The questions must be answered in writing within a stipulated time.

interstate commerce Commerce that moves between states or that affects commerce between states.

intervention The act of others to join as parties to an existing lawsuit.

intestacy statute A state statute that specifies how a deceased's property will be distributed if he or she dies without a will or if the last will is declared void and there is no prior valid will.

intestate The state of having died without leaving a will.

intoxicated person A person who is under contractual incapacity because of ingestion of alcohol or drugs to the point of incompetence.

intrastate offering exemption An exemption from registration that permits local businesses to raise capital from local investors to be used in the local economy without the need to register with the SEC.

involuntary petition A petition filed by creditors of a debtor that alleges that the debtor is not paying his or her debts as they become due.

issued shares Shares that have been sold by a corporation.

joint and several liability Tort liability of partners together and individually. A plaintiff can sue one or more partners separately. If successful, the plaintiff can recover the entire amount of the judgment from any or all of the defendant-partners.

joint custody A custody arrangement that gives both parents responsibility for making major decisions concerning the child.

joint liability Liability of partners for contracts and debts of the partnership. A plaintiff must name the partnership and all of the partners as defendants in a lawsuit.

joint marital debts Debts incurred during the marriage for joint needs.

joint tenancy A form of co-ownership that includes the right of survivorship.

joint venture An arrangement in which two or more business entities combine their resources to pursue a single project or transaction.

joint venture corporation A corporation owned by two or more joint venturers that is created to operate a joint venture.

joint venture partnership A partnership owned by two or more joint venturers that is formed to operate a joint venture.

joint will A will that is executed by two or more testators.

judicial branch The part of the U.S. government that interprets the law. It consists of the Supreme Court and other federal courts.

judicial decision A decision about an individual lawsuit issued by a federal or state court.

judicial dissolution Dissolution of a corporation through a court proceeding instituted by the state.

jurisprudence The philosophy or science of law.

jury instructions Instructions given by the judge to the jury that inform them of the law to be applied in the case.

Just Compensation Clause A clause of the U.S. Constitution that requires the government to compensate the property owner, and possibly others, when the government takes property under its power of eminent domain.

Kantian ethics A moral theory which says that people owe moral duties that are based on universal rules, such as the categorical imperative "Do unto others as you would have them do unto you." Also known as *duty ethics*.

key-person life insurance Life insurance purchased and paid for by a business that insures against the death of owners and other key executives and employees of the business.

land pollution Pollution of the land that is generally caused by hazardous waste being disposed of in an improper manner.

land sales contract An arrangement in which the owner of real property sells property to a purchaser and extends credit to the purchaser.

landlord An owner who transfers a leasehold.

Lanham Act An amended federal statute that (1) establishes the requirements for obtaining a federal mark and (2) protects marks from infringement.

larceny The taking of another's personal property other than from his or her person or building.

law That which must be obeyed and followed by citizens, subject to sanctions or legal consequences; a body of rules of action or conduct prescribed by controlling authority and having binding legal force.

lease A transfer of the right to the possession and use of named goods for a set term in return for certain consideration. A transfer of the right to the possession and use of real property for a set term in return for certain consideration; the rental agreement between a landlord and a tenant. The transfer of the right to use real property for a specified period of time.

leasehold A tenant's interest in property.

legal insanity A state of contractual incapacity, as determined by law.

legal value Support for a contract when either (1) the promisee suffers a legal detriment or (2) the promisor receives a legal benefit.

legally enforceable contract A contract in which if one party fails to perform as promised, the other party can use the court system to enforce the contract and recover damages or other remedy.

legislative branch The part of the U.S. government that makes federal laws. It is known as Congress (the Senate and the House of Representatives).

lessee A person who acquires the right to possession and use of goods under a lease.

lessor A person who transfers the right of possession and use of goods under a lease.

libel A false statement that appears in a letter, newspaper, magazine, book, photograph, movie, video, and so on.

license A contract that transfers limited rights in intellectual property and informational rights. A document that grants a person the right to enter upon another's property for a specified and usually short period of time.

licensee A party who is granted limited rights in or access to intellectual property or informational rights owned by a licensor.

licensee's damages Monetary damages that a licensee may recover from a licensor who breaches a contract.

licensing A business arrangement that occurs when the owner of intellectual property (the *licensor*) contracts to permit another party (the *licensee*) to use the intellectual property.

licensing agreement A detailed and comprehensive written agreement between a licensor and a licensee that sets forth the express terms of their agreement.

licensing statute A statute that requires a person or business to obtain a license from the government prior to engaging in a specified occupation or activity.

licensor An owner of intellectual property or informational rights who transfers rights in the property or information to the licensee.

licensor's damages Monetary damages that a licensor may recover from a licensee who breaches a contract.

life estate An interest in real property for a person's lifetime; upon that person's death, the interest will be transferred to another party.

life insurance A form of insurance in which the insurer is obligated to pay a specific sum of money upon the death of the insured.

limited liability The liability of LLC members for the LLC's debts, obligations, and liabilities only to the extent of their capital contributions.

limited liability company (LLC) An unincorporated business entity that combines the most favorable attributes of general partnerships, limited partnerships, and corporations.

limited liability limited partnership (LLLP) A special type of limited partnership that has both general partners and limited partners where both the general and limited partners have limited liability and are not personally liable for the debts of the LLLP.

limited liability of limited partners The limited liability of limited partners of a limited partnership only up to their capital contributions to the limited partnership; limited partners are not personally liable for the debts and obligations of the limited partnership.

limited liability of shareholders A general rule of corporate law which provides that generally shareholders are liable only to the extent of their capital contributions for the contracts and debts of their corporation and are not personally liable for the contracts and debts of the corporation.

limited liability partnership (LLP) A special form of partnership in which all partners are limited partners, and there are no general partners.

limited partners Partners in a limited partnership who invest capital but do not participate in management and are not personally liable for partnership debts beyond their capital contributions.

limited partnership A type of partnership that has two types of partners: (1) general partners and (2) limited partners.

limited partnership agreement A document that sets forth the rights and duties of general and limited partners; the terms and conditions regarding the operation, termination, and dissolution of a partnership; and so on.

limited-jurisdiction trial court A court that hears matters of a specialized or limited nature.

line of commerce The products or services that will be affected by a merger, including those that consumers use as substitutes. If an increase in the price of one product or service leads consumers to purchase another product or service, the two products are substitutes for each other.

lineal descendants Children, grandchildren, great-grandchildren, and so on of a testator.

liquidated damages Damages that parties to a contract agree in advance should be paid if the contract is breached. Damages that will be paid upon a breach of contract that are established in advance.

liquidation preference The right to be paid a stated dollar amount if a corporation is dissolved and liquidated.

litigation The process of bringing, maintaining, and defending a lawsuit.

living trust A method for holding property during a person's lifetime and distributing the property upon that person's death. Also called a grantor's trust or a revocable trust.

living will A document that states which life-saving measures the signor does and does not want, and can specify that he or she wants such treatments withdrawn if doctors determine that there is no hope of a meaningful recovery.

long-arm statute A statute that extends a state's jurisdiction to nonresidents who were not served a summons within the state.

lost property Property that the owner leaves somewhere due to negligence, carelessness, or inadvertence.

Magnuson-Moss Warranty Act A federal statute that regulates written warranties on consumer products.

mailbox rule A rule that states that an acceptance is effective when it is dispatched, even if it is lost in transmission. Also known as the acceptance-upon-dispatch rule.

main purpose exception An exception to the Statute of Frauds which states that if the main purpose of a transaction and an oral collateral contract is to provide pecuniary benefit to the guarantor, the collateral contract does not have to be in writing to be enforced.

maker of a CD The financial institution that issues a CD (borrower).

maker of a note The party who makes a promise to pay (borrower).

malicious prosecution A lawsuit in which the original defendant sues the original plaintiff. In the second lawsuit, the defendant becomes the plaintiff and vice versa.

manager-managed LLC An LLC that has designated in its articles of organization it is a manager-managed LLC and whose non-manager members give their management rights over to designated managers.

marine insurance Insurance that owners of a vessel can purchase to insure against loss or damage to the vessel and its cargo caused by perils on the water.

Marine Protection, Research, and Sanctuaries Act A federal statute that extends limited environmental protection to the oceans.

marital property Property acquired during the course of marriage using income earned during the marriage, and separate property that has been converted to marital property.

mark The collective name for trademarks, service marks, certification marks, and collective marks that can be trademarked.

market extension merger A merger between two companies in similar fields whose sales do not overlap.

marketable title Title to real property that is free from any encumbrances or other defects that are not disclosed but would affect the value of the property. Also called good title.

marriage A legal union between spouses that confers certain legal rights and duties upon the spouses and upon the children born of the marriage.

marriage license A legal document issued by a state which certifies that two people are married.

master limited partnership A form of limited partnership that is listed on stock exchanges and is publicly traded to provide liquidity.

material breach A breach that occurs when a party renders inferior performance of his or her contractual duties.

maximizing profits A theory of social responsibility that says a corporation owes a duty to take actions that maximize profits for shareholders.

means test A new test added by the 2005 act that applies to debtors who have family incomes that exceed the state's median income for families of the same size.

mechanic's lien A contractor's, laborer's, and material person's statutory lien that makes the real property to which services or materials have been provided security for the payment of the services and materials.

mediation A form of ADR in which the parties use a mediator to propose a settlement of their dispute.

meeting of the creditors A meeting of the creditors in a bankruptcy case that must occur within a reasonable time after an order for relief. The debtor must appear at this meeting.

meeting the competition defense A defense provided in Section 2(b) that says a seller may lawfully engage in price discrimination to meet a competitor's price.

member An owner of an LLC.

member-managed LLC An LLC that has not designated it is a manager-managed

LLC in its articles of organization and is managed by its members.

mens rea "Evil intent"—the possession of the requisite state of mind to commit a prohibited act.

merchant A person who (1) deals in the goods of the kind involved in a transaction or (2) by his or her occupation holds himself or herself out as having knowledge or skill peculiar to the goods involved in the transaction.

merchant protection statutes Statutes that allow merchants to stop, detain, and investigate suspected shoplifters without being held liable for false imprisonment if (1) there are reasonable grounds for the suspicion, (2) suspects are detained for only a reasonable time, and (3) investigations are conducted in a reasonable manner.

merger A situation in which one corporation is absorbed into another corporation and ceases to exist.

merger clause A clause in a contract that stipulates that it is a complete integration and the exclusive expression of the parties' agreement. Also known as an integration clause.

midnight deadline The midnight of the next banking day following the banking day on which the bank received an "on them" check for collection.

minor A person who has not reached the age of majority.

minor breach A breach that occurs when a party renders substantial performance of his or her contractual duties.

minor's duty of restoration A rule which states that a minor is obligated only to return the goods or property he or she has received from the adult in the condition it is in at the time of disaffirmance.

mirror image rule A rule which states that for an acceptance to exist, the offeree must accept the terms as stated in the offer.

misdemeanor A less serious crime; not inherently evil but prohibited by society. Many crimes against property are misdemeanors.

mislaid property Property that an owner voluntarily places somewhere and then inadvertently forgets.

misuse A defense that relieves a seller of product liability if the user abnormally misused the product. Products must be designed to protect against foreseeable misuse.

mitigation A nonbreaching party's legal duty to avoid or reduce damages caused by a breach of contract.

mixed sale A sale that involves the provision of a service and a good in the same transaction.

monetary damages An award of money.

Money Laundering Control Act A federal statute that makes it a crime to (1) knowingly engage in a money transaction through a financial institution involving property from an unlawful activity worth more than $10,000 and (2) knowingly engage in a *financial transaction* involving the proceeds of an unlawful activity.

search warrant A warrant issued by a court that authorizes the police to search a designated place for specified contraband, articles, items, or documents. A search warrant must be based on probable cause.

monopoly power The power to control prices or exclude competition, measured by the market share the defendant possesses in the relevant market.

moral minimum A theory of social responsibility that says a corporation's duty is to make a profit while avoiding causing harm to others.

moral obligation A sense of honor that prompts a person to make a promise. Promises made out of a sense of moral obligation lack consideration.

mortgage An interest in real property given to a lender as security for the repayment of a loan. A collateral arrangement in which a property owner borrows money from a creditor, who uses real estate as collateral for repayment of the loan.

mortgagee The creditor in a mortgage transaction.

mortgagor The owner-debtor in a mortgage transaction.

motion for summary judgment A motion which asserts that there are no factual disputes to be decided by the jury and that the judge can apply the proper law to the undisputed facts and decide the case without a jury. These motions are supported by affidavits, documents, and deposition testimony.

motion for judgment on the pleadings A motion which alleges that if all the facts presented in the pleadings are taken as true, the party making the motion would win the lawsuit when the proper law is applied to these asserted facts.

motivation test A test that determines whether an agent's motivation in committing an intentional tort is to promote the principal's business; if so, the principal is liable for any injury caused by the tort.

mutual benefit bailment A bailment for the mutual benefit of the bailor and bailee. The bailee owes a duty of ordinary care to protect the bailed property.

mutual mistake of fact A mistake made by both parties concerning a material fact that is important to the subject matter of a contract.

mutual mistake of value A mistake that occurs if both parties know the object of the contract but are mistaken as to its value.

mutual wills A situation in which two or more testators execute separate wills that leave their property to each other on the condition that the survivor leave the remaining property on his or her death as agreed by the testators. Also known as reciprocal wills.

national ambient air quality standards (NAAQS) Standards for certain pollutants set by the EPA that protect (1) human beings (primary level) and (2) vegetation, matter, climate, visibility, and economic values (secondary level).

national courts The courts of individual nations.

National Environmental Policy Act (NEPA) A federal statute which mandates that the federal government consider the adverse impact a federal government action would have on the environment before the action is implemented.

National Labor Relations Board (NLRB) A federal administrative agency that oversees union elections, prevents employers and unions from engaging in illegal and unfair labor practices, and enforces and interprets certain federal labor laws.

necessaries of life Food, clothing, shelter, medical care, and other items considered necessary to the maintenance of life. Minors must pay the reasonable value of necessaries of life for which they contract.

negligence A tort related to defective products in which the defendant has breached a duty of due care and caused harm to the plaintiff. Failure of a corporate director or officer to exercise the duty of care while conducting the corporation's business. Negligence in which the accountant breaches the duty of reasonable care, knowledge, skill, and judgment that he or she owes to a client when providing auditing and other accounting services to the client. Also known as *accountant malpractice*.

negligence per se A tort in which the violation of a statute or an ordinance constitutes the breach of the duty of care.

negligent infliction of emotional distress A tort that permits a person to recover for emotional distress caused by the defendant's negligent conduct.

negotiable instrument A special form of contract that satisfies the requirements established by Article 3 of the UCC. Also called commercial paper or instrument.

negotiation The transfer of a negotiable instrument by a person other than the issuer to a person who thereby becomes a holder.

No Electronic Theft Act (NET Act) A federal statute that makes it a crime for a person to willfully infringe on a copyright work that exceeds $1,000 in retail value.

no evidence of forgery, alteration, or irregularity requirement A requirement that says a holder cannot become an HDC to an instrument that is apparently forged or altered or is so otherwise irregular or incomplete as to call into question its authenticity.

Noerr **doctrine** A doctrine which says that two or more persons can petition the executive, legislative, or judicial branch of the government or administrative agencies to enact laws or take other action without violating antitrust laws.

no-fault automobile insurance An automobile insurance system used by some states in which the driver's insurance company pays for any injuries or death the driver suffers in an accident, no matter who caused the accident.

no-fault divorce A divorce recognized by the law of a state whereby neither party is blamed for the divorce.

nominal damages Damages awarded when the nonbreaching party sues the breaching party even though no financial loss has resulted from the breach. Nominal damages are usually $1 or some other small amount.

nonattainment area A geographical area that does not meet established air quality standards.

nonconforming uses Uses and buildings that already exist in a zoned area that are permitted to continue even though they do not fit within new zoning ordinances.

noncupative will An oral will that is made before a witness during the testator's last illness. Also known as a dying declaration or deathbed will.

non-intent crime A crime that imposes criminal liability without a finding of mens rea (intent).

nonnegotiable contract A contract that fails to meet the requirements of a negotiable instrument and, therefore, is not subject to the provisions of UCC Article 3.

nonpossessory interest A situation in which a person holds an interest in another person's property without actually owning any part of the property.

non-price vertical restraints Restraints of trade that are unlawful under Section 1 of the Sherman Act if their anticompetitive effects outweigh their procompetitive effects.

nonrestrictive indorsement An indorsement that has no instructions or conditions attached to the payment of the funds.

North American Free Trade Agreement (NAFTA) A treaty that has removed or reduced tariffs, duties, quotas, and other trade barriers between the United States, Canada, and Mexico.

note A debt security with a maturity of five years or less. An instrument that evidences a borrower's debt to the lender.

notice of dishonor The formal act of letting the party with secondary liability to pay a negotiable instrument know that the instrument has been dishonored.

novation agreement An agreement that substitutes a new party for one of the original contracting parties and relieves the exiting party of liability on the contract. Also known as simply a novation.

Nuclear Regulatory Commission (NRC) A federal agency that licenses the construction and opening of commercial nuclear power plants.

Nutrition Labeling and Education Act A federal statute that requires food manufacturers to place on food labels that disclose nutritional information about the food.

objective rule A rule which states that if an engagement is broken off, the prospective bride must return the engagement ring, regardless of which party broke off the engagement.

objective theory of contracts A theory that says the intent to contract is judged by the reasonable person standard and not by the subjective intent of the parties.

obligation An action a party to a sales or lease contract is required by law to carry out.

obscene speech Speech that (1) appeals to the prurient interest, (2) depicts sexual conduct in a patently offensive way, and (3) lacks serious literary, artistic, political, or scientific value.

Occupational Safety and Health Act A federal act enacted in 1970 that promotes safety in the workplace.

offensive speech Speech that is offensive to many members of society. It is subject to time, place, and manner restrictions.

offer "The manifestation of willingness to enter into a bargain, so made as to justify another person in understanding that his assent to that bargain is invited and will conclude it." (Section 24 of the Restatement (Second) of Contracts).

offeree The party to whom an offer to enter into a contract is made.

offeror The party who makes an offer to enter into a contract.

officers Employees of a corporation who are appointed by the board of directors to manage the day-to-day operations of the corporation.

Oil Pollution Act A federal statute that requires the oil industry to take measures to prevent oil spills and to readily respond to and clean up oil spills.

Older Workers Benefit Protection Act (OWBPA) A federal statute that prohibits age discrimination in employee benefits.

one-year "on sale" doctrine A doctrine that says a patent may not be granted if the invention was used by the public for more than one year prior to the filing of the patent application.

one-year rule A rule which states that an executory contract that cannot be performed by its own terms within one year of its formation must be in writing.

operating agreement An agreement entered into among members that governs the affairs and business of the LLC and the relations among members, managers, and the LLC.

order A decision issued by an administrative law judge.

order for relief An order that occurs upon the filing of either a voluntary petition or an unchallenged involuntary petition, or an order that is granted after a trial of a challenged involuntary petition.

order paper An instrument that is negotiated by (1) delivery and (2) indorsement.

order to pay A drawer's unconditional order to a drawee to pay a payee.

ordinance Law enacted by local government bodies, such as cities and municipalities, counties, school districts, and water districts.

organizational meeting A meeting that must be held by the initial directors of a corporation after the articles of incorporation are filed.

original tenor The original amount for which the drawer wrote a check.

outside director A member of a board of directors who is not an officer of the corporation.

overdraft The amount of money a drawer owes a bank after it has paid a check despite the drawer's account having insufficient funds.

parol evidence Any oral or written words outside the four corners of a written contract.

parol evidence rule A rule that says if a written contract is a complete and final statement of the parties' agreement, any prior or contemporaneous oral or written statements that alter, contradict, or are in addition to the terms of the written contract are inadmissible in court regarding a dispute over the contract. There are several exceptions to this rule.

part performance An equitable doctrine that allows the court to order an oral contract for the sale of land or transfer of another interest in real property to be specifically performed if it has been partially performed and performance is necessary to avoid injustice.

partially disclosed agency An agency in which a contracting third party knows that the agent is acting for a principal but does not know the identity of the principal.

participating preferred stock Stock that allows the stockholder to participate in the profits of the corporation along with the common stockholders.

partnership agreement A written agreement that partners sign. Also called articles of partnership.

partnership at will A partnership created with no fixed duration.

partnership for a term A partnership created for a fixed duration.

past consideration A prior act or performance. Past consideration (e.g., prior acts) will not support a new contract. New consideration must be given.

patent infringement Unauthorized use of another's patent. A patent holder may recover damages and other remedies against a patent infringer.

payable on demand or at a definite time requirement A requirement that a negotiable instrument be payable either on demand or at a definite time.

payee of a CD The party to whom a CD is made payable; usually the depositor (lender).

payee of a check The party to whom a check is written.

payee of a draft The party who receives the money from a draft.

payee of a note The party to whom a promise to pay is made (lender).

payer bank The bank where the drawer has a checking account and on which a check is drawn.

penal code A collection of criminal statutes.

per capita distribution A distribution of an estate in which each grandchild and great-grandchild of the deceased inherits equally with the children of the deceased.

per se rule A rule that is applicable to restraints of trade considered inherently anti-competitive. Once this determination is made about a restraint of trade, the court will not permit any defenses or justifications to save it.

per stirpes distribution A distribution of an estate in which grandchildren and great-grandchildren of the deceased inherit by representation of their parent.

perfect tender rule A rule that says if the goods or tender of a delivery fail in any respect to conform to the contract, the buyer may opt either (1) to reject the whole shipment, (2) to accept the whole shipment, or (3) to reject part and accept part of the shipment.

periodic tenancy A tenancy created when a lease specifies intervals at which payments are due but does not specify how long the lease is for.

permanency requirement A requirement of negotiable instruments that says they must be in a permanent state, such as written on ordinary paper.

personal articles floater An addition to a homeowners' policy that covers specific valuable items.

personal defense A defense that can be raised against enforcement of a negotiable instrument by an ordinary holder but not against an HDC.

personal liability of general partners The unlimited personal liability of general partners of a limited partnership for the debts and obligations of the general partnership.

personal property Tangible property such as automobiles, furniture, and equipment, and intangible property such as securities, patents, and copyrights.

personal satisfaction test A subjective test that applies to contracts involving personal taste and comfort.

petition for certiorari A petition asking the Supreme Court to hear a case.

petition for divorce A document filed with the proper state court that commences a divorce proceeding.

petition A document filed with a bankruptcy court that starts a bankruptcy proceeding.

physical or mental examination A court-ordered examination of a party to a lawsuit before trial to determine the extent of the alleged injuries.

picketing The action of strikers walking in front of an employer's premises, carrying signs announcing their strike.

piercing the corporate veil A doctrine that says if a shareholder dominates a corporation and uses it for improper purposes, a court of equity can disregard the corporate entity and hold the shareholder personally liable for the corporation's debts and obligations. Also called the *alter ego doctrine*.

plaintiff The party who files a complaint.

plan of reorganization A plan that sets forth a proposed new capital structure for a debtor to assume when it emerges from Chapter 11 reorganization bankruptcy.

plea bargain An agreement in which the accused admits to a lesser crime than charged.

In return, the government agrees to impose a lesser sentence than might have been obtained had the case gone to trial.

pleadings The paperwork that is filed with the court to initiate and respond to a lawsuit.

police power Power that permits states and local governments to enact laws to protect or promote the public health, safety, morals, and general welfare.

policy An insurance contract.

portability requirement A requirement of negotiable instruments that says they must be able to be easily transported between areas.

postdated check A check that a drawer does not want cashed until sometime in the future.

power of attorney An express agency agreement that is often used to give an agent the power to sign legal documents on behalf of the principal.

power of sale A power stated in a mortgage or deed that permits foreclosure without court proceedings and sale of the property through an auction.

precedent A rule of law established in a court decision. Lower courts must follow the precedent established by higher courts.

preemption doctrine The concept that federal law takes precedence over state or local law.

preemptive rights Rights that give existing shareholders the option of subscribing to new shares being issued in proportion to their current ownership interests.

preexisting duty Something a person is already under an obligation to do. A promise lacks consideration if a person promises to perform a preexisting duty.

preferred stock A type of equity security that is given certain preferences and rights over common stock.

preferred stockholder A person who owns preferred stock.

prefiling period A period of time that begins when the issuer first contemplates issuing securities and ends when the registration statement is filed. The issuer may not condition the market during this period.

premises liability The liability of landlords and tenants to persons injured on their premises.

premium Money paid to an insurance company.

prenuptial agreement A contract entered into prior to marriage that specifies how property will be distributed upon the termination of the marriage or death of a spouse. Also called a premarital agreement.

presentment A demand for acceptance or payment of an instrument made upon the maker, acceptor, drawee, or other payer by or on behalf of the holder.

presentment across the counter A situation in which a depositor physically presents a check for payment at the payer bank instead of depositing an "on them" check for collection.

presentment warranties Three warranties that a person who presents a draft or check for payment or acceptance makes to a drawee or an acceptor who pays or accepts the instrument in good faith: (1) The presenter has good title to the instrument or is authorized to obtain payment or acceptance of the person who has good title; (2) the instrument has not been materially altered; and (3) the presenter has no knowledge that the signature of the maker or drawer is unauthorized.

presentment warranty A guarantee in which each prior transferor warrants that a check has not been altered.

pretrial motion A motion a party can make to try to dispose of all or part of a lawsuit prior to trial.

price-fixing A restraint of trade that occurs when competitors in the same line of business agree to set the price of the goods or services they sell, raising, depressing, fixing, pegging, or stabilizing the price of a commodity or service.

primary liability Absolute liability to pay a negotiable instrument, subject to certain universal (real) defenses.

principal A person who authorizes an agent to sign a negotiable instrument on his or her behalf.

principal–agent relationship A relationship formed when an employer hires an employee and gives that employee authority to act and enter into contracts on his or her behalf.

Privacy Act A federal act which states that federal administrative agencies can maintain only information about an individual that is relevant and necessary to accomplish a legitimate agency purpose.

private corporation A corporation formed to conduct privately owned business.

private placement exemption An exemption from registration that permits issuers to raise capital from an unlimited number of accredited investors and no more than 35 nonaccredited investors without having to register the offering with the SEC.

Private Securities Litigation Reform Act of 1995 A federal statute that limits a defendant's liability to its proportionate degree of fault.

Privileges and Immunities Clause A clause that prohibits states from enacting laws that unduly discriminate in favor of their residents.

privity of contract The state of two specified parties being in a contract.

pro rata rule A rule that says shares must be purchased on a pro rata basis if too many shares are tendered.

probability of a substantial lessening of competition The probability that a merger will substantially lessen competition or create a monopoly, in which case the court may prevent the merger under Section 7 of the Clayton Act.

probate The process of a deceased's property being collected, debts and taxes being paid, and the remainder of the estate being distributed. Also called settlement of the estate.

probate court A specialized state court that supervises the administration and settlement of estates.

procedural due process A category of due process which requires that the government give a person proper notice and hearing of the legal action before that person is deprived of his or her life, liberty, or property. Due process that requires the respondent to be given proper and timely notice of the allegations or charges against him or her and an opportunity to present evidence on the matter.

product defect Something wrong, inadequate, or improper in the manufacture, design, packaging, warning, or instructions about a product.

product disparagement False statements about a competitor's products, services, property, or business reputation. Also known as trade libel, product disparagement and slander of title.

product liability The liability of manufacturers, sellers, and others for the injuries caused by defective products.

product liability insurance Insurance that protects sellers and manufacturers against injuries caused by defective products.

production of documents A request by one party to another party to produce all documents relevant to the case prior to the trial.

professional corporation A corporation formed by lawyers, doctors, or other professionals.

professional malpractice The liability of a professional who breaches his or her duty of ordinary care.

professional malpractice insurance Insurance that insures professionals against liability for injuries caused by their negligence. Also known as malpractice insurance.

profit A document that grants a person the right to remove something from another's real property. Also known as profit-à-prendre.

profit corporation A corporation created to conduct a business for profit that can distribute profits to shareholders in the form of dividends.

promise to pay A maker's (borrower's) unconditional and affirmative undertaking to repay a debt to a payee (lender).

promissory estoppel An equitable doctrine that prevents the withdrawal of a promise by a promisor if it will adversely affect a promisee who has adjusted his or her position in justifiable reliance on the promise. An equitable doctrine that permits enforcement of oral contracts that should have been in writing. It is applied to avoid injustice. Also known as *equitable estoppel*.

promissory note A two-party negotiable instrument that is an unconditional written promise by one party to pay money to another party.

promoter A person or persons who organize and start a corporation, negotiate and enter into contracts in advance of its formation, find the initial investors to finance the corporation, and so forth.

promoters' contracts A collective term for such things as leases, sales contracts, contracts to purchase property, and employment contracts entered into by promoters on behalf of the proposed corporation prior to its actual incorporation.

proof of claim A document required to be filed by a creditor that states the amount of his or her claim against the debtor.

proof of interest A document required to be filed by an equity security holder that states the amount of his or her interest against the debtor.

proper dispatch The proper addressing, packaging, and posting of an acceptance.

prospectus A written disclosure document that must be submitted to the SEC along with the registration statement and given to prospective purchasers of the securities.

provisional credit A situation in which a collecting bank gives credit to a check in the collection process prior to its final settlement. Provisional credits may be reversed if the check does not clear.

proximate cause A point along a chain of events caused by a negligent party after which this party is no longer legally responsible for the consequences of his or her actions. Also called legal cause.

proxy A written document that a shareholder signs, authorizing another person to vote his or her shares at the shareholders' meetings in the event of the shareholder's absence. Also called a *proxy card*.

proxy contest A contest in which opposing factions of shareholders and managers solicit proxies from other shareholders; the side that receives the greatest number of votes wins the proxy contest.

proxy statement A document that fully describes (1) the matter for which a proxy is being solicited, (2) who is soliciting the proxy, and (3) any other pertinent information.

publicly held corporation A corporation that has many shareholders and whose securities are often traded on national stock exchanges.

punitive damages Monetary damages that are awarded to punish a defendant who either intentionally or recklessly injured the plaintiff.

qualified individual with a disability A person who (1) has a physical or mental impairment that substantially limits one or more of his or her major life activities, (2) has a record of such impairment, or (3) is regarded as having such impairment.

qualified indorsement An indorsement that includes the notation "without recourse" or similar language that disclaims liability of the indorser.

qualified indorser An indorser who signs a qualified indorsement to an instrument.

qualified indorsers Those who disclaim liability and are not secondarily liable on instruments they endorse.

quasi in rem jurisdiction Jurisdiction that allows a plaintiff who obtains a judgment in one state to try to collect the judgment by attaching property of the defendant located in another state.

quasi-contract (implied-in-law contract) An equitable doctrine whereby a court may award monetary damages to a plaintiff for providing work or services to a defendant even though no actual contract existed. The doctrine is intended to prevent unjust enrichment and unjust detriment.

quiet title action An action brought by a party, seeking an order of the court declaring who has title to disputed property. The court "quiets title" by its decision.

quorum The required number of shares that must be represented in person or by proxy to hold a shareholders' meeting. The RMBCA establishes a majority of outstanding shares as a quorum.

Racketeer Influenced and Corrupt Organizations Act (RICO) A federal act that provides for both criminal and civil penalties for racketeering.

radiation pollution Emissions from radioactive wastes that can cause injury and death to humans and other life and can cause severe damage to the environment.

ratification A situation in which a principal accepts an agent's unauthorized contract. The act of a minor after the minor has reached the age of majority by which he or she accepts a contract entered into when he or she was a minor.

rational basis test A test that is applied to classifications not involving a suspect or protected class.

reaffirmation agreement An agreement entered into by a debtor with a creditor prior to discharge, whereby the debtor agrees to pay the creditor a debt that would otherwise be discharged in bankruptcy. Certain requirements must be met for a reaffirmation agreement to be enforced.

real property The land itself, as well as buildings, trees, soil, minerals, timber, plants, crops, fixtures and other things permanently affixed to the land or buildings.

reasonable person test An objective test that applies to commercial contracts and contracts involving mechanical fitness.

receiving stolen property To (1) knowingly receive stolen property and (2) intend to deprive the rightful owner of that property.

record date A date specified in corporate bylaws that determines whether a shareholder may vote at a shareholders' meeting.

recording statute A state statute that requires a mortgage or deed of trust to be recorded in the county recorder's office of the county in which the real property is located.

red light doctrine A doctrine that says a holder cannot qualify as an HDC if he or she has notice of an unauthorized signature or an alteration of the instrument or any adverse claim against or defense to its payment.

redeemable preferred stock Stock that permits a corporation to buy back the preferred stock at some future date.

reformation An equitable doctrine that permits the court to rewrite a contract to express the parties' true intentions.

registered agent A person or corporation that is empowered to accept service of process on behalf of a corporation.

registration statement A document that an issuer of securities files with the SEC that contains required information about the issuer, the securities to be issued, and other relevant information.

Regulation A A regulation that permits the issuer to sell securities pursuant to a simplified registration process.

Regulation Z A regulation that sets forth detailed rules for compliance with the TILA.

regulatory statute A licensing statute enacted to protect the public.

regulatory statutes Statutes such as environmental laws, securities laws, and antitrust laws that provide for criminal violations and penalties.

rejection Express words or conduct by the offeree that rejects an offer. Rejection terminates the offer.

release of lien A written document signed by a contractor, subcontractor, laborer, or material person, waiving his or her statutory lien against real property. Also known as a *lien release*.

relevant geographical market A relevant market that is defined as the area in which the defendant and its competitors sell the product or service.

relevant product or service market A relevant market that includes substitute products or services that are reasonably interchangeable with the defendant's products or services.

religious discrimination Discrimination against a person solely because of his or her religion or religious practices.

remainder A right of possession that returns to a third party upon the expiration of a limited or contingent estate.

remainder beneficiary of a living trust A person who receives the assets of a living trust upon the death of the grantor.

remainder beneficiary of a trust A person or an entity to receive the trust corpus upon the termination of a trust.

renters' insurance Insurance that renters purchase to cover loss or damage to their possessions.

replacement cost insurance Insurance that pays the cost to replace the damaged or destroyed property up to the policy limits.

replevin An action by a buyer or lessor to recover scarce goods wrongfully withheld by a seller or lessor.

reply A document filed by the original plaintiff to answer the defendant's cross-complaint.

res ipsa loquitur A tort in which the presumption of negligence arises because (1) the defendant was in exclusive control of the situation and (2) the plaintiff would not have suffered injury but for someone's negligence. The burden switches to the defendant to prove that he or she was not negligent.

resale price maintenance A *per se* violation of Section 1 of the Sherman Act that occurs when a party at one level of distribution enters into an agreement with a party at another level to adhere to a price schedule that either sets or stabilizes prices.

rescission An action to rescind (undo) a contract. Rescission is available if there has been a material breach of contract, fraud, duress, undue influence, or mistake.

residuary gift A gift of an estate left after the debts, taxes, and specific and general gifts have been given.

Resource Conservation and Recovery Act (RCRA) A federal statute that authorizes the EPA to regulate facilities that generate, treat, store, transport, and dispose of hazardous wastes.

respondeat superior A rule that says an employer is liable for the tortious conduct of its employees or agents while they are acting within the scope of its authority.

Restatement of the Law of Contracts A compilation of model contract law principles drafted by legal scholars. The Restatement is not law.

restitution The return of goods or property received from the other party to rescind a contract. If the actual goods or property are not available, a cash equivalent must be made.

restrictive indorsement An indorsement that contains some sort of instruction from the indorser.

resulting trust A trust that is implied from the conduct of the parties.

revenue-raising statute A licensing statute with the primary purpose of raising revenue for the government.

reverse discrimination Discrimination against a group that is usually thought of as a majority.

reversion A right of possession that returns to the grantor after the expiration of a limited or contingent estate.

Revised Article 3 A comprehensive revision of the UCC law of negotiable instruments that reflects modern commercial practices.

Revised Model Business Corporation Act (RMBCA) A 1984 revision of the MBCA that arranges the provisions of the act more logically, revises the language to be more consistent, and makes substantial changes in the provisions.

Revised Uniform Limited Partnership Act (RULPA) A 1976 revision of the ULPA that provides a more modern, comprehensive law for the formation, operation, and dissolution of limited partnerships.

revocation Termination of a will. Withdrawal of an offer by the offeror which terminates the offer.

revocation of acceptance Reversal of acceptance.

reward An award given for performance of some service or attainment. To collect a reward, the offeree must (1) have knowledge of the reward offer prior to completing the requested act and (2) perform the requested act.

right of first refusal An agreement that requires a selling shareholder to offer his or her shares for sale to the other parties to the agreement before selling them to anyone else.

right of redemption A right that allows the mortgagor to redeem real property after default and before foreclosure. It requires the mortgagor to pay the full amount of the debt incurred by the mortgagee because of the mortgagor's default.

right to cover The right of a buyer or lessee to purchase or lease substitute goods if a seller or lessor fails to make delivery of the goods or repudiates the contract or if the buyer or lessee rightfully rejects the goods or justifiably revokes their acceptance.

right to dispose of goods The right to dispose of goods in a good faith and commercially reasonable manner. A seller or lessor who is in possession of goods at the time the buyer or lessee breaches or repudiates a contract may in good faith resell, release, or otherwise dispose of the goods in a commercially reasonable manner and recover damages, including incidental damages, from the buyer or lessee.

right to participate in management A situation in which, unless otherwise agreed, each partner has a right to participate in the management of a partnership and has an equal vote on partnership matters.

right to reclaim goods The right of a seller or lessor to demand the return of goods from the buyer or lessee under specified situations.

right to recover damages for breach of contract A seller's or lessor's right to recover damages measured as the difference between the contract price (or rent) and the market price (or rent) at the time and place the goods were to be delivered, plus incidental damages, from a buyer or lessee who repudiates the contract or wrongfully rejects tendered goods.

right to recover goods from an insolvent seller or lessor The right of a buyer or lessee who has wholly or partially paid for goods before they are received to recover the goods from a seller or lessor who becomes insolvent within 10 days after receiving the first payment; the buyer or lessee must tender the remaining purchase price or rent due under the contract.

right to recover the purchase price or rent A seller's or lessor's right to recover the contracted-for purchase price or rent

from the buyer or lessee (1) if the buyer or lessee fails to pay for accepted goods, (2) if the buyer or lessee breaches the contract and the seller or lessor cannot dispose of the goods, or (3) if the goods are damaged or lost after the risk of loss passes to the buyer or lessee.

right to reject nonconforming goods or improperly tendered goods A situation in which a buyer or lessee rejects goods that do not conform to the contract. If the goods or the seller's or lessor's tender of delivery fails to conform to the contract, the buyer or lessee may (1) reject the whole, (2) accept the whole, or (3) accept any commercial unit and reject the rest.

right to stop delivery of goods in transit The right of a seller or lessor to stop delivery of goods in transit if he or she learns of the buyer's or lessee's insolvency or if the buyer or lessee repudiates the contract, fails to make payment when due, or gives the seller or lessor some other right to withhold the goods.

right to withhold delivery A seller's or lessor's right to refuse to deliver goods to a buyer or lessee upon breach of a sales or lease contract by the buyer or lessee or the insolvency of the buyer or lessee.

robbery The taking of personal property from another person by the use of fear or force.

Rule 10b-5 A rule adopted by the SEC to clarify the reach of Section 10(b) against deceptive and fraudulent activities in the purchase and sale of securities.

rule of reason A rule which holds that only unreasonable restraints of trade violate Section 1 of the Sherman Act. The court must examine the pro- and anticompetitive effects of a challenged restraint.

Racketeer Influenced and Corrupt Organizations Act (RICO) A federal act that provides for both criminal and civil penalties for securities fraud.

Safe Drinking Water Act A federal statute that authorizes the EPA to establish national primary drinking water standards.

sale on approval A type of sale in which there is no actual sale unless and until the buyer accepts the goods.

sale or return contract A contract in which the seller delivers goods to a buyer with the understanding that the buyer may return them if they are not used or resold within a stated or reasonable period of time.

sale The passing of title from a seller to a buyer for a price. Also called a *conveyance*.

Sarbanes-Oxley Act A federal act that imposes new rules that affect public accountants. The act: created the Public Company

Accounting Oversight Board (PCAOB); requires public accounting firms to register with the PCAOB; separates audit services and certain nonaudit services provided by accountants to clients; requires an audit partner of the accounting firm to supervise an audit and approve an audit report prepared by the firm and requires a second partner of the accounting firm to review and approve the audit report; and prohibits employment of an accountant by a previous audit client for certain positions for a period of one year following the audit.

satisfaction The performance of an accord.

scienter Intentional conduct. Scienter is required for there to be a violation of Section 10(b) and Rule 10b-5. Knowledge that a representation is false or that it was made without sufficient knowledge of the truth.

secondary boycott picketing A type of picketing in which a union tries to bring pressure against an employer by picketing the employer's suppliers or customers.

secondary liability Liability on a negotiable instrument that is imposed on a party only when the party primarily liable on the instrument defaults and fails to pay the instrument when due.

"secondary meaning" A brand name that has evolved from an ordinary term.

Section 1 of the Sherman Act A section that prohibits contracts, combinations, and conspiracies in restraint of trade.

Section 2 of the Sherman Act A section that prohibits monopolization and attempts or conspiracies to monopolize trade.

Section 2(a) of the Robinson-Patman Act A section that prohibits direct and indirect price discrimination by sellers of a commodity of a like grade and quality, where the effect of such discrimination may be to substantially lessen competition or to tend to create a monopoly in any line of commerce.

Section 3 of the Clayton Act An act that prohibits tying arrangements involving sales and leases of goods.

Section 5 of the Federal Trade Commission Act A section that prohibits unfair methods of competition and unfair or deceptive acts or practices in or affecting commerce.

Section 5 of the FTC Act A provision in the FTC Act that prohibits unfair and deceptive practices.

Section 7 of the Clayton Act A section which provides that it is unlawful for a person or business to acquire the stock or assets of another "where in any line of commerce or in any activity affecting commerce in any

section of the country, the effect of such acquisition may be substantially to lessen competition, or to tend to create a monopoly."

Section 7 of the NLRA A law that gives employees the right to join together to form a union.

Section 8(a) of the NLRA A law that makes it an unfair labor practice for an employer to interfere with, coerce, or restrain employees from exercising their statutory right to form and join

Section 10(b) A provision of the Securities Exchange Act of 1934 that prohibits the use of manipulative and deceptive devices in the purchase or sale of securities in contravention of the rules and regulations prescribed by the SEC.

Section 10(b) A section of the Securities Exchange Act of 1934 that prohibits any manipulative or deceptive practice in connection with the purchase or sale of a security.

Section 11 A provision of the Securities Act of 1933 that imposes civil liability on persons who intentionally defraud investors by making misrepresentations or omissions of material facts in the registration statement or who are negligent for not discovering the fraud.

Section 11(a) A section of the Securities Act of 1933 that imposes civil liability on accountants and others for (1) making misstatements or omissions of material facts in a registration statement or (2) failing to find such misstatements or omissions.

Section 12 A provision of the Securities Act of 1933 that imposes civil liability on any person who violates the provisions of Section 5 of the act.

Section 14(a) A provision of the Securities Exchange Act of 1934 that gives the SEC the authority to regulate the solicitation of proxies.

Section 14(e) A provision of the Williams Act that prohibits fraudulent, deceptive, and manipulative practices in connection with a tender offer.

Section 16(b) A section of the Securities Exchange Act of 1934 that requires that any profits made by a statutory insider on transactions involving short-swing profits belong to the corporation.

Section 18(a) A section of the Securities Exchange Act of 1934 that imposes civil liability on any person who makes false or misleading statements in any application, report, or document filed with the SEC.

Section 24 A provision of the Securities Act of 1933 that imposes criminal liability on any person who willfully violates the 1933 act or the rules or regulations adopted thereunder.

Section 24 A section of the Securities Act of 1933 that makes it a criminal offense for any person to (1) willfully make any untrue statement of material fact in a registration statement filed with the SEC, (2) omit any material fact necessary to ensure that the statements made in the registration statement are not misleading, or (3) willfully violate any other provision of the Securities Act of 1933 or rule or regulation adopted thereunder.

Section 32 A provision of the Securities Exchange Act of 1934 that imposes criminal liability on any person who willfully violates the 1934 act or the rules or regulations adopted thereunder.

Section 32(a) A section of the Securities Exchange Act of 1934 that makes it a criminal offense for any person willfully and knowingly to make or cause to be made any false or misleading statement in any application, report, or other document required to be filed with the SEC pursuant to the Securities Exchange Act of 1934 or any rule or regulation adopted thereunder.

Section 552 of the Restatement (Second) of Torts A rule which says that an accountant is liable only for negligence to third parties who are members of a limited class of intended users of the client's financial statements. It provides a broader standard for holding accountants liable to third parties for negligence than does the Ultramares doctrine.

section of the country A division of the country that is based on the relevant geographical market; the geographical area that will feel the direct and immediate effects of a merger.

secured credit Credit that requires security (collateral) that secures payment of the loan.

Securities Act of 1933 A federal statute that primarily regulates the issuance of securities by corporations, partnerships, associations, and individuals.

Securities and Exchange Commission (SEC) The federal administrative agency that is empowered to administer federal securities laws. The SEC can adopt rules and regulations to interpret and implement federal securities laws.

Securities Exchange Act of 1934 A federal statute that primarily regulates the trading in securities.

security (1) An interest or instrument that is common stock, preferred stock, a bond, a debenture, or a warrant; (2) an interest or instrument that is expressly mentioned in securities acts; and (3) an investment contract.

self-incrimination   A person being a witness against himself or herself. The Fifth Amendment prevents self-incrimination in any criminal case.

seller's or lessor's cancellation   A seller or lessor has the right to cancel a sales or lease contract if the buyer or lessee rejects or revokes acceptance of the goods, fails to pay for the goods, or repudiates the contract in part or in whole.

separate property   Property owned by a spouse prior to marriage, as well as inheritances and gifts received by a spouse during the marriage.

service mark   A mark that distinguishes the services of the holder from those of its competitors.

service of process   A summons being served on the defendant to obtain personal jurisdiction over him or her.

settlement agreement   A written document signed by divorcing parties that evidences their agreement settling property rights and other issues of their divorce.

settlement conference   A hearing before a trial in order to facilitate the settlement of a case. Also called a pretrial hearing.

settlor   A person who creates a trust. Also known as a trustor or transferor.

sex discrimination   Discrimination against a person solely because of his or her gender.

sexual harassment   Lewd remarks, touching, intimidation, posting of indecent materials, and other verbal or physical conduct of a sexual nature that occurs on the job.

share exchange   A situation in which one corporation acquires all the shares of another corporation, and both corporations retain their separate legal existence.

shareholder resolution   A resolution that a shareholder who meets certain ownership requirements may submit to other shareholders for a vote. Many shareholder resolutions concern social issues.

shareholder voting agreement   An agreement between two or more shareholders that stipulates how they will vote their shares.

shipment contract   A contract that requires the seller to ship the goods to the buyer via a common carrier. A sales contract that requires the seller to send the goods to the buyer but not to a specifically named destination. The buyer bears the risk of loss during transportation.

short-form merger   A merger between a parent corporation and a subsidiary corporation that does not require the vote of the shareholders of either corporation or the board of directors of the subsidiary corporation.

sight draft   A draft payable on sight. Also called a demand draft.

signature   Any name, word, or mark used in lieu of a written signature; any symbol that is (1) handwritten, typed, printed, stamped, or made in almost any other manner and (2) executed or adopted by a party to authenticate a writing.

signature liability   Liability in which a person cannot be held contractually liable on a negotiable instrument unless his or her signature appears on the instrument. Also called contract liability.

signature requirement   A requirement which states that a negotiable instrument must be signed by the drawer or maker. Any symbol executed or adopted by a party with a present intent to authenticate a writing qualifies as his or her signature.

signer   A person signing an instrument who acts in the capacity of (1) a maker of notes or certificates of deposit, (2) a drawer of drafts or checks, (3) a drawee who certifies or accepts checks or drafts, (4) an indorser who indorses an instrument, (5) an agent who signs on behalf of others, or (6) an accommodation party.

slander   Oral defamation of character.

small claims court   A court that hears civil cases involving small dollar amounts.

small offering exemption   An exemption from registration that permits the sale of securities not exceeding $1 million during a 12-month period.

social contract   A moral theory that says each person is presumed to have entered into a social contract with all others in society to obey moral rules that are necessary for people to live in peace and harmony.

Social Security   A federal system that provides limited retirement and death benefits to covered employees and their dependents.

sole proprietorship   A form of business in which the owner is actually the business; the business is not a separate legal entity.

special federal courts   Federal courts that hear matters of specialized or limited jurisdiction.

special indorsement   An indorsement that contains the signature of the indorser and specifies the person (indorsee) to whom the indorser intends the instrument to be payable. It creates order paper.

special shareholders' meetings   Meetings of shareholders that may be called to consider and vote on important or emergency issues, such as a proposed merger or amending the articles of incorporation.

specific duty standard   An OSHA standard that addresses a safety problem of a specific duty nature (e.g., requirement for a safety guard on a particular type of equipment).

specific gift   A gift of a specifically named piece of property.

specific performance   A decree of the court that orders a seller or lessor to perform his or her obligations under the contract; usually occurs when the goods in question are unique, such as art or antiques. A remedy that orders the breaching party to perform the acts promised in the contract. Specific performance is usually awarded in cases in which the subject matter is unique, such as in contracts involving land, heirlooms, and paintings.

spousal support   Payments made by one divorced spouse to the other divorced spouse. Also called *alimony*.

stakeholder interest   A theory of social responsibility that says a corporation must consider the effects its actions have on persons other than its shareholders.

stale check   A check that has been outstanding for more than six months.

standard fire insurance form   A standard fire insurance policy that protects the homeowner from loss caused by fire, lightning, smoke, and water damage.

standing to sue   Some stake in the outcome of a lawsuit.

stare decisis   Latin: "to stand by the decision." Adherence to precedent.

state action exemptions   Business activities that are mandated by state law and are therefore exempt from federal antitrust laws.

state administrative agencies   Administrative agencies that states create to enforce and interpret state law.

state median income   For any size family, income for which half of the state's families of this size have incomes above this figure and half of the state's families of this size have incomes less than this figure.

State Supreme Court   The highest court in a state court system; it hears appeals from intermediate appellate state courts and certain trial courts.

statement of disassociation   A document filed with the secretary of state that gives constructive notice that a member has disassociated from an LLC.

statement of opinion   A commendation of goods, made by a seller or lessor, that does not create an express warranty. Also known as puffing.

statement of policy   A statement issued by an administrative agency that announces a proposed course of action that the agency intends to follow in the future.

statute   Written law enacted by the legislative branch of the federal and state governments that establishes certain courses of conduct that must be adhered to by covered parties.

statute of frauds   A state statute that requires certain types of contracts to be in writing.

statute of limitations   A statute that establishes the period during which a plaintiff must bring a lawsuit against a defendant. A statute that establishes the time period during which a lawsuit must be brought; if the lawsuit is not brought within this period, the injured party loses the right to sue. A statute that requires an injured person to bring an action within a certain number of years from the time that he or she was injured by a defective product.

statute of repose   A statute that limits the seller's liability to a certain number of years from the date when the product was first sold.

statute of wills   A state statute that establishes the requirements for making a valid will.

statutory exemptions   Exemptions from antitrust laws that are expressly provided in statutes enacted by Congress.

stock dividend   Additional shares of stock distributed as a dividend.

stop-payment order   An order by a drawer of a check to the payer bank not to pay or certify a check.

straight voting   A system in which each shareholder votes the number of shares he or she owns on candidates for each of the positions open. Also called noncumulative voting.

strict liability   A tort doctrine that makes manufacturers, distributors, wholesalers, retailers, and others in the chain of distribution of a defective product liable for the damages caused by the defect, *irrespective of fault*. Liability without fault.

strict scrutiny test   A test that is applied to classifications based on race.

strike   A cessation of work by union members in order to obtain economic benefits or correct an unfair labor practice.

sublease   A situation in which a tenant transfers only some of his or her rights under the lease.

sublessee   The new tenant in a sublease situation.

sublessor   The original tenant in a sublease situation.

substantial performance   Performance by a contracting party that deviates only slightly from complete performance.

substantive due process   A category of due process which requires that government statutes, ordinances, regulations, or other laws be clear on their face and not overly broad in scope.

substantive rule   A rule issued by an administrative agency that has the force of law and to which covered persons and businesses must adhere.

subsurface rights   Rights to the earth located beneath the surface of the land.

suicide clause   A clause in a life insurance contract which provides that if an insured commits suicide before a stipulated date, the insurance company does not have to pay the life insurance proceeds.

summons   A court order directing the defendant to appear in court and answer the complaint.

superseding or intervening event   An event for which a defendant is not responsible. The defendant is not liable for injuries caused by the superseding or intervening event.

supervening event or intervening event   An alteration or a modification of a product by a party in the chain of distribution that absolves all prior sellers from strict liability.

supervening illegality   The enactment of a statute, regulation, or court decision that makes the object of an offer illegal. This action terminates the offer.

supramajority voting requirement   A requirement that a greater than majority of shares constitutes a quorum of the vote of the shareholders.

Supremacy Clause   A clause of the U.S. Constitution which establishes that the U.S. Constitution and federal treaties, laws, and regulations are the supreme law of the land.

surety arrangement   An arrangement in which a third party promises to be primarily liable with the borrower for the payment of the borrower's debt.

taking for value requirement   A requirement that says a holder must give value for a negotiable instrument in order to qualify as an HDC.

taking in good faith requirement   A requirement that says a holder must take the instrument in good faith in order to qualify as an HDC.

taking without notice of defect requirement   A requirement that says a person cannot qualify as an HDC if he or she has notice that the instrument is defective in certain ways.

tangible property   All real property and physically defined personal property, such as buildings, goods, animals, and minerals.

target corporation   The corporation that is proposed to be acquired in a tender offer situation.

Tax Reform Act of 1976   An act that imposes criminal liability on accountants and others who prepare federal tax returns if they (1) willfully understate a client's tax liability, (2) negligently understate the tax liability, or (3) aid or assist in the preparation of a false tax return.

tax sale   A method of transferring property ownership that involves a lien on property for unpaid property taxes. If the lien remains unpaid after a certain amount of time, a tax sale is held to satisfy the lien.

tenancy at sufferance   A tenancy created when a tenant retains possession of property after the expiration of another tenancy or a life estate without the owner's consent.

tenancy at will   A tenancy created by a lease that may be terminated at any time by either party.

tenancy by the entirety   A form of co-ownership of real property that can be used only by married couples.

tenancy for years   A tenancy created when a landlord and a tenant agree on a specific duration for a lease.

tenancy in common   A form of co-ownership in which the interest of a surviving tenant in common passes to the deceased tenant's estate and not to the co-tenants.

tenant   The party to whom a leasehold is transferred.

tender of delivery   The obligation of a seller to transfer and deliver goods to the buyer or lessee in accordance with a sales or lease contract.

tender of performance   An unconditional and absolute offer by a contracting party to perform his or her obligations under a contract. Also known as tender.

tender offer   An offer that an acquirer makes directly to a target corporation's shareholders in an effort to acquire the target corporation.

tender offeror   The party that makes a tender offer.

Term LLC   An LLC that has a specified term of duration.

testamentary trust   A trust created by a will; the trust comes into existence when the settlor dies.

testator or testatrix   A person who makes a will.

thermal pollution   Heated water or material discharged into waterways that upsets the ecological balance and decreases the oxygen content.

time draft   A draft payable at a designated future date.

time instrument   An instrument payable (1) at a fixed date, (2) on or before a stated date, (3) at a fixed period after sight, or (4) at a time readily ascertainable when the promise or order is issued. An instrument that specifies a definite date for payment of the instrument.

time note A note payable at a specific time.

tippee A person who receives material nonpublic information from a tipper.

tipper A person who discloses material nonpublic information to another person.

title Legal, tangible evidence of ownership of goods.

Title I of the ADA A title of a federal statute that prohibits employment discrimination against qualified individuals with disabilities in regard to job application procedures, hiring, compensation, training, promotion, and termination.

Title I of the Landrum-Griffin Act Labor's "bill of rights," which gives each union member equal rights and privileges to nominate candidates for union office, vote in elections, and participate in membership meetings.

Title III of the Americans with Disabilities Act A federal statute that prohibits discrimination on the basis of disability in places of public accommodation by private entities.

Title VII of the Civil Rights Act of 1964 A title of a federal statute enacted to eliminate job discrimination based on five protected classes: race, color, religion, sex, and national origin.

title insurance Insurance that owners of real property purchase to ensure that they have clear title to the property.

tort of misappropriation of the right to publicity An attempt by another person to appropriate a living person's name or identity for commercial purposes.

tortfeasor A person who intentionally or unintentionally (negligently) causes injury or death to another person. A person liable to persons he or she injures and to the heirs of persons who die because of his or her conduct.

toxic substances Chemicals used by agriculture, industry, business, mining, and households that cause injury to humans, birds, animals, fish, and vegetation.

Toxic Substances Control Act A federal statute that authorizes the EPA to regulate toxic substances.

trade acceptance A sight draft that arises when credit is extended (by a seller to a buyer) with the sale of goods. The seller is both the drawer and the payee, and the buyer is the drawee.

trade secret A product formula, pattern, design, compilation of data, customer list, or other business secret.

trade secrets Ideas that make a franchise successful but that do not qualify for trademark, patent, or copyright protection.

trademark A distinctive mark, symbol, name, word, motto, or device that identifies the goods of a particular business.

trademark infringement Unauthorized use of another's mark. The holder may recover damages and other remedies from the infringer.

trademark or service mark A distinctive mark, symbol, name, word, motto, or device that identifies the goods or services of a particular franchisor.

transfer Any passage of an instrument other than its issuance and presentment for payment.

transfer warranties Any of the following five implied warranties: (1) The transferor has good title to the instrument or is authorized to obtain payment or acceptance on behalf of one who does have good title; (2) all signatures are genuine or authorized; (3) the instrument has not been materially altered; (4) no defenses of any party are good against the transferor; and (5) the transferor has no knowledge of any insolvency proceeding against the maker, the acceptor, or the drawer of an unaccepted instrument.

Treaty Clause A clause of the U.S. Constitution which states that the president "shall have the power . . . to make treaties, provided two-thirds of the senators present concur."

treaty A compact made between two or more nations. The first source of international law, consisting of an agreement or a contract between two or more nations that is formally signed by an authorized representative and ratified by the supreme power of each nation.

trier of fact The jury in a jury trial; the judge where there is not a jury trial.

trust A legal arrangement established when one person transfers title to property to another person to be held and used for the benefit of a third person.

trust corpus Property and assets held in trust. Also known as trust res.

trustee A legal representative of the debtor's estate. A person named in a living will to administer the trust assets. This is usually the grantor. A person or an entity that holds legal title to a trust corpus and manages the trust for the benefit of the beneficiary or beneficiaries.

Truth-in-Lending Act (TILA) A federal statute that requires creditors to make certain disclosures to debtors in consumer

transactions and real estate loans on the debtor's principal dwelling.

tying arrangement A restraint of trade in which a seller refuses to sell one product to a customer unless the customer agrees to purchase a second product from the seller.

U.S. Constitution The fundamental law of the United States of America. It was ratified by the states in 1788.

U.S. courts of appeals The federal court system's intermediate appellate courts.

U.S. district courts The federal court system's trial courts of general jurisdiction.

U.S. Supreme Court The highest court in the United States, located in Washington, DC. The Supreme Court was created by Article III of the U.S. Constitution.

U.S. trustee A federal government official who is responsible for handling and supervising many of the administrative tasks of a bankruptcy case.

UCC Statute of Frauds Section 2-201(1) A section of the Uniform Commercial Code which states that sales contracts for the sale of goods costing $500 or more must be in writing.

UCC Statute of Frauds Section 2A-201(1) A section of the Uniform Commercial Code which states that lease contracts involving payments of $1,000 or more must be in writing.

UCC Statute of Frauds A rule that requires all contracts for the sale of goods costing $500 or more and lease contracts involving payments of $1,000 or more to be in writing.

UCC statute of limitations A rule which provides that an action for breach of any written or oral sales or lease contract must commence within four years after the cause of action accrues. The parties may agree to reduce the limitations period to one year.

ultra vires **act** An act by a corporation that is beyond its express or implied powers.

ultramares doctrine A rule which says that an accountant is liable only for negligence to third parties who are in privity of contract or in a privity-like relationship.

unauthorized signature A signature made by a purported agent without authority from the purported principal.

unconditional Not conditional or limited. Promises to pay and orders to pay must be unconditional in order for them to be negotiable.

unconditional promise or order to pay requirement A requirement that says a negotiable instrument must contain either an unconditional promise to pay (note or CD) or an unconditional order to pay money. A "medium of exchange authorized or adopted by a domestic or foreign government" [UCC 1-201(24)].

unconscionable contract   A contract that courts refuse to enforce in part or at all because it is so oppressive or manifestly unfair as to be unjust.

undisclosed agency   An agency in which a contracting third party does not know of either the existence of the agency or the principal's identity.

undue influence   A situation in which one person takes advantage of another person's mental, emotional, or physical weakness and unduly persuades that person to enter into a contract; the persuasion by the wrongdoer must overcome the free will of the innocent party.

unduly burden interstate commerce   A concept which says that states may enact laws that protect or promote the public health, safety, morals, and general welfare, as long as the laws do not unduly burden interstate commerce.

unenforceable contract   A contract in which the essential elements to create a valid contract are met but there is some legal defense to the enforcement of the contract.

Uniform Commercial Code (UCC) A comprehensive statutory scheme which includes laws that cover aspects of commercial transactions. A model act that includes comprehensive laws that cover most aspects of commercial transactions. All the states have enacted all or part of the UCC as statutes.

Uniform Computer Information Transactions Act (UCITA)   A model state law that creates contract law for the licensing of information technology rights.

Uniform Computer Information Transactions Act (UCITA)   A model act that establishes uniform legal rules for the formation and enforcement of electronic contracts and licenses.

Uniform Franchise Offering Circular (UFOC)   A uniform disclosure document that requires a franchisor to make specific presale disclosures to prospective franchisees.

Uniform Gifts to Minors Act and Uniform Transfers to Minors Act   Acts that establish procedures for adults to make gifts of money and securities to minors.

Uniform Limited Liability Company Act (ULLCA)   A model act that provides comprehensive and uniform laws for the formation, operation, and dissolution of LLCs.

Uniform Partnership Act (UPA)   A model act that codifies partnership law.

Most states have adopted the UPA in whole or in part.

Uniform Simultaneous Death Act   An act which provides that if people who would inherit property from each other die simultaneously, each person's property is distributed as though he or she had survived.

unilateral contract   A contract in which the offeror's offer can be accepted only by the performance of an act by the offeree; a "promise for an act."

unilateral mistake   A mistake in which only one party is mistaken about a material fact regarding the subject matter of a contract.

unilateral refusal to deal   A unilateral choice by one party not to deal with another party. This does not violate Section 1 of the Sherman Act because there is not concerted action.

uninsured motorist coverage   Automobile insurance that provides coverage to a driver and passengers who are injured by an uninsured motorist or a hit-and-run driver.

unintentional tort   A doctrine that says a person is liable for harm that is the foreseeable consequence of his or her actions. Also known as negligence.

union shop   A workplace where an employee must join the union within a certain number of days after being hired.

United Nations (UN)   An international organization created by a multilateral treaty in 1945 to promote social and economic cooperation among nations and to protect human rights.

universal defense   A defense that can be raised against both holders and HDCs. Also called a real defense.

unlawful detainer action   A legal process that a landlord must complete to evict a holdover tenant.

unprotected speech   Speech that is not protected by the First Amendment and may be forbidden by the government.

unqualified indorsement   An indorsement whereby the indorser promises to pay the holder or any subsequent indorser the amount of the instrument if the maker, drawer, or acceptor defaults on it.

unqualified indorser   An indorser who signs an unqualified indorsement to an instrument.

unqualified indorsers   Those who are secondarily liable on negotiable instruments they endorse.

unreasonable search and seizure   Any search and seizure by the government that violates the Fourth Amendment.

unsecured credit   Credit that does not require any security (collateral) to protect the payment of the debt.

usury law   A law that sets an upper limit on the interest rate that can be charged on certain types of loans.

utilitarianism   A moral theory that dictates that people must choose the action or follow the rule that provides the greatest good to society.

valid contract   A contract that meets all the essential elements to establish a contract; a contract that is enforceable by at least one of the parties.

variance   An exception that permits a type of building or use in an area that would not otherwise be allowed by a zoning ordinance.

venue   A concept that requires lawsuits to be heard by the court with jurisdiction that is nearest the location in which the incident occurred or where the parties reside.

vertical merger   A merger that integrates the operations of a supplier and a customer.

vertical restraint of trade   A restraint of trade that occurs when two or more parties on different levels of distribution enter into a contract, combination, or conspiracy to restrain trade.

violation   A crime that is neither a felony nor a misdemeanor that is usually punishable by a fine.

visitation rights   Rights of a non-custodial parent to visit with the child for limited periods of time.

void contract   A contract that has no legal effect; a nullity.

void title   A situation in which a thief acquires no title to goods he or she steals. Also known as a void leasehold interest.

voidable contract   A contract in which one or both parties have the option to avoid their contractual obligations. If a contract is avoided, both parties are released from their contractual obligations.

voidable title   A title that a purchaser has if the goods were obtained by (1) fraud, (2) a check that is later dishonored, or (3) impersonation of another person. Also known as *voidable leasehold interest.*

voir dire   The process whereby prospective jurors are asked questions by the judge and attorneys to determine whether they would be biased in their decisions.

voluntary dissolution   Dissolution of a corporation that has begun business or issued shares upon recommendation of the board of directors and a majority vote of the shares entitled to vote.

voluntary petition   A petition filed by a debtor that states that the debtor has debts.

voting trust   An arrangement in which the shareholders transfer their stock certificates to a trustee who is empowered to vote the shares.

warranty A seller's or lessor's express or implied assurance to a buyer or lessee that the goods sold or leased meet certain quality standards.

warranty disclaimer A statement that negates express and implied warranties.

warranty against interference A warranty in which the lessor warrants that no person holds a claim or an interest in the goods that arose from an act or omission of the lessor that will interfere with the lessee's enjoyment of his or her leasehold interest. An automatic warranty of a seller or lessor who is a merchant who regularly deals in goods of the kind sold or leased which warrants that the goods are delivered free of any third-party patent, trademark, or copyright claim. Also known as the *warranty against infringements*.

warranty of no security interests A warranty in which sellers of goods warrant that the goods they sell are delivered free from any third-party security interests, liens, or encumbrances that are unknown to the buyer.

warranty of good title A warranty in which the seller warrants that he or she has valid title to the goods being sold and that the transfer of title is rightful.

water pollution Pollution of lakes, rivers, oceans, and other bodies of water.

wetlands Areas that are inundated or saturated by surface water or ground water that support vegetation typically adapted for life in such conditions.

will A declaration of how a person wants his or her property to be distributed upon death.

winding up The process of liquidating a partnership's assets and distributing the proceeds to satisfy claims against the partnership.

winding up and liquidation The process by which a dissolved corporation's assets are collected, liquidated, and distributed to creditors, shareholders, and other claimants.

Williams Act An amendment to the Securities Exchange Act of 1934 made in 1968 that specifically regulates tender offers.

World Wide Web An electronic connection of millions of computers that support a standard set of rules for the exchange of information.

work-related test A test that determines whether an agent committed an intentional tort within a work-related time or space; if so, the principal is liable for any injury caused by the agent's intentional tort.

workers' compensation Compensation paid to workers and their families when workers are injured in connection with their jobs.

Worker Adjustment and Retraining Notification (WARN) Act A federal act that requires employers with 100 or more employees to give their employees 60 days' notice before engaging in certain plant closings or layoffs.

workers' compensation insurance Insurance that compensates employees for work-related injuries.

work product immunity A state statute which provides that an accountant's work papers cannot be used against a client in a court action.

World Trade Organization (WTO) An international organization of more than 130 member nations created to promote and enforce trade agreements among member nations.

writ of certiorari An official notice that the Supreme Court will review a case.

writ of garnishment An order of the court that orders that wages, bank accounts, or other property of the breaching party

held by third persons be paid to the non-breaching party to satisfy a judgment.

writ of attachment An order of the court that enables a government officer to seize property of the breaching party and sell it at auction to satisfy a judgment.

wrongful dishonor A situation in which there are sufficient funds in a drawer's account to pay a properly payable check, but the bank does not do so.

wrongful termination The termination of an agency contract in violation of the terms of the agency contract. The nonbreaching party may recover damages from the breaching party.

wrongful dissolution A situation in which a partner withdraws from a partnership without having the right to do so at that time.

wrongful disassociation When a member withdraws from (1) a term LLC prior to the expiration of the term or (2) an at-will LLC when the operating agreement eliminates a member's power to withdraw.

wrongful termination Termination of a franchise without just cause.

writ of certiorari An official notice that the Supreme Court will review a case.

WTO panel A body of three WTO judges that hears trade disputes between member nations and issues a "panel report."

WTO appellate body A panel of seven judges selected from WTO member nations that hears and decides appeals from decisions of the dispute-settlement body.

WTO dispute settlement body A board composed of one representative from each WTO member nation that reviews panel reports.

zoning ordinances Local laws that are adopted by municipalities and local governments to regulate land use within their boundaries.

Index